Building Regression Models with SAS®

A Guide for Data Scientists

Robert N. Rodriguez

The correct bibliographic citation for this manual is as follows: Rodriguez, Robert N. 2023. *Building Regression Models with SAS®: A Guide for Data Scientists*. Cary, NC: SAS Institute Inc.

Building Regression Models with SAS®: A Guide for Data Scientists

Contents

Quick Guide to Key Procedures

Table 1   SAS 9 Procedures for Building Regression Models

Procedure	Model	Introduction	Example
GLMSELECT	General linear models including least squares regression	page 50	page 56
QUANTSELECT	Quantile regression	page 143	page 146
HPLOGISTIC	Logistic regression	page 163	page 174
HPGENSELECT	Generalized linear models	page 197	page 201
GAMPL	Generalized additive models	page 228	page 230
HPSPLIT	Classification and regression trees	page 274	page 276
ADAPTIVEREG	Multivariate adaptive regression splines	page 302	page 304

Table 2   SAS Viya Procedures for Building Regression Models

Procedure	Model	Introduction	Example
REGSELECT	General linear models including least squares regression	page 77	page 81
QTRSELECT	Quantile regression	page 155	page 156
LOGSELECT	Logistic regression	page 183	page 187
GENSELECT	Generalized linear models	page 215	page 216
GAMMOD	Generalized additive models	page 239	page 239
GAMSELECT	Generalized additive models	page 244	page 246
PHSELECT	Proportional hazards models	page 259	page 261
TREESPLIT	Classification and regression trees	page 282	page 283

Preface

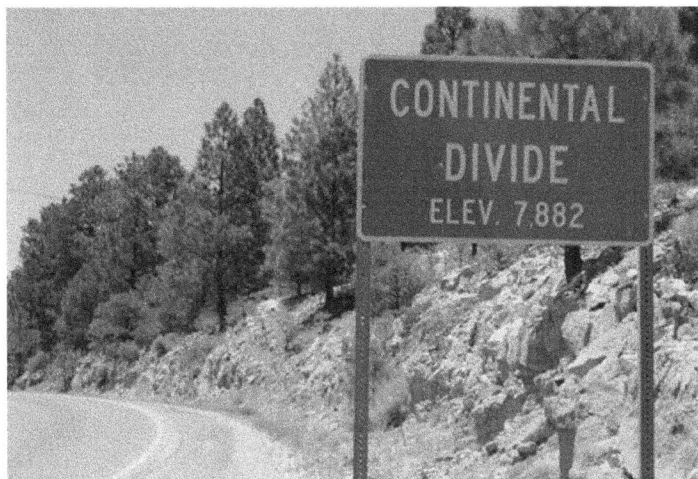

If you travel in the western mountains of the United States, you will eventually encounter the Continental Divide. When a thunderstorm drops its contents on the divide, a portion flows eastward to the Mississippi River and then to the Atlantic Ocean; the other portion flows westward to the Pacific Ocean. During the 1800s, the Great Divide, as it is known, was the highest hurdle faced by settlers trekking across the American frontier until the construction of railways.

Great divides are also encountered in scientific fields, where philosophical differences impede practical applications until they are eventually resolved—often by breakthroughs in technology. In the field of statistics, the great divide of the 20th century was the disagreement between proponents of frequentist and Bayesian approaches. Today, objective Bayesian methods are widely accepted due to computational advances in the 1990s.

Machine learning has created a new divide for the practice of statistics, which relies heavily on data from well-designed studies for modeling and inference. Statistical methods now vie with algorithms that learn from large amounts of observational data. In particular, the new divide influences how regression models are viewed and applied. While statistical analysts view regression models as platforms for inference, data scientists view them as platforms for prediction. And while statistical analysts prefer to specify the effects in a model by drawing on subject matter knowledge, data scientists rely on algorithms to determine the form of the model.

This book equips both groups to cross the divide and find value on the other side by presenting SAS procedures that build regression models for prediction from large numbers of candidate effects. It introduces statistical analysts to methods of predictive modeling drawn from supervised learning, and at the same time it introduces data scientists to a rich variety of models drawn from statistics.

Throughout, the book uses the term *model building* because the procedures provide far more than sequential methods for model selection such as stepwise regression. The procedures also provide shrinkage methods, methods for model averaging, methods for constructing spline effects, and methods for building trees.

Motivation for the Book

The need for this book originated some years ago with the introduction of SAS/STAT procedures that were specifically designed to build regression models for prediction. The first was the GLMSELECT procedure, which builds general linear models (Cohen 2006). It not only equips analysts with modern methods for prediction but also provides the scalability that is essential in data mining and business analytics, where the number of observations can be in the millions and the number of potential predictors can be in the tens of thousands.

The GLMSELECT procedure was followed by a series of procedures that build other types of models. For instance, the HPLOGISTIC procedure builds logistic regression models, and the HPGENSELECT procedure builds generalized linear models.

Naturally, with so many new tools to choose from, SAS users began to ask questions such as the following:

> How is the GLMSELECT procedure different from the GLM and REG procedures?
>
> What methods are available for model validation?
>
> Should I switch from the GAM procedure to the GAMPL procedure?
>
> Can I trust the p-values and confidence intervals I get when I select a model?

Because SAS is a global company, I had opportunities to answer these questions in presentations at customer sites, user events, and conferences on six continents. During this odyssey, I discussed the new procedures with business analysts, data scientists, researchers, university faculty, and students. As I listened to their questions, I realized they could benefit from a book that served as a guide to the procedures. I also recognized that there were two audiences for this book.

Audiences for the Book

Many of the people I met during my odyssey were SAS users with experience in applied statistics. They were familiar with the GLM and GENMOD procedures for analyzing general linear models and generalized linear models. However, they were now working on projects where they had to build predictive models from large databases—and that was unfamiliar territory.

For this audience, adopting the model building procedures is mostly a matter of learning the concepts of predictive modeling, which differ considerably from the concepts of statistical modeling. The syntax of the procedures is not a challenge because they implement MODEL and CLASS statements similar to those of the GLM procedure.

I also met SAS users who had graduated from programs in business analytics and data science where machine learning is emphasized. They knew the basics of linear regression and logistic regression but were not acquainted with more specialized regression models. Nonetheless, they understood the concepts of predictive modeling because they were familiar with supervised learning.

For this second audience, adopting the model building procedures involves learning about regression models that are considerably more versatile than standard linear and logistic regression. With quantile regression and generalized additive models, for instance, it is possible to gain insights that cannot be obtained with conventional regression models.

Knowledge Prerequisites for the Book

This book assumes you know the basics of regression analysis. It uses standard matrix notation for regression models but explains the concepts and methods behind the procedures without mathematical derivations.

For readers who want to dive into the technical aspects of concepts and algorithms, explanations are given in appendices which use calculus and linear algebra at the level expected by master of science programs in data science and statistics.

The book also assumes you know enough about SAS to write a program that reads data and runs procedures. If you are new to SAS or need a refresher, an excellent primer is *The Little SAS Book* by Delwiche and Slaughter (2019).

Software Prerequisites for the Book

This book covers regression model building procedures in SAS 9 and SAS Viya. In order to run the examples that illustrate the procedures in SAS 9, you need SAS 9.4 with SAS/STAT installed. In order to run all the examples, you need SAS Viya with SAS Visual Statistics installed.

If you have questions about the software in this book, contact SAS Technical Support at https://support.sas.com. You can enter a request or problem at Submit a Support Request. Other questions related to this book can be directed to the book website at https://support.sas.com/rodriguez.

What the Book Does Not Cover

Regression analysis is a vast subject. This book does not cover the use of regression models for statistical inference, nor does it cover the basics of regression analysis. It is not a substitute for introductory textbooks such as Rawlings, Pantula, and Dickey (1998); Sheather (2009); Montgomery, Peck, and Vining (2012); and Fox (2016).

Furthermore, this book does not cover predictive or prognostic models in clinical research, biostatistics, and epidemiology. In those areas, the data typically come from carefully designed studies, the model variables are specified based on scientific knowledge, and the models are crafted by checking model assumptions, transforming variables, imputing missing data, and applying diagnostic techniques. The book *Regression Modeling Strategies* by Harrell (2015) gives a thorough exposition of these methods, and it discusses problems with automatic model selection that are echoed here. Another recommended book is *Clinical Prediction Models* by Steyerberg (2019).

Moreover, this book does not cover the breadth of methods now available for supervised learning or statistical learning. For the latter, the definitive text is *The Elements of Statistical Learning* by Hastie, Tibshirani, and Friedman (2009). Another useful text is *An Introduction to Statistical Learning* by James et al. (2021).

Finally, this book is not a substitute for the procedure documentation in *SAS/STAT User's Guide* and *SAS Visual Statistics: Procedures*. The documentation contains details of features, methods, and options that are not covered in this book. SAS documentation is available at https://support.sas.com/en/documentation.html.

Acknowledgments

During the writing of this book, I benefited extensively from technical reviews provided by SAS developers who are highly knowledgeable about different aspects of regression modeling. I thank Ralph Abbey, Weijie Cai, Fang Chen, Bob Derr, Bruce Elsheimer, Gordon Johnston, David Kessler, Michael Lamm, Warren Kuhfeld, Pushpal Mukhopadhyay, Ying So, Clay Thompson, Randy Tobias, Yingwei Wang, and Yonggang Yao.

I also received expert advice from SAS staff who work in the areas of Technical Support (Cyrus Bradford, Phil Gibbs, and David Schlotzhauer), the Output Delivery System (David Kelley and Dan O'Connor), and ODS Graphics (Dan Heath, Prashant Hebbar, and Lingxiao Li).

My thanks also go to Joseph Gardiner (Michigan State University), Aric LaBarr (North Carolina State University), Simon Sheather (University of Kentucky), Besa Smith (ICONplc and Analydata), and Tyler Smith (National University), who read the manuscript and sent me detailed comments that led to significant improvements.

Tim Arnold, Bob Derr, Warren Kuhfeld, and Ed Porter patiently answered questions about the LaTeX system with which I typeset the book. I am also grateful to Ed Huddleston, who meticulously formatted the references so that I could manage them with BibTeX, and to Jennifer Evans and Karissa Wrenn, who pointed me to online research tools that were indispensable.

I also extend thanks to Gary McDonald, who showed me the merits of ridge regression at a time when it had not yet gained acceptance; Richard Cutler, who taught me much about classification and regression trees; and Robert Cohen, who introduced me to model averaging and to parallel computing techniques that underpin the scalability of the procedures.

This book would not have come about without the guidance of Catherine Connolly, my editor at SAS Press, nor could it have been completed without the expertise of Suzanne Morgen, my copy editor.

It is a special pleasure to acknowledge assistance from three members of my family. My daughter-in-law Kayla provided technical advice for one of the examples. My daughter Susan, who is a champion of correct English usage, often pointed out how I could improve my writing. And my wife Sandra listened carefully whenever I mentioned a problem with the book and invariably helped me think about it in ways that proved useful.

Chapter 1
Introduction

Contents

This book is about SAS procedures that use algorithmic methods to build a variety of regression models for prediction. The following introduction explains the origins of the methods, the benefits of the procedures, and how to read the book.

Model Building at the Crossroads of Machine Learning and Statistics

The procedures in this book combine regression models from the field of statistics with predictive modeling methods from the field of machine learning. The two fields take very different approaches to model building:

- In machine learning, models are computational algorithms. Large amounts of data are used to train predictive models that can have hundreds of thousands of parameters. Models are assessed by how well they generalize—in other words, how well they predict new data not seen during training. The internal complexity of machine learning models cannot be grasped by the human mind but enables them to excel at prediction by capturing intricate relationships among myriad variables. Although these models lend themselves to automation, their reliability rests squarely on the quality of the data and the selection of model features.

- In statistics, models are assumptions about the process that generates the data. Statistical modeling relies on scientific and business knowledge to decide which variables and effects to include in the model. Statistical modeling employs algorithms to estimate model parameters, to determine how well the model agrees with the data, and to make inferences about the process. Unlike machine learning models, which attempt to capture reality in its entirety, statistical models are simplified descriptions of reality; this makes them valuable for understanding which variables affect the response. Furthermore, statistical models distinguish between signal and noise, and they quantify uncertainty in their results by incorporating a probability distribution for noise.

Statistical Learning: A Blend of Two Cultures

The approaches followed by statistics and machine learning remained far apart in practice until data mining drew them together in the 1990s. Companies in the retail, insurance, financial, and telecommunications sectors began using machine learning methods to find patterns in large customer and transactional databases. Concurrently, companies began using statistical models for regression and classification to predict outcomes and make business decisions. Banks, for example, adopted this combination of approaches for credit and market risk analysis, fraud detection, and gaining insights about customers.

In a 2001b paper written for statisticians, Leo Breiman at the University of California, Berkeley, referred to the statistical approach as the "data modeling culture" and the machine learning approach as the "algorithmic modeling culture." Over time, the paper convinced many statisticians that they too needed a broader set of methods to solve real world problems in settings where large amounts of data are available and the goal is prediction rather than inference.

Breiman's thinking predated the growth of business analytics and the advent of data science. Today, the methods for algorithmic modeling that he advocated—in particular, random forests—are widely accepted by statisticians and are standard tools for data scientists.

During the last 20 years, powerful new methods have emerged from the area of statistical learning, which combines the goals of statistical modeling with concepts from supervised and unsupervised learning (Hastie, Tibshirani, and Friedman 2009; James et al. 2021; Hastie, Tibshirani, and Wainwright 2015).

Overview of Procedures for Building Regression Models

The procedures in this book build the following regression models:

- standard regression models
- general linear models
- quantile regression models
- logistic regression models
- generalized linear models
- generalized additive models
- proportional hazards regression models
- tree models for classification and regression
- models based on multivariate adaptive regression splines

The procedures provide algorithmic methods for building predictive and explanatory regression models when there are many candidate predictors to choose from. These methods include the following:

- sequential selection methods such as forward and stepwise regression
- shrinkage methods such as the lasso
- dimension reduction methods such as principal components regression
- model averaging
- recursive partitioning for constructing tree models
- multivariate adaptive regression splines

Figure 1.1 is a high-level view of the procedures in this book categorized by the models they build. Each model is explained by a chapter in the book, and for most models there is a procedure in SAS 9 and a procedure in SAS Viya. For instance, Chapter 5 explains how to build general linear models with the GLMSELECT procedure in SAS 9 and the REGSELECT procedure in SAS Viya.

Figure 1.1 Procedures in SAS 9 and SAS Viya for Building Regression Models

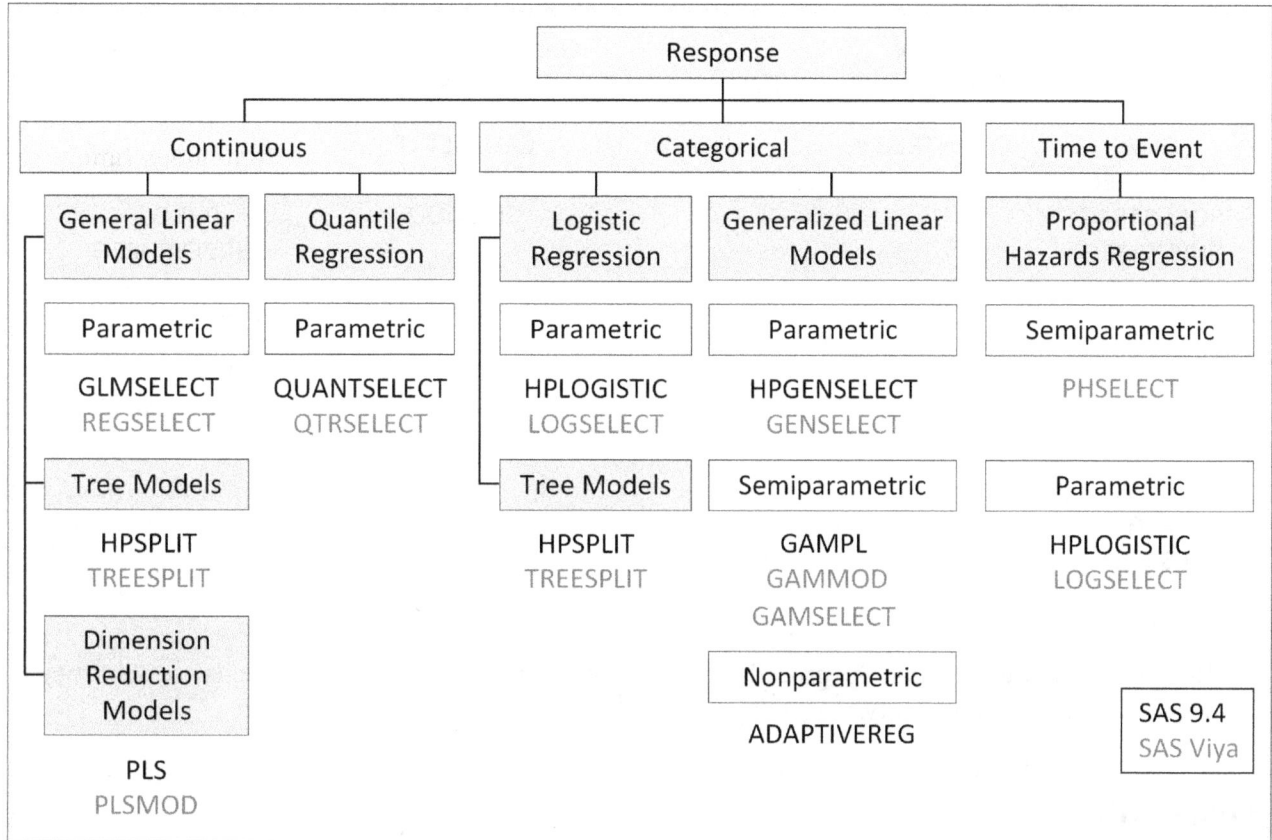

Practical Benefits

Both data scientists and statistical analysts will benefit from the models and procedures in this book:

- If you are a data scientist, you are undoubtedly familiar with linear regression and logistic regression as basic models for supervised learning. The specialized models presented here give you valuable alternatives for prediction. For instance, by applying quantile regression to customer lifetime value, you can predict the 10th, 50th, and 90th percentiles of the response, which can give you important insights about customer behavior.

- If you are a statistical analyst, you might be familiar with the SAS/STAT regression procedures in Figure 1.2 (not covered in this book), which fit models for statistical analysis. The model building procedures share various features with the statistical analysis procedures, which will help you get started with predictive modeling. For instance, if you have used the GENMOD procedure to analyze generalized linear models, you will encounter the same basic syntax in the HPGENSELECT procedure, which builds generalized linear models for prediction.

Figure 1.2 Procedures in SAS 9 for Statistical Analysis of Fitted Regression Models

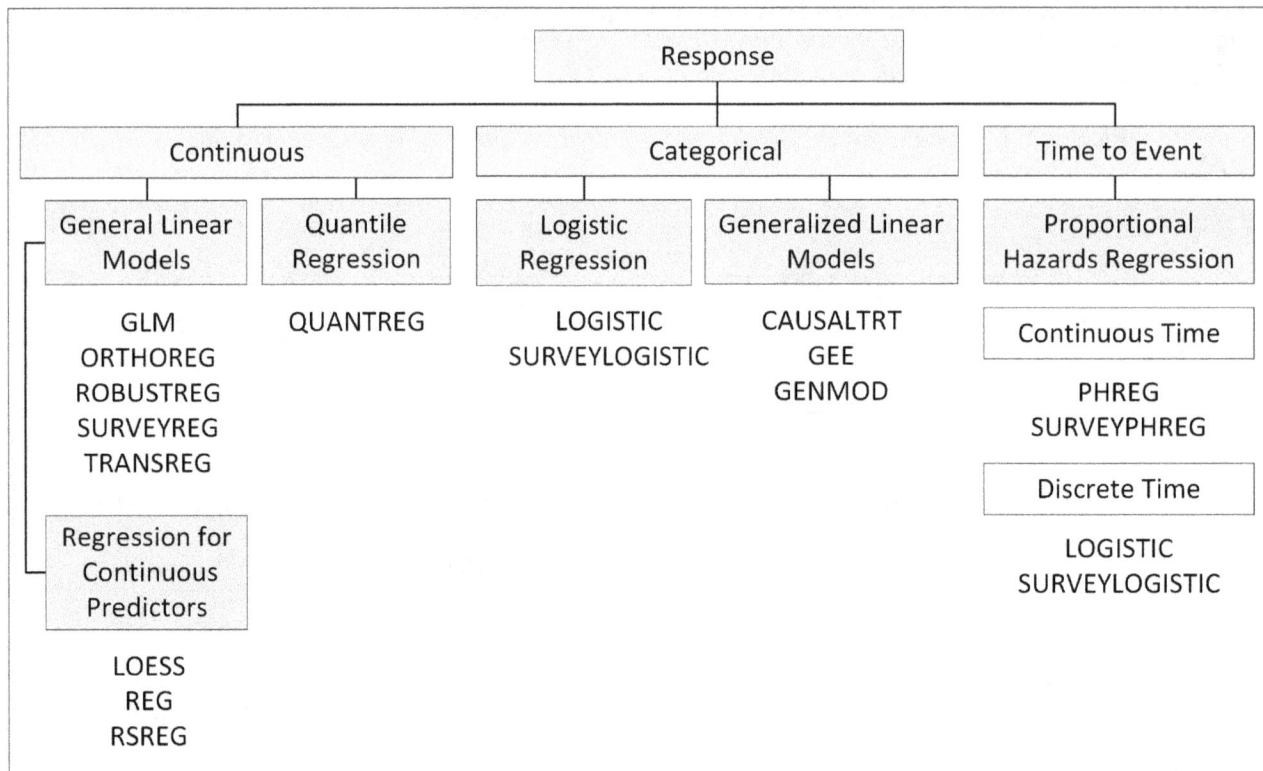

		Response		

Continuous		Categorical		Time to Event

General Linear Models	Quantile Regression	Logistic Regression	Generalized Linear Models	Proportional Hazards Regression
GLM ORTHOREG ROBUSTREG SURVEYREG TRANSREG	QUANTREG	LOGISTIC SURVEYLOGISTIC	CAUSALTRT GEE GENMOD	Continuous Time
				PHREG SURVEYPHREG
Regression for Continuous Predictors				Discrete Time
LOESS REG RSREG				LOGISTIC SURVEYLOGISTIC

Regardless of your training, the procedures in this book provide three major benefits: scalability, versatility, and interpretability.

Scalability

The procedures are designed to build models with large data; they provide high-performance computing on a single machine by exploiting all the available cores and threads. The procedures in SAS Viya can also run on a cluster of machines that distribute the data and the computations. With this much computational power, you can readily explore different combinations of models, model building methods, and selection criteria to determine which ones provide the best predictive performance for your work.

Versatility

With the procedures in this book, you can predict variables that are continuous, categorical, or the time to an event. Most of the procedures provide the following features:
- specification of candidate effects that can be continuous variables, categorical variables, classification effects, or spline effects
- a variety of parameterizations for classification levels
- assessment of prediction error based on validation, cross validation, and information criteria
- partitioning of data into training, validation, and testing roles
- tables and graphs for understanding the model building process
- facilities for saving the final model and scoring future data

Interpretability

All of the models in this book are interpretable. Most have a linear or additive structure that describes how the inputs are combined to predict the response. Parameter estimates and model summaries can yield valuable insights, especially when interpreted with the help of business or scientific knowledge. Other models—for instance, tree models—produce rules you can readily understand.

When Does Interpretability Matter?

The interpretability of a model is essential when it is used to make critical decisions. In the biopharmaceutical, insurance, and banking industries, interpretability is a regulatory requirement.

Interpretability is also essential for avoiding algorithmic bias, an ethical concern in any endeavor that relies on black box models—models whose internal working cannot be ascertained—to make life-changing decisions. There is growing evidence that black box models can be seriously biased.

One example, reported in *The Wall Street Journal*, is a complex algorithm deployed by a large hospital to identify patients with diabetes, heart disease, and other chronic conditions who could benefit from having health care workers monitor their status. A 2019 research study discovered the algorithm was giving priority to healthier white patients over sicker black patients because it used cost to rank patients. As it turned out, health care spending was less for black patients than it was for white patients with similar conditions (Evans and Mathews 2019; Obermeyer et al. 2019).

The COVID-19 pandemic accentuated the importance of interpretability. Predictive models for case counts and hospitalizations were at the forefront of medical efforts and policy making, and the reliability of these models was hotly debated in social media. Across the globe, there was an unprecedented need for models that could be understood by the general public (Stuart et al. 2020).

Can Interpretable Models Match the Accuracy of Black Box Models?

Although machine learning algorithms are only superficially understood by humans, they are often preferred over regression models because they can achieve higher predictive accuracy. Nonetheless, it is not unusual for evaluations of machine learning methods to conclude that the accuracy of logistic regression is comparable to that of support vector machines, neural nets, and random forests.

That was the finding of a recent study in *JAMA Neurology*, which compared algorithms for predicting the likelihood of freedom from seizure for patients after their first prescribed antiseizure medication (Chiang and Rao 2022; Hakeem et al. 2022). Likewise, an editorial in *Nature Medicine* concerning misuse of machine learning in clinical research recognized that it is unlikely to improve over statistical models in problems where the effects of strong predictors, chosen on the basis of prior research, are inherently linear (Volovici et al. 2022).

Cynthia Rudin, a prominent computer scientist at Duke University, and her colleagues have provided compelling examples to demonstrate that an interpretable model is not necessarily less accurate than a black box model (Rudin and Radin 2019; Rudin, Wang, and Coker 2020). They recommend against the use of black box models for high-stakes decisions unless no interpretable model with the same level of accuracy can be constructed. They conclude, "It is possible that an interpretable model can always be constructed—we just have not been trying" (Rudin and Radin 2019, p. 7).

Explanation Models

Rudin (2019) distinguishes between models (such as regression models) that are inherently interpretable and so-called explanation models used to elucidate black box models in machine learning. An explanation model can only approximate the original model (otherwise it would not be necessary), which raises the question of which model to trust. Reliance on two models that can disagree complicates the decision-making process. And even if an explanation model makes predictions that are identical to those of the black box model, the explanation that it offers could well be incorrect in the sense that it incorporates a different set of features in the data. This can occur, for instance, if the features happen to be correlated with those of the black box model. In fact, highly correlated variables are common in large databases.

Explanatory Models

The field of statistics uses the term *explanatory model*—not to be confused with explanation model!—for models that yield understanding about the process generating the data. The most valuable explanatory models are simple—they incorporate only the most relevant variables in the data, and they give you meaningful parameter estimates. On the other hand, the most valuable *predictive models* minimize prediction error when applied to future data, whether or not the parameter estimates have meaning. The two kinds of models are fundamentally different, and they require distinct approaches.

When Should You Use the Procedures in This Book?

You should use the procedures in this book when you are faced with many potential predictors and you need to build a regression model that not only generalizes well to future data but is also interpretable.

If interpretability is not a concern, you should also consider random forests, neural networks, gradient boosting, and other methods of supervised learning. These lie outside the scope of this book but are available in SAS Enterprise Miner, which runs in SAS 9, and SAS Visual Data Mining and Machine Learning, which runs in SAS Viya.

Comparison with Regression Procedures for Statistical Analysis

If you need to evaluate the statistical significance of effects in a regression model, you should not use the model building procedures because the p-values and confidence limits they compute are unadjusted for the process of model selection. Instead, you should use one of the many procedures available in SAS/STAT for statistical analysis of regression models whose effects are fully specified based on domain knowledge. Those procedures, listed in Figure 1.2, are not covered in this book.

Among the procedures for statistical analysis, the REG, LOGISTIC, and PHREG procedures provide limited features for effect selection. These features are superseded by modern model building capabilities available in the GLMSELECT, HPLOGISTIC, and PHSELECT procedures, respectively.

Table 1.1 compares regression procedures that build models with those that analyze models.

Table 1.1   Comparison of Regression Procedures for Model Building and Statistical Analysis

Characteristics	Procedures for Building Regression Models	Procedures for Fitting and Analyzing Regression Models
Goal	Prediction of future observations	Inference about model parameters
Model effects	Selected from candidates	Specified by analyst
Types of effects	Continuous, classification, polynomial, spline	Continuous, classification, polynomial, spline
Uses of training data	Estimation and model selection	Estimation
Parameter estimates	Subject to various types of bias	Unbiased if model is assumed to include true effects
p-values, confidence intervals	Unadjusted for model selection	Valid
Model fit diagnostics	No	Yes
Model validation methods	Yes	No
Model prediction	Applies to future data	Applies only to training data

How to Read This Book

The chapters of this book are organized into two parts:

- Part I is about building standard regression models and general linear models. It spans six chapters because so many methods are available for these models.

- Part II is about building specialized models. It provides a chapter for each type of model.

Part I begins by discussing concepts that play a role throughout the book. Chapter 2 explains the fundamentals of building predictive models, Chapter 3 explains issues associated with model building, and Chapter 4 explains methods for building generalized linear models.

Each of the subsequent chapters introduces the procedures that build a particular model. The chapter describes important characteristics of the model, summarizes essential procedure options, and presents examples that illustrate options and interpret the output. The examples are drawn from actual scenarios, but the data have been simplified to circumvent the many steps of data preparation that are inevitable in practice.

You can read the chapters independently of each other. However, if you are not familiar with model selection, you should start with Chapters 2, 3, and 4.

Two sets of appendices cover supplementary topics:

- Appendices in Part III cover algorithms and computational methods for readers who would like a deeper understanding of those aspects.

- Appendices in Part IV cover topics common to all of the procedures: methods for scoring data, coding schemes for categorical predictors, and the use of ODS graphics.

Programs, Data Sets, and Macros

Programs and data sets for the examples are available on the website for this book, which you can access at support.sas.com/rodriguez.

In a number of situations, the book fills gaps in procedure functionality by providing SAS macros which you can use in your own work. The macros are available on the book website.

Conventions

The book gives you many tips for running the procedures in your own programs. These are shown as follows:

Programming Tip: Suggestions in boxes like this one will save you time and work!

The SAS code for each example is presented in blocks consisting of statements that involve multiple steps and procedure options. In some situations, to focus attention on a critical option that might easily be overlooked, the option is highlighted as in the following example:

```
proc glmselect plots=coefficients data=Stores;
   class Region(param=reference ref='Midwest')
         Training(param=reference ref='None');
   model CloseRate = Region Training X1-X20 L1-L6 P1-P6 /
       selection=lasso( adaptive  choose=sbc stop=sbc showstepL1);
run;
```

Throughout the book, you will encounter road warning signs in the margins. These are placed to alert you to unavoidable problems, common misunderstandings, and potential tripping points. When you see these signs, slow down and read carefully!

Part I

General Linear Models

Chapter 2
Building General Linear Models: Concepts

Contents

This chapter explains the concepts behind methods available in the GLMSELECT and related procedures for building general linear models. As explained in Chapter 4, these methods build predictive models from candidate predictors (features) in observational data.

For each method, the procedures provide tuning options that determine the predictive ability of the final model. Because no one combination of methods and options works well in every situation, the concepts explained here will help you decide which combinations to apply in your work.

If you have used the GLM procedure to analyze general linear models, you have encountered a number of concepts related to statistical inference: normally distributed errors, unbiasedness and minimum variance of least squares estimates, measures for goodness of fit, analysis of variance, and degrees of freedom. Analysis of this type provides results about the model parameters—in particular, estimates, confidence intervals, and hypothesis tests—and quantifies the uncertainty in the results.

A much different cast of concepts takes the stage when your goal is prediction rather than inference and you use algorithmic methods to select the effects in the model. Goodness of fit no longer plays a leading role; in fact, overfitting the training data is avoided because it does not produce models that generalize well to unseen data. Biased parameter estimation now plays a positive role; by allowing small amounts of bias, penalized least squares methods provide benefits such as stable regression coefficients and parsimonious models. Moreover, prediction error cannot be minimized without a tradeoff between prediction bias and prediction variance. Tuning a method to minimize prediction error involves even more concepts, some drawn from machine learning and some with deep theoretical roots in the field of statistics.

You will find it helpful to refer back to this chapter when you need to learn more about concepts mentioned in subsequent chapters. A number of topics covered here apply not only to procedures for building general linear models, but also to procedures for building other classes of models presented in Part II of this book.

Example: Predicting Network Activity

The following example illustrates several conceptual issues that arise when you build a regression model for the purpose of prediction.

The cybersecurity analytics division at a large corporation uses predictive models for network activity to identify unusual changes in traffic. A plot of activity measurements taken during a particular time period, shown in Figure 2.1, reveals an increasing trend with a number of up-and-down variations. Some of these are expected in the normal behavior of the network, while others could be due to noise.

Figure 2.1 Regression Models for Network Activity

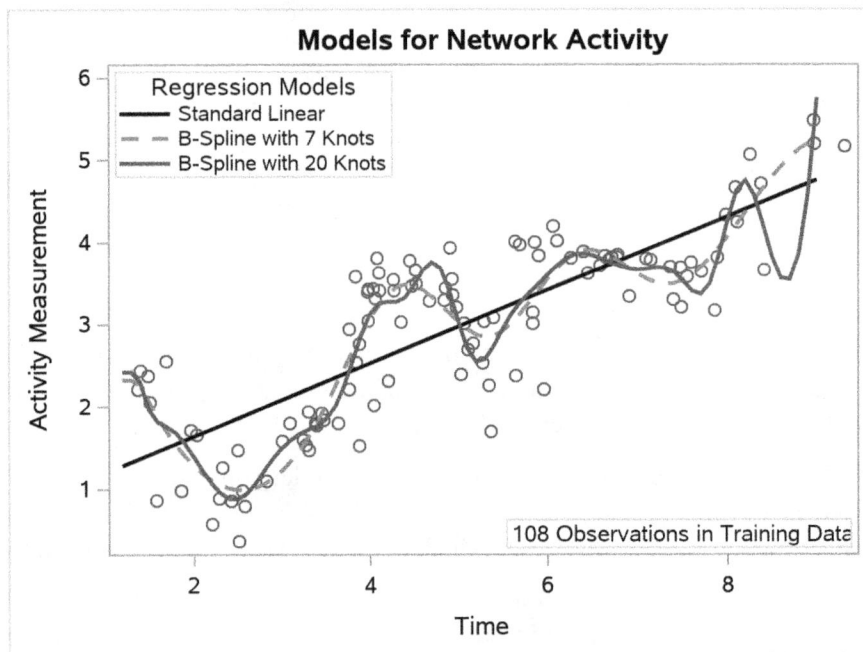

Analysts used the data to train three different regression models[†] for network activity:

- a standard linear regression model with time as the predictor variable
- a model that expresses time as a spline effect with 7 knots
- a model that expresses time as a spline effect with 20 knots

All three models are linear smoothers that accommodate the up-and-down variation with different degrees of flexibility. The question is, which model has the best predictive ability?

The standard regression model is the smoothest of the three. It is insensitive to small changes in the data that would result from measuring activity during other time periods with similar characteristics,

---

[†]The GLMSELECT procedure was used to fit all three models. The SAS program for this example is available on the website for this book, which you can access at support.sas.com/rodriguez. Appendix F, "Spline Methods," explains the terminology of splines and how you can incorporate spline effects when building regression models with the procedures in this book.

and so it has the lowest variance of the three models. On the other hand, it has the highest bias because it does not approximate any of the local variation in the data.

Compared with the standard regression model, the two spline models have higher variance but lower bias. They do a much better job of fitting the training data, as indicated by their R^2 measures.

Output 2.1 Assessment of Model Fit

Model Fit with Training Data (108 Observations)

Model	R-square
Standard Linear	0.64003
B-Spline with 7 Knots	0.83438
B-Spline with 20 Knots	0.85643

It is tempting to conclude that the 20-knot model is the best predictive model because it minimizes the error in predicting activity in the training data. This error, which is sometimes called resubstitution error, is biased downward because it is computed from the same data that were used to train the model. Compared with the 7-knot model, the 20-knot model might be accommodating more noise than signal.

Ideally, you should assess predictive performance with independent test data not involved in training the model. As it happens, such data are available and were used to compute the mean squared prediction error (MSPE) for each model. The 7-knot model has the lowest prediction error (0.30752), as shown in Output 2.2.

Output 2.2 Assessment of Model Performance

Model Performance with Test Data (98 Observations)

Model	MSE Prediction
Standard Linear	0.48022
B-Spline with 7 Knots	0.30752
B-Spline with 20 Knots	0.38791

Essential Aspects of Regression Model Building

Although the preceding example involves only one predictor variable, it demonstrates three essential aspects of building a regression model from a large number of candidate predictors.

First, regression models are approximations to reality. None of the models in this example are correct or true; instead, they have different levels of predictive ability that could be improved by including additional variables and applying different algorithms. The expression "true model" has meaning in mathematical assumptions and simulation studies, but it is an oxymoron in the context of model building because regression models are simplifications of reality, as discussed by Burnham and Anderson (2002, Sec. 1.2.5).

Second, building a good predictive model involves making a reasonable tradeoff between low bias and low variance, as achieved by the 7-knot model in this example. Models with low bias, such as the 20-knot model, can closely approximate the training data, but they are more apt to accommodate noise along with actual effects, and this can undermine their ability to make accurate predictions with new data. Models with low variance, such as the standard regression model, are limited in the number of effects they can include, which can hamper their predictive ability, but they require relatively less data for parameter estimation. Table 2.1 summarizes the differences between models with low bias and models with low variance.

Table 2.1 Comparison of Regression Models

Models with Low Bias	Models with Low Variance
Provide flexibility for fitting data	Provide simplicity for interpretation
Contain more effects	Contain fewer effects
Have more degrees of freedom	Have fewer degrees of freedom
Require more observations to estimate	Require fewer observations to estimate
Tend to overfit noise in the data	Tend to underfit signal in the data
Risk including spurious effects	Risk omitting useful effects

Third, selecting a good predictive model requires a valid measure of predictive performance. In this example, the measure is the mean square prediction error computed from test data, but in practice there is seldom enough data for both training and testing, and so alternative approaches are needed.

These and other aspects of regression model building have been studied for 60 years. In 1976, Ronald Hocking, a statistician at Mississippi State University, reviewed the methods for variable selection that were available at that time. His paper, which is still worth reading, spanned 49 pages and listed 170 references (Hocking 1976). Today, such a survey would be a herculean task because so many more models and algorithms are available.

Notation and Terminology for General Linear Models

The general linear model for a continuous response variable $\mathbf{y}$ is

$$\mathbf{y} = \beta_0 + \beta_1 \mathbf{x}_1 + \cdots + \beta_p \mathbf{x}_p + \boldsymbol{\epsilon}$$

where $\mathbf{x}_1, \ldots, \mathbf{x}_p$ are the predictors, $\beta_0, \beta_1, \ldots, \beta_p$ are the model parameters, and $\boldsymbol{\epsilon}$ is an error term. The corresponding model for the value of $\mathbf{y}$ in the ith observation of the data is

$$y_i = \beta_0 + \beta_1 x_{i1} + \cdots + \beta_p x_{ip} + \epsilon_i, \quad i = 1, \ldots, n$$

where the x_{ij} denotes the values of $\mathbf{x}_1, \ldots, \mathbf{x}_p$, and the errors ϵ_i are assumed to be independent with a mean of 0 and a constant variance σ^2. When prediction rather than inference is the goal, it is not necessary to assume that the errors are normally distributed.

Throughout this book, n denotes the number of observations and p denotes the number of predictors $\mathbf{x}_1, \ldots, \mathbf{x}_p$ in a general linear model and in classes of models, such as generalized linear models, that involve a linear predictor. Including β_0, which is called the intercept parameter, the total number of parameters is $p + 1$.

The conditional expectation or average of $\mathbf{y}$ at a point $(\mathbf{x}_1, \ldots, \mathbf{x}_p)$ is

$$E(\mathbf{y} \mid \mathbf{x}_1, \ldots, \mathbf{x}_p) = \beta_0 + \beta_1 \mathbf{x}_1 + \cdots + \beta_p \mathbf{x}_p$$

A general linear model expresses the deviation of $\mathbf{y}$ from its conditional expectation:

$$\mathbf{y} = E(y \mid \mathbf{x}_1, \ldots, \mathbf{x}_p) + \epsilon$$

The conditional expectation is better known as the regression function, and the parameters $\beta_1, \ldots, \beta_p$ are referred to as the regression coefficients.

The conditional expectation provides the best pointwise prediction of $\mathbf{y}$ in the sense that it minimizes the expected squared error loss function of the prediction error:

$$E(\mathbf{y} \mid \mathbf{x}_1, \ldots, \mathbf{x}_p) = \underset{c}{\operatorname{argmin}} \; E([\, \mathbf{y} - c \,]^2 \mid \mathbf{x}_1, \ldots, \mathbf{x}_p)$$

The concept of a loss function occurs throughout statistics and supervised learning, where it serves to penalize estimation error and prediction error. Different loss functions are associated with the various classes of models in this book. The squared error loss function is closely associated with general linear models. In statistical analysis, it underlies the method of least squares, which was introduced by Carl Friedrich Gauss and Adrien-Marie Legendre over two centuries ago (Stigler 1981), and it is the optimization criterion for least squares estimation of the parameters.

Modeling Nonlinearity

There is a misconception that linear models apply only when the relationship between the predictors and the response is linear. In fact, the linearity of a general linear model is *in the parameters* rather than the predictors. For example, each of the following is a linear model:

$$y_i = \beta_0 + \beta_1 x_{i1} + \beta_2 x_{i2} + \epsilon_i$$
$$y_i = \beta_0 + \beta_1 x_{i1} + \beta_2 x_{i2} + \beta_3 x_{i3} + \epsilon_i \quad \text{where } x_{i3} = x_{i1} x_{i2}$$
$$y_i = \beta_0 + \beta_4 x_{i4} + \beta_5 x_{i5} + \epsilon_i \qquad \text{where } x_{i4} = \log(x_{i1}), \; x_{i5} = x_{i2}^2$$

These examples show that you can model nonlinear relationships by including predictors that are nonlinear transformations of other predictors. The example on page 12 shows that you can also model nonlinear relationships with spline effects. As explained in Appendix F, a spline effect is represented by a set of predictors, $\mathbf{x}_{j_1}, \mathbf{x}_{j_2}, \ldots, \mathbf{x}_{j_q}$, and a corresponding set of coefficients, $\beta_{j_1}, \beta_{j_2}, \ldots, \beta_{j_q}$.

Interpreting the Parameters

When you fit a general linear model that is fully specified and your data come from a planned study such as a designed experiment or a randomized clinical trial, the predictors are typically orthogonal—they vary independently of each other—because their levels have been assigned by the experimenter, and they systematically represent the x-space for the population or process that you are studying. Because of the orthogonality, you can interpret the parameter β_j as the average increase in y associated with a unit increase in the predictor $\mathbf{x}_j$ when all of the other predictors are held constant.

This interpretation does not apply if you fit a model with data from an observational study because the variables will almost always exhibit some correlation. Their values will be random rather than fixed, and they will not necessarily represent the entire x-space. And if you select the model algorithmically, the size of β_j and even its sign can change during the process of selection, depending on which other predictors happen to be in the model at a particular step. As a consequence, β_j cannot be compared across models.

Effects in a General Linear Model

General linear models provide much greater versatility than standard linear regression models. The predictors $x_1, \ldots, x_p$ in standard regression are typically data variables that are numeric and continuous, but they can also represent transformations of these variables, such as log and power transformations. In addition, the predictors in general linear models can represent classification effects, interaction effects, and constructed effects (such as spline effects) formed from data variables. The effects of data variables are referred to as main effects because they affect the response directly and independently of each other. Other types of effects extend the ways in which the variables affect the response.

This distinction between standard regression models and general linear models is not universal. Some books consider classification effects together with continuous variables as predictors in regression models. In SAS, the inclusion of classification effects is part of the definition of a general linear model, whether or not they are used in interactions or other effects.

Keep in mind that the number of predictors is greater than or equal to the number of effects. For instance, the main effect of a continuous variable is represented by a single predictor, but the spline effect of a continuous variable is represented by multiple predictors, depending on the number of knots. On the other hand, if (say) reference cell coding is used, the main effect of a classification variable with m levels is represented by $m - 1$ predictors (see Appendix I). The interaction effect of two classification variables, one with m_1 levels and one with m_2 levels, is represented by $(m_1 - 1)(m_2 - 1)$ predictors.

Parameter Estimation

The methods for building a general linear model presented in Part I of this book estimate the model parameters using ordinary least squares and penalized least squares. In order to understand these two approaches, it helps to express the model in matrix form:

$$\mathbf{y}_{n \times 1} = \beta_0 \mathbf{1} + \beta_1 \mathbf{x}_1 + \cdots + \beta_p \mathbf{x}_p + \boldsymbol{\epsilon} = \mathbf{X}_{n \times (p+1)} \boldsymbol{\beta}_{(p+1) \times 1} + \boldsymbol{\epsilon}_{n \times 1}$$

Here $\boldsymbol{\beta}$ is the parameter vector $(\beta_0, \beta_1, \ldots, \beta_p)'$, and $\mathbf{X}$ is the matrix $[\mathbf{1} \; \mathbf{x}_1 \cdots \mathbf{x}_p]$. The vector $\mathbf{1}$, which consists of 1's and corresponds to the intercept term, together with the p predictors constitute the columns of the model matrix $\mathbf{X}$. The model matrix is also referred to as the design matrix, even when the values of the predictors are random rather than assigned.

The ordinary least squares (OLS) estimator of $\boldsymbol{\beta}$ minimizes the sum of squared differences between the observed and predicted values of the response:

$$\hat{\boldsymbol{\beta}}_{\text{OLS}} = \operatorname*{argmin}_{\beta_0, \ldots, \beta_p} \sum_{i=1}^{n} (y_i - \beta_0 - \sum_{j=1}^{p} x_{ij} \beta_j)^2 = \operatorname*{argmin}_{\boldsymbol{\beta}} \| \mathbf{y} - \mathbf{X} \boldsymbol{\beta} \|_2^2$$

Here $\| \mathbf{y} - \mathbf{X} \boldsymbol{\beta} \|_2$ denotes the ℓ_2 norm of $\mathbf{y} - \mathbf{X} \boldsymbol{\beta}$. The ℓ_2 (Euclidean) norm of a vector $\mathbf{z} = (z_1, \ldots, z_m)'$ is defined as

$$\| \mathbf{z} \|_2 = (\mathbf{z}'\mathbf{z})^{\frac{1}{2}} = \left(\sum_{i=1}^{m} z_i^2 \right)^{\frac{1}{2}}$$

The least squares minimization problem has a unique solution assuming that $\mathbf{X}$ is of full rank, which means that its columns are linearly independent. The predictors can be correlated—which is inevitable with observational data—but not to the extent that any one predictor is a linear function of the others. In other words, there can be no redundancy in the information contributed by the predictors. The OLS estimator can then be written as

$$\hat{\boldsymbol{\beta}}_{\text{OLS}} = (\mathbf{X}'\mathbf{X})^{-1}\mathbf{X}'\mathbf{y}$$

This expression is convenient for theoretical purposes, but it is not a recipe for computing $\hat{\boldsymbol{\beta}}_{\text{OLS}}$ because inverting $\mathbf{X}'\mathbf{X}$ is notoriously inefficient and inaccurate. In practice, $\hat{\boldsymbol{\beta}}_{\text{OLS}}$ is computed by solving the system of normal equations

$$\mathbf{X}'\mathbf{X}\boldsymbol{\beta} = \mathbf{X}'\mathbf{y}$$

that results from taking the derivative of $\|\mathbf{y} - \mathbf{X}\boldsymbol{\beta}\|^2$ with respect to $\boldsymbol{\beta}$ and setting it to zero. Appendix A describes numerical algorithms commonly used to solve the system, including the sweep algorithm implemented by procedures in Part I of this book.

The estimate $\hat{\beta}_j$, known as the partial regression coefficient for $\mathbf{x}_j$, represents the additional contribution of $\mathbf{x}_j$ to the response after $\mathbf{x}_j$ has been adjusted for the other predictors. As explained in Appendix A, the adjustment allows for correlation in the predictors, which is inevitable with observational data.

When you specify the model prior to estimation and it includes all of the true effects, $\hat{\boldsymbol{\beta}}_{\text{OLS}}$ is unbiased (its expectation $E(\hat{\boldsymbol{\beta}}_{\text{OLS}})$ is equal to $\boldsymbol{\beta}$), and its variance matrix is

$$\text{Var}(\hat{\boldsymbol{\beta}}_{\text{OLS}}) \stackrel{\text{def}}{=} E\left[(\hat{\boldsymbol{\beta}}_{\text{OLS}} - \boldsymbol{\beta})'(\hat{\boldsymbol{\beta}}_{\text{OLS}} - \boldsymbol{\beta})\right] = (\mathbf{X}'\mathbf{X})^{-1}\sigma^2$$

The diagonal elements of $\text{Var}(\hat{\boldsymbol{\beta}}_{\text{OLS}})$ are the variances of the coefficient estimates $\hat{\beta}_j$. However, when you select the model algorithmically, $\hat{\boldsymbol{\beta}}_{\text{OLS}}$ is subject to various types of bias; see page 35.

The Hat Matrix

Given the least squares estimator $\hat{\boldsymbol{\beta}}_{\text{OLS}}$, the predicted response is

$$\hat{\mathbf{y}} = \mathbf{X}\hat{\boldsymbol{\beta}}_{\text{OLS}} = \mathbf{P}\mathbf{y}$$

where $\mathbf{P} = \mathbf{X}(\mathbf{X}'\mathbf{X})^{-1}\mathbf{X}'$. The matrix $\mathbf{P}$ is called the hat matrix because it transforms $\mathbf{y}$ to $\hat{\mathbf{y}}$. Appendix B illustrates the geometry of the transformation, which is referred to as a projection in linear algebra.

The hat matrix is helpful for exploring models. The ith diagonal element of $\mathbf{P}$ (denoted by $\mathbf{P}_{ii}$) is related to the distance of the ith row of $\mathbf{X}$ from the center of the $\mathbf{X}$-space. Larger values of $\mathbf{P}_{ii}$ correspond to data points that are farther from the center.

The diagonal elements appear in the definitions of influence statistics, such as Cook's D and DFFITS, which are covered in standard courses on regression and are available with the REG procedure. Although influence statistics are not discussed in this book, the *sum* of $\mathbf{P}_{11}, \mathbf{P}_{22}, \ldots, \mathbf{P}_{nn}$ (called the trace of $\mathbf{P}$) plays a role as a measure of model flexibility; see page 22.

Residuals

The vector of residual values can be expressed in terms of $\mathbf{P}$ as

$$\mathbf{r} = (y_1 - \hat{y}_1, y_2 - \hat{y}_2, \dots, y_n - \hat{y}_n)' = \mathbf{y} - \hat{\mathbf{y}} = \mathbf{y} - \mathbf{P}\mathbf{y} = (\mathbf{I} - \mathbf{P})\,\mathbf{y}$$

where $\mathbf{I}$ denotes the identity matrix. Using basic linear algebra, Appendix B explains that $\mathbf{r}$ is orthogonal (perpendicular) to $\hat{\mathbf{y}}$. This implies that the residuals corresponding to a particular set of predictors contain no information that can further improve the model fit as measured by the error sum of squares or the R-square statistic (see page 25).

On the other hand, the residuals contain information that will improve the fit if the model is augmented with a new predictor that is not a linear function of the original predictors. The residuals for the augmented model can be used to incorporate yet another predictor, and so on. This is essentially how models are built by forward selection, which is one of the methods discussed in Chapter 4.

When you fit a specified model, the orthogonality of $\mathbf{r}$ and $\hat{\mathbf{y}}$ makes it possible for you to assess the fit and identify outliers by examining the residuals. If you plot the residuals against the predictors, you can also identify transformations of the predictors, such as splines, that improve the fit by contributing additional columns to $\mathbf{X}$. You can request residual plots with the REG procedure; they are not provided by other model building procedures discussed in this book because they are not practical with large numbers of observations.

Limitations of Ordinary Least Squares Estimation

Least squares estimates of $\beta_1, \dots, \beta_p$ obtained with data for which n is much greater than p—described as tall data—typically have low variances. Models trained by using such estimates can have good predictive accuracy. On the other hand, when n is only slightly greater than p, or when there is collinearity in the columns of the model matrix, least squares estimates can have high variances and result in poor prediction.

Data for which p is much greater than n are called wide or high dimensional. They occur in biomarker studies where expressions of tens of thousands of genes are measured on hundreds of patient samples. When p is greater than n, the least squares estimator is not unique; in fact, the least squares minimization problem has infinitely many solutions. When p is less than n and the predictors are collinear (see page 85) or if p is only slightly less than n, the least squares estimator is not stable.

Penalized Least Squares Estimation

The limitations of OLS regression can be overcome by alternatives, such as ridge regression and the lasso, that penalize or constrain the regression coefficients. Penalization reduces the flexibility of a model—but it does so in ways that are beneficial.

Ridge regression estimates β by adding an ℓ_2 penalty to the sum of squares:

$$\hat{\beta}_{\text{ridge}} = \underset{\beta}{\operatorname{argmin}}\{\,\|\,\mathbf{y} - \mathbf{X}\beta\,\|_2^2 + k\|\beta\|_2^2\,\} = \underset{\beta}{\operatorname{argmin}}\left\{\sum_{i=1}^{n}(y_i - \mathbf{x}_i'\beta)^2 + k\sum_{j=1}^{p}\beta_j^2\right\}, \quad k > 0$$

The lasso estimates $\boldsymbol{\beta}$ by adding an ℓ_1 penalty to the sum of squares:

$$\hat{\boldsymbol{\beta}}_{\text{lasso}} = \underset{\boldsymbol{\beta}}{\text{argmin}}\{ \| \mathbf{y} - \mathbf{X}\boldsymbol{\beta} \|_2^2 + \lambda \| \boldsymbol{\beta} \|_1 \}, \quad \lambda \geq 0$$

where $\|\boldsymbol{\beta}\|_1$ denotes the ℓ_1 (absolute value) norm of $\boldsymbol{\beta}$. The ℓ_1 norm of a vector $\mathbf{z} = (z_1, \ldots, z_m)'$ is defined as

$$\| \mathbf{z} \|_1 = \sum_{i=1}^{m} |z_i|$$

The penalty is called a regularizer, and the tuning parameters k and λ control the amount of the penalty. Regularization, also known as penalization, is a fundamental concept in supervised and unsupervised learning. In regression models, penalized estimators exchange small amounts of bias in $\hat{\boldsymbol{\beta}}$ for improvements in predictive accuracy that outweigh the bias. Penalization also contributes to interpretability.

Ridge regression shrinks the estimates $\hat{\beta}_1, \ldots, \hat{\beta}_p$ toward zero relative to the OLS estimates, which stabilizes the estimates and makes them more interpretable when there is collinearity; see page 98. The lasso also shrinks $\hat{\beta}_1, \ldots, \hat{\beta}_p$ toward zero, but in a different way. Furthermore, by setting some of the estimates to zero, the lasso acts as a model selection method and produces models that are sparse; see page 42. Sparseness is especially helpful when working with a large number of predictors, and an advantage of the lasso is that it can be applied with high-dimensional data.

Maximum Likelihood Estimation

When the parameter estimates for a general linear model are obtained by ordinary least squares estimation or penalized least squares estimation, it is not necessary to assume the responses are normally distributed. Normality is assumed when the model is used for statistical analysis. That type of analysis, performed by the GLM procedure, lies outside the scope of this book.

Logistic regression models, generalized linear models, and generalized additive models—discussed in Part II of this book—always assume a parametric distribution for the response. For instance, binary logistic models assume a binary distribution or a binomial distribution. The parameter estimates for these models are obtained by maximum likelihood estimation, and so a brief description of this approach is given here.

Maximum likelihood estimation, introduced by Ronald Fisher[†] beginning in 1912, is one of the most influential methods in the field of statistics. Likelihood-based inference can be viewed as a compromise between Bayesian and frequentist approaches, as pointed out by Bradley Efron in a 1998 paper based on his R. A. Fisher Lecture at the 1996 Joint Statistical Meetings.

[†]Fisher made numerous fundamental contributions to theoretical and applied statistics, including regression analysis, design of experiments, multivariate analysis, nonparametric analysis, and multivariate analysis. In addition to maximum likelihood, he named concepts such as parameter, statistic, variance, information, efficiency, and optimality that are entrenched in the vocabulary of 21st century statistics (Pawitan 2001, p. 17). Leonard Savage noted in his 1970 R. A. Fisher Lecture that it is easier to list the few areas of statistics in which Fisher took no interest than those in which he did (Savage 1976, p. 449).

Suppose that $\mathbf{y} = (y_1, y_2, \ldots, y_n)'$ is a sample of n independent univariate observations with a parametric density function $f_{\boldsymbol{\theta}}(y)$, where $\boldsymbol{\theta}$ denotes an unknown parameter. As a function of $\boldsymbol{\theta}$,

$$L(\boldsymbol{\theta}; y) \equiv f_{\boldsymbol{\theta}}(y)$$

is called the likelihood function.

Because the observations are independent, the likelihood function for the sample is

$$L(\boldsymbol{\theta}; \mathbf{y}) = \prod_{i=1}^{n} f_{\boldsymbol{\theta}}(y_i)$$

In practice, it is simpler to work with the log-likelihood function:

$$\mathcal{L}(\boldsymbol{\theta}; \mathbf{y}) \equiv \sum_{i=1}^{n} \log(f_{\boldsymbol{\theta}}(y_i))$$

The maximum likelihood estimator (MLE) of $\boldsymbol{\theta}$ is

$$\hat{\boldsymbol{\theta}}_{\mathrm{MLE}} = \underset{\boldsymbol{\theta}}{\mathrm{argmax}}\{\mathcal{L}(\boldsymbol{\theta}; \mathbf{y})\}$$

This is the value of $\boldsymbol{\theta}$ for which the observed data have the highest probability of occurrence under the assumed model.

For many regression models, the shape of $\mathcal{L}(\boldsymbol{\theta}; \mathbf{y})$ is concave in $\boldsymbol{\theta}$, and $\hat{\boldsymbol{\theta}}_{\mathrm{MLE}}$ can be obtained by finding the derivative of $\mathcal{L}(\boldsymbol{\theta}; \mathbf{y})$ with respect to $\boldsymbol{\theta}$, setting it to 0, and solving for $\boldsymbol{\theta}$. The derivative is called the score function.

For example, consider a general linear model $\mathbf{y} = \mathbf{X}\boldsymbol{\beta} + \boldsymbol{\epsilon}$, for which $\epsilon_1, \ldots, \epsilon_n$ are independent and normally distributed with an unknown variance σ^2. The log-likelihood function is

$$\mathcal{L}(\boldsymbol{\beta}, \sigma^2; \mathbf{y}) = \frac{-n \log(2\pi\sigma^2)}{2} - \frac{1}{2\sigma^2} \sum_{i=1}^{n} (y_i - \mathbf{x}_i'\boldsymbol{\beta})^2 = \frac{-n \log(2\pi\sigma^2)}{2} - \frac{1}{2\sigma^2} \| \mathbf{y} - \mathbf{X}\boldsymbol{\beta} \|_2^2$$

where $\mathbf{x}_i'$ is the ith row of $\mathbf{X}$. Taking derivatives with respect to $\boldsymbol{\beta}$ and σ^2 and setting them to zero leads to explicit solutions for the maximum likelihood estimators:

$$\hat{\boldsymbol{\beta}}_{\mathrm{MLE}} = (\mathbf{X}'\mathbf{X})^{-1}\mathbf{X}'\mathbf{y}$$

$$\widehat{\sigma^2}_{\mathrm{MLE}} = \frac{1}{n}\sum_{i=1}^{n}(y_i - \mathbf{x}_i'\hat{\boldsymbol{\beta}})^2 = \frac{1}{n}\| \mathbf{y} - \mathbf{X}\hat{\boldsymbol{\beta}}_{\mathrm{MLE}} \|_2^2$$

Here, $\hat{\boldsymbol{\beta}}_{\mathrm{MLE}}$ happens to be identical to $\hat{\boldsymbol{\beta}}_{\mathrm{OLS}}$, and the MLE of σ^2 is the average squared error.

For generalized linear models, MLEs must be computed numerically by applying algorithms that are described in Appendix D. For generalized additive models, the computation of MLEs and penalized MLEs requires more highly specialized algorithms that are described in Appendix G.

Regardless of the estimation method, building a good predictive model involves a tradeoff between the bias and the variance of the prediction, and it requires ways to assess and minimize predictive error. These topics are discussed in the sections that follow.

The Bias-Variance Tradeoff for Prediction

The mean squared prediction error (MSPE) of a general linear model for a future response y^* at an input $\mathbf{x}^* = (x_1^*, \ldots, x_p^*)'$ is

$$\text{MSPE} = E[(y^* - \hat{y}^*)^2] = E[(y^* - \mathbf{x}^{*\prime}\hat{\boldsymbol{\beta}})^2]$$

Also known as generalization error, MSPE is a simplified version of the expected mean squared prediction error for a test sample.

Suppose that for any observation, the true relationship between the response y and the predictor $\mathbf{x}$ is $y = f(\mathbf{x}) + \epsilon$, where f is an unknown function and ϵ is a random error with expectation 0 and variance σ^2. For simplicity, assume $\hat{\boldsymbol{\beta}}$ is a least squares estimate of $\boldsymbol{\beta}$ obtained from a fully specified model with design matrix $\mathbf{X}$, and assume $\epsilon^* = y^* - \hat{y}^*$ has the same distribution as ϵ. Since $\hat{\boldsymbol{\beta}}$ is unbiased, MSPE can be decomposed into three terms:

$$\text{MSPE} = E[(f(\mathbf{x}^*) + \epsilon^* - \mathbf{x}^{*\prime}\hat{\boldsymbol{\beta}})^2] = E[(f(\mathbf{x}^*) - \mathbf{x}^{*\prime}\boldsymbol{\beta} + \mathbf{x}^{*\prime}(\boldsymbol{\beta} - \hat{\boldsymbol{\beta}}) + \epsilon^*)^2]$$

$$= E(f(\mathbf{x}^*) - \mathbf{x}^{*\prime}\boldsymbol{\beta})^2 + \mathbf{x}^{*\prime}\text{Var}(\hat{\boldsymbol{\beta}})\mathbf{x}^* + \text{Var}(\epsilon^*)$$

$$= \underbrace{(f(\mathbf{x}^*) - \mathbf{x}^{*\prime}\boldsymbol{\beta})^2}_{\text{Squared Prediction Bias}} + \underbrace{\mathbf{x}^{*\prime}(\mathbf{X}'\mathbf{X})^{-1}\mathbf{x}^*\sigma^2}_{\text{Prediction Variance}} + \underbrace{\sigma^2}_{\text{Irreducible Variance}}$$

To understand the meaning of the first two terms, imagine that multiple data sets are generated by the same process, and multiple predictions for y^* are obtained by training the same model with these data sets. Prediction bias measures how closely the average of the predictions $\hat{y}^*$ approximates $f(\mathbf{x})$. Prediction variance measures the dispersion of the predictions from their average.

Unlike the third term (σ^2), which is fixed, the expressions for the first two terms involve the model matrix $\mathbf{X}$ and the parameter $\boldsymbol{\beta}$, and so they depend on the form of the model. Since the first two terms are positive, the only way to minimize MSPE is by finding a model that reduces prediction bias and prediction variance. As it turns out, these terms operate like the seats on a children's seesaw; when one goes down, the other goes up.

You can reduce prediction bias by including more effects with predictive value in the model—in other words, by increasing the number of predictors p. For instance, if f is highly nonlinear, a model with spline effects will have less bias than a model with only main effects, which will underfit f (recall the network data example on page 12). However, the prediction variance of the spline model will be greater than that of the main effects model. In general, the prediction variance will increase as more effects are included, *regardless of whether they contribute predictive value*. For any general linear model, if the parameters are estimated using least squares, the prediction variance will increase monotonically with p, assuming a fixed number of observations n (Miller 2002, pp. 4–5).

Instead of building a general linear model, you could reduce bias with a more complex model built with a different method of supervised learning. However, you would not avoid the seesaw behavior. Highly complex models have low prediction bias because they allow more flexibility for fitting features of f, but they tend to accommodate noise and overfit the training data. Simpler, more restricted models have lower prediction variance, but they tend to underfit f. Both of these tendencies can inflate MSPE, and so the question becomes how to make the right tradeoff between prediction bias and prediction variance—in other words, how to balance the seesaw.

Estimation bias in $\hat{\beta}$ is usually undesirable when the goal is statistical inference. On the other hand, when the goal is good predictive performance, a small amount of prediction bias is tolerable and can be traded for a lower prediction variance that reduces the overall MSPE.

The methods for building general linear models discussed in Chapter 5 and Chapter 6 minimize MSPE by finding the optimal value of a tuning parameter (such as λ for the lasso or k for ridge regression) that controls the flexibility of the model. As flexibility increases, MSPE will at first decrease because the earliest effects to be selected will likely be useful for prediction. Eventually, as more effects are introduced, MSPE will increase because overfitting will be more likely and the decrease in prediction bias will be overtaken by the increase in prediction variance. The preferred models—those with minimum MSPE—will typically be somewhere in the middle.

In practice, the bias-variance tradeoff is more complicated than indicated by the three-term decomposition of MSPE because model selection methods are subject to selection bias, which is explained on page 35. This is not the only complication. A completely automated selection method—without benefit of subject matter knowledge—might have a large bias and a large prediction variance. And even a model with many effects that are known to be useful can suffer from bias if the function f is sufficiently complex. You might need an entirely different type of model with more flexibility.

Finally, note that the decomposition of MSPE applies to a future response y^* in a single observation with a particular value of $\mathbf{x}^*$. Predictive models should minimize prediction error over a range of values of $\mathbf{x}$, which might be random in some cases.

In practice, building a general linear model requires measures of prediction error and methods of selection that balance model flexibility by minimizing these measures. These topics are addressed on page 25, following an explanation of how flexibility is summarized by degrees of freedom.

Model Flexibility and Degrees of Freedom

A general linear model with good predictive ability must be flexible enough to avoid prediction error due to high bias, yet not so flexible that prediction error is inflated by high variance. The degrees of freedom for a model quantifies its flexibility and provides a convenient way to compare different models for the same data. For instance, Output 2.3 compares the three models for network activity presented on page 12.

Output 2.3 Degrees of Freedom for Network Activity Models

Model Degrees of Freedom with Training Data (108 Observations)

Model	Degrees of Freedom
Standard Linear	1
B-Spline with 7 Knots	10
B-Spline with 20 Knots	23

The standard regression model is the least flexible; it has only one degree of freedom. The B-spline model with 20 knots is the most flexible; it has 23 degrees of freedom. The question becomes how to determine the degrees of freedom for different types of models.

Degrees of Freedom for Least Squares Models

Few topics in the field of statistics are as elusive as degrees of freedom. Instructors for introductory courses struggle to explain it in ways their students can grasp when they are learning about *t* tests. In fact, the theory behind degrees of freedom for hypothesis tests falls well outside the scope of a beginning course; it is explained in courses on linear models and textbooks such as Searle (1971), where it is related to the analysis of variance.

For a least squares regression model whose effects are specified, analysis of variance quantifies how well the model explains the total variation in **y**. Based on the orthogonal geometry of least squares illustrated in Figure B.1 on page 322, the squared length of **y** can be decomposed into two terms:

$$\underbrace{\|\mathbf{y}\|_2^2}_{\text{Length squared}} = \underbrace{\mathbf{y}'\mathbf{I}\mathbf{y}}_{\text{Total sum of squares}} = \underbrace{\mathbf{y}'\mathbf{P}\mathbf{y}}_{\text{Model sum of squares}} + \underbrace{\mathbf{y}'(\mathbf{I}-\mathbf{P})\mathbf{y}}_{\text{Residual sum of squares}}$$

Here, **I** denotes the identity matrix and **P** denotes the hat matrix $\mathbf{X}(\mathbf{X}'\mathbf{X})^{-1}\mathbf{X}'$, which is explained on page 17. The three matrices **I**, **P**, and **I** − **P** are projection matrices as defined on page 322.

For any projection matrix **A**, the degrees of freedom associated with a sum of squares of the form **y**'**Ay** is defined as the rank of **A** (the maximum number of linearly independent columns or rows), which is the dimension of the projection space. Because **A** is idempotent, its rank is equal to its trace, denoted by tr(**A**), which is the sum of its diagonal elements. It follows that the degrees of freedom associated with the three sums of squares are related as follows:

$$n = \underbrace{\text{tr}(\mathbf{I})}_{\text{Total degrees of freedom}} = \underbrace{\text{tr}(\mathbf{P})}_{\text{Model degrees of freedom}} + \underbrace{\text{tr}(\mathbf{I}-\mathbf{P})}_{\text{Residual degrees of freedom}}$$

Based on this definition, the degrees of freedom for the model is the same as the maximum number of linearly independent columns in the model matrix **X**, including the column of 1's that represents the intercept. Assuming no linear dependencies, it can be shown that the trace of **P** is simply $p + 1$, the number of columns of **X**. However, the column of 1's is not counted in the model degrees of freedom when the total sum of squares is adjusted or corrected for the mean. For instance, there are two columns (**1** and $\mathbf{x}_1$) in the matrix for the standard linear regression model on page 12, but the degrees of freedom for this model is 1 in Output 2.3 and in the analysis of variance table shown in Output 2.4.

Output 2.4 ANOVA Table for Standard Linear Model in Output 2.1

Least Squares Model (No Selection)

Analysis of Variance

Source	DF	Sum of Squares	Mean Square	F Value	Pr > F
Model	1	84.56424	84.56424	188.47	<.0001
Error	106	47.56196	0.44870		
Corrected Total	107	132.12620			

Assuming an adjustment for the mean, different types of effects in the model contribute different numbers of columns to the model matrix:

- A continuous predictor contributes one column.

- A polynomial effect of degree d for a continuous predictor contributes d columns.

- A B-spline effect for a continuous predictor contributes a number of columns that is determined by the degree of the spline and the number of knots (see page 353 in Appendix F).

- A categorical predictor with m levels contributes $m - 1$ or m columns, depending on the coding scheme used to represent the information in the predictor (see Appendix I).

- If (say) reference coding is used, the interaction effect of two categorical predictors, one with m_1 levels and one with m_2 levels, contributes $(m_1 - 1)(m_2 - 1)$ columns.

In the statistical analysis of a general linear model, which is available with the GLM procedure, the degrees of freedom serves as a mathematical parameter that determines F distributions used for testing hypotheses about linear estimable functions of the parameters as well as the overall model; these tests are based on sums of squares.

Such tests are not valid in models that are selected because the distributions of the test statistics are unknown for the final selected model. Indeed, if your model is built for prediction, the parameters might be of no interest. Nonetheless, the degrees of freedom serves as a measure of flexibility and as a tuning parameter for sequential selection methods and all subsets regression.

Effective Degrees of Freedom

For a general linear model trained with penalized least squares estimation, the rank definition of degrees of freedom does not apply because the model prediction cannot be characterized as a linear projection. Instead, for penalized methods, analogues of degrees of freedom, called *effective degrees of freedom*, provide a basis for comparing and selecting models.

Effective degrees of freedom are defined for the lasso method (page 44) and for ridge regression (page 99). They are also defined for linear smoothers such as smoothing splines (page 356). Each of these methods has its own tuning parameter that determines the amount of shrinkage or smoothing by controlling the penalization. Tuning parameters operate on different scales, which complicates their specification. However, because there is a one-to-one relationship between a tuning parameter and the effective degrees of freedom, it is possible to express shrinkage and smoothing on the degrees-of-freedom scale, which is both consistent and intuitive.

Effective degrees of freedom have also been devised for generalized additive models, which involve smoothing and are discussed in Chapter 11. See "Effective Degrees of Freedom" on page 372.

Amount of Fitting

The interpretations of degrees of freedom discussed so far apply to a given model. For data-driven model building methods such as the lasso and least angle regression (page 44) that proceed along a solution path, the degrees of freedom can also be interpreted as the amount of fitting done at any stage. This quantity is not well-defined for sequential selection and best-subset regression (page 40). For the former, it is believed to be greater than $p + 1$, and it is a topic of theoretical investigation (Zou, Hastie, and Tibshirani 2007).

Assessment and Minimization of Prediction Error

For a general linear model, the ideal measure of predictive ability is the mean (average) squared prediction error for test data that are representative of data for which predictions are to be computed, but were not used to train the model:

$$\text{ASE}_{\text{test}} = \frac{1}{T} \sum_{t=1}^{T} \left(y_t^{\text{test}} - \hat{y}_t^{\text{test}} \right)^2 = \frac{1}{T} \sum_{t=1}^{T} \left(y_t^{\text{test}} - x_t^{\text{test}\,\prime} \hat{\boldsymbol{\beta}} \right)^2$$

Here T denotes the number of test observations. This approach, which estimates MSPE, requires a large amount of test data that is not needed for training. Usually, this requirement is not realistic, and so other measures of prediction error must be employed for model selection.

It is tempting to choose a model that minimizes the average squared error of prediction for the training data:

$$\text{ASE}_{\text{train}} = \frac{1}{n} \sum_{i=1}^{n} (y_i - \hat{y}_i)^2$$

where $\sum_{i=1}^{n} (y_i - \hat{y}_i)^2$ is the error (residual) sum of squares for the model, commonly denoted by SSE, and n is the number of observations in the training data. This is equivalent to maximizing the R-square statistic, which measures how well the model fits the training data:

$$R^2 \equiv 1 - \frac{\text{error sum of squares}}{\text{total sum of squares}} = 1 - \frac{\sum_{i=1}^{n} (y_i - \hat{y}_i)^2}{\sum_{i=1}^{n} (y_i - \bar{y})^2} = 1 - \frac{\text{ASE}_{\text{train}}}{\frac{1}{n} \sum_{i=1}^{n} (y_i - \bar{y})^2} = 1 - \frac{\text{ASE}_{\text{train}}}{s_y^2}$$

where s_y^2 is the sample variance of the response. You can minimize $\text{ASE}_{\text{train}}$ by including all potential effects in the model. However, this leads to models that are overly complex and do not generalize well to future data because training error always underestimates prediction error. This problem arises with most—if not all—supervised learning methods, and the training error rate (also called the apparent error rate) can severely underestimate the test error rate.

To understand this phenomenon, consider the simplified case in which a general linear model is used to predict the responses y_i^* at n future observations for which the inputs, $x_i^* = (x_{i1}^*, \ldots, x_{ip}^*)$, $i = 1, \ldots, n$, are the *same* as those in the training data. The errors ϵ_i^* in the predictions y_i^* are assumed to have the same distribution as the errors ϵ_i in the training data.[†] The analogue of $\text{ASE}_{\text{train}}$ for future observations, called the out-of-sample prediction error, is

$$\text{ASE}_{\text{out}} = \frac{1}{n} \sum_{i=1}^{n} \left(y_i^* - \hat{y}_i^* \right)^2$$

Assuming the form of the model is determined independently of the training data, it can be shown that the expected out-of-sample prediction error is

$$E(\text{ASE}_{\text{out}}) = E(\text{ASE}_{\text{train}}) + \frac{2}{n} \sigma^2 (p + 1) > E(\text{ASE}_{\text{train}})$$

[†]Predictive models of this type are referred to as fixed (Thompson 1978); they are more applicable to experimental data than observational data.

The term $(2/n)\sigma^2(p + 1)$ is called the *optimism* in the model. It could well be called false optimism because it is the amount by which the expected training error underestimates the expected prediction error; see Efron (1986) and Hastie, Tibshirani, and Friedman (2009, Sec. 7.4) for an in-depth analysis.

For fixed n and σ^2, optimism increases with p because adding more predictors allows the model to adjust to noise in the data without necessarily improving its predictive ability. For fixed n and p, optimism increases with σ^2 because greater noise masks poor predictive ability. On the other hand, for fixed p and σ^2, optimism decreases with n because adding observations exposes inadequacies in the model.

When you build a model with the GLMSELECT and REGSELECT procedures, you can choose from various methods that address the issues of model optimism and overfitting by minimizing a valid measure of prediction error or by penalizing model flexibility (complexity). These methods, listed in Table 2.2, are explained in the remainder of this section.

Table 2.2 Methods for Minimizing Prediction Error During Model Selection

Method	Criterion Minimized
Mallows' C_P statistic	Estimate of expected mean squared prediction error
Information criteria	$n \log(\text{ASE}_\text{train})$ plus penalty for model flexibility
External validation	Squared error of prediction in data withheld from training data
Cross validation	Squared error of prediction in hold-out partitions within training data

Mallows' C_P Statistic

The C_P statistic is a widely used measure of prediction error for a general linear model. It was proposed in 1964 by Colin Mallows[†] at Bell Laboratories, who defined it as

$$C_P \equiv \frac{\text{SSE}}{\hat{\sigma}^2} + 2p' - n = \frac{n\text{ASE}}{\hat{\sigma}^2} + 2p' - n$$

where $p' = p + 1$ is the number of parameters $\beta_0, \ldots, \beta_p$, and where $\hat{\sigma}^2$ is an unbiased estimate of σ^2 obtained from a model that contains all of the candidate effects under consideration.

Mallows (1973) derived C_P as an estimate of J_P, the standardized total expected prediction error for a set of n observations based on a candidate model with p predictors:

$$J_P = \frac{1}{\sigma^2} \sum_{i=1}^{n} (\mathbf{x}_i'\hat{\boldsymbol{\beta}} - \mathbf{x}_i'\boldsymbol{\beta})^2$$

[†]Mallows chose the letter C in honor of a collaborator, Cuthbert Daniel, who was a pioneer in the application of statistical methods to problems in industry. Years later, in a conversation with two colleagues, Lorraine Denby and Jim Landwehr, Mallows recalled that he first considered the approach with Daniel in 1963, but did not think it was a good idea at the time (Denby, Landwehr, and Mallows 2013). Only after C_P was discussed by Gorman and Toman (1966) and Daniel and Wood (1971) did Mallows write his 1973 paper, which turned out to be his most influential publication.

where x_i' is the ith row of $\mathbf{X}$. The quantity J_P is a version of the expected out-of-sample prediction error $E(\text{ASE}_{\text{out}})$, which is discussed on page 25; it is scaled by σ^2 rather than n.

If the model is correctly specified or overspecified, SSE is an unbiased estimate of $(n - p')\sigma^2$, and so C_P is approximately equal to p'. On the other hand, if relevant effects are omitted from the model, then the expected value of C_P is greater than p'.

Mallows recommended plotting C_P versus p as a way to examine models comprised of different subsets of the candidate variables. He stated that "the greatest value of the device [plot] is that it helps the statistician to examine some aspects of the structure of his data and helps him to recognize the ambiguities that confront him" (Mallows 1973, p. 669).

Mallows did not advocate selecting the model with the smallest value of C_P; in fact, he emphasized that this can be unreliable, especially when the data are not adequate to support a single model (Mallows 1973, 1995). He stated that "the ambiguous cases where the 'minimum C_P rule' will give bad results are exactly those where a large number of subsets are close competitors for the honor" (Mallows 1973, p. 671).

Despite Mallows' concerns, statistical software that was developed during the late 1970s adopted C_P (along with measures described in the next section) as a selection criterion because it was convenient computationally. At the same time, C_P gained acceptance in textbooks as a criterion for automatic model selection.

The hands-on investigative approach to model development that Mallows recommended is fundamentally different from the automated approach of supervised learning, which can produce predictive models that are highly accurate if given the right data. However, assembling the right data is far more difficult than running an algorithm. As pointed out on page 5, black box models that are unknowingly built with the wrong data can have severe consequences, and so today's data scientists are well advised to heed Mallows' recommendation by examining the structure and ambiguities of their data.

The C_P statistic is available in the GLMSELECT and REGSELECT procedures as option for selecting a predictive model (see page 52). If you use this option, be sure to request coefficient progression plots and fit criteria plots, which can help you to identify competing models, as discussed in "Understanding the Selection Process" on page 61.

Different expressions for C_P appear in papers and books on regression analysis, which can be confusing. The GLMSELECT and REGSELECT procedures compute the statistic as

$$C_P = \frac{\text{SSE}}{\hat{\sigma}^2} + 2p - n$$

Replacing p' with p changes the value of C_P, but it does not alter the minimization of C_P. Model selection can also be based on minimizing $\text{ASE}_{\text{train}} + \frac{2}{n}\hat{\sigma}^2(p + 1)$. This expression, which some authors refer to as C_P, penalizes training error for model flexibility with an estimate of model optimism as defined on page 26.

Mallows (1973, Sec. 5) extended the definition of C_P to ridge regression by replacing p (which is the degrees of freedom for OLS regression) with the effective degrees of freedom for ridge regression. Minimizing C_P provides a way to select the ridge parameter, as illustrated in "Alternative Methods for Selecting the Ridge Parameter" on page 103. Extensions of C_P are available for the lasso and related methods in the GLMSELECT and REGSELECT procedures. Unlike the information criteria discussed in the next section, C_P does not extend to models that involve likelihood estimation, such as logistic regression.

Criteria Based on Information Theory

The GLMSELECT and REGSELECT procedures provide four criteria for selecting general linear models that are collectively known as information criteria because they are derived from information theory. These criteria are listed in Table 2.3. Although they differ from C_P in their derivations, they are similar in the sense that they penalize model goodness-of-fit (ASE_train) for model flexibility.

Table 2.3 Information Criteria for Selecting General Linear Models

Criterion	Source	Common Label	SAS Label
Akaike's information criterion	Akaike (1973)	AIC	AIC
Corrected Akaike's information criterion	Hurvich and Tsai (1989)	AICC	AICC
Sawa Bayesian information criterion	Sawa (1978)		BIC
Schwarz Bayesian information criterion	Schwarz (1978)	BIC	SBC

The Schwarz Bayesian criterion is labeled as SBC in the documentation, syntax, and output of the procedures, but it is more commonly labeled as BIC in textbooks and papers. This book uses the label SBC for consistency with the software, and it notes the distinction when necessary to avoid confusion.

The GLMSELECT and REGSELECT procedures compute the criteria as follows:

$$\text{AIC} = n \log(\text{ASE}_\text{train}) + 2p + n + 2$$

$$\text{AICC} = n \log(\text{ASE}_\text{train}) + \frac{n(n+p)}{n-p-2}$$

$$\text{BIC} = n \log(\text{ASE}_\text{train}) + \frac{2(p+2)\hat{\sigma}^2}{\text{ASE}_\text{train}} - 2\left(\frac{\hat{\sigma}^2}{\text{ASE}_\text{train}}\right)^2$$

$$\text{SBC} = n \log(\text{ASE}_\text{train}) + p \log(n)$$

As with Mallows' C_P, $\hat{\sigma}^2$ is determined using the largest fitted model.

When model selection is based on one of these criteria, the model is chosen by determining a set of p effects for which the criterion is minimized. You might encounter different versions of these formulas in other references and software. For instance, the equation for AIC that is shown here involves the term $n + 2$, which does not appear in the reduced equation for AIC on page 324. Typically, such discrepancies do not affect the minimization with respect to p. When you compare models with these criteria, what matters is their relative differences and not their actual values.

Appendix C explains the motivation for Akaike's information criterion. Akaike (1973, p. 620) noted that when his approach is applied to the selection of OLS regression models, it is essentially equivalent to using Mallows' C_P. As noted earlier, C_P is limited to this situation, whereas AIC is not. SAS procedures for building logistic regression models and other types of models that involve likelihood estimation provide versions of AIC that adapt to the particular form of the likelihood.

Cross validation, an alternative to using information criteria that is described on page 31, was introduced around the same time as AIC, but it took much longer to gain acceptance because it is computationally intensive, whereas AIC and AICC are easily implemented in software that already does maximum likelihood estimation.

Comparisons of Information Criteria

In contrast to AIC and AICC, which were developed by extending the framework for likelihood estimation, BIC and SBC were developed in a Bayesian model selection framework. The criterion SBC, introduced in 1978 by Gideon Schwarz, is an asymptotic approximation of $-2 \log \text{Pr}(\text{model } g | \text{data})$, where $\text{Pr}(\text{model } g | \text{data})$ is the Bayesian posterior probability of model g.

Neath and Cavanaugh (2012) note that model selection based on SBC is consistent for large n, meaning that with a probability of one it will select the candidate model with the correct structure or the model with the fewest effects that is closest to the true model in terms of Kullback-Leibler distance. As with AIC, the Bayesian criteria involve a likelihood function, and for a general linear model this is defined by assuming that the errors are normally distributed.

Unlike Mallows' C_P, the information criteria are not estimates of prediction error, but like C_P they balance model flexibility and model parsimony. Whereas flexibility (more effects) improves the fit to the training data and captures subtle relationships, parsimony (fewer effects) avoids overfitting and improves prediction and interpretability. All of these criteria involve $\text{ASE}_{\text{train}}$ in a term that measures lack of fit, and they all involve a term in p that penalizes flexibility. The penalty term for AIC is $2p$, whereas the penalty term for SBC is $p \log(n)$.

Which Criterion Should You Use?

There are different points of view concerning which criterion to apply. The recommendations provided by experts are based on theoretical properties of the criteria, but they are not entirely in agreement.

Burnham and Anderson (2002, p. 270) note that SBC (which they refer to as BIC) is more conservative than AIC, in the sense of leading to models with fewer effects.

Hastie, Tibshirani, and Friedman (2009, p. 235) state, "For model selection purposes, there is no clear choice between AIC and BIC [SBC in this book]. What this means is that given a family of models, including the true model, the probability that BIC will select the correct model approaches one as the sample size $N \to \infty$. This is not the case for AIC, which tends to choose models which are too complex as $N \to \infty$. On the other hand, for finite samples, BIC often chooses models that are too simple, because of its heavy penalty on complexity."

Cavanaugh and Neath (2019) recommend AIC and AICC when the goal is prediction because they are asymptotically efficient. They recommend SBC (referred to as BIC) when the goal is discovery of the most important effects because for large n it favors the candidate model that is most probable based on the data.

Burnham and Anderson (2002, p. 66) compare AIC with AICC and recommend using AICC when n/p is less than around 40.

Simonoff (2003, p. 46) concludes, "AIC and AICC have the desirable property that they are efficient model selection criteria. What this means is that as the sample gets larger, the error obtained in making predictions using the model chosen using these criteria becomes indistinguishable from the error obtained using the best possible model among all candidate models. That is, in this large-sample predictive sense, it is as if the best approximation was known to the data analyst. Other criteria, such as the Bayesian Information Criterion, BIC, ... do not have this property."

Criticisms of Information Criteria

Some experts have expressed misgivings about applying information criteria to model selection. When asked about AIC and SBC, Colin Mallows replied, "What I don't like about . . . these procedures is that they are blind. They don't look at the data. They just say this is the way to get a good prediction model. Whereas with C_P, the idea is that you do look at the plot and see whether a unique subset is indicated, or whether . . . you have a collection of subsets that do about equally well, and you can't choose between them, and you should do something else" (Denby, Landwehr, and Mallows 2013, p. 343). As an alternative, Mallows suggested model averaging, which is discussed in Chapter 7.

Breiman (1992) pointed out that asymptotic results for criteria such as C_P, AIC, and BIC assume a predetermined sequence of models and lead to biased results with finite n because they do not adjust for data-driven selection.

Harrell (2015, p. 69) notes that AIC used with stepwise selection does not solve the problem of selection bias (see page 35). He adds that AIC works successfully when the progression of candidate models is defined by a single parameter, as is the case with shrinkage methods, which keep all of the candidate effects in the model.

The adjusted R-square statistic

$$1 - \frac{(n-1)(1-R^2)}{n-p} = 1 - \frac{(n-1)\text{ASE}_{\text{train}}}{(n-p)s_y^2}$$

is often used to compare standard regression models with different numbers of predictors. It is not an information criterion, but it is comparable in the sense that it penalizes model flexibility.

External Validation Method for Estimating Prediction Error

If you have sufficient data, you can take advantage of features in the GLMSELECT and REGSELECT procedures that partition the observations into as many as three disjoint subsets: training data, validation data, and test data. The procedures estimate parameters of candidate models based on the training data, and they directly assess prediction error based on the validation data. The final selected model is the one that minimizes average squared error computed from the validation data. You can use the test data to assess the final model based on observations that were uninvolved in model selection.

There are no precise guidelines for deciding how many observations to allocate to each partition. Hastie, Tibshirani, and Friedman (2009, p. 222) suggest a typical split of 50% for training, with 25% each for validation and testing.

Allocating the right data to each split is not simply a decision about sample size; it is much like preparing a fair exam that measures how much students have learned in a statistics course. The exam problems should not depart from concepts that were taught, but neither should they duplicate homework exercises. Likewise, validation and test data should have an underlying structure similar to that of the training data, with enough differences to yield realistic measures of predictive ability.

Even if the allocation is made fairly, the estimate of prediction error based on the validation data will tend to be biased higher than the true error for the model because it is trained on only a portion of the data.

Cross Validation Methods for Estimating Prediction Error

As an alternative to external validation, you can use cross validation, which provides nearly unbiased estimates of prediction error by synthesizing validation data. This approach was systematized in the 1970s by the work of Stone (1974) and Geisser (1975). Cross validation was introduced around the same time as Akaike's information criterion and is even more general although seemingly less principled. The GLMSELECT and REGSELECT procedures provide two ways to apply cross validation during model building: *m*-fold cross validation and leave-one-out cross validation.

m-Fold Cross Validation

m-fold cross validation splits the training data into *m* approximately equal parts, one of which is held out as a test set. Each candidate model is trained on the remaining *m* − 1 parts and then used to compute ASE$_{\text{test}}$ on the test set. This process is repeated for each of the *m* parts in turn, and the total of the *m* ASE$_{\text{test}}$ values (the CVPRESS statistic) is used to estimate the prediction error for the model. The model selected is the one with the smallest error estimate.

Hastie, Tibshirani, and Friedman (2009, Ch. 7) point out that cross validation estimates the expected squared error of prediction over the joint distribution of the x_j and y, rather than the conditional expected test error over an independent test sample where the training sample is fixed.

The main advantages of *m*-fold cross validation are its simplicity and its high level of generality; it can be used with many forms of supervised learning. See page 74 for an application of *m*-fold cross validation to all subsets regression.

Leave-One-Out Cross Validation

Leave-one-out cross validation computes the predictive residual sum of squares (PRESS) statistic, which was introduced by Allen (1971, 1974). For the *i*th observation, each candidate model is trained on the other $n - 1$ observations and used to compute a prediction $\hat{y}_{-i}$ for y_i. The PRESS statistic for the model is generally defined as

$$\text{PRESS(p)} = \sum_{i=1}^{n} (y_i - \hat{y}_{-i})^2$$

The model selected is the one with the smallest prediction error. Like *m*-fold cross validation, leave-one-out cross validation can be applied with different model building methods. One of these is ridge regression; see page 98.

For model building methods that use least squares estimation, the PRESS statistic is computed as

$$\text{PRESS(p)} = \sum_{i=1}^{n} \frac{(y_i - \hat{y}_i)^2}{(1 - P_{ii})^2}$$

where P_{ii} is the *i*th diagonal element of the hat matrix $\mathbf{P} = \mathbf{X}(\mathbf{X'X})^{-1}\mathbf{X'}$. Larger values of P_{ii}, known as the leverage of the *i*th observation, inflate the training error $(y_i - \hat{y}_i)^2$. Intuitively, this makes sense because $\hat{y}_i$ is more likely to overfit y_i when $\hat{y}_i$ depends heavily on y_i, and the covariance between the two quantities is $\text{Cov}(\hat{\mathbf{y}}, \mathbf{y}) = \sigma^2\mathbf{P}$, so that $\text{Cov}(\hat{y}_i, y_i) = \sigma^2 P_{ii}$. Breiman and Spector (1992) referred to this form of cross validation as "partial cross validation" because unlike *m*-fold cross validation, the model selection method is not re-applied to each group of observations that is set aside.

Comparison of Cross-Validation Methods

Breiman and Spector (1992) concluded that m-fold cross validation with $m = 5$ is more effective for model selection than leave-one-out cross validation. Leave-one-out cross validation minimizes the bias of the validation approach (page 30) by training the model on almost all the observations. It can be computationally expensive and tends to produce estimates of prediction error with a higher variance than those obtained with m-fold cross validation (James et al. 2021, Sec. 5.1.3). For a reasonable compromise between bias and variance, different experts recommend $m = 5$ or $m = 10$.

Bootstrap Estimates of Prediction Error

The bootstrap, introduced in 1979 by Bradley Efron at Stanford University, is a general approach to statistical inference that provides confidence intervals and estimates of standard errors and bias without requiring the assumption of a parametric distribution. Given a data set with n observations, the nonparametric bootstrap operates by drawing n observations with replacement from the data and then repeating this many times to form a series of B bootstrap samples. The concept behind the bootstrap is an analogy: the bootstrap samples are related to the original sample in the same way that the original sample is related to the population.

The bootstrap provides a way to assess the predictive error of a model. Variations of this method have been proposed by Efron (1983), Efron (1986), and Efron and Tibshirani (1997). For a helpful introduction, see Efron and Tibshirani (1993, Ch. 17).

Unlike the methods in Table 2.2, the bootstrap does not serve well to minimize prediction error during model selection because it is computationally intensive. Nonetheless, you can use the bootstrap to estimate the prediction error of the final selected model, as illustrated on page 68 and page 172.

Summary

Building a general linear model for prediction requires concepts that differ fundamentally from those required for statistical analysis of a fitted model. Table 2.4 summarizes these differences.

Table 2.4 Concepts Involved in Fitting and Building General Linear Models

Concept	Fitting for Inference	Building for Prediction
Purpose of the model	Understanding the process that generated the data	Predicting future responses with data from the same process
Determination of effects in the model	Specified by the analyst based on subject knowledge	Selected from the data by model building methods and algorithms
Theoretical approach	Unbiased estimation of the model parameters	Minimization of the mean square error for prediction
Main requirement	Valid model assumptions	Reasonable tradeoff between bias and variance of the prediction
Parameter estimation	Least squares	Least squares, penalized least squares
Assessment of prediction error	Average square error for training data, R-square statistic	Mallows' C_P statistic, information criteria, external validation, cross validation

Chapter 3
Building General Linear Models: Issues

Contents

Since the 1970s when stepwise regression entered statistical practice, experts have warned about problems with data-driven model selection that can lead to incorrect or misleading results. The rapid adoption of statistical computing software in the 1980s led to additional concerns that data analysis done by algorithms would displace sound statistical thinking. At meetings of the American Statistical Association, George Box, J. Stuart Hunter, Oscar Kempthorne, Donald Marquardt, Fred Mosteller, John Tukey, and other leaders discussed the scientific value of explanatory models created by algorithms. Not surprisingly, some of the issues they discussed have resurfaced in the field of machine learning.

This chapter points out issues you should be aware of when you build a general linear model because they affect the predictive ability of the model as well as its interpretation. These issues also arise when you build models discussed in Part II of this book.

Problems with Data-Driven Model Selection

Most of the problems associated with model selection are consequences of using the same data to determine the form of the model and to estimate the model parameters. These problems are fundamentally unavoidable, but they can be mitigated with appropriate model building methods.

Underfitting and Overfitting

Underfitting, also known as omission bias, occurs when a model building method leaves out effects that have predictive value. Underfitting biases the prediction. As explained in "The Bias-Variance Tradeoff for Prediction" on page 21, adding useful effects to the model reduces the bias of the prediction, but it also increases the variance. In fact, the variance increases even if the additional effects have no predictive value (Miller 2002, Section 1.2).

Overfitting occurs when a model building method includes spurious effects (effects with no predictive value). Overfitting inflates the variance of the prediction. It cannot be avoided without incurring underfitting, and underfitting cannot be avoided without incurring overfitting.

As explained in Chapter 2, the procedures in this book provide methods and criteria designed to minimize prediction error by providing a good tradeoff between bias and variance.

Inadequate Feature Engineering

Feature engineering is the process of generating candidate predictors from hundreds or thousands of raw variables in large databases; it is a preliminary step in large-scale applications of machine learning and data mining such as credit scoring and fraud detection. Domain knowledge is necessary to avoid mistakes such as treating redundant variables as potential predictors (which introduces collinearity); mislabeling variables (for instance, designating variables that measure outcomes as inputs); and transforming variables in ways that are unnecessary (which also leads to collinearity).

Feature engineering done by experts is so time-consuming that automating the process has become a holy grail for machine learning (Domingos 2012). The risk of automation is that it can inadvertently produce candidate predictors that are irrelevant or biased (see page 5). None of the model building methods in this book can compensate for poor choices of inputs.

Over-Reliance on a Single Selection Criterion

The methods in this book build a single model that optimizes the criterion for choosing the model (see Table 2.2). There will often be other models with nearly the same criterion value—so close that with a small change in the data, any of them could be selected. You can identify closely competing models by examining criterion plots such as those on page 62 and page 219.

Resampling is a general-purpose method for evaluating competing models and justifying the best model. The idea is to draw a large number of bootstrap samples from the data, repeat the selection process in each sample, and compute quantities such as measures of prediction error and inclusion frequencies for the predictors (Heinze, Wallisch, and Dunkler 2017). Resampling methods require extra work and can be computationally expensive. Macros for bootstrap evaluation of prediction error are presented in Chapter 5 and Chapter 9. The computation of bootstrap inclusion frequencies is discussed in Chapter 7.

An alternative for deciding among competing models is to select one of the sparser models. Yet another alternative is model averaging, which is explained in Chapter 7.

Selection Based on Significance Tests

A longstanding criticism of sequential selection concerns the use of F tests and χ^2 tests to determine the order in which effects enter or leave the model and when to stop the selection. The problem with this approach is that the test statistics do not have F and χ^2 distributions; in fact, their actual distributions are unknown. Pope and Webster (1972) cautioned that when terms associated with hypothesis tests, such as Type I error and F distribution, are applied to methods such as stepwise regression, they are misrepresentations; they give users a false sense of security about the selected model.

The use of significance levels to control the operation of sequential selection was introduced in the early 1970s; it became popular because it is simple and seemingly legitimized by statistical theory. This approach was implemented in the STEPWISE procedure and its successor, the REG procedure, for lack of better alternatives at the time that these procedures were developed. However, there is no theoretical justification for the default levels that the REG procedure provides for stepwise regression (0.15 for a variable to enter the model and 0.15 for a variable to leave).

In some applications it is possible to select useful models by treating the levels as numerical tuning parameters. However, this must be done in an ad hoc fashion since there are no generally recommended guidelines for determining appropriate levels. For example, in a tutorial article about issues of variable selection in transplantation research, Heinze and Dunkler (2017) suggest that backward elimination with a level of 0.157 can be a good starting point for obtaining prognostic models, but they quickly add that other choices might be more appropriate.

Because there is no one level that works in general, and because selection based on significance tests is so easily misinterpreted, this method is not recommended here. Instead, this book emphasizes modern methods designed to minimize measures of prediction error as discussed in Chapter 2.

Treating the Selected Model as a Specified Model

Regardless of which method you use, avoid treating the final model as if were a fully specified model based on subject matter knowledge. When the final model is used for inferential analysis, it leads to p-values that are too small, estimated coefficients $\hat{\beta}_j$ that are biased upward, and confidence intervals that are too narrow (Harrell 2015, Sec. 4.3). If stepwise regression is to be used, Harrell recommends a preliminary global test of no regression, so that effect selection proceeds only if the test is significant.

Business analysts and scientific researchers often use model selection to reduce the number of predictors and then eliminate insignificant effects from the selected model based on p-values and confidence intervals that are displayed with parameter estimates. However, as noted throughout this book, these quantities are not adjusted to account for the steps of the selection process, and so they cannot be relied upon.

Eliminating a predictor from a model sets its regression coefficient to zero, which can lead to a suboptimal model in the sense that it overrides the maximum likelihood estimate (Heinze and Dunkler 2017). Furthermore, because regression coefficients depend on which other predictors are in the model (see page 17), eliminating a predictor can cause the coefficient for a different predictor to move closer to zero, changing its status from significant to insignificant (Heinze and Dunkler 2017).

High Collinearity

High collinearity (strong correlation) of candidate predictors is common in observational data and undermines sequential selection methods and the lasso. Chapter 6 presents methods that deal with collinearity.

Selection Bias

Among the various issues associated with model selection, the most insidious is selection bias; it is not obvious, and it fundamentally affects every method for data-driven model selection. Selection bias is a type of overfitting that results from using the same data to estimate model parameters that were used to select the effects in the model. The data values at each step must be more extreme in order to satisfy the selection criterion, which leads to parameter estimates that are biased high in absolute value. This reduces the predictive ability of the final model and clouds its interpretation.

The next example demonstrates a simple case of selection bias; it is patterned after a simulation presented in Miller (2002, Section 6.2).

Example: Simulation of Selection Bias

The following statements simulate 200 data sets, each with 12 observations, that contain two predictor variables (X1 and X2) and a response variable (Y).

```
%let NDataSets = 200;  /* Number of data sets */
%let NObs      = 12;   /* Sample size         */
data Make (keep=x1 x2 y DataSet);
   call streaminit(219921);
   do DataSet=1 to &NDataSets;
      do i = 1 to &Nobs;
         z1 = rand("Normal"); z2 = rand("Normal"); z3 = rand("Normal");
         x1 = z1;
         x2 = -3*z1  + 4*z2;
         y  = 1 + z1 + 2*z2 + z3;
         output;
      end;
   end;
run;
```

In the complete program for this example, which is available on the book website, the REG procedure fits two models for each data set:

Model 1: $y = \beta_{0_1} + \beta_1 x_1 + \epsilon_1$

Model 2: $y = \beta_{0_2} + \beta_2 x_2 + \epsilon_2$

The model selected is the one for which the residual sum of squares (RSS) is smaller. For both models, the actual regression coefficients and error variances are the same. Figure 3.1 compares the distribution of $\hat{\beta}_1$ from all 200 data sets with the distribution of $\hat{\beta}_1$ from data sets for which Model 1 was selected. For the latter, the average $\hat{\beta}_1$ is clearly biased upward.

Figure 3.1 Distributions of Estimates of β_1 for 200 Simulated Data Sets

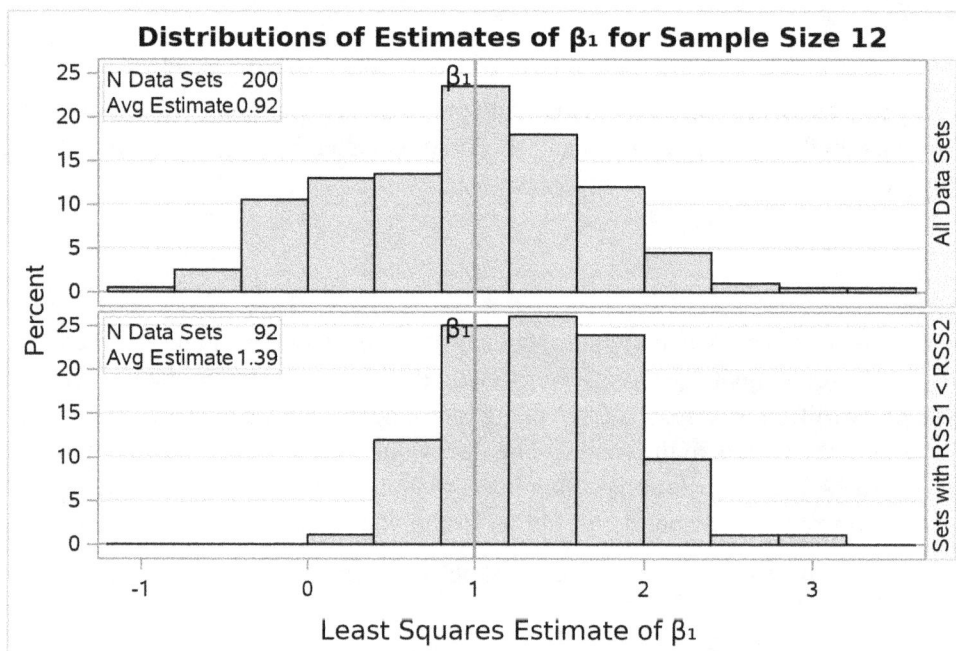

Figure 3.2 compares the same two distributions for 500 data sets, each generated with 1200 observations. Because of the larger sample, the variances of the two distributions are smaller than those in Figure 3.1, but the average $\hat{\beta}_1$ for the selected data sets is still biased.

Figure 3.2 Distributions of Estimates of β_1 for 500 Simulated Data Sets

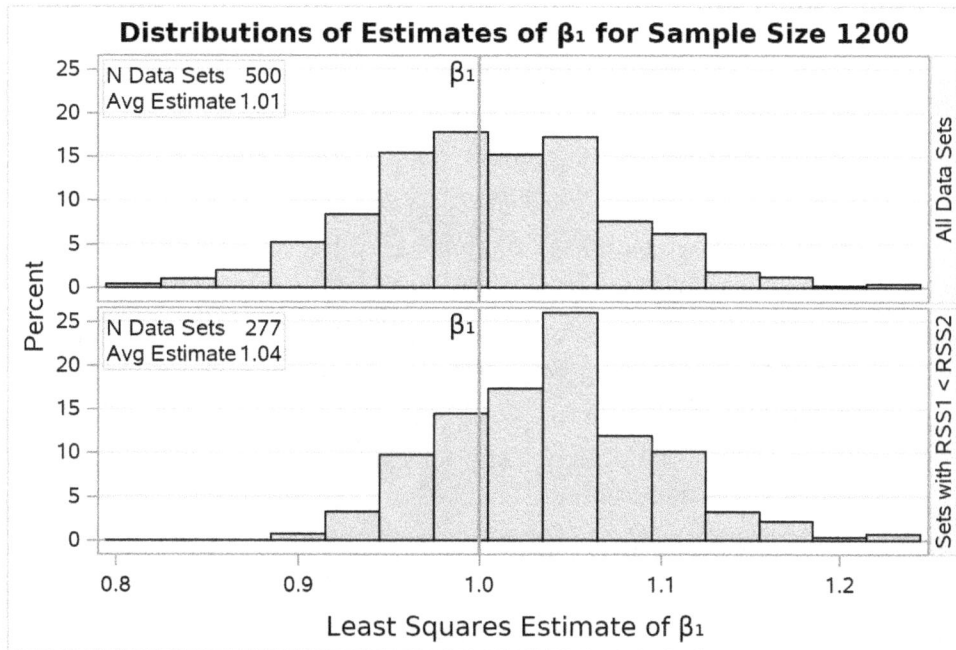

Selection bias cannot be eliminated by increasing the number of observations. In theory, it could be avoided by using independent data to estimate the parameters at each stage, but doing so would require so much data that it is impractical. Shrinkage methods provide a way to deal with the upward bias in the estimated coefficients.

Freedman's Paradox

In a brief but thought-provoking 1983 paper, David Freedman at the University of California analyzed selection bias in the extreme situation where the choice of candidate predictors is not informed by subject matter knowledge, there is little or no relationship between the predictors and the response, and the number of predictors (p) is of the same order as the number of observations (n).

Using simulated data in which the predictors were pure noise, Freedman repeatedly fitted two regression models. In the second model the only predictors included were those that were significant at the level $\alpha = 0.25$ in the first model. Consistently, a higher number of predictors were significant at $\alpha = 0.05$ in the second pass than in the first pass, appearing to show a relationship between the predictors and the response. This problem, known as Freedman's paradox, can occur even if there is a weak relationship between the predictors and the response.

To avoid misleading results in problems where n is not much greater than p, Lukacs, Burnham, and Anderson (2010) recommend a model averaging approach which is discussed in Chapter 7.

Summary

Table 3.1 summarizes the issues discussed in this chapter.

Table 3.1 Problems Associated with Regression Model Building

Problem	Consequences	Remedies
Underfitting, omission bias	Prediction bias resulting from leaving useful effects out of the model	Use methods that minimize prediction error through bias-variance tradeoff
Overfitting	Prediction variance resulting from including spurious effects in the model	Use methods that minimize prediction error through bias-variance tradeoff
Inadequate feature engineering	Overfitting, high prediction variance, collinearity, no interpretability	Understand the meaning and relevance of candidate variables
Over-reliance on one selection criterion	Failure to find the most useful model among those with near-optimal values of the selection criterion	Examine criterion and coefficient progression plots; select sparsest or most interpretable model
Selection based on significance tests	Entry or deletion of effects based on F tests that are statistically invalid	Adopt more effective criteria available in the procedures
Treating the selected model as if specified	p-values and confidence limits for parameters are not valid	Avoid post-selection inference and further selection based on p-values
High collinearity of predictors	Unstable OLS estimates of β_j; degraded performance of sequential selection methods and lasso	Collinearity diagnostics; ridge regression, elastic net, other methods in Chapter 6
Selection bias	Bias in $\hat{\beta}_j$ caused by estimation with the same data used to select the model	No real remedy; shrinkage methods and model averaging can help

The article by Heinze and Dunkler (2017) is a lucid introduction to problems that complicate the analysis of models obtained with variable selection. Heinze, Wallisch, and Dunkler (2017) provide an extensive review of issues associated with the selection of explanatory models in life sciences applications, and they provide helpful recommendations.

Writing for medical researchers, Sauerbrei et al. (2020) discuss issues encountered in building descriptive regression models, strategies for variable selection, ways to select functional forms for continous variables, and methods for combining the selection of functions and variables. They conclude there is not yet enough evidence to recommend such methods.

Chapter 4
Building General Linear Models: Methods

Contents

This chapter describes sequential selection and shrinkage methods for building general linear models that are available in the GLMSELECT and REGSELECT procedures; it also describes best-subset regression, which is available in the REG and REGSELECT procedures.

Table 4.1 lists all the methods for building general linear models discussed in Part I of this book. Most of the sequential and shrinkage methods extend to specialized models discussed in Part II.

Table 4.1   Methods for Building General Linear Models

Method	SAS 9 Procedure	SAS Viya Procedure	Example
Best-subset regression ($k < \approx 40$)	REG	REGSELECT	page 74
Sequential selection			
Forward selection	GLMSELECT	REGSELECT	page 56
Forward swap selection	REG	REGSELECT	page 81
Backward elimination	GLMSELECT	REGSELECT	page 60
Stepwise selection	GLMSELECT	REGSELECT	page 60
Shrinkage			
Ridge regression	REG		page 98
Lasso	GLMSELECT	REGSELECT	page 66
Least angle regression	GLMSELECT	REGSELECT	
Adaptive lasso	GLMSELECT	REGSELECT	page 72
Folded concave penalization		REGSELECT	
Group lasso	GLMSELECT		page 72
Elastic net	GLMSELECT	REGSELECT	page 106
Adaptive elastic net		REGSELECT	
Dimension reduction			
Variable clustering	VARCLUS	GVARCLUS	page 93
Principal components regression	PLS	PLSMOD	page 109
Partial least squares regression	PLS	PLSMOD	page 114
Model averaging			
Bootstrap model averaging	GLMSELECT		page 121
Averaging with Akaike weights	GLMSELECT		page 127

Best-Subset Regression

Best-subset regression, also known as all subsets regression, fits all possible least squares regression models from a set of k candidate predictors. This method is available in the REG and REGSELECT procedures. For each model size p, it finds the best model based on a criterion such as R^2, adjusted R^2, or C_P. There are k models that contain one predictor, $k(k-1)/2$ models that contain two predictors, and, in general, $k!/(j!(k-j)!)$ models that contain j predictors. The total number of possible models is 2^k.

In order to find the best model, which is a combinatorial optimization problem, the procedures implement the algorithm of Furnival and Wilson (1974). With standard computational resources, solutions are feasible only for k less than around 40 or 50. For larger k, you can use the sequential selection methods discussed next, although they are not guaranteed to find the best model for each size. However, even when best-subset regression is feasible, the model that is overall the best in terms of R^2 will not have the lowest prediction error, as explained on page 25. Chapter 5 addresses this problem by using cross validation to select the model size p; see page 74.

Sequential Selection Methods

As implemented by the GLMSELECT and REGSELECT procedures, forward selection, backward elimination, stepwise selection, and forward swap selection build a model by starting with a set of candidate effects and selecting those that minimize an appropriate measure of prediction error. At each step of the selection process, the current model is updated by including or removing the predictors that correspond to a single effect.

Forward selection and backward elimination are greedy algorithms; they make the choice that is best at each step and do not allow for choices that might be better in the long run. Stepwise regression and forward swap selection are slightly less greedy. The order in which effects enter or leave the model should not be interpreted as a measure of their importance.

You control the operation of sequential selection methods by specifying a select criterion, a choose criterion, and a stop criterion. The select criterion determines which effect is added or discarded at each step, the choose criterion determines the final selected model, and the stop criterion determines when the process terminates. Table 2.2 on page 26 summarizes the criteria provided by the procedures, which either measure prediction error or penalize model complexity.

Unlike best-subset regression, sequential selection methods do not evaluate the choose criterion for all of the 2^k models that can be formed from subsets of a set of k candidate predictors. Consequently, these methods do not necessarily identify the model with the best value of the choose criterion. Forward selection, for instance, fits at most $1 + k(k+1)/2$ models, which is much smaller than 2^k.[†] Despite their relatively narrow search, sequential selection methods can produce models whose criterion values are reasonably close to the best possible value. You can gain insights about the selection process by specifying options in the procedures that provide information about the top 10 candidate effects for inclusion or exclusion at each step; see page 61.

[†]This is not an accurate comparison because the models considered by forward selection are reasonable choices and not a random sample. An unrestricted search through a vast set of candidate models risks overfitting the training data while incurring a high computational cost.

Sequential selection methods use least squares estimation to train candidate models but differ in how they form the model at each step, as discussed next.

Forward Selection

Forward selection begins by initializing the current model to the null model, which consists of the intercept term and no effects. At each step, it computes the residuals from the current model and fits the residuals with all of the candidate models that increment the current model by a single effect. The candidate model that best predicts the residuals by yielding the maximum improvement in the selection criterion then becomes the current model. The selection terminates when the stop criterion is satisfied. Among all the current models selected at the various steps, the final selected model is the one with the best value of the choose criterion.

Forward selection is computationally efficient and can be used when the number of candidate predictors k is greater than n. However, the number of predictors corresponding to the effects in the final selected model cannot exceed $n - 1$ because ordinary least squares (OLS) estimation is not available at that point.

Backward Elimination

Backward elimination begins by initializing the current model to the model that consists of the intercept term and all of the candidate effects. At each step, it constructs all of the candidate models that decrease the current model by a single effect. Backward elimination cannot be used when k is greater than n.

This method is preferred over forward selection in some fields such as biostatistics (Sauerbrei et al. 2020, p. 4) where the full model is plausible based on specialized knowledge. A drawback of backward elimination is that it might not be feasible if the full model is very large.

Stepwise Selection

Stepwise selection was introduced by Efroymson (1960). It begins in the same way as forward selection, but after the second step it allows an effect to be added or deleted from the current model. The model selected at the jth step is not necessarily nested within the model selected at the $(j + 1)$st step, as is the case with forward selection.

Forward Swap Selection

Forward swap selection begins in the same way as forward selection, but starting with the second step it makes pairwise swaps of all effects in the current model with effects out of the current model in order to improve the value of the select criterion. It tries to find the model with the best value among models consisting of one effect, the model with the best value among models consisting of two effects, and so on, but it is not guaranteed to find the model with the best value for each model size. Forward swap selection evaluates all swaps before any swap is made, whereas the stepwise method can remove the worst effect without considering what is possible by adding the best remaining effect.

Shrinkage Methods

Shrinkage methods—also called penalization methods—can provide more predictive accuracy and stability than sequential selection methods because they operate smoothly and simultaneously on all of the available effects.

Ridge regression, lasso methods, and least angle regression shrink the estimates of the regression coefficients $\beta_1, \ldots, \beta_p$ toward zero and away from their least squares estimates. The amount of shrinkage is controlled by a tuning parameter.

To use one of the shrinkage methods in the GLMSELECT and REGSELECT procedures, you specify a choose criterion and a stop criterion. The procedures find the value of the tuning parameter that optimizes the choose criterion, and they apply the stop criterion to determine the number of steps before the process terminates. Different types of criteria are available as explained on page 26.

Shrinkage methods reduce prediction variance at the cost of some bias, and they improve on the predictive accuracy of least squares regression as measured by mean squared error. The particular benefits of a shrinkage method depend on the way it penalizes the estimates of the coefficients:

- The lasso applies an ℓ_1 penalty, which results in a sparse, more interpretable model, as explained in the next section.

- Ridge regression applies an ℓ_2 penalty, which stabilizes the estimates when there is collinearity in the predictors. See page 98 for an explanation.

- The elastic net applies both an ℓ_1 penalty and an ℓ_2 penalty as a compromise between the lasso and ridge regression. See page 46 for an explanation.

The Lasso Method

The lasso, which stands for least absolute shrinkage and selection operator, was introduced by Robert Tibshirani in 1996 as a method for avoiding the instability of sequential selection methods while providing more interpretability than ridge regression.

Tibshirani (2011) explains how the idea for the lasso was influenced by Leo Breiman, who had made the case for methods that not only shrink the OLS estimates but also set some to zero. Breiman (1995) proposed the nonnegative garrotte as one such method. It provides better prediction accuracy than best-subset regression, but because it depends on the sizes and signs of the OLS estimates, it suffers from problems of collinearity encountered with OLS regression, which are explained in Chapter 6.

The lasso estimates β by adding an ℓ_1 penalty to the sum of squares of the residuals:

$$\hat{\beta}_{\text{lasso}} = \underset{\beta}{\text{argmin}} \left\{ \| \mathbf{y} - \mathbf{X}\beta \|_2^2 + \lambda \sum_{j=1}^{p} |\beta_j| \right\}, \quad \lambda \geq 0$$

This is equivalent to solving the constrained minimization problem

$$\min_{\beta_1, \ldots, \beta_p} \| \mathbf{y} - \mathbf{X}\beta \|_2^2 \quad \text{subject to} \quad \sum_{j=1}^{p} |\beta_j| \leq t, \quad t \geq 0$$

Because the lasso is not invariant to linear transformations of the predictors $x_1, \ldots, x_p$, they are first centered by their means and standardized so that $\sum_{i=1}^{n} x_{ij} = 0$ and $(1/n) \sum_{i=1}^{n} x_{ij}^2 = 1$ for $j = 1, \ldots, p$. Sets of predictors corresponding to classification variables or effects with multiple degrees of freedom are split, allowing them to enter or leave the model independently of each other.

The penalization parameter t controls the amount of shrinkage in $\hat{\boldsymbol{\beta}}_{\text{lasso}}$, which constrains the model by limiting how well it can fit the data. If t is zero, all of the estimated regression coefficients are zero and the model consists of an intercept term estimated by $\hat{\beta}_0 = (1/n) \sum_{i=1}^{n} y_i$. If t is larger than $\|\hat{\boldsymbol{\beta}}_{\text{OLS}}\|_1$, then $\hat{\boldsymbol{\beta}}_{\text{lasso}}$ coincides with $\hat{\boldsymbol{\beta}}_{\text{OLS}}$. As t increases away from zero, the lasso acts as a model selection method by setting some of the estimates of $\beta_1, \ldots, \beta_p$ to zero. Predictors are added to the model and can be removed due to the way in which the diamond-shaped constraint region for the coefficients intersects with the elliptical contours of the residual sum of squares.

In the special case where the model matrix is orthonormal ($\mathbf{X}'\mathbf{X}$ is the identity matrix $\mathbf{I}$), the lasso estimate of β_j for a fixed value of t has the soft threshold form

$$\hat{\beta}_j = \text{sign}(\tilde{\beta}_j) \left(|\tilde{\beta}_j| - \gamma \right)^+, \quad j = 1, \ldots, p$$

where $\tilde{\beta}_j$ is the OLS estimate and the constant γ is determined by the condition $\sum_{j=1}^{p} |\hat{\beta}_j| = t$; see Tibshirani (1996, Sec. 2.2). The lasso shrinks all of the coefficients toward zero by the same amount, setting smaller coefficients to zero and selecting the predictors corresponding to larger coefficients. The ridge regression estimate of β_j in this case is

$$\hat{\beta}_j = \frac{1}{1 + \gamma} \tilde{\beta}_j, \quad j = 1, \ldots, p$$

Ridge regression shrinks all of the coefficients by the same proportion, setting none of them to zero.

As t increases and the lasso adds a predictor to the model, its coefficient grows linearly in absolute value from zero until the next step, where another predictor enters or leaves. Output 5.18 on page 67 illustrates the coefficient progression for an example in which the lasso selects three predictors. Note that the slopes change at each step. For comparison, Output 5.5 on page 59 illustrates the progression for the same example using forward selection. There the coefficients are OLS estimates, which jump in and do not change from one step to the next (the lines connecting each coefficient to zero are plot artifacts).

As t decreases, the smooth nature of the shrinkage performed by the lasso enables it to better exploit the bias-variance tradeoff explained on page 21, and it equips the lasso to improve on the predictive accuracy of sequential selection methods.

Finding the optimal amount of shrinkage involves computing $\hat{\boldsymbol{\beta}}_{\text{lasso}}$ for a series of values of t. In general, the minimization problem has no simple closed form solution. Tibshirani (1996) obtained the solution with quadratic programming, but since then better, more scalable algorithms have emerged, including the LARS algorithm (Efron et al. 2004), a homotopy method (Osborne, Presnell, and Turlach 2000a, b), and simple coordinate descent (Hastie, Tibshirani, and Friedman 2009, Sec. 3.8.6).

The GLMSELECT and REGSELECT procedures compute the lasso solution path with the LARS algorithm, which contributes a shrinkage method of its own, referred to as least angle regression (LAR). The letter S in the abbreviation LARS indicates that it covers LAR, the lasso, and forward stagewise selection, a related method that is not discussed here.

Unlike ridge regression, the lasso assumes that the coefficients for some of the effects are zero. Tibshirani (1996) concluded that the lasso does better than ridge regression in situations with a small to moderate number of moderately sized effects, while ridge regression does considerably better than the lasso with a large number of small effects. Best-subset selection does better than the lasso and ridge regression with a small number of large effects. Across the board, no one method is uniformly superior.

Because the lasso and ridge regression are shrinkage methods, they can provide better prediction accuracy than selection methods. But compared with ridge regression, an advantage of selection methods and the lasso is that the models they produce are easier to interpret.

If t is small enough, the lasso can be used with data for which p is greater than n, an advantage over OLS regression it shares with ridge regression. Since its inception in 1996, applications of the lasso have grown in high-dimensional settings, such as the analysis of microarray data, where p is much greater than n, and in settings where a sparse or relatively small set of effects is believed to play an important role.

Although Tibshirani did not use the word *sparse* in his 1996 paper, the lasso does well with sparse problems because of the particular way in which the ℓ_1 penalty constrains the parameter estimates. Many different techniques for sparse statistical modeling have stemmed from the lasso approach during the past 20 years. The book by Hastie, Tibshirani, and Wainwright (2015) provides an in-depth overview.

Least Angle Regression Method

The least angle regression (LAR) method was introduced by Bradley Efron, Trevor Hastie, Iain Johnstone and Robert Tibshirani in 2004. It initializes $\hat{\beta}_1, \ldots, \hat{\beta}_p$ to zero and standardizes the predictors, so that $\sum_{i=1}^{n} x_{ij} = 0$, and $(1/n) \sum_{i=1}^{n} x_{ij}^2 = 1$. As with the lasso, sets of predictors corresponding to classification variables or effects with multiple degrees of freedom are split, allowing them to enter or leave the model independently of each other.

Like forward selection, the LAR method first finds the predictor, say x_{j_1}, most correlated in absolute value with the initial residual $r_0 = y - \bar{y}$. Forward selection would project r on the subspace spanned by x_{j_1} and set $\hat{\beta}_{j_1}$ to the OLS estimate $\sum_{i=1}^{n} x_{ij_1} r_i$, so that the correlation between $x_{j_1} \hat{\beta}_{j_1}$ and the residual $r_1 = y - x_{j_1} \hat{\beta}_{j_1}$ would be zero.

In contrast, the LAR method moves $\hat{\beta}_{j_1}$ from zero toward the OLS estimate. Concurrent with this increase, the residual changes and the correlation decreases. The step finishes when another predictor, say x_{j_2}, is equally correlated with the current residual.

The method then projects the current residual $y - x_{j_1} \hat{\beta}_{j_1}$ on the subspace spanned by x_{j_1} and x_{j_2}, and it moves $\hat{\beta}_{j_1}$ and $\hat{\beta}_{j_2}$ toward their joint least squares coefficients in a direction that is equiangular between x_{j_1} and x_{j_2}, so that their correlations with the current residual remain equal but decrease. This step finishes when a third predictor matches those correlations. The process terminates, reaching the full least squares solution, after $\min(p, n - 1)$ steps.

With a slight modification, this approach yields an efficient algorithm for producing the lasso solution path. Given the same set of candidate effects, the lasso can take more steps than LAR because it allows a predictor to leave as well as enter.

The degrees of freedom for the LAR and lasso methods is

$$\mathrm{df}(\hat{\mathbf{y}}) \equiv \frac{1}{\sigma^2} \sum_{i=1}^{n} \mathrm{Cov}(\hat{y}_i, y_i)$$

This definition, which extends to adaptive model fitting, is based on Stein's unbiased risk estimation theory (Stein 1981) and work by Efron et al. (2004). For the LAR method, $\mathrm{df}(\hat{\mathbf{y}})$ is equal to k after k steps (Hastie, Tibshirani, and Wainwright 2015, p. 18), and so Mallows' C_P statistic can be used to choose the number of steps. By comparison, $\mathrm{df}(\hat{\mathbf{y}})$ is greater than k for sequential selection methods, although it is difficult to assess.

For the lasso, Zou, Hastie, and Tibshirani (2007) showed that the number of nonzero coefficients is an unbiased estimate of the degrees of freedom and is a good approximation for $\mathrm{df}(\hat{\mathbf{y}})$ anywhere in the solution path. This opens the door for using C_P, AIC, and SBC (also known as BIC) as model selection criteria for the lasso. Cross validation is also recommended for model selection with the LAR and lasso methods.

Along with the LAR method, the GLMSELECT and REGSELECT procedures provide a hybrid version of LAR that uses the LARS algorithm to select the effects in the model but estimates the coefficients using OLS. The hybrid version was suggested by Efron et al. (2004, p. 421) to provide a more familiar looking model.

The LAR method is appealing because of its computational efficiency and geometric interpretability. On the other hand, its reliance on equal correlation make it vulnerable to collinearity in the predictors. Hastie, Tibshirani, and Friedman (2009, Sec. 3.4) provide a deeper explanation of the lasso and LAR methods.

The Adaptive Lasso Method

The adaptive lasso method is one of many variants of the lasso method; it was proposed by Zou (2006) to deal with sparse situations in which the lasso is inconsistent, which means it does not necessarily select the correct effects as n increases.

For positive γ, the adaptive lasso method defines a coefficient weight vector

$$\hat{\mathbf{w}} = (\hat{w}_1, \ldots, \hat{w}_p)' = 1/\|\hat{\boldsymbol{\beta}}\|^{\gamma}$$

where $\hat{\boldsymbol{\beta}}$ is a root-n-consistent pilot estimator of $\boldsymbol{\beta}$. Both γ and $\hat{\boldsymbol{\beta}}$ are tuning parameters specified by the user.

The adaptive lasso estimator is

$$\hat{\boldsymbol{\beta}}_{\mathrm{adapt}} = \underset{\boldsymbol{\beta}}{\mathrm{argmin}} \left\{ \|\mathbf{y} - \mathbf{X}\boldsymbol{\beta}\|_2^2 + \lambda \sum_{j=1}^{p} |\hat{w}_j \beta_j| \right\}, \quad \lambda \geq 0$$

Zou (2006) showed that if $\hat{\mathbf{w}}$ is chosen appropriately, the adaptive lasso can have oracle properties; it identifies the right effects with the optimal estimation rate as n increases. Zou suggested using $\hat{\boldsymbol{\beta}}_{\mathrm{OLS}}$ as a choice for $\hat{\boldsymbol{\beta}}$ or using $\hat{\boldsymbol{\beta}}_{\mathrm{ridge}}$ if collinearity is a problem. For $p \geq n$, univariate regression estimates can be used.

The adaptive lasso method is a two-stage approach; it begins with an initial estimate of $\hat{\beta}$ that reduces the bias of large estimates $\hat{\beta}_j$. The GLMSELECT and REGSELECT procedures provide the ability to specify a customized initial estimate with an input data set. By default, the procedures use $\hat{\beta}_{\text{OLS}}$ and $\gamma = 1$.

The Group Lasso Method

The group lasso method, introduced by Yuan (2006), extends the lasso by allowing it to select entire effects with multiple degrees of freedom—in other words, effects associated with sets of columns in the model matrix. Rather than splitting the columns for a particular effect, the group lasso method forces them to be collectively included or excluded from the model.

Suppose there are J groups of columns and β_{G_j} is the set of coefficients corresponding to the jth group. The group lasso estimator is

$$\hat{\beta}_{\text{group}} = \underset{\beta}{\text{argmin}} \left\{ \| \mathbf{y} - \mathbf{X}\beta \|_2^2 + \lambda \sum_{j=1}^{J} \sqrt{|G_j|} \|\beta_{G_j}\|_2 \right\}, \quad \lambda \geq 0$$

Here $|G_j|$ denotes the number of parameters that correspond to the jth group. If $|G_j| = 1$, then $\sqrt{|G_j|}\|\beta_{G_j}\|_2 = |\beta_{G_j}|$. Furthermore, if $|G_j| = 1$ for $j = 1, \ldots, J$, the group lasso estimator reduces to the lasso estimator.

The group lasso method selects effects in such a way that some of the estimates $\hat{\beta}_{G_j}$ are zero, while the elements of the remaining estimates $\hat{\beta}_{G_j}$ are all nonzero. This is a consequence of the ℓ_2 constraint in the penalization term.

The solution path for the group lasso is not piecewise linear as it is for the lasso. The GLMSELECT procedure solves the optimization problem for the group lasso with a method proposed by Nesterov (2013) that corresponds to a specified value of λ. Since the optimal λ is unknown, the search is based on a sequence of regularization parameters $\rho, \rho^2, \rho^3, \ldots$, where ρ is a positive value less than one that is specified by the user. At the kth step, the group lasso uses $\lambda = \rho^k$. The group lasso does not necessarily include or exclude one effect. With the GLMSELECT procedure, you can specify λ directly, or you can specify ρ.

The Elastic Net Method

The elastic net method was introduced by Zou and Hastie (2005) to overcome several limitations of the lasso; in particular, the lasso does not handle correlated predictors as well as ridge regression when n is greater than p. The elastic net method compromises between the lasso and ridge regression by penalizing both the sum of the absolute values of the regression coefficients and the sum of the squared regression coefficients:

$$\min_{\beta_0,\ldots,\beta_p} \sum_{i=1}^{n} \left(y_i - \beta_0 - \sum_{j=1}^{p} x_{ij}\beta_j \right)^2 \quad \text{subject to} \quad \sum_{j=1}^{p} |\beta_j| \leq t_1 \text{ and } \sum_{j=1}^{p} \beta_j^2 \leq t_2$$

If t_1 is a large value, the method reduces to ridge regression. If t_2 is a large value, the method reduces to the lasso method.

The elastic net method offers advantages over the lasso method in three situations (Zou and Hastie 2005; Hastie, Tibshirani, and Wainwright 2015):

- The elastic net method can select more than n variables when the number of parameters p exceeds n. The lasso method can select at most n variables.

- The elastic net method can achieve better prediction when the predictors are highly correlated and n exceeds p.

- The elastic net method can handle groups of highly correlated variables more effectively (Hastie, Tibshirani, and Wainwright 2015, Ch. 4).

See page 106 in Chapter 6 for more details.

The SCAD Penalization Method

Fan and Li (2001) introduced an alternative to the lasso that replaces the absolute value penalty function $\lambda|\beta|$ with the smoothly clipped absolute deviation (SCAD) penalty function

$$P^{\text{SCAD}}(\beta; \lambda, \alpha) = \begin{cases} \lambda|\beta| & \text{if } |\beta| \leq \lambda \\ \left(2\alpha\lambda|\beta| - \lambda^2 - \beta^2\right)/(2(\alpha-1)) & \text{if } \lambda < |\beta| < \alpha\lambda \\ \lambda^2(\alpha+1)/2 & \text{if } |\beta| \geq \alpha\lambda \end{cases}$$

where λ and α are tuning parameters with $\lambda > 0$ and $\alpha > 2$. The SCAD estimator is

$$\hat{\boldsymbol{\beta}}_{\text{SCAD}} = \underset{\boldsymbol{\beta}}{\text{argmin}} \left\{ \frac{1}{2}\|\mathbf{y} - \mathbf{X}\boldsymbol{\beta}\|_2^2 + n \sum_{j=1}^{p} P^{\text{SCAD}}(\beta_j; \lambda, \alpha) \right\}$$

Figure 4.1 compares the lasso penalty with the SCAD penalty and the minimax concave penalty (MCP) (see page 48) with $\lambda = 1$ and $\alpha = 4$,

Figure 4.1 SCAD Penalty and Minimax Concave Penalty with $\lambda = 1$ and $\alpha = 4$

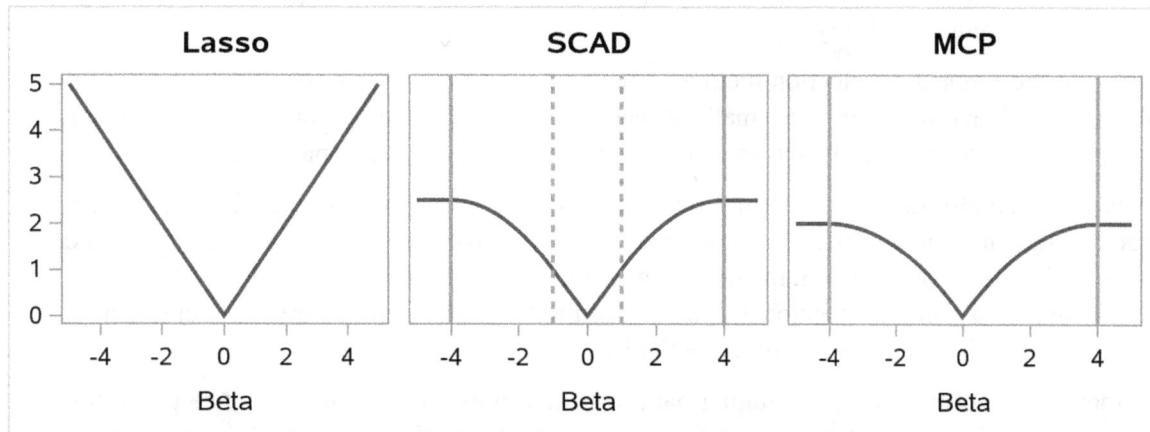

For $|\beta| \leq \lambda$, the SCAD penalty is identical to the lasso penalty. For $|\beta| > \lambda$, the SCAD penalty increases quadratically until it becomes a constant for $|\beta| > \alpha\lambda$. Unlike the lasso penalty, the SCAD

penalty is neither convex nor concave; it is called a folded concave penalty because it is concave for $\beta < 0$ and concave for $\beta > 0$. Like the adaptive lasso method (see page 45), the SCAD penalization method mitigates the bias of the lasso method by shrinking the larger coefficient estimates less severely, but it does so in a single stage rather than two stages.

The Minimax Concave Penalty Method

The minimax concave penalty (MCP) method, introduced by Zhang (2010), is a folded concave penalty method like the SCAD penalization method, and it has a similar motivation. The MCP function is

$$P^{\text{MCP}}(\beta; \lambda, \alpha) = \begin{cases} \lambda|\beta| - 2\beta^2\alpha & \text{if } |\beta| \le \alpha\lambda \\ \alpha\lambda^2/2 & \text{if } |\beta| > \alpha\lambda \end{cases}$$

As illustrated in Figure 4.1, the slope of the MCP begins to decrease for $|\beta| > 0$, whereas the slope for the SCAD penalty does not begin to decrease until $|\beta|$ reaches λ and the slope for the lasso penalty remains constant.

The MCP estimator is

$$\hat{\boldsymbol{\beta}}_{\text{MCP}} = \underset{\boldsymbol{\beta}}{\text{argmin}} \left\{ \frac{1}{2}\|\mathbf{y} - \mathbf{X}\boldsymbol{\beta}\|_2^2 + n\sum_{j=1}^{p} P^{\text{MCP}}(\beta_j; \lambda, \alpha) \right\}$$

Summary

Among the methods presented in this chapter, no single method stands above the rest.

Best-subset regression finds the best model in terms of a criterion such as R^2, but it does not easily extend to models with classification effects or to models with more than around 40 continuous predictors.

Sequential selection methods do not have these limitations, but they can be overly sensitive to small changes in the data that induce large changes in the effects that are selected. This makes it more difficult to rely on the model for explanatory purposes, and it complicates the process of building a model with good predictive ability.

In contrast to the sequential selection methods, the lasso method operates smoothly on all of the available effects; it automatically sets small estimated coefficients to zero, which produces models that are sparser and can provide better predictive performance, and it is computationally efficient.

However, the lasso also has its limitations, which include a tendency to produce biased estimates for large coefficients. The adaptive lasso method, the group lasso method, the elastic net method, and the folded concave penalization methods deal with these limitations by modifying the penalty function for the lasso. The optimization techniques required by these methods are considerably more complex and expensive than those of other methods.

All the methods involve at least one tuning parameter that must be chosen to balance prediction bias and variance. For best-subset regression and sequential selection methods, this parameter is the model size; for shrinkage methods, it is the parameters that control the optimization. Chapter 5 explains features of the GLMSELECT, REG, and REGSELECT procedures that deal with the issue of choosing the tuning parameter.

Chapter 5
Building General Linear Models: Procedures

Contents

This chapter introduces two procedures that build general linear models: the GLMSELECT procedure in SAS 9 and its counterpart in SAS Viya, the REGSELECT procedure. In addition, this chapter describes the use of the REG procedure in SAS 9 for building models with best-subset regression.

The chapter helps you get started with the procedures by presenting examples that illustrate their syntax and output. To make the best use of the procedures, you should have some understanding of concepts, issues, and methods presented in Chapter 2, Chapter 3, and Chapter 4, respectively.

This chapter begins with a detailed explanation of the GLMSELECT procedure. Because the REGSELECT procedure shares many features with the GLMSELECT procedure, only the differences between the two procedures are explained.

Many features of the GLMSELECT procedure are also available in procedures for building specialized models that are introduced in Part II of this book.

Introduction to the GLMSELECT Procedure

The GLMSELECT procedure fits and builds general linear models for prediction. It is closely related to two other SAS/STAT procedures: the GLM procedure, which fits general linear models for statistical inference, and the REG procedure, which fits and builds regression models. Unlike the GLM procedure, the REG procedure is limited to models with predictors that are numeric.

If you are a longtime user of the REG procedure, you might have wished that it had a CLASS statement so that you could incorporate categorical predictors in your models. Not only does the GLMSELECT procedure have a CLASS statement, but it also improves greatly on the model building capability of the REG procedure:

- The GLMSELECT procedure implements modern methods for building models that are parsimonious and provide good predictive performance. The REG procedure lacks methods that protect against overfitting the training data.

- By default, the REG procedure uses significance levels for F tests as the criteria for sequential model selection. These criteria are no longer recommended, as discussed on page 34. Instead, the GLMSELECT procedure provides criteria that minimize prediction error or penalize model complexity; see page 25 in Chapter 2.

- The GLMSELECT procedure provides newer methods, such as the lasso and model averaging, that are not available in the REG procedure.

During the design of the GLMSELECT procedure, the developers debated its name. Should it be REGSELECT to emphasize new capability for building regression models? Or should it be GLMSELECT to emphasize capability for building general linear models? GLMSELECT was chosen, and REGSELECT was later chosen for the corresponding procedure in SAS Viya.

Table 5.1 shows how the GLMSELECT, REG, and GLM procedures complement each other.

Table 5.1 Recommended Uses of the GLMSELECT, REG, and GLM Procedures

GLMSELECT Procedures	REG Procedure	GLM Procedure
Fitting general linear models with specified effects (continuous or categorical)	Fitting regression models with numeric predictors	Fitting general linear models with specified effects (continuous or categorical)
Computing p-values, confidence limits, tests for β_js in fitted general linear models	Computing p-values, confidence limits, tests for β_js in fitted regression models	Inference, including tests for effects, estimates of linear functions of β_js, tests for linear contrasts of β_js
	Exploring regression models with diagnostics, influence statistics	
Building general linear models		
Model averaging		
	Best-subset regression ($k < \approx 40$)	
	Ridge regression	

Specifying the Candidate Effects and the Selection Method

When you use the GLMSELECT procedure to build a regression model, you specify the candidate effects in the MODEL, CLASS, and EFFECT statements.

As with other SAS/STAT modeling procedures, the CLASS statement names the classification variables; it enables you to specify classification variables without constructing dummy variables for their levels. You can use the PARAM= option to specify parameterization methods for these variables, which are explained in Appendix I, and you can specify them individually for each variable. The default is GLM coding when the PARAM= option is not specified with any individual variable; otherwise, the default is effect coding.

The MODEL statement names the response variable and the candidate effects, which can include main effects, interactions, and other effects that are formed from continuous or classification variables. The candidate effects can also be constructed effects such as splines and polynomials, which you define with the EFFECT statement, as explained in Appendix F. You specify the method of selection or shrinkage with the SELECTION= option in the MODEL statement. For instance, the following statements (taken from the example that begins on page 56) request forward selection from two classification variables and 20 continuous variables:

```
proc glmselect data=Stores;
   class Region Training;
   model CloseRate = Region Training X1-X20 /
      selection=forward(choose=sbc select=sbc stop=sbc);
run;
```

Table 5.2 summarizes the methods available with the SELECTION= option.

Table 5.2 Selection and Shrinkage Methods in the GLMSELECT Procedure

Method	Description	SELECTION=*keyword*
Forward selection	Starts with the intercept and adds effects	FORWARD
Backward elimination	Starts with the full model and deletes effects	BACKWARD
Stepwise selection	Starts with the intercept; effects are added and can be deleted (Efroymson 1960)	STEPWISE
Least angle regression	Starts with no effects and adds effects; at each step, $\hat{\beta}_j$s are shrunk toward zero (Efron et al. 2004)	LAR
Hybrid LAR	Uses LAR to select effects and OLS to estimate coefficients (Efron et al. 2004)	LAR(LSCOEFFS)
Lasso	Constrains sum of $|\beta_j|$s; some $\hat{\beta}_j$s are set to zero (Tibshirani 1996)	LASSO
Adaptive lasso	Constrains sum of weighted $|\beta_j|$s; some $\hat{\beta}_j$s are set to zero (Zou 2006)	LASSO(ADAPTIVE)
Group lasso	Constrains sum of Euclidean norms of β_js corresponding to effects; all $\hat{\beta}_j$s for the same effect are set to zero or are nonzero (Yuan and Lin 2006)	GROUPLASSO
Elastic net	Constrains sum of $|\beta_j|$s and sum of β_j^2s; some $\hat{\beta}_j$s are set to zero (Zou and Hastie 2005)	ELASTICNET
No selection	Fits fully specified model	NONE

Controlling the Selection Method

The GLMSELECT procedure provides three ways to control the operation of the methods in Table 5.2, which you specify with suboptions in parentheses after the SELECTION= option:

- CHOOSE= specifies the criterion for choosing the model. This criterion is evaluated at each step of the selection process. The final selected model is the model with the best value of this criterion.

- SELECT= specifies the criterion for determining which effect enters or leaves at each step of the forward, backward, and stepwise methods. This is the effect that gives the maximum improvement in the specified criterion, with the exception of the SL criterion, which bases the determination on the significance level of an approximate test.

  Do not confuse the SELECT= suboption with the SELECTION= option. Also note that the SELECT= suboption does not apply to shrinkage methods.

- STOP= specifies the criterion for terminating the selection process. This suboption is ignored if you use the STEPS=k option in the MODEL statement to specify the precise number of steps or if you use the MAXSTEPS=k suboption to specify the maximum number of steps.

  If you specify STOP=NONE and do not specify STEPS=k or MAXSTEPS=k, then no stopping criterion is applied; the process terminates when there are no further models to consider.

The CHOOSE= criteria fall into two categories:

- Criteria that estimate the prediction error of the model: Mallows' C_P statistic (see page 26), the predicted residual sum of squares based on cross validation, and the average squared error for validation data (see page 31).

- Criteria that penalize the complexity of the model: adjusted R-square (see page 30), AIC, AICC, BIC, and SBC (see page 28).

Table 5.3 lists the criteria you can request with the CHOOSE= suboption.

Table 5.3 Criteria Available with the CHOOSE= Suboption

Suboption	Criterion
ADJRSQ	Adjusted R-square statistic
AIC	Akaike's information criterion
AICC	Corrected Akaike's information criterion
BIC	Sawa Bayesian information criterion
CP	Mallows' C_P statistic
CV	Predicted residual sum of squares with internal m-fold cross validation
CVEX	Predicted residual sum of squares with external m-fold cross validation
PRESS	Predicted residual sum of squares with leave-one-out cross validation
SBC	Schwarz Bayesian information criterion
VALIDATE	Average squared error for validation data if data are partitioned

When you specify CHOOSE=ADJRSQ, the model chosen is the one with the largest adjusted *R*-square statistic. Otherwise, the model chosen is the one with the smallest value of the criterion. Not all of the criteria in Table 5.3 are available with every selection method. For details, see the chapter on the GLMSELECT procedure in the *SAS/STAT 15.1 User's Guide*.

Table 5.4 lists the criteria you can request with the SELECT= suboption.

Table 5.4   Criteria Available with the SELECT= Suboption

Suboption	Criterion
ADJRSQ	Adjusted *R*-square statistic
AIC	Akaike's information criterion
AICC	Corrected Akaike's information criterion
BIC	Sawa Bayesian information criterion
CP	Mallows' C_P statistic
CV	Predicted residual sum of squares with internal *m*-fold cross validation
PRESS	Predicted residual sum of squares with leave-one-out cross validation
RSQUARE	*R*-square statistic
SBC	Schwarz Bayesian information criterion
SL	Significance level (not recommended)
VALIDATE	Average square error for validation data

With the SELECT=SL option, the significance level (*p*-value) of an *F* test is used to assess the contribution of a candidate effect to the model fit. You can specify the threshold levels for an effect to enter or stay with the SLENTRY= and SLSTAY= suboptions for the METHOD= option. The default levels are both 0.05. Because these levels are not meaningful as probabilities, the SELECT=SL option is not recommended (see "Problems with Data-Driven Model Selection" on page 33); it is provided for backward compatibility with the REG procedure.

Table 5.5 lists criteria you can request with the STOP= suboption. Except for STOP=*m*, selection stops when the criterion for the model at the next step would not improve.

Table 5.5   Criteria Available with the STOP= Suboption

Suboption	Criterion
m	Selection stops when model has *m* effects
ADJRSQ	Adjusted *R*-square statistic
AIC	Akaike's information criterion
AICC	Corrected Akaike's information criterion
BIC	Sawa Bayesian information criterion
CP	Mallows' C_P statistic
CV	Predicted residual sum of squares with internal *m*-fold cross validation
L1	Lasso regularization parameter
PRESS	Predicted residual sum of squares with leave-one-out cross validation
SBC	Schwarz Bayesian information criterion
SL	Significance level (not recommended)
VALIDATE	Average square error for validation data

Which Selection Methods and Criteria Should You Use?

You should not rely on the defaults for the SELECTION= option and the CHOOSE=, SELECT=, and STOP= suboptions; they are by no means guaranteed to produce models with good predictive performance. In fact, no single combination of selection methods and criteria is uniformly the most effective in practice.

Validation Based on Independent Data

The preferred approach is to find a set of effects that minimizes prediction error when applied to validation or test data that the training process has not encountered. Training error is not a reliable estimate of prediction error, as explained on page 25.

If you can spare enough observations to set aside for validation, you can build a model by computing its average square error (ASE) from the validation portion:

$$\text{ASE}_{\text{val}} = \frac{1}{m} \sum_{i=1}^{m} (y_i^{\text{val}} - \hat{y}_i^{\text{val}})^2$$

where m is the number of observations in the validation data. You can request this approach by specifying VALIDATE with the CHOOSE=, SELECT=, or STOP= options. For example, if you specify CHOOSE=VALIDATE, the GLMSELECT procedure computes ASE from the validation data at each step, and it selects the model at the first step where ASE_{val} is minimized. You can use the PARTITION statement to allocate part of the DATA= data set for validation, or you can specify an independent data set for validation with the VALDATA= option in the PROC GLMSELECT statement.

Alternatives to Independent Validation

When you do not have enough observations for independent validation, you can use the CHOOSE=, SELECT=, and STOP= suboptions to request criteria that are computed from the training data. These include AIC, AICC, BIC, and SBC, which penalize model complexity; Mallows' C_P statistic, which estimates the expected mean square error of prediction (see page 26); and m-fold cross validation and leave-one-out cross validation, which estimate prediction error (see page 31).

Recommendations for Applying *m*-fold Cross Validation

Although m-fold cross validation is one of the better alternatives, it can easily be done incorrectly, especially if there are patterns or trends in the data that might be confounded with the folds. With the CVMETHOD= suboption, which you specify after the METHOD= option, you can request different ways to create the folds, including random assignment.

There are subtle but important differences in the m-fold cross validation methods provided by the CHOOSE=CV and CHOOSE=CVEX suboptions in Table 5.3.

The internal m-fold cross validation method provided by the CV suboption correctly mimics how forward selection, backward elimination, and stepwise selection are applied to independent validation data because the candidate models at each step all have the same number of effects (independently of the data) and because the effect estimates are based on OLS using all of the training folds.

However, this method is not applicable with the lasso and elastic net methods, which obtain the regularization parameter λ from a solution path determined from the training data. Consequently, with the lasso and elastic net methods, you should specify CHOOSE=CVEX to request external m-fold cross validation.

In *each* of the m steps, this method first determines a solution path from the $m-1$ training folds and then computes a penalized estimate $\hat{\beta}$ and a predicted residual sum of squares for each value of λ in the path. The m different paths are then combined into a single path, and the predicted residual sums of squares are added at distinct parameters along this path to form an estimate of the prediction error (CVEXPRESS) for each value of λ. The model corresponding to the value of λ with the smallest CVEXPRESS is then selected. This procedure is computationally more expensive than internal cross validation, but it properly applies cross validation to the entire lasso method, which avoids reuse of the response data. It also uses the shrinkage estimates obtained with penalized least squares.

External m-fold cross validation does not apply to the group lasso method because the solution path for that method is specified by the user rather than determined from the data.

Recommendations for Applying Leave-One-Out Cross Validation

Leave-one-out cross validation, requested with the PRESS suboption, avoids the difficulties of choosing the folds for m-fold cross validation, but it has other drawbacks as discussed on page 32. Also, note that leave-one-out cross validation is not available with the elastic net and group lasso methods; it is available with the lasso and LAR methods if you specify the LSCOEFFS suboption so that OLS coefficients are computed at each step.

Comparing Selection Criteria

To help you understand whether selection criteria other than the one you specified might lead to a different model, the GLMSELECT procedure produces a plot that displays multiple criteria for each step of the selection process. For instance, see Output 5.8 on page 62. You can request this plot by specifying PLOTS=CRITERIA or PLOTS=ALL in the MODEL statement.

Forced Inclusion of Model Effects

Based on subject matter knowledge, you might want some effects to be included in the final model regardless of how others are selected.

If you are using forward selection, backward elimination, or stepwise selection, you can specify the suboption INCLUDE=m to force inclusion of the first m effects in the MODEL statement. For instance, the following statements[†] build a model consisting of Region, Training, and X1, together with predictors selected from X2 through X20:

```
proc glmselect data=Stores;
   class Region Training;
   model CloseRate = Region Training X1-X20 /
      selection=forward( include=3  choose=sbc select=sbc stop=sbc);
run;
```

[†]The book highlights code to differentiate options or point out options that are easily overlooked.

Example: Predicting the Close Rate of Retail Stores

The following example is used in this chapter to illustrate methods available in the GLMSELECT and REGSELECT procedures. It is revisited in Chapter 8, "Building Quantile Regression Models," and in Appendix H, "Methods for Scoring Data."

Within the retail industry, the close rate for a store is the percentage of shoppers entering a store who make a purchase. Analytics groups in large retail companies build regression models to identify factors that are good predictors of close rate. Models that are interpretable as well as accurate are especially valuable because they yield insights for understanding customer behavior.

The close rates for 500 home improvement stores are saved in a data set named Stores. Each observation provides information about a store. The variables are the response CloseRate and the following candidate predictors:

- A categorical variable Region, which indicates the marketing region and has values **East**, **West**, **South**, and **Midwest**
- A categorical variable Training, which provides the level of customer service training at the store and has values **None**, **In Progress**, and **Complete**
- Continuous variables X1, ..., X20, which measure 20 general characteristics of each store, such as its floor size and number of associates
- Continuous variables P1, ..., P6, which measure six promotional activities, such as advertising and sales
- Continuous variables L1, ..., L6, which measure special layouts of items in six departments

In practice, the data available for predicting close rates are much larger. The data in Stores have been cleaned and transformed to simplify the example.

Example: Building a Model with Forward Selection

The following statements use the GLMSELECT procedure to build a model for close rate by using the forward selection method:

```
ods graphics on;
proc glmselect plots=coefficients data=Stores;
   class Region(param=reference ref='Midwest' split)
         Training(param=reference ref='None');
   model CloseRate = Region Training X1-X20 L1-L6 P1-P6 /
      selection=forward(choose=sbc select=sbc stop=sbc);
run;
```

The DATA= option in the procedure statement specifies the input data set. The PLOTS= option requests graphs that visualize the selection process and help you interpret the results. The graphs are automatically produced by ODS Graphics, as explained in Appendix J. The ON and OFF options in the ODS GRAPHICS statement enable and disable the creation of graphs. You do not need to sandwich every procedure invocation between **ods graphics on;** and **ods graphics off;** statements—this is a common misconception.

Programming Tip: Enable procedures to create graphs by placing `ods graphics on;` at the top of your program.

The CLASS statement lists the predictor variables that are classification variables; it behaves like the CLASS statement in the GLM procedure and other statistical modeling procedures. The PARAM= option specifies how the values of classification variables are parameterized (coded) in the model matrix **X**. Here, because reference-cell coding is specified for Region and Training, the parameter estimates for their main effects (if selected) will estimate the differences between the effects of the non-reference levels and the effect of the level specified with the REF= option. In particular, if one of these reference-based parameters is not selected, this implies that the difference between that level of the variable and the reference level is not important for predictive purposes.

In general, the interpretation of the parameter estimates for the selected model depends on the coding scheme, and so it is important to choose a scheme that is meaningful. Appendix I, "Coding Schemes for Categorical Predictors," describes parameterizations that are commonly used. For complete details, see the chapter on Shared Concepts and Topics in the *SAS/STAT 15.1 User's Guide*.

The SPLIT option is available in a number of model selection procedures. It allows the columns of the model matrix that are associated with a classification effect to be selected independently of each other rather than as a group. Here, for instance, the column for `South` can be selected independently of the columns for `East` and `North`.

The SPLIT option contributes interpretability to a selected model with classification effects. However, splitting a large number of effects with many levels can greatly increase the number of candidate predictors, making it more difficult to select the true effects if the number of observations is small.

The MODEL statement lists the response variable, the candidate predictor effects, and options after the slash that specify and customize the selection method. Here the SELECTION= option requests forward selection. Table 5.2 lists other methods you can request.

Customizing the Forward Selection Method

The GLMSELECT procedure provides many ways to customize model building methods. Here, the CHOOSE=SBC suboption specifies SBC as the criterion for choosing the model.[†] At each step of the selection process, an effect is added to the model and the SBC statistic is evaluated for the current model:

$$\text{SBC} = n \log\left(\frac{\text{SSE}}{n}\right) + p \log(n)$$

where SSE is the error sum of squares. Like other information criteria, SBC penalizes for the number of effects, or to be precise, the number of predictors (p) that represent the effects in the model matrix **X**. The selected model is the model for which SBC is the smallest.

The SELECT=SBC suboption specifies that the effect added at each step is the one that decreases SBC the most. Note that SELECT=SBC is the default for the forward, backward, and stepwise methods. It does not apply to other methods.

[†]The Schwarz Bayesian information criterion SBC is called BIC in many references. See page 28.

The STOP=SBC suboption specifies that selection is to stop at the step where the next step would yield a model that has a larger value of SBC. Here, this happens to be the default stopping criterion because SELECT=SBC is specified.

There is no particular reason to prefer SBC in this example; it is used purely for illustration. AIC would be equally valid as a choice for an information criterion. Alternative methods for model selection are illustrated later in this example.

Interpreting the Results

The GLMSELECT statements on page 56 produce a series of tables and a plot, beginning with Output 5.1, which lists the criteria for the selection process.

Output 5.1 Model Information

Data Set	WORK.STORES
Dependent Variable	CloseRate
Selection Method	Forward
Select Criterion	SBC
Stop Criterion	SBC
Choose Criterion	SBC
Effect Hierarchy Enforced	None

Effect hierarchy refers to the requirement that for any term to be selected, all effects contained in the term must also be in the model (this is called strong hierarchy). For instance, effect hierarchy allows a two-way interaction effect to be included only if the corresponding main effects are included. By default, the GLMSELECT procedure does not maintain model hierarchy, but in this example it is not relevant since there are no contained effects in the model. If your model includes interactions that contain main effects, you can control how the model hierarchy requirement is applied with the HIERARCHY= option in the MODEL statement. See page 179, where this option is used with the HPLOGISTIC procedure.

Output 5.2 lists the levels of the classification variables.

Output 5.2 Class Level Information

Class Level Information		
Class	**Levels**	**Values**
Region	4	* East Midwest South West
Training	3	Complete InProgress None
* Associated Parameters Split		

Output 5.3 lists the number of candidate effects. This can be very large if, for instance, you select a model from all of the main effects and their two-way interactions.

Output 5.3 Dimensions

Dimensions	
Number of Effects	35
Number of Effects after Splits	37
Number of Parameters	38

At each step of the selection process, SBC is evaluated, and the model that yields the minimal value of SBC is chosen. Output 5.4 shows that the minimum is reached at Step 15, when L2 enters the model.

Output 5.4 Selection Summary of Forward Selection Using SBC

		Forward Selection Summary		
Step	Effect Entered	Number Effects In	Number Parms In	SBC
0	Intercept	1	1	631.5807
1	X2	2	2	360.0538
2	X4	3	3	137.2902
3	Region_South	4	4	81.3798
4	L1	5	5	69.1589
5	P5	6	6	58.8027
6	L5	7	7	48.5608
7	P3	8	8	39.3333
8	P4	9	9	32.8399
9	L6	10	10	29.2646
10	L3	11	11	24.8623
11	P6	12	12	23.4529
12	P2	13	13	21.2727
13	L4	14	14	18.2626
14	P1	15	15	17.1062
15	L2	16	16	16.8729*
		* Optimal Value of Criterion		

The coefficient progression plot in Output 5.5, requested with the PLOTS= option, shows the standardized coefficients of the effects selected at each step along with the change in SBC.

Output 5.5 Coefficient Progression for Forward Selection

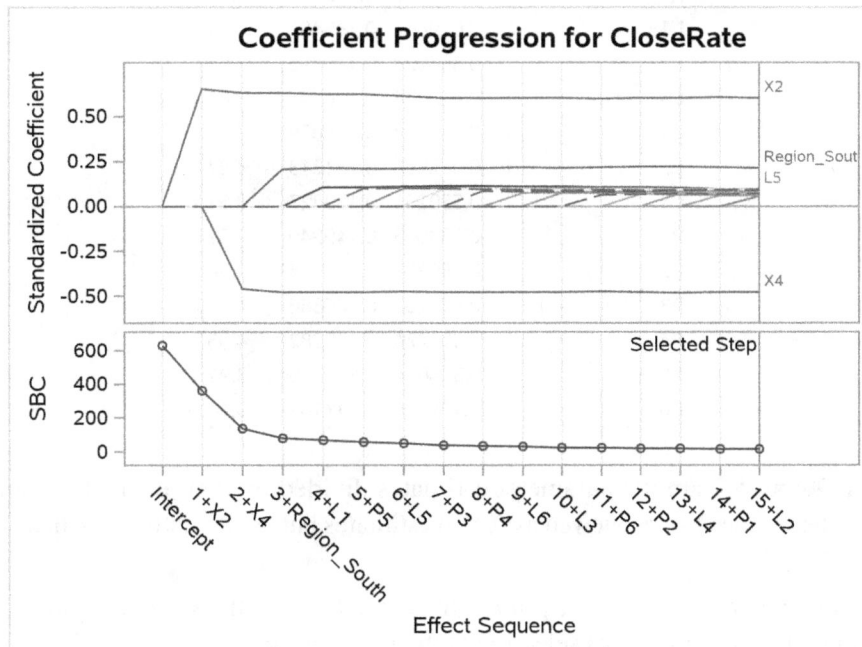

In this example, SBC decreases quickly when X2, X4, and Region_South are selected. Then it decreases only slightly after Step 4, when L1 is selected. The small effects could be actual effects, or they could be noise. The fact that all of these effects measure promotional activities and special layouts suggests they are true predictors of close rate.[†] Output 5.6 lists the effects and fit statistics for the selected model.

Output 5.6 Effects and Fit Statistics for the Selected Model

Effects: Intercept Region_South X2 X4 L1 L2 L3 L4 L5 L6 P1 P2 P3 P4 P5 P6

Root MSE	0.93585
Dependent Mean	61.39824
R-Square	0.7573
Adj R-Sq	0.7498
AIC	451.43918
AICC	452.70889
SBC	16.87291

Output 5.7 shows the parameter estimates. The estimates for Region_South, X2, and X4 are larger than the estimates for the other predictors. You should interpret the sizes of the estimates with care, since the predictors are not necessarily on the same scale. You can request the display of standardized estimates in the table by specifying the option STB in the MODEL statement.

Output 5.7 Parameter Estimates with Forward Selection

Parameter Estimates

Parameter	DF	Estimate	Standard Error	t Value
Intercept	1	59.563030	0.181698	327.81
Region_South	1	0.852461	0.091167	9.35
X2	1	3.959738	0.150641	26.29
X4	1	-3.015353	0.142871	-21.11
L1	1	0.629862	0.149481	4.21
L2	1	0.366923	0.146395	2.51
L3	1	0.412324	0.146743	2.81
L4	1	0.469072	0.144829	3.24
L5	1	0.602895	0.141213	4.27
L6	1	0.530262	0.139327	3.81
P1	1	0.392566	0.149940	2.62
P2	1	0.485213	0.144584	3.36
P3	1	0.592262	0.146886	4.03
P4	1	0.602274	0.148382	4.06
P5	1	0.574614	0.146799	3.91
P6	1	0.462066	0.147162	3.14

The t values in Output 5.7 are the parameter estimates divided by their estimated standard errors $(\hat{\beta}_j / \widehat{SE}(\hat{\beta}_j))$. The t values can be viewed as scaled estimates but not as statistics with a t distribution.

[†] After examining a progression plot, you might decide to rerun the selection with fewer or more steps. Specifying STOP=k terminates selection at the first step for which the model has k effects.

Unlike the GLM procedure, the GLMSELECT procedure does not report *p*-values by default because they are not appropriate when computed from selected models. If you fit a fully specified model, you can specify the SHOWPVALUES option in the MODEL statement to request *p*-values.

In this example, if you specify STOP=NONE instead of STOP=SBC, forward selection continues beyond Step 15 and terminates at Step 36, where it runs out of candidate effects. The global minimum of SBC turns out to be the local minimum reached at Step 15, and so the same model is chosen. In general, specifying STOP=NONE can result in a lower global minimum and a model with more effects. For this reason, some experts recommend specifying STOP=NONE when the number of candidate effects *p* is small and STOP=*k* when *p* is large (where *k* is less than *p*).

To assess the sensitivity of the selection process to the selection method, the following statements build the model with stepwise selection and backward elimination:

```
proc glmselect plots=coefficients data=Stores;
   class Region(param=reference ref='Midwest' split)
         Training(param=reference ref='None');
   model CloseRate = Region Training X1-X20 L1-L6 P1-P6 /
      selection= stepwise (choose=sbc select=sbc stop=sbc);
run;
```

```
proc glmselect plots=coefficients data=Stores;
   class Region(param=reference ref='Midwest' split)
         Training(param=reference ref='None');
   model CloseRate = Region Training X1-X20 L1-L6 P1-P6 /
      selection= backward (choose=sbc select=sbc stop=sbc);
run;
```

In this example, both of the selected models (not shown) are identical to the model selected with the forward method, and the effect sequences for the stepwise and forward methods are identical. This suggests that the signal-to-noise ratio in the data is fairly strong.

In general, you should expect to obtain different models with different methods and different selection criteria. Stepwise selection is often regarded as better than forward selection because it checks the contribution of each effect to determine whether it should stay in the model. However, because sequential selection methods form only one candidate model at each step, they do not generally identify the model with the best value of the criterion for each model size (see page 41).

Blind reliance on a single method is to be avoided. A useful strategy is to apply different methods and criteria and examine a set of contender models. It is also helpful to gain an understanding of the selection process by taking advantage of options that are explained in the next section.

Understanding the Selection Process

The GLMSELECT procedure provides various options that request details about each step of the selection process, as illustrated by the following statements:

```
proc glmselect  plots=all  data=Stores;
   class Region(param=reference ref='Midwest' split)
         Training(param=reference ref='None');
   model CloseRate = Region Training X1-X20 L1-L6 P1-P6 /
      selection=forward(choose=sbc select=sbc stop=sbc)
               stats=all  details=all ;
run;
```

The option PLOTS=ALL requests two plots in addition to the coefficient progression plot in Output 5.5. The panel in Output 5.8 displays seven different criteria for each step of the selection process. This is helpful for understanding whether different criteria might lead to different model selections. In this example, the selected model is the same regardless of the criterion.

Output 5.8 Comparison of Fit Criteria at Each Step

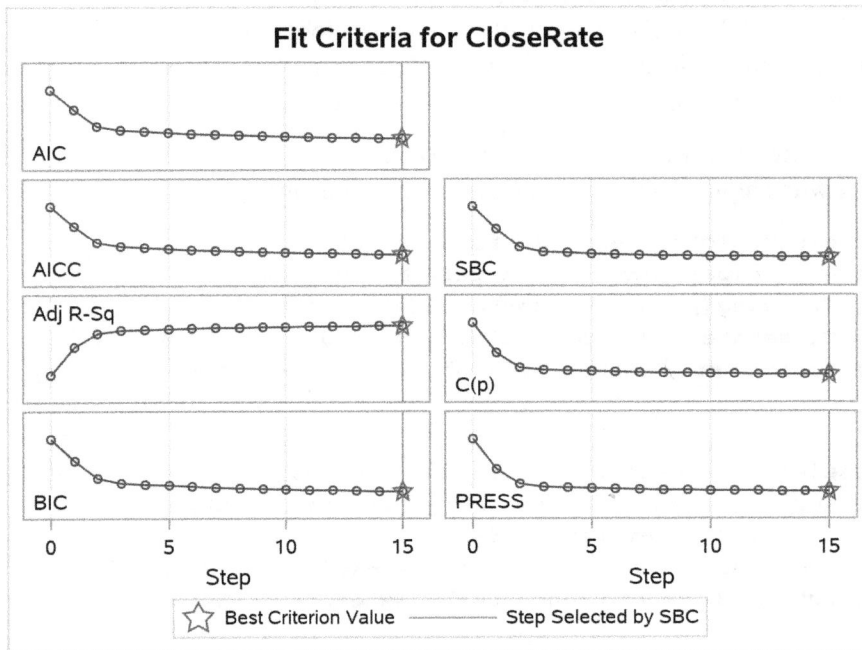

The plot in Output 5.9 displays the ASE at each step of the selection process.

Output 5.9 Average Squared Error at Each Step

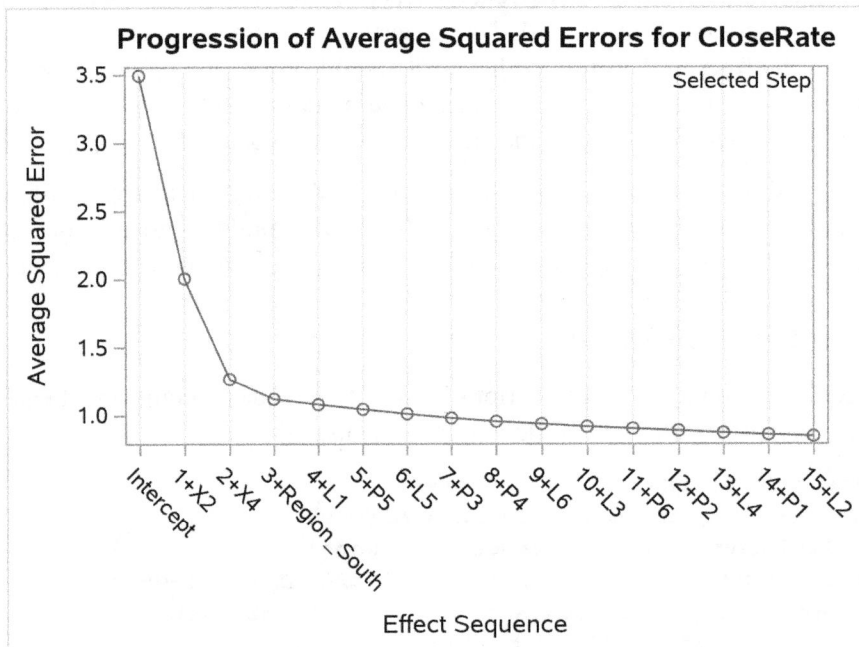

The option STATS=ALL produces a table (not shown) of the values plotted in Output 5.8 and Output 5.9. The option DETAILS=ALL provides complete details for each step of the selection process, which include the following:

- An analysis of variance for the current model

- Fit statistics for the current model

- Parameter estimates for the current model

- Criterion values and plot for the best 10 entry candidates

Output 5.10 shows the criterion plot for Step 15. The best entry candidate is L2, followed by X6.

Output 5.10 Plot of Best 10 Entry Candidates at Step 15

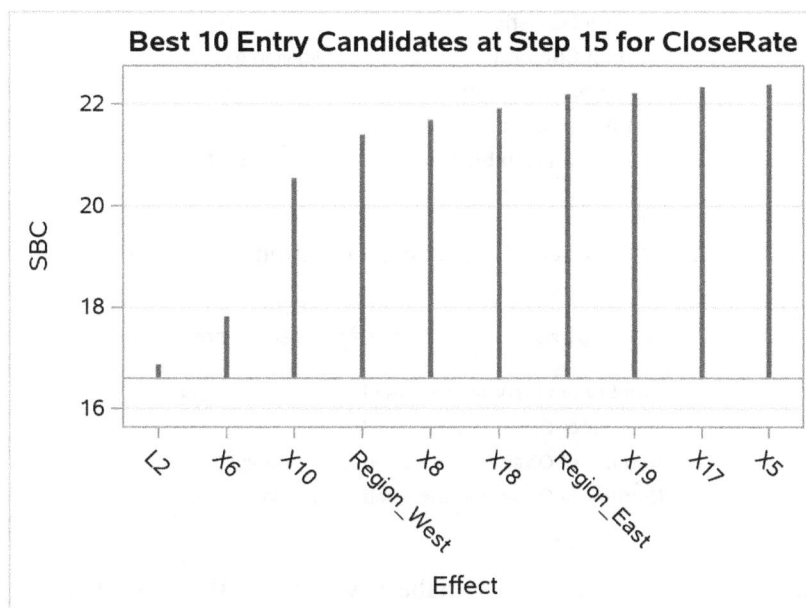

Terminating Selection Based on ASE Computed from Validation Data

Instead of using an information criterion such as SBC to terminate forward selection, you can use the ASE computed from data set aside for validation. Of course, n must be large enough to partition the data and leave sufficient observations for training.

The PARTITION statement assigns observations in the input data set to disjoint subsets for the purposes of training, validation, and testing. The following statements specify that 30% of the observations in Stores are to be randomly chosen for validation and 70% are to be used for training:

```
proc glmselect plots=(aseplot criteria) data=Stores seed=13551;
   class Region(param=reference ref='Midwest' split)
         Training(param=reference ref='None');
   model CloseRate = Region Training X1-X20 L1-L6 P1-P6 /
      selection=forward(choose=sbc select=sbc stop=validate);
   partition fraction(validate=0.3);
run;
```

The SEED= option specifies an integer used to start the random number generator for the partitioning. When you do not provide a seed, it is generated from the time on your computer's clock, and so your results will differ the next time you run the procedure.

Programming Tip: To make your results reproducible, specify and save the seed.

Output 5.11 lists the criteria for the selection process.

Output 5.11 Model Information Using Partitioning

Data Set	WORK.STORES
Dependent Variable	CloseRate
Selection Method	Forward
Select Criterion	SBC
Stop Criterion	Validation ASE
Choose Criterion	SBC
Effect Hierarchy Enforced	None
Random Number Seed	13551

Output 5.12 shows the number of observations in each partition.

Output 5.12 Numbers of Observations

Number of Observations Read	500
Number of Observations Used	500
Number of Observations Used for Training	363
Number of Observations Used for Validation	137

The model chosen is the one with the best (smallest) value of SBC. At each step of the selection process, the effect that is added is the one that most decreases SBC. The process stops when the next step would result in an increase in ASE computed from the validation data. Output 5.13 shows that this occurs at Step 3, when Region_South enters the model. The selected model is sparse compared with the model previously selected with SBC as the stop criterion (see Output 5.4).

Output 5.13 Selection Summary of Forward Selection Using Partitioning

	Forward Selection Summary					
Step	Effect Entered	Number Effects In	Number Parms In	SBC	ASE	Validation ASE
0	Intercept	1	1	450.0121	3.3989	3.7436
1	X2	2	2	259.3022	1.9775	2.0751
2	X4	3	3	98.0614	1.2479	1.3243
3	Region_South	4	4	59.5638*	1.1042	1.1653*
	* Optimal Value of Criterion					

Output 5.14 compares ASE with four other criteria whose best values also occur at Step 3.

Output 5.14 Comparison of Fit Criteria Using Partitioning

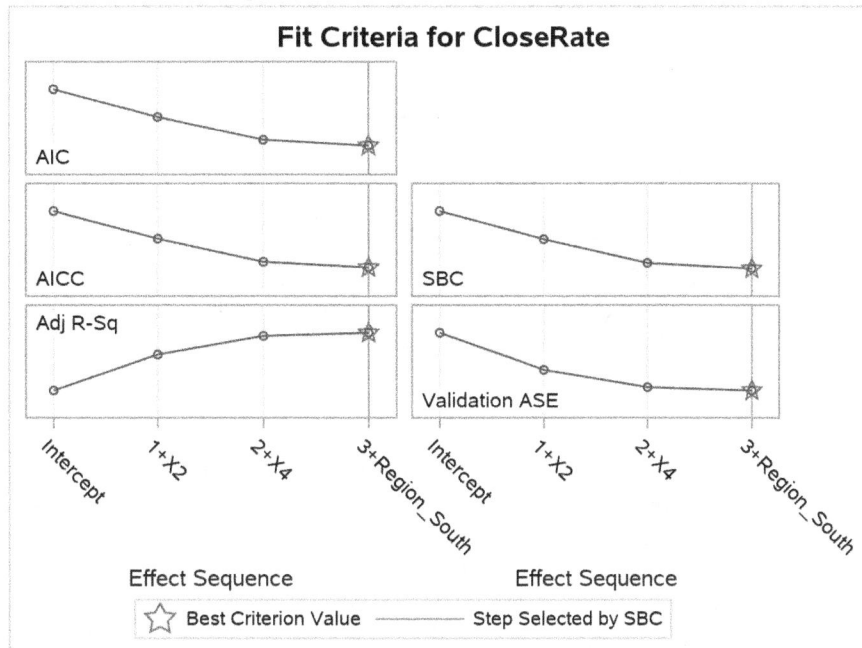

Output 5.15 shows that ASE decreases monotonically for both the training data (lower series) and the validation data (upper series).

Output 5.15 ASE Plot

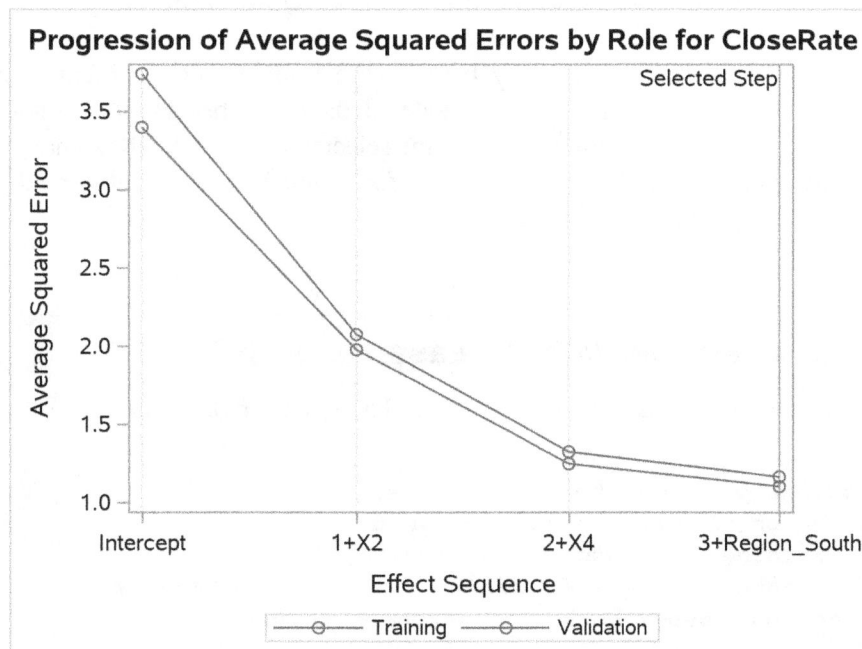

The values of ASE for the training data are only slightly less than the values for the validation data, which indicates that bias and variance are well balanced. High bias (underfitting) is characterized by high training error that is close to validation error; this might be remedied by adding features. High variance (overfitting) is characterized by low training error that is much lower than validation error; this might be remedied with more data or by performing regularization.

Output 5.16 shows the parameter estimates.

Output 5.16 Parameter Estimates for Model Selected with Forward Selection and Partitioning

		Parameter Estimates		
Parameter	DF	Estimate	Standard Error	t Value
Intercept	1	61.087012	0.067018	911.50
Region_South	1	0.820985	0.120137	6.83
X2	1	4.029965	0.198469	20.31
X4	1	-3.019392	0.190098	-15.88

With the GLMSELECT procedure—as with other model building procedures in this book—it is possible to customize the selection method by specifying many different combinations of suboptions. This does not mean that all these combinations are effective. Here, for instance, it is possible to specify CHOOSE=VALIDATE and SELECT=VALIDATE along with STOP=VALIDATE:

```
proc glmselect plots=(ASEPlot Criteria) data=Stores seed=13551;
   class Region(param=reference ref='Midwest' split)
         Training(param=reference ref='None');
   model CloseRate = Region Training X1-X20 L1-L6 P1-P6 /
      selection=forward( choose=validate  select=validate  stop=validate) ;
   partition fraction(validate=0.3);
run;
```

With this combination, the procedure uses ASE based on the training data to build the model. Clearly ASE decreases monotonically as more effects are added to the model because it does not penalize for p as do SBC and other information criteria, and so the selected model is likely to include predictors that represent noise. In practice, there is no substitute for understanding the relative advantages and disadvantages of different selection methods.

Example: Building a Model with the Lasso and SBC

The following statements use the lasso method to build a model for CloseRate:

```
proc glmselect plots=coefficients data=Stores;
   class Region(param=reference ref='Midwest')
         Training(param=reference ref='None');
   model CloseRate = Region Training X1-X20 L1-L6 P1-P6 /
      selection= lasso(choose=sbc stop=sbc showstepL1) ;
run;
```

In order to determine the regularization parameter λ for the ℓ_1 penalty (see page 42), this example uses SBC as the choose and stop criteria. These are the same criteria used with forward selection in the example on page 56.

The SELECT= suboption does not apply with lasso selection. The procedure uses the LAR algorithm to produce a sequence of regression models in which one parameter is added at each step.

When you request the lasso method and the model contains classification effects, these effects are automatically split. The columns of the model matrix **X** that correspond to a classification effect are then selected independently of each other. It is not necessary to specify the SPLIT option in the CLASS statement, as is the case with forward selection.

Output 5.17 shows that the minimum SBC is reached at Step 3. In contrast to the forward method, which selects a model with 15 effects (see Output 5.4), the lasso method selects a sparse model with three effects. For each step, the table includes the value of the regularization parameter (labeled L1 Ratio), as requested by the SHOWSTEPL1 option.

Output 5.17 Selection Summary for the Lasso

	LASSO Selection Summary				
Step	Effect Entered	Effect Removed	Number Effects In	SBC	L1 Ratio
0	Intercept		1	631.5807	1.0000
1	X2		2	530.0953	0.7385
2	X4		3	222.3215	0.2877
3	Region_South		4	136.4781*	0.1679
	* Optimal Value of Criterion				

The coefficient progression plot in Output 5.18 visualizes the selection.

Output 5.18 Coefficient Progression for the Lasso

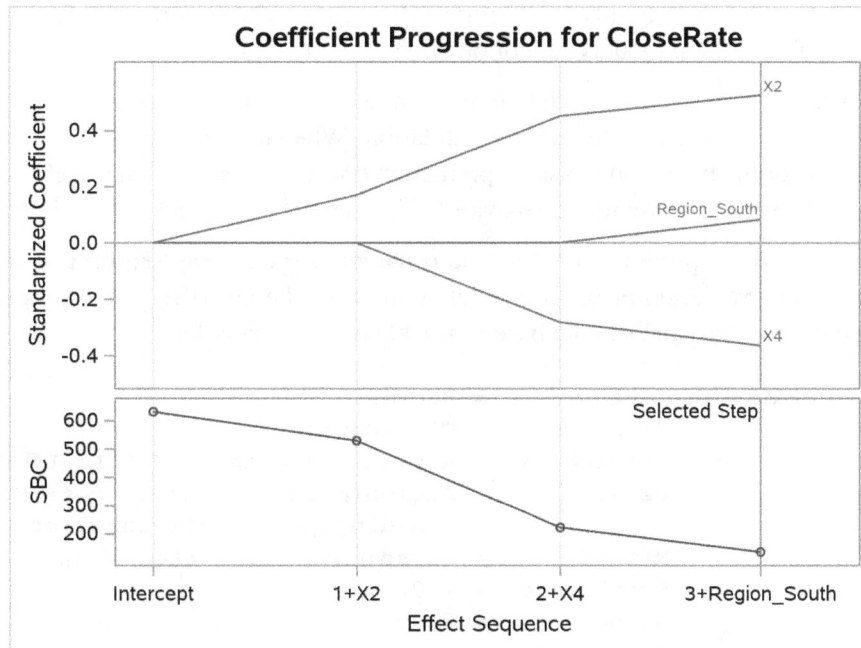

Output 5.19 shows the fit statistics for the selected model.

Output 5.19 Fit Statistics for Model Selected with the Lasso

Root MSE	1.12259
Dependent Mean	61.39824
R-Square	0.6421
Adj R-Sq	0.6399
AIC	621.61972
AICC	621.74117
SBC	136.47815

Output 5.20 shows the parameter estimates. Because the lasso method shrinks the estimates, they are closer to zero than the corresponding estimates obtained with forward selection (Output 5.7).

Output 5.20 Parameter Estimates for Model Selected with the Lasso

Parameter Estimates		
Parameter	DF	Estimate
Intercept	1	61.257017
Region_South	1	0.344869
X2	1	3.453344
X4	1	-2.290891

Bootstrap Estimation of the Prediction Error

In this example, the model obtained with the lasso method is sparse compared with the model obtained with the forward selection method in the example on page 56. You might wonder, which model has the better predictive ability? Although SBC was the choose criterion for both methods, the values of SBC for the final models cannot be directly compared.

The preferred way to compare the models is to compute their mean square errors of prediction (MSPE) from test data not used for training or validation. When test data are not available, you can use cross validation or the bootstrap to assess prediction error, as explained on page 31 and page 32. The GLMSELECT procedure provides cross validation (see Table 5.3) but not the bootstrap.

The website for this book provides a SAS macro named %BootstrapPredError that uses the bootstrap to estimate prediction error for models built with the GLMSELECT procedure.[†] The following statement requests an estimate based on 100 bootstrap samples:

```
%BootstrapPredError( Data        = Stores,
                     Response     = CloseRate,
                     Predictors   = Region Training X1-X20 L1-L6 P1-P6,
                     Class        = Region(param=reference ref='Midwest' split)
                                    Training(param=reference ref='None'),
                     Method       = lasso(choose=sbc stop=sbc),
                     NReplicates  = 100,
                     Seed         = 556985,
                     ShowTable    = 1,
                     Out          = LassoResults )
```

[†]To use this macro, download the file *BootstrapPredError.sas* and include the macro definition at the beginning of your SAS program.

Note that the first four macro parameters duplicate the specification of the lasso method on page 66.

There are different versions of the bootstrap for assessing prediction error; the one implemented by the macro is described by Efron and Tibshirani (1993, Sec. 17.6). The macro produces the table in Output 5.21.

Output 5.21 Lasso Estimates of Prediction Error

Estimation of Prediction Error for CloseRate Using 100 Bootstrap Samples

Description	Estimate
Average squared prediction error for training data	1.25012
Simple bootstrap estimate of prediction error	1.21995
Apparent prediction error from bootstrap samples	1.20049
Bootstrap estimate of optimism	0.01946
Refined bootstrap estimate of prediction error	1.26958

In general, the prediction error for the training data (ASE_{train}) underestimates the prediction error for future data, as explained on page 25. The simple bootstrap estimate in Output 5.21 is obtained by training the model on each of the bootstrap samples, applying the model to the original sample, and averaging the prediction errors. This estimate is improved upon by estimating the optimism, which is the amount by which the expected training error underestimates the expected prediction error (see page 26).

The optimism is estimated as the average of the differences between the bootstrap model prediction errors on the original sample and the bootstrap model prediction errors on their respective samples. The refined bootstrap estimate is then computed by adding the estimated optimism to ASE_{train}. This approach improves on the precision of the simple estimate by fixing the predictor values in the original sample for ASE_{train} and by averaging over the predictor values in the bootstrap samples to estimate the optimism.

Output 5.22 compares the results in Output 5.21 with the results obtained by applying the macro to the model obtained with forward selection.

Output 5.22 Comparison of Prediction Errors

Description	Lasso	Forward
Average squared prediction error for training data	1.25012	0.84779
Simple bootstrap estimate of prediction error	1.21995	0.91288
Apparent prediction error from bootstrap samples	1.20049	0.81720
Bootstrap estimate of optimism	0.01946	0.09568
Refined bootstrap estimate of prediction error	1.26958	0.94347

The model obtained with forward selection has a smaller refined bootstrap estimate of prediction error, most likely because it includes more effects that are predictive of close rate than the sparse model obtained with the lasso.

Programming Tip: Use the `%BootstrapPredError` macro to estimate and compare the prediction errors of models built with the GLMSELECT procedure.

Recommendations for Writing Your Own Bootstrap Program

Because the power of the bootstrap lies in its generality, you might want to write programs that apply it in other situations. The code for the **%BootstrapPredError** macro illustrates four techniques that you should consider for computational efficiency:

- Use the SURVEYSELECT procedure to generate the bootstrap samples.

- For computational efficiency, process the bootstrap samples as BY groups within a data set.

- Disable the display of unnecessary tables and graphs, which slows processing, by specifying

  ```
  ods select none;
  ```

- If the model building procedure provides a PARTITION statement, interweave copies of the original sample (indicated by Original=1 in the macro) with the bootstrap samples (indicated by Original=0). Then use the ROLEVAR= option to specify that models trained with the bootstrap samples are to be tested on the original sample:

  ```
  partition rolevar=Original(train='0' test='1');
  ```

Programming Tip: Write efficient programs that implement the bootstrap by applying the techniques used in the **%BootstrapPredError** macro.

Example: Building a Model with the Lasso and Cross Validation

The GLMSELECT procedure provides various approaches for determining the value of the lasso parameter λ to minimize prediction error. The example on page 66 uses SBC as the criterion. An alternative is 5-fold external cross validation with random assignment of observations to folds, as requested by the following statements:

```
proc glmselect plots=coefficients data=Stores seed=59915;
   class Region(param=reference ref='Midwest')
         Training(param=reference ref='None');
   model CloseRate = Region Training X1-X20 L1-L6 P1-P6 / cvmethod=random(5)
      selection=lasso(choose=cvex maxsteps=15 showstepL1);
run;
```

Output 5.23 shows that this approach produces the same sparse model as selection based on SBC (see Output 5.17). This is not surprising because the number of observations is large and the effects of X2, X4, and Region_South are fairly strong.

Output 5.23 Selection Summary for the Lasso with Cross Validation

				LASSO Selection Summary			
Step	Effect Entered	Effect Removed	Number Effects In	SBC	CVEX PRESS	L1 Ratio
0	Intercept		1	631.5807	3.5092	1.0000
1	X2		2	530.0953	2.8071	0.7385
2	X4		3	222.3215	1.5081	0.2877
3	Region_South		4	136.4781*	1.2767*	0.1679
			* Optimal Value of Criterion			

With small data sets, cross validation can lead to values of λ that are too small and models that include too many effects. You can specify a value of λ with the L1= suboption of the LASSO option and then estimate the prediction error with the %BootstrapPredError macro, as discussed on page 68.

Example: Building a Model with the Lasso and Validation Data

Because there are enough observations in Stores to partition the data into subsets for training and validation, it is possible to select λ by minimizing the average squared error (ASE) computed from the validation data. The following statements apply this approach:

```
proc glmselect plots=coefficients data=Stores seed=59915;
   class Region(param=reference ref='Midwest')
         Training(param=reference ref='None');
   model CloseRate = Region Training X1-X20 L1-L6 P1-P6 /
      selection=lasso(choose=validate maxsteps=15 showstepL1);
   partition fraction(validate=0.3);
run;
```

The MAXSTEPS= option limits the number of steps to 15.

The selection summary in Output 5.24 shows that the validation ASE reaches a minimum at Step 4, when the variable L1 enters the model.

Output 5.24 Selection Summary for the Lasso with Cross Validation

							Validation	
Step	Effect Entered	Effect Removed	Number Effects In		SBC	ASE	ASE	L1 Ratio
0	Intercept		1		454.4413	3.4764	3.5358	1.0000
1	X2		2		397.8583	2.9226	2.9130	0.7792
2	X4		3		185.2375	1.5928	1.5201	0.3294
3	Region_South		4		126.1827	1.3299	1.2853	0.2223
4	L1		5		95.6445*	1.2019	1.2034*	0.1651

* Optimal Value of Criterion

Output 5.25 shows the parameter estimates.

Output 5.25 Parameter Estimates with the Lasso and Validation ASE

Parameter	DF	Estimate
Intercept	1	61.076754
Region_South	1	0.486272
X2	1	3.371467
X4	1	-2.396170
L1	1	0.231850

Here, the model contains the effects in the models previously selected with SBC and 5-fold cross validation (see Output 5.17 and Output 5.23), and it is nearly as sparse.

Example: Building a Model with the Adaptive Lasso

As explained on page 45, an advantage of the adaptive lasso method over the lasso method is that it has the oracle property, which means it can identify the right effects with the optimal estimation rate as n increases.

The following statements use the adaptive lasso method to build a model for CloseRate:

```
proc glmselect plots=coefficients data=Stores;
   class Region(param=reference ref='Midwest')
         Training(param=reference ref='None');
   model CloseRate = Region Training X1-X20 L1-L6 P1-P6 /
      selection=lasso( adaptive  choose=sbc stop=sbc showstepL1);
run;
```

Output 5.26 shows that the minimum SBC is reached at Step 3.

Output 5.26 Selection Summary for the Adaptive Lasso Method

		LASSO Selection Summary			
Step	Effect Entered	Effect Removed	Number Effects In	SBC	L1 Ratio
0	Intercept		1	631.5807	1.0000
1	X2		2	466.8434	0.5662
2	X4		3	152.5955	0.1020
3	Region_South		4	86.4979*	0.0253
		* Optimal Value of Criterion			

Although the adaptive lasso method selects the same effects as the lasso method on page 71, Output 5.27 shows that the parameter estimates are different (see Output 5.20).

Output 5.27 Parameter Estimates for Model Selected with the Adaptive Lasso Method

Parameter Estimates		
Parameter	DF	Estimate
Intercept	1	61.162661
Region_South	1	0.622748
X2	1	4.041475
X4	1	-2.857911

Example: Building a Model with the Group Lasso

The group lasso method is a variation of the lasso method that constrains the sum of squares in such a way that all parameters in a group are simultaneously included or excluded at each step. The parameters in a group correspond to multiple columns in the model matrix that define classification effects and other effects; see page 46. The GLMSELECT procedure constructs a solution path for the group lasso that follows a sequence of regularization parameters $\rho, \rho^2, \rho^3, \ldots$, where $0 < \rho < 1$. At the kth step, the penalization parameter is ρ^k.

The following statements use the group lasso method to build a model for CloseRate:

```
proc glmselect plots=coefficients data=Stores;
   class Region(param=reference ref='Midwest')
         Training(param=reference ref='None');
   model CloseRate = Region Training X1-X20 L1-L6 P1-P6 /
      selection= grouplasso (choose=sbc stop=sbc steps=20  rho=0.9 );
run;
```

Here, the groups are the classification effects of Region and Training. You specify ρ with the RHO= suboption, for which the default is 0.9. The STEPS= option forces the selection to take 20 steps. Output 5.28 shows that the minimum SBC is reached at Step 20. The group effect of Region enters at Step 16.

Output 5.28 Coefficient Progression for the Group Lasso

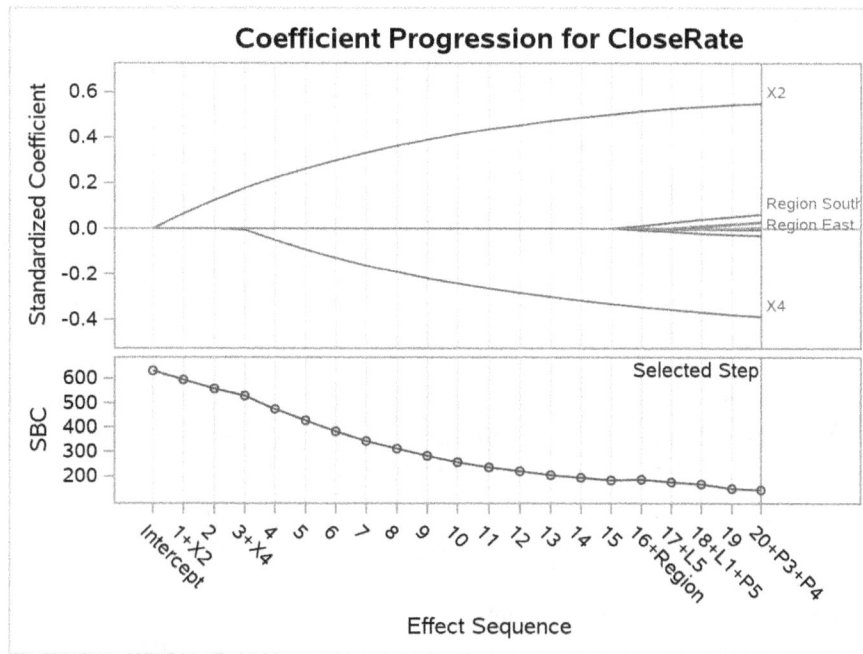

Output 5.29 shows the parameter estimates.

Output 5.29 Parameter Estimates for Model Selected with the Group Lasso

Parameter Estimates		
Parameter		**Estimate**
Intercept		61.148381
Region	East	-0.132166
Region	South	0.248748
Region	West	-0.026287
X2		3.598613
X4		-2.457087
L1		0.181035
L5		0.180026
P3		0.044313
P4		0.021653
P5		0.157236

Because the group lasso is a shrinkage method, these estimates are closer to zero than the corresponding estimates in Output 5.7.

Without the STEPS= option in this example, the group lasso would select a sparser model with only X2 and X4. The lasso selects these two variables and Region_South (see Output 5.20). This suggests that the **South** level of Region should be distinguished, although the **East** and **North** levels can be grouped together with the reference level **Midwest** for the purpose of prediction.

It is informative to try different combinations of the RHO= and STEPS= options because the behavior of the group lasso is sensitive to the value of ρ. Smaller values lead to bigger steps, which tend to pick up noise effects.

Using the REG Procedure for Best-Subset Regression

As noted on page 50, the sequential selection methods provided by the GLMSELECT and REGSELECT procedures supersede those of the REG procedure. Nonetheless, the REG procedure provides two model building methods, best-subset regression and ridge regression, that are not available in the GLMSELECT procedure. Best-subset regression, illustrated here, is explained on page 40 of Chapter 4. Ridge regression is explained on page 98 of Chapter 6.

Example: Finding the Best Model for Close Rate

Because the REG procedure does not handle classification effects, the following statements fit all of the models for CloseRate that are possible with the 32 numeric predictors in Stores. For reuse, the names of these predictors are first saved in a macro variable.

```
%let CVars = X1   X2   X3   X4   X5   X6   X7 X8 X9 X10 X11 X12 X13 X14
             X15 X16 X17 X18 X19 X20 P1 P2 P3 P4 P5 P6 L1 L2 L3 L4 L5 L6;
```

```
proc reg data=Stores outest=ParmEst;
    model CloseRate = &CVars / selection=rsquare best=1;
quit;
```

The SELECTION=RSQUARE option specifies the criterion for *best* as the highest value of R^2 among models of a given size. The data set ParmEst saves the parameter estimates.

The procedure displays a table of the predictors for the best models of each size in which the maximum number of models for each size is determined by the BEST= option. Output 5.30 shows the portion of the table for $p = 1, 2, 3, 14, 15, 18$, where p is the size (the number of predictors).

Output 5.30 Models with Highest R^2 (partial list)

Number in Model	R-Square	Variables in Model
1	0.4262	X2
2	0.6370	X2 X4
3	0.6488	X2 X4 P5
14	0.7134	X2 X4 P1 P2 P3 P4 P5 P6 L1 L2 L3 L4 L5 L6
15	0.7169	X2 X4 X6 P1 P2 P3 P4 P5 P6 L1 L2 L3 L4 L5 L6
18	0.7219	X1 X2 X4 X6 X10 X11 P1 P2 P3 P4 P5 P6 L1 L2 L3 L4 L5 L6

The term *best model* can be misleading. Models that best—most closely—fit the training data do not provide the best predictive ability, nor do they necessarily provide the best interpretability. Here, since R^2 increases with p, a model with $p = 32$ has the highest R^2 and the lowest training error. However, this model will not have the lowest prediction error (see page 25), and a smaller model might well be more interpretable.

When prediction is the goal, you should treat p as a tuning parameter. As explained on page 31, m-fold cross validation gives you a way to determine the value of p that minimizes prediction error. Although the REG procedure does not provide this method, you can apply it with the %BestSubsetCV macro, which is available on the book website. The following statement requests 10-fold cross validation:

```
%BestSubsetCV( Data = Stores,
              Response = CloseRate, Predictors = &CVars,
              NFolds = 10, Seed = 17537,
              OutCV = CVResults, ShowPlot = 1)
```

The NFOLDS= option specifies the number of folds. The SEED= option specifies the seed for random assignment of observations to folds. The OUTCV= option saves the results in the data set CVResults, and the SHOWPLOT= option requests the plot shown in Output 5.31.

Output 5.31 Selection of Model Size Using Cross Validation

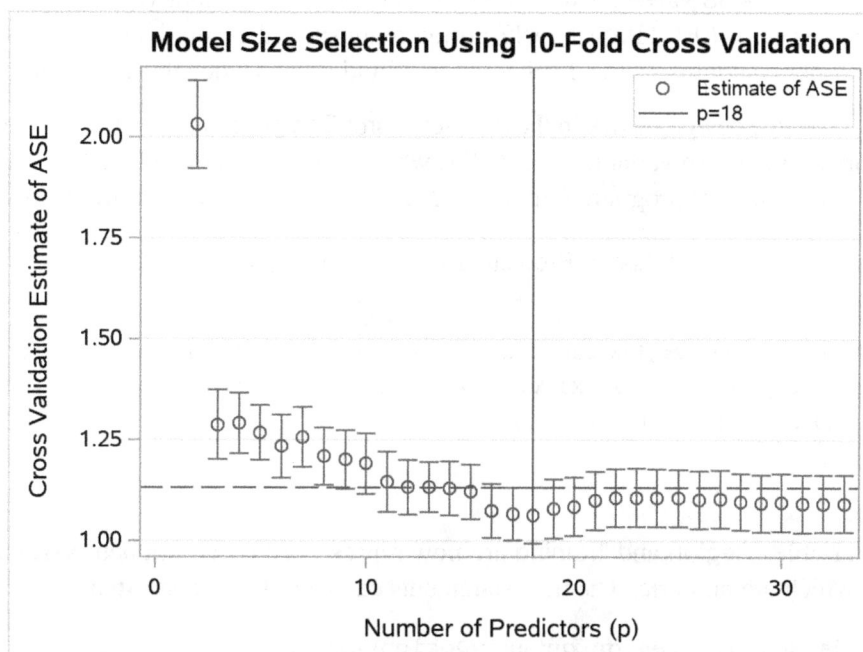

The estimated average square error (ASE) for prediction is minimized by the model with 18 predictors, and it is approximately minimized by models with p near 18. Note that the predictors for the model with $p = 14$ match the continuous predictors in the model selected earlier with forward selection (see Output 5.7).

Breiman's one-standard-error rule (Breiman et al. 1984) favors the model with 15 predictors because it is the simplest model whose estimate for ASE is within one standard error above the minimum estimate, which is indicated by the dashed line in Output 5.31. Several other models produce nearly the same estimate of ASE. Because sparseness favors predictive accuracy and interpretability, the models with 11 and 12 predictors are also strong contenders.

Example: Best-Subset Regression with Categorical Predictors

There are two categorical variables in the data set Stores, Region and Training, which the previous example excluded because the REG procedure only accepts numeric variables. You can work around this limitation by following these two steps:

1. Use the GLMSELECT procedure to obtain the design matrix for the full model (see page 16). You can also use the GLMMOD and TRANSREG procedures in SAS/STAT.

2. Specify the design matrix as the input data for the REG procedure.

The following statements carry out the first step:

```
proc glmselect data=Stores  outdesign=StoresDesign noprint ;
   class Region(param=reference ref='Midwest'  split )
         Training(param=reference ref='None'  split );
   model CloseRate = Region Training X1-X20 L1-L6 P1-P6 /  selection=none ;
run;
```

Note that all of the CLASS variables must be split into their component variables, also known as dummy variables. The SELECTION=NONE option requests a fitted model for all of the variables. The NOPRINT option suppresses the display of tables and graphs since these are not needed here.

The procedure saves the design matrix in the data set StoresDesign. It automatically saves the names of the predictors in the macro variable _GLSIND1, which you can examine by adding the statement **%put &=_GLSIND1;** to your program. Output 5.32 shows what this writes to the SAS log.

Output 5.32 List of Predictors Corresponding to Model Matrix

```
 _GLSIND1=Region_East Region_South Region_West Training_Complete
Training_InProgress X1 X2 X3 X4 X5 X6 X7 X8 X9 X10 X11 X12 X13 X14 X15 X16 X17
X18 X19 X20 L1 L2 L3 L4 L5 L6 P1 P2 P3 P4 P5 P6
```

The CLASS variables Region and Training are now represented by component variables, such as Region_East, which are numeric. The next statements carry out the second step:

```
proc reg data=StoresDesign outest=DesignParmEst;
    model CloseRate = &_GLSIND1 / selection=rsquare best=1;
quit;
```

The REG procedure produces a table (not shown here) similar to the one in Output 5.30. You can request *m*-fold cross validation by calling the **%BestSubsetCV** macro with Data=StoresDesign and Predictors=&_GLSIND1.

When you use this workaround, keep in mind that the component variables for a given classification effect will not generally appear together in the models found by the REG procedure. Also, the number of component variables for a large number of classification effects with many levels can easily exceed the feasibility limit for best-subset regression.

Introduction to the REGSELECT Procedure

The REGSELECT procedure in SAS Viya fits and builds general linear models. It provides functionality comparable to that of the GLMSELECT and REG procedures in SAS/STAT. Because the REGSELECT procedure was developed specifically for SAS Viya, it can run on a cluster of machines that distribute the data and the computations.

When you use the REGSELECT procedure you specify candidate effects with MODEL, CLASS, and EFFECTS statements, which are similar to those of the GLMSELECT procedure. You request data partitioning with the PARTITION statement, which is similar to that of the GLMSELECT procedure.

However, there are important differences in the REGSELECT procedure:

- You request model selection and selection methods with the SELECTION statement in the REGSELECT procedure. The GLMSELECT procedure does not have a SELECTION statement; instead, you request model selection and selection methods with the MODEL statement.

- The selection methods available in the REGSELECT procedure do not currently include the group lasso, which is available in the GLMSELECT procedure.

- The selection methods available in the REGSELECT procedure include forward swap, adaptive elastic net, best-subset selection, the MCP method, and the SCAD method, which are not available in the GLMSELECT procedure.

- The STOPHORIZON= option specifies the number of consecutive steps at which the STOP= criterion must worsen for a local extremum to be detected. The default is 3. Setting STOPHORIZON=1 matches the behavior of the GLMSELECT procedure.

- The DISPLAY statement replaces the ODS SELECT statement for specifying displayed output.[†]

- The DISPLAYOUT statement, which creates CAS tables from displayed output, provides functionality comparable to that of the ODS OUTPUT statement.[‡]

- The STORE statement saves results that you can process with the ASTORE procedure. In particular, you can use the SCORE statement in the ASTORE procedure to score observations with models built by the REGSELECT procedure (see page 384).

[†]The DISPLAY statement serves the same purpose as the ODS SELECT statement but is preferable because it eliminates unnecessary communication with the grid.

[‡]The DISPLAYOUT statement creates a CAS table that is based on the displayed output, whereas the ODS OUTPUT statement creates a SAS data set. The ODS OUTPUT statement might be preferred in some situations because the ordering of the rows in CAS tables is not fixed. For instance, to save tables with parameter estimates and covariance matrix estimates for reuse in a DATA step program in SAS 9, you would need to make sure that the row ordering of the two tables is the same. The likelihood of a change in row ordering is small in most cases, but because it is a possibility, a better alternative would be to create SAS data sets directly with the ODS OUTPUT statement.

The REGSELECT procedure produces the following results which apply to fully specified models:

- Parameter estimates tables that display *p*-values by default. The *p*-values should be ignored when you build a model because they are not adjusted for the selection process.

- A model ANOVA (analysis of variance) table that displays tests computed with Type III sums of squares for each effect. You can request this table with the SS3 option.

- Observationwise residual and influence diagnostics, which you can request in the OUTPUT statement.

- Variance inflation factors and tolerance values, which you can request with the VIF and TOL options to accompany the parameter estimates.

Table 5.6 summarizes methods you can request with the SELECTION statement. The CHOOSE=, SELECT=, and STOP= suboptions with these methods mirror those of the GLMSELECT procedure.

Table 5.6 Effect Selection Methods in the REGSELECT Procedure

Method	Description	METHOD=*keyword*
Best-subset regression	Uses the branch-and-bound method (Furnival and Wilson 1974)	BESTSUBSET
Forward selection	Starts with the intercept and adds effects	FORWARD
Forward swap selection	Extends forward selection; before adding an effect, makes all pairwise swaps of one effect in the model and one out of the model to improve the selection criterion	FORWARDSWAP
Backward elimination	Starts with the full model and deletes effects	BACKWARD
Stepwise selection	Starts with the intercept; effects are added and can be deleted	STEPWISE
Least angle regression	Starts with no effects and adds effects; at each step, $\hat{\beta}_j$s shrink toward zero (Efron et al. 2004)	LAR
Hybrid LAR	Uses LAR to select effects and OLS to estimate coefficients (Efron et al. 2004)	LAR (LSCOEFFS)
Lasso	Constrains sum of $|\beta_j|$s; some $\hat{\beta}_j$s are set to zero (Tibshirani 1996)	LASSO
Adaptive lasso	Constrains sum of weighted $|\beta_j|$s; some $\hat{\beta}_j$s are set to zero (Zou 2006)	LASSO (ADAPTIVE)
Elastic net	Constrains sums of $|\beta_j|$s and β_j^2s; some $\hat{\beta}_j$s are set to zero (Zou and Hastie 2005)	ELASTICNET
Adaptive elastic net	Constrains sums of weighted $|\beta_j|$s and β_j^2s; some $\hat{\beta}_j$s are set to zero (Zou and Zhang 2009)	ELASTICNET (ADAPTIVE)
MCP	Uses minimum concave penalty (Zhang 2010)	MCP
SCAD	Uses smoothly clipped absolute deviations (Fan and Li 2001)	SCAD
No selection	Fits fully specified model	NONE

Example: Defining a CAS Session and Loading Data

The REGSELECT procedure—like other procedures in SAS Viya—runs on the Cloud Analytics Services (CAS) server and operates on in-memory tables referred to as CAS tables. In order to use the procedure, a CAS server must be available. Your system administrator can provide instructions for starting and terminating a server. You can define a CAS session and a CAS engine libref that connects to the server as follows:

```
cas mysession;
libname mycas cas sessref=mysession;
```

The next two examples use the REGSELECT procedure to build models with the data in Stores. First, however, the data must be loaded into memory. The following DATA step creates a CAS table named mycas.Stores.

```
data mycas.Stores;
   set Stores;
run;
```

This is not the only approach you can take. The CASUTIL procedure provides a more efficient alternative for loading large amounts of data; see page 184 for an example.

Example: Differences from the GLMSELECT Procedure

This example illustrates several differences between the REGSELECT and GLMSELECT procedure. In most cases, the results produced by the two procedures will agree, but you can expect some differences due to the ways in which the procedures implement certain algorithms. Furthermore, there are differences in syntax that you should anticipate if you are moving your work from SAS 9 to SAS Viya and are converting from the GLMSELECT procedure to the REGSELECT procedure.

The example on page 63 uses the GLMSELECT procedure to build a model with the following statements:

```
proc glmselect plots=(aseplot criteria) data=Stores seed=13551;
   class Region(param=reference ref='Midwest' split)
         Training(param=reference ref='None');
   model CloseRate = Region Training X1-X20 L1-L6 P1-P6 /
      selection=forward(choose=sbc select=sbc stop=validate);
   partition fraction(validate=0.3);
run;
```

The next statements use the REGSELECT procedure to rebuild the model with the same method:

```
proc regselect data=mycas.Stores;
   class Region(param=reference ref='Midwest' split)
         Training(param=reference ref='None');
   model CloseRate = Region Training X1-X20 L1-L6 P1-P6;
   selection method=forward(choose=sbc select=sbc stop=validate)
         stophorizon=1  plots=(criteria);
   partition fraction(validate=0.3 seed=13551);
run;
```

Note the differences in the syntax of the REGSELECT procedure:

- You specify the selection method in the SELECTION statement rather than the MODEL statement.
- You specify the PLOTS= option in the SELECTION statement rather than the procedure statement. Some plot options are different.
- You specify the SEED= option in the PARTITION statement rather than the procedure statement.
- You use the STOPHORIZON= option to specify the number of steps at which the stopping criterion must decrease in order for a local minimum to be detected. Since the default number is three, STOPHORIZON=1 is specified here to match the behavior of the GLMSELECT procedure.

The numbers of observations in the training and validation partitions are shown in Output 5.33.

Output 5.33 Partition Information for Model Selected by REGSELECT Procedure

Number of Observations Read	500
Number of Observations Used	500
Number of Observations Used for Training	354
Number of Observations Used for Validation	146
Number of Observations Used for Testing	0

The partition sizes do not quite match those in Output 5.12 even though the same seed is specified in both procedures. The reason for this is that the REGSELECT procedure does not handle random partitioning in exactly the same way as the GLMSELECT procedure.

Output 5.34 shows the parameter estimates for the final model.

Output 5.34 Parameter Estimates for Model Selected by REGSELECT Procedure

Parameter Estimates					
Parameter	DF	Estimate	Standard Error	t Value	Pr > |t|
Intercept	1	60.795643	0.112399	540.89	<.0001
Region_South	1	0.828372	0.112621	7.36	<.0001
X2	1	3.820854	0.183188	20.86	<.0001
X4	1	-2.888462	0.180528	-16.00	<.0001
L1	1	0.636020	0.187910	3.38	0.0008
P3	1	0.626724	0.180314	3.48	0.0006
P4	1	0.628534	0.183192	3.43	0.0007
P5	1	0.656612	0.183811	3.57	0.0004
P6	1	0.556406	0.182053	3.06	0.0024

The model selected by the REGSELECT procedure has five more effects (L1, P3, P4, P5, and P6) than the model selected by the GLMSELECT procedure (see Output 5.16). This is not surprising because the training data sets used to build the two models are not the same. In fact, if you apply different combinations of selection methods and criteria with the same training data, you will find that almost all of the final models include the strong effects of Region_South, X2, and X4, while some include the weaker effects of promotional and layout variables.

Example: Building a Model with Forward Swap Selection

Forward swap selection, which is available in the REGSELECT procedure but not the GLMSELECT procedure, is the same as the MAXR (maximum *R*-square improvement) method in the REG procedure when the selection criterion is *R*-square. This example compares forward swap selection and forward selection by using the two methods to build models for CloseRate.

The following statements apply forward selection:

```
proc regselect data=mycas.Stores;
    class Region(param=reference ref='Midwest' split)
          Training(param=reference ref='None');
    model CloseRate = Region Training X1-X20 L1-L6 P1-P6;
    selection method= forward (choose=sbc select=sbc stop=sbc);
run;
```

Output 5.35 shows the selection steps. The minimum SBC is reached at Step 15, when L2 enters the model.

Output 5.35 Selection Summary for Forward Selection

Selection Details

	Selection Summary		
Step	Effect Entered	Number Effects In	SBC
0	Intercept	1	631.5807
1	X2	2	360.0538
2	X4	3	137.2902
3	Region_South	4	81.3798
4	L1	5	69.1589
5	P5	6	58.8027
6	L5	7	48.5608
7	P3	8	39.3333
8	P4	9	32.8399
9	L6	10	29.2646
10	L3	11	24.8623
11	P6	12	23.4529
12	P2	13	21.2727
13	L4	14	18.2626
14	P1	15	17.1062
15	L2	16	16.8729*
16	X6	17	17.3638
17	X10	18	20.4921
18	X8	19	24.8278
	* Optimal Value Of Criterion		

Output 5.36 lists the effects in the final model.

Output 5.36 Effects Selected with Forward Selection

Selected Effects: Intercept Region_South X2 X4 L1 L2 L3 L4 L5 L6 P1 P2 P3 P4 P5 P6

The next statements apply forward swap selection with the same criteria:

```
proc regselect data=mycas.Stores;
   class Region(param=reference ref='Midwest' split)
         Training(param=reference ref='None');
   model CloseRate = Region Training X1-X20 L1-L6 P1-P6;
   selection method= forwardswap (choose=sbc select=sbc stop=sbc)
      stophorizon=1 plots=coefficients;
run;
```

Output 5.37 shows that the minimum SBC is reached at Step 16, when L2 enters the model.

Output 5.37 Selection Summary for Forward Swap Selection

Selection Details

	Selection Summary			
Step	Effect Entered	Effect Removed	Number Effects In	SBC
0	Intercept		1	631.5807
1	X2		2	360.0538
2	X4		3	137.2902
3	Region_South		4	81.3798
4	L1		5	69.1589
5	P5		6	58.8027
6	L5		7	48.5608
7	P3		8	39.3333
8	P4		9	32.8399
9	L6		10	29.2646
10	L3		11	24.8623
11	P6		12	23.4529
12	P2		13	21.2727
13	L4	L3	13	19.8539
14	L3		14	18.2626
15	P1		15	17.1062
16	L2		16	16.8729*

* Optimal Value Of Criterion

Note that forward swap selection removes L3 at Step 13 but adds it back at Step 14.

Output 5.38 lists the effects in the final model.

Output 5.38 Effects Selected with Forward Swap Selection

Selected Effects: Intercept Region_South X2 X4 L1 L2 L3 L4 L5 L6 P1 P2 P3 P4 P5 P6

As with stepwise selection, the advantage of forward swap selection is that it is more flexible than forward selection. However, in this case the final model happens to be the same as the one obtained with forward selection.

Using the Final Model to Score New Data

When you build a predictive model, you need to be able to use it to compute the responses for new data. SAS provides a variety of methods for this task, which is called scoring. The data to be scored should not have been used to train the model; they should be reasonably similar to the training data, and they must contain the same variables with the same set of levels as the training data.

Appendix H explains different methods for scoring. Not every method is available with every procedure, and each method has its advantages and disadvantages.

The missing response method is the only method available with all of the model building procedures in this book. You include the observations to be scored—with their response values set to missing—in the input data set. The procedure scores these observations and saves them, together with the training observations, in an output data set. The disadvantage of this method is that the scoring model is not portable; you must rebuild it whenever you score new data.

Example: Scoring with the Missing Response Method

This example illustrates the missing response method with the model for close rate that was built with the GLMSELECT procedure on page 56. The following statements rebuild the model and score data for additional stores provided in the data set NewStores.

```
data NewStores; set NewStores;  CloseRate = . ;  Use = 'Score'; run;
data Stores;    set Stores;                       Use = 'Train'; run;
data Combine;   set NewStores Stores; run;

proc glmselect data=Combine;
   class Region(param=reference ref='Midwest' split)
         Training(param=reference ref='None');
   model CloseRate = Region Training X1-X20 L1-L6 P1-P6 /
      selection=forward(choose=sbc select=sbc stop=sbc);
   output out=Results Predicted=p_CloseRate;
run;

proc print data=Results(where=(Use='Score') obs=3) noobs;
   var StoreID x1-x3 l1-l2 p1-p2 Region Training p_CloseRate;
run;
```

Output 5.39 shows a partial listing of Results. The variable p_CloseRate contains the predicted values.

Output 5.39 Partial Listing of Results

StoreID	X1	X2	X3	L1	L2	P1	P2	Region	Training	p_CloseRate
601	-0.340	-0.268	0.376	0.451	0.633	0.094	-0.122	East	None	58.3912
602	0.466	0.225	-0.069	0.021	0.093	0.496	0.107	East	InProgress	60.5080
603	0.436	0.469	-0.250	0.193	0.557	-0.225	-0.316	East	None	62.1660

Appendix H provides examples of other, more practical, scoring methods you can apply with the GLMSELECT procedure: the SCORE statement method (page 382), the PLM procedure method (page 383), and the CODE statement method (page 387).

Summary

The GLMSELECT and REGSELECT procedures provide modern tools for building general linear models for predictive applications. You should use these tools instead of the model selection methods in the REG procedure, which are limited and outdated.

Nonetheless, best-subset regression and ridge regression—available in the REG procedure but not in the GLMSELECT procedure—remain useful for building regression models. The REG procedure also provides diagnostic measures and plots that are useful for exploring models you have built with the GLMSELECT and REGSELECT procedures.

A major limitation of the REG procedure is that the predictors must be numeric variables. When you use the procedure for best-subset regression and some of the predictors are categorical variables, you can work around this limitation by providing the design matrix for the model as the input data set.

Table 5.7 compares the features of the three procedures.

Table 5.7 Features of the GLMSELECT, REG, and REGSELECT Procedures

Feature	GLMSELECT	REG	REGSELECT
Fits regression models	Yes	Yes	Yes
Fits general linear models	Yes	No	Yes
Builds regression models	Yes	Outdated	Yes
Builds general linear models	Yes	No	Yes
Modern criteria	Yes	No	Yes
Data partitioning	Yes	No	Yes
Candidate effects			
Continuous predictors	Yes	Yes	Yes
Categorical predictors	Yes	No	Yes
Interaction effects	Yes	No	Yes
Polynomial effects	Yes	Indirectly	Yes
Spline effects	Yes	No	Yes
Model averaging	Yes	No	No
Best-subset regression	No	Yes ($k < \approx 40$)	Yes
Ridge regression	No	Yes	No
Model fit statistics	Yes	Yes	Yes
p-values for parameters of full models	Yes (option)	Yes (default)	Yes (default)
Tests of linear hypotheses for full models	No	Yes	No
Residual diagnostics	No	Yes	Yes
Influence statistics	No	Yes	Yes
Collinearity diagnostics	No	Yes	Yes
Diagnostic plots	No	Yes	No

Chapter 6
Building General Linear Models: Collinearity

Contents

This chapter explains approaches for dealing with collinearity when you build a general linear model. Some of these approaches apply to other classes of models, such as logistic regression, that involve a linear predictor and are discussed later in the book.

Collinearity occurs when some predictors in the model contribute no information about the response because they are linear—or nearly linear—combinations of other predictors. For instance, if two predictors X1 and X2 are highly correlated (with a Pearson correlation near 1 or −1), then X2 can be expressed as aX1 + b, and so it is a surrogate for X1. In other words, including either predictor in the model will give the same predicted value for the response. The linear combinations can involve more than two predictors, and the term *multicollinearity* is sometimes used for this situation.

Collinearity is hard to avoid when you build models with observational data. If your goal is to identify which predictors or effects are important in a business or scientific sense, collinearity allows meaningful predictors to be replaced by irrelevant predictors. Collinearity also induces instability in the estimates of regression coefficients. Indeed, the estimates can vary so much that they have the wrong sign.

If your goal is prediction, then some collinearity is not necessarily a problem provided future data have the same linear dependency structure as your training data. However, you should avoid prediction at points outside the x-space for the training data (page 15). This might be difficult because the subspaces spanned by sets of collinear predictors can be very narrow. Points that fall within the individual ranges of these predictors might actually lie far from these subspaces.

Collinearity undermines sequential selection methods based on least squares estimation. It also causes problems for the lasso and the LARS method, as noted in Chapter 6.

Example: Modeling the Effect of Air Pollution on Mortality

During the 1970s, concerns about air pollution in American cities led to studies that modeled the effects of pollutants on mortality and motivated regulations to improve air quality. The work of Lester Lave and Eugene Seskin, two environmental economists at Carnegie Mellon University, was particularly influential (Lave and Seskin 1970, 1977). Not only did it gain the attention of policymakers, but it also motivated deeper analysis by researchers in universities and the auto industry.

Assuming an association between air pollution and mortality, Lave and Seskin used data from Standard Metropolitan Statistical Areas (SMSAs) and least squares regression to quantify the effects of pollutant levels. To allow for other factors, their models included variables that measured weather and socioeconomic conditions. The magnitudes of the regression coefficients were of special interest.

Several investigators found that the least squares estimates were unstable due to correlation (non-orthogonality) of the variables. At General Motors Research Laboratories, Gary McDonald and Richard Schwing established the effectiveness of ridge regression for stabilizing the estimates in a study that was one of the first major applications of this method (McDonald and Schwing 1973).

This chapter uses data compiled by Lave and Seskin to illustrate a variety of methods—including ridge regression—that are useful for building general linear models for prediction when there is a high degree of collinearity in the variables. Although Lave and Seskin's models were explanatory, predictive models now play a role in air pollution studies that examine health effects over time and across geographic areas. Today, for example, researchers are investigating a possible link between rising rates of Parkinson's disease in regions of the world where sulfur dioxide emissions have increased during the past 50 years (Dorsey, Okun, and Tanner 2021).

Lave and Seskin's data, which were corrected and reanalyzed by Thibodeau et al. (1980) and Gibbons and McDonald (1980), provide measurements on the total mortality rate (TMR) and 60 predictors of TMR for 108 SMSAs in 1960. Table 6.1 describes the variables, which are saved in a SAS data set named AirPollution108.

Table 6.1   Variables in Data Set AirPollution108

Variable	Description
	Response Variable
TMR	Unadjusted total mortality (per 100,000)
	Air Pollution Measures
SMin	Smallest biweekly sulfate reading ($\mu g/m^3 \times 10$)
SMean	Arithmetic mean of biweekly sulfate readings ($\mu g/m^3 \times 10$)
SMax	Largest biweekly sulfate reading ($\mu g/m^3 \times 10$)
PMin	Smallest biweekly suspended particulate reading ($\mu g/m^3$)
PMean	Arithmetic mean of biweekly suspended particulate readings ($\mu g/m^3$)
PMax	Largest biweekly suspended particulate reading ($\mu g/m^3$)
	Socioeconomic Variables
PM2	SMSA population density (per square mile $\times 0.1$)
GE65	Percentage of SMSA population at least 65 years old ($\times 10$)

Table 6.1 *continued*

Variable	Description
PNOW	Percentage of nonwhites in SMSA population (×10)
POOR	Percentage of SMSA families with income below the poverty level (×10)
POP	SMSA population (×10, 000)

Occupation Mix Characteristics

Variable	Description
UNEMP	Unemployed
MALE	Male
AGRI	Agriculture
CONST	Construction
MFGD	Durable goods manufacturing
MFGND	Non-durable goods manufacturing
TRANS	Transportation, communication, other public utilities
TRADE	Wholesale and retail trade
FIN	Finance, insurance, real estate
EDUC	Educational services
PUBADM	Public administration
WHICO	Percentage of employed persons in white collar occupations
USETRN	Percentage of employed persons who use public transportation to work

Climate Characteristics

Variable	Description
TEMPMIN	Average daily minimum temperature (°F ×10)
TEMPMAX	Average daily maximum temperature (°F ×10)
DEG	Heating degree days (× 0.1)
PREC	Total precipitation (in ×10)
HUMIDAM	Average percent relative humidity at 1 AM
HUMIDPM	Average percent relative humidity at 1 PM
WIND	Average hourly wind speed (mph ×10)
RAIN	Number of days with at least 0.01 in of precipitation
SNOW	Number of days with at least 1 in of snow or sleet
FOG	Number of days with heavy fog
MAX90	Number of days with maximum temperature 90° and above
MAX32	Number of days with maximum temperature 32° and below
MIN32	Number of days with minimum temperature 32° and below
MIN0	Number of days with minimum temperature 0° and below

Heating Equipment

Variable	Description
STEAM_HE	Steam or hot water heating equipment (percentage of total housing units ×10)
WAF_HE	Warm air furnace heating equipment (percentage of total housing units ×10)
FLOOR_HE	Floor, wall, pipeless furnace heating equipment (percentage of total housing units ×10)
ELEC_HE	Built-in electric units heating equipment (percentage of total housing units ×10)
FLUE_HE	Other means with flue heating equipment (percentage of total housing units ×10)
WOFL_HE	Other means without flue heating equipment (percentage of total housing units ×10)
NONE_HE	Without heating equipment (percentage of total housing units ×10)

Heating Fuel

Variable	Description
GAS_HF	Utility gas heating fuel (percentage of occupied housing units ×10)
OIL_HF	Fuel oil, kerosene, etc heating fuel (percentage of occupied housing units ×10)

Table 6.1 *continued*

Variable	Description
COAL_HF	Coal or coke heating fuel (percentage of occupied housing units ×10)
ELEC_HF	Electricity heating fuel (percentage of occupied housing units ×10)
BGAS_HF	Bottled, tank, or LP gas heating fuel (percentage of occupied housing units ×10)
OTHER_HF	Other heating fuel (percentage of occupied housing units ×10)
NONE_HF	Without heating fuel (percentage of occupied housing units ×10)

Water Heating Fuel

Variable	Description
GAS_WF	Utility gas water heating fuel (percentage of occupied housing units ×10)
ELEC_WF	Electricity water heating fuel (percentage of occupied housing units ×10)
COAL_WF	Coal or coke water heating fuel (percentage of occupied housing units ×10)
BGAS_WF	Bottled, tank, or LP gas water heating fuel (percentage of occupied housing units ×10)
OIL_WF	Fuel oil, kerosene, or other water heating fuel (percentage of occupied housing units ×10)
OTHER_WF	Other water heating fuel (percentage of occupied housing units ×10)
NONE_WF	Without water heating fuel (percentage of occupied housing units ×10)

Air Conditioning

Variable	Description
WO_AC	Percentage of occupied housing units without air conditioning (×10)

The next statement saves the names of the 60 predictors in a macro variable named AP60Predictors:

```
%let AP60Predictors =
SMin       SMean     SMax     PMin      PMean    PMax     PM2      GE65      PNOW      POOR
POP        UNEMP     MALE     AGRI      CONST    MFGD     MFGND    TRANS     TRADE     FIN
EDUC       PUBADM    WHICO    USETRN    TEMPMIN  TEMPMAX  DEG      PREC      HUMIDAM   HUMIDPM
WIND       RAIN      SNOW     FOG       MAX90    MAX32    MIN32    MIN0      STEAM_HE  WAF_HE
FLOOR_HE   ELEC_HE   FLUE_HE  WOFL_HE   NONE_HE  GAS_HF   OIL_HF   COAL_HF   ELEC_HF   BGAS_HF
OTHER_HF   NONE_HF   GAS_WF   ELEC_WF   COAL_WF  BGAS_WF  OIL_WF   OTHER_WF  NONE_WF   WO_AC;
```

You can display the value of a macro variable in the SAS log by submitting a %PUT statement:

```
%put &=AP60Predictors;
```

The equal sign after the ampersand indicates that the name of the macro variable is to be shown as well as its value. Output 6.1 shows how this information appears in the SAS log:

Output 6.1 Result of the %PUT Statement

```
AP60PREDICTORS=SMin     SMean    SMax    PMin     PMean    PMax     PM2     GE65
PNOW      POOR POP      UNEMP    MALE    AGRI     CONST    MFGD     MFGND   TRANS
TRADE     FIN EDUC      PUBADM   WHICO   USETRN   TEMPMIN TEMPMAX DEG      PREC
HUMIDAM   HUMIDPM WIND     RAIN     SNOW    FOG      MAX90    MAX32    MIN32 MIN0
  STEAM_HE WAF_HE FLOOR_HE ELEC_HE FLUE_HE WOFL_HE NONE_HE GAS_HF   OIL_HF
COAL_HF   ELEC_HF   BGAS_HF OTHER_HF NONE_HF GAS_WF   ELEC_WF COAL_WF BGAS_WF
OIL_WF OTHER_WF NONE_WF   WO_AC
```

Programming Tip: When you build models with many predictors, save their names in macro variables and provide them in MODEL statements.

Detecting Collinearity

You can find pairs of collinear predictors by examining a correlation matrix and looking for off-diagonal correlations that are high in absolute value. However, the collinearity of three or more predictors is usually not evident in a correlation matrix, and so detecting multicollinearity requires an eigendecomposition of the $X'X$ matrix. The next two sections present tools for detecting these forms of collinearity.

Finding High Pairwise Correlations

The CORR procedure computes correlation matrices; see page 97 for an example. You can use the following statements to obtain the 60×60 correlation matrix (not shown) for the predictors in AirPollution108:

```
proc corr noprob nosimple data=AirPollution108;
   var &AP60Predictors;
run;
```

However, it is difficult to spot all the high correlations in a 60×60 matrix.

The `%HighCorr` macro[†] gives you much more readable information by listing all the correlations r_{ij} between two different variables for which $|r_{ij}|$ is greater than a specified cutoff. For instance, the following statements list the correlations greater than or equal to 0.9:

```
%HighCorr(Data=AirPollution108, VarList=&AP60Predictors, MinAbsCorr=0.9,
          DisplayTable=1,        OutHighCorr=HighCorrelations)
```

Output 6.2 displays the table that is requested with the DisplayTable= option. The information in the table is saved in a data set named with the OutHighCorr= option.

Output 6.2 Highest Correlations Among 60 Predictors in AirPollution108

8 Pairwise Correlations >= 0.9 in Absolute Value

Variable 1	Variable 2	Correlation
ELEC_HE	ELEC_HF	0.99019
DEG	MIN32	0.94084
TEMPMIN	TEMPMAX	0.92832
GAS_HF	GAS_WF	0.91595
GAS_HF	OIL_HF	-0.90256
TEMPMIN	MIN32	-0.92572
TEMPMAX	DEG	-0.95129
TEMPMIN	DEG	-0.97790

[†]This macro and others described in this chapter are available on the website for this book. To use this macro, download the file *HighCorrMacro.sas* and define the macro in your SAS program with a statement such as `%include 'HighCorrMacro.sas';` The macro header explains the options.

Keep in mind that a correlation coefficient measures the strength of the linear relationship between two variables. There is no universal definition of a high correlation; this depends on the application, and the cutoff 0.9 is specified here purely for illustration. The macro makes it convenient to try different cutoffs.

> **Programming Tip:** When p is large, use the `%HighCorr` macro instead of the CORR procedure to obtain a concise list of predictors with high pairwise correlations.

Excluding predictors with high correlations from a model does not generally solve the problem of collinearity, but it is a good way to start. In this example, since ELEC_HE is almost perfectly correlated with ELEC_HF, it is reasonable to exclude one of them, say ELEC_HE. And since DEG is highly correlated with TEMPMAX, TEMPMIN, and MIN32, it is reasonable to exclude DEG. Of course, based on Output 6.2, other predictors might be excluded.

The next statement assigns a list of the remaining 58 predictors to the macro variable AP58Predictors for subsequent use:

```
%let AP58Predictors =
SMin    SMean   SMax    PMin     PMean    PMax     PM2      GE65     PNOW
POOR    POP     UNEMP   MALE     AGRI     CONST    MFGD     MFGND    TRANS
TRADE   FIN     EDUC    PUBADM   WHICO    USETRN   TEMPMIN  TEMPMAX  PREC
HUMIDAM HUMIDPM WIND    RAIN     SNOW     FOG      MAX90    MAX32    MIN32
MIN0    STEAM_HE WAF_HE FLOOR_HE FLUE_HE WOFL_HE  NONE_HE  GAS_HF   OIL_HF
COAL_HF ELEC_HF BGAS_HF OTHER_HF NONE_HF GAS_WF   ELEC_WF  COAL_WF  BGAS_WF
OIL_WF  OTHER_WF NONE_WF WO_AC;
```

Finding Collinearity with Eigenvalues

Technically, collinearity occurs when some linear function of the columns of the model matrix $\mathbf{X}$ is exactly equal to the zero vector $\mathbf{0}$. When this occurs, the minimization problem for least squares estimation does not have a unique solution (see page 16).

A more complicated form of collinearity occurs if the linear function is nearly equal to $\mathbf{0}$. There can be one or more linear functions of this type; these are called near-singularities. Although $\mathbf{X'X}$ is invertible and the least squares estimator $\hat{\beta}_{OLS} = (\mathbf{X'X})^{-1}\mathbf{X'y}$ exists, the variance matrix $\text{Var}(\hat{\beta}) = (\mathbf{X'X})^{-1}\sigma^2$ is unstable. Small changes in $\mathbf{y}$ can cause large changes in the estimated coefficients $(\hat{\beta}_1, \ldots, \hat{\beta}_p)$, which can be hard to interpret because they have high standard errors. There can also be large swings in the coefficients as predictors are added or removed from the model.

You can diagnose collinearity by examining the eigenvalues of $\mathbf{X'X}$. Because this matrix is square, symmetric, and positive semi-definite,[†] it can be represented as $\mathbf{X'X} = \mathbf{VDV'}$, where $\mathbf{D}$ is a $p \times p$ diagonal matrix whose elements are the eigenvalues $\lambda_1, \ldots, \lambda_p$ with $\lambda_1 \geq \lambda_2 \geq \cdots \geq \lambda_p \geq 0$. This follows from the singular value decomposition for $\mathbf{X}$, which is explained in Appendix A on page 316.

[†] A square, symmetric matrix $\mathbf{A}$ is positive semi-definite if $\mathbf{x'Ax} \geq 0$ for all vectors $\mathbf{x}$ and some vector $\mathbf{x'Ax} = 0$ for some $\mathbf{x} \neq \mathbf{0}$.

The p columns of $\mathbf{V}$ are the eigenvectors $\mathbf{v}_j$ corresponding to the eigenvalues. The eigenvectors have the property that $\mathbf{X}'\mathbf{X}\mathbf{v}_j = \lambda_j\mathbf{v}_j$. Furthermore, they are mutually orthogonal ($\mathbf{v}'_j\mathbf{v}_k = 0, j \neq k$), and they have unit length:

$$\|\mathbf{v}_j\|_2 = (\mathbf{v}'_j\mathbf{v}_j)^{\frac{1}{2}} = 1, \quad j = 1, \ldots, p$$

It follows that $\mathbf{V}'\mathbf{V} = \mathbf{I}$ and $\mathbf{V}'\mathbf{X}'\mathbf{X}\mathbf{V} = \mathbf{D}$.

Eigenvalues are useful for diagnosing collinearity in two ways. First, the number of nonzero eigenvalues is equal to the rank of $\mathbf{X}'\mathbf{X}$. If the rank is less than p, then $\mathbf{X}'\mathbf{X}$ is not invertible and $\hat{\boldsymbol{\beta}}_{\mathrm{OLS}}$ does not exist. Second, if all the eigenvalues are positive but $\mathbf{X}$ is nearly collinear, then at least one of the eigenvalues will be nearly zero. Small eigenvalues inflate the variance–covariance matrix of $\hat{\boldsymbol{\beta}}_{\mathrm{OLS}}$:

$$\mathrm{Var}(\hat{\boldsymbol{\beta}}_{\mathrm{OLS}}) = \sigma^2(\mathbf{X}'\mathbf{X})^{-1} = \sigma^2\mathbf{V}'\mathbf{D}^{-1}\mathbf{V}$$

where the diagonal elements of $\mathbf{D}^{-1}$ are $1/\lambda_1, \ldots, 1/\lambda_p$. In particular, small eigenvalues inflate the variances of the regression coefficients:

$$\mathrm{Var}(\hat{\beta}_j) = \sigma^2 \sum_{k=1}^{p} \frac{\mathbf{V}(j,k)^2}{\lambda_k}, \quad j = 1, \ldots, p$$

where $\mathbf{V}(j, k)$ is the element of $\mathbf{V}$ in the jth row and kth column. Small eigenvalues also inflate the expected squared distance between $\hat{\boldsymbol{\beta}}_{\mathrm{OLS}}$ and $\boldsymbol{\beta}$, which is $\sigma^2 \sum_{j=1}^{p}(1/\lambda_j)$.

Computing Eigenvalues with the REG Procedure

You can obtain a table of the 58 eigenvalues for the predictors in AP58Predictors by specifying the COLLIN option in the REG procedure:

```
proc reg data=AirPollution108;
    model TMR = &AP58Predictors / collin;
    ods output CollinDiag = DiagnosticsAP108;
quit;
```

The table has 58 rows, which list the eigenvalues in decreasing order, and it has 61 columns. Output 6.3 displays the upper left portion of the table.

Output 6.3 Partial Table of Collinearity Diagnostics for 58 Predictors

| | | | | Collinearity Diagnostics | | | | | |
| | | | | | Proportion of Variation | | | | |
Number	Eigenvalue	Condition Index	Intercept	Smin	SMean	SMax	PMin	PMean	PMax
1	41.52162	1.00000	9.35211E-13	0.00002414	0.00000768	0.00001143	0.00001209	0.00000363	0.00001144
2	4.49224	3.04022	2.56287E-14	0.00015136	0.00004760	0.00005133	0.00001426	0.00000126	1.825149E-7
3	2.35863	4.19573	1.70386E-13	0.00000101	0.00000108	0.00000571	0.00003846	0.00001327	0.00004216
4	1.77089	4.84219	1.31044E-13	0.00003090	0.00011901	0.00011142	0.00002784	0.00000221	6.438776E-7
5	1.37040	5.50444	4.20206E-14	0.00024046	0.00008045	0.00007221	0.00030995	0.00008350	0.00023805
6	1.11017	6.11564	2.00942E-13	0.00008249	0.00000845	0.00004722	0.00001200	0.00001955	0.00008793
7	0.80257	7.19278	1.57066E-13	0.00151	0.00000522	0.00001225	0.00006602	0.00000113	0.00000328
8	0.72959	7.54395	1.16504E-13	0.00668	0.00057258	0.00057296	3.065073E-7	0.00000546	0.00002574

The condition index for the jth eigenvalue is the largest eigenvalue divided by λ_j. Condition indices between 30 and 100 indicate moderate to strong collinearity, and indices greater than 100 indicate serious collinearity (Rawlings, Pantula, and Dickey 1998, p. 371).

In addition to i, λ_i, and the condition index, the ith row shows—for each of the 58 predictors—the proportion of $\text{Var}(\hat{\beta}_j)$ that is associated with λ_i:

$$\text{Variance decomposition proportion} = \frac{\mathbf{V}(j,i)^2/\lambda_i}{\sum_{k=1}^{p}\mathbf{V}(j,k)^2/\lambda_k}, \quad j = 1,\ldots,p$$

For the jth predictor, a high proportion in the ith row reveals a strong association between the variance of $\hat{\beta}_j$ and the ith eigenvalue.

You can identify important collinearities by finding combinations of high condition indices and large variance decomposition proportions. None are evident in the part of the table that is shown in Output 6.3, but they exist elsewhere in the table.

Finding Collinearities with the VDPScreen Macro

Finding all of the combinations that represent important collinearities is difficult when the number of predictors is more than around 10. Instead, you can use the %VDPScreen macro, available on the book website, to extract a more readable portion of the table. The following statement displays only those predictors involved in near-singularities for which the condition index is greater than 100 and the variance decomposition proportion is greater than 0.5:

```
%VDPScreen( Data = AirPollution108,
          Response = TMR, Predictors = &AP58Predictors,
          MinCondIndex = 100, MinProportion = 0.5,
          OutScreen = ResultsAP108, Showtable = 1)
```

The table produced by the macro is shown in Output 6.4.

Output 6.4 Selected Variance Decomposition Proportions

Predictors with Variance Decomposition Proportion >= 0.5

Component Number	Eigenvalue	Condition Index	Predictors with Proportion >=0.5					
47	.004103190	100.59						
48	.003252600	112.99						
49	.003088357	115.95						
50	.001937228	146.40						
51	.001329368	176.73	TRADE					
52	.001004719	203.29	WHICO					
53	.000789357	229.35						
54	.000231874	423.17	MALE					
55	.000159646	509.99	TEMPMIN	MIN32				
56	.000077817	730.47	TEMPMAX					
57	.000039854	1020.71	STEAM_HE	WAF_HE	FLOOR_HE	FLUE_HE	WOFL_HE	
58	.000000006	82399.92	GAS_WF	ELEC_WF	COAL_WF	BGAS_WF	OIL_WF	OTHER_WF
			NONE_WF					
59	.000000001	181421.00	Intercept	GAS_HF	OIL_HF	COAL_HF	ELEC_HF	BGAS_HF
			OTHER_HF	NONE_HF				

Output 6.4 reveals collinearities involving sets of variables within the categories of occupation, temperature, heating equipment, water heating fuel, and heating fuel; see Table 6.1. This is not surprising; nearly all the predictors in this study are partially redundant with others that measure aspects of the same phenomenon.

Here, the minimum value for the condition index (specified with the MinCondIndex= option) and the minimum value for the variance decomposition proportion (specified with the MinProportion= option) are intended for illustration. In practice, you should try various combinations of these values.

Programming Tip: When *p* is large, use the `%VDPScreen` macro to explore collinearity.

There is no easy way to eliminate complex collinearities, although you can sometimes do so by excluding or averaging some of the predictors. The rest of this chapter illustrates approaches for dealing with collinearity that offer different degrees of interpretability and predictive ability.

Dimension Reduction Using Variable Clustering

Variable clustering, available in the VARCLUS procedure, provides a way to reduce the dimension of data sets without losing too much information. When you build regression models with many candidate predictors, clustering can help you identify those that are highly related and possibly redundant; by eliminating them, you can sometimes reduce collinearity. As illustrated here, you can also treat the cluster components as a reduced set of predictors.

This approach is unsupervised; it does not risk over- or underfitting the model. However, it involves several tuning parameters—in particular, the number of clusters—and the results will vary depending on how you choose these parameters.

The VARCLUS procedure uses algorithms that assign numeric variables to clusters. For each cluster, the procedure computes a component that is a linear combination of the variables in the cluster. Cluster components differ from standard principal components (see page 109); they are rotated to make them more interpretable, but they do not explain as much variance because they are not uncorrelated.

The next example uses the VARCLUS procedure to cluster the 58 predictors in AirPollution108. You can determine an appropriate number of clusters by creating multiple sets of clusters, each with a different number of clusters, and then comparing them with measures computed by the procedure.

The following statements request five sets of clusters for which the number of clusters ranges from 10 to 14:

```
proc varclus data=AirPollution108 minclusters=10 maxclusters=14
             outstat=ClusterStat random=155219;
   var &AP58Predictors;
   ods output RSquare=RSqClusters;
run;
```

For each set of clusters, the procedure lists the predictors in each of the clusters. Output 6.5 shows the predictors that form Clusters 4 and 5 in the set of 12 clusters.

Output 6.5 R^2 Measures for Clusters 4 and 5 in Set of 12

Cluster	Variable	R-squared with Own Cluster	Next Closest	1-R**2 Ratio	Variable Label
Cluster 4	**PNOW**	0.6807	0.2481	0.4247	Percent of nonwhites in SMSA population (x 10)
	POOR	0.8389	0.3379	0.2433	Percent of SMSA families with income below the poverty level (x 10)
	OTHER_HF	0.7010	0.1510	0.3522	Other heating fuel (% occupied housing units x 10)
	NONE_WF	0.8371	0.1750	0.1974	Without water heating fuel (% occupied housing units x 10)
Cluster 5	**PREC**	0.4741	0.2356	0.6880	Total precipitation (inches x 10)
	HUMIDAM	0.7774	0.1403	0.2589	Average percent relative humidity at 1 AM
	HUMIDPM	0.5837	0.0741	0.4496	Average percent relative humidity at l PM
	RAIN	0.6338	0.3076	0.5288	Number of days with at least 0.01 in precipitation
	FOG	0.3388	0.0978	0.7328	Number of days with heavy fog

For each predictor, the table provides R^2_{own}, the squared correlation of the predictor with its own cluster component (the larger this measure, the higher the correlation). The table also provides R^2_{next}, the next-highest squared correlation of the predictor with a cluster component (the smaller this measure, the better the separation). Small values of the $1 - R^2$ ratio, which is defined as $(1 - R^2_{own})/(1 - R^2_{next})$, indicate good clustering.

The set of 12 clusters explains 62% of the variance; among them, 9 clusters contain predictors that measure aspects of the same topic, as shown in the following table.

Table 6.2 Interpretation of Clusters

Cluster	Topic	Score Variable
1	Cold weather	Clus1
2	Heating	Clus2
3	Sulfate readings and population	Clus3
4	Poverty	Clus4
5	Precipitation	Clus5
8	Particulates	Clus8
10	Occupation	Clus10
11	Heating and air conditioning	Clus11
12	Trade and manufacturing	Clus12

Keep in mind that variable clustering does not necessarily form clusters that are interpretable. Furthermore, the results will vary depending on the seed for random initialization of cluster components and other options.

Using Cluster Components as Predictors

You can treat the components for the 12 clusters as a reduced set of predictors. The following statements fit a model by using 12 score variables (named Clus1 to Clus12) produced by the SCORE procedure from coefficients in the OUTSTAT= data set that was created by the VARCLUS procedure:

```
proc score data=AirPollution108 out=DataScores108 type=score
          score=ClusterStat(where=(_NCL_=12));
   var &AP58Predictors;
run;

proc glmselect data=DataScores108;
   model TMR=Clus1-Clus12 / selection=none;
run;
```

The SELECTION=NONE option requests a fitted model instead of a selected model. Output 6.6 shows the parameter estimates.

Output 6.6 Parameter Estimates for Model Using 12 Score Variables as Predictors

Least Squares Model (No Selection)

		Parameter Estimates			
Parameter	DF	Estimate	Standard Error	t Value	Pr > |t|
Intercept	1	186.245856	192.397176	0.97	0.3355
Clus1	1	-0.075050	0.296122	-0.25	0.8005
Clus2	1	-0.115129	0.074612	-1.54	0.1261
Clus3	1	0.257453	0.202824	1.27	0.2074
Clus4	1	-0.035232	0.253706	-0.14	0.8898
Clus5	1	1.005441	0.385311	2.61	0.0105
Clus6	1	1.941832	0.638588	3.04	0.0030
Clus7	1	-0.235346	0.278397	-0.85	0.4000
Clus8	1	-0.281121	0.200374	-1.40	0.1639
Clus9	1	0.417461	0.111745	3.74	0.0003
Clus10	1	-0.554668	0.261858	-2.12	0.0368
Clus11	1	-0.547950	0.230557	-2.38	0.0195
Clus12	1	1.182780	0.288681	4.10	<.0001

The *t*-values and *p*-values shown here are valid because the model is fitted rather than selected. The estimates for six of the score variables (Clus5, Clus6, Clus9, Clus10, Clus11, and Clus12) are significant. You can explain four of these variables with the help of Table 6.2. For instance, Clus5 is related to precipitation and Clus10 is related to occupation. As noted earlier, clustering deals well with variable redundancy, but it does not generally lead to models that are explainable.

Checking for Collinearity

Although clustering reduces the dimension of the predictor space from 58 to 12, there is some collinearity in the score variables. Again, you can examine this with the %VDPScreen macro:

```
%VDPScreen( Data          = DataScores108, Response = TMR,
            Predictors    = Clus1 Clus2 Clus3 Clus4  Clus5  Clus6
                            Clus7 Clus8 Clus9 Clus10 Clus11 Clus12,
            MinProportion = 0.3, MinCondIndex  = 10,
            OutScreen = ResultsClus, Showtable = 1)
```

The table produced by the macro is shown in Output 6.7.

Output 6.7 Variance Decomposition Proportions for Clus1, ..., Clus12

Predictors with Variance Decomposition Proportion >= 0.3

Component Number	Eigenvalue	Condition Index	Predictors with Proportion >=0.3			
8	0.081561	10.8920				
9	0.075370	11.3305	Clus8			
10	0.043183	14.9690	Clus11			
11	0.032372	17.2887	Clus4	Clus10		
12	0.008733	33.2866	Clus1	Clus2	Clus5	Clus11
13	0.001664	76.2565	Intercept	Clus6		

Not surprisingly, Clus1 (cold weather), Clus2 (heating), Clus5 (precipitation), and Clus11 (heating and air conditioning) are involved in a collinearity. This suggests that you could combine some of the clusters and refit the model.

Using Cluster Representatives as Predictors

Instead of treating the cluster components as predictors, you can select representative predictors from each cluster. Good representatives are those whose $1 - R^2$ ratios are the lowest in each cluster. The **%ClusterReps** macro, available on the book website, extracts these representatives from the data set RSqClusters that was created by the VARCLUS procedure:

```
%ClusterReps( Data = RSqClusters, NClusters = 12, NLowestRatios = 1,
              OutRsquare = RsqSelected, ShowTable = 1,
              VarListName = RepPredictors, NVarListName = NRepPredictors)
```

The table produced by the macro is shown in Output 6.8.

Output 6.8 R^2 Measures for Representative Predictors

Representative Predictors from 12 Clusters

Predictor	Label	Cluster	RSq Own Cluster	RSq Next Closest	1 - RSq Ratio
MAX32	Number of days with maximum temperature 32 and below	Cluster 1	0.8207	0.3118	0.2605
GAS_WF	Utility gas water heating fuel (% occupied housing units x 10)	Cluster 2	0.9329	0.1583	0.0798
PM2	SMSA population density (per square mile x 0.1)	Cluster 3	0.6867	0.1070	0.3508
NONE_WF	Without water heating fuel (% occupied housing units x 10)	Cluster 4	0.8371	0.1750	0.1974
HUMIDAM	Average percent relative humidity at 1 AM	Cluster 5	0.7774	0.1403	0.2589
UNEMP	Unemployed	Cluster 6	0.5578	0.0404	0.4609
BGAS_WF	Bottled, tank, or LP gas water heating fuel (% occupied housing units x 10)	Cluster 7	0.5192	0.0772	0.5210
PMean	Arithmetic mean of biweekly suspended particulate readings (microg/m**3)	Cluster 8	0.9429	0.1828	0.0699
OIL_WF	Fuel oil, kerosine, etc water heating fuel (% occupied housing units x 10)	Cluster 9	0.8578	0.1496	0.1672
WHICO	Percent of employed persons in white collar occupations	Cluster 10	0.7199	0.3338	0.4205
WOFL_HE	Other means without flue heating equipment (% total housing units x 10)	Cluster 11	0.7478	0.4327	0.4445
TRADE	Wholesale and retail trade	Cluster 12	0.7475	0.2033	0.3170

The macro saves the names of the representatives in the macro variable RepPredictors, which you can specify with the `%HighCorr` macro to find the highest correlations among the representatives:

```
%HighCorr(Data=AirPollution108, VarList=&RepPredictors, MinAbsCorr=0.4,
        DisplayTable=1, OutHighCorr=HighCorrReps)
```

Output 6.9 displays the table produced by the macro.

Output 6.9 Highest Correlations Among Representative Predictors

5 Pairwise Correlations >= 0.4 in Absolute Value

Variable 1	Variable 2	Correlation
NONE_WF	WOFL_HE	0.43871
WHICO	TRADE	0.41985
MAX32	NONE_WF	-0.43702
GAS_WF	OIL_WF	-0.45074
MAX32	WOFL_HE	-0.52752

Output 6.9 shows moderate pairwise collinearity in the representative predictors. To examine multicollinearity, you can specify RepPredictors in the `%VDPScreen` macro:

```
%VDPScreen( Data = AirPollution108,
            Response = TMR, Predictors = &RepPredictors,
            MinProportion = 0.3, MinCondIndex  = 10,
            OutScreen = ResultsReps, Showtable = 1)
```

The table produced by the macro is shown in Output 6.10.

Output 6.10 Variance Decomposition Proportions for Representative Variables

Predictors with Variance Decomposition Proportion >= 0.3

Component Number	Eigenvalue	Condition Index	Predictors with Proportion >=0.3		
8	0.071057	11.6737	PMean		
9	0.065620	12.1477	UNEMP		
10	0.047035	14.3483	GAS_WF	WOFL_HE	
11	0.010087	30.9833	HUMIDAM	TRADE	
12	0.004963	44.1694	WHICO	TRADE	
13	0.001720	75.0375	Intercept	HUMIDAM	WHICO

These results demonstrate that variable clustering can reduce multicollinearity while providing a certain amount of interpretability. However, variable clustering does not eliminate multicollinearity.

If you apply variable clustering with more than a few thousand variables, you will find that the algorithms in the VARCLUS procedure are not scalable. Lee et al. (2008) described a two-stage approach to overcoming this barrier.

Dimension reduction based on variable clustering was not available when Gibbons and McDonald (1980) analyzed the data in AirPollution108. Instead, they applied stepwise selection to reduce the number of predictors so that best-subset regression would be feasible with the remaining set.

Ridge Regression

Ridge regression was introduced by Arthur Hoerl in the early 1960s to remedy instabilities in ordinary least squares (OLS) regression coefficients that occur when there is collinearity in the predictors. The coefficients can be too large in absolute value and their signs can be incorrect, contradicting subject matter knowledge.

Hoerl, who was working in the chemical process industry, had previously developed an approach called ridge analysis for optimizing processes involving multiple independent variables. This method provides graphs that trace the ridges of a quadratic response surface, which are paths of steepest ascent and descent. Hoerl recognized that the residual sum of squares (RSS) for OLS regression has a similar quadratic form, with the regression estimator $\hat{\boldsymbol{\beta}}$ in place of the process variables:

$$\text{RSS} = (\mathbf{y} - \hat{\mathbf{y}})'(\mathbf{y} - \hat{\mathbf{y}}) = \mathbf{y}'\mathbf{y} - 2\hat{\boldsymbol{\beta}}\mathbf{X}'\mathbf{y} + \hat{\boldsymbol{\beta}}'(\mathbf{X}'\mathbf{X})\hat{\boldsymbol{\beta}}$$

This enabled him to apply ridge analysis to the problem of minimizing RSS (Hoerl 1962). The application became known as ridge regression, although ridge analysis itself never gained broad acceptance in the area of response surface methodology.[†] Hoerl, together with Robert Kennard, laid the theoretical foundation for ridge regression in Hoerl and Kennard (1970a, b).

The Ridge Estimator

The ridge estimator $\hat{\boldsymbol{\beta}}_{\text{ridge}}$ constrains the sizes of the regression coefficients by solving a minimization problem that adds an ℓ_2 penalty on the coefficients to the sum of squares of the residuals:

$$\hat{\boldsymbol{\beta}}_{\text{ridge}} = \underset{\boldsymbol{\beta}}{\text{argmin}} \left\{ \| \mathbf{y} - \mathbf{X}\boldsymbol{\beta} \|_2^2 + k\|\boldsymbol{\beta}\|_2^2 \right\} = \underset{\boldsymbol{\beta}}{\text{argmin}} \left\{ \sum_{i=1}^{n}(y_i - \mathbf{x}_i'\boldsymbol{\beta})^2 + k \sum_{i=1}^{n} \beta_j^2 \right\}, \quad k > 0$$

This is a convex optimization problem with a unique solution for every value of the Lagrange multiplier k. The solution, called the ridge estimator, has a closed form:

$$\hat{\boldsymbol{\beta}}_{\text{ridge}} = (\mathbf{X}'\mathbf{X} + k\mathbf{I})^{-1}\mathbf{X}'\mathbf{y}$$

The components of $\hat{\boldsymbol{\beta}}_{\text{ridge}}$ estimate $\beta_1, \ldots, \beta_p$ and are called the ridge coefficients. To obtain $\hat{\boldsymbol{\beta}}_{\text{ridge}}$, the predictors $\mathbf{x}_1, \ldots, \mathbf{x}_p$ are centered by their means, and so the estimate of β_0 is not penalized but is simply the average response $\bar{y} = (1/n) \sum_{i=1}^{n} y_i$. The predictors are also standardized to avoid scale dependences in the ridge coefficients.

As k approaches zero, $\hat{\boldsymbol{\beta}}_{\text{ridge}}$ approaches the least squares estimator $\hat{\boldsymbol{\beta}}_{\text{OLS}} = (\mathbf{X}'\mathbf{X})^{-1}\mathbf{X}'\mathbf{y}$, which exists provided that $\mathbf{X}$ is of full rank; see page 16. Hoerl and Kennard (1970b, Sec. 2) showed that the length of the ridge estimator ($\| \hat{\boldsymbol{\beta}}_{\text{ridge}} \|_2$) is less than the length of the OLS estimator ($\| \hat{\boldsymbol{\beta}}_{\text{OLS}} \|_2$)

[†]Roger Hoerl, the son of Arthur Hoerl, explained this twist in a 1985 retrospective paper. In a 2020 issue of *Technometrics* that highlighted ridge regression, he related the story behind the 1970 papers. Roger Hoerl's accounts are well worth reading because they illustrate how persistence and careful thinking about a problem in one field (chemical engineering) resulted in a broadly applicable statistical method that continues to serve in many fields.

and approaches zero as k increases, forcing the ridge coefficients toward zero. Interestingly, the word "shrink" does not appear in the 1970 papers[†]; only later did ridge regression come to be viewed as a shrinkage method.

Some of the ridge coefficients can change sign and cross zero as k increases, but they are never set to zero. Since all of the predictors remain in the model, ridge regression does not serve as an effect selection method, but it can identify active effects if a subset of the ridge coefficients is clearly dominant. In practice, the main issue is how to choose the parameter k. This is discussed on page 100.

The ridge estimator is biased because

$$E[\hat{\boldsymbol{\beta}}_{\text{ridge}}] = \boldsymbol{\beta} - k(\mathbf{X}'\mathbf{X} + k\mathbf{I})^{-1}\boldsymbol{\beta}, \quad k > 0$$

However, by allowing a small amount of bias, the ridge estimator gains an improvement in total mean squared error over that of the OLS estimator, which compensates for the bias. Hoerl and Kennard (1970b, Sec. 4) showed that the total mean (expected) squared error of the ridge estimator is

$$\underbrace{E[(\hat{\boldsymbol{\beta}}_{\text{ridge}} - \boldsymbol{\beta})'(\hat{\boldsymbol{\beta}}_{\text{ridge}} - \boldsymbol{\beta})]}_{\text{Total Mean Squared Error}} = \underbrace{\sigma^2 \sum_{j=1}^{p} \lambda_j/(\lambda_j + k)^2}_{\text{Total Variance}} + \underbrace{k^2\boldsymbol{\beta}'(\mathbf{X}'\mathbf{X} + k\mathbf{I})^{-2}\boldsymbol{\beta}}_{\text{Total Squared Bias}}$$

The quantities $\lambda_1, \ldots, \lambda_p$ are the eigvenvalues of $\mathbf{X}'\mathbf{X}$, which are all positive (see page 90). For positive k, the total variance is less than that of the OLS estimator (σ^p). It decreases sharply as k increases, producing the improvement in mean squared error for a range of k values. Within this range, the mean squared error decreases to a minimum.

There is also a bias-variance tradeoff in the mean squared error for prediction (MSEP), which is discussed on page 21. Here, the issue is the flexibility (complexity) of the model, which is measured by the effective degrees of freedom for ridge regression:

$$\text{df}(k) = \text{rank}(\mathbf{X}(\mathbf{X}'\mathbf{X} + k\mathbf{I})^{-1}\mathbf{X}') = \text{tr}(\mathbf{X}(\mathbf{X}'\mathbf{X} + k\mathbf{I})^{-1}\mathbf{X}') = \sum_{j=1}^{p} \frac{\lambda_j^2}{\lambda_j^2 + k}$$

As k increases, the degrees of freedom decreases. The predicted response for ridge regression can be expressed as

$$\hat{\mathbf{y}}_{\text{ridge}} = \mathbf{X}\hat{\boldsymbol{\beta}}_{\text{ridge}} = \sum_{j=1}^{p} \mathbf{u}_j \frac{\lambda_j}{\lambda_j + k} \mathbf{u}_j'\mathbf{y}$$

where $\mathbf{u}_1, \ldots, \mathbf{u}_p$ are an orthonormal basis for the column space of $\mathbf{X}$ and correspond to the eigenvalues. Because of the orthogonality, $\hat{\mathbf{y}}_{\text{ridge}}$ can be interpreted as the sum of predictions from p independent regression models, each with a single predictor $\mathbf{u}_j$. The product $\mathbf{u}_j'\mathbf{y}$ is the OLS regression coefficient, and $\lambda_j/(\lambda_j + k)$ is the amount by which ridge regression shrinks the coefficient.

[†]The concept of shrinkage was already established by that point. Charles Stein, a mathematical statistician at Stanford University, demonstrated in 1956 that shrinkage can improve the mean squared error of a multivariate sample mean whose dimension is at least three. James and Stein (1961) introduced a particular shrinkage estimator that always achieves a mean squared error less than that of the OLS estimator. These results were landmarks in the field of statistics, but shrinkage estimation did not gain acceptance in practice until much later. The concept is central to the lasso and its variants, and it continues to evolve in the area of statistical learning.

In short, ridge regression applies different amounts of shrinkage to the OLS coefficients, depending on the eigenvalues. It applies the largest amounts to the coefficients that correspond to the smallest eigenvalues. As explained on page 90, those are the eigenvalues most associated with collinearity and the problems it presents for OLS regression.

Ridge Regression Using the REG Procedure

Ridge regression is available with the REG procedure, as illustrated by this example, which uses the 12 representative predictors for TMR in Output 6.8. These predictors are moderately collinear, as shown in Output 6.9 and Output 6.10. To request ridge regression, you specify a list of ridge parameters k with the RIDGE= option:

```
ods graphics on;
proc reg data=AirPollution108 outest=Parms(rename=(_RIDGE_=k)) outstb outvif
         ridge=0 to 1 by 0.1
         plots(only)=ridge(unpack VIFaxis=log varsperplot=12);
   model TMR = &RepPredictors / vif;
quit;

proc print data=Parms(where=((_TYPE_="RIDGE") or (_TYPE_="RIDGESTB"))) noobs;
   var k Intercept &RepPredictors;
run;
```

Usually, $k = 1$ will serve as the maximum value in the RIDGE= list. You might find that much smaller values are appropriate, especially with a large number of predictors.

Programming Tip: Specify different lists with the RIDGE= option to find the most useful range.

By default, the procedure displays a table, shown in Output 6.11, of the OLS parameter estimates.

Output 6.11 Parameter Estimates for OLS Regression

Model: MODEL1
Dependent Variable: TMR

		Parameter Estimates				
Variable	DF	Parameter Estimate	Standard Error	t Value	Pr > |t|	Variance Inflation
Intercept	1	377.22361	219.76031	1.72	0.0893	0
MAX32	1	0.07105	0.59555	0.12	0.9053	2.67753
GAS_WF	1	0.02009	0.06415	0.31	0.7548	2.94443
PM2	1	0.32036	0.27301	1.17	0.2436	1.64871
NONE_WF	1	0.06436	0.25972	0.25	0.8048	2.47780
HUMIDAM	1	3.30626	1.58300	2.09	0.0394	1.61725
UNEMP	1	2.31552	0.88890	2.60	0.0107	1.35832
BGAS_WF	1	0.06671	0.54898	0.12	0.9035	1.42276
PMean	1	0.27986	0.33616	0.83	0.4072	1.62870
OIL_WF	1	0.52477	0.10208	5.14	<.0001	1.95060
WHICO	1	-0.78188	0.30200	-2.59	0.0111	2.41770
WOFL_HE	1	-0.19709	0.09979	-1.98	0.0512	3.17268
TRADE	1	2.24357	0.58370	3.84	0.0002	1.69797

For each value of k specified with the RIDGE= option, the procedure computes a set of unstandardized ridge estimates that are saved in the data set Parms and are partially listed in Output 6.12. The estimates for $k = 0$ match those in Output 6.11 for OLS regression.

Output 6.12 Partial Listing of Data Set Parms

k	_TYPE_	Intercept	MAX32	GAS_WF	PM2	NONE_WF	UNEMP	OIL_WF	WHICO	PMean
0.0	RIDGE	377.22	0.07105	0.02009	0.32036	0.06436	2.31552	0.52477	-0.78188	0.27986
0.0	RIDGESTB	0.00	0.01428	0.03931	0.11022	0.02854	0.22208	0.52522	-0.29447	0.07772
0.1	RIDGE	486.10	0.25271	-0.02171	0.33653	0.02464	2.20010	0.43192	-0.61441	0.20434
0.1	RIDGESTB	0.00	0.05079	-0.04249	0.11578	0.01093	0.21101	0.43229	-0.23140	0.05675
0.2	RIDGE	559.15	0.28948	-0.03691	0.32922	0.00653	2.03660	0.37435	-0.52748	0.15745
0.2	RIDGESTB	0.00	0.05818	-0.07222	0.11326	0.00289	0.19533	0.37466	-0.19866	0.04373
0.3	RIDGE	612.69	0.29350	-0.04363	0.31556	-0.00368	1.88097	0.33374	-0.47093	0.12579
0.3	RIDGESTB	0.00	0.05899	-0.08537	0.10856	-0.00163	0.18040	0.33403	-0.17736	0.03493

A natural question is, how does one choose the value of k? Many solutions have been proposed for this problem, beginning with Hoerl and Kennard (1970a), who suggested plotting the standardized ridge coefficients as a function of k. They named this the *ridge trace*. Output 6.13 shows the ridge trace plot for this example, which was requested with the PLOTS=RIDGE option.

Output 6.13 Ridge Trace Plot

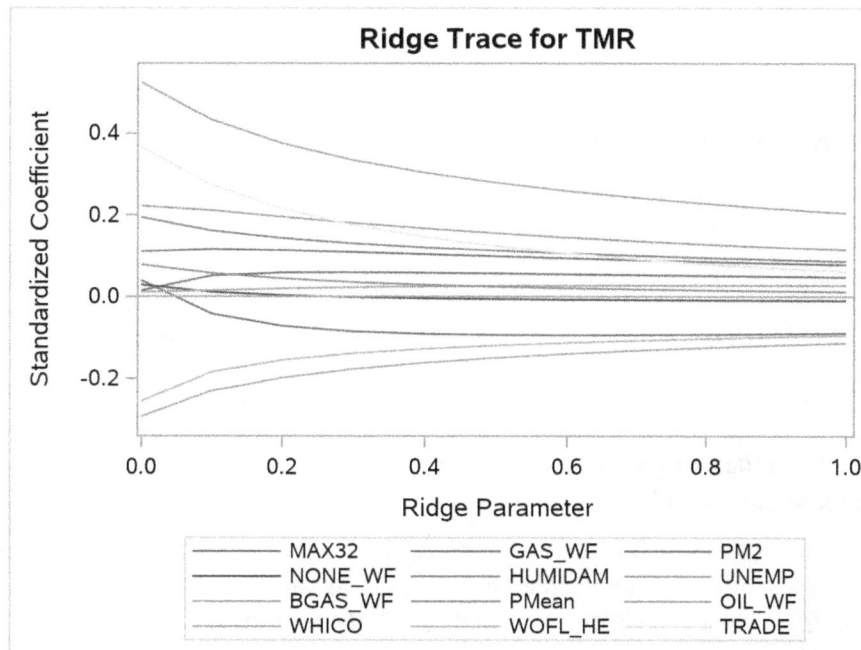

The coefficients at $k = 0$ correspond to OLS regression; the unstandardized OLS coefficients are shown in Output 6.11. As k increases, the ridge coefficients shrink to zero, corresponding to the intercept-only model.

Hoerl and Kennard recommended choosing the smallest k for which the coefficients are stable and have proper signs. Here, the coefficients begin to stabilize between 0.1 and 0.2. The coefficients for GAS_WF and NONE_WF change sign between 0 and 0.1. Both of these predictors are correlated with other predictors; see Output 6.9.

When you specify PLOTS=RIDGE, the REG procedure produces a companion plot, shown in Output 6.14, of the variance inflation factors (VIF$_j$) for each predictor.

Output 6.14 Variance Inflation Factor Plot

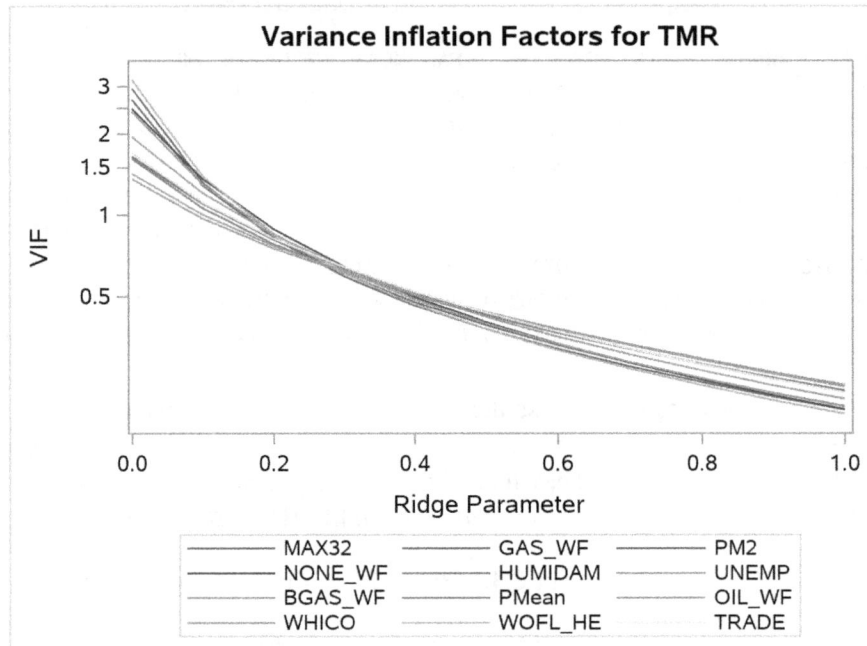

Interpreting Variance Inflation Factors

The variance inflation factors VIF$_1$, . . ., VIF$_p$ are the factors by which the variances of the least squares estimates $\hat{\beta}_1$, . . ., $\hat{\beta}_p$ increase due to collinearity (Marquardt 1970). For the jth predictor, VIF$_j$ is the jth diagonal element of the matrix

$$(\mathbf{X'X} + k\mathbf{I})^{-1}\mathbf{X'X}(\mathbf{X'X} + k\mathbf{I})^{-1}$$

where the columns of $\mathbf{X}$ are first centered by their means and scaled by their standard deviations.

In Output 6.14, the variance inflation factors decrease to one between $k = 0.1$ and $k = 0.2$, after which they decrease further, indicating overshrinkage of $\hat{\beta}_1$, . . ., $\hat{\beta}_p$.

For $k = 0$, VIF$_j$ simplifies to $1/(1 - R_j^2)$, where R_j^2 is the value of R^2 from the regression of the jth predictor $\mathbf{x}_j$ on the other predictors. These values are included in the parameter estimates table shown in Output 6.11 when you specify VIF in the MODEL statement.

If there is a near-singularity that involves $\mathbf{x}_j$, then VIF$_j$ will be large, but if $\mathbf{x}_j$ is orthogonal to the other predictors, then VIF$_j$ will be one. Values greater than 10 are often regarded as a sign of severe collinearity, based on a comment by Marquardt (1970, p. 610). This cutoff is not a substitute for the eigenvalue analysis discussed on page 90; if applied blindly, it can lead to remedies that do more harm than good, as pointed out by O'Brien (2007) and other authors.

Output 6.13 and Output 6.14 indicate that the small amounts of bias introduced by $k = 0.1$ and $k = 0.2$ produce coefficients that are fairly stable. The standardized coefficients of PMean in Output 6.12 are considerably smaller in magnitude than those of UNEMP, OIL_WF, and WHICO.

Alternative Methods for Selecting the Ridge Parameter

Trace plots and VIF plots are helpful for understanding the effects of collinearity, but their interpretation is nonetheless subjective. When prediction is the goal, you can apply the criteria explained in "Assessment and Minimization of Prediction Error" on page 25 to choose k. These criteria are not available in the REG procedure, but you can use two macros that are available on the book website:

- The **%RidgeSelect** macro produces plots of Mallows' C_P, AIC, SBC, and estimates of prediction error based on leave-one-out cross validation and generalized cross validation (Craven and Wahba 1979).

- The **%RidgeCrossVal** macro produces plots of the average square error (ASE) of prediction based on m-fold cross validation.

With these plots you can identify the values of k that minimize the various criteria. Both macros save the minimizing values of k in output data sets and macro variables, which make it convenient to access this information programmatically.

The following statement uses the **%RidgeSelect** macro to request a series of plots that show how the predictive ability of the ridge regression model for TMR varies with k:

```
%RidgeSelect(Data=AirPollution108,
          Response=TMR, Predictors=&RepPredictors, KMax=0.6, NKInc=20,
          OutEst=RidgeEstimates, OutSel=RidgeKSelections,
          CpPlot=1, InfPlot=1, LOOCVPlot=1, DFPlot=1)
```

Output 6.15 shows how Mallows' C_P statistic, explained on page 26, varies with k. The smallest C_P occurs at $k = 0.1048$.

Output 6.15 Selection of k Based on C_P

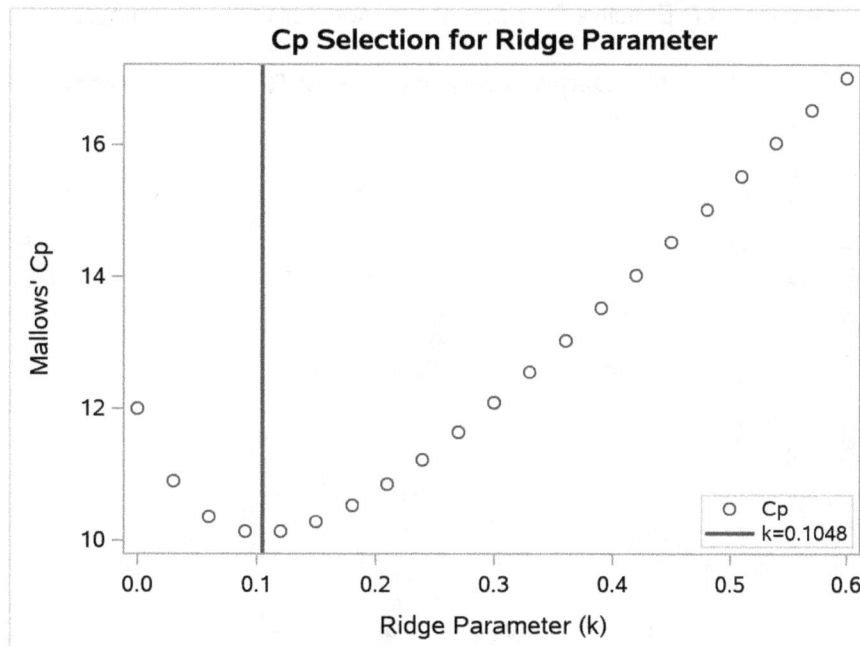

Output 6.16 shows how AIC and SBC (also known as BIC) vary with k. The smallest AIC occurs at $k = 0.0914$; the smallest SBC occurs at $k = 0.3744$.

Output 6.16 Selections of k Based on AIC and SBC

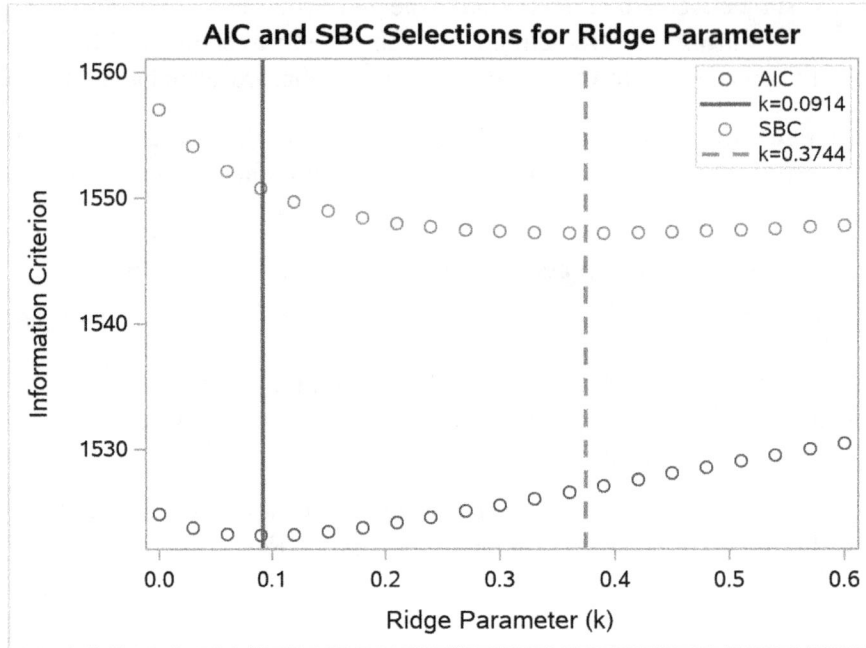

Compared with AIC, SBC generally tends to choose models that are simpler (see page 29). Here, SBC favors a model whose coefficients are closer to zero.

Output 6.17, requested with the DFPlot=1 option, shows how the effective degrees of freedom for ridge regression (see page 99) decreases as k increases.

Output 6.17 Effective Degrees of Freedom for Ridge Regression

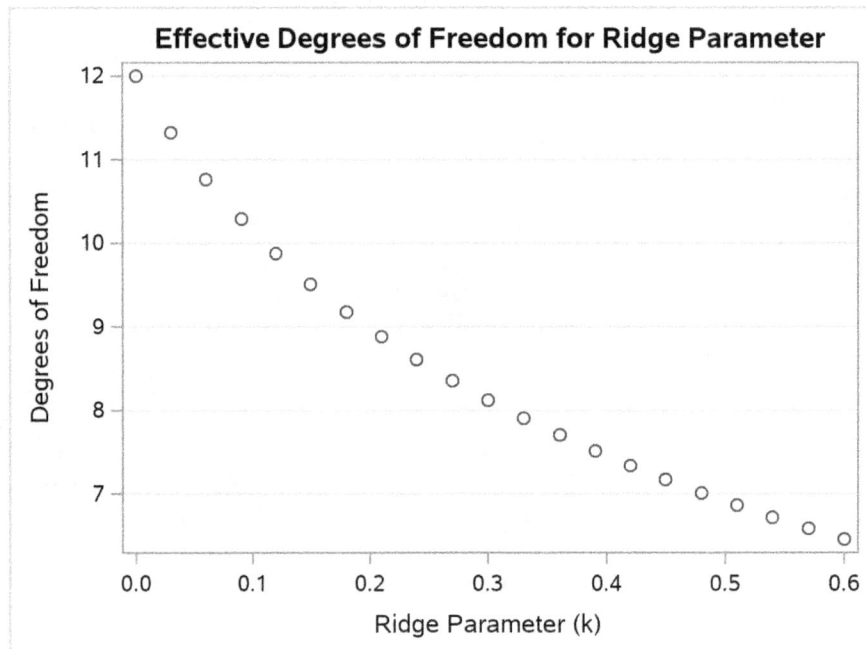

At $k = 0$, which corresponds to the OLS regression model, the degrees of freedom is 12. At $k = 0.0914$, the degrees of freedom for the ridge regression model is 10.3, and at $k = 0.3744$ it is 7.5.

Output 6.18 shows how estimates of prediction error computed with leave-one-out cross validation (LOOCV) and generalized cross validation (GCV) vary with k.

Output 6.18 Selections of k Based on Leave-One-Out and Generalized Cross Validation

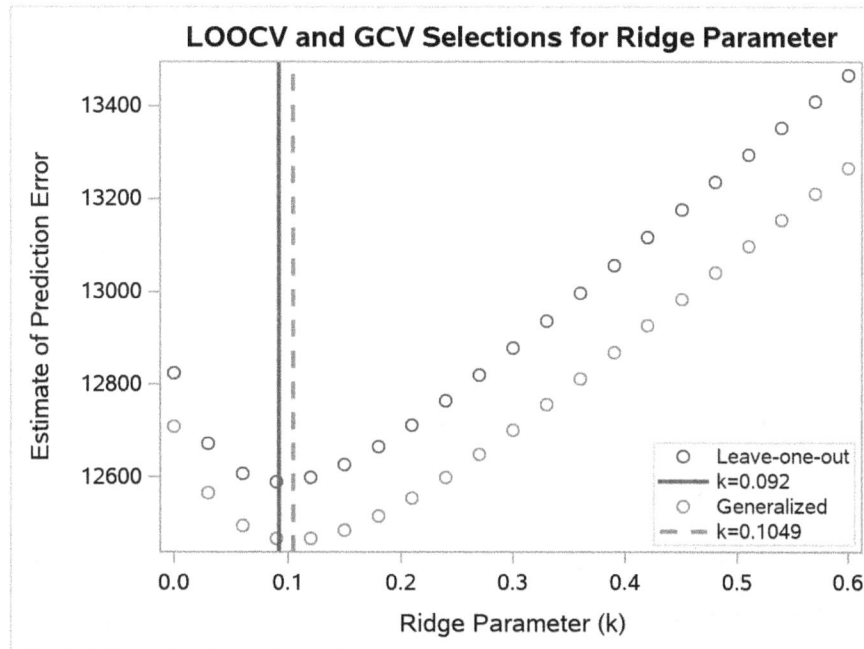

As explained in "Cross Validation Methods for Estimating Prediction Error" on page 31, LOOCV is computationally expensive, but in the case of ridge regression, it can be computed efficiently with a singular value decomposition of the **X** matrix. GCV, introduced by Craven and Wahba (1979), is an approximation to LOOCV that extends to other regression methods involving squared error loss. Here, the two methods agree closely. The smallest LOOCV estimate occurs at $k = 0.092$, and the smallest GCV estimate occurs at $k = 0.1049$.

Output 6.19 displays the various selections of k that are saved in the data set RidgeKSelections.

Output 6.19 Selected Values of Ridge Parameter k

kLOOCV	MinLOOCV	kGCV	MinGCV	kAIC	MinAIC	kSBC	MinSBC	kCp	MinCP
0.092017	12589.18	0.10492	12465.16	0.091434	1523.16	0.37438	1547.23	0.10481	10.1181

The `%RidgeCrossVal` macro estimates the prediction error for ridge regression by using m-fold cross validation; see page 31. The following statement requests 10-fold cross validation:

```
%RidgeCrossVal(Data=AirPollution108,
               Response=TMR, Predictors=&RepPredictors,
               KMax=0.6, NKInc=20,
               NFolds=10, Seed=599103,
               OutCV=CVResults, Plot=1, ShowSE=1)
```

Output 6.20 shows how the error estimates vary with k. The smallest estimate occurs at $k = 0.15$. However, taking into account the standard errors, requested with the ShowSE= option, this estimate cannot be distinguished from estimates for smaller values of k that were selected with other methods.

Output 6.20 Selection of k Based on 10-Fold Cross Validation

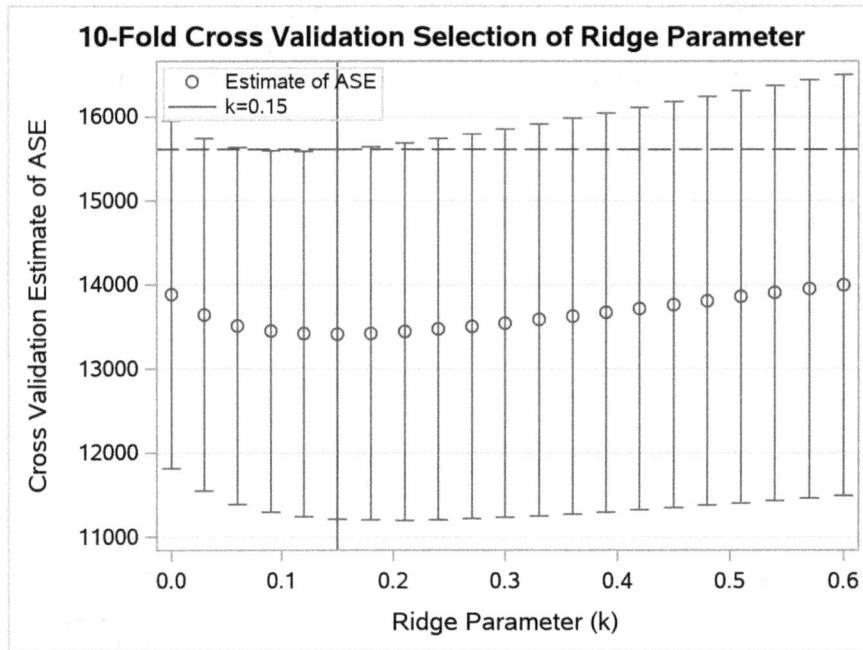

In summary, all but one of the approaches agree on $k = 0.1$ as the best value for minimizing prediction error. The SBC approach favors $k = 0.37$, but it is generally recommended for discovery of important effects rather than prediction; see page 29.

The Elastic Net Method

The elastic net method is a generalization of the lasso method that estimates the regression coefficients by solving a doubly penalized least squares problem:

$$\hat{\boldsymbol{\beta}}_{\text{naive}} = \underset{\boldsymbol{\beta}}{\arg\min} \left\{ \| \mathbf{y} - \mathbf{X}\boldsymbol{\beta} \|_2^2 + \lambda_1 \|\boldsymbol{\beta}\|_1 + \lambda_2 \|\boldsymbol{\beta}\|_2^2 \right\}, \quad \lambda_1 > 0, \ \lambda_2 > 0$$

The solution $\hat{\boldsymbol{\beta}}_{\text{naive}}$ is referred to as the naive elastic net estimator. The optimization criterion reduces to the ridge regression criterion if λ_1 is zero, and it reduces to the lasso criterion if λ_2 is zero. By blending two penalties, the elastic net method incorporates useful features of the lasso and ridge regression. However, these come with the expense of greater computational complexity.

The elastic net and ridge regression are both shrinkage methods, but unlike ridge regression, the elastic net sets some coefficients to zero, and so it serves as a model selection method. This is an advantage when you work with a large number of candidate predictors because the final model is easier to interpret.

The elastic net method offers two advantages over the lasso:

- If p is greater than n, it can select as many as p predictors; the lasso can select at most n predictors.

- It can do grouped selection in the sense that coefficients for a group of highly correlated variables will tend to be similar. Ridge regression also has this property. The lasso tends to select just one predictor in a group.

Like the lasso, the elastic net method centers and standardizes the columns of $\mathbf{X}$. It also splits effects that correspond to multiple columns. As in ridge regression, the response is centered by its mean so that the estimate of β_0 is not penalized but is simply the average response.

For fixed values of λ_1 and λ_2, the elastic net criterion can be rewritten as $\| \mathbf{y}^* - \mathbf{X}^* \boldsymbol{\beta}^* \|_2^2 + \gamma \| \boldsymbol{\beta}^* \|_1$, where $\gamma = \lambda_1 / \sqrt{1 + \lambda_2}$ and

$$\mathbf{y}^*_{n+p} = \begin{pmatrix} \mathbf{y} \\ \mathbf{0} \end{pmatrix}, \quad \mathbf{X}^*_{(n+p) \times p} = \frac{1}{\sqrt{1 + \lambda_2}} \begin{pmatrix} \mathbf{X} \\ \sqrt{\lambda_2} \, \mathbf{I} \end{pmatrix}, \quad \boldsymbol{\beta}^* = \sqrt{1 + \lambda_2} \, \boldsymbol{\beta}$$

As a result, $\hat{\boldsymbol{\beta}}_{\text{naive}}$ can be obtained as the solution to a lasso optimization problem with augmented data. For fixed λ_2, the coefficients follow the same piecewise linear path as the lasso coefficients.

The elastic net was introduced by Hui Zou and Trevor Hastie (2005). They found that the naive elastic net can create bias that is unnecessary and does not reduce variance. To correct for this, they defined the elastic net estimator

$$\hat{\boldsymbol{\beta}}_{\text{elastic net}} = (1 + \lambda_2) \hat{\boldsymbol{\beta}}_{\text{naive}}$$

as a scaled version of the naive elastic net estimator. Based on simulations, they conjectured that "whenever ridge regression improves on OLS regression, the elastic net will improve on the lasso" (Zou and Hastie 2005, p. 312).

The Elastic Net Method Using the GLMSELECT Procedure

The elastic net method is available in the GLMSELECT procedure, as illustrated by this example, which applies it to selecting a model for TMR from the 58 predictors that were identified on page 90.

The following statements build the model:

```
proc glmselect plots=coefficients data=AirPollution108;
   model TMR = &AP58Predictors /
      selection=elasticnet(steps=16 choose=sbc enscale);
run;
```

The STEPS= option specifies the number of selection steps. The CHOOSE= option specifies SBC as the criterion for choosing the model; it is evaluated at each step, and the model with the smallest value is chosen. The ENSCALE option requests the estimator $\hat{\boldsymbol{\beta}}_{\text{elastic net}}$.

By default, the procedure does a grid search for λ_2, and for each value of λ_2 it uses the choose criterion to determine the best value of λ_1.

Output 6.21 shows the coefficient progression plot requested with the PLOTS= option.

Output 6.21 Coefficient Progression with Elastic Net

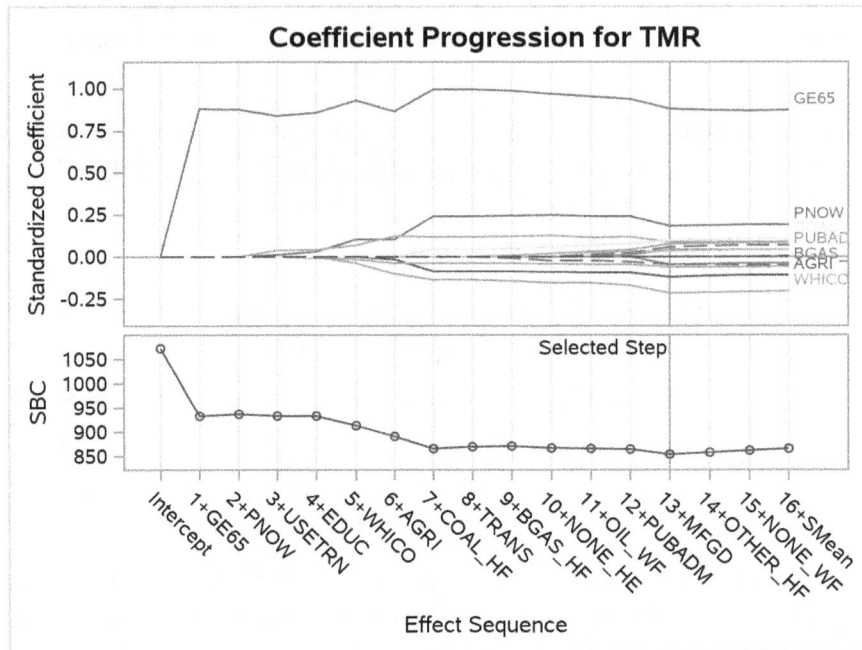

The minimum value of SBC is attained at Step 13, and there is a local minimum at Step 7.

For prediction, the sparser models at Step 4 and Step 7 should be considered. The next statements build the model at Step 7:

```
proc glmselect plots=coefficients data=AirPollution108;
   model TMR = &AP58Predictors /
       selection=elasticnet(steps=7 choose=sbc enscale);
run;
```

Output 6.22 shows the parameter estimates.

Output 6.22 Parameter Estimates for Model at Step 7

Selected Model

Parameter Estimates		
Parameter	DF	Estimate
Intercept	1	453.454338
GE65	1	6.729838
PNOW	1	0.325261
AGRI	1	-0.759711
EDUC	1	-0.315355
WHICO	1	-0.356141
USETRN	1	0.294104
COAL_HF	1	0.058278

Interestingly, none of these predictors are related to air pollution or climate characteristics. The only predictor related to heating is COAL_HF.

Principal Components Regression

Principal components regression takes a different approach to the problem of collinearity. Instead of selecting a subset of the predictors, it builds the model from derived linear combinations of all the predictors. These combinations, called principal components,[†] have two special properties: they are uncorrelated with each other, and they correspond to the p eigenvalues of $\mathbf{X}'\mathbf{X}$. By including only the principal components for the q largest eigenvalues, this approach eliminates the components corresponding to small eigenvalues that cause most of the collinearity. The central question is how to determine the tuning parameter q.

As explained on page 90, the matrix $\mathbf{X}'\mathbf{X}$ can be factorized as

$$\mathbf{X}'\mathbf{X} = \mathbf{V}\mathbf{D}\mathbf{V}'$$

where $\mathbf{D}$ is a diagonal matrix whose elements are the eigenvalues $\lambda_1 \geq \lambda_2 \geq \cdots \geq \lambda_p \geq 0$. The columns of $\mathbf{X}$ represent the predictors, which are usually centered and scaled to have a mean of 0 and a standard deviation of 1.

The eigenvectors corresponding to the eigenvalues are the columns $\mathbf{v}_j$ of the matrix $\mathbf{V}$. They are mutually orthogonal ($\mathbf{v}'_j\mathbf{v}_k = 0$, $j \neq k$) and have unit length ($\|\mathbf{v}\|_2 = (\mathbf{v}'_j\mathbf{v}_j)^{\frac{1}{2}} = 1$, $j = 1, \ldots, p$). The eigenvectors define the *directions* of the principal components.

The principal components themselves are p new variables or features that are derived as linear combinations of the predictors:

$$\mathbf{t}_j = \mathbf{X}\mathbf{v}_j = \mathbf{v}_j(1)\mathbf{x}_1 + \cdots + \mathbf{v}_j(p)\mathbf{x}_p, \quad j = 1, \ldots, p$$

where $\mathbf{v}_j(k)$ denotes the kth element of $\mathbf{v}_j$. The coefficients $\mathbf{v}_j(k)$ are referred to as loadings. A different principal component is associated with each of the eigenvectors, and the components are ordered in the same way as the eigenvectors: the first component $\mathbf{t}_1$ is associated with λ_1, the second component $\mathbf{t}_2$ is associated with λ_2, and so on. The value of $\mathbf{t}_j$ for the ith observation is referred to as its score on the jth principal component, and $\mathbf{t}_j$ is referred to as a score variable.

The first eigenvector $\mathbf{v}_1$ points in the direction of maximum variation among the predictors. Among all normalized linear combinations of $\mathbf{x}_1, \ldots, \mathbf{x}_p$, the first principal component $\mathbf{t}_1$ has the largest sample variance:

$$\mathrm{Var}(\mathbf{t}_1) = \mathrm{Var}(\mathbf{X}\mathbf{v}_1) = \mathrm{E}(\mathbf{v}'_1\mathbf{X}'\mathbf{X}\mathbf{v}_1) = \lambda_1$$

The second principal component $\mathbf{t}_2$ lies along a direction orthogonal to that of $\mathbf{t}_1$, and it has the next largest sample variance (λ_2). All of the principal components are uncorrelated with each other, and the sum of their variances equals the sum of the variances of the predictors.

To clarify these concepts, consider an example with only two predictors. Output 6.23 shows a scatter plot of SMin and SMax, two of the pollution variables in AirPollution108. The data are plotted in units of standard deviations from the mean.

[†]Principal component analysis is an unsupervised learning method for understanding linear relationships among a set of continuous variables. It was introduced in the field of statistics by Karl Pearson (1901) and Harold Hotelling (1936) There are four procedures in SAS for general principal component analysis: the PRINCOMP, PRINQUAL, and HPPRINCOMP procedures in SAS/STAT and the PCA procedure in SAS Viya.

Output 6.23 Scatter Plot of SMin and SMax

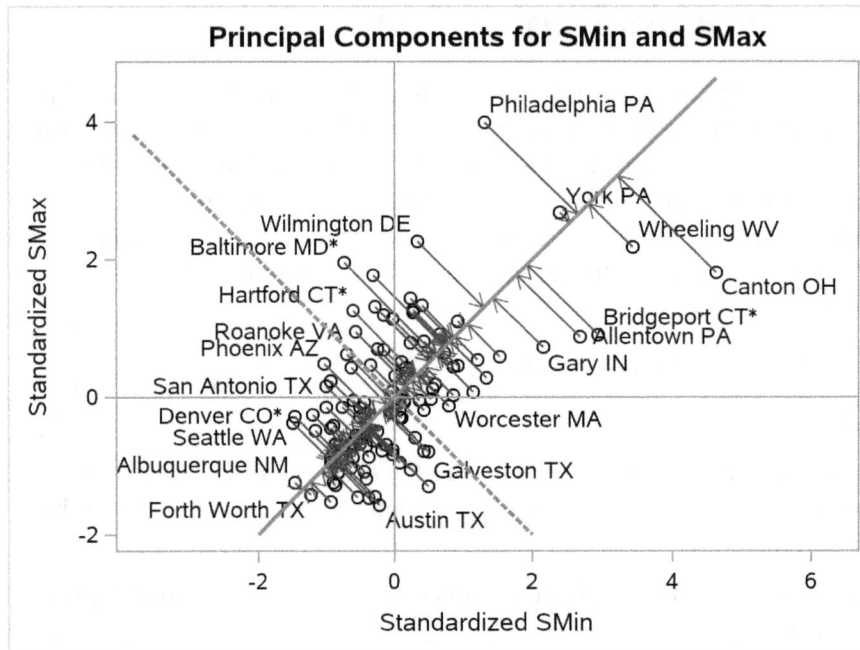

In this example there are two eigenvectors: $\mathbf{v}'_1 = (1/\sqrt{2}, 1/\sqrt{2})$ and $\mathbf{v}'_2 = (-1/\sqrt{2}, 1/\sqrt{2})$. The solid diagonal line represents the first principal component:

$$t_1 = \frac{1}{\sqrt{2}}(\text{SMin} - \text{mean}(\text{SMin}))/\text{std}(\text{SMin}) + \frac{1}{\sqrt{2}}(\text{SMax} - \text{mean}(\text{SMax}))/\text{std}(\text{SMax})$$

The scores for this component are the distances to the origin of the projections of the data points on the line. For instance, the score for Canton is 4.53, and the score for Albuquerque is −1.90. The direction of the line maximizes the variance of these distances; it also minimizes the variance of the lengths of the projection arrows, which is the reconstruction error of the first component.

The dashed diagonal line represents the second principal component. Together, the two lines form the principal component axes for the data.

The assumption behind principal components regression is that the directions of largest variation in the predictors are the most useful for modeling the variation in the response, and so the model is built by treating the first q principal components as a new set of predictors:

$$\hat{\mathbf{y}} = \bar{y}\mathbf{1} + \hat{\theta}_1\mathbf{t}_1 + \cdots + \hat{\theta}_q\mathbf{t}_q$$

Principal Components Regression Using the PLS Procedure

Principal components regression is available in the PLS and PLSMOD procedures, which are primarily intended for partial least squares (PLS), a general approach to linear predictive modeling. Partial least squares regression is discussed on page 114.

The following statements use the PLS procedure to build a principal components regression model for TMR from the 58 predictors in AP58Predictors:

```
proc pls data=AirPollution108 method=pcr cv=random(seed=311994001);
   model TMR = &AP58Predictors;
run;
```

The METHOD=PCR option requests principal components regression. The PLS procedure does not require that the predictors be numeric variables; you can specify effects for a general linear model by providing CLASS and EFFECTS statements in combination with the MODEL statement.

The procedure extracts principal components from the predictors and regresses the response on each of the components. Since the components are uncorrelated, the model is formed by summing these regressions. Extracting too many components leads to overfitting; see page 21. To avoid this, the procedure extracts 15 components by default and selects the model with the first q components that minimize an estimate of prediction error obtained by cross validation. The CV=RANDOM option requests 10-fold cross validation in which the folds are selected at random. Other methods are available, including leave-one-out cross validation; see page 31.

Output 6.24 shows that 12 components (referred to as factors) minimize the root mean predictive residual sum of squares (PRESS) statistic.

Output 6.24 Selection of Number of Principal Components

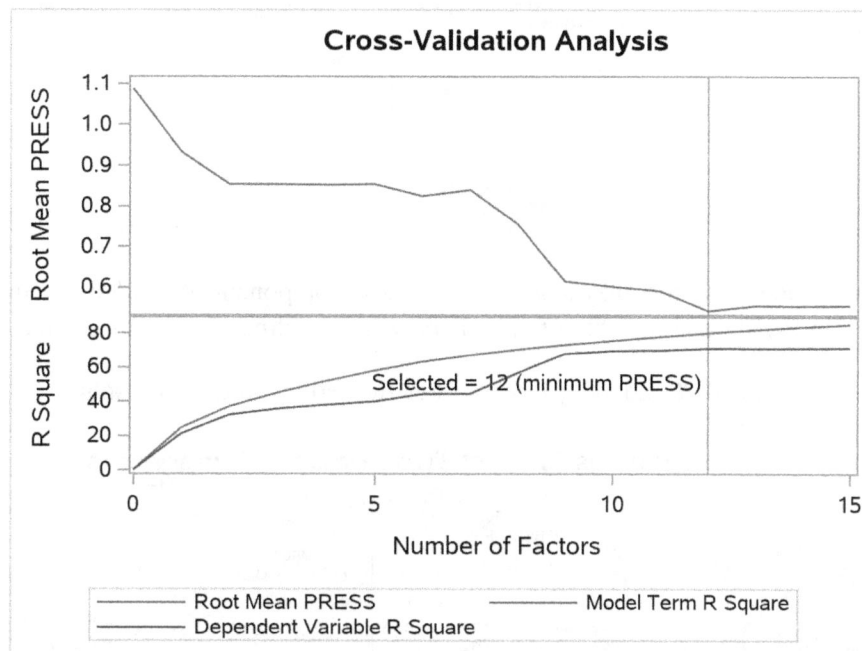

The model with $q = 8$ components achieves nearly the same minimum and should have a smaller prediction variance. You can request this model by specifying NFAC=8:

```
ods output XLoadings=PCRLoadings ParameterEstimates=PCRParmEst;
proc pls data=AirPollution108 method=pcr cv=random(seed=311994001) nfac=8
         details;
   model TMR = &AP58Predictors / solution;
   output out=Scores xscore=Score predicted=pred;
run;
```

The procedure produces a Percent Variation table (not shown here), which indicates that the eight components capture 70% of the variation in the predictors and 57% of the variation in TMR.

Output 6.25 reveals how the SMSAs are differentiated by their scores on the first two components. SMSAs in the southern part of the United States lie in the upper left quadrant, those in the west lie in the lower left quadrant, those in the midwest lie in the lower right quadrant, and those in the east lie in the upper right quadrant.

Output 6.25 Score Plot for First Two Principal Components

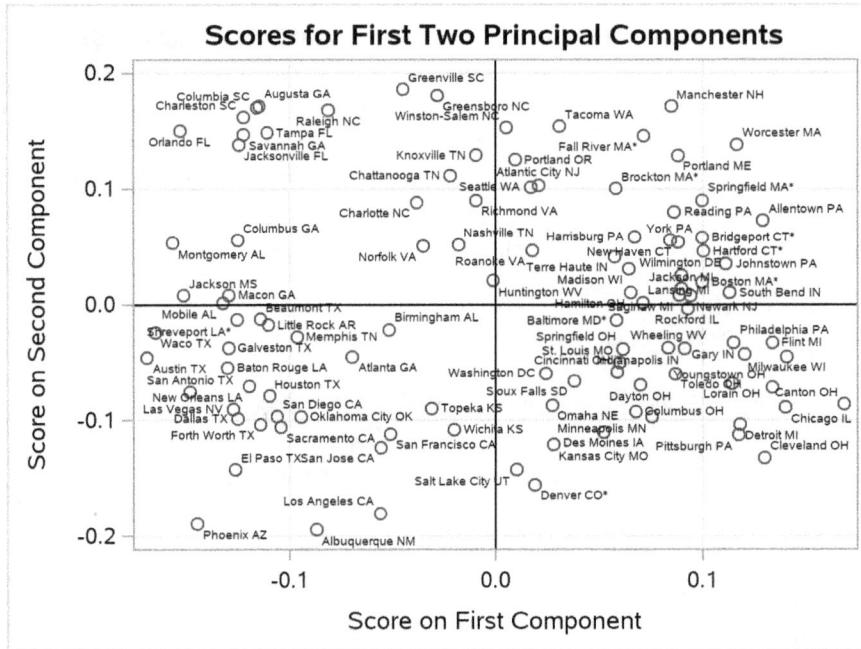

You can identify which predictors play a large role in these components by examining their loadings, which are saved in PCRLoadings. Output 6.26 displays the loadings for the first two components.

Output 6.26 Loading Plot for First Two Principal Components

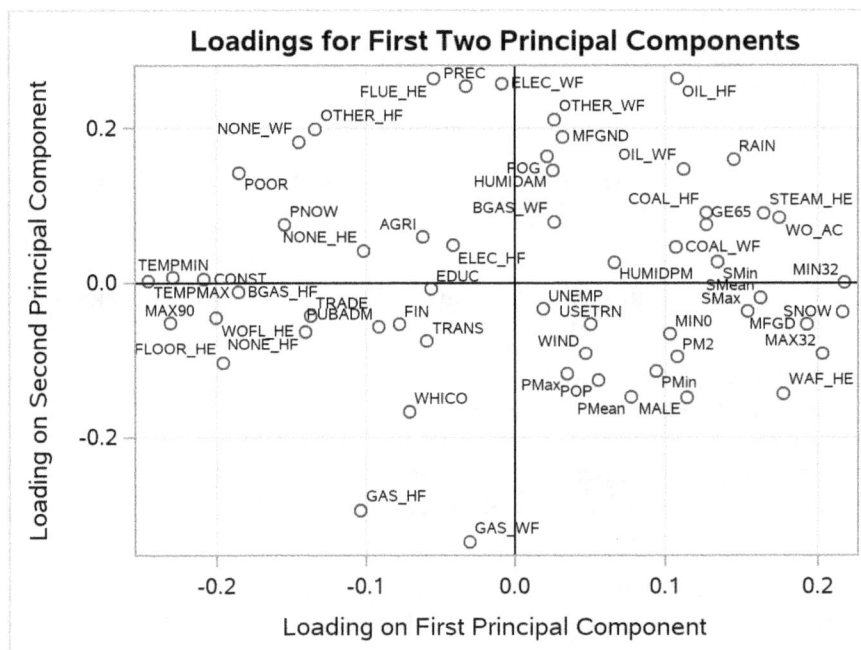

Predictors such as TEMPMIN, PREC, and SNOW that measure climate characteristics (see Table 6.1) have high loadings. Predictors that measure air pollution have smaller loadings and lie in the lower right quadrant. The loadings for sulfate readings are similar, as are the loadings for particulates.

The book website provides a short SAS program that created the plots in Output 6.25 and Output 6.26 from the data sets Scores and PCRLoadings. Score plots and loading plots for the first few components can often be interpreted with subject knowledge. However, the primary advantage of principal components regression is its predictive ability, which draws from all of the variables.

There are two approaches to predicting or scoring the response variable in data that were not used to train the model. The PLS procedure scores observations with missing values of the response variable before saving them in the OUT= data set. This is inefficient if scoring is done repeatedly because the model must be retrained each time. A better approach expresses the model on page 110 in terms of the original p predictors and uses the parameter estimates for scoring:

$$\hat{y} = \hat{\beta}_0 + \hat{\beta}_1 x_1 + \cdots + \hat{\beta}_p x_p$$

Here $\hat{\beta}_0 = \bar{y}$ and $\hat{\beta}_k = \sum_{j=1}^{q} \hat{\theta}_j v_j(k), k = 1, \ldots, p$. The SOLUTION option requests a table of the estimates $\hat{\beta}_0, \ldots, \hat{\beta}_q$, which are saved here in the data set PCRParmEst.

With estimates in data sets created by the REG and VARCLUS procedures, you can use the SCORE procedure to predict responses for new observations; see page 94. This will not work with estimates in a data set created by the PLS procedure unless you first transpose it into the form required by the SCORE procedure. The %PLSRegScore macro, available on the book website, does this for you.

The following statements use the macro to predict TMR for nine SMSAs in AirPollutionTest that were not included in AirPollution108:

```
%PLSRegScore( Data=AirPollutionTest, ParameterEstimates=PCRParmEst,
             Predictors=&AP58Predictors, Response=TMR,
             PredResponse=PCRPred, PredData=PCRPred)

title "Prediction with Principal Components Regression (MSPE=&MSEPredPLS.)";
proc print data=PCRPred noobs;
   var SMSA TMR PCRPred;
run;
```

Output 6.27 shows the predicted responses and the mean squared prediction error (MSPE).

Output 6.27 Predicted Values of TMR for 9 SMSAs Using Principal Components Regression

Prediction with Principal Components Regression (MSPE=46671.43)

SMSA	TMR	PCRPred
Fresno CA	845	810.49
Miami FL	897	1424.11
Duluth MN	1117	1043.91
Jersey City NJ	1199	1255.07
New York NY	1046	1273.96
Scranton PA	1400	1223.58
Wilkes Barre PA	1282	1201.19
Providence RI	1096	981.85
Charleston WV	780	952.83

> **Programming Tip:** Use the `%PLSRegScore` macro to score data using parameter estimates for regression models built with the PLS procedure.

Partial Least Squares Regression

The PLS procedure, used for principal components regression in the previous section, provides a variety of linear predictive methods, including partial least squares (PLS) regression, which accommodates multiple response variables and extracts factors that explain variation in both the predictors and the responses.

Partial least squares was originally introduced as a method for econometric path modeling by Herman Wold (1966), a statistician and econometrician. The version of partial least squares provided by the PLS procedure is sometimes called predictive partial least squares or 2-block PLS. It was developed during the 1980s by Svante Wold (the son of Herman Wold), Harald Martens,[†] Bruce Kowalski, and others in what is now the field of chemometrics. It also has applications to the analysis of genomic and proteomic data (Boulesteix and Strimmer 2006) and to multivariate process monitoring.[‡]

The assumption behind PLS regression is that a relatively small number of latent (unobserved) components are responsible for the behavior of a complex system and can be represented by factors that serve for prediction. The factors, much like principal components, are computed as projections on the observed **X**- and **Y**-variables. For this reason, Svante Wold noted that PLS can be interpreted as an acronym for "projection to latent structures." PLS regression works with a large number of predictors that are correlated, and the number of observations (n) can be considerably less than the number of predictors (p).

In chemometrics, PLS regression is used, for example, to model the relationship between near-infrared spectral measurements and the chemical compositions of samples. The predictors are absorbance measurements at hundreds of wavelength channels, which are highly collinear, and the responses are concentrations of specific compounds. The model, which is trained (calibrated) with a few dozen reference samples, serves two purposes: it predicts the concentrations of new samples, and it provides a description of the spectral measurements. As a technique for multivariate calibration, PLS regression provides practical advantages compared with least squares regression, inverse least squares regression, and principal components regression (Haaland and Thomas 1988).

[†]Martens and Wold described their early efforts and collaboration in two papers, Martens (2001) and Wold (2001). Martens was stung by the negative reaction of statisticians for whom his technique seemed more like a Rube Goldberg contraption than a bona fide statistical modeling approach. He persisted because he realized that PLS answered real scientific questions in a way that no other statistical method could.

During the 1990s, statisticians gained an appreciation for partial least squares, largely through Gordon Research Conferences on Statistics in Chemistry and Chemical Engineering. One of the PLS experts who participated in these meetings was Sijmen de Jong, the inventor of the SIMPLS algorithm (De Jong 1993), which is widely used for PLS regression and is implemented in the PLS procedure.

[‡]The MVPMODEL, MVPDIAGNOSE, and MVPMONITOR procedures in SAS/QC provide methods for this purpose.

PLS factors are linear combinations of the predictors (the columns of X) and the response variables (the columns of Y). They are extracted one step at a time. Before starting, the X- and Y-variables are usually centered and scaled to have a mean of 0 and a standard deviation of 1. At the first step, PLS finds the specific linear combination $t = Xw$ of the predictors that has maximum covariance $t'u$ with some linear combination $u = Yq$ of the responses. The vector t is the first PLS factor; it is called a score vector, and w is its associated weight vector. The vectors p and c are proportional to u_1 and v_1 in the singular value decomposition of $X'Y$ (see page 316).

PLS then projects X and Y in the direction of t by forming two new matrices:

$$\hat{X} = tp', \quad \text{where } p' = (t't)^{-1}t'X$$

$$\hat{Y} = tc', \quad \text{where } c' = (t't)^{-1}t'Y$$

Note that $\hat{X} = t(t't)^{-1}t'X$ and $\hat{Y} = t(t't)^{-1}t'Y$. These expressions have the same form as the hat projection for OLS regression, which is explained in Appendix B, "Least Squares Geometry."

At the second step, PLS moves X and Y orthogonally to their projections by replacing them with their residual matrices:

$$X \leftarrow X - \hat{X}$$

$$Y \leftarrow Y - \hat{Y}$$

The orthogonality of these matrices is like that of the projection and residual vectors for OLS regression; see Figure B.1 on page 322 of Appendix B. After orthogonalizing, PLS extracts a second factor in the same way as in the first step. This process is repeated until the appropriate number of factors has been extracted based on cross validation to avoid overfitting. If the number of factors is greater than or equal to the rank of X, then the result is equivalent to OLS regression.

In PLS regression, there are two sets of scores: the t combinations, which are called X-scores, and the u combinations, which are called Y-scores. These represent directions chosen so that the relationship between the pairs of scores at each step is as strong as possible. Unlike principal components regression, which chooses directions of X-scores to explain as much of the predictor variation as possible, PLS regression chooses directions associated with high variation in the X-space but bends them toward directions of accurate prediction in the Y-space.

PLS regression has proved successful in chemometric applications, where it is essential to model X- and Y-blocks of data. The PLS approach also provides diagnostic tools for interpreting both models; these are available in the PLS procedure but are not discussed here.

PLS regression is not well known among statisticians and data scientists because it does not fit neatly into mainstream approaches. Nonetheless, it can make a valuable addition to your portfolio of model building methods.

Partial Least Squares Regression Using the PLS Procedure

The following statements use the PLS procedure to build a partial least squares regression model for TMR from the 58 predictors in AP58Predictors:

```
ods output XLoadings=PLSLoadings ParameterEstimates=PLSParmEst;
proc pls data=AirPollution108 method=pls cv=random(seed=311994001) details;
   model TMR = &AP58Predictors / solution;
   output out=PLSScores xscore=Score;
run;
```

The METHOD=PLS option requests partial least squares regression. By default, the procedure extracts 15 factors. Output 6.28 shows that four factors minimize the root mean PRESS statistic.

Output 6.28 Selection of Number of Factors

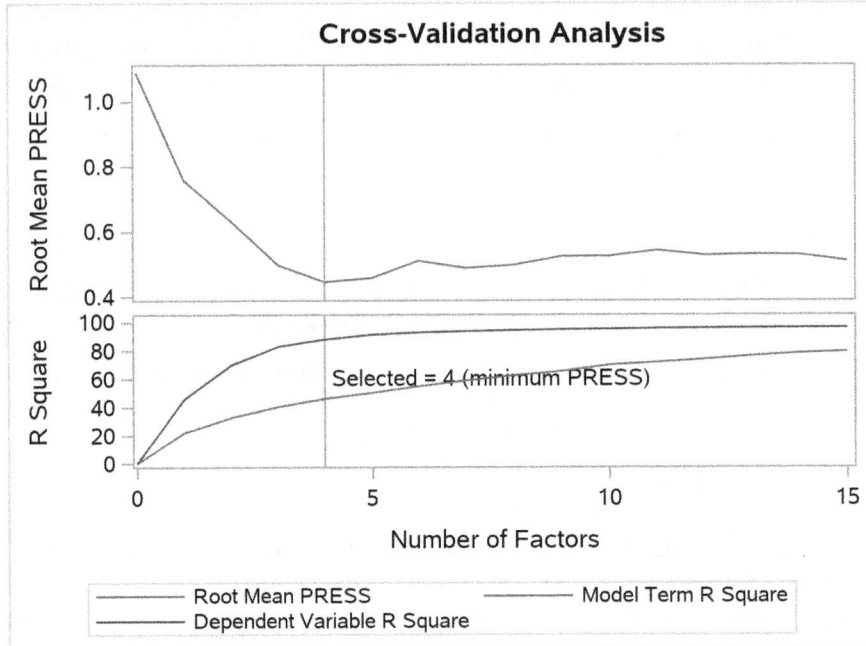

The procedure produces a Percent Variation table (not displayed) that shows that the four factors capture 46% of the variation in the model effects and 88% of the variation in TMR.

The data set PLSScores saves the scores on the factors as variables named Score1, ..., Score4. Output 6.29 shows that the scores on the first two factors differentiate the SMSAs geographically much like the scores on the first two principal components in Output 6.25.

Output 6.29 Score Plot for First Two PLS Factors

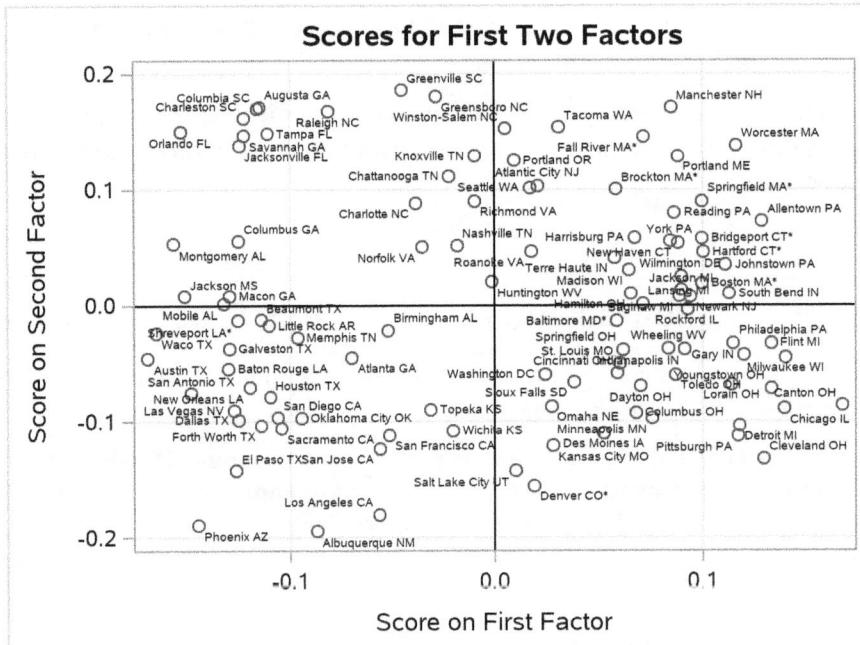

Likewise, the loadings for the first two factors (not shown) are similar to the loadings for the first two components in Output 6.26.

The following statements use the `%PLSRegScore` macro to predict TMR for the nine SMSAs in AirPollutionTest by using the parameter estimates for the PLS model that were saved in PLSParmEst:

```
%PLSRegScore( Data=AirPollutionTest, ParameterEstimates=PLSParmEst,
              Predictors=&AP58Predictors, Response=TMR,
              PredResponse=PLSPred, PredData=PLSPred)

title "Prediction with Partial Least Squares Regression (MSPE=&MSEPredPLS.)";
proc print data=PLSPred noobs;
   var SMSA TMR PLSPred;
run;
```

The MSPE in Output 6.30 is 58% less than the MSPE for principal components regression in Output 6.27 .

Output 6.30 Predicted Values of TMR for 9 SMSAs Using Partial Least Squares Regression

Prediction with Partial Least Squares Regression (MSPE=27254.82)

SMSA	TMR	PLSPred
Fresno CA	845	906.57
Miami FL	897	1286.17
Duluth MN	1117	1261.99
Jersey City NJ	1199	1141.29
New York NY	1046	1166.03
Scranton PA	1400	1243.98
Wilkes Barre PA	1282	1206.41
Providence RI	1096	1052.62
Charleston WV	780	919.10

Conclusions for Air Pollution Example

Each approach presented in this chapter produces a different model with the data in AirPollution108. The high collinearity in the 58 candidate predictors makes it easy for one subset of predictors to substitute for another. Furthermore, the signal-to-noise level of the data is low. Many factors now known to influence mortality are not represented.

Gibbons and McDonald (1980) were not able to settle on a single model. They used stepwise regression to reduce the number of predictors to 46 so that best-subset regression could be applied, noting that this was not guaranteed to identify the model with the best value of the R^2 criterion. They found models with 7, 11, 18, and 22 variables that provided good fits. None included the six measures of air pollution. After forcing these measures into the models, they estimated a 0.45% reduction in mortality rate associated with a 50% reduction in the six measures. This agreed closely with other published results.

When the 18-variable model identified by Gibbons and McDonald is used to predict TMR for the data in AirPollutionTest, the MSPE is 60360.88. This is considerably larger than the values of MSPE in Output 6.27 and Output 6.30, but, of course, those results were obtained with different approaches.

Summary

In general, you should expect different results with the model building approaches in this chapter because they deal with collinearity in distinct ways. Table 6.3 summarizes how these approaches compare.

Table 6.3 Characteristics of Model Building Approaches

Model Building Approach	Reduces Dimension	Penalizes Estimate	Shrinks OLS Estimate	Selects Model
Variable clustering	Yes	No	No	No
Best-subset regression ($k < \approx 40$)	No	No	No	Yes
Best-subset regression with predictors representing clusters	Yes	No	No	Yes
Ridge regression	No	Yes	Yes	No
Elastic net	No	Yes	Yes	Yes
Principal components regression	Yes (directed)	Yes	Yes	No
Partial least squares regression	Yes (directed)	Yes	Yes, but expands in some directions	No

Keep in mind that no one approach is superior to the others, and because of collinearity, the parameter estimates for a model do not necessarily indicate its predictive ability.

There are some similarities among ridge regression, principal components regression, and partial least squares regression. All three shrink the regression coefficients in directions of low variance, but unlike principal components regression, PLS regression involves the response in the extraction of factors, and these factors are not the same as principal components.

Frank and Friedman (1993) compared ridge regression, principal components regression, and PLS regression. They found that—with the same number of factors—PLS regression has less bias but more variance than principal components regression, and they concluded that "it is not clear which solution would be better in any given situation." Garthwaite (1994) provided an interpretation of PLS regression in the context of a single response and compared it with OLS regression, forward selection, principal components regression, and a Stein shrinkage method. He concluded that PLS regression is useful with a large number of predictors, especially when the error variance is large.

In short, there is no single best way to proceed when you identify collinearity in your data. If you know that collinearity is inherent in the process you are modeling, you can eliminate predictors that are involved in simple forms of collinearity (Hocking 1983, p. 224). Otherwise, this is not recommended.

The good news is that you can choose from a number of useful approaches. Experimenting with a variety of approaches will give you a better understanding of how they operate and will help you decide which ones are most appropriate for your work.

Chapter 7
Building General Linear Models: Model Averaging

The methods for building general linear models presented in Chapter 5 form a series of candidate models and select the model that optimizes a criterion for predictive ability. It is tempting to refer to the selected model as the "best model," but this is misleading for several reasons:

- Among the candidate models, there will often be some whose values of the selection criterion are nearly the same as those of the final model. Some of these models might be more useful than the selected model because they are sparser or more explainable.

- Applying a different criterion might result in the selection of a different model.

- If you are using a sequential selection method, relatively small changes in the data can sometimes lead to a different model.

In other words, you can easily be faced with many models to consider.

This dilemma, called *model uncertainty*, was recognized 30 years ago when highly automated methods for building predictive models were adopted for data mining (Chatfield 1995). The most reliable way to judge competing models is to compare their predictive performance on independent data that were not involved in training. However, this is not always possible, and there is no single recommended alternative.

Model averaging, the topic of this chapter, deals with the dilemma by averaging the predictions from a set of competing general linear models that are weighted in some fashion. Averaging reduces the risk of relying on a single model for prediction. And by smoothing the results of sequential selection methods, averaging reduces their sensitivity to small changes in the data.

Approaches to Model Averaging

Model averaging is rooted in multimodel inference,[†] which is used in biological and medical research where scientific knowledge is often expressed as a set of plausible models that are specified independently of each other.

There are various approaches to model averaging. Bayesian model averaging (not discussed here) is favored by some experts because it is derived from a foundation of Bayesian principles. It is computationally complex and requires prior probabilities for the models (Raftery, Madigan, and Hoeting 1997; Hoeting et al. 1999). Frequentist model averaging, the approach explained here, requires weights for the models but is computationally simpler.

This chapter explains how you can use the GLMSELECT procedure to perform model averaging with bootstrap frequency weights. The chapter also explains how you can use the GLMSELECT procedure in conjunction with a macro to perform model averaging with Akaike weights.

Using the GLMSELECT Procedure for Model Averaging

The MODELAVERAGE statement in the GLMSELECT procedure provides options for bootstrap averaging of general linear models, which is done by resampling the data many times, selecting a model with each sample, and computing the averages of the parameter estimates of these models. In the same way that you use the GLMSELECT procedure to select a single model, you specify the response and a set of candidate effects or predictors, $x_1, x_2, \ldots, x_p$, in the MODEL statement, together with a selection method. Table 5.2 on page 51 lists the methods available with the SELECTION= option.

Each selected model is linear in a potentially different set of selected predictors. The parameter estimates can be averaged by setting the estimate $\hat{\beta}_j^{(b)}$ for x_j in the bth bootstrap model to zero if x_j is not selected for that model. With this convention, the model average prediction from B bootstrap samples can be written as

$$\hat{\mathbf{y}}^{(\text{avg})} = \frac{1}{B} \sum_{b=1}^{B} \hat{\mathbf{y}}^{(b)} = \frac{1}{B} \sum_{b=1}^{B} \mathbf{X} \hat{\boldsymbol{\beta}}^{(b)} = \mathbf{X} \hat{\beta}_j^{(\text{avg})}$$

where

$$\hat{\beta}_j^{(\text{avg})} = \frac{1}{B} \sum_{b=1}^{B} \hat{\beta}_j^{(b)}, \quad j = 1, \ldots, p$$

If $\hat{\beta}_j^{(b)}$ is set to zero for one or more models, the average estimate $\hat{\beta}_j^{(\text{avg})}$ shrinks toward zero, which helps to counteract selection bias (see page 35). Since the average estimates do not shrink all the way to zero, bootstrap model averaging (like ridge regression) does not do model selection, nor does it necessarily produce a sparse model.

[†]The book by Burnham and Anderson (2002) provides a clear exposition of information-theoretic methods for model selection and multimodel inference.

With bootstrap model averaging, the number of distinct bootstrap models is typically less than the number of bootstrap samples. The average prediction $\hat{y}^{(avg)}$ weights the predictions of the distinct models by their bootstrap selection frequencies divided by B. Likewise, the average parameter estimates weight the parameter estimates for the distinct models by the proportions of samples in which the models are selected (Buckland, Burnham, and Augustin 1997).

When you use the MODELAVERAGE statement, the bootstrap selection frequencies indicate the stability of the final selected model (Sauerbrei 1999, Sec. 4.1). Similarly, the bootstrap inclusion frequencies for the predictors indicate their relative importance.

Bootstrap Model Averaging with Stepwise Regression

This example illustrates bootstrap model averaging using the observations for 108 standard metropolitan statistical areas (SMSAs) in the data set AirPollution108, which is introduced in Chapter 6 on page 86. The response variable TMR is the total mortality rate, and the predictors are saved in the macro variable AP58Predictors, as explained on page 90. The collinearity of the predictors, which is discussed in Chapter 6, is not considered here.

The following statements build a single model for TMR by using the stepwise regression method with SBC as the choose criterion. Stepwise regression is described on page 41, and SBC (also known as BIC) is described on page 28.

```
ods graphics on;
proc glmselect data=AirPollution108 plots=coefficients;
   model TMR = &AP58Predictors /
      selection=stepwise(choose=sbc select=sbc stop=sbc);
run;
```

The plot in Output 7.1 shows the selection process. The effect of CONST is included at Step 3, removed at Step 7, and included back at Step 10. The minimum value of SBC is achieved at Step 11.

Output 7.1 Coefficient Progression for Stepwise Selection

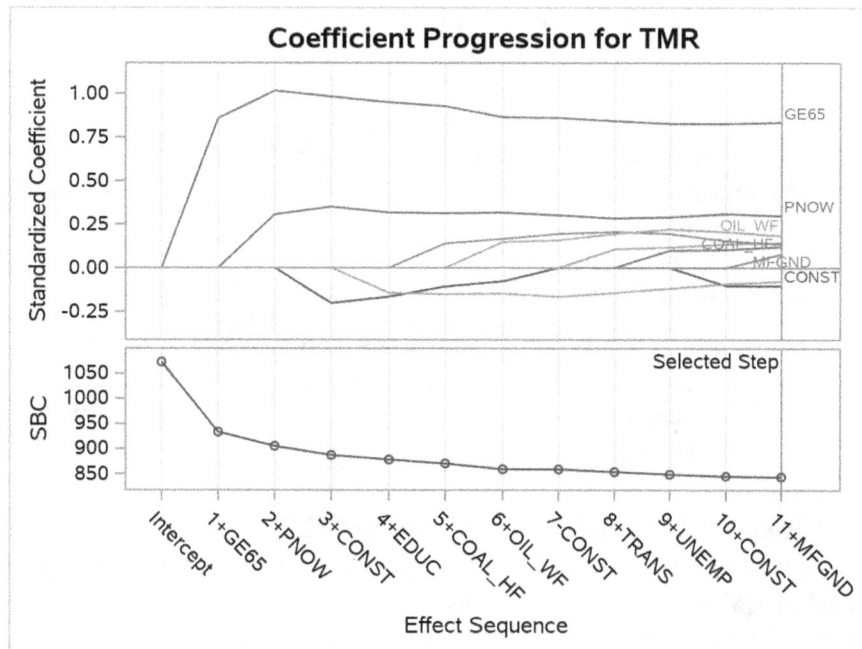

Output 7.2 shows the parameter estimates for the final selected model.

Output 7.2 Parameter Estimates with Stepwise Selection

			Standard	
Parameter	DF	Estimate	Error	t Value
Intercept	1	296.007876	43.434277	6.82
GE65	1	5.629469	0.258820	21.75
PNOW	1	0.400920	0.047180	8.50
UNEMP	1	1.262314	0.332272	3.80
CONST	1	-1.018319	0.355993	-2.86
MFGND	1	0.175419	0.074602	2.35
TRANS	1	0.987692	0.221598	4.46
EDUC	1	-0.682309	0.289837	-2.35
COAL_HF	1	0.167571	0.042205	3.97
OIL_WF	1	0.183289	0.036621	5.01

Parameter Estimates

None of the six predictors in Table 6.1 that measure air pollution are included, which raises two questions: is it reasonable to conclude that the parameter estimates for these predictors are all zero, and how frequently would this result occur if stepwise regression were to be repeated with different data for the same metropolitan areas? Bootstrap model averaging answers these questions.

The following statements repeat the previous step, adding the MODELAVG statement and various options (highlighted) to request 100 bootstrap samples from the observations in AirPollution108.

```
proc glmselect  data=AirPollution108  seed=896753
                plots=( EffectSelectPct(minpct=25 order=ascending)
                        ParmDist(minpct=25 order=descending) ) ;
     model TMR = &AP58Predictors /
                selection=stepwise(choose=sbc select=sbc stop=sbc);
     modelAverage  nsamples=100
                tables=( EffectSelectPct(minpct=25 order=descending)
                         ModelSelectFreq(best=8) ParmEst(all) ) ;
run;
```

The SEED= option specifies the seed for random generation of the samples, and the NSAMPLES= option specifies the number of samples (the default is 100). As shown in Output 7.3, all of the observations are sampled with replacement.

Output 7.3 Information about Bootstrap Sampling

Model Averaging Information	
Sampling Method	Unrestricted (with replacement)
Sample Percentage	100
Number of Samples	100

Output 7.4 shows the graph requested with the PLOTS=EFFECTSELECTPCT option. The bars represent percentages of samples for which the selected model includes the predictors. For instance, PNOW is included in 91% of the models. For brevity, only predictors included in at least 25% of the models are shown. You can view the percentages as measures of variable importance.

Output 7.4 Selection Percentages for Effects

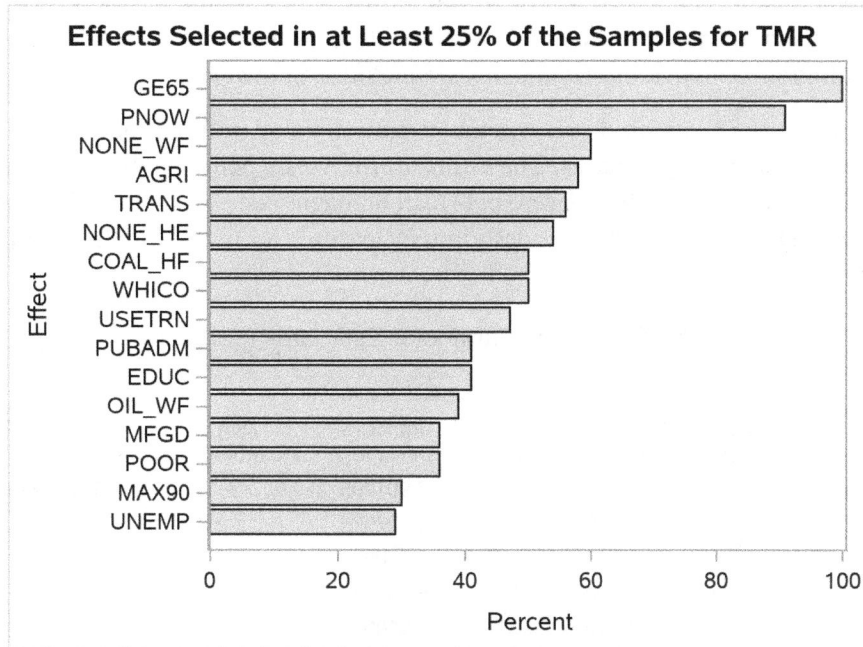

The TABLES=EFFECTSELECTPCT option requests a table, shown in Output 7.5, of the selection percentages for the models. The BEST=8 suboption requests the best eight models ranked by their frequency scores.

Output 7.5 Model Selection Frequencies

				Model Selection Frequency
Times Selected	Selection Percentage	Number of Effects	Frequency Score	Effects in Model
1	1.00	10	1.59	Intercept GE65 PNOW POOR UNEMP EDUC USETRN COAL_HF OIL_WF NONE_WF
1	1.00	9	1.58	Intercept GE65 PNOW UNEMP TRANS TRADE EDUC COAL_HF OIL_WF
1	1.00	10	1.58	Intercept GE65 PNOW UNEMP AGRI EDUC MIN0 NONE_HE COAL_HF OIL_WF
1	1.00	11	1.57	Intercept PMin GE65 PNOW AGRI TRANS WHICO NONE_HE COAL_HF OTHER_HF OIL_WF
1	1.00	10	1.57	Intercept SMax GE65 PNOW AGRI TRANS WHICO COAL_HF OIL_WF WO_AC
1	1.00	10	1.56	Intercept PMin GE65 PNOW AGRI EDUC FLOOR_HE NONE_HE BGAS_HF NONE_WF
1	1.00	11	1.56	Intercept GE65 PNOW POOR UNEMP TRANS TRADE EDUC USETRN OIL_WF NONE_WF
1	1.00	12	1.56	Intercept GE65 PNOW POOR UNEMP TRANS PUBADM WHICO COAL_HF ELEC_HF OIL_WF NONE_WF

The frequency score for the bth model (s_b) is the sum of its selection frequency and its average selection fraction. The selection frequency (m_b) is the number of samples for which the model is selected. Suppose that $f_j, j = 1, \ldots, p$, is the proportion of models that include the predictor x_j, and suppose that the bth model consists of the predictors $x_{b_1}, x_{b_2}, \ldots, x_{b_{p_b}}$. The frequency score is

$$s_b = m_b + \frac{1}{p_b}\left(f_{b_1} + f_{b_2} + \cdots + f_{b_{p_b}}\right), \quad b = 1, \ldots, B$$

In this example, $m_b = 1$ for the eight top-ranked models. The frequency score adjusts for the different numbers of predictors in each model and the different frequencies with which these predictors are selected. The scores for the top-ranked models are very close. None of these models include variables that measure pollution, although these variables are included in lower-ranked models.

The TABLES=PARMEST option displays a table, partially shown in Output 7.6, of the average parameter estimates for all the predictors. The estimates for the six pollution variables (SMin, SMean, SMax, PMin, PMean, and PMax) are nonzero but small in magnitude compared with the estimates for GE65 and PNOW. The table also provides descriptive measures for the distributions of the estimates across samples.

Output 7.6 Average Parameter Estimates (partial list)

		Average Parameter Estimates					
Parameter	Number Non-zero	Non-zero Percentage	Mean Estimate	Standard Deviation	25th Quantile	50th Quantile	75th Quantile
Intercept	100	100.00	377.621501	277.901905	259.022791	371.041695	528.219923
SMin	9	9.00	0.009716	0.127576	0	0	0
SMean	8	8.00	0.019585	0.090551	0	0	0
SMax	11	11.00	0.015203	0.052244	0	0	0
PMin	16	16.00	0.063130	0.310921	0	0	0
PMean	15	15.00	0.069290	0.205204	0	0	0
PMax	10	10.00	-0.004872	0.045009	0	0	0
PM2	6	6.00	0.011349	0.064183	0	0	0
GE65	100	100.00	6.143246	0.641668	5.687487	6.114283	6.602173
PNOW	91	91.00	0.323574	0.142634	0.248444	0.338652	0.416450

The PLOTS=PARMDIST option displays the distributions of the parameter estimates in a series of panels, the first of which is shown in Output 7.7.

Output 7.7 Distributions of Parameter Estimates (First Panel)

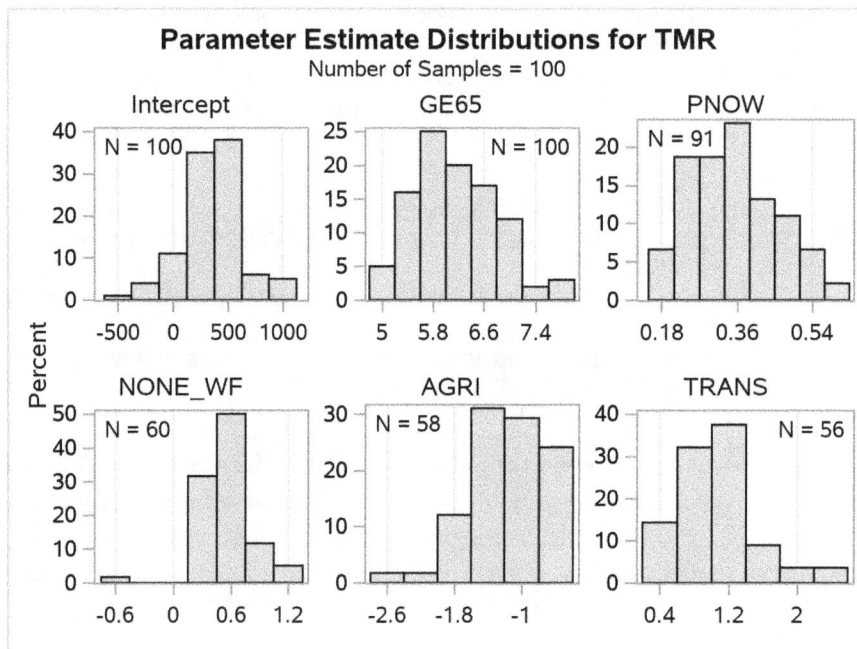

Refitting to Build a Parsimonious Model

The model obtained on page 124 contains all 58 predictors in AP58Predictors. Output 7.4 shows that the selection percentages for the predictors decline linearly after a sharp drop following the percentages for GE65 and PNOW. To obtain a parsimonious model, you can request a refit:

```
proc glmselect data=AirPollution108 seed=896753 plots=(ParmDistribution);
   model TMR = &AP58Predictors /
      selection=stepwise(choose=sbc select=sbc stop=sbc);
   modelAverage nsamples=100  refit(minpct=65 nsamples=1000) alpha=0.05;
   code file='ModelAvgScoreCode.sas';
run;
```

The REFIT option requests a model built by drawing 1000 bootstrap samples, fitting a model for each sample (with no selection), and averaging the parameter estimates for these models. The MINPCT= option determines the degree of sparsity; an effect is included in each model only if it occurred in at least 65% of the models selected in the initial round. Alternatively, you can specify the BEST=n option to include the n most frequently selected effects in the initial round.

Here, the refit model contains GE65 and PNOW. Output 7.8 shows their average parameter estimates.

Output 7.8 Average Parameter Estimates for Refit Model

Refit Model Averaging Results

	Average Parameter Estimates				
Parameter	Mean Estimate	Standard Deviation	2.5th Quantile	50th Quantile	97.5th Quantile
Intercept	265.530369	61.387479	148.679452	268.325858	375.288893
GE65	7.003104	0.660252	5.821136	6.964721	8.253970
PNOW	0.429866	0.086604	0.267590	0.425976	0.602324

Output 7.9 shows the distributions of the parameter estimates.

Output 7.9 Distributions of Parameter Estimates for Refit

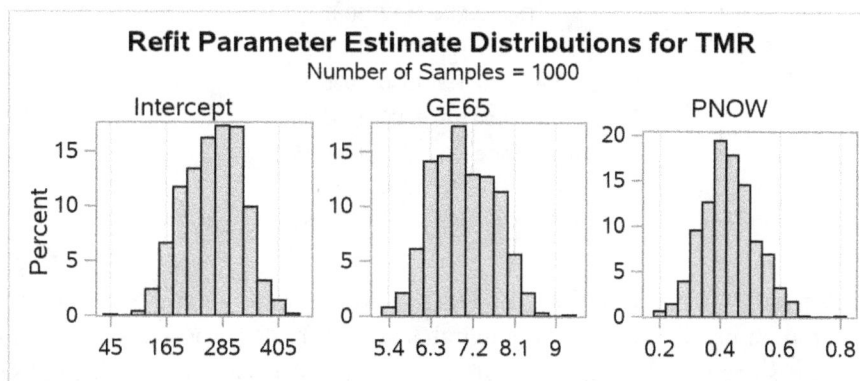

If you specify MINPCT=20, which is the default, the refit model will contain the intercept and 22 effects, none of which are variables that measure pollution.

The CODE statement writes and saves DATA step code you can use to predict values of the response with the refit model. The following statements use the code saved in *ModelAvgScoreCode.sas* to score the observations for the metropolitan areas in AirPollutionTest:

```
data RefitPred;
   set AirPollutionTest;
   %inc 'ModelAvgScoreCode.sas';
run;
```

The predicted values are saved in a variable named P_TMR. The following statements compute the mean squared prediction error (MSPE):

```
data RefitPred; set RefitPred;
   SqError = (TMR-P_TMR )**2;
run;

proc means data=RefitPred;
   var SqError;
   output out=MSEPred (drop=_TYPE_ _FREQ_) mean=ASE;
run;

data MSEPred; set MSEPred;
   if _N_ = 1 then call symputx('MSERefit', put(ASE, BEST8.), 'g' );
run;

title "Prediction with Refit Model (MSPE=&MSERefit.)";
proc print data=RefitPred noobs;
   var SMSA TMR P_TMR;
run;
```

Output 7.10 displays the predicted values and the MSPE, which is smaller than the MSPE of 27254.82 obtained with partial least squares regression; see Output 6.30 on page 117.

Output 7.10 Predicted Values of TMR for 9 SMSAs Using Refit Model

Prediction with Refit Model (MSPE=22873.41)

SMSA	TMR	P_TMR
Fresno CA	845	865.02
Miami FL	897	1029.89
Duluth MN	1117	1067.32
Jersey City NJ	1199	1016.51
New York NY	1046	996.42
Scranton PA	1400	1100.62
Wilkes Barre PA	1282	1044.16
Providence RI	1096	1037.90
Charleston WV	780	780.68

This approach to building a parsimonious model treats the number of times a predictor is initially selected as a measure of its importance. Although this approach often succeeds, it can fail if there are predictors that act as surrogates for each other in their contributions to the model. In this situation, as pointed out by Cohen (2009, p. 21), it is possible that none of the predictors appears in a large enough percentage of bootstrap models to be considered important, even though every model contains at least one of these predictors.

Model Averaging with Akaike Weights

Lukacs, Burnham, and Anderson (2010) proposed model averaging with Akaike weights as a way to deal with the problem of Freedman's paradox, an extreme form of selection bias in which irrelevant effects appear to be important (see page 37). Using simulation, they demonstrated that this problem results in poor coverage (averaging 41.9%) of 95% confidence intervals for parameters obtained with stepwise selection. The coverage obtained with their model averaging approach is near the nominal 95% level.

Model averaging with Akaike weights is applicable to prediction as well as inference. It assumes there are relevant predictors to be found, and it compares competing models by their values of Akaike's information criterion (AIC) or AICC, a bias-corrected version of AIC that is recommended when n/p is less than around 40 (Burnham and Anderson 2002, p. 66). See "Criteria Based on Information Theory" on page 28 for an explanation of these criteria.

If there are R candidate models, they can be ranked by their AIC differences:

$$\Delta_r = \text{AIC}_r - \min_{1 \leq r \leq R} \text{AIC}_r, \quad r = 1, \ldots, R$$

This difference (computed in the same way for AICC) is zero for the model with the lowest value of AIC, which is the model selected when you specify AIC as the choose criterion in the GLMSELECT procedure. The larger the value of Δ_r, the less support there is for the rth model compared with the selected model. Table 7.1 shows rules of thumb given by Burnham and Anderson (2002, p. 70) for interpreting Δ_r, particularly for models whose effects are nested within each other.

Table 7.1 Interpretation of Akaike Differences

Δ_r	**Level of Support for Model r**
0-2	Substantial
4-7	Considerably less
>10	Essentially none

They recommend that the differences be reported and emphasize that it is the differences in AIC that matter rather than the actual values of AIC.

Akaike (1979) showed that the likelihood of the rth model is

$$\Pr[g_r \,|\, \mathbf{x}] = w_r = \frac{\exp\left(-\frac{1}{2}\Delta_r\right)}{\sum_{r=1}^{R} \exp\left(-\frac{1}{2}\Delta_r\right)}, \quad r = 1, \ldots, R$$

This is the conditional probability, given the data, that the rth model is the best of the R models in terms of their relative Kullback-Leibler distances (see page 324). The probability w_r is called the Akaike weight because it serves to weight the model in model averaging.

Lukacs, Burnham, and Anderson (2010) proposed the model averaging estimator

$$\hat{\beta}_j^{(\text{AIC})} = \frac{1}{R} \sum_{r=1}^{B} w_r \hat{\beta}_j^{(r)}, \quad j = 1, \ldots, p$$

The parameter $\beta_j^{(r)}$ is assumed to be zero for a predictor x_j that is not included in the rth model. Consequently, $\hat{\beta}_j^{(\text{AIC})}$ shrinks the estimate of β_j for a weak or spurious predictor.

The next example shows how you can apply Akaike weights to average the predictions and parameter estimates for models that are sequentially selected with AIC or AICC as the selection criterion. The data in AirPollution108 are used here because they fit the profile of samples studied by Freedman (1983) and Lukacs, Burnham, and Anderson (2010), for which n is only twice as large as p.

The following statements request forward selection with AICC as the choose criterion:

```
proc glmselect data=AirPollution108 plots=Coefficient;
   ods output ParameterEstimates = StepEst(keep=Step Parameter Estimate)
              SelectionSummary    = StepSum(keep=Step EffectEntered AICC);
   model TMR = &AP58Predictors /
       selection=forward(choose=aicc select=aicc stop=13)
       stats=aicc details=steps(parmest);
run;
```

The STOP= option determines the number of models that are evaluated. Output 7.11 shows that AICC is minimized at Step 12.

Output 7.11 Coefficient Progression for Forward Selection

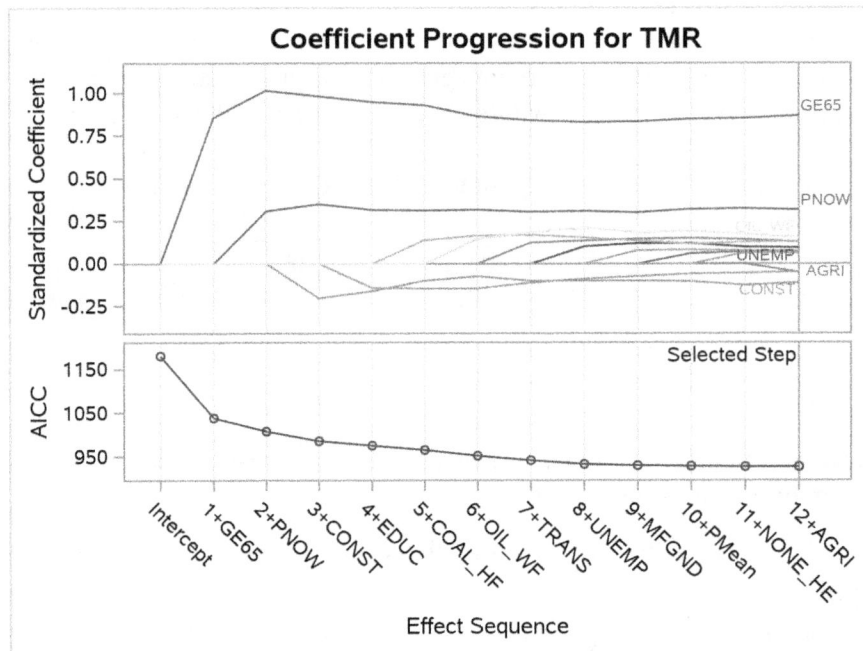

The values of AICC for the models at Steps 10 and 11 are very close to the minimum, and so it is worth considering the parameter estimates and predictions obtained by averaging these quantities for the models at Steps 10 through 12.

The GLMSELECT procedure does not provide model averaging with Akaike weights, but it does create data sets that save the parameter estimates and values of AICC for each model. As explained next, you can use the %ICWeightParmEst macro, available on the book website, to read these data sets and perform the averaging.

In the preceding statements, the DETAILS= option requests tables (not shown) of the parameter estimates for the model at each step, and the PARAMETERESTIMATES= option in the ODS OUTPUT statement saves the estimates in StepEst. The STATS=AICC option specifies that the values of AICC for the models are to be displayed in selection summary tables (not shown), and the SELECTIONSUMMARY= option in the ODS OUTPUT statement saves these values in StepSum.

Output 7.12 and Output 7.13 show the structures of the two data sets that are saved. The variable Step serves as a common index for the models, the parameter estimates, and the AICC values.

Output 7.12 Partial Listing of Parameter Estimates Saved in StepEst

Step	Parameter	Estimate
0	Intercept	898.879630
1	Intercept	420.630004
1	GE65	5.797616
2	Intercept	279.520395
2	GE65	6.857605
2	PNOW	0.411208

Output 7.13 Partial Listing of Step Selection Summary Saved in StepSum

Step	EffectEntered	AICC
0	Intercept	1180.3573
1	GE65	1038.1313
2	PNOW	1007.0599
3	CONST	986.3845
4	EDUC	975.5540

The following statement uses the `%ICWeightParmEst` macro to compute an Akaike weight for each model and average the parameter estimates across models:

```
%ICWeightParmEst( ParameterEstimates  = StepEst(where=(Step>=10 AND Step<13)),
                  SelectionSummary     = StepSum(where=(Step>=10 AND Step<13)),
                  Criterion            = AICC,
                  WtdParmEstimates     = WtdEstimates,
                  ModelWeights         = ModelWts,
                  DisplayParmEst       = 1, DisplayWeights = 1 )
```

The WHERE clause for Step designates the models included in the average. The model differences (Δ_r) and weights (w_r) are saved in ModelWts, and they are displayed in Output 7.14.

Output 7.14 Akaike Weights for Models in Steps 10 to 14

AICC Weights for Averaged Models

Step	EffectEntered	AICC	MinAICC	Delta	ModelWt
10	PMean	928.1559	927.0427	1.11321	0.23122
11	NONE_HE	927.2408	927.0427	0.19815	0.36536
12	AGRI	927.0427	927.0427	0.00000	0.40342

Based on Table 7.1, there is substantial support for the models at Steps 10 and 11.

The averaged estimates $\hat{\beta}_j^{(AIC)}$ are saved in WtdEstimates, and they are displayed in Output 7.15.

Output 7.15 Parameter Estimates Averaged with Akaike Weights

Parameter Estimates for Model Averaged with AICC Weights

Parameter	WtdEstimate
Intercept	264.018589
PMean	0.230658
GE65	5.804908
PNOW	0.426344
UNEMP	1.048268
CONST	-1.170278
MFGND	0.168457
TRANS	0.936614
EDUC	-0.472741
COAL_HF	0.155885
OIL_WF	0.169415
NONE_HE	1.112896
AGRI	-0.477581

Output 7.16 shows the estimates for the selected model, which are similar.

Output 7.16 Parameter Estimates for Selected Model

Parameter Estimates

Parameter	DF	Estimate	Standard Error	t Value
Intercept	1	269.923032	49.244351	5.48
PMean	1	0.222701	0.117257	1.90
GE65	1	5.871766	0.265518	22.11
PNOW	1	0.423759	0.047683	8.89
UNEMP	1	0.951762	0.348922	2.73
AGRI	1	-0.477581	0.300073	-1.59
CONST	1	-1.129070	0.384682	-2.94
MFGND	1	0.162610	0.073312	2.22
TRANS	1	0.857732	0.228820	3.75
EDUC	1	-0.421397	0.297481	-1.42
NONE_HE	1	1.158428	0.595636	1.94
COAL_HF	1	0.162550	0.043364	3.75
OIL_WF	1	0.153881	0.039043	3.94

Programming Tip: Use the `%ICWeightParmEst` macro to average the parameter estimates of candidate models by using Akaike weights.

To predict the response with the estimates in WtdEstimates, you can use the `%ModelAvgScore` macro, which is also available on the book website. The following statements compute predicted values of TMR for the nine SMSAs in the data set AirPollutionTest:

```
%ModelAvgScore( Data                = AirPollutionTest,
                ParameterEstimates = WtdEstimates,
                Response           = TMR,
                PredResponse       = PredTMR,
                PredData           = WtdPredictions )

title "Predictions of TMR Using Akaike Weights (MSPE=&MSEModelAvg.)";
proc print data=WtdPredictions noobs;
   var SMSA TMR PredTMR;
run;
```

The predicted values are shown in Output 7.17.

Output 7.17 Weighted Predictions from Models at Steps 10 to 12

Predictions of TMR Using Akaike Weights (MSPE=22380.12)

SMSA	TMR	PredTMR
Fresno CA	845	815.71
Miami FL	897	1309.05
Duluth MN	1117	1133.61
Jersey City NJ	1199	1180.06
New York NY	1046	1146.59
Scranton PA	1400	1291.74
Wilkes Barre PA	1282	1234.74
Providence RI	1096	1101.21
Charleston WV	780	857.74

The MSPE is slightly less than the MSPE obtained with the refit model in Output 7.10.

Programming Tip: Use the `%ModelAvgScore` macro to compute average predictions with Akaike weights.

The approach illustrated in this example can also be carried out with SBC as the information criterion used to compute the weights (Buckland, Burnham, and Augustin 1997, p. 605). The `%ICWeightParmEst` macro accepts the same information criteria as the SELECT= option in the GLMSELECT procedure.

To apply model averaging as proposed by Lukacs, Burnham, and Anderson (2010) for a set of general linear models that are provided *independently*, follow these steps:

1. Fit each model with the GLMSELECT procedure and save the information criteria and parameter estimates in data sets specified with the FITSTATISTICS= and PARAMETERESTIMATES= options in an ODS OUTPUT statement.

2. Compute an Akaike weight for each model by combining the data sets with the fit statistics and using the equation for the weight on page 127.

3. Merge the likelihoods with the parameter estimates and average the estimates across models with the MEANS procedure, specifying the weights in the WEIGHT statement.

Summary

Automated selection methods often identify a set of competing models whose values of the selection criterion are numerically close to that of the optimal value. Instead of assuming a single best model, model averaging combines the parameter estimates and predictions from a set of competing models by computing their weighted averages. This approach can be useful with sequential selection methods, which are sensitive to small changes in the data.

The GLMSELECT procedure implements bootstrap model averaging, which weights the predictions by bootstrap selection frequencies. Bootstrap model averaging offers three benefits:

- The average parameter estimates shrink toward zero, which mitigates selection bias.

- The percentages of the effects selected in a specified proportion of the bootstrap samples serve as measures of effect importance.

- A parsimonious and more interpretable model can be obtained by refitting a preliminary model and including only those effects that had higher selection percentages.

As an alternative to bootstrap model averaging, you can apply model averaging with Akaike weights, which are computed by the GLMSELECT procedure during model selection. This form of model averaging also mitigates selection bias. You can use the `%ICWeightParmEst` macro to average the parameter estimates and the `%ModelAvgScore` macro to average the predictions.

A drawback of model averaging is that it does not naturally extend to generalized linear models and other models presented in Part II of this book.

Part II

Specialized Regression Models

Chapter 8
Building Quantile Regression Models

Contents

This chapter introduces two procedures for building quantile regression models: the QUANTSELECT procedure in SAS 9 and its counterpart in SAS Viya, the QTRSELECT procedure. They provide features for specifying candidate effects and methods for selecting models that parallel those of the GLMSELECT and REGSELECT procedures.

Quantile regression, which models the conditional quantiles of a continuous response, was developed in the mid 1970s by Roger Koenker (then at Bell Laboratories) and Gilbert Bassett (University of Illinois at Chicago). It has since proved its value in financial risk management, fraud detection, customer lifetime value analysis, predictive maintenance, and other areas where important questions are answered by modeling percentiles of key indicators—especially in the tails of their distributions.[†] Quantile regression produces results not readily obtained with least squares regression because it models heterogeneous response distributions.

Quantile regression is computationally expensive compared with least squares regression, and for this reason its early applications were limited to data with at most a few hundred observations. Although this barrier has been broken by modern algorithms and computational power, there is a lingering misconception that quantile regression is not practical with large data, and it is often overlooked in courses on regression analysis and supervised learning.

The QUANTSELECT and QTRSELECT procedures make it convenient to build quantile regression models with large observational data. And with sufficiently large amounts of data, these procedures can build quantile process regression models that provide information about the entire set of conditional distributions of the response.

[†]In a 2017 interview, Koenker recalled that his landmark paper with Bassett (Koenker and Bassett 1978) was initially rejected because modeling percentiles other than the 50th did not seem useful.

For readers who are unfamiliar with quantile regression, this chapter begins with basic concepts and describes the QUANTREG procedure for fitting fully specified quantile regression models.

What Is a Quantile?

Introductory courses in data science and statistics emphasize the importance of summarizing the distribution of a variable with a set of descriptive measures rather than a single number. Early in the course, students learn to compute percentiles—such as the 5th, 25th, 50th, 75th, and 95th—along with means and standard deviations. Later, students learn about least squares regression for modeling the mean of a response variable. At that point a natural question to ask is, "Why not also model the percentiles of the response distribution?"

Quantile regression provides models for percentiles that can be used for prediction and inference, in much the same way that standard regression provides models for means. The technical details of quantile regression fall outside the scope of a basic course, and advanced courses on regression focus on models for the mean because of their wide applicability. Nonetheless, quantile regression is a practical alternative to standard regression in situations that require a more complete description of the response distribution.

If you are unfamiliar with quantile regression you might wonder, "What is the difference between a quantile and a percentile?" The two terms are simply different labels for the same quantity. Whereas a percentile is labeled by a percent between 0 and 100, a quantile is labeled by the corresponding proportion between 0 and 1, which is called the quantile level. For instance, the 0.75 quantile is the same as the 75th percentile.

The term *percentile* is commonly used in statistical practice, while the term *quantile* is preferred in statistical theory, where the quantile level is interpreted as a probability. The level itself is often denoted by the Greek letter τ. For instance, the level of the 0.75 quantile is $\tau = 0.75$.

How Does Quantile Regression Compare With Ordinary Least Squares Regression?

Quantile regression is most often used to model one or more conditional quantiles of the distribution of a continuous response y given a set of predictors $x_1, \ldots, x_p$. The conditional quantile at level τ is denoted by $Q_\tau(y \mid x_1, \ldots, x_p)$. In contrast, ordinary least squares (OLS) regression models the conditional expectation $E(y \mid x_1, \ldots, x_p)$ and assumes that the conditional variance $\text{Var}(y \mid x_1, \ldots, x_p)$ is a constant (σ^2). When statistical inference is the goal, OLS regression assumes that the errors in the model are normally distributed. Quantile regression does not assume a parametric distribution, and it does not necessarily assume a constant variance.

Figure 8.1 displays an example of regression data for 500 bank customers. The response is the customer lifetime value (CLV), and the predictor is the maximum balance of the customer's account. Both the conditional mean and the conditional variance of CLV increase with maximum balance.

The line shown in Figure 8.1 represents a least squares regression model. The curves represent the conditional distributions of CLV for four different values of maximum balance. The distributions are slightly skewed, and there is no reason to assume they are normal distributions. Clearly the quantiles (percentiles) of these distributions—and not just their means—vary with maximum balance.

Figure 8.1 Least Squares Regression Fit for Customer Lifetime Value

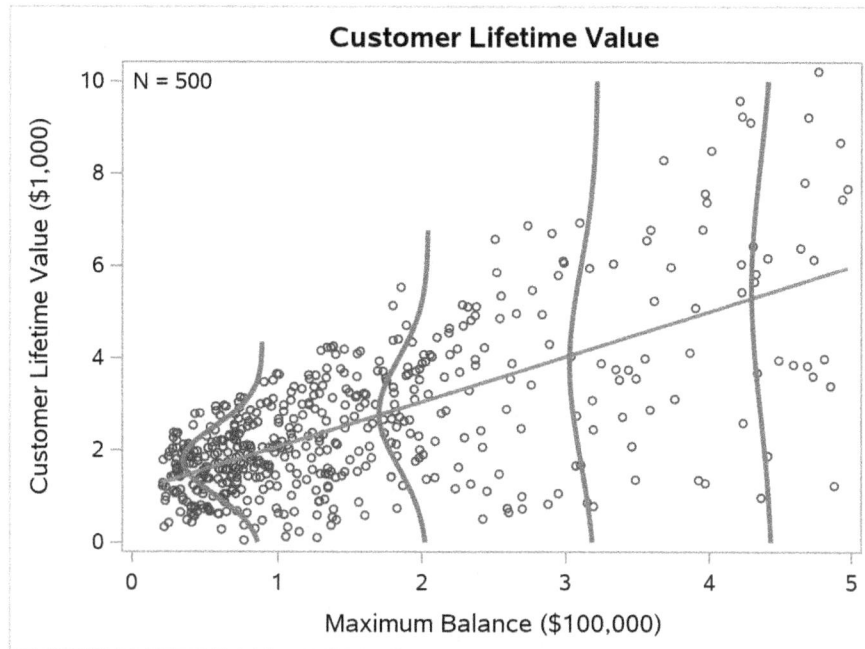

Quantile regression answers questions that require modeling the conditional distributions of a response. For instance, to improve the bank's strategy for customer retention, it might be useful to develop predictive models for the 10th, 50th, and 90th percentiles of CLV.

Figure 8.2 displays quantile regression models for the levels 0.1, 0.5, and 0.9 or, equivalently, the 10th, 50th, and 90th percentiles.

Figure 8.2 Regression Models for Quantile Levels 0.1, 0.5, and 0.9

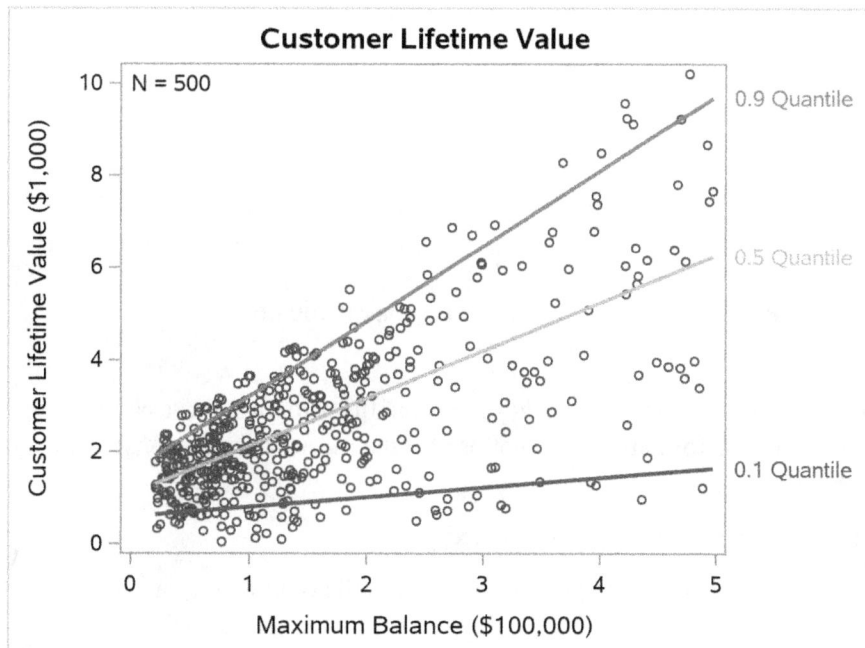

From a modeling perspective, the quantile level τ is the proportion of the population that is associated with a quantile. The conditional quantile is the value of y below which the proportion of the conditional response population is τ. If you prefer to think in terms of a probability model for y, then τ is the probability $\Pr[y \leq Q_\tau(y \mid x_1, \ldots, x_p)]$.

By fitting quantile regression models for a grid of values of τ in the interval $(0,1)$, you can approximate the entire set of conditional distributions. The optimal grid choice depends on the data. The more data you have, the more detail you can model in the conditional distributions.

The models in Figure 8.2 are linear, which might suggest that quantile regression is not sufficiently flexible for nonlinear dependencies. You can accommodate nonlinearity by including terms for polynomial or spline effects in the model, just as you would in a standard regression model.

Quantile regression gives you a principled alternative to the recommended practice of applying transformations prior to fitting a standard regression model. Well-chosen transformations lead to better models, but depending on the data it can be difficult to find a simple transformation (such as the log function) for which the transformed responses reasonably satisfy the assumption of constant variance. This is evident in Figure 8.3, where the variance of log(CLV) increases for maximum balances near 100,000 USD and the conditional distributions are asymmetric.

Figure 8.3 Least Squares Regression Fit for log(CLV)

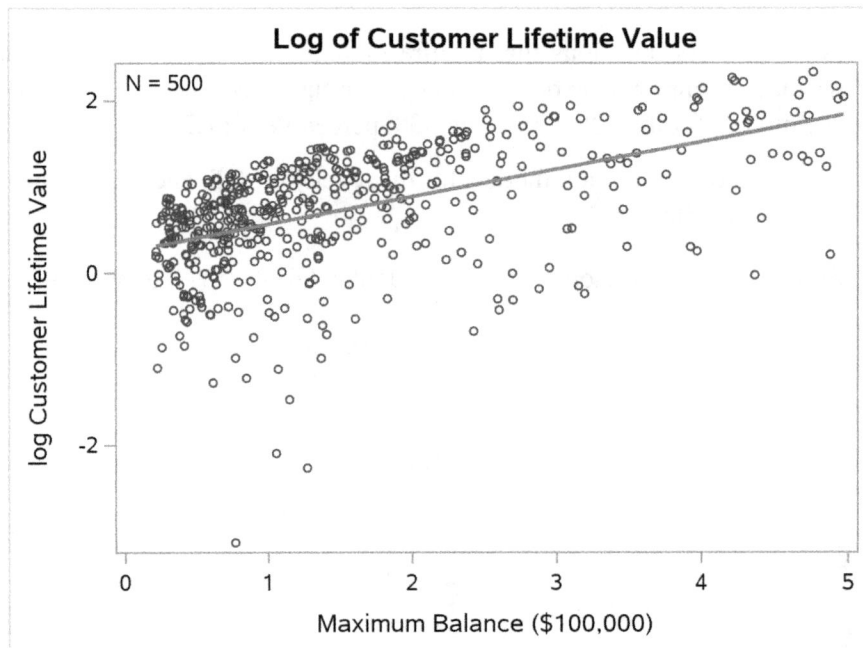

Even when a monotone transformation $h(y)$ reasonably satisfies the assumptions for standard regression, the inverse transformation does not predict the mean of the response in the untransformed scale:

$$E(y \mid x_1, \ldots, x_p) \neq h^{-1}(E(h(y) \mid x_1, \ldots, x_p))$$

In contrast, the inverse transformation can be applied to the predicted quantiles of the transformed response:

$$Q_\tau(y \mid x_1, \ldots, x_p) = h^{-1}(Q_\tau(h(y) \mid x_1, \ldots, x_p))$$

Table 8.1 summarizes key differences between OLS regression and quantile regression.

Table 8.1   Comparison of Ordinary Least Squares Regression and Quantile Regression

OLS Regression	Quantile Regression
Predicts the conditional mean	Predicts conditional quantiles
Applies when n is small	Needs sufficient data
Often assumes normality	Is distribution agnostic
Does not preserve the conditional mean under monotone transformation	Preserves conditional quantiles under monotone transformation
Is sensitive to response outliers	Is robust to response outliers
Is computationally inexpensive	Is computationally intensive

The books by Koenker (2005) and Hao and Naiman (2007) provide comprehensive introductions to the theory and applications of quantile regression.

Fitting Fully Specified Quantile Regression Models

The QUANTREG procedure in SAS/STAT fits quantile regression models for which the effects are fully specified; it provides features for model exploration, and it supports statistical inference by computing p-values, confidence intervals, and tests for model parameters. In many ways the QUANTREG procedure mirrors the functionality of the REG procedure for standard least squares regression.

Least squares regression models the expectation of the response for the ith observation:

$$E(y_i) = \beta_0 + \beta_1 x_{i1} + \cdots + \beta_p x_{ip}, \quad i = 1, \ldots, n$$

The parameters β_j are estimated by solving the least squares minimization problem

$$\min_{\beta_0, \ldots, \beta_p} \sum_{i=1}^{n} \left(y_i - \beta_0 - \sum_{j=1}^{p} x_{ij} \beta_j \right)^2$$

In contrast, quantile regression models the quantile of the response at level τ:

$$Q_\tau(y_i) = \beta_0(\tau) + \beta_1(\tau) x_{i1} + \cdots + \beta_p(\tau) x_{ip}, \quad i = 1, \ldots, n$$

The parameters $\beta_j(\tau)$ are estimated by solving the minimization problem

$$\min_{\beta_0(\tau), \ldots, \beta_p(\tau)} \sum_{i=1}^{n} \rho_\tau \left(y_i - \beta_0(\tau) - \sum_{j=1}^{p} x_{ij} \beta_j(\tau) \right)$$

where $\rho_\tau(r) = \tau \max(r, 0) + (1 - \tau) \max(-r, 0)$. The function $\rho_\tau(r)$ is referred to as the check loss, because it resembles a check mark when plotted as a function of r.

For each quantile level τ that you specify, the solution to the minimization problem yields a different set of regression coefficients. When two quantile levels are sufficiently close, it is possible (depending on the data) for them to share the same parameter estimates. Median regression is the special case of quantile regression for which $\tau = 0.5$. The function $2\rho_{0.5}(r)$ is the absolute value function.

Example: Predicting Quantiles for Customer Lifetime Value

Returning to the illustration on page 137, suppose that the goal is to predict low, medium, and high customer lifetime values (CLVs) based on 15 variables (X1, ..., X15) that include the maximum balance, the average overdraft, and the total credit card amount that was used. There is evidence that different parts of the distribution of CLV correspond to subpopulations of customers with different profiles of these predictors.

Assume that low, medium, and high values are represented by the 10th, 50th, and 90th percentiles of the conditional distribution of CLV or, equivalently, the quantiles at levels 0.1, 0.5, and 0.9. The following statements use the QUANTREG procedure to model these quantiles:

```
proc quantreg data=CLV ci=resampling;
    model CLV = x1-x15 / quantlev=0.1 0.5 0.9;
run;
```

The MODEL statement lists the response variable and the predictors. A CLASS statement and an EFFECT statement are also available for specifying classification variables and constructed effects such as polynomials and splines. The QUANTLEV= option specifies the levels for quantiles to be modeled, and the CI= option requests confidence intervals computed by Markov chain marginal bootstrap resampling.

The QUANTREG procedure produces a variety of tables, including those in Output 8.1 and Output 8.2, which show the parameter estimates for the quantiles at levels 0.1 and 0.9.

Output 8.1 Parameter Estimates for Quantile Level 0.1

The QUANTREG Procedure
Quantile Level = 0.1

Parameter	DF	Estimate	Standard Error	95% Confidence Limits		t Value	Pr > |t|
Intercept	1	9.9046	0.0742	9.7587	10.0504	133.40	<.0001
X1	1	0.8503	0.0554	0.7413	0.9592	15.34	<.0001
X2	1	0.9471	0.0679	0.8136	1.0806	13.94	<.0001
X3	1	0.9763	0.0504	0.8773	1.0754	19.36	<.0001
X4	1	0.9256	0.0725	0.7831	1.0681	12.77	<.0001
X5	1	0.6670	0.0521	0.5646	0.7694	12.80	<.0001
X6	1	0.2905	0.0603	0.1720	0.4090	4.82	<.0001
X7	1	0.2981	0.0675	0.1654	0.4308	4.41	<.0001
X8	1	0.2094	0.0603	0.0908	0.3280	3.47	0.0006
X9	1	-0.0633	0.0520	-0.1654	0.0389	-1.22	0.2244
X10	1	0.0129	0.0706	-0.1258	0.1516	0.18	0.8550
X11	1	0.1084	0.0569	-0.0033	0.2202	1.91	0.0572
X12	1	-0.0249	0.0627	-0.1481	0.0983	-0.40	0.6910
X13	1	-0.0505	0.0503	-0.1494	0.0483	-1.00	0.3157
X14	1	0.2009	0.0731	0.0572	0.3446	2.75	0.0062
X15	1	0.1623	0.0746	0.0157	0.3089	2.18	0.0301

Output 8.2 Parameter Estimates for Quantile Level 0.9

				Parameter Estimates			
				95% Confidence Limits			
Parameter	**DF**	**Estimate**	**Standard Error**			**t Value**	**Pr > |t|**
Intercept	1	10.1007	0.1379	9.8297	10.3716	73.25	<.0001
X1	1	0.0191	0.1419	-0.2596	0.2979	0.13	0.8928
X2	1	0.9539	0.1375	0.6837	1.2240	6.94	<.0001
X3	1	0.0721	0.1196	-0.1628	0.3071	0.60	0.5465
X4	1	1.1171	0.1508	0.8208	1.4133	7.41	<.0001
X5	1	-0.0317	0.1681	-0.3621	0.2986	-0.19	0.8503
X6	1	0.1096	0.1764	-0.2371	0.4563	0.62	0.5348
X7	1	0.2428	0.1517	-0.0553	0.5410	1.60	0.1102
X8	1	-0.0743	0.1489	-0.3668	0.2183	-0.50	0.6181
X9	1	0.0918	0.1469	-0.1969	0.3804	0.62	0.5324
X10	1	-0.2426	0.1794	-0.5952	0.1099	-1.35	0.1769
X11	1	0.9099	0.1662	0.5833	1.2365	5.47	<.0001
X12	1	0.7759	0.1377	0.5054	1.0463	5.64	<.0001
X13	1	0.5380	0.1468	0.2495	0.8265	3.66	0.0003
X14	1	0.6897	0.1438	0.4071	0.9723	4.80	<.0001
X15	1	1.0145	0.1330	0.7531	1.2758	7.63	<.0001

The results in Output 8.1 and Output 8.2 are different. For example, the estimate for X1 is significant in the model for the 0.1 quantile, but it is not significant in the model for the 0.9 quantile. In general, quantile regression produces a different set of parameter estimates and predictions for each quantile level. However, when two quantile levels are sufficiently close, it is possible for them to share the same parameter estimates and predictions.

Example: Fitting a Quantile Process Model for Customer Lifetime Value

The model for quantile regression is

$$Q_\tau(y \mid x_1, \ldots, x_p) = \beta_0(\tau) + \beta_1(\tau)\, x_1 + \cdots + \beta_p(\tau)\, x_p$$

where the subscript τ refers to one or more individual quantile levels. With sufficient data, you can use quantile regression to model the entire set of quantiles for the continuum of levels in the interval (0,1). This approach—referred to as quantile process regression—treats the quantile as a continuous function of τ. To emphasize the dependence on τ, the quantile process model is written as

$$Q_y(\tau \mid x_1, \ldots, x_p) = \beta_0(\tau) + \beta_1(\tau)\, x_1 + \cdots + \beta_p(\tau)\, x_p, \quad 0 < \tau < 1$$

Quantile process regression requires more data and greater computational resources than quantile regression, but it has many potential applications because it enables you to model the entire set of conditional distributions.

This example fits a quantile process model with the QUANTREG procedure and uses it to explore the effects of predictors on different parts of the response distribution. The procedure provides three ways to fit a quantile process model, which you specify with the QUANTLEV= option. The first way is to specify a grid of evenly spaced levels between 0 and 1:

```
proc quantreg data=CLV ci=resampling;
   model CLV = x1-x15 / quantlev=0.02 to 0.98 by 0.02;
   ods output ParameterEstimates=Estimates;
run;
```

For each level in the grid, the procedure fits a quantile regression model and saves the parameter estimates and confidence limits in a data set named Estimates.

When the number of levels does not exceed the number of observations n, the parameter estimates for the quantile levels should be different from each other. However, in practice it might not be obvious how to specify a grid that is fine enough to capture important features of the response distribution, and yet not so fine that adjacent levels share the same parameter estimates. The second way to fit a quantile process model avoids this problem; you can specify QUANTLEV=PROCESS, which requests a search for the optimal grid:

```
proc quantreg data=CLV ci=resampling;
   model CLV = x1-x15 / quantlev=process plot=quantplot;
run;
```

The optimal grid will depend on the data and is usually not evenly spaced. However, it is computationally expensive when n and p are large. The third way is less expensive; you can specify QUANTLEV=FQPR(N=m), which requests a fast quantile process regression method proposed by Yao (2017) that approximates quantile process regression on a grid of m evenly spaced levels.

In the preceding MODEL statement, the PLOT=QUANTPLOT option requests panels of quantile process plots that display parameter estimates for the intercept term and all the predictors. These plots help you to identify which predictors are associated with different parts of the response distribution. Output 8.3 displays the second of four panels that are produced. The plot for X5 shows lower confidence limits that are greater than zero for quantile levels less than 0.35. In other words, X5 has a significant, positive effect on the lower tail of the distribution for CLV in the level range (0.07, 0.35).

Output 8.3 Quantile Process Plots (Panel 2)

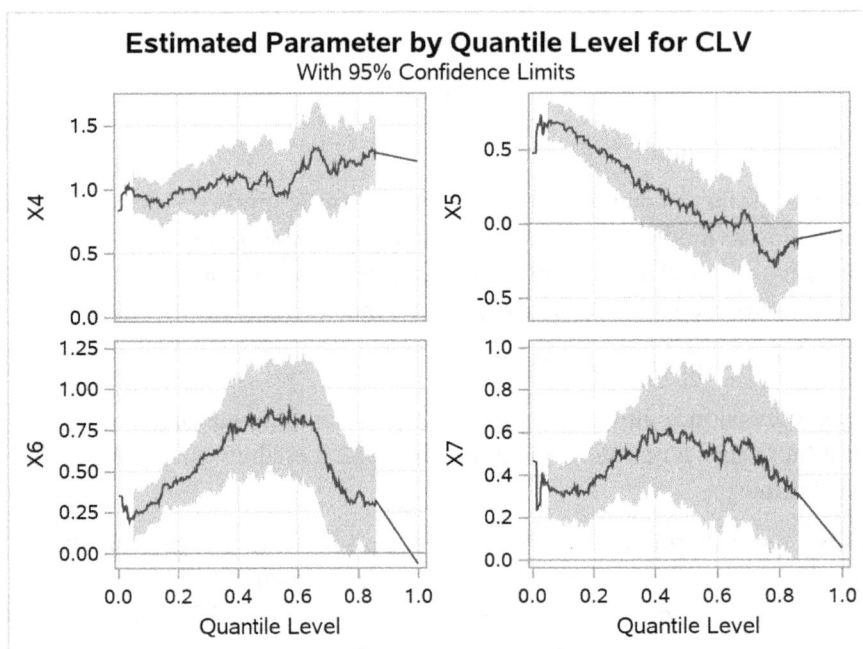

Introduction to the QUANTSELECT Procedure

The QUANTSELECT procedure builds quantile regression models and quantile process models that are useful for prediction and data exploration. Like the GLMSELECT procedure, which builds general linear models, it selects model effects from a set of candidates. The QUANTSELECT procedure does not compute confidence intervals or hypothesis tests because these are not appropriate for selected models. Inferential results for fully specified models are available in the QUANTREG procedure.

When you use the QUANTSELECT procedure to build a model, you specify the candidate effects in the MODEL statement. The QUANTSELECT procedure provides the same versatile syntax for effect specification that is available in the GLMSELECT procedure. Not only can the predictors $x_1, \ldots, x_p$ represent the main effects of variables that are continuous or categorical, but they can also represent interaction effects or constructed effects such as polynomial effects and spline effects.

For instance, consider the following statements:

```
proc quantselect data=Stores;
   class Region Training;
   effect SpX1 = spline(X1);
   model CloseRate = Region Training Region*Training SpX1 P1-P6 /
      quantlev=0.1 0.5 0.9
      selection=forward(choose=sbc select=sbc stop=sbc);
   effect
run;
```

The CLASS statement identifies two classification variables, Region and Training. The EFFECT statement constructs a spline effect from the continuous variable X1. The MODEL statement requests forward selection from 10 candidate effects: the main and interaction effects of Region and Training, the spline effect of X1, and the main effects of the six continuous variables P1, ..., P6. The SELECTION= option specifies the selection method, and the QUANTLEV= option specifies the quantile levels.

Overfitting and other issues that undermine the predictive accuracy of general linear models are equally problematic when you build quantile regression models. The QUANTSELECT procedure provides effect selection methods and criteria that parallel most of those provided by the GLMSELECT procedure. Table 8.2 summarizes the available methods.

Table 8.2   Effect Selection Methods in the QUANTSELECT Procedure

Method	Description	SELECTION=*keyword*
Forward selection	Starts with the intercept and adds effects	FORWARD
Backward elimination	Starts with the full model and deletes effects	BACKWARD
Stepwise selection	Starts with the intercept; effects are added and can be deleted.	STEPWISE
Lasso	Constrains sum of $|\beta_j|$s; some $\hat{\beta}_j$s are set to 0.	LASSO
Adaptive lasso	Constrains sum of weighted $|\beta_j|$s; some $\hat{\beta}_j$s are set to 0.	LASSO(ADAPTIVE)
No selection	Fits fully specified model	NONE

Forward selection, backward elimination, and stepwise regression reduce the number of effects in the model. Here, the lasso method modifies the lasso method of Tibshirani (1996) by minimizing the sum of check losses rather than the sum of squares, while penalizing the sum of absolute values of the coefficients. Similarly, the adaptive lasso method modifies the adaptive lasso method of Zou (2006).

Both lasso methods leave all the effects in the model but restrict the parameter estimates in such a way that some are set to zero while others shrink toward zero. The QUANTSELECT procedure uses lasso methods only to determine which effects to include in the model at each step; the model at that step is then refitted without penalizing the estimation, and the parameter estimates and selection criteria are based on the refitted model. If the model contains CLASS variables or constructed effects, they are split into predictors corresponding to individual columns of the design matrix.

For each selection method, the QUANTSELECT procedure provides multiple criteria and options you can use to control and visualize the process of model selection. You control how effects are selected by specifying suboptions in parentheses after the SELECTION= option:

- CHOOSE= specifies the criterion for choosing the model. This criterion is evaluated at each step of the selection process; the final selected model is the model with the best value of this criterion.

- SELECT= specifies the criterion for determining which effect enters or leaves at each step of the forward, backward, and stepwise methods. This effect gives the maximum improvement in the specified criterion. Do not confuse the SELECT= suboption with the SELECTION= option.

- STOP= specifies the criterion for terminating the selection process. This option is ignored if you use the MAXSTEPS=m option to specify the maximum number of steps. If you specify STOPHORIZON=k together with the STOP= option, the process looks ahead for k steps to decide whether an extreme value of the stop criterion is achieved.

These criteria are counterparts of the more familiar criteria used by the GLMSELECT procedure to select effects in general linear models (see page 52). The counterpart of the R-square statistic is

$$R1(\tau) = 1 - \frac{D(\tau)}{D_0(\tau)}$$

where $D(\tau)$ is the sum of check losses

$$D(\tau) = \sum_{i=1}^{n} \rho_\tau(y_i - \mathbf{x}_i' \hat{\boldsymbol{\beta}}(\tau))$$

and $D_0(\tau)$ is the sum of check losses for the intercept-only model. The counterpart of the adjusted R-square statistic is

$$\text{ADJR1}(\tau) = 1 - \frac{(n-1)D(\tau)}{(n-p)D_0(\tau)}$$

The counterparts of the information criteria AIC, AICC, and SBC are $\text{AIC}(\tau)$, $\text{AICC}(\tau)$, and $\text{SBC}(\tau)$, which are derived by assuming that the model errors follow an asymmetric Laplace distribution (Koenker 2005, pp. 133-138). Koenker (2005, sec. 4.9) discusses $\text{AIC}(\tau)$ and $\text{SBC}(\tau)$, which he refers to as SIC.

Table 8.3 lists the criteria you can request with the CHOOSE= suboption. Not all of these criteria are available with every selection method.

Table 8.3   Criteria Available with the CHOOSE= Suboption

Suboption	Criterion
ADJR1	Adjusted quantile regression R-square statistic
AIC	Akaike's information criterion
AICC	Corrected Akaike's information criterion
SBC	Schwarz Bayesian information criterion
VALIDATE	Average check loss (ACL) for validation data

When you specify CHOOSE=ADJR1, the model chosen is the one with the largest value of the adjusted R1 statistic. Otherwise, the model chosen is the one with the smallest value of the criterion. Note that SBC is called BIC in many books and papers; see page 28.

Table 8.4 lists the criteria you can request with the SELECT= suboption.

Table 8.4   Criteria Available with the SELECT= Suboption

Suboption	Criterion
ADJR1	Adjusted quantile regression R-square statistic
AIC	Akaike's information criterion
AICC	Corrected Akaike's information criterion
SBC	Schwarz Bayesian information criterion
SL	Significance level (not recommended)
VALIDATE	Average check loss for validation data

If you provide validation data, the default is VALIDATE; otherwise, the default is SBC. The SL suboption is provided simply for compatibility with older software. In modern practice, the use of statistical tests to determine which effects enter or leave is not recommended because the distributions and significance levels associated with such tests do not have valid interpretations; see page 33.

Table 8.5 lists the criteria you can request with the STOP= suboption. Except for STOP=m, selection stops when the criterion for the model at the next step would not improve.

Table 8.5   Criteria Available with the STOP= Option

Option	Criterion
m	Selection stops when model has m effects
ADJR1	Adjusted quantile regression R-square statistic
AIC	Akaike's information criterion
AICC	Corrected Akaike's information criterion
SBC	Schwarz Bayesian information criterion
VALIDATE	Average check loss for validation data

Example: Building Quantile Regression Models for Close Rate

This example illustrates the use of the QUANTSELECT procedure to build quantile regression models with the data in Stores, which were introduced on page 56. In Chapter 5 the data were used to build general linear models for the conditional average of the close rate by selecting effects from the following candidates:

- A categorical variable Region, which indicates the marketing region
- A categorical variable Training, which provides the level of customer service training
- Continuous variables X1, ..., X20, which measure 20 general characteristics of each store
- Continuous variables P1, ..., P6, which measure six promotional activities
- Continuous variables L1, ..., L6, which measure special layouts of items in six departments

Here the data are used to build quantile regression models for conditional percentiles of the close rate distribution. The close rate for a store is considered to be low if it is less than the 10th percentile for stores that have the same combination of predictor values. Likewise, a close rate is considered to be high if it is greater than the 90th percentile for stores that have the same combination of predictor values. Models that predict high close rates can inform strategic decisions, while models that predict low close rates can aid efforts to improve store performance.

The following statements use the QUANTSELECT procedure to build models for the quantiles at levels 0.1 and 0.9:

```
proc quantselect data=Stores plots=(Coefficients Criteria) seed=219531;
   class Region(param=reference ref='Midwest' split)
         Training(param=reference ref='None');
   model CloseRate = Region Training X1-X20 L1-L6 P1-P6 / quantlev=0.1 0.9
      selection=forward(choose=sbc select=sbc stop=validate stophorizon=3);
   partition fraction(validate=0.3);
run;
```

The PARAM= option in the CLASS statement specifies how the values of Region and Training are parameterized in the design matrix (see page 56 for details). The SPLIT option allows the design matrix columns associated with Region to be selected independently of each other. The SELECTION= option in the MODEL statement specifies the forward method with a stop horizon of 3 and the same criteria that are used to model the conditional mean of CloseRate in the example on page 63. The PARTITION statement reserves 30% of the data for validation.

Interpreting the Results

Output 8.4 shows the numbers of observations used for training and validation.

Output 8.4 Numbers of Observations

Number of Observations Read	500
Number of Observations Used	500
Number of Observations Used for Training	363
Number of Observations Used for Validation	137

Output 8.5 shows the levels of the classification variables.

Output 8.5 Class Level Information

Class	Levels	Values
Class Level Information		
Region	4	* East Midwest South West
Training	3	Complete In Progress None
* Associated Parameters Split		

Output 8.6 shows the number of candidate effects and the number of associated parameters.

Output 8.6 Number of Effects and Number of Parameters

Dimensions	
Number of Effects	35
Number of Parameters	38

Output 8.7 summarizes the selection process for quantile level 0.1.

Output 8.7 Selection Summary for Quantile Level 0.1

Quantile Level = 0.1

		Number					
	Effect	Effects				Validation	Adjusted
Step	Entered	In	AIC	AICC	SBC	ACL	R1
0	Intercept	1	-845.9958	-845.9848	-842.1014	0.3150	0.0000
1	X2	2	-1065.0464	-1065.0131	-1057.2576	0.2113	0.2604
2	X4	3	-1315.0443	-1314.9774	-1303.3610	0.1545	0.4759
3	Region_South	4	-1373.6174	-1373.5056	-1358.0398	0.1436	0.5165
4	P2	5	-1411.3530	-1411.1849	-1391.8810	0.1340	0.5410
5	P1	6	-1456.5509	-1456.3150	-1433.1845	0.1196	0.5687
6	P3	7	-1542.1025	-1541.7870	-1514.8417	0.1072	0.6166
7	P5	8	-1570.0416	-1569.6349	-1538.8864	0.1059	0.6310
8	P4	9	-1581.4071	-1580.8971	-1546.3574	0.1050*	0.6367
9	L1	10	-1592.9229	-1592.2979	-1553.9789*	0.1093	0.6424
10	L5	11	-1593.6025*	-1592.8504*	-1550.7641	0.1108	0.6427*
* Optimal Value Of Criterion							

The stop criterion (validation ACL) decreases starting at Step 1 and reaches a minimum at Step 8. The process stops after Step 11 because the criterion at Step 8 is smaller than the criteria at Steps 9, 10, and 11, which are the three extended steps specified by STOPHORIZON=3. The final selected model is the model at Step 9, which includes L1 and minimizes the selection criterion (SBC). For comparison, the selection summary includes the criteria AIC, AICC, and adjusted R1, all of which would include one more effect (L5).

The progression plot in Output 8.8 visualizes the selection process for quantile level 0.1. The variables X2, X4, and Region_South are the first to enter the model, followed by five of the six promotion measures and two of the six layout measures.

Output 8.8 Coefficient Progression for Quantile Level 0.1

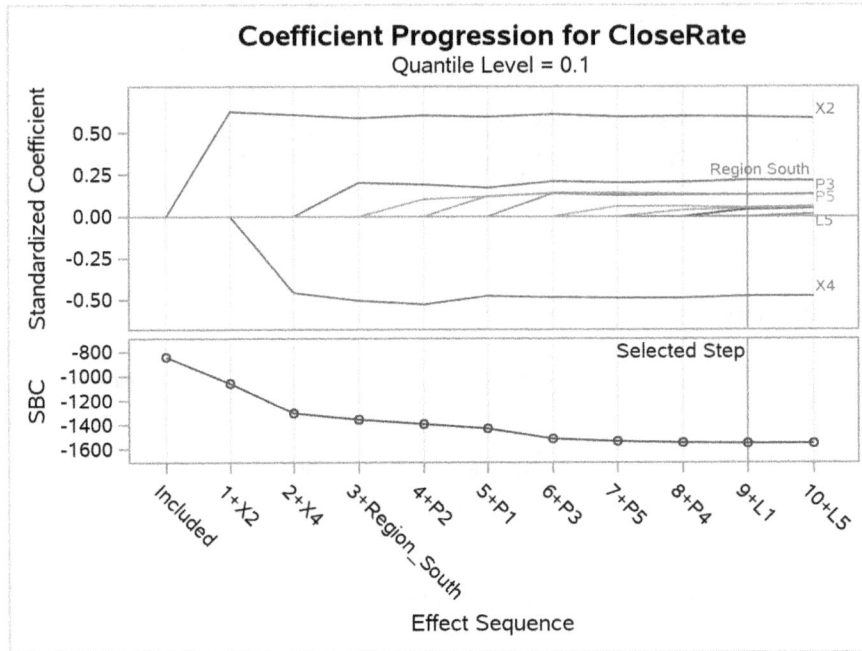

Output 8.9 shows the parameter estimates for the selected model for quantile level 0.1.

Output 8.9 Parameter Estimates for Selected Model for Quantile Level 0.1

	Parameter Estimates		
Parameter	DF	Estimate	Standardized Estimate
Intercept	1	59.972591	0
Region South	1	0.852213	0.215396
X2	1	3.891180	0.594825
X4	1	-3.005504	-0.478659
L1	1	0.264792	0.040557
P1	1	0.834461	0.129170
P2	1	0.794731	0.127051
P3	1	0.807001	0.127255
P4	1	0.302373	0.047208
P5	1	0.346196	0.053684

Unlike the parameter estimates tables in Output 8.1 and Output 8.2, the table in Output 8.9 does not display confidence limits for the regression coefficients or *p*-values. Inferential results are not applicable here because the final selected model cannot be treated as if it were a fully specified model.

The procedure produces the same series of tables and graphs for each quantile level that you specify in the MODEL statement. The progression plot in Output 8.10 visualizes the selection process for quantile level 0.9. The process stops at Step 12. The variables X2, X4, and Region_East are the first to enter the model; they are eventually followed by all six of the layout variables, L1 through L6.

Output 8.10 Coefficient Progression for Quantile Level 0.9

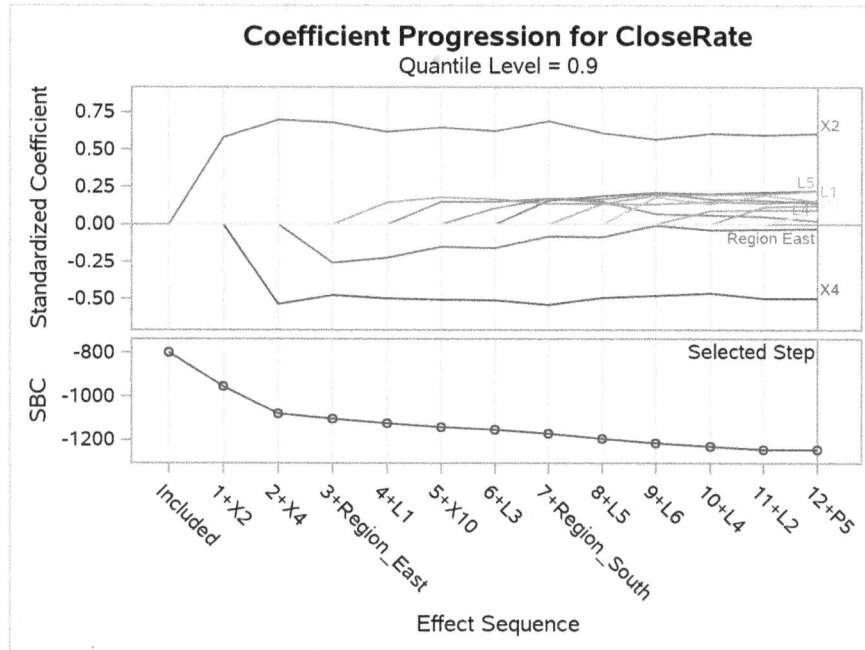

Output 8.11 shows the parameter estimates for the final model for quantile level 0.9.

Output 8.11 Parameter Estimates for Selected Model for Quantile Level 0.9

Parameter	DF	Estimate	Standardized Estimate
Intercept	1	59.739162	0
Region East	1	-0.132357	-0.032417
Region South	1	0.879524	0.222299
X2	1	3.953394	0.604335
X4	1	-3.130735	-0.498604
X10	1	0.125662	0.019988
L1	1	1.043174	0.159777
L2	1	0.796149	0.123183
L3	1	0.890926	0.139295
L4	1	0.571799	0.091854
L5	1	1.372780	0.223090
L6	1	0.933061	0.155231
P5	1	0.480492	0.074509

In summary, X2, X4, and Region_South are selected in the models for the 10th and 90th percentiles; these variables have large effects on store performance. However, the two models tell different stories. Five promotional measures (P1 through P5) are selected in the model for the 10th percentile, indicating that these measures are predictors of low performance. All six layout measures (L1 through L6) are selected in the model for the 90th percentile, indicating that special layouts are predictors of high performance. These insights would be difficult to gain with OLS regression methods.

Example: Building a Quantile Process Model for Close Rate

Quantile process regression was introduced on page 141, where the QUANTREG procedure was used to fit a fully specified quantile process model. The following statements use the QUANTSELECT procedure to build a quantile process model by using the forward selection method:

```
proc quantselect data=Stores outdesign=StoresDesign seed=337295;
   class Region(param=reference ref='Midwest' split)
         Training(param=reference ref='None');
   model CloseRate = Region Training X1-X20 L1-L6 P1-P6 / quantlev=process
      selection=forward(choose=sbc select=sbc stop=validate stophorizon=3);
   partition fraction(validate=0.3);
   output out=Predictions predicted=PredCloseRate quantlevel=ObsLevel;
run;
```

The QUANTLEV=PROCESS option requests an accurate model based on a set of levels $0 < \tau_1 < \ldots < \tau_u \ldots < \tau_U < 1$ that is determined algorithmically to represent the continuum of levels in $(0,1)$. Alternatively, you can specify QUANTLEV=PROCESS(NTAU=m) to request an approximate model that is based on m equally spaced levels in $(0,1)$. Building a quantile process model is computationally intensive because it involves fitting a quantile regression model at each of many steps. In SAS/STAT 14.3 and later releases, you can specify QUANTLEV=FQPR to request a fast quantile process regression method due to Yao (2017), which is statistically equivalent to the method behind QUANTLEV=PROCESS.

The QUANTSELECT procedure provides the same set of selection methods for building quantile process models that it provides for building quantile regression models (see page 145). The criteria for selecting quantile process models are integrals of the corresponding criteria for selecting quantile regression models. The SELECT= criterion here is SBC $= \int_0^1 \text{SBC}(\tau) \, d\tau$. At each step of the forward selection process—and for each effect that is a candidate for inclusion—the procedure fits a quantile regression model for each τ_u and computes SBC(τ_u). The procedure then computes SBC for the candidate effect. Among the candidate effects at each step, the effect selected for inclusion is the one that minimizes SBC.

Interpreting the Results

Output 8.12 displays the fit statistics for the final selected quantile process model, and Output 8.13 lists the effects in the model.

Output 8.12 Fit Statistics for Final Selected Quantile Process Model

The QUANTSELECT Procedure

Fit Statistics	
Objective Function	83.31945
R1	0.53775
Adj R1	0.51654
AIC	-1086.44647
AICC	-1084.77776
SBC	-1025.04279
ACL (Train)	0.24291
ACL (Validate)	0.25954

Output 8.13 Effects in Final Selected Quantile Process Model

Selected Effects: Intercept Region_South X2 X4 L1 L2 L3 L4 L5 L6 P1 P2 P3 P4 P5 P6

Unlike the quantile regression models that were selected for $\tau = 0.1$ and $\tau = 0.9$ in the previous example, this model includes all the variables that measure special layouts and promotional activities. Output 8.14 displays the parameter estimates.

Output 8.14 Parameter Estimates for Final Selected Quantile Process Model

Parameter Estimates			
Parameter	DF	Estimate	Standardized Estimate
Intercept	1	59.628427	0
Region South	1	0.880207	0.221799
X2	1	3.825823	0.581359
X4	1	-3.150172	-0.512150
L1	1	0.575155	0.088316
L2	1	0.314287	0.048659
L3	1	0.407959	0.062978
L4	1	0.513572	0.082822
L5	1	0.537103	0.086992
L6	1	0.559931	0.091895
P1	1	0.471916	0.072762
P2	1	0.610474	0.096155
P3	1	0.361515	0.056155
P4	1	0.317615	0.049644
P5	1	0.616329	0.096597
P6	1	0.515154	0.079945

The parameter for the jth effect is $\beta_j = \int_0^1 \beta_j(\tau)\,d\tau$, where $\beta_j(\tau)$ is the parameter for the jth effect in the quantile regression model for level τ:

$$Q_\tau(y \mid x_1, \ldots, x_p) = \beta_0(\tau) + \beta_1(\tau)\,x_1 + \cdots + \beta_p(\tau)\,x_p$$

The estimate of β_j is computed by summing $\hat{\beta}_j(\tau_1), \ldots, \hat{\beta}_j(\tau_U)$. The interpretation of the β_js is not obvious, but it can be shown that

$$\beta_0 + \beta_1 x_1 + \cdots + \beta_p x_p = \int_0^1 \beta_0(\tau)\,d\tau \ + \ x_1 \int_0^1 \beta_1(\tau)\,d\tau \ + \ \cdots \ + \ x_p \int_0^1 \beta_p(\tau)\,d\tau$$

$$= \int_0^1 Q_y(\tau \mid x_1, \ldots, x_p)\,d\tau = E\left(y \mid x_1, \ldots, x_p\right)$$

In other words, the $\hat{\beta}_j$s are the regression coefficients in a model for the conditional *expectation* of CloseRate. They are comparable to the parameter estimates for the general linear models for CloseRate in Output 5.7 on page 60 and in Output 5.16 on page 66. In practice, quantile process regression is not an efficient way to build a predictive model for a conditional expectation, and so the $\hat{\beta}_j$s in Output 8.14 have limited use.

On the other hand, the level-specific estimates $\hat{\beta}_j(\tau_u)$ yield valuable information about the conditional distribution of a response variable. Features for obtaining such results are not available in the QUANTSELECT procedure, but they are available in the QUANTREG procedure.

For instance, you can create quantile process plots for the effects in Output 8.13 with the PLOT=QUANTPLOT option in the QUANTREG procedure (see page 142). This requires that you refit the final selected quantile process model by specifying its effects in the MODEL statement for the QUANTREG procedure.

To facilitate model reuse, the QUANTSELECT procedure creates macro variables that save the names of the effects in selected models (Intercept is not saved). When you specify a list of levels with the QUANTLEV= option, the procedure creates macro variables named _QRSINDT1, _QRSINDT2, and so on. When you specify QUANTLEV=PROCESS, the procedure creates a single macro variable named _QRSIND. Ordinarily, you could refit the quantile process model as follows:

```
proc quantreg data=Stores ci=resampling;
   class Region(param=reference ref='Midwest' split)
         Training(param=reference ref='None');
   model CloseRate = &_QRSIND / quantlev=process plot=quantplot;
run;
```

However, the CLASS statement for the QUANTREG procedure does not currently support the parameterization options in the CLASS statement for the QUANTSELECT procedure on page 150. You can circumvent this limitation by replacing Stores with the design matrix that was created with the OUTDESIGN= option and saved in StoresDesign.

```
proc quantreg data=StoresDesign ci=resampling;
   model CloseRate = &_QRSIND / quantlev=process plot=quantplot;
run;
```

This works because the design matrix represents the classification effects with numeric columns that are coded as specified by the CLASS statement in the QUANTSELECT procedure. The QUANTREG procedure produces four panels of quantile process plots that display the parameter estimates for the effects. The panel in Output 8.15 shows that P3 and P1 positively affect the lower tail of the distribution of CloseRate, while L3 and L6 positively affect the upper tail. The confidence limits are not adjusted for the selection process and should not be interpreted as significance tests.

Output 8.15 Quantile Process Plots (Panel 3)

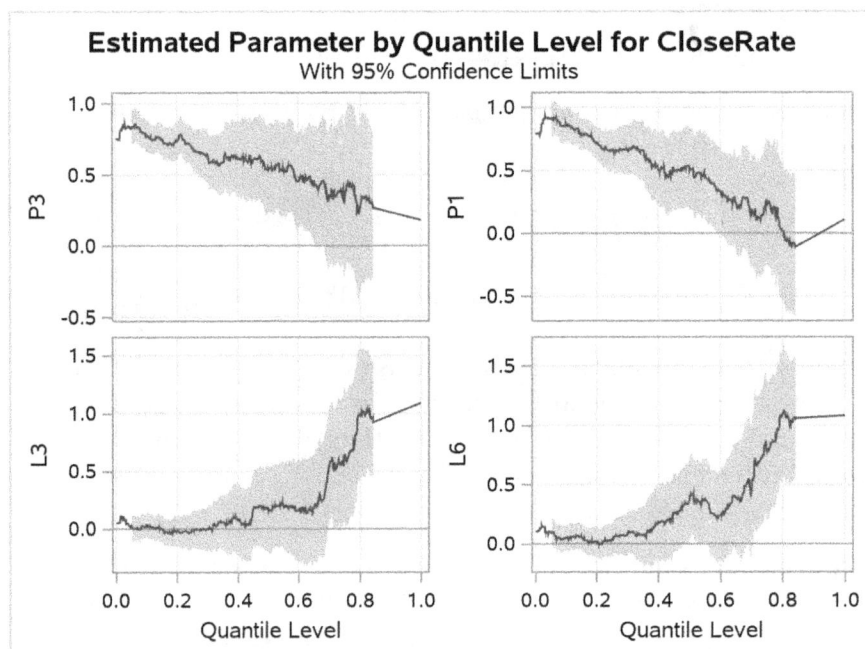

Example: Ranking Store Performance with Conditional Distributions

This example uses the quantile process model that was obtained with the QUANTSELECT procedure on page 150 to estimate conditional distributions of CloseRate and rank the performance of stores.

Until now, quantile process regression has been presented as a method of modeling the complete set of conditional quantiles of a response y:

$$Q_y(\tau \mid x_1, \ldots, x_p) = \beta_0(\tau) + \beta_1(\tau)x_1 + \cdots + \beta_p(\tau)x_p, \quad 0 < \tau < 1$$

Quantile process regression is also a method of modeling the complete set of conditional distribution functions of y. For any random variable Y with a continuous distribution, the cumulative distribution function $F(y) = \Pr[Y \leq y]$ and the quantile function $Q(\tau)$ are inverses of each other:

$$Q(\tau) = F^{-1}(\tau) = \min\{y : F(y) \geq \tau\}, \quad 0 < \tau < 1$$
$$F(y) = Q^{-1}(y) = \min\{\tau : Q(\tau) \geq y\}, \quad ; \ -\infty < y < \infty$$

Similarly, by inverting the conditional quantile process model for a response variable, you can obtain a model for its conditional distribution function:

$$\Pr[Y \leq y \mid x_1, \ldots, x_p] = F(y \mid x_1, \ldots, x_p) = Q_y^{-1}(\tau \mid x_1, \ldots, x_p) = \tau$$

The two models are summarized in Table 8.6. The key to understanding their relationship is that a quantile level τ can be interpreted as a cumulative probability.

Table 8.6 Comparison of Models for Conditional Quantiles and Conditional Distributions

Model	Predictors	Input Parameter	Response
Conditional quantile	$x_1, \ldots, x_p$	Level τ (probability)	Quantile (y)
Conditional distribution	$x_1, \ldots, x_p$	y (quantile)	Probability (τ)

Conditional distribution models have many potential applications because they provide complete information about a response. One such application is ranking subjects—such as stores, customers, or patients—by their predicted quantile levels.

For instance, consider the two stores whose observations numbers are 126 and 142 in the partition of Stores that was used to train the quantile process model. You could compare their close rates by where they fall in the sample (marginal) distribution for all stores. This would not take into account the effects of the quantile process model; see Output 8.13. It is more informative to base the comparison on the two conditional distributions that the model predicts for stores with the same effect profiles as Stores 126 and 142.

You can use the QUANTREG procedure to compute and plot these distributions, as illustrated by the following statements that refit the quantile process model:

```
proc quantreg data=StoresDesign(where=(_ROLE_='TRAIN'));
   model CloseRate = &_QRSIND / quantlev=fqpr;
   conddist obs=126 142 plot=cdfplot;
run;
```

The CONDDIST statement inverts the model and computes the predicted conditional distributions of CloseRate given the values of the effect variables in observations 126 and 142. The PLOT= option requests plots of these distributions.

Interpreting the Results

Output 8.16 shows the distributions (labeled *126* and *142*) together with the marginal distribution (labeled *TrainObs*).

Output 8.16 Conditional and Marginal Distributions of CloseRate

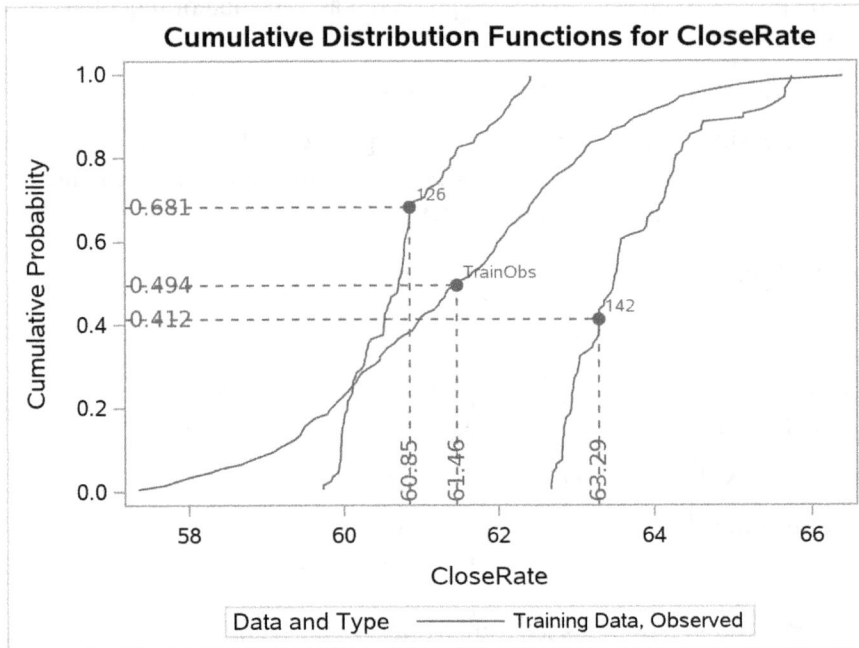

The three distributions differ in location, scale, and shape.

Output 8.17 lists the quantile levels of the two stores based on the three distributions.

Output 8.17 Conditional and Marginal Quantile Levels for Selected Stores

The QUANTREG Procedure
Conditional Distribution Analysis 1

Conditional Distribution Estimates

Data	Type	Label	Response Value	Quantile Level Regression	Sample
Training	Observed	TrainObs	61.46157	0.4936	0.4936
Training	Fit for Obs	126	60.85211	0.6814	0.3805
Training	Fit for Obs	142	63.29210	0.4123	0.8411

Store 142 has a higher close rate (63.3) than that of Store 126 (60.9). Compared with all the stores, Store 142 is at the 84th percentile, while Store 126 is only at the 38th percentile. A very different conclusion emerges if the comparison is based on the conditional distributions: Store 142 is only at the 41st percentile, while Store 126 is at the 68th percentile.

Note that if you only need the observation quantile levels, you can use the QUANTSELECT procedure to compute and save them in a data set specified with an OUTPUT statement, as illustrated on page 150.

Introduction to the QTRSELECT Procedure

The QTRSELECT procedure fits and builds quantile regression models in SAS Viya. It provides functionality comparable to that of the QUANTREG and QUANTSELECT procedures in SAS/STAT. Because the QTRSELECT procedure was developed specifically for SAS Viya, it can run on a cluster of machines that distribute the data and the computations.

When you use the QTRSELECT procedure, you specify models with MODEL, CLASS, and EFFECTS statements, which are similar to those of the QUANTSELECT procedure. You request data partitioning with the PARTITION statement, which is similar to that of the QUANTSELECT procedure. Nonetheless, there are some differences in the QTRSELECT procedure:

- You request model selection and selection methods with the SELECTION statement in the QTRSELECT procedure. The QUANTSELECT procedure does not have a SELECTION statement; instead, with that procedure you request model selection and selection methods with the MODEL statement.

- The selection methods available in the QTRSELECT procedure do not include the lasso, which is available in the QUANTSELECT procedure.

- Tables of parameter estimates produced by the QTRSELECT procedure display *p*-values (see Output 8.18). These *p*-values are valid when you fit a model with a fully specified set of effects, but you should disregard them when you build a model from candidate effects, because they are not adjusted for the selection process.

- The QTRSELECT procedure does not currently support quantile process regression, which is available in the QUANTREG and QUANTSELECT procedures.

- The STB option requests standardized regression coefficients, which are not available in the QUANTREG and QUANTSELECT procedures.

- The DISPLAY statement replaces the ODS SELECT statement for specifying displayed output. The DISPLAYOUT statement, which creates CAS tables from displayed output, provides functionality comparable to that of the ODS OUTPUT statement.

- The STORE statement saves results that you can process with the ASTORE procedure. For instance, with the SCORE statement in the ASTORE procedure, you can score observations with models built by the QTRSELECT procedure.

Table 8.7 summarizes the methods you can request with the SELECTION statement.

Table 8.7 Effect Selection Methods in the QTRSELECT Procedure

Method	Description	METHOD=*keyword*
Forward selection	Starts with the intercept and adds effects	FORWARD
Backward elimination	Starts with the full model and deletes effects	BACKWARD
Stepwise selection	Starts with the intercept; effects are added and can be deleted	STEPWISE
No selection	Fits fully specified model	NONE

Example: Building Quantile Regression Models for Close Rate

The example on page 146 used the QUANTSELECT procedure to build quantile regression models for close rates at the levels 0.1 and 0.9:

```
proc quantselect data=Stores plots=(Coefficients Criteria) seed=219531;
   class Region(param=reference ref='Midwest' split)
         Training(param=reference ref='None');
   model CloseRate = Region Training X1-X20 L1-L6 P1-P6 / quantlev=0.1 0.9
      selection=forward(choose=sbc select=sbc stop=validate stophorizon=3);
   partition fraction(validate=0.3);
run;
```

This example illustrates how to build these models using the QTRSELECT procedure.

To run a procedure in SAS Viya, you must create a CAS (Cloud Analytic Services) session, and your data must be in a CAS table that is accessible in your session. Here it is assumed that a CAS engine libref named mycas has been set up and that the data in Stores have been loaded into a CAS table named Stores.

The following statements use the QTRSELECT procedure to build the models:

```
proc qtrselect data=mycas.Stores;
   class Region(param=reference ref='Midwest' split)
         Training(param=reference ref='None');
   model CloseRate = Region Training X1-X20 L1-L6 P1-P6 / quantiles=0.1 0.9;
    selection method=forward(choose=sbc select=sbc stop=validate)
            stophorizon=3 plots=(Coefficients Criteria) ;
   partition fraction(validate=0.3  seed=219531 );
run;
```

There are several differences between the statements for the two procedures:

- In the QTRSELECT procedure, the selection method is specified with the SELECTION statement. In the QUANTSELECT procedure, the selection method is specified with the SELECTION= option in the MODEL statement.

- The PLOTS= option in the QTRSELECT procedure is in the SELECTION statement rather than the procedure statement.

- The SEED= option is in the PARTITION statement rather than the procedure statement.

Interpreting the Results

The QTRSELECT procedure produces tables and graphs much like those produced by the QUANTSELECT procedure in the example on page 146. However, there are some quantitative differences in these results even though the selection criteria and random seeds are identical.

For instance, the parameter estimates shown in Output 8.18, which the QTRSELECT procedure computes for quantile level 0.1, are slightly different from those shown in Output 8.9, which the QUANTSELECT procedure computed.

Output 8.18 Parameter Estimates for Selected Model for Quantile Level 0.1

The QTRSELECT Procedure

Quantile Level = 0.1
Selected Model

		Parameter Estimates			
Parameter	DF	Estimate	Standard Error	t Value	Pr > |t|
Intercept	1	60.00478	0.01575	3809.19	<.0001
Region_South	1	0.83484	0.01753	47.61	<.0001
X2	1	3.92508	0.02482	158.14	<.0001
X4	1	-3.11484	0.02035	-153.05	<.0001
L1	1	0.14161	0.03277	4.32	<.0001
P1	1	0.82497	0.03267	25.25	<.0001
P2	1	0.85602	0.02664	32.13	<.0001
P3	1	0.82066	0.03125	26.27	<.0001
P4	1	0.13512	0.04050	3.34	0.0009
P5	1	0.38974	0.04722	8.25	<.0001

These differences occur because the QTRSELECT procedure was developed to take advantage of the distributed environment that SAS Viya provides, and so it does not handle random partitioning in exactly the same way as the QUANTSELECT procedure.

Summary

Quantile regression is highly versatile because it uses a general linear model for the conditional quantiles of a response without assuming that the response has a parametric distribution or a constant variance. By comparison, OLS regression is computationally less expensive, but it only models the conditional mean and assumes a constant variance.

Quantile regression yields valuable insights in applications where answers to important questions lie in modeling the tails of the conditional distribution. Such insights would otherwise be difficult to obtain with OLS regression.

Although quantile regression is most often used to model specific conditional quantiles of the response, it can also predict the quantile levels of observations while adjusting for the effects of covariates. This provides a way to rank the performance of entities while taking into account their individual characteristics.

With sufficiently rich data, quantile process regression estimates the entire set of conditional distributions of the response, allowing the shapes of the distributions to depend on the predictors. Quantile process plots reveal the effects of predictors on different parts of the response distribution.

When quantile regression was introduced in 1978, model fitting with more than a few hundred observations and a dozen variables was not practical and model selection was out of the question. Today, the optimization techniques and computational power of the QUANTSELECT procedure make it possible to build models with hundreds of thousands of observations and hundreds of variables. By distributing the data and the computations, the QTRSELECT procedure makes it possible to build models with even larger data.

Chapter 9
Building Logistic Regression Models

Contents

This chapter introduces two procedures for building logistic regression models: the HPLOGISTIC procedure in SAS 9 and its newer counterpart in SAS Viya, the LOGSELECT procedure.

In statistical analysis, logistic regression is used to model the association between a categorical response variable and a set of explanatory variables; it is also used to predict the probabilities of the levels of the response variable. If the response variable has two levels, which is often the case, it is referred to as a binary or dichotomous response. The level of interest is called the event, and its complement is called the nonevent. Some examples of events are hospitalization due to COVID-19, payment of a mortgage, or a fraudulent transaction. Binary logistic regression models the probability of the event with a Bernoulli distribution.

In supervised learning, logistic regression is viewed as a method for classification along with methods such as support vector machines, trees, random forests, and neural networks. In classification problems, the response variable has a finite number of levels, and the goal is to find a rule that correctly assigns levels to future observations. Binary logistic regression is applied to classification by specifying a cutoff for the predicted probability of the event.

The HPLOGISTIC and LOGSELECT procedures build three types of binary logistic regression models: logit models, probit models, and complementary log-log models. These procedures also build logistic regression models for polytomous response variables, which have more than two levels. If the levels are ordered, the procedures build cumulative logit models, which generalize binary logit models. If the levels are unordered, the procedures build generalized logit models. In both cases, a multinomial distribution is assumed for the probabilities of the levels.

Training a logistic regression model is computationally more expensive than training a general linear model because it involves maximum likelihood estimation of the regression parameters, which requires multiple passes through the data. Building a logistic regression model is even more expensive because the parameters must be estimated multiple times at each step of the process, and the cost increases even further with the size of the data. The HPLOGISTIC and LOGSELECT procedures provide the performance needed for model building by running algorithms in parallel.

This chapter illustrates the capabilities of the procedures with two examples that involve large data. In the first example, the data are short and wide; the number of predictors p is much larger than the number of observations n. In the second, the data are tall and narrow; n is much larger than p.

Comparison of Procedures for Logistic Regression

The LOGISTIC procedure is the primary procedure in SAS for fitting logistic regression models with specified effects. Along with parameter estimates, p-values, and model fit statistics, it provides postfit statistical analysis, such as estimates of contrasts in the model parameters and tests of hypotheses. The LOGISTIC procedure also provides several sequential methods for model selection, but these are not recommended for reasons that are discussed in "Problems with Data-Driven Model Selection" on page 33. And because the procedure is single-threaded, its performance does not scale well with large data.

In contrast, the HPLOGISTIC and LOGSELECT procedures are designed for building predictive models from massive amounts of observational data, such as data with tens of thousands of predictors and millions of observations. These procedures provide the following advantages:

- The ability to define candidate effects with MODEL and CLASS statements that are similar to those in the LOGISTIC procedure.

- The ability to specify regression spline effects, polynomial effects, and other constructed effects in the set of candidate effects. In the LOGSELECT procedure, this is done with the EFFECT statement, which is also available in the LOGISTIC procedure.

- Model building with sequential selection methods and the lasso method, which is available in the LOGSELECT procedure. Although the lasso method is not provided by the HPLOGISTIC procedure, it is provided for logistic regression by the HPGENSELECT procedure; see Chapter 10.

- Model selection with information criteria (AIC, AICC, and SBC) that help to avoid overfitting by penalizing model complexity. This approach is discussed in "Criteria Based on Information Theory" on page 28.

- Model selection based on partitioning the data into training and validation sets. This approach is discussed in "External Validation Method for Estimating Prediction Error" on page 30.

- The ability to specify prior event probabilities for the purpose of computing posterior predicted event probabilities. When you know what percentage of the population has a rare event and you oversample that event, specifying event prevalences in the population as prior probabilities gives posterior probabilities that also reflect the population.

- Multithreaded computation, which results in much faster performance compared with model selection using the LOGISTIC procedure. The LOGSELECT procedure can also perform computations with data distributed across multiple computers in a cloud environment.

- A choice of optimization techniques for computing maximum likelihood estimates of the regression parameters. This is useful because no one technique works equally well in every problem. See "Computational Algorithms" on page 327 of Appendix D.

Programming Tip: When your goal is prediction, take advantage of the improved model building capability in the HPLOGISTIC and LOGSELECT procedures. When your goal is inference, use the LOGISTIC procedure.

Basic Concepts of Binary Logistic Regression

Binary logistic regression is the most common form of logistic regression.[†] It assumes a Bernoulli distribution for a response with two levels in which the probability of the event of interest depends on the values of the predictors for each observation.

For instance, consider a hospital patient database in which the response y is assigned the value 1 in the event that a patient is diagnosed with asthma, and the value 0 otherwise. The probability of the event for the ith patient is denoted by

$$\pi_i \equiv \Pr[y_i = 1 \mid \mathbf{x_1} = x_{i1}, \ldots, \mathbf{x_p} = x_{ip}], \quad i = 1, \ldots, n$$

where $\mathbf{x}_1, \ldots, \mathbf{x}_p$ are p predictors that provide demographic, geographic, and medical information about the patient. Of course, the observed values of y are 0's and 1's rather than probabilities.

The form of the linear logistic regression model for π_i is

$$\text{logit}(\pi_i) \equiv \log\left(\frac{\pi_i}{1 - \pi_i}\right) = \beta_0 + \beta_1 x_{i1} + \cdots + \beta_p x_{ip} = \mathbf{x}_{[i]}\boldsymbol{\beta}, \quad i = 1, \ldots, n$$

where $\boldsymbol{\beta} = (\beta_0, \beta_1, \ldots, \beta_p)'$ is the vector of regression parameters, $\mathbf{x}_{[i]} = [1 \; x_{i1} \; \ldots \; x_{ip}]$ is the ith row of the model matrix $\mathbf{X}$, and $\mathbf{x}_{[i]}\boldsymbol{\beta}$ is referred to as the linear predictor.

By inverting the logit transformation, π_i can be expressed as the logistic function of the linear predictor:

$$\pi_i = \frac{\exp(\mathbf{x}_{[i]}\boldsymbol{\beta})}{1 + \exp(\mathbf{x}_{[i]}\boldsymbol{\beta})}, \quad i = 1, \ldots, n$$

Although the linear predictor is not bounded, π_i must be between 0 and 1.

The logit transformation is referred to as a link function because it connects the mean of the response distribution ($E(y_i) = \Pr(y_i = 1) = \pi_i$) with the linear predictor. Link functions, together with response distributions and linear predictors, are the defining elements of generalized linear models, which are discussed in Chapter 10. Linear logistic regression is a particular type of generalized linear model.

Binary logistic regression models can be formulated with other link functions such as the probit function $\Phi^{-1}(\pi_i)$ and the complementary log-log function $\log(-\log(1 - \pi_i))$. The logit link is usually preferred because the model can then be expressed in terms of the odds of the event:

$$\text{odds} \equiv \frac{\pi_i}{1 - \pi_i} = \exp(\mathbf{x}_{[i]}\boldsymbol{\beta}) = \exp(\beta_0)\exp(\beta_1)^{x_{i1}} \cdots \exp(\beta_p)^{x_{ip}}$$

[†]Francois Pierre Verhulst introduced the logistic function between 1838 and 1847 as a mathematical model for population growth, and a century later, Joseph Berkson introduced this function in bioassay (Cramer 2002).
In 1958, David R. Cox, then at Birkbeck College, London, formulated an inferential approach to modeling binary data that laid the cornerstone for modern logistic regression and established the roles of the logistic function and the logit function. Many years later, Professor Cox recalled that this approach did not gain much attention until it was implemented in software (Reid 1994).

The odds of the event are always nonnegative; they are greater than 1 when the event is more likely than the complementary event (called the nonevent), and they are less than 1 when the event is less likely than the nonevent. For instance, if the probability of the event is 0.75, then the probability of the nonevent is 0.25, and the odds of the event are $0.75/0.25 = 3$. This means you can expect to see three events for every nonevent in observations that are independent of each other.

For a binary logistic regression model defined with the logit link function, the odds increase by $\exp(\beta_j)$ with a unit increase in x_{ij}, assuming the other predictors remain fixed. Equivalently, the log of the odds, called the log odds, increases by β_j with a unit increase in x_{ij}, assuming that all the other predictors remain fixed. These interpretations are helpful if your model is fully specified and your data come from a planned study, such as a randomized clinical trial, in which the predictors are controlled. However, these interpretations do not necessarily apply if you are working with observational data because the predictors might be highly correlated; see page 15.

Maximum Likelihood Estimation

Like the LOGISTIC procedure, the HPLOGISTIC and LOGSELECT procedures use the method of maximum likelihood to estimate the regression parameters.

For example, in a binary logistic regression model where the levels of the response variable are 0 and 1, the Bernoulli distribution of the response for the ith observation is

$$\Pr[y_i = k] = \pi_i^k (1 - \pi_i)^{1-k}, \quad k = 0, 1; \quad i = 1, \ldots, n$$

where π_i is a function of $\boldsymbol{\beta}$, as shown on page 161. Given this model, the probability of the observed data $\mathbf{y} = (y_1, \ldots, y_n)'$ as a function of $\boldsymbol{\beta}$ is the likelihood function:

$$L(\boldsymbol{\beta}; \mathbf{y}) = \prod_{i=1}^{n} \pi_i^{y_i} (1 - \pi_i)^{1-y_i} = \prod_{i=1}^{n} \left(\frac{\exp(\mathbf{x}_{[i]} \boldsymbol{\beta})}{1 + \exp(\mathbf{x}_{[i]} \boldsymbol{\beta})} \right)^{y_i} \left(\frac{1}{1 + \exp(\mathbf{x}_{[i]} \boldsymbol{\beta})} \right)^{1-y_i}$$

The likelihood function captures the uncertainty in the data by showing where $\boldsymbol{\beta}$ is most likely to fall in the parameter space. It is simpler to work with the log-likelihood function:

$$\mathcal{L}(\boldsymbol{\beta}; \mathbf{y}) \equiv \log L(\boldsymbol{\beta}; \mathbf{y}) = \sum_{i=1}^{n} y_i \mathbf{x}_{[i]} \boldsymbol{\beta} - \sum_{i=1}^{n} \log(1 + \exp(\mathbf{x}_{[i]} \boldsymbol{\beta}))$$

If the ith observation is weighted by a positive weight w_i and the weights are scaled so they sum to n, the log-likelihood function is written as

$$\mathcal{L}(\boldsymbol{\beta}; \mathbf{y}) = \sum_{i=1}^{n} w_i y_i \mathbf{x}_{[i]} \boldsymbol{\beta} - \sum_{i=1}^{n} w_i \log(1 + \exp(\mathbf{x}_{[i]} \boldsymbol{\beta}))$$

In general, the maximum likelihood estimator of $\boldsymbol{\beta}$ is $\hat{\boldsymbol{\beta}}_{\mathrm{MLE}} = \underset{\boldsymbol{\beta}}{\operatorname{argmax}} \{\mathcal{L}(\boldsymbol{\beta}; \mathbf{y})\}$.

Unlike the estimator for least squares regression, $\hat{\boldsymbol{\beta}}_{\mathrm{MLE}}$ cannot be expressed in a closed form. The procedures compute $\hat{\boldsymbol{\beta}}_{\mathrm{MLE}}$ using iterative algorithms that require multiple passes through the data. Because these algorithms are computationally expensive, the scalability of the procedures is essential when you build models with large data.

Appendix D explains the algorithms and two data patterns, called complete separation and quasi-separation, for which the maximum likelihood estimate does not exist.

Introduction to the HPLOGISTIC Procedure

The HPLOGISTIC procedure is the recommended procedure in SAS/STAT for fitting and building logistic regression models with large data when the goal is prediction or exploration.

What Does the *HP* Stand For?

The prefix *HP* stands for high performance. It appears in the names of analytical procedures in SAS 9 that were engineered to run either on the server where SAS is installed or in distributed mode on a cluster of computers. The distributed mode of the HP procedures has been superseded by the distributed capability of newer procedures in SAS Viya. Nonetheless, the HP procedures continue to be available in single-server mode. They provide excellent computational performance because they are multithreaded and exploit all the cores available (Cohen and Rodriguez 2013).

High-performance statistical procedures are included with SAS/STAT and are documented in *SAS/STAT 15.1 User's Guide*. A subset of these procedures are designed for building accurate predictive models with large data; they are *not* intended to provide all the methods for inferential analysis that are available in traditional SAS/STAT procedures.

In addition to the HPLOGISTIC procedure, this book discusses the following high-performance procedures:

- The HPGENSELECT procedure for building generalized linear models; see Chapter 10.

- The GAMPL procedure for fitting generalized additive models; see Chapter 11. The GAMPL procedure was named HPGAMPL during development, but the prefix *HP* was then dropped.

- The HPSPLIT procedure for building classification and regression trees; see Chapter 13.

Three other high-performance procedures, HPPLS, HPQUANTSELECT, and HPREG, are not discussed in this book. They correspond to the PLS, QUANTSELECT, and GLMSELECT procedures in SAS/STAT, respectively, but because the latter have more capabilities they are presented instead. The high-performance procedures operate like other SAS procedures, except that they require an XML stream for user-defined formats; see page 176.

Specifying the Candidate Effects

When you use the HPLOGISTIC procedure to build a model, you specify the candidate effects with the MODEL and CLASS statements. As with other modeling procedures, the CLASS statement lists variables that should be treated as categorical (the response variable does not need to be included). You specify the method of selection with the SELECTION statement.

For instance, the following statements (taken from a later example on page 174) request forward selection with the information criterion SBC:

```
proc hplogistic data=Hospitals;
   class Region Sex RaceCategory DischargeStatus;
   model Asthma(event='Yes') = Region Age Sex RaceCategory DischargeStatus
                               DaysOfCare NumberBeds / link=logit;
   selection method=forward(choose=sbc select=sbc stop=sbc);
run;
```

The procedure fits all of the effects in the MODEL statement if you specify METHOD=NONE or if you omit the SELECTION statement.

The LINK= option specifies the link function. The logit link is commonly used with binary logistic regression, and it is the default in that situation.

The EVENT= option specifies the event category (the level you are interested in modeling) for a binary response variable. If you do not provide the EVENT= option, the default event category is the first ordered category of the response. If, for instance, the levels of the response are 0 and 1, the default event category is 0. This is not what you might expect in applications where the event of interest is indicated by a value of 1. To avoid confusion, make it a practice to specify the event.

Programming Tip: Use the EVENT= option to designate the response category that is modeled.

Selection Methods

Table 9.1 summarizes the methods available with the METHOD= option in the SELECTION statement.

Table 9.1 Selection Methods in the HPLOGISTIC Procedure

Method	Description	METHOD=*keyword*
Forward selection	Starts with no effects in the model and adds effects	FORWARD
Backward elimination	Starts with all effects in the model and deletes effects	BACKWARD
Fast backward elimination	Starts with all effects in the model and deletes effects without refitting the model; applies with SELECT=SL	BACKWARD(FAST)
Stepwise selection	Starts with no effects in the model and adds effects; effects already in the model do not necessarily stay	STEPWISE
No selection	Fits fully specified model	NONE

Controlling the Methods of Selection

The HPLOGISTIC procedure provides three ways to control the operation of the methods in Table 9.1, which you specify with suboptions in parentheses after the METHOD= option:

- CHOOSE= specifies the criterion for choosing the model. This criterion is evaluated at each step of the selection process. The final selected model is the model with the best value of this criterion.

- SELECT= specifies the criterion for determining which effect enters or leaves at each step. This is the effect that gives the maximum improvement in the specified criterion.

- STOP= specifies the criterion for terminating the selection process. This suboption is ignored if you use the MAXSTEPS=k suboption to specify the maximum number of steps. The STOPHORIZON=k option in the SELECTION statement specifies the number of consecutive steps at which the criterion must worsen to detect a local minimum; the default is three steps.

Table 9.2 lists the criteria you can request with these suboptions.

Table 9.2   Criteria for Controlling Selection

Criterion	Suboption *keyword*
Akaike's information criterion (AIC)	AIC
Corrected Akaike's information criterion (AICC)	AICC
Schwarz Bayesian information criterion (SBC or BIC)	SBC
Significance level of score test	SL (not a CHOOSE= suboption)
Average square error for validation data (ASE)	VALIDATE (not a SELECT= suboption)

The information criteria are computed by an approximation that is computationally efficient, as explained on page 332 of Appendix D.

For consistency with the LOGISTIC procedure, the default criterion for all three suboptions is the significance level of an approximate chi-square test statistic. You can specify the levels for an effect to enter or stay with the SLENTRY= and SLSTAY= suboptions for the METHOD= option. This criterion is not recommended; see "Problems with Data-Driven Model Selection" on page 33.

The preferred approach for building a model that generalizes well to future data is to find a set of effects that minimizes prediction error when applied to validation or test data that the training process has not encountered. For instance, if you specify CHOOSE=VALIDATE, the HPLOGISTIC procedure computes the average square error (ASE) from the validation data at each step, and it selects the model at the first step where ASE_{val} is minimized. You use the PARTITION statement to allocate part of the DATA= data set for validation. Training error is not a reliable estimate of prediction error, as explained on page 25. When there are not enough data for independent validation, consider using an information criterion; see page 28.

No one combination of selection methods and criteria is uniformly the most effective. To learn how different methods perform, try various alternatives with your data. Performance varies depending on the size and shape of the data, the signal-to-noise ratios of effects, and issues such as missingness and collinearity. The problem of separation (see page 162) tends to occur with a large number of candidates, and backward elimination will sometimes fail in that situation.

Link Functions

Table 9.3 summarizes the link functions available with the LINK= option in the MODEL statement.

Table 9.3   Link Functions in the HPLOGISTIC Procedure

LINK=*keyword*	**Link Function**	$g(\mu) = \eta =$
CLOGLOG | CLL	Complementary log-log	$\log(-\log(1-\mu))$
GLOGIT | GENLOGIT	Generalized logit	varies with number of levels
LOGIT	Logit	$\log(\mu/(1-\mu))$
LOGLOG	Log-log	$-\log(-\log(\mu))$
PROBIT	Probit	$\Phi^{-1}(\mu)$

Here μ denotes the mean of the response distribution, and $\Phi^{-1}(\cdot)$ denotes the quantile function of the standard normal distribution.

If the response variable has more than two categories, the HPLOGISTIC procedure fits a model with a cumulative link function based on the specified link. However, if you specify LINK=GLOGIT, the procedure assumes a generalized logit model for nominal (unordered) response categories, regardless of the number of categories.

Summarizing the Predictive Ability of Binary Logistic Regression

When you build a binary logistic regression model using the PARTITION statement, the HPLOGISTIC procedure cross-classifies the observations within each partition by the observed and classified values of the response y. Otherwise, the procedure cross-classifies the observations in the training data. If the predicted probability of the event for the ith observation ($\hat{\pi}_i$) exceeds a specified cutpoint z in $(0, 1)$, the observation is classified as 1; otherwise, it is classified as 0.

The matrix in Table 9.4 defines the number of observations for the four possible cross-classifications.

Table 9.4 Decision Matrix

Actual Response	**Classify as 1**	**Classify as 0**	**Total**
$y = 1$ (event)	n_{11} true positives	n_{10} false negatives	n_1
$y = 0$ (nonevent)	n_{01} false positives	n_{00} true negatives	n_0

The procedure summarizes the predictive ability of the model with statistics that are derived from this matrix. Sensitivity (n_{11}/n_1) is the proportion of event responses that are classified as events; specificity ($1 - n_{01}/n_0$) is the proportion of nonevent responses that are classified as nonevents. The correct classification rate is ($n_{11} + n_{00}$)/n, and the misclassification rate is $1 - (n_{11} + n_{00})/n$. The positive predictive value is $n_{11}/(n_{11} + n_{01})$, and the negative predictive value is $n_{00}/(n_{10} + n_{00})$.

The procedure computes the values for a receiver operating characteristic (ROC) curve by moving the cutpoint z from 0 to 1 and selecting those values where sensitivity and specificity change. A plot of the curve shows sensitivity as a function of $1 -$ specificity. The area under the curve (AUC) is identical to the concordance index c, which estimates the probability that the predictions and outcomes are concordant; this means that observations with larger values of y have larger values of $\hat{\pi}$ (Harrell et al. 1982).

Ideally, the value of AUC should be nearly 1; in practice, values over 0.75 might be acceptable depending on the context. On the other hand, a value exactly equal to 1 corresponds to the problem of separation, which is discussed on page 329.

In addition to c, the procedure provides three other association statistics that measure predictive power: Somers' D (Gini coefficient), Goodman-Kruskal gamma, and Kendall's tau-a.

The procedure also computes the average square error:

$$\text{ASE} = \frac{1}{n} \sum_{i=1}^{n} (y_i (1 - \hat{\pi}_i)^2 + (1 - y_i)\hat{\pi}_i^2)$$

This is also known as the Brier score for binary predictions; it is one of various loss functions used for binary classification. Lower scores (near 0) are preferable, but a low score does not necessarily indicate a good predictive model if the classes are highly imbalanced because the event rarely occurs.

Example: Simulated RNA Sequencing Data

RNA sequencing (RNA-Seq) technology reveals the quantity of RNA in a biological sample. This method directly sequences source material and quantifies gene expression. The genes in an RNA-Seq data set can number in the tens of thousands, but the number of samples is usually between 30 and 300 because of cost. The material is often sampled from two classes of cells that correspond to the presence or absence of a disease. The expression levels serve as candidate predictors for building binary logistic regression models used to classify new samples.

In a 2009 SAS Global Forum paper, Robert Cohen showed that a general linear model selected with the GLMSELECT procedure can produce a useful classifier for simulated data from microarrays (now replaced by RNA-Seq technology). General linear models do not meet the requirements of binary logistic regression (see page 161), but they can identify relevant predictors in a first pass.

This example revisits Cohen's simulation, replacing the GLMSELECT procedure with the HPLOGISTIC procedure, which was added to SAS/STAT in 2013.

Simulating the Data

The following program simulates training and test data sets named Train and Test, each with 5,000 candidate predictors, 10 actual predictors, and only 200 observations. Typically, far more observations are needed to find all the relevant predictors.

```
%let NTest  = 200;
%let NTrain = 200;
%let NVars  = 5000;

data Train Test;
   drop j LinPred;
   array x{&NVars};
   call streaminit(89995);
   do ObsNum=1 to &NTest + &NTrain;

      /* Assign predictors randomly */
      do j=1 to &nVars; x{j}=ranuni(1); end;

      /* Form linear predictor that depends on x1-x10 */
      LinPred = 11*x1 - 10*x2 + 9*x3 - 8*x4 + 7*x5 -6*x6 + 5*x7 - 4*x8
                + 3*x9 - 2*x10;

      /* Compute true probability, avoiding large arguments for exp */
      if LinPred < 1 then TrueProb1 = exp(LinPred) / (1.0 + exp(LinPred));
      else                TrueProb1 = 1.0 / (1.0 + exp(-LinPred));

      /* Assign response values of 0 or 1 based on true probability */
      y = ( TrueProb1 > rand("Uniform") );
      if ObsNum <= &nTrain then output Train; else output Test;
   end;
run;
```

The response variable y has two values, 0 and 1. The probability of the event $y = 1$ is saved in the variable TrueProb1. This probability is generated from an additive logistic regression model in which the true predictors are x1 through x10 in decreasing order of importance.

Classification Based on an Oracle Model

For subsequent use, the following statements define a macro that assigns the observations in a data set into two classes, 0 and 1, based on whether the predicted event probability is less than or greater than 0.5. The macro compares the assigned class with the response y and displays the percentages of observations that are classified correctly and incorrectly.

```
%macro Classify(Data, ClassVar, PredProb);
data &Data;
   length &ClassVar $9;
   set &Data;
   yClassified = ( &PredProb > 0.5 );
   if y = yClassified then &ClassVar = 'Correct'; else &ClassVar = 'Incorrect';
run;
proc freq data=&Data;
   table &ClassVar / nocum;
run;
%mend;
```

To provide a baseline for comparison with models that are built later in this example, the next statements fit an oracle model with the true predictors and assess the results with the macro:

```
proc hplogistic data=Train;
   model y(event='1') = x1-x10;
   output out=TrainOut(keep=y OracleModelPred1) copyvars=(y) p=OracleModelPred1;
   code file='ScoreStmts.sas';
run;

data TestOut(rename=(P_y1=OracleModelPred1) keep=y P_y1);
   set Test;
   %inc 'ScoreStmts.sas';
run;

%Classify(TrainOut, Train, OracleModelPred1)
%Classify(TestOut,  Test,  OracleModelPred1)
```

The OUTPUT statement saves the predicted probabilities of the event $y = 1$ for the training data as values of OracleModelPred1 in the data set TrainOut. The COPYVARS= option copies y from Train to TrainOut. The CODE statement generates DATA step code for scoring and saves it in *ScoreStmts.sas*. This code is then used to compute the predicted probabilities for the data in Test, which are saved as values of OracleModelPred1 in the data set TestOut.

Output 9.1 shows that the oracle model misclassifies 5.5% of the training data (which is too optimistic) and 12.5% of the test data (which is realistic). Of course, models selected from all 5,000 candidate predictors will have much higher percentages of misclassification.

Output 9.1 Training and Test Set Classification Percentages for Oracle Model

Train	Frequency	Percent
Correct	189	94.50
Incorrect	11	5.50

Test	Frequency	Percent
Correct	175	87.50
Incorrect	25	12.50

Classification Based on a Model Selected with the Stepwise Method and Validation

The following statements use the HPLOGISTIC procedure to select a model by using the stepwise method with validation as the choose criterion:

```
proc hplogistic data=Train;
   model y(event='1') = x1-x&NVars / association ctable=ROCValues;
   selection method=stepwise(choose=validate select=sbc stop=validate
                             maxsteps=20);
   output out=trainOut(keep=y ModelPred1) copyvars=(y) p=ModelPred1;
   partition fraction(validate=0.2 test=0.2 seed=15531);
   code file='ScoreStmts.sas'; ods output Association=AssocStat;
run;
```

The PARTITION statement randomly assigns the observations to training, validation, and testing roles in the proportions 0.6, 0.2, and 0.2, respectively. At each step, the procedure uses the SBC criterion to determine which predictor enters or leaves. The process stops when ASE computed from the validation data reaches a minimum based on a default stop horizon of three steps. The procedure chooses the model with the smallest validation ASE. Output 9.2 summarizes the steps.

Output 9.2 Effect Selection Summary

	Selection Summary			
Step	Effect Entered	Number Effects In	SBC	Validation ASE
0	Intercept	1	151.85	0.2423
1	x1	2	127.69	0.2397
2	x2	3	115.17	0.1996*
3	x3	4	102.34	0.2148
4	x4226	5	94.0292	0.2995
5	x5	6	81.3128*	0.2493

* Optimal Value of Criterion

The selected model contains the two strongest predictors (x1 and x2) and none of the noise variables; it is too sparse, but this is to be expected considering the dimensions of the data. Output 9.3 shows the fit statistics for the partitions. A default cutpoint of 0.5 is used to compute the misclassification error and the true negative and true positive fractions (see page 166).

Output 9.3 Fit Statistics

Partition Fit Statistics			
Statistic	Training	Validation	Testing
Area under the ROCC	0.8561	0.7754	0.8307
Average Square Error	0.1466	0.1996	0.1656
Hosmer-Lemeshow Test	0.9753	0.1328	0.6390
Misclassification Error	0.2232	0.3191	0.2683
R-Square	0.3416	0.1341	0.2715
Max-rescaled R-Square	0.4672	0.1811	0.3754
McFadden's R-Square	0.3181	0.1067	0.2467
Mean Difference	0.3693	0.2854	0.3649
Somers' D	0.7121	0.5508	0.6614
True Negative Fraction	0.6829	0.4737	0.7143
True Positive Fraction	0.8310	0.8214	0.7407

Output 9.4 shows the association statistics.

Output 9.4 Association Statistics

	Association Statistics			
Role	Concordance Index	Somers' D	Gamma	Tau-a
Training	0.856063	0.712126	0.712126	0.333494
Validation	0.775376	0.550752	0.551789	0.271045
Testing	0.830688	0.661376	0.661376	0.304878

The next statements use the SGPLOT procedure and the data set ROCValues, requested with the CTABLE= option, to produce the plot shown in Output 9.5. The data set AssocStat furnishes the area under the curve, which is displayed on the plot.

```
data _null_;
   set AssocStat(where=(role=3)); /* 3 corresponds to test */
   call symputx('AUC', put(C,5.3));
run;

proc sgplot data=ROCValues(where=(role=3)) aspect=1 noautolegend;
   lineparm x=0 y=0 slope=1 / lineattrs=(color=red);
   series x=FPF y=TPF;
   inset 'Area under curve=&AUC.' / position=bottomright;
   xaxis values=(0 to 1 by 0.25) grid offsetmin=.05 offsetmax=.05;
   yaxis values=(0 to 1 by 0.25) grid offsetmin=.05 offsetmax=.05;
run;
```

Output 9.5 Receiver Operating Characteristic Curve for Test Data

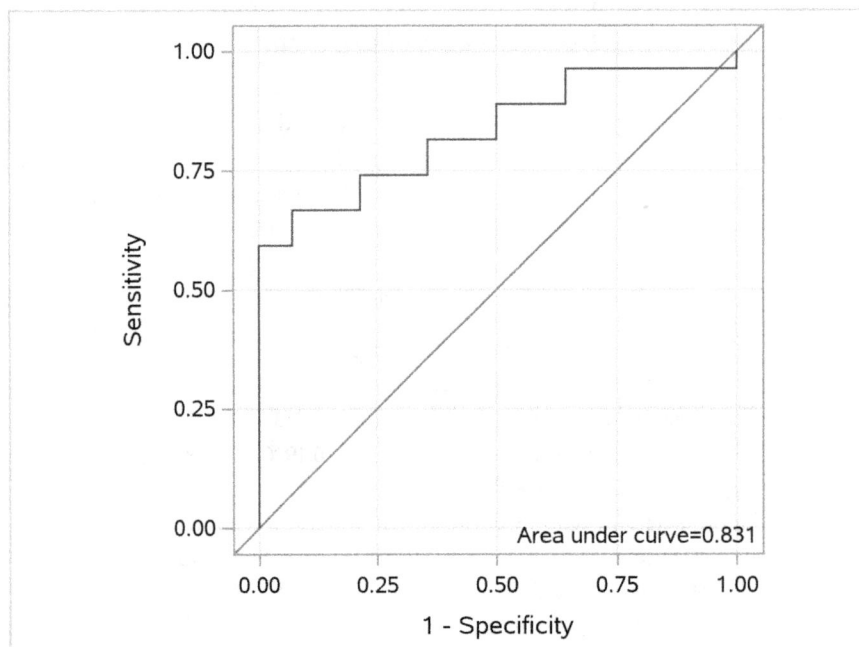

The AUC of 0.831 corresponds to the concordance index c in Output 9.4. A value of 0.5 would indicate that the model prediction is no better than a random guess.

The following statements use the `%Classify` macro and the data set Test to compute the misclassification error for the selected model, which is shown in Output 9.6.

```
data TestOut(rename=(P_y1=ModelPred1) keep=y P_y1);
   set Test;
   %inc 'ScoreStmts.sas';
run;
%Classify(TestOut, Test, ModelPred1)
```

Output 9.6 Test Set Classification Percentages for Selected Model

Test	Frequency	Percent
Correct	148	74.00
Incorrect	52	26.00

The percentage incorrectly classified (26.0%) agrees with the misclassification error (0.2683) shown in Output 9.3 for the test partition of the data in Train.

Classification Based on a Model Selected with the Stepwise Method and SBC

When the data are insufficient to hold out observations for validation and testing, you can use one of the information criteria listed in Table 9.2. The following statements select a model by using the stepwise method with SBC as the choose, select, and stop criteria:

```
ods output Association=AssocStat;
proc hplogistic data=Train;
   model y(event='1') = x1-x&NVars / association;
   selection method=stepwise(choose=sbc select=sbc stop=sbc maxsteps=20);
   code file='ScoreStmts.sas';
   performance details;
run;
```

As shown in Output 9.7, the selected model includes the five most relevant predictors and four noise variables. In contrast to the model selected in Output 9.2, this model is not sparse enough.

Output 9.7 Selected Effects

Selected Effects: Intercept x1 x2 x3 x4 x5 x300 x1487 x2075 x3605

The next statements use the model to score the observations in Test and classify the results:

```
data TestOut(rename=(P_y1=ModelPred1) keep=y P_y1);
   set Test;
   %inc 'ScoreStmts.sas';
run;
%Classify(TestOut, Test, ModelPred1)
```

Output 9.8 shows that the percentage of incorrectly classified observations is 24.5%.

Output 9.8 Test Set Classification Percentages for Selected Model

Test	Frequency	Percent
Correct	151	75.50
Incorrect	49	24.50

Bootstrap Assessment of Prediction Error

When test data are not available, you can assess the prediction error of a selected model with cross validation, which is described on page 31. Leave-one-out cross validation is nearly unbiased, but it can be variable. An alternative approach is the bootstrap, which is described in "Bootstrap Estimates of Prediction Error" on page 32.

Efron (1983) proposed several bootstrap estimators of prediction error. One of these is the optimism estimator, which is implemented for general linear models by the `%BootstrapPredError` macro in Chapter 5; see page 68. Another estimator is the .632 estimator:

$$\widehat{\mathrm{Err}}^{(.632)} = 0.368\,\overline{\mathrm{err}} + 0.632\,\widehat{\mathrm{Err}}^{(1)}$$

Here $\overline{\mathrm{err}}$ is the apparent error rate, also known as the resubstitution error rate, which is the misclassification error computed from the training data. This rate is biased downward from the true error rate, as explained on page 25. The quantity $\widehat{\mathrm{Err}}^{(1)}$ is the leave-one-out bootstrap estimate, which predicts the error at the ith observation only from bootstrap samples that do not contain that observation. The leave-one-out bootstrap is a smoothed version of leave-one-out cross validation (LOOCV); it reduces the variance of LOOCV by averaging.

The .632 estimator is intended to balance the downward bias of the apparent error rate with the upward bias of the leave-one-out bootstrap estimate. The weights 0.368 and 0.632 were chosen because approximately 63.2% of the n observations in the data are represented in a bootstrap sample.

The .632 estimator can be biased downward with classification rules such as nearest neighbors for which $\overline{\mathrm{err}} = 0$. For this reason, Efron and Tibshirani (1997) introduced a refinement called the .632+ estimator:

$$\widehat{\mathrm{Err}}^{(.632+)} = (1 - \hat{\omega})\,\overline{\mathrm{err}} + \hat{\omega}\,\widehat{\mathrm{Err}}^{(1)}$$

where

$$\hat{\omega} = \frac{0.632}{1 - 0.368\hat{R}}$$

$$\hat{R} = \frac{\widehat{\mathrm{Err}}^{(1)} - \overline{\mathrm{err}}}{\hat{\gamma} - \overline{\mathrm{err}}}$$

$$\hat{\gamma} = \hat{p}_1(1 - \hat{q}_1) + (1 - \hat{p}_1)\hat{q}_1$$

$\hat{p}_1$ = proportion of responses equal to 1

$\hat{q}_1$ = proportion of predictions equal to 1

You can compute the .632 and .632+ estimators with the `%Bootstrap632Plus` macro, which is available on the book website. The macro assumes, as in Efron and Tibshirani (1997, p. 549), that the response variable y takes two values, 0 and 1, and it assigns a discrepancy of 1 to an observation if the actual and classified values of y do not match.

The following statement requests .632 and .632+ bootstrap estimates of the prediction error for the model selected in the previous section:

```
%Bootstrap632Plus(Data=Train, Response=y, Event='1', Predictors=x1-x&NVars,
                  Method=stepwise(criterion=sbc choose=sbc stop=sbc
                                  maxsteps=20),
                  Cutoff=0.5, NReplicates=50, Seed=65589,
                  Showtable=1, Out=Results)
```

The first five parameters duplicate the specification of the stepwise method in the HPLOGISTIC procedure statements on page 171. The cutoff probability is 0.5, which means that responses in the training data and bootstrap samples are assigned a value of 1 if the predicted probability is greater than or equal to 0.5. The number of bootstrap samples is 50. Output 9.9 shows the results.

Output 9.9 Bootstrap Estimates of Prediction Error Rates

Estimates of Error Rate for Prediction of y(event='1')

Samples	Cutoff	Proportion of Responses Equal to Event Level	Proportion of Predictions Equal to Event Level	Apparent Error Rate	Leave-one-out Bootstrap Rate	.632 Rule Error Rate	.632+ Rule Error Rate
50	0.5	0.63	0.625	0.075	0.31491	0.22662	0.27063

The apparent error rate is much smaller than the .632 and .632+ estimates, which are consistent with the incorrect classification percentage in Output 9.8. The leave-one-out bootstrap rate is larger than both estimates.

The macro invokes the HPLOGISTIC procedure once to select the model from the training data and once to select a model from each bootstrap sample and score the training data. The second invocation processes the samples as BY groups. As discussed on page 70, BY processing avoids rerunning the procedure for each sample, which would be very inefficient.

Output 9.10 shows a breakdown of the time used by the second invocation of the HPLOGISTIC procedure. Most of it was spent evaluating candidate models.

Output 9.10 Timing Results for HPLOGISTIC Procedure

Procedure Task Timing		
Task	Seconds	Percent
Data Read and Variable Levelization	4.44	0.37%
Effect Levelization	0.65	0.05%
Candidate Evaluation	1074.41	90.47%
Candidate Model Fit	104.66	8.81%
Full Model Fit	2.38	0.20%
Computation of Summary Table	0.54	0.05%
Computation of Scores	0.54	0.05%

In total, the macro took 20 minutes to run on the author's computer. That is reasonable considering that the selection process—which is computationally intensive to begin with—was repeated for each of the 50 bootstrap samples.

In general, the high performance of the HPLOGISTIC procedure makes it feasible to assess prediction error with the bootstrap in model-building applications where it might otherwise be out of reach due to the dimensions of the data.

Programming Tip: Use the `%Bootstrap632Plus` macro to estimate and compare the prediction errors of models built with the HPLOGISTIC procedure.

Customizing the %Bootstrap632Plus Macro

As noted earlier, the `%Bootstrap632Plus` macro applies the same penalty to false positive classifications and false negative classifications. If this is not appropriate for your work, you can modify the code for the macro by assigning different penalties to the internal variable Discrepancy. The assignment must be done in two places.

If you are using SAS Viya, you can modify the macro for use in a SAS client session by replacing the HPLOGISTIC procedure with the LOGSELECT procedure, which is introduced on page 183. This enables the computations to be distributed.

Writing Your Own Bootstrap Programs

In order to apply the bootstrap in your work, you might find it necessary to write a customized program. A paper presented by Isaiah Lankham and Matthew Slaughter at SAS Global Forum 2021 provides a helpful and highly detailed explanation of SAS programming techniques for efficient bootstrap implementation (Lankham and Slaughter 2021). The paper illustrates these techniques by implementing the bootstrap estimate of optimism for concordance in binary logistic regression.

Example: Hospital Discharge Data

This example illustrates the use of the HPLOGISTIC procedure to build a binary logistic regression model for data that are large and tall ($p << n$).

The example uses a data set named Hospitals that is a subset of data collected by the National Center for Health Statistics in three National Hospital Discharge Surveys (NHDS), conducted in 2008, 2009, and 2010. The NHDS data were intended for analysis of hospital utilization in the United States. There are 308,243 observations in Hospitals, each of which represents a patient. The variables are listed in Table 9.5.

Table 9.5 Variables in Data Set Hospitals

Variable	Description	Type
AdmissionSource	Source of admission	Categorical (9 levels)
AdmissionType	Type of admission	Categorical (5 levels)
Age	Age	Continuous (≥ 18)
Asthma	Asthma diagnosis (event)	Categorical (2 levels)
DaysOfCare	Days of care	Continuous
DischargeStatus	Discharge status	Categorical (7 levels)
HospitalOwner	Hospital ownership	Categorical (3 levels)
MaritalStatus	Marital status	Categorical (6 levels)
NHDSWeight	Sampling weight	Continuous
NumberBeds	Number of beds	Categorical (5 levels)
PriPaySource	Principal expected source of payment	Categorical (11 levels)
RaceCategory	Race category	Categorical (4 levels)
Region	Geographic region	Categorical (5 levels)
Sex	Sex	Categorical (2 levels)

The data in Hospitals were the focus of a case study presented by Tyler Smith and Besa Smith at SAS Global Forum in 2019, developed to provide realistic classroom exercises for students learning to analyze health-related data. The data contain medical and demographic information (but no identifiers or confidential information) for patients from discharge records; they are available in public-use data files at https://www.cdc.gov/nchs/nhds/nhds_questionnaires.htm.

Smith and Smith (2019) define a discharge diagnosis of asthma as an event of interest and present logistic regression as a method for investigating the association between asthma diagnosis and geographic region while adjusting for other variables.

Formatting the Categorical Variables

When you build models with categorical variables, formatting their levels with descriptors will help you interpret the results. The next statements define formats for the categorical variables in Hospitals:

```
proc format;
    value Admiss_fmt     1='Emergency' 2='Urgent' 3='Elective' 4='Newborn'
                         9='Not available' ;
    value Discharge_fmt 1='Routine' 2='Left' 3='Tfr to short term'
                         4='Tfr to long term' 5='Alive' 6='Dead' 9='Unknown';
    value Marital_fmt    1='Married' 2='Single' 3='Widowed' 4='Divorced'
                         5='Separated' 6-9='Not stated';
    value NBed_fmt       1='6-99' 2='100-199' 3='200-299' 4='300-499'
                         5='500 and over';
    value Owner_fmt      1='Proprietary' 2='Government' 3='Nonprofit/Church';
    value Pay_fmt        1='Workers Comp' 2='Medicare' 3='Medicaid'
                         4='Other gov' 5='BCBS' 6='HMO/PPO' 7='Other private'
                         8='Self pay' 9='No charge' 10-99='Other';
    value Race_fmt       1='White' 2='Black/AfAmerican' 3='Asian' 0='Other';
    value Region_fmt     1='Northeast' 2='Midwest' 3='South' 4='West';
    value Sex_fmt        1='Male' 2='Female';
    value Source_fmt     1='Physician referral' 2='Clinical referral'
                         3='HMO referral' 4='Tfr from hospital'
                         5='Tfr from nursing facility' 6='Tfr from other'
                         7='Emergency room' 8='Court' 9-99='Other';
    value YN_fmt         0='No' 1='Yes';
run;
```

The next step assigns formats to the variables:

```
data Hospitals; set Hospitals;
    format AdmissionSource Source_fmt. AdmissionType Admiss_fmt.
           Asthma YN_fmt.               DischargeStatus Discharge_fmt.
           HospitalOwner Owner_fmt.     MaritalStatus Marital_fmt.
           NumberBeds NBed_fmt.         PriPaySource Pay_fmt.
           RaceCategory Race_fmt.       Region Region_fmt.
           SecPaySource Pay_fmt.        Sex Sex_fmt. ;
run;
```

Here, because the FORMAT statement is used in the DATA step, the association of formats with variables is permanently saved in Hospitals. If you assign formats with the FORMAT statement in a procedure step, the association is temporary; it affects only the results from that procedure.

Programming Tip: To aid interpretability, assign descriptive formats to your categorical variables.

Creating an XML Stream for the Formats

High-performance procedures handle user-defined formats slightly differently from other SAS procedures. You must create a file (called an XML stream) that contains the formats and pass the file reference to the procedure with the FMTLIBXML= option. The **%Make_XMLSTREAM** macro generates this file:

```
%macro Make_XMLStream(name=tempxml);
    filename &name 'fmt.xml';
    libname   &name XML92 xmltype=sasfmt tagset=tagsets.XMLsuv;
    proc format cntlout=&name..allfmts;
    run;
%mend;
```

The **%Delete_XMLSTREAM** macro deletes the file:

```
%macro Delete_XMLStream(fref);
    %let rc=%sysfunc(fdelete(&fref));
%mend;
```

The next statement creates an XML stream named *HospFmts* that is used later on page 178:

```
%Make_XMLStream(name=HospFmts);
```

Saving the Model Information in Macro Variables

Prior to building models with many candidate effects, it is helpful to save their names in macro variables that you can specify in CLASS and MODEL statements. This makes the statements more readable and facilitates reuse of model information in your programs.

The next statement creates a macro variable named ClassVars that saves the names of the categorical variables in Hospitals with their reference levels:

```
%let ClassVars =
AdmissionSource(ref='Physician referral') AdmissionType(ref='Elective')
DischargeStatus(ref='Routine')            HospitalOwner(ref='Proprietary')
MaritalStatus(ref='Married')              NumberBeds(ref='6-99')
PriPaySource(ref='Medicaid')              RaceCategory(ref='White')
Region(ref='Northeast')                   Sex(ref='Male');
```

The REF= values are used for reference parameterization of the variable levels, which is a method for parameterizing or coding the levels. Appendix I explains the various parameterizations that are available with procedures in this book.

The next statement creates a macro variable named Predictors that defines candidate effects, two of which are interactions:

```
%let Predictors = AdmissionSource AdmissionType Age Age*Sex DaysOfCare
                  DischargeStatus HospitalOwner MaritalStatus NumberBeds
                  PriPaySource RaceCategory Region Region*RaceCategory Sex;
```

Programming Tip: For convenience and reusability, save lists of variables and effects in macro variables.

Partitioning the Data for Training, Validation, and Testing

The data set Hospitals contains more than enough observations to apply model selection with the validation method. The following statements use the SURVEYSELECT procedure to randomly allocate 50% of the observations to training, 25% to validation, and 25% to testing. The variable Role identifies the purpose of each partition.

```
proc surveyselect data=Hospitals out=Hospitals rep=1
                  method=srs samprate=0.50 seed=59931 outall;
run;
data Hospitals(drop=Selected);
   set Hospitals;
   if        Selected = 1 then Role = 0;  /* hold out        */
   else if Selected = 0 then Role = 1;  /* use for training */
run;

proc surveyselect data=Hospitals(where=(Role=0)) out=Hospitals0 rep=1
                  method=srs samprate=0.50 seed=35911 outall;
run;
data Hospitals0(drop=Selected);
   set Hospitals0;
   if        Selected = 1 then Role = 2;  /* use for validation */
   else if Selected = 0 then Role = 3;  /* use for testing    */
run;

data Hospitals; set Hospitals(where=(Role=1)) Hospitals0; run;
proc sort data=Hospitals; by Role; run;
```

Incorporating the Weights

The weight variable NHDSWeight plays an important role because the data are not a simple random sample of discharges from all hospitals in the United States. Instead, the surveys were based on a three-stage stratified sampling design. In the first two stages, hospitals or geographic areas were selected from a list (sampling frame). Discharges were then selected within the sampled hospitals using systematic random sampling. As a result, discharges were included from the sampled population with different probabilities. The sampling weights given by NHDSWeight are the reciprocals of the inclusion probabilities. For each observation, the weight is the number of population units it represents.

Whether you fit or build a logistic regression model with these data, the weights should be taken into account. If you fit a model, use the SURVEYLOGISTIC procedure because it provides valid inference by estimating variances of estimators that incorporate the weights and the sample design. The SURVEYLOGISTIC procedure does not provide model selection, but for that purpose you can use the HPLOGISTIC procedure with a WEIGHT statement. This incorporates the weights as multipliers in the likelihood function.

In order to use the weights in NHDSWeight to build a model[†] with the HPLOGISTIC procedure, they must be rescaled so they sum to the number of samples in each partition rather than the number of population units. This requirement comes from the form of the weighted log-likelihood on page 162, which the procedure uses to estimate the regression coefficients.

[†]The general question of how to incorporate survey weights in model selection lies outside the scope of this book. The approach taken here is simplified.

The following statements rescale the weights:

```
proc means data=Hospitals;
   var NHDSWeight;
   output out=SumWt(drop=_TYPE_ rename=(_FREQ_=NSample))
               sum(NHDSWeight)=SumNHDSWeight;
   by Role;
run;

data Hospitals(drop=NSample SumNHDSWeight);
   set Hospitals;
   by Role;
   if first.Role then set SumWt;
   retain NSample SumNHDSWeight;
   SelectionWt = NHDSWeight*(NSample/SumNHDSWeight);
run;
```

The rescaled weights are saved in a variable named SelectionWt that can be specified with the WEIGHT statement in the HPLOGISTIC procedure.

Building a Model with the Stepwise Method and Validation ASE

The following statements build a model for asthma diagnosis by using the stepwise method with validation ASE as the choose criterion:

```
proc hplogistic data=Hospitals fmtlibxml=HospFmts;
   class &Classvars / param=ref;
   model Asthma(event='Yes') = &Predictors / association cutpoint=0.12;
   weight SelectionWt;
   selection method=stepwise(choose=validate select=sbc stop=validate)
           hierarchy=single;
   partition rolevar=Role(train='1' validate='2' test='3');
run;
```

The macro variables Classvars and Predictors enhance the readability of the statements. The PARAM=REF option requests the reference method of parameterization for the classification variables (see Appendix I). High-performance statistical procedures with a CLASS statement only support reference parameterization and GLM parameterization (the default). The PARTITION statement requests data partitioning based on the values of Role.

Interpreting the Results

Output 9.11 displays the number of observations for each level of Asthma.

Output 9.11 Response Profile

		Response Profile			
Ordered		Total			
Value	Asthma	Frequency	Training	Validation	Testing
1	No	291620	146376.6	73144.52	73222.83
2	Yes	16623	7744.434	3916.479	3838.166

You are modeling the probability that Asthma='Yes'.

Output 9.12 displays the formatted levels and reference levels of the CLASS variables.

Output 9.12 Class Level Information

Class Level Information

Class	Levels	Reference Value	Values
AdmissionSource	9	Physician referral	Clinical referral Court Emergency room HMO referral Other Physician referral Tfr from hospital Tfr from nursing facility Tfr from other
AdmissionType	3	Elective	Elective Emergency Urgent
DischargeStatus	7	Routine	Alive Dead Left Routine Tfr to long term Tfr to short term Unknown
HospitalOwner	3	Proprietary	Government Nonprofit/Church Proprietary
MaritalStatus	6	Married	Divorced Married Not stated Separated Single Widowed
NumberBeds	5	6-99	100-199 200-299 300-499 500 and over 6-99
PriPaySource	10	Medicaid	BCBS HMO/PPO Medicaid Medicare No charge Other Other gov Other private Self pay Workers Comp
RaceCategory	4	White	Asian Black/AfAmerican Other White
Region	4	Northeast	Midwest Northeast South West
Sex	2	Male	Female Male

Output 9.13 shows the effects that were added or removed at each step of the selection.

Output 9.13 Selection Summary

Selection Summary

Step	Effect Entered	Effect Removed	Number Effects In	SBC	Validation ASE
0	Intercept		1	61429	0.04824
1	Sex		2	60984	0.04808
2	DischargeStatus		3	60673	0.04796
3	RaceCategory		4	60417	0.04790
4	AdmissionType		5	60264	0.04781
5	Region		6	60161	0.04776
6	Age		7	60062	0.04772
7	Age*Sex		8	60003	0.04771
8	NumberBeds		9	59994	0.04768
9	MaritalStatus		10	59986	0.04769
10	HospitalOwner		11	59983	0.04768*
11		NumberBeds	10	59982*	0.04770

* Optimal Value of Criterion

During the selection, model hierarchy was enforced because HIERARCHY=SINGLE was specified. This requires that for any term to enter the model, all model effects that are contained in the term must be present. Here, for instance, the interaction effect AGE*SEX was permitted to enter only after the main effects of AGE and SEX entered. Subsequently, the main effects of AGE and SEX could have been removed only after AGE*SEX was removed. By default, the procedure does not apply model hierarchy unless the backward elimination method is used.

Output 9.14 lists the effects that were selected. One of these is Region.

Output 9.14 Selected Effects

Selected Effects:	Intercept AdmissionType Age Age*Sex DischargeStatus HospitalOwner MaritalStatus NumberBeds RaceCategory Region Sex

Output 9.15 shows the fit statistics for each of the partitions.

Output 9.15 Fit Statistics for Partitioned Data

Partition Fit Statistics			
Statistic	Training	Validation	Testing
Area under the ROCC	0.6334	0.6235	0.6289
Average Square Error	0.04712	0.04768	0.04673
Hosmer-Lemeshow Test	4.09E-6	0.000024	0.000043
Misclassification Error	0.05949	0.06063	0.06056
R-Square	0.01148	0.01061	0.01130
Max-rescaled R-Square	0.03493	0.03206	0.03456
McFadden's R-Square	0.02898	0.02654	0.02870
Mean Difference	0.01639	0.01459	0.01742
Somers' D	0.2667	0.2470	0.2579
True Negative Fraction	0.9889	0.9886	0.9872
True Positive Fraction	0.02570	0.01966	0.02814

An observation is classified as an event if the predicted probability of the event is greater than or equal to the value specified with the CUTPOINT= option; otherwise, it is classified as a nonevent. The cutpoint affects the misclassification rate and the true positive and true negative fractions; see page 166. Here, the similarity of the statistics for the training and testing partitions is reassuring.

Output 9.16 shows the estimates for the first 10 parameters in the selected model. These are listed in the order in which the candidate effects were specified in the MODEL statement and not in the order of effect selection.

Output 9.16 Effect Estimates (partial list)

Effect	Parameter	Estimate
Intercept	Intercept	-2.1791
AdmissionType	AdmissionType Emergency	0.2947
AdmissionType	AdmissionType Urgent	-0.1055
Age	Age	-0.01455
Age*Sex	Age*Sex Female	0.01118
DischargeStatus	DischargeStatus Alive	-0.2369
DischargeStatus	DischargeStatus Dead	-0.8871
DischargeStatus	DischargeStatus Left	0.3876
DischargeStatus	DischargeStatus Tfr to long term	-0.5281
DischargeStatus	DischargeStatus Tfr to short term	-0.4980

With reference parameterization, you interpret the estimate for the intercept as the log odds of being discharged with an asthma diagnosis, assuming the classification effects are all at the reference levels shown in Output 9.12 and the continuous variables are all set to zero. The estimate for each level of a classification effect is the increment (which can be positive or negative) in the log odds. For instance, the estimate −0.2369 for DischargeStatus Alive is the decrease in the log odds for that level compared with DischargeStatus Routine, assuming the other classification effects are at their reference levels and the continuous variables are set to zero. Of course, these interpretations are conditional on the selected model.

Output 9.17 shows the association statistics for each of the partitions.

Output 9.17 Association Statistics for Partitioned Data

	Association Statistics			
	Concordance			
Role	Index	Somers' D	Gamma	Tau-a
Training	0.633361	0.266723	0.268209	0.027129
Validation	0.623478	0.246957	0.248335	0.025121
Testing	0.628930	0.257860	0.259316	0.026564

The concordance index for the testing partition (0.629) corresponds to the area under the ROC curve, which is not shown.

Building a Model with the Stepwise Method and SBC as the Choose Criterion

For comparison, the following statements build a second model by using the stepwise method with SBC instead of validation ASE as the choose criterion:

```
proc hplogistic data=Hospitals fmtlibxml=HospFmts;
   class &Classvars / param=ref;
   model Asthma(event='Yes') = &Predictors / association cutpoint=0.12;
   weight SelectionWt;
   selection method=stepwise(choose=sbc select=sbc stop=sbc) hierarchy=single;
   partition rolevar=Role(train='1' validation='2' test='3');
run;
```

Here, the observations in the validation set are not used to select the model.

As shown in Output 9.18, the predictor NumberBeds enters at Step 8 and is removed at Step 11.

Output 9.18 Effect Selection Summary

	Selection Summary			
Step	Effect Entered	Effect Removed	Number Effects In	SBC
0	Intercept		1	61429
1	Sex		2	60984
2	DischargeStatus		3	60673
3	RaceCategory		4	60417
4	AdmissionType		5	60264
5	Region		6	60161
6	Age		7	60062
7	Age*Sex		8	60003
8	NumberBeds		9	59994
9	MaritalStatus		10	59986
10	HospitalOwner		11	59983
11		NumberBeds	10	59982*

* Optimal Value of Criterion

The selected effects, which are listed in Output 9.19, include Region. They do not include NumberBeds but are otherwise the same as the effects listed in Output 9.14. The similarity of the two models is not surprising considering the large numbers of observations in the training and validation partitions.

Output 9.19 Selected Effects

Selected Effects: Intercept AdmissionType Age Age*Sex DischargeStatus HospitalOwner MaritalStatus RaceCategory Region Sex

Output 9.20 shows the first ten parameter estimates for the effects in the model.

Output 9.20 Parameter Estimates (partial list)

Effect	Parameter	Estimate
Intercept	Intercept	-2.2930
AdmissionType	AdmissionType Emergency	0.2821
AdmissionType	AdmissionType Urgent	-0.09939
Age	Age	-0.01453
Age*Sex	Age*Sex Female	0.01139
DischargeStatus	DischargeStatus Alive	-0.2318
DischargeStatus	DischargeStatus Dead	-0.8890
DischargeStatus	DischargeStatus Left	0.3886
DischargeStatus	DischargeStatus Tfr to long term	-0.5223
DischargeStatus	DischargeStatus Tfr to short term	-0.4618

Output 9.21 shows the fit statistics for each of the partitions.

Output 9.21 Fit Statistics for Partitioned Data

Partition Fit Statistics			
Statistic	Training	Validation	Testing
Area under the ROCC	0.6325	0.6217	0.6289
Average Square Error	0.04713	0.04770	0.04675
Hosmer-Lemeshow Test	3.885E-7	0.000209	0.01980
Misclassification Error	0.05999	0.06096	0.06068
R-Square	0.01118	0.01018	0.01094
Max-rescaled R-Square	0.03403	0.03077	0.03347
McFadden's R-Square	0.02822	0.02547	0.02779
Mean Difference	0.01605	0.01420	0.01723
Somers' D	0.2650	0.2435	0.2578
True Negative Fraction	0.9885	0.9881	0.9871
True Positive Fraction	0.02415	0.02196	0.02814

The values of these statistics for the test data—and in particular, the AUC and the misclassification error—are nearly identical to the corresponding values in Output 9.15.

At this point, the XML stream that contains the user-defined formats is no longer needed. The following statement deletes the stream:

```
%Delete_XMLStream(HospFmts);
```

Introduction to the LOGSELECT Procedure

The LOGSELECT procedure in SAS Viya fits and builds logistic regression models. It provides functionality comparable to that of the HPLOGISTIC procedure in SAS/STAT, and so it involves the same basic concepts (see page 161) and computes the same statistics for assessing predictive ability (see page 166). The relative advantages of the LOGISTIC, HPLOGISTIC, and LOGSELECT procedures are described on page 160. Because the LOGSELECT procedure was developed specifically for SAS Viya, it can run on a cluster of machines that distribute the data and the computations.

When you use the LOGSELECT procedure to build a model, you specify the model with MODEL and CLASS statements, the selection method with a SELECTION statement, and data partitioning with a PARTITION statement. These statements are similar to those of the HPLOGISTIC procedure. Nonetheless, there are some differences in the LOGSELECT procedure:

- The selection methods include the group lasso.

- The CLASS statement offers a full set of methods for parameterization.

- The EFFECT statement specifies polynomial, spline, and other constructed effects.

- The ODDSRATIO statement specifies variables for which odds ratios are computed.

- The PLOTS= option in the SELECTION statement requests coefficient progression plots and model fit criterion plots. ODS Graphics must be enabled before you can request plots.

- The DISPLAY statement replaces the ODS SELECT statement for specifying displayed output. The DISPLAYOUT statement, which creates CAS tables from displayed output, provides functionality comparable to that of the ODS OUTPUT statement.

- The STORE statement saves results you can process with the ASTORE procedure. In particular, you can use the SCORE statement in the ASTORE procedure to score observations with models built by the LOGSELECT procedure (see page 384).

Table 9.6 summarizes the methods available with the SELECTION statement.

Table 9.6   Effect Selection Methods in the LOGSELECT Procedure

Method	Description	METHOD=*keyword*
Forward selection	Starts with no effects in the model and adds effects	FORWARD
Backward elimination	Starts with all effects in the model and deletes effects	BACKWARD
Fast backward elimination	Starts with all effects in the model and deletes effects without refitting the model; applies with SELECT=SL	BACKWARD(FAST)
Stepwise selection	Starts with no effects in the model and adds effects; effects already in the model do not necessarily stay	STEPWISE
Group lasso	Minimizes $-\mathcal{L}(\boldsymbol{\beta}; \mathbf{y})$ using a constraint that forces all parameters for the same effect to be included or excluded	LASSO
No selection	Fits fully specified model	NONE

Example: Simulated RNA Sequencing Data (continued)

The example introduced on page 167 simulated RNA sequencing data saved in the data set Train. The data are wide; there are 5,000 candidate predictors and only 200 observations. Among the candidate predictors, only x1 through x10 are actual predictors; the remainder are noise variables.

On page 171, the HPLOGISTIC procedure was used to select a classification model for the event $y = 1$ with the stepwise method and SBC as the choose criterion. Output 9.22 lists the effects that were selected.

Output 9.22 Effects Selected with the Stepwise Method and SBC

Selected Effects:	Intercept x1 x2 x3 x4 x5 x300 x1487 x2075 x3605

The order in which variables are listed in Output 9.22 is determined by the order in which the candidate predictors were listed in the MODEL statement on page 171—it should not be interpreted as their order of importance.

Assessing Variable Importance with Bootstrap Inclusion Frequencies

One way to assess variable importance is to draw a large number of bootstrap samples from the data set Train, repeat the model selection for each sample, and determine for each variable the percentage of samples for which it is selected in a model.[†] The LOGSELECT procedure, like the HPLOGISTIC procedure, provides the computational performance needed for this approach.

The following statements use the SURVEYSELECT procedure to draw 100 bootstrap samples:

```
%let NSamples=100;
proc surveyselect data=Train out=TrainBoot outall reps=&NSamples
                  samprate=1 method=urs seed=558543;
run;
```

The samples are saved in the data set TrainBoot, which resides in the WORK library. It contains a variable named Replicate that indexes the samples and a variable named NumberHits that counts the number of times an observation in Train is included in each sample.

In order to read the data in TrainBoot with the LOGSELECT procedure, they must first be loaded into memory on SAS Cloud Analytic Services. The following statements assign the libref mycas to in-memory tables on the CAS server and use the CASUTIL procedure to load TrainBoot into a CAS table named mycas.TrainBoot:

```
libname mycas cas;
proc casutil;
   load data=work.TrainBoot;
quit;
```

[†]This is similar to the selection percentage approach that is illustrated on page 122 for a standard regression model. Model averaging, as presented in Chapter 7 for general linear models, is not feasible with logistic regression due to the nonlinearity of the link function.

The next statements build logistic regression models for the bootstrap samples:

```
proc logselect data=mycas.TrainBoot;
   model y(event='1') = x1-x&NVars;
   selection method=stepwise(criterion=sbc choose=sbc stop=sbc maxsteps=10);
   displayout ParameterEstimates = ParmEst;
   freq NumberHits;
   by Replicate;
run;
```

The MODEL and SELECTION statements are identical to those on page 171. The variable Replicate serves as a BY variable, and the variable NumberHits serves as a FREQ variable. The DISPLAYOUT statement saves the parameter estimates in a CAS table named ParmEst; this statement is analogous to the ODS OUTPUT statement.

The next statements sort the observations in ParmEst by parameter, count the number of times that each effect is selected, and plot the frequencies:

```
proc sort data=mycas.ParmEst out=ParmEstSorted; by parameter; run;
proc freq data=ParmEstSorted order=freq;
   tables parameter / out=PredictorFreq(rename=(count=NSelections));
run;


title "Frequency of Effect Selections";
proc sgplot data=PredictorFreq(where=((NSelections GE 5) AND
                                       (Parameter NE "Intercept")));
   yaxis discreteOrder = data;
   xaxis grid;
   hbar Parameter / freq=NSelections;
run;
```

Output 9.23 shows the effects selected for at least five of the 100 models.

Output 9.23 Effects Selected for at Least Five Models

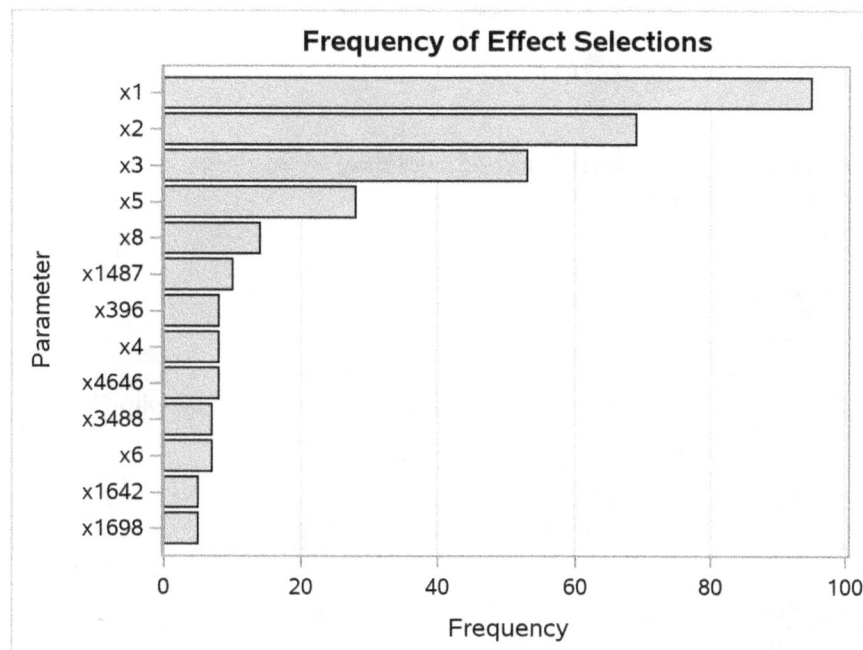

The variable x8, which is relevant but not listed in Output 9.22, is selected more often than x1487, which is listed there. Although frequency selection does not identify all of the relevant variables, Output 9.23 suggests a sparse model with predictors x1, x2, x3, x5, and x8. The following statements fit this model and use it to score the test data in Test:

```
proc logselect data=mycas.TrainBoot;
    model y(event='1') = x1 x2 x3 x5 x8;
    code file='SparseModel5Vars.sas';
run;

data TestOut(rename=(P_y=ModelPred1) keep=y P_y); set Test;
    %inc 'SparseModel5Vars.sas';
run;
```

The next statement uses the %Classify macro, defined on page 168, to produce a table with the classification percentages of observations in Test.

```
%Classify(TestOut, Test, ModelPred1)
```

The table is shown in Output 9.24.

Output 9.24 Test Set Classification Percentages for Sparse Model with Five Predictors

Test	Frequency	Percent
Correct	157	78.50
Incorrect	43	21.50

The percentage of incorrect classifications (21.5%) is somewhat less than the percentage (24.5%) shown in Output 9.8 for the original model selected with the stepwise method and SBC.

Output 9.23 also suggests a model with only four predictors: x1, x2, x3, and x5. The following statements fit this model, use it to score the data in Test, and produce a table of classification percentages:

```
proc logselect data=mycas.TrainBoot;
    model y(event='1') = x1 x2 x3 x5;
    code file='SparseModel4Vars.sas';
run;

data TestOut(rename=(P_y=ModelPred1) keep=y P_y); set Test;
    %inc 'SparseModel4Vars.sas';
run;

%Classify(TestOut, Test, ModelPred1)
```

The table is shown in Output 9.25.

Output 9.25 Test Set Classification Percentages for Sparse Model with Four Predictors

Test	Frequency	Percent
Correct	165	82.50
Incorrect	35	17.50

The percentage of incorrect classifications (17.5%) is considerably less than the percentage for the original model and closer to the percentage (12.5%) shown in Output 9.1 for the oracle model.

Example: Hospital Discharge Data (continued)

The example introduced on page 174 uses the HPLOGISTIC procedure and the data set Hospitals to build two models for asthma diagnosis with the stepwise method and validation ASE and SBC as the choose criteria. For comparison, this example uses the LOGSELECT procedure to build a model with the backward elimination method and SBC as the choose criterion. This involves two preliminary steps: making the user-defined formats available to the CAS server and loading the data.

Working with User-Defined Formats in SAS Viya

On page 175, the FORMAT procedure is used to define formats for the classification variables in Hospitals. In SAS Viya, user-defined formats are not directly available to a CAS server. You can make them available by using the FORMAT procedure as follows:

```
proc format casfmtlib="casformats";
   value YN_fmt          0='No' 1='Yes';
   value Sex_fmt         1='Male' 2='Female';
   ... additional VALUE statements ...
run;
```

The CASFMTLIB= option adds a format library named casformats to the CAS session.

Loading the Data into a CAS Table

The next statements use the CASUTIL procedure to load the data in Hospitals into a CAS table named mycas.Hospitals and assign formats to the classification variables:

```
proc casutil;
   format AdmissionType Admiss_fmt.       AdmissionSource Source_fmt.
          Asthma YN_fmt.                   DischargeStatus Discharge_fmt.
          HospitalOwner Owner_fmt.         MaritalStatus Marital_fmt.
          NumberBeds NBed_fmt.             PriPaySource Pay_fmt.
          RaceCategory Race_fmt.           Region Region_fmt.
          SecPaySource Pay_fmt.            Sex Sex_fmt. ;

   load data=work.Hospitals;
quit;
```

Building a Model with Backward Elimination and SBC as the Choose Criterion

The following statements build the model:

```
proc logselect data=mycas.Hospitals association;
   class &Classvars / param=reference;
   model Asthma(event='Yes') = &Predictors / link=logit;
   selection method=backward(choose=sbc select=sbc stop=sbc);
   partition rolevar=Role(train='1' validate='2' test='3');
   weight NHDSWeight / normalize ;
run;
```

The original example created the macro variables ClassVars and Predictors on page 176. The NORMALIZE option scales the weights in NHDSWeight, which eliminates the need to this in a preliminary step as on page 178.

Interpreting the Results

Backward elimination starts with all of the candidate effects in the model and deletes effects at each step. Here, as shown in Output 9.26, the selection terminates when the stop criterion SBC reaches a local minimum based on a default stop horizon of three steps. You can specify the horizon with the STOPHORIZON= option in the SELECTION statement.

Output 9.26 Selection Summary for Backward Elimination

Selection Details

Step	Effect Removed	Number Effects In	SBC
0		15	60118.7293
1	PriPaySource	14	60040.9780
2	AdmissionSource	13	59994.6494
3	RaceCategory*Region	12	59989.0133
4	DaysOfCare	11	59982.6025
5	NumberBeds	10	59982.3005*
6	MaritalStatus	9	59998.2688
7	HospitalOwner	8	60004.5469
8	Age*Sex	7	60061.9691

Selection Summary

* Optimal Value Of Criterion

Output 9.27 shows that the selected effects are the same as those selected with the stepwise method in Output 9.19. This is not surprising considering the large number of observations in the training partition.

Output 9.27 Selected Effeccts

Selected Effects: Intercept AdmissionType Age Age*Sex DischargeStatus HospitalOwner MaritalStatus RaceCategory Region Sex

Output 9.28 shows the association statistics for the three partitions.

Output 9.28 Association Statistics

Description	Training	Validation	Testing
Concordance Index (AUC)	0.6325	0.6217	0.6289
Somers' D	0.2650	0.2435	0.2578
Gamma	0.2651	0.2435	0.2579
Tau-a	0.0270	0.0248	0.0266
Pairs	1.20798E9	302030498	305878874
Percent Concordant	63.2418	62.1621	62.8793
Percent Discordant	36.7369	37.8169	37.0993
Percent Tied	0.0213	0.0210	0.0214

Association of Predicted Probabilities and Observed Responses

The values of the concordance index (area under the ROC curve) and Somers' D match the corresponding values obtained with the stepwise method, which are shown in Output 9.21.

Summary of Procedure Features

Table 9.7 compares the features of the LOGISTIC, HPLOGISTIC, and LOGSELECT procedures.

Table 9.7 Comparison of Procedures for Logistic Regression

Feature	LOGISTIC	HPLOGISTIC	LOGSELECT
Primary purpose	Statistical analysis of fully specified models[†]	Building predictive models and scoring with large data	Building predictive models and scoring with large data
MODEL and CLASS statements	Yes	Yes	Yes
Parameterization methods for classification variables	Full set	GLM, reference	Full set
Default parameterization	Effect	GLM	GLM
SPLIT option for classification variables	No	No	Yes
EFFECT statement for splines and other constructed effects	Yes	No	Yes
Model building methods	Sequential, best-subset	Sequential	Sequential, lasso,
Model selection criteria	Limited	Information, validation	Information, validation
Selection plots	No	No	Yes
Data partitioning	No	Yes	Yes
Classification tables and association statistics	Yes	Yes	Yes
ROC curves	Displayed	Computed	Computed
Model fit statistics	Yes	Yes	Yes
p-values for parameters	Yes	Yes	Yes
Goodness-of-fit tests	Yes (extensive)	Yes	Yes
Postfit analyses: contrasts, estimates of model effects, least squares means, odds ratios	Yes	No	Limited
Residual diagnostics	Yes	No	Yes
Influence statistics	Yes	No	Yes
Diagnostic and fit plots	Yes	No	No
Computational operation	Single thread	Multiple threads	Multiple threads, distributed

[†]Use the SURVEYLOGISTIC procedure for analysis that incorporates complex survey sample designs.

Chapter 10
Building Generalized Linear Models

Contents

This chapter introduces two procedures for building generalized linear models: the HPGENSELECT procedure in SAS 9 and its newer counterpart in SAS Viya, the GENSELECT procedure.

The class of generalized linear models includes models with a variety of response distributions. Logistic regression models and Poisson regression models belong to this class, as do standard regression models with a normally distributed response.

Generalized linear models and the term *generalized linear model* were introduced fifty years ago by John Nelder and Robert Wedderburn at Rothamsted Experimental Station (Nelder and Wedderburn 1972).[†] Until then, data analysts had dealt with nonnormal response distributions by applying specialized regression methods (such as probit analysis for binary responses) or by transforming the response in order to meet the requirements for standard regression: additivity of effects and normally distributed errors with a constant variance. In practice, these requirements are rarely met by a single transformation, and so this approach was never a general solution.

Generalized linear models were a breakthrough because they replaced disparate methods and ad hoc transformations with a unified framework in which the analyst specifies a response distribution and selects a link function that relates the mean of the distribution to a linear predictor of the form $\beta_0 + \beta_1 x_1 + \cdots + \beta_p x_p$. Instead of forcing the data into the confined structure of standard regression, the new framework expanded this structure to accommodate a broad range of data.

Along with this framework, Nelder and Wedderburn provided methods for estimating the regression parameters $\beta_0, \beta_1, \ldots, \beta_p$ and for performing statistical analysis. With these tools, the effects in generalized linear models could be explored and assessed in ways that were already well established for the analysis of general linear models.

[†]Rothamsted, located in Harpenden, England, is the oldest agricultural research institution in the world. It has been called the birthplace of modern data analysis because it is where Ronald Fisher developed fundamental concepts of modern statistics while analyzing data obtained from crop trials (Rothamsted Research 2019). Several generations of influential statisticians have held positions in the Rothamsted statistics department, which was founded by Fisher in 1919.

Generalized linear models gained popularity in the mid-1980s not only because of their versatility but also because they became available in statistical software. Today, they are well-established in statistical practice, and they have become indispensable for analyzing categorical outcomes in medical research and for determining rates in the insurance industry.

Generalized linear models are sometimes confused with general linear models, which are discussed in Part I of this book. In fact, general linear models with normally distributed responses are a type of generalized linear model.[†]

Procedures for Generalized Linear Models

The GENMOD procedure is the primary procedure in SAS for fitting and analyzing generalized linear models with specified effects. In addition to parameter estimates, *p*-values, and model fit statistics, it provides many features for postfit statistical analysis, such as estimation of contrasts in the model parameters and tests of hypotheses concerning the parameters.

The HPGENSELECT and GENSELECT procedures do not replicate the inferential features of the GENMOD procedure. Instead, they were designed to fit and build generalized linear models with large data for the purpose of prediction, and they provide the following features:

- The ability to define candidate effects with MODEL and CLASS statements similar to those of the GENMOD procedure.

- The ability to specify regression spline effects, polynomial effects, and other constructed effects in the set of candidate effects. This is available with the EFFECT statement in the GENSELECT procedure.

- Model building with sequential selection methods and the group lasso method (see page 46).

- Model selection based on information criteria (AIC, AICC, and SBC) that avoid overfitting by penalizing model complexity. This approach is discussed in "Criteria Based on Information Theory" on page 28.

- Model selection based on partitioning the data into training and validation sets. This approach is discussed in "External Validation Method for Estimating Prediction Error" on page 30.

- Multithreaded computation for faster performance. The GENSELECT procedure can also perform computations with data distributed across multiple computers in a cloud environment.

Programming Tip: When your goal is prediction, take advantage of the model building capability in the HPGENSELECT and GENSELECT procedures. When your goal is inference, use the GENMOD procedure.

[†]In a 2003 interview with Stephen Senn, John Nelder recounted the introduction of generalized linear models and acknowledged that choosing a different name would have avoided confusion (Senn and Nelder 2003). He also noted that the 1972 paper, which appeared in the *Journal of the Royal Statistical Society*, was earlier rejected by another prominent journal, presumably because it did not contain enough theorems.

Basic Concepts of Generalized Linear Models

Generalized linear models extend the class of general linear models. As explained in Chapter 5, the general linear model for the ith observation is

$$y_i = \beta_0 + \beta_1 x_{i1} + \cdots + \beta_p x_{ip} + \epsilon_i, \quad i = 1, \ldots, n$$

where y_i is the value of a continuous response variable $\mathbf{y}$, the quantities x_{ij} are the values of the predictors $\mathbf{x}_1, \ldots, \mathbf{x}_p$, and the error term ϵ_i has a mean of 0 and a constant variance σ^2. When the goal is prediction rather than inference, it is not necessary to assume that ϵ_i (or equivalently, y_i) is normally distributed. However, in both situations, $y_1, \ldots, y_n$ are assumed to be independent.

In a generalized linear model, y_i is assumed to have a distribution in the exponential family that can be continuous or discrete, and $y_1, \ldots, y_n$ are assumed to be independent. The model for the expected value of y_i is

$$\mu_i \equiv E(y_i) = g^{-1}(\beta_0 + \beta_1 x_{i1} + \cdots + \beta_p x_{ip})$$

where $g(\cdot)$ is an invertible function. The model is usually expressed as

$$g(\mu_i) = \eta_i \equiv \beta_0 + \beta_1 x_{i1} + \cdots + \beta_p x_{ip}$$

For instance, suppose that y_i has two values, 0 and 1, with a Bernoulli distribution. Then

$$\mu_i = E[y_i] = \Pr[y_i = 1 \mid \mathbf{x}_1 = x_{i1}, \ldots, \mathbf{x}_p = x_{ip}], \quad i = 1, \ldots, n$$

When $g(\cdot)$ is chosen to be the logit function, the model can be written as

$$\mathrm{logit}(\mu_i) \equiv \log\left(\frac{\mu_i}{1 - \mu_i}\right) = \beta_0 + \beta_1 x_{i1} + \cdots + \beta_p x_{ip}, \quad i = 1, \ldots, n$$

This is the binary logistic regression model described on page 161. In fact, the entire class of logistic regression models constitutes one type of generalized linear model.

Components of Generalized Linear Models

A generalized linear model consists of three components:

- A specified parametric distribution for y_i. This distribution, which is selected from the exponential family of distributions, is called the *random component*.

- A linear predictor:

  $$\eta_i \equiv \beta_0 + \beta_1 x_{i1} + \cdots + \beta_p x_{ip}, \quad i = 1, \ldots, n$$

  This is called the *systematic component*. A linear predictor can include the same types of effects as those in a general linear model.

- A specified function $g(\cdot)$ that is smooth, invertible, and connects μ_i, the mean of the response distribution, with η_i, the linear predictor:

  $$g(\mu_i) = \eta_i = \beta_0 + \beta_1 x_{i1} + \cdots + \beta_p x_{ip}, \quad i = 1, \ldots, n$$

  This function is called the *link function* because it provides the relationship between the random component and the systematic component.

Table 10.1 lists examples of the three components.

Table 10.1 Components of Generalized Linear Models

Component	Examples
Response distribution	Binary (Bernoulli), binomial, exponential, gamma, geometric, inverse Gaussian, multinomial, negative binomial, normal, Poisson, Tweedie
Link function	Log, logit, log-log, complementary log-log, probit, reciprocal, reciprocal square
Linear predictor	Effects that involve continuous or classification variables, such as main effects, interactions, and spline effects

Many books have been written about the statistical theory and inferential applications of generalized linear models, which lie outside the scope of this chapter. To learn more, see McCullagh and Nelder (1989), Dobson (1990), Firth (1991), Pawitan (2001, Ch. 6), McCulloch, Searle, and Neuhaus (2008), Frees (2010), Agresti (2013, Ch. 4), Agresti (2015), and Goldburd et al. (2020). The books by Dobson (1990) and Goldburd et al. (2020) are written at an introductory level.

Response Distributions

The response distributions that you can specify for a generalized linear model are characterized as members of the exponential family. This is a broad class of distributions; it includes the distributions listed in Table 10.1. The exponential family is sometimes confused with the exponential distribution, which happens to be one member of the family. Appendix E explains how the exponential family is defined, and it provides information about distributions in the family that are available in the HPGENSELECT and GENSELECT procedures.

If y_i has a distribution in the exponential family and μ_i denotes the mean (expectation) of y_i, it can be shown that the variance of y_i is equal to $\phi V(\mu_i)$, where ϕ is called the *dispersion parameter* and $V(\cdot)$ is called the *variance function*. Table 10.2 lists the variance functions associated with standard distributions in the exponential family.

Table 10.2 Variance Functions for Distributions in the Exponential Family

Distribution Type	Distribution	$V(\mu)$	Notes
Continuous	normal	1	
Continuous	gamma	μ^2	
Continuous	exponential	μ^2	
Continuous	inverse Gaussian	μ^3	
Continuous	Tweedie	μ^p	$1 < p < 2$
Discrete	binary (Bernoulli)	$\mu(1-\mu)$	
Discrete	binomial	$\mu(1-\mu)/n$	n is the number of trials
Discrete	negative binomial	$\mu(1+k\mu)$	$k > 0$ allows larger variance than Poisson
Discrete	geometric	$\mu + \mu^2$	
Discrete	Poisson	μ	

Unlike the mean μ_i, which is allowed to vary across observations, the dispersion parameter is treated as a constant. However, because of the flexibility provided by the variance function, the variance itself need not be constant (as is the case in a general linear model).

For the normal distribution, the variance function is a constant; the variance is equal to ϕ (usually denoted by σ^2), and it is functionally independent of the mean. For the binary and binomial distributions, the variance function is quadratic with a maximum at $\mu = 1/2$. For the other distributions in Table 10.2 the variance is an increasing function of the mean.

Selecting a Response Distribution

Because the mean and variance are the two most important characteristics of a response distribution, knowing the variance function can help you select a distribution that is appropriate for a particular application. For instance, the variance function for the gamma distribution is $V(\mu) = \mu^2$, which makes it a candidate for modeling data in insurance rating, where higher expected risks are often associated with higher variances (Goldburd et al. 2020, Sec. 2.2).

Skewness is also a consideration in selecting a response distribution. With the exception of the normal distribution, which is symmetric, all of the distributions in Table 10.2 are right-skewed. Some of these distributions can accommodate varying degrees of skewness.

The following distributions are not listed in Table 10.2 but are available in the procedures:

- The multinomial distribution, used if the response is categorical and has more than two levels. This distribution belongs to the multivariate exponential family; see page 344.

- The zero-inflated negative binomial distribution (see page 346) and the zero-inflated Poisson distribution (see page 349), which are available in the HPGENSELECT procedure. As extensions of the negative binomial distribution and the Poisson distribution, they are used to model overdispersed data in which the frequency of zeros exceeds the mean-variance relationships in Table 10.2.

Link Functions

Table 10.3 lists link functions available in the HPGENSELECT and GENSELECT procedures. As usual, $\Phi^{-1}(\cdot)$ denotes the quantile function of the standard normal distribution.

Table 10.3   Link Functions

Function	$g(\mu) = \eta =$
Complementary log-log	$\log(-\log(1 - \mu))$
Generalized logit	varies with number of response levels
Identity	μ
Inverse	$1/\mu$
Inverse square	$1/\mu^2$
Log	$\log(\mu)$
Logit	$\log(\mu/(1 - \mu))$
Log-log	$-\log(-\log(\mu))$
Probit	$\Phi^{-1}(\mu)$

The procedures provide a default link function for each response distribution, but it is by no means the best link function for every application. When possible, you should choose a link function that makes the model more interpretable or matches the scale of the predictors.

For instance, in generalized linear models for insurance ratemaking, a log link is often chosen when the logs of continuous predictors are included in the model:

$$\log(\mu) = \beta_0 + \beta_1 x_1 + \cdots + \beta_p x_p$$

The mean of the response can then be expressed as

$$\mu = \exp(\beta_0) \exp(\beta_1 x_1) \cdots \exp(\beta_p x_p)$$

Goldburd et al. (2020, Sec. 2.4) illustrate this with an example involving a single predictor x_1 that is the amount of insurance for a property. If β_1 is 0.62 and the base amount is 100,000 USD, the relativity factor for 200,000 USD is $200^{0.62} / 100^{0.62} = 1.54$. In other words, a property with 200,000 USD of insurance has an expected outcome that is 54% more than that of a property with 100,000 USD of insurance.

Linear Predictors and Offsets

In the linear predictor for a generalized linear model, $x_1, \ldots, x_p$ can represent continuous or categorical variables. The effects of these variables are called main effects because they affect the response directly and independently of each other. The predictors can also represent classification effects, interaction effects, and constructed effects such as polynomial and spline effects formed from data variables. In other words, $x_1, \ldots, x_p$ have exactly the same interpretation as the predictors for a general linear model (see page 14).

The predictors in a generalized linear model can also include a special numeric variable, called the *offset variable*, that has a fixed coefficient of 1:

$$g(\mu_i) = \beta_0 + \beta_1 x_1 + \cdots + \beta_p x_p + x_{\text{offset}}$$

Typically, this variable provides a measure of exposure that adjusts the mean of the response variable. For instance, suppose the response variable is the number of motor vehicle fatalities for different sections of an interstate highway system, and suppose that the offset variable is the log of the number of miles traveled by vehicles in each section during the same period of time. With a log link for the response, the model becomes

$$\log \left(\frac{\text{average number of fatalities}}{\text{total vehicle-miles}} \right) = \beta_0 + \beta_1 x_1 + \cdots + \beta_p x_p$$

Offset variables are useful in models where the response mean varies with time or some other measure of risk. Such models occur in epidemiology, medical research, environmental studies, customer behavior modeling, insurance rating, and financial risk analysis. The scale of the offset should match that of the linear predictor. For instance, you should provide the offset variable on a log scale if you specify a log link.

The variance of the response variable might well increase with the measure of exposure. You can account for this by selecting a distribution with an appropriate variance function from Table 10.2. There are applications, such as modeling the frequency of insurance claims, where the variance decreases as exposure increases, but the mean does not change. For these situations, Goldburd et al. (2020, p. 18) note that a weight variable (not an offset variable) is appropriate.

Introduction to the HPGENSELECT Procedure

The HPGENSELECT procedure is the recommended procedure in SAS/STAT for fitting and building generalized linear models with large data when the goal is prediction or exploration. Like the HPLOGISTIC procedure, the HPGENSELECT procedure is a high-performance procedure. Characteristics of high-performance procedures are explained on page 163.

Specifying the Candidate Effects

When you use the HPGENSELECT procedure to build a model, you specify the candidate effects with the MODEL and CLASS statements and the method of selection with the SELECTION statement. You specify the distribution and the link function with the DISTRIBUTION= and LINK= options in the MODEL statement. For instance, the following statements (taken from a later example on page 203) build a model for the mean of ClaimAmount by assuming it has a gamma distribution:

```
proc hpgenselect data=ClaimSeverity;
   class Education Deductible CreditScore Citations MultipleVehicles;
   model ClaimAmount = Education Deductible StdHouseIncome AgePolicyHolder
                       CreditScore Citations Multiple Vehicles  /
                       distribution=gamma link=log;
   selection method=stepwise(choose=validate select=sl stop=sbc);
   partition fraction(validate=0.25 seed=59883);
run;
```

When the response has a binomial distribution, you define the model with the events/trials syntax in the MODEL statement. For instance, consider data in which each observation provides information about bank transfers that occur independently during a five-minute interval. A trials variable named NTransactions records the number of bank transfers during each interval, and an events variable named NLargeTransactions records the number that involve more than 10,000 USD. The following statements build a model for the probability of a large transaction:

```
proc hpgenselect data=Transactions;
   class Region Origin Destination DayOfWeek Holiday
   model NLargeTransactions / NTransactions = TimeOfDay Region Origin
      Destination DayOfWeek Holiday / distribution=binomial link=logit;
   selection method=backward(choose=aic select=sl stop=aic);
run;
```

Because the events/trials syntax is also available in the HPLOGISTIC procedure, you could build this model as follows:

```
proc hplogistic data=Transactions;
   class Region Origin Destination DayOfWeek Holiday
   model NLargeTransactions / NTransactions = TimeOfDay Region Origin
      Destination DayOfWeek Holiday / link=logit;
   selection method=backward(choose=aic select=sl stop=aic);
run;
```

The HPGENSELECT procedure fits all of the effects in the MODEL statement if you specify METHOD=NONE or if you omit the SELECTION statement.

Specifying the Selection Method

Table 10.4 summarizes the methods available with the METHOD= option in the SELECTION statement.

Table 10.4 Selection Methods in the HPGENSELECT Procedure

Method	Description	METHOD=*keyword*
Forward selection	Starts with no effects in the model and adds effects	FORWARD
Backward elimination	Starts with all effects in the model and deletes effects	BACKWARD
Stepwise selection	Starts with no effects in the model and adds effects; effects already in the model do not necessarily stay	STEPWISE
Group lasso	Uses the group lasso method	LASSO
No selection	Fits fully specified model	NONE

Controlling the Methods of Selection

The HPGENSELECT procedure provides three ways to control the operation of the methods in Table 10.4, which you specify with suboptions in parentheses after the METHOD= option:

- CHOOSE= specifies the criterion for choosing the model. This criterion is evaluated at each step of the selection process. The final selected model is the model with the best value of this criterion.

- SELECT= specifies the criterion for determining which effect enters or leaves at each step. This suboption does not apply with the group lasso method. With the other methods, the only suboption available[†] is SELECT=SL, which selects the effect with the smallest observed significance level (p-value) for an approximate chi-square test. This test is roughly similar to the F test that is provided in the GENMOD procedure for comparing a model and a submodel; here, an F statistic is not computed because the scale parameter is not re-estimated.

  You can specify the threshold levels for an effect to enter or stay with the SLENTRY= and SLSTAY= suboptions for the METHOD= option. The default levels are both 0.05. You should treat these levels as tuning parameters and avoid interpreting them as probabilities; see "Problems with Data-Driven Model Selection" on page 33.

- STOP= specifies the criterion for terminating the selection process.

For the group lasso method, the LASSOSTEPS= option specifies the maximum number of steps, and the LASSORHO= option specifies ρ for the regularization parameter sequence $m\rho, m\rho^2, m\rho^3, \ldots$, where m is computed as the smallest regularization parameter that produces a model in which all regression parameters are equal to zero; see page 72. You specify these options in the procedure statement rather than the MODEL statement. For other methods, the MAXSTEPS= suboption for the METHOD= option specifies the maximum number of steps.

[†]Suboptions for information criteria are not available with the SELECT= option because they would require each candidate submodel to be refitted. This is prohibitively expensive for large data.

Table 10.5 lists the criteria you can request with the CHOOSE= suboption.

Table 10.5 Criteria Available with the CHOOSE= Suboption

Suboption	Criterion
AIC	Akaike's information criterion (Akaike 1974)
AICC	Corrected Akaike's information criterion (Hurvich and Tsai 1989)
SBC I BIC	Schwarz Bayesian information criterion Schwarz (1978)
VALIDATE	Average square error for validation data if data are partitioned

These criteria are likelihood-based analogues of the information criteria for general linear models that are discussed on page 28. They are computed as follows:

$$AIC = -2\mathcal{L}(\hat{\beta}; y) + 2p$$

$$AICC = \begin{cases} -2\mathcal{L}(\hat{\beta}; y) + 2pn/(n - p - 1) & \text{when } n > p + 2 \\ -2\mathcal{L}(\hat{\beta}; y) + 2p(p + 2) & \text{otherwise} \end{cases}$$

$$BIC = -2\mathcal{L}(\hat{\beta}; y) + p \log(n)$$

where p denotes the number of parameters in the candidate model, n denotes the number of observations, and $\mathcal{L}(\hat{\beta}; y)$ is the log-likelihood function evaluated at the maximum likelihood estimate of the regression parameters. Appendix E explains how this estimate is computed.

Table 10.6 lists criteria you can request with the STOP= suboption.

Table 10.6 Criteria Available with the STOP= Suboption

Suboption	Criterion
AIC	Akaike's information criterion (Akaike 1974)
AICC	Corrected Akaike's information criterion (Hurvich and Tsai 1989)
SBC I BIC	Schwarz Bayesian information criterion (Schwarz 1978)
SL	Significance level of approximate chi-square test

With the STOP=SL suboption, when you use the forward selection or stepwise method, selection stops at the step where the significance level of the candidate for entry is greater than the SLENTRY= threshold level. When you use the backward elimination or stepwise method, selection stops at the step where the significance level of the candidate for removal is greater than the SLSTAY= threshold level. The default levels are both 0.05, but larger values might be preferable. Again, you should treat these levels as tuning parameters; they are not meaningful probabilities.

No one combination of selection methods and criteria is uniformly the most effective. With large data, the preferred approach for building a model is to find a set of effects that minimizes prediction error when applied to test data that the training process has not encountered. If you specify CHOOSE=VALIDATE, the HPGENSELECT procedure computes the average square error (ASE) from the validation data at each step, and it selects the model at the first step where ASE_{val} is minimized. You use the PARTITION statement to allocate part of the DATA= data set for validation. Training error is not a reliable estimate of prediction error, as explained on page 25.

When there are insufficient data for independent validation, consider using the sequential selection methods in Table 10.4 in combination with one of the information criteria. For an explanation of these criteria, see "Criteria Based on Information Theory" on page 28. In some situations, the group lasso can provide better predictive accuracy; see "Shrinkage Methods" on page 42.

Specifying the Distribution and the Link Function

Table 10.7 lists the response distributions you can specify with the DISTRIBUTION= option. For more information about these distributions, see Appendix E.

Table 10.7   Distributions and Default Link Functions

Response Distribution	DISTRIBUTION= keyword	Default Link Function	Characteristics of Response Data
Binary (Bernoulli)	BINARY	Logit	Binary, typically 1s and 0s
Binomial	BINOMIAL	Logit	Count of k events in n trials
Gamma	GAMMA	Inverse	Continuous over $(0, \infty)$
Inverse Gaussian	INVERSEGAUSSIAN	Inverse square	Continuous over $(0, \infty)$
Multinomial (nominal)	MULTINOMIAL	Generalized logit	Categorical with nominal levels
Multinomial (ordinal)	MULTINOMIAL	Logit	Categorical with ordered levels
Negative binomial	NEGATIVEBINOMIAL	Log	Count $k = 0, 1, \ldots$
Normal (Gaussian)	NORMAL	Identity	Continuous over $(-\infty, \infty)$
Poisson	POISSON	Log	Count $k = 0, 1, \ldots$
Tweedie	TWEEDIE	Log	Typically continuous over $(0, \infty)$ with positive probability of 0
Zero-inflated negative binomial	ZINB	Log for counts, logit for 0s	Count $k = 0, 1, \ldots$ with inflated probability of $k = 0$
Zero-inflated Poisson	ZIP	Log for counts, logit for 0s	Count $k = 0, 1, \ldots$ with inflated probability of $k = 0$

Table 10.8 lists link functions you can specify with the LINK= option. For the binary, binomial, and multinomial distributions, the only link functions available are the defaults shown in Table 10.7.

Table 10.8   Link Functions

LINK=	Link Function	$g(\mu) = \eta =$
CLOGLOG	Complementary log-log	$\log(-\log(1 - \mu))$
GLOGIT	Generalized logit	varies with number of response levels
IDENTITY	Identity	μ
INV	Inverse	$1/\mu$
INV2	Inverse square	$1/\mu^2$
LOG	Logarithm	$\log(\mu)$
LOGIT	Logit	$\log(\mu/(1 - \mu))$
LOGLOG	Log-log	$-\log(-\log(\mu))$
PROBIT	Probit	$\Phi^{-1}(\mu)$

Example: Modeling the Severity of Insurance Claims

In the property insurance industry, analysts build generalized linear models to create and update rating (pricing) plans that account for various sources of variability and risk. These models provide the interpretability needed to satisfy regulatory requirements. They also provide the versatility needed to predict various targets: claim severity (monetary loss per claim), claim frequency (the number of claims per measure of exposure), pure premium (monetary loss per exposure), and loss ratio (loss per premium). Hundreds of potential predictor variables are available, ranging from demographic characteristics of customers to geospatial variables.

Table 10.9 describes predictors used by examples in this chapter and Chapter 11.

Table 10.9 Candidate Predictor Variables in Examples

Variable	Description	Type
AgePolicyholder	Age of policyholder	Continuous
AreaType	Type of geographic area	Categorical (4 levels)
Citations	Traffic citations	Categorical (3 levels)
CreditScore	Credit score	Continuous
Deductible	Level of deductible	Categorical (3 levels)
DriverAge	Age of driver	Continuous
Education	Educational attainment	Categorical (8 levels)
GarageParked	Vehicle parked in garage	Categorical (2 levels)
Gender	Gender	Categorical (2 levels)
Homeowner	Policyholder owns home	Categorical (2 levels)
StdHouseIncome	Household income (standardized)	Continuous
LicenseYrs	Years with driver license	Continuous
LatPolicyholder	Latitude of policyholder	Continuous
LonPolicyholder	Longitude of policyholder	Continuous
MaritalStatus	Marital status	Categorical (5 levels)
MultipleVehicles	More than one vehicle	Categorical (2 levels)
NDrvConvict	Number driver convictions	Categorical (2 levels)
NumberAtFault	Number of at fault accidents	Categorical (3 levels)
NumberNoFault	Number of no-fault accidents	Categorical (9 levels)
NYoungDrvrs	Number of drivers 18-21	Categorical (5 levels)
PolicyYears	Years policy has been held	Continuous
Rating	Rating category	Categorical (4 levels)
TookCourse	Accident prevention course	Categorical (2 levels)
Transaction	Type of last transaction	Categorical (3 levels)
VehicleOwned	Vehicle owned or financed	Categorical (2 levels)
VehicleType	Vehicle type	Categorical (8 levels)
VehicleUse	Vehicle use	Categorical (2 levels)
WorkStatus	Work status	Categorical (3 levels)

The following example builds a gamma regression model for the mean of claim severity using a data set named ClaimSeverity with information about auto insurance policyholders in a mid-Atlantic region of the United States. Each observation represents a policyholder. The dollar amounts given by the response variable ClaimAmount are scaled. The candidate predictors include demographic variables that describe the policyholder and variables that describe the vehicle associated with the policyholder.

The example begins by formatting the categorical variables in ClaimSeverity and creating macro variables with information that will be specified in the CLASS and MODEL statements of the HPGENSELECT procedure.

Formatting the Categorical Variables

The following statements define and assign formats for the categorical variables:

```
proc format;
    value AType    1='City'  2='Town'  3='Village'  4='Rural';
    value Cite     1='None'  2='One'  3-5='Multiple';
    value Conv     0='None' 1='1 or more';
    value Cred     800-850='800 to 850'   750-799='750 to 799'
                   700-749='700 to 749'   650-699='650 to 699'
                   600-649='600 to 649'   550-599='550 to 599'
                   500-549='500 to 549'   300-499='300 to 499';
    value Ded      0='None' 1='Low' 2='High';
    value EdLev    1='No HS diploma' 2='HS diploma' 3='Some college'
                   4='Associate'      5='Bachelor'      6='Master'
                   7='Professional'   8='Doctorate';
    value MStat    1='Married'  2='Widowed'  3='Divorced'  4='Separated'
                   5='Never Married';
    value RType    1='U'   2='V'   3='W'   4='X';
    value TType    1='New' 2='Modify' 3='Renew';
    value VType    1='Crossover'  2='Pickup'  3='Small'  4='SUV'
                   5='Midsized'   6='Luxury'  7='Van'    8='Large';
    value VUse     1='Pleasure'   2='Commuting';
    value WStat    1='Full Time'  2='Part Time'  3='Not Working';
    value YN       1='Yes'  0='No';
run;


data ClaimSeverity;
    set ClaimSeverity;
    format AreaType AType.      Citations Cite.       CreditScore Cred.
           Deductible Ded.      Education EdLev.       GarageParked YN.
           Homeowner YN.        MaritalStatus MStat.  MultipleVehicles YN.
           Rating RType.        TookCourse YN.        Transaction TType.
           VehicleOwned YN.     VehicleType VType.    VehicleUse VUse.
           WorkStatus WStat. ;
run;
```

Programming Tip: To aid interpretability, assign descriptive formats to your categorical variables.

High-performance procedures such as the HPGENSELECT procedure handle user-defined formats slightly differently from other SAS procedures. You must create a file (called an XML stream) that contains the formats and pass the file reference to the procedure with the FMTLIBXML= option. As explained on page 176, the following statement creates a stream named *ClmsFmts*:

```
%Make_XMLStream(name=ClmsFmts);
```

Saving Model Information in Macro Variables

When you build models with a large number of candidate effects, it is helpful to save their names in macro variables you can provide in CLASS and MODEL statements. This makes the statements more readable, and it facilitates reuse of model information in your programs.

The next statement creates a macro variable named ClassVars that saves the names of the categorical variables together with their reference levels:

```
%let ClassVars = AreaType(ref='Rural')              Citations(ref='None')
                 CreditScore(ref='300 to 499')      Deductible(ref='None')
                 Education(ref='No HS diploma')      GarageParked(ref='No')
                 Gender(ref='F')                     Homeowner(ref='No')
                 MaritalStatus(ref='Married')        MultipleVehicles(ref='No')
                 Rating(ref='U')                     TookCourse(ref='No')
                 Transaction(ref='New')              VehicleOwned(ref='No')
                 VehicleType(ref='Small')            VehicleUse(ref='Pleasure')
                 WorkStatus(ref='Not Working');
```

The levels are to be used by the reference method of parameterization, which is specified in the CLASS statement (see Appendix I).

The next statement creates a macro variable named Candidates that saves the names of variables that are potentially predictive of claim severity:

```
%let Candidates = AgePolicyHolder AreaType Citations CreditScore
                  Education GarageParked Gender Homeowner MaritalStatus
                  MultipleVehicles Rating StdHouseIncome TookCourse
                  VehicleOwned VehicleType VehicleUse WorkStatus;
```

Programming Tip: For convenience and reusability, save lists of variables and effects in macro variables.

Building a Gamma Regression Model

The gamma distribution and the inverse Gaussian distribution are often used to model claim severity. These distributions are explained on page 339 and page 338, respectively.

The following statements assume a gamma distribution for ClaimAmount and build a model for the mean by using the stepwise method with validation ASE as the choose criterion:

```
proc hpgenselect data=ClaimSeverity fmtlibxml=ClmsFmts;
   class &ClassVars / param=ref;
   model ClaimAmount = &Candidates / distribution=gamma link=log;
   selection method=stepwise(choose=validate select=sl stop=sbc);
   partition fraction(validate=0.25 seed=59883);
run;
```

High-performance statistical procedures with a CLASS statement support only two types of parameterization: reference parameterization and GLM parameterization (the default). The PARTITION statement requests a partition of the data in which 25% of the observations are randomly assigned to validation and 75% to training.

Programming Tip: You can reproduce a data partition by saving and reusing the SEED= value.

Interpreting the Results

The output produced by the HPGENSELECT procedure begins with Output 10.1, which displays the distribution, the link function, and the optimization technique used to compute maximum likelihood estimates of the parameters.

Output 10.1 Model Information

Model Information	
Data Source	WORK.CLAIMSEVERITY
Response Variable	ClaimAmount
Class Parameterization	Reference
Distribution	Gamma
Link Function	Log
Optimization Technique	Newton-Raphson with Ridging
Seed	59883

The ridged Newton–Raphson technique, which is the default, is explained on page 327. You can request other techniques with the TECHNIQUE= option in the procedure statement; see page 328.

Output 10.2 displays the selection method and criteria. At each step, ASE is computed on the validation data. The selected model is the smallest model at any step with the lowest ASE.

Output 10.2 Selection Information

Selection Information	
Selection Method	Stepwise
Select Criterion	Significance Level
Stop Criterion	SBC
Choose Criterion	Validation ASE
Effect Hierarchy Enforced	None
Entry Significance Level (SLE)	0.05
Stay Significance Level (SLS)	0.05
Stop Horizon	3

By default, effect hierarchy is not applied with the stepwise method; you can request it with the HIERARCHY= option in the SELECTION statement. Here, it would not make a difference because all of the candidate effects are main effects.

Output 10.3 displays the number of observations in each partition.

Output 10.3 Number of Observations

Number of Observations			
Description	Total	Training	Validation
Number of Observations Read	30360	22853	7507
Number of Observations Used	30360	22853	7507

Output 10.4 displays the formatted levels and the reference levels for the classification variables. The levels were defined on page 202.

Output 10.4 Class Level Information

		Reference	
Class	Levels	Value	Values
AreaType	4	Rural	City Rural Town Village
Citations	3	None	Multiple None One
CreditScore	8	300 to 499	300 to 499 500 to 549 550 to 599 600 to 649 650 to 699 700 to 749 750 to 799 800 to 850
Deductible	3	None	High Low None
Education	8	No HS diploma	Associate Bachelor Doctorate HS diploma Master No HS diploma Professional Some college
GarageParked	2	No	No Yes
Gender	2	F	F M
Homeowner	2	No	No Yes
MaritalStatus	5	Married	Divorced Married Never Married Separated Widowed
MultipleVehicles	2	No	No Yes
Rating	4	U	U V W X
TookCourse	2	No	No Yes
Transaction	3	New	Modify New Renew
VehicleOwned	2	No	No Yes
VehicleType	8	Small	Crossover Large Luxury Midsized Pickup SUV Small Van
VehicleUse	2	Pleasure	Commuting Pleasure
WorkStatus	3	Not Working	Full Time Not Working Part Time

Output 10.5 shows the effects that entered at each step of the selection; none were removed.

Output 10.5 Selection Summary

	Effect	Number		Validation	p
Step	Entered	Effects In	SBC	ASE	Value
0	Intercept	1	101834.787	11.2569	.
1	AreaType	2	99264.204	10.6357	<.0001
2	AgePolicyHolder	3	97896.382	10.3875	<.0001
3	VehicleType	4	97707.712	10.3157	<.0001
4	Homeowner	5	97533.598*	10.2683	<.0001
5	WorkStatus	6	97542.105	10.2607*	0.0033
6	VehicleOwned	7	97547.512	10.2621	0.0311

* Optimal Value of Criterion

Output 10.6 explains that the model at Step 5 was selected because the ASE computed from the validation data reached a minimum, and it lists the effects that were selected.

Output 10.6 Selection Reason and Selected Effects

The model at step 5 is selected where Validation ASE is 10.26067.

Selected Effects: Intercept AgePolicyHolder AreaType Homeowner VehicleType WorkStatus

Output 10.7 displays the fit statistics for each partition.

Output 10.7 Fit Statistics

Fit Statistics		
	Training	Validation
-2 Log Likelihood	97382	31923
AIC (smaller is better)	97414	31955
AICC (smaller is better)	97414	31955
BIC (smaller is better)	97542	32066
Pearson Chi-Square	15039	4724.85
Pearson Chi-Square/DF	0.6585	0.6307
Average Square Error	10.9597	10.2607

Output 10.8 displays the maximum likelihood estimates, explained in Appendix D, for the regression parameters and the dispersion parameter ϕ in the final model (see page 339 for the definition of ϕ).[†]

Output 10.8 Parameter Estimates

Parameter	DF	Estimate	Standard Error	Chi-Square	Pr > ChiSq
Intercept	1	0.326115	0.028292	132.8614	<.0001
AgePolicyHolder	1	0.012620	0.000317	1580.4026	<.0001
AreaType City	1	0.577484	0.018921	931.4844	<.0001
AreaType Town	1	0.040750	0.020014	4.1454	0.0417
AreaType Village	1	0.091743	0.045983	3.9806	0.0460
Homeowner Yes	1	-0.140030	0.010387	181.7481	<.0001
VehicleType Crossover	1	0.005467	0.016670	0.1075	0.7430
VehicleType Large	1	0.057650	0.067725	0.7246	0.3946
VehicleType Luxury	1	0.317200	0.026748	140.6342	<.0001
VehicleType Midsized	1	-0.095553	0.022327	18.3150	<.0001
VehicleType Pickup	1	0.005044	0.018769	0.0722	0.7881
VehicleType SUV	1	-0.026667	0.021988	1.4709	0.2252
VehicleType Van	1	0.027441	0.027641	0.9856	0.3208
WorkStatus Full Time	1	-0.017610	0.010479	2.8239	0.0929
WorkStatus Part Time	1	-0.047476	0.013972	11.5454	0.0007
Dispersion	1	1.945832	0.016875	.	.

With reference parameterization, the intercept is the average severity, assuming all classification variables are at their reference levels and all continuous variables are set to zero. The estimate for each classification level is the increment (positive or negative) in the average. For instance, the estimate 0.577484 for Area Type City is the increment for that level compared with Area Type Rural, assuming other classification effects are at their reference levels and continuous variables are set to zero. The estimate 0.012620 for AgePolicyHolder is the increase for one year of age, assuming classification effects are at their reference levels and other continuous variables are set to zero.

The *p*-values shown here are not adjusted for the selection process; see "Problems with Data-Driven Model Selection" on page 33.

[†]When you fit a gamma regression model with the GENMOD procedure, it produces a Parameter Estimates table with a scale parameter that is equal to the inverse of the dispersion parameter.

Example: Modeling the Frequency of Insurance Claims

This example builds a zero-inflated Poisson regression model for the frequency of insurance claims using a data set named ClaimFrequency with information about 20,361 auto insurance policyholders. The response variable is NumberClaims, the number of claims submitted during a period of time that varies by policyholder and is given by the variable Exposure. The candidate predictors happen to be the same as those in the previous example, and so the formats created on page 202 can be reused.

```
data ClaimFrequency;
   set ClaimFrequency;
   format AreaType AType.      Citations Cite.        CreditScore Cred.
          Deductible Ded.      Education EdLev.        GarageParked YN.
          Homeowner YN.        MaritalStatus MStat.   MultipleVehicles YN.
          Rating RType.        TookCourse YN.         Transaction TType.
          VehicleOwned YN.     VehicleType VType.     VehicleUse VUse.
          WorkStatus WStat. ;
run;
```

Pre-Partitioning the Data for Training, Validation, and Testing

The number of observations in ClaimFrequency is clearly sufficient to build the model with the validation ASE criterion. The PARTITION statement of the HPGENSELECT procedure could again be used to randomly assign observations for training and validation, as on page 203. However, the model built here will be compared with a Poisson regression model built with the GENSELECT procedure on page 216, and the PARTITION statement of that procedure does a different random assignment (even with the same SEED= value). By pre-partitioning the data, the comparisons can be based on the same partitions.

The following program uses the SURVEYSELECT procedure to randomly allocate 50% of the observations to training, 25% to validation, and 25% to testing. To identify the partitions, the program creates a variable named Role, which is used on page 208 and on page 217.

```
proc surveyselect data=ClaimFrequency out=ClaimFrequency rep=1
                  method=srs samprate=0.50 seed=852937 outall;
run;

data ClaimFrequency(drop=Selected); set ClaimFrequency;
   if      Selected = 1 then Role = 0;
   else if Selected = 0 then Role = 1;    /* use for training */
run;

proc surveyselect data=ClaimFrequency(where=(Role=0)) out=ClaimFrequency0
                  rep=1 method=srs samprate=0.50 seed=35911 outall;
run;

data ClaimFrequency0(drop=Selected); set ClaimFrequency0;
   if      Selected = 1 then Role = 2;    /* use for validation */
   else if Selected = 0 then Role = 3;    /* use for testing    */
run;

data ClaimFrequency; set ClaimFrequency(where=(Role=1)) ClaimFrequency0; run;

proc sort data=ClaimFrequency; by Role; run;
```

Building a Zero-Inflated Poisson Regression Model

In the insurance industry, the Poisson and negative binomial distributions are commonly used to build generalized linear models for claim frequencies (Goldburd et al. 2020, p. 21). In some applications, the number of zero counts is greater than the number predicted by these distribution. The HPGENSELECT procedure provides zero-inflated Poisson and zero-inflated negative binomial distributions, described in Appendix E, that model the probability of observing additional zero counts.

Here, because some claims are not reported, it is reasonable to think that there might be zero inflation in the distribution of NumberClaims, and so this example builds a zero-inflated Poisson model. A follow-up example on page 217 builds a Poisson model and compares the two models.

When you build a zero-inflated Poisson model, you provide two sets of candidate effects because the linear predictor has two components:

- The zero component is the linear predictor for a binary logistic regression model that predicts the probability that an observation inflates the zero count (see page 349). You specify the candidate effects for this predictor in the ZEROMODEL statement.

- The Poisson component is a linear predictor for the mean of the Poisson distribution of the counts, some of which are zero. You specify the candidate effects for this predictor with the MODEL statement.

In this example, experience suggests two different sets of candidates for the components. For instance, Deductible is a candidate for the zero component because a high deductible amount could deter the submission of a claim. On the other hand, NYoungDrvrs is a candidate for the Poisson component because the risk of a claim might be higher for policies that cover younger drivers.

The macro variable ZCandidates saves the names of candidates for the zero component:

```
%let ZCandidates = Citations Deductible StdHouseIncome VehicleOwned
                   WorkStatus;
```

The macro variable PCandidates saves the names of candidates for the Poisson component:

```
%let PCandidates = AgePolicyHolder AreaType CreditScore Education
                   GarageParked Gender MaritalStatus MultipleVehicles
                   NumberNoFault NYoungDrvrs Rating TookCourse
                   VehicleUse;
```

The following statements build the model using forward selection with the validation ASE criterion. The DISTRIBUTION=ZIP option specifies the zero-inflated Poisson distribution. Because the partition was pre-determined, the variable Role is specified with the ROLEVAR= option in the PARTITION statement and the SEED= option is not used.

```
proc hpgenselect data=ClaimFrequency fmtlibxml=ClmsFmts;
   class &ClassVars / param=ref;
   model NumberClaims = &PCandidates /  distribution=zip  link=log
                                        offset=logExposure ;
   zeromodel &ZCandidates / link=logit;
   selection method=forward(choose=validate select=sl stop=sbc);
   code file='ZIPModelScore.sas';
   partition  rolevar=Role(train='1' validate='2' test='3') ;
run;
```

The model predicts the mean of the claim frequency adjusted by time—in other words, the mean of NumberClaims divided by Exposure. Here, the OFFSET= variable is logExposure rather than Exposure because a log link function is specified and the offset variable should be on the same scale as the link function; see page 196. The CODE statement generates DATA step code for scoring new data with the final model.

Interpreting the Results

Output 10.9 shows the number of observations in each of the partitions.

Output 10.9 Numbers of Observations

Number of Observations				
Description	Total	Training	Validation	Testing
Number of Observations Read	20361	10180	5091	5090
Number of Observations Used	20361	10180	5091	5090

Output 10.10 lists the variables that entered the model during forward selection.

Output 10.10 Selection Summary

Selection Summary					
Step	Effect Entered	Number Effects In	SBC	Validation ASE	p Value
0	Intercept	1			
	Intercept_Zero	2	27519.4872	1.5157	.
1	NYoungDrvrs	3	27482.2074	1.5055	<.0001
2	Deductible_Zero	4	27460.5614	1.5085	<.0001
3	StdHouseIncome_Zero	5	27425.7005	1.5114	<.0001
4	VehicleOwned_Zero	6	27412.7951	1.5063	<.0001
5	AgePolicyHolder	7	27409.8521*	1.5077	<.0001
6	AreaType	8	27422.8838	1.5049*	0.0001
7	NumberNoFault	9	27426.4748	1.5060	0.0006

* Optimal Value of Criterion

At each step, candidate variables in both the MODEL and the ZEROMODEL statements were evaluated. The suffix _Zero designates variables selected from candidates in the ZEROMODEL statement. The model at Step 6 was chosen because the validation ASE reached a minimum at that point.

Output 10.11 displays the effects in the final model, which include intercept terms for the zero and Poisson components, as well as effects selected from the candidates.

Output 10.11 Selected Effects

Selected Effects:	Intercept AgePolicyHolder AreaType NYoungDrvrs Intercept_Zero Deductible_Zero StdHouseIncome_Zero VehicleOwned_Zero

Output 10.12 shows the fit statistics for the final model for each of the partitions.

Output 10.12 Fit Statistics

Fit Statistics			
	Training	Validation	Testing
-2 Log Likelihood	27321	13571	13727
AIC (smaller is better)	27343	13593	13749
AICC (smaller is better)	27343	13593	13750
BIC (smaller is better)	27423	13665	13821
Pearson Chi-Square	10073	4930.46	5103.81
Pearson Chi-Square/DF	0.9905	0.9706	1.0049
Average Square Error	1.5734	1.5049	1.5937

The statistic -2 Log Likelihood and the information statistics are explained on page 199. Pearson's chi-square is $\chi^2 = \sum_i^n (y_i - \mu_i)^2 / V(\mu_i)$. The statistic Pearson Chi-Square/DF is χ^2 divided by the degrees of freedom. For each statistic, a smaller value indicates a better fit.

Output 10.13 shows the parameter estimates for the Poisson component.

Output 10.13 Parameter Estimates for Poisson Component

Parameter Estimates					
Parameter	DF	Estimate	Standard Error	Chi-Square	Pr > ChiSq
Intercept	1	0.988442	0.048955	407.6643	<.0001
AgePolicyHolder	1	-0.002047	0.000579	12.4966	0.0004
AreaType City	1	0.077713	0.039324	3.9053	0.0481
AreaType Town	1	0.001755	0.041896	0.0018	0.9666
AreaType Village	1	0.142157	0.092230	2.3757	0.1232
NYoungDrvrs	1	0.056050	0.008122	47.6173	<.0001

With reference parameterization, you interpret the estimate for Intercept as the log of the mean adjusted frequency (LMAF), assuming all classification effects are at their reference levels (see Output 10.4) and all continuous variables are set to zero. The estimate 0.077713 for Area Type City is the increase in LMAF for the City level of AreaType compared with the Rural level, assuming that AgePolicyHolder and NYoungDrvrs are set to zero.

Output 10.14 shows the parameter estimates for the zero component.

Output 10.14 Parameter Estimates for Zero Inflation Component

Zero-Inflation Parameter Estimates					
Parameter	DF	Estimate	Standard Error	Chi-Square	Pr > ChiSq
Intercept_Zero	1	-1.623032	0.124273	170.5694	<.0001
Deductible_Zero High	1	0.979997	0.162566	36.3402	<.0001
Deductible_Zero Low	1	0.144293	0.129999	1.2320	0.2670
StdHouseIncome_Zero	1	0.247496	0.035447	48.7495	<.0001
VehicleOwned_Zero Yes	1	-0.441211	0.098199	20.1875	<.0001

The estimate for Intercept_Zero is the log odds of the event that an observation inflates the zero count, assuming all classification variables are at their reference levels and all continuous variables are set to zero. The estimate 0.979997 for Deductible_Zero High is the increase in log odds for the High level of Deductible compared with the None level, assuming that Deductible_Zero and VehicleOwned_Zero are at their reference levels and StdHouseIncome_Zero is set to zero.

Checking for Convergence of the Optimization Method

The HPGENSELECT and HPLOGISTIC procedures provide a variety of optimization techniques for computing maximum likelihood estimates of the parameters; these are explained on page 327. The Model Information table indicates which method was used (see Output 10.1). The default is Newton–Raphson optimization with ridging. You might seldom need an alternative, but in any case it is good practice to make sure that the convergence criterion for the method was satisfied. You can do this by examining the Convergence Status note that is displayed near the end of the output. Output 10.15 shows the note for this example.

Output 10.15 Confirmation of Convergence

Convergence criterion (ABSGCONV=1E-7) satisfied.

You can tune this criterion with the FCONV= option in the procedure statement, which also provides options for related convergence criteria.

Programming Tip: When you build models with methods that involve maximum likelihood estimation, be sure to check for convergence.

Scoring New Data with the Selected Model

The following statements use the code created by the CODE statement and saved in *ZIPModelScore.sas* to score new observations provided in the data set NewClaimFrequency.

```
data ZIPPredictions;
   set NewClaimFrequency;
   %inc 'ZIPModelScore.sas';
run;
```

The scored observations are saved in a data set named ZIPPredictions, which is partially listed in Output 10.16. The variable P_NumberClaims provides the predicted values of NumberClaims.

Output 10.16 Observations Scored with the Zero-Inflated Poisson Model

P_NumberClaims	NumberClaims	AgePolicyHolder	AreaType	Citations	Deductible	NumberNoFault	NYoungDrvrs
0.22968	0	55	Town	None	None	0	1
1.05765	0	23	Town	None	Low	0	0
1.39087	0	40	Town	None	Low	0	1

Programming Tip: By using code created with a CODE statement, you can score any data set that contains all the predictor variables and the offset variable for the model.

Example: Modeling the Cost of Insurance Claims

This example builds a Tweedie regression model for the cost of insurance claims using a data set named ClaimCost with information about 550,222 auto insurance policyholders.

The variable CostOfClaims provides the cost of a policyholder's claims during a period of time measured by the variable Exposure. The distribution of CostOfClaims has a positive probability at zero because a large number of policyholders did not submit claims, and it is continuous for claims greater than zero. The Tweedie distribution, described on page 340 of Appendix E, is often used to model data of this type.

The data set contains 10 candidate predictor variables, described in Table 10.9, whose names are saved in the macro variable CostCandidates:

```
%let CostCandidates = Deductible DriverAge Gender LicenseYrs
                      MultipleVehicles NDrvConvict NumberAtFault
                      PolicyYears Rating Transaction;
```

The following statements assign formats defined on page 202 to five of the candidate variables:

```
data ClaimCost;
   set ClaimCost;
   format Deductible Ded.  MultipleVehicles YN.  NDrvConvict Conv.
          Rating RType.    Transaction TType. ;
run;
```

The next statements use the HPGENSELECT procedure to build a Tweedie regression model for the mean claim cost by using stepwise regression with the validation ASE criterion:

```
proc hpgenselect data=ClaimCost fmtlibxml=ClmsFmts;
   class Deductible(ref='None') Gender(ref='F') MultipleVehicles(ref='No')
         Rating(ref='U') Transaction(ref='New') / param=ref;
   model CostOfClaims = &CostCandidates / link=log offset=logExposure
                        dist=Tweedie(eql optmethod=eqllhood) ;
   selection method=stepwise(choose=validate select=sl stop=sbc);
   partition fraction(validate=0.25 seed=59883);
   performance details;
run;
```

The DIST= option requests the Tweedie distribution, and the LINK= option requests the log link. The model predicts the mean of claim frequency adjusted by time. However, the variable specified with the OFFSET= option is logExposure rather than Exposure because the offset variable should have the same scale as the link function; see page 196.

Parameter estimates for Tweedie regression models require specialized techniques to compute. You can request these with the following suboptions for the DIST=TWEEDIE option:

- The EQL suboption requests estimation based on the extended quasi-likelihood function rather than the log-likelihood function (see page 341).

- The OPTMETHOD= suboption requests an optimization method that uses the extended quasi-likelihood for a sample of the data, followed by the log-likelihood for the full data. This is the default. For alternatives, see Table E.2 in Appendix E.

Interpreting the Results

Output 10.17 shows the levels of the classification variables.

Output 10.17 Class Level Information

Class	Levels	Reference Value	Values
Deductible	3	None	High Low None
Gender	2	F	F M
MultipleVehicles	2	No	No Yes
Rating	4	U	U V W X
Transaction	3	New	Modify New Renew

Output 10.18 shows the effects that entered at each step of the selection; none were removed.

Output 10.18 Selection Summary

Step	Effect Entered	Number Effects In	SBC	Validation ASE	p Value
0	Intercept	1	1379263.66	478683.069	.
1	Transaction	2	1378441.04	478510.644	<.0001
2	MultipleVehicles	3	1377698.91	478504.405	<.0001
3	LicenseYrs	4	1377444.40	478495.437*	<.0001
4	Rating	5	1377088.76	478525.144	<.0001
5	Deductible	6	1376905.15	478547.927	<.0001
6	PolicyYears	7	1376791.11	478566.775	<.0001
7	DriverAge	8	1376780.67	478585.328	<.0001
8	NumberAtFault	9	1376780.52*	478583.424	0.0003

* Optimal Value of Criterion

Output 10.19 explains that the model at Step 3 was selected because ASE computed from the validation data reached a minimum, and it lists the effects in this model.

Output 10.19 Selection Reason and Selected Effects

The model at step 3 is selected where Validation ASE is 478495.4.

Selected Effects: Intercept LicenseYrs MultipleVehicles Transaction

Output 10.20 shows how many observations were used at each stage of the optimization method for computing the parameter estimates.

Output 10.20 Stages of Optimization

Optimization Stage	Optimization Type	Sampling Percentage	Observations Used
1	Quasilikelihood	18.92	75273
2	Quasilikelihood	100.00	281112

Output 10.21 shows the fit statistics for the selected model.

Output 10.21 Fit Statistics

Fit Statistics		
	Training	Validation
-2 Log Likelihood	1377357	462827
AIC (smaller is better)	1377371	462841
AICC (smaller is better)	1377371	462841
BIC (smaller is better)	1377444	462907
Pearson Chi-Square	5.8031E8	3.5693E8
Pearson Chi-Square/DF	2064.39	3798.81
Average Square Error	382000	478495

Output 10.22 shows the parameter estimates for the selected model. Here, Dispersion and Power are the dispersion parameter ϕ and the power parameter p for the Tweedie distribution; see page 340.

Output 10.22 Parameter Estimates

Parameter Estimates					
Parameter	DF	Estimate	Standard Error	Chi-Square	Pr > ChiSq
Intercept	1	5.302392	0.032427	26737.4404	<.0001
LicenseYrs	1	-0.010075	0.000612	270.8052	<.0001
MultipleVehicles Yes	1	-0.386685	0.014181	743.5755	<.0001
Transaction Modify	1	0.307674	0.031319	96.5111	<.0001
Transaction Renew	1	-0.082409	0.030808	7.1553	0.0075
Dispersion	1	25.004774	0.067160	.	.
Power	1	1.811783	0.000493	.	.

With reference parameterization, the intercept is the average cost, assuming that the classification effects are at the reference levels shown in Output 10.17 and the continuous variables are set to zero. The estimate -0.010075 for LicenseYrs is the decrease in average cost for a one-year increase in this predictor, assuming that MultipleVehicles and Transaction are at their reference levels.

Output 10.23 shows that the HPGENSELECT procedure took about 80 seconds.

Output 10.23 Timing

Procedure Task Timing		
Task	Seconds	Percent
Reading and Levelizing Data	0.33	0.43%
Candidate evaluation	1.08	1.41%
Candidate model fit	34.13	44.73%
Final model fit	2.68	3.51%
Performing Model Selection	38.09	49.91%

At this point, the XML stream that contains the user-defined formats is no longer needed. The following statement deletes the stream:

```
%Delete_XMLStream(ClmsFmts);
```

Introduction to the GENSELECT Procedure

The GENSELECT procedure in SAS Viya fits and builds generalized linear models. It provides functionality comparable to that of the HPGENSELECT procedure in SAS/STAT, and it shares the same concepts (see page 193). Because the GENSELECT procedure was developed specifically for SAS Viya, it can run on a cluster of machines that distribute the data and the computations.

When you use the GENSELECT procedure to build a model, you specify the model with MODEL and CLASS statements, the selection method with a SELECTION statement, and data partitioning with a PARTITION statement. These statements are similar to those of the HPGENSELECT procedure.

However, there are some differences in the GENSELECT procedure:

- The selection methods include fast backward elimination.

- Information criteria can be specified with the SELECT= suboption for forward selection, backward elimination, and stepwise selection.

- The CLASS statement offers a full set of methods for parameterization.

- The EFFECT statement specifies polynomial, spline, and other constructed effects.

- The zero-inflated Poisson and zero-inflated negative binomial distributions are not available.

- The PLOTS= option in the SELECTION statement requests coefficient progression plots.

- The DISPLAY statement replaces the ODS SELECT statement for specifying displayed output. The DISPLAYOUT statement, which creates CAS tables from displayed output, provides functionality comparable to that of the ODS OUTPUT statement.

- The STORE statement saves results you can process with the ASTORE procedure. In particular, you can use the SCORE statement in the ASTORE procedure to score observations with models built by the GENSELECT procedure (see page 384).

Table 10.10 summarizes the methods available with the SELECTION statement.

Table 10.10   Effect Selection Methods in the GENSELECT Procedure

Method	Description	METHOD=*keyword*
Forward selection	Starts with no effects in the model and adds effects	FORWARD
Backward elimination	Starts with all effects in the model and deletes effects	BACKWARD
Fast backward	Starts with all effects in the model and deletes effects	BACKWARD(FAST)
Stepwise selection	Starts with no effects in the model and adds effects; effects already in the model do not necessarily stay	STEPWISE
Group lasso	Minimizes $-\mathcal{L}(\boldsymbol{\beta}; \mathbf{y})$ using a constraint that forces all parameters for the same effect to be included or excluded	LASSO
No selection	Fits fully specified model	NONE

Example: Modeling the Frequency of Insurance Claims

This example revisits the one introduced on page 207. There, the HPGENSELECT procedure was used to build a predictive model for the frequency of insurance claims by assuming a zero-inflated Poisson distribution. For comparison, this example assumes a Poisson distribution.

The data set ClaimFrequency is again used here with the same training, validation, and testing partitions created on page 207. The variable Role identifies the partitions. The frequency of insurance claims is provided by the variable NumberClaims.

Preliminary Steps

Working with these data in the CAS (Cloud Analytic Services) environment requires some preliminary steps.

User-defined formats are not directly available to a CAS server. The following statements re-create the formats that were defined on page 202 and make them visible to the CAS server:

```
proc format casfmtlib="casformats";
   value AType   1='City'  2='Town'  3='Village'  4='Rural';
   value Cite    1='None'  2='One'   3-5='Multiple';
   value Conv    0='None' 1='1 or more';
   ... additional VALUE statements ...
   value YN      1='Yes'  0='No';
run;
```

The CASFMTLIB= option adds a format library named *casformats* to the CAS session.

The following statement assigns the libref mycas to in-memory tables on the CAS server:

```
libname mycas cas;
```

Here, mycas refers to the active caslib. A caslib is associated with a data source; it is similar to a libref in SAS, but it operates on the CAS server and enables you to read and write tables from CAS. The active caslib is the default location for reading and writing in-memory data sets; it is created for you when you start a CAS session.

The next statements use the CASUTIL procedure to upload the data in ClaimFrequency to a CAS table named mycas.ClaimFrequency. These statements also assign the formats to the classification variables that will be used as candidate predictors.

```
proc casutil;
   format AreaType AType.       Citations Cite.        CreditScore Cred.
          Deductible Ded.       Education EdLev.       GarageParked YN.
          Homeowner YN.         MaritalStatus MStat.   MultipleVehicles YN.
          Rating RType.         TookCourse YN.         Transaction TType.
          VehicleOwned YN.      VehicleType VType.     VehicleUse VUse.
          WorkStatus WStat. ;
   load data=work.ClaimFrequency;
quit;
```

Programming Tip: Submit the FORMAT statement before the LOAD statement.

Building a Poisson Regression Model

The macro variable AllCandidates saves the names of candidate predictors that are to be specified with the MODEL statement in the GENSELECT procedure:

```
%let AllCandidates = AgePolicyHolder AreaType Citations CreditScore Deductible
                     Education GarageParked Gender Homeowner MaritalStatus
                     MultipleVehicles NumberNoFault NYoungDrvrs Rating
                     StdHouseIncome TookCourse VehicleOwned VehicleType
                     VehicleUse WorkStatus;
```

This list combines the candidates for the zero-inflated Poisson model that were specified with the MODEL and ZEROMODEL statements on page 208.

The following statements build a model for claim frequency by using the forward selection method with the validation ASE criterion:

```
ods graphics on / attrpriority=none;
proc genselect data=mycas.ClaimFrequency;
   class &ClassVars / param=ref;
   model NumberClaims = &AllCandidates / distribution=poisson link=log
                                         offset=logExposure;
   selection method=forward(choose=validate select=sl stop=sbc)
             plots=(coefficients fitbyrole criteria(unpack)) ;
   partition rolevar=Role(train='1' validate='2' test='3');
run;
```

With the exception of the ODS GRAPHICS statement and the PLOTS= option, these statements are similar to those in the HPGENSELECT procedure on page 208. The DISTRIBUTION= option specifies the Poisson distribution, and the LINK= option specifies the log link. The model predicts the mean of claim frequency adjusted by time. The adjustment variable logExposure is specified with the OFFSET= option for scale compatibility with the link function.

The option ATTRPRIORITY=NONE in the ODS GRAPHICS statement requests an ODS style that distinguishes the lines in plots requested with the PLOTS= option by symbols, colors, and line patterns; see "Distinguishing Groups in Graphs" on page 400 in Appendix J. By default, the lines are distinguished only by their colors.

Programming Tip: Specify ATTRPRIORITY=NONE to distinguish elements of your graphs when you use black-and-white printing.

Interpreting the Results

Output 10.24 confirms that the number of observations in each partition is the same as in Output 10.9.

Output 10.24 Numbers of Observations

Number of Observations				
Description	Total	Training	Validation	Testing
Number of Observations Read	20361	10180	5091	5090
Number of Observations Used	20361	10180	5091	5090

Output 10.25 lists the variables that entered the model during forward selection. The minimum validation ASE was reached at Step 6, when AreaType entered the model. At subsequent steps, the validation ASE increases slightly.

Output 10.25 Selection Summary

		Selection Summary			
Step	**Effect Entered**	**Number Effects In**	**SBC**	**Validation ASE**	**p Value**
0	Intercept	1	28218.6262	1.5156	.
1	NYoungDrvrs	2	28180.4831	1.5055	<.0001
2	StdHouseIncome	3	28149.8575	1.5088	<.0001
3	Deductible	4	28139.7212	1.5115	<.0001
4	VehicleOwned	5	28128.1446	1.5056	<.0001
5	AgePolicyHolder	6	28122.1683*	1.5070	<.0001
6	AreaType	7	28130.6929	1.5044*	0.0003
7	NumberNoFault	8	28133.9264	1.5054	0.0136
8	MultipleVehicles	9	28137.9115	1.5063	0.0224
		* Optimal Value Of Criterion			

Output 10.26 displays the effects that were selected. These are essentially the same effects shown in Output 10.11 for the zero-inflated Poisson model, where Deductible, StdHouseIncome, and VehicleOwned are predictors for the zero component.

Output 10.26 Selected Effects

Selected Effects: Intercept AgePolicyHolder AreaType Deductible NYoungDrvrs StdHouseIncome VehicleOwned

The PLOTS=COEFFICIENTS option requests the coefficient progression plot in Output 10.27.

Output 10.27 Coefficient Progression with Forward Selection

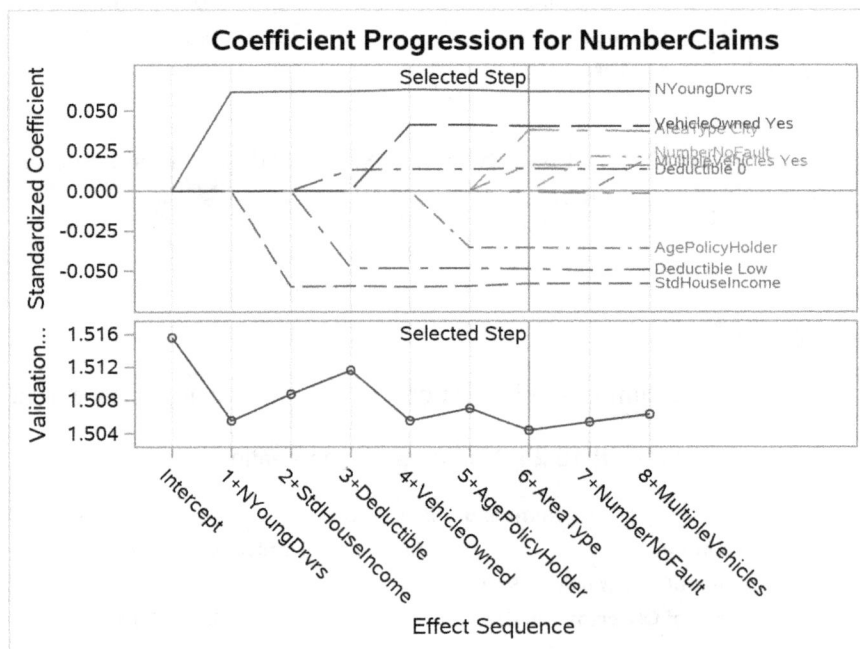

The plot in Output 10.28, requested by the PLOTS=FITBYROLE option, shows the progression of ASE for each of the three partitions. The values of ASE for the test data are larger than those for the training data, as explained in "Assessment and Minimization of Prediction Error" on page 25.

Output 10.28 Average Squared Error by Step

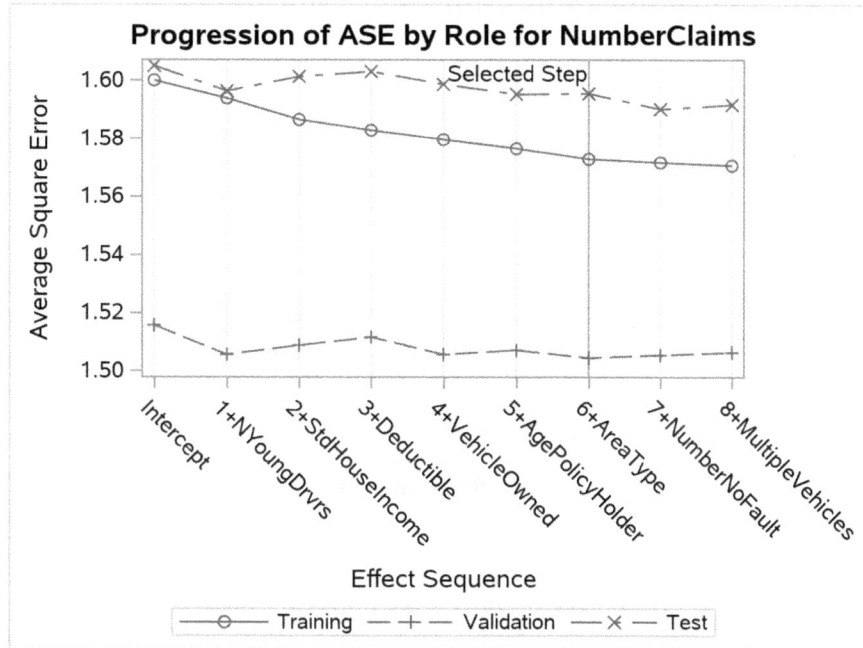

The PLOTS=CRITERIA option requests the plots in Output 10.29, Output 10.30, and Output 10.31. By default, these plots are combined in a panel to facilitate comparison. Here, the UNPACK suboption requests that they be produced individually, which makes them easier to read.

Output 10.29 Validation Average Squared Error by Step

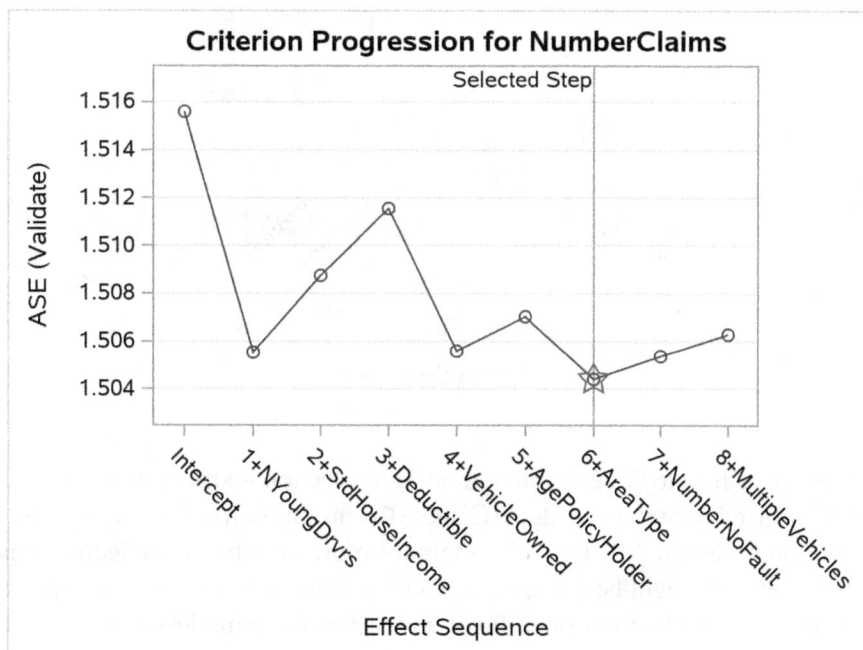

Output 10.30 Akaike's Information Criterion by Step

Criterion Progression for NumberClaims

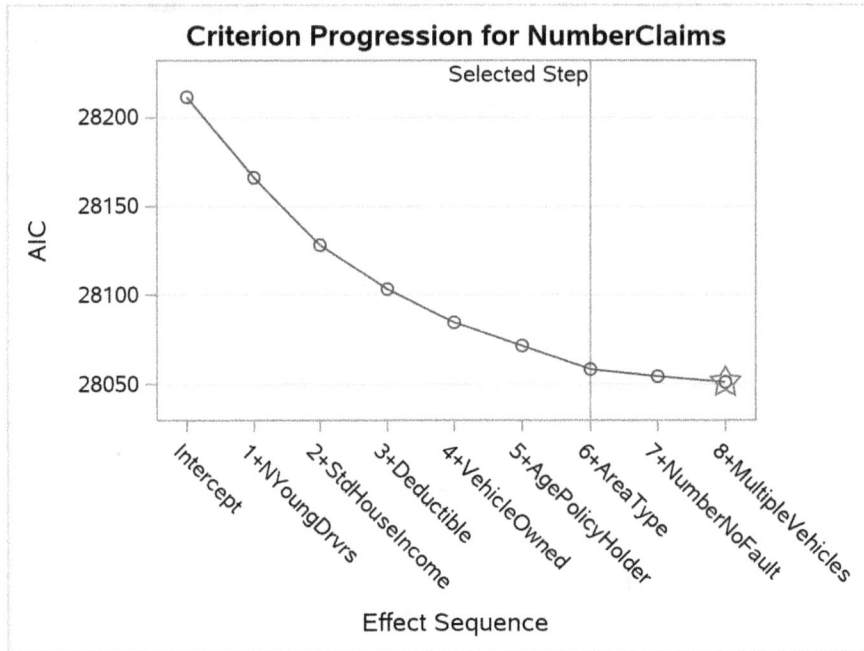

Output 10.31 Schwarz Bayesian Information Criterion by Step

Criterion Progression for NumberClaims

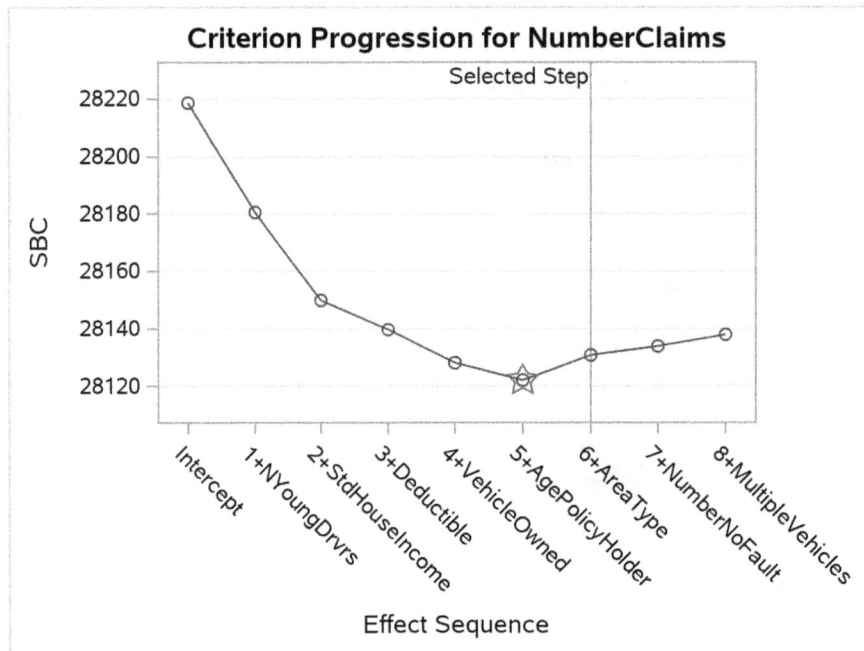

The criteria in these plots lead to three different models if selection is strictly based on their minimum values. ASE is minimized at Step 6, while AIC and SBC are minimized at Steps 8 and 5. As noted on page 29, selection based on AIC typically includes more effects than selection based on SBC. The model with five effects might be preferred because it is the sparsest, but without subject matter knowledge there is no compelling reason to favor any one of these models (see page 34).

Programming Tip: Examine the progressions for various criteria rather than basing your model selection entirely on the minimum of a single criterion.

Output 10.32 shows the fit statistics for the selected Poisson model.

Output 10.32 Fit Statistics

Fit Statistics			
Description	Training	Validation	Testing
-2 Log Likelihood	28038	13889	14101
AIC (smaller is better)	28058	13909	14121
AICC (smaller is better)	28058	13909	14121
SBC (smaller is better)	28131	13974	14186
Average Square Error	1.57282	1.50440	1.59539

You can use AIC to compare how well two generalized linear models fit the same training data. The models need not have the same distribution or the same number of effects, and they need not be nested (Burnham and Anderson 2002, p. 88). For the zero-inflated Poisson model, AIC is 27343 (see Output 10.12); for the Poisson model, AIC is 28058. This indicates that the zero-inflated Poisson model provides a better fit.

The ASE for the test data (1.59539) is nearly the same as the ASE (1.5937) for the zero-inflated Poisson model. This indicates that the two models have the same predictive ability, which is not surprising since they have the same effects.

Output 10.33 shows the parameter estimates for the selected model.

Output 10.33 Parameter Estimates

Parameter Estimates					
Parameter	DF	Estimate	Standard Error	Chi-Square	Pr > ChiSq
Intercept	1	0.772374	0.045972	282.2689	<.0001
AgePolicyHolder	1	-0.002084	0.000535	15.1632	<.0001
AreaType City	1	0.079113	0.036484	4.7021	0.0301
AreaType Town	1	-0.001268	0.038859	0.0011	0.9740
AreaType Village	1	0.159651	0.086381	3.4159	0.0646
Deductible 0	1	0.039201	0.024716	2.5154	0.1127
Deductible Low	1	-0.174183	0.036043	23.3542	<.0001
NYoungDrvrs	1	0.052656	0.007552	48.6126	<.0001
StdHouseIncome	1	-0.057613	0.009563	36.2970	<.0001
VehicleOwned Yes	1	0.084751	0.018789	20.3468	<.0001

With reference parameterization, you interpret the estimate for Intercept as the log of the mean adjusted frequency (LMAF), assuming the categorical variables are at their reference levels and the continuous variables are set to zero. The estimate -0.002084 for AgePolicyHolder is the decrease in LMAF for each year of age, assuming that AreaType, Deductible, and VehicleOwned are at their reference levels and that NYoungDrvrs and StdHouseIncome are set to zero. The effect of AgePolicyHolder is re-examined in Chapter 11 by fitting a generalized additive model; see page 239.

Summary of Procedure Features

Table 10.11 Comparison of the GENMOD, HPGENSELECT, and GENSELECT Procedures

Feature	GENMOD	HPGENSELECT	GENSELECT
Primary purpose	Statistical analysis of fully specified models	Building predictive models with large data	Building predictive models with large data
Parameterization methods for classification variables	Full set	GLM, reference	Full set
Default parameterization	GLM	GLM	GLM
SPLIT option for CLASS variables	No	No	Yes
EFFECT statement for splines and other constructed effects	No	No	Yes
Scale parameter	See page 335	ϕ if applicable	ϕ if applicable
Zero-inflated Poisson and negative binomial distributions	Yes	Yes	No
Scale for Poisson overdispersion	Yes	No	No
Default link for gamma	Inverse	Inverse	Log
Default link for inverse Gaussian	Inverse square	Inverse square	Log
User-defined links, distributions	Yes	No	No
Model building methods	None	Sequential, lasso	Sequential, lasso
Model selection criteria	None	AIC, AICC, SBC, validation ASE	AIC, AICC, SBC, validation ASE
Data partitioning	No	Yes	Yes
Selection plots	No	No	Yes
Model fit statistics	Yes	Yes	Yes
p-values for parameters	Yes	Yes	Yes
Goodness-of-fit tests	Yes	Yes	Yes
Postfit analyses: contrasts, estimates of model effects, least squares means, odds ratios	Yes	No	Limited
Correlated responses	Yes	No	No
Exact Poisson, logistic regression	Yes	No	No
Bayesian analysis	Yes	No	No
Residual diagnostics	Yes	No	Yes
Influence statistics	Yes	No	Yes
Diagnostic and fit plots	Yes	No	No
Computational operation	Single thread	Multiple threads	Multiple threads, distributed

Chapter 11
Building Generalized Additive Models

Contents

This chapter introduces three procedures for working with generalized additive models: the GAMPL procedure in SAS 9 and the GAMMOD and GAMSELECT procedures in SAS Viya. The GAMPL and GAMMOD procedures fit models, while the GAMSELECT procedure fits and builds models. The chapter also compares these procedures with the GAM procedure in SAS 9.

Generalized additive models were developed in the late 1980s by Trevor Hastie and Robert Tibshirani, both now at Stanford University (Hastie and Tibshirani 1986, 1987). Their 1990 book *Generalized Additive Models* explains the theory and provides computational methods.

Generalized additive models extend the framework of generalized linear models, discussed in Chapter 10, by incorporating smooth functions of continuous predictors that represent unknown nonlinear relationships between the mean of the response distribution and the predictors. These functions are called smooth effects or spline effects because they are typically estimated with splines. They contribute flexibility to the model that can reduce bias (see "The Bias-Variance Tradeoff for Prediction" on page 21). Plots of smooth components are valuable for interpreting the model and exploring the data; in some cases, they can suggest simpler parametric models.

By incorporating distributions in the exponential family, generalized additive models also extend the framework of additive models, which have the form

$$y = \mu + f_1(x_1) + f_2(x_2) + \cdots + f_p(x_p) + \epsilon$$

where y has a continuous distribution, the functions $f_j(\cdot)$ are typically smooth univariate functions, and the errors are assumed to be independent with $E(\epsilon) = 0$ and $\mathrm{Var}(\epsilon) = \sigma^2$. Examples of additive models are linear regression models in which $f_j(x_j) = \beta_j x_j$, general linear models in which all the terms are main effects of classification variables, and univariate smoothers such as local regression (loess) and splines. Terms for second-order or higher-order interactions can be included when there is reason to believe that complex effects are present. However, the order cannot be increased without eventually encountering the curse of dimensionality (see page 366).

Generalized additive models are semiparametric. Along with spline effects, which are nonparametric, they include the same types of parametric effects that characterize general linear models and generalized linear models. The parametric effects describe how the response varies globally—across the entire range of the data—as a function of the predictors. The spline effects describe how the response varies locally, near particular data points.

Example: Predicting Network Activity (revisited)

Figure 11.1 displays network activity data presented on page 12 of Chapter 2. The points exhibit local variation including several undulations. The curve represents a generalized additive model obtained with the GAMPL procedure by specifying a spline effect for time.

Figure 11.1 Generalized Additive Model for Network Activity

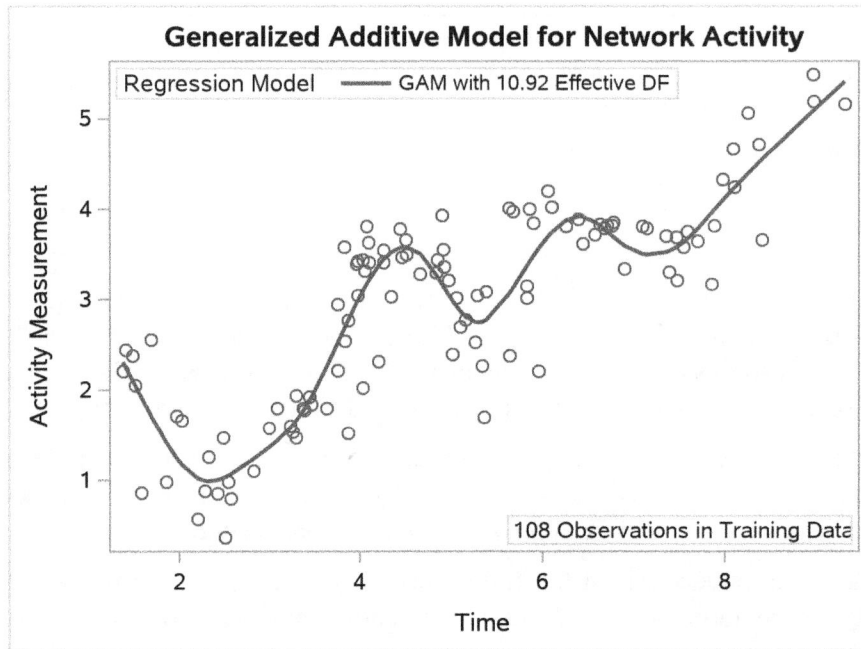

Although the model is flexible enough to capture the undulations, it is not so wiggly that it overfits the data or impedes interpretability. The flexibility is measured by the effective degrees of freedom for the model, which is 10.92 as shown in Figure 11.2.

Figure 11.2 Model Fit Statistics

Fit Statistics	
Penalized Log Likelihood	-66.20216
Roughness Penalty	0.36555
Effective Degrees of Freedom	10.91876
Effective Degrees of Freedom for Error	97.00338
AIC (smaller is better)	153.87628
AICC (smaller is better)	156.58520
BIC (smaller is better)	183.16181
GCV (smaller is better)	0.24108

The flexibility of a generalized additive model—or conversely, its smoothness—is determined algorithmically. The number of knots for each spline effect does not need to be specified, as it was for the two B-spline models discussed in Chapter 2; see Figure 2.1 on page 12.

Algorithmic Requirements of Generalized Additive Models

Generalized additive models requires algorithms that are considerably more complex than the techniques used to fit generalized linear models. In addition to estimating the parameters for linear effects, fitting a generalized additive model involves estimating a set of smooth functions $f_j(\cdot)$ and determining an appropriate amount of smoothness for each estimate.

Hastie and Tibshirani introduced an iterative algorithm called local scoring that is based on the backfitting method for estimating the components of an additive model; it generalizes the Fisher scoring method for computing maximum likelihood estimates of the parameters in a generalized linear model (see page 328).

Local scoring is computationally expensive because it fits models for each of the predictors at each step of the iteration. Its performance was more than adequate for early applications of generalized additive models in medical research and other areas, where the data had hundreds of observations and around a dozen predictors. However, local scoring does not perform well with much larger data encountered in data mining and predictive analytics. In those areas, local scoring has been superseded by algorithms that are more complex and provide the necessary scalability.

The GAMPL and GAMMOD procedures implement newer algorithms developed largely by Simon Wood, now at the University of Bristol, and explained in his 2006 book *Generalized Additive Models*. Fortunately, you do not need to know the details of how these algorithms work in order to use the procedures. Nonetheless, a basic understanding is helpful for selecting options that control the algorithms, and so an overview is provided in Appendix G, "Algorithms for Generalized Additive Models."

The procedures in this chapter implement splines as the building blocks for estimating the smooth functions $f_j(\cdot)$. As with the algorithms, you do not need to know the details of splines in order to use the procedures, but a basic understanding of spline types is helpful for deciding which options to select. An overview is provided in Appendix F, "Spline Methods."

Procedures for Generalized Additive Models

The work of Hastie and Tibshirani motivated the development of the GAM procedure in SAS/STAT, which fits generalized additive models by using local scoring and a combination of univariate smoothing splines, local regression (loess) smoothers, and bivariate thin-plate smoothing splines. The amount of smoothness is chosen by cross validation.

The GAM procedure performs well for data with dozens of variables and tens of thousands of observations. Nonetheless, it lacks the performance needed for large-data applications such as mortgage repayment modeling and insurance ratemaking.

The GAMPL and GAMMOD procedures, which supersede the GAM procedure, are designed to fit models with data in which the number of predictors can be in the thousands and the number of observations can be in the millions. To construct spline terms, these procedures use thin-plate regression splines which are relatively inexpensive to compute. Instead of local scoring, they use a penalized likelihood approach in which the penalty controls the roughness of the model fit (Wood 2003, 2004, 2008, 2011, 2012).

The GAMPL and GAMMOD procedures provide the following features:

- Response distributions in the exponential family of distributions (see Appendix E) and multiple link functions.

- Specification of parametric and spline effects with MODEL and CLASS statements.

- Construction of the basis expansions for spline terms that depend on one or more continuous variables by using thin-plate regression splines, with options for determining how the expansions are formed and options for controlling the maximum roughness of splines.

- Model fitting based on penalized likelihood estimation of the regression parameters, given a fixed set of smoothing parameters for the spline terms.

- Two methods for finding the best smoothing parameters for spline effects: outer iteration (Wood 2006, Sec. 4.7) and performance iteration (Gu and Wahba 1991; Wood 2004).

- Bayesian posterior prediction limits and tests of the total contributions of spline terms.

- Plots for spline components.

- Multithreaded computation for faster performance. The GAMMOD procedure also performs computations with data distributed across multiple computers in a cloud environment.

The GAMSELECT procedure is primarily intended for selecting the effects in a generalized additive model; it provides the following features:

- Response distributions in the exponential family of distributions (see Appendix E) and multiple link functions.

- Specification of candidate parametric and spline effects with MODEL and CLASS statements.

- Model selection through the SELECTION statement, which provides two methods for determining which spline effects should be kept in the model: componentwise functional gradient descent, also known as boosting, and shrinkage based on penalized likelihood optimization.

- Data partitioning for training, testing, and validation through the PARTITION statement.

- Plots for spline components.

- Multithreaded computation for faster performance. The procedure also performs computations with data distributed across multiple computers in a cloud environment.

Table 11.1 compares the design characteristics of the procedures. For a more detailed comparison, see Table 11.9 on page 250.

Table 11.1   Design Differences in Procedures for Generalized Additive Models

Procedure	Purpose	Data Size	Availability
GAM	Fitting models for exploration, inference	Small to moderate	SAS 9
GAMPL	Fitting models for exploration, inference	Large	SAS 9
GAMMOD	Fitting models for exploration, inference	Large, distributed	SAS Viya
GAMSELECT	Building models for prediction	Large, distributed	SAS Viya

Components of Generalized Additive Models

As explained in Chapter 10, a generalized linear model consists of three components:

- A parametric response distribution from the exponential family. See Appendix E, "Distributions for Generalized Linear Models."

- A linear parametric predictor:

$$\eta_i = \beta_0 + \beta_1 x_{i1} + \cdots + \beta_p x_{ip}, \quad i = 1, \ldots, n$$

- A link function $g(\cdot)$, which connects μ_i, the mean of the response distribution, with η_i, the linear predictor:

$$g(\mu_i) = \eta_i \equiv \beta_0 + \beta_1 x_{i1} + \cdots + \beta_p x_{ip}$$

Generalized additive models retain these components but replace η_i with the additive predictor

$$\eta_i = f_1(x_{i1}) + \cdots + f_p(x_{ip}), \quad i = 1, \ldots, n$$

where $f_1(\cdot,), \ldots, f_p(\cdot,)$ are smooth functions of continuous variables. These nonparametric effects are typically functions of a single variable but can also be functions of several variables. Since the additive predictor can also include linear parametric effects of continuous and categorical variables, it can be expressed more generally as

$$\eta_i = \underbrace{\beta_0 + \beta_1 x_{i1} + \cdots + \beta_p x_{ip}}_{\text{Linear parametric effects}} + \underbrace{f_1(x_{i(p+1)}) + \cdots + f_q(x_{i(p+q)})}_{\text{Smooth nonparametric effects}}, \quad i = 1, \ldots, n$$

Each $f_j(x_j)$ is represented by a spline effect that is a linear combination of N_j basis functions:

$$S_j(x_j) = \beta_{j_1} b_{j_1}(x_j) + \cdots + \beta_{j N_j} b_{j N_j}(x_j), \quad j = p + 1, \ldots, p + q$$

As explained in Appendix F, each basis function involves a power of x_j and is equal to zero outside of an interval determined by a value called a knot. The functions expand the model matrix $\mathbf{X}$ in the same way that the terms $1, x_j, x_j^2, x_j^3, \ldots$ of a polynomial effect for x_j add a set of columns to $\mathbf{X}$—but with superior numerical properties. The parameters $\beta_{j_1}, \ldots, \beta_{j N_j}$ control the smoothness of the spline and must be estimated. Unlike the parameters $\beta_0, \ldots, \beta_p$, they cannot be interpreted independently of each other. The number of basis functions N_j and the number of knots can grow with the number of observations.

Table 11.2 summarizes the components of a generalized additive model.

Table 11.2 Components of Generalized Additive Models

Component	Description
Linear parametric effects	Effects involving continuous or classification variables
Nonparametric effects	Spline terms involving one or more continuous variables
Link function	Logit, log, log-log, complementary log-log, identity, inverse, inverse square, probit
Distribution	Binary, binomial, gamma, inverse Gaussian, normal, Poisson, Tweedie

Introduction to the GAMPL Procedure

The GAMPL procedure is the recommended procedure in SAS/STAT for fitting generalized additive models with large data; it is a high-performance procedure, as explained on page 163. The name GAMPL is an alias for the original name HPGAMPL; the prefix HP, which stands for high performance, was dropped during development. The suffix PL stands for penalized likelihood.

Specifying the Effects

The MODEL and CLASS statements of the GAMPL procedure are similar to those of the HPGENSELECT procedure with two important differences. In the MODEL statement, you specify parametric effects with the PARAM option and nonparametric effects with the SPLINE options. For instance, the following statements (taken from a later example on page 230) fit a generalized additive model for the mean of ClaimAmount:

```
proc gampl data=ClaimSeverity;
   class AreaType Homeowner VehicleType WorkStatus;
   model ClaimAmount = param(AreaType Homeowner VehicleType WorkStatus)
                       spline(AgePolicyHolder)
                       / distribution=gamma link=log;
run;
```

The option `PARAM(AreaType Homeowner VehicleType WorkStatus)` specifies the main effects of the classification variables AreaType, Homeowner, VehicleType, and WorkStatus. The option `SPLINE(AgePolicyHolder)` specifies a smooth nonparametric effect for AgePolicyHolder that is represented by a spline term. By default, the procedure uses an optimization algorithm to determine the amount of smoothing for this effect, and the maximum degrees of freedom is 10.

Specifying the Distribution and the Link Function

Table 11.3 lists response distributions you can specify with the DISTRIBUTION= option.

Table 11.3   Distributions and Default Link Functions

Response Distribution	DISTRIBUTION= keyword	Default Link Function	Characteristics of Response Data
Binary (Bernoulli)	BINARY	Logit	Binary, typically 1s and 0s
Binomial	BINOMIAL	Logit	Count of k events in n trials
Gamma	GAMMA	Inverse	Continuous over $(0, \infty)$
Inverse Gaussian	INVERSEGAUSSIAN	Inverse square	Continuous over $(0, \infty)$
Negative binomial	NEGATIVEBINOMIAL	Log	Count $k = 0, 1, \ldots$
Normal (Gaussian)	NORMAL	Identity	Continuous over $(-\infty, \infty)$
Poisson	POISSON	Log	Count $k = 0, 1, \ldots$
Tweedie	TWEEDIE	Log	Typically continuous over $(0, \infty)$ with positive probability of 0

Table 11.4 lists link functions you can specify with the LINK= option.

Table 11.4 Link Functions

LINK=	**Link Function**	$g(\mu) = \eta =$
CLOGLOG	Complementary log-log	$\log(-\log(1-\mu))$
GLOGIT	Generalized logit	varies with number of response levels
IDENTITY	Identity	μ
INV	Inverse	$1/\mu$
INV2	Inverse square	$1/\mu^2$
LOG	Logarithm	$\log(\mu)$
LOGIT	Logit	$\log(\mu/(1-\mu))$
LOGLOG	Log-log	$-\log(-\log(\mu))$
PROBIT	Probit	$\Phi^{-1}(\mu)$

For the binary and binomial distributions, you can specify a logit, probit, complementary log-log, or log-log link function. For the gamma, inverse Gaussian, and normal distributions you can specify a log link function instead of the default link function. For the Poisson and Tweedie distributions, only the log link function is recommended.

Specifying the Method for Selecting Smoothing Parameters

The GAMPL procedure provides two methods for determining optimal smoothing parameters for spline effects, which you can request with the METHOD= option in the MODEL statement; these are described in "Searching for the Optimal λ" on page 371 of Appendix G. You request the outer iteration method by specifying METHOD=OUTER and the performance iteration method by specifying METHOD=PERFORMANCE. The performance iteration method is the default.

You use the CRITERION= option in the MODEL statement to specify the evaluation criterion for selecting smoothing parameters (see page 370). Table 11.5 lists the available criteria.

Table 11.5 Options for Model Evaluation Criteria

Criterion	**Notation**	**CRITERION=keyword**
Generalized cross validation	$V_g(\lambda)$	GCV
Unbiased risk estimator	$V_u(\lambda)$	UBRE
Generalized approximate cross validation	$V_a(\lambda)$	GACV

The default criterion is GCV for distributions that have a nontrivial dispersion parameter ϕ. As explained in Appendix E, these are the normal, inverse Gaussian, gamma, and Tweedie distributions. The default criterion is UBRE for distributions that have a dispersion parameter $\phi \equiv 1$. These are the binary, binomial, negative binomial, and Poisson distributions.

The default value of the tuning parameter γ (see page 370) is 1. You can specify a value greater than 1 with a GAMMA= suboption such as CRITERION=GCV(GAMMA=1.5).

Example: Modeling the Severity of Insurance Claims

The example on page 201 uses the data set ClaimSeverity and the HPGENSELECT procedure to build a generalized linear model for the severity of insurance claims by assuming a gamma distribution for the response variable ClaimAmount. The candidate variables are described in Table 10.9. The selected variables, shown in Output 10.6 on page 205, are AgePolicyHolder, AreaType, Homeowner, VehicleType, and WorkStatus.

This example explores the relationship between the mean of ClaimAmount and AgePolicyHolder by fitting a generalized additive model with a nonparametric effect for AgePolicyHolder. The variables AreaType, Homeowner, VehicleType, and WorkStatus are still assumed to have linear parametric effects.

Formatting the Categorical Variables

The following steps define and assign formats for the categorical variables:

```
proc format;
   value AType    1='City'  2='Town'  3='Village'  4='Rural';
   value VType    1='Crossover'  2='Pickup'  3='Small'  4='SUV'
                  5='Midsized'   6='Luxury'  7='Van'     8='Large';
   value WStat    1='Full Time' 2='Part Time' 3='Not Working';
   value YN       1='Yes'  0='No';
run;

data ClaimSeverity; set ClaimSeverity;
   format AreaType AType. Homeowner YN. VehicleType VType. WorkStatus WStat.;
run;
```

High-performance procedures such as the GAMPL procedure handle user-defined formats slightly differently from other SAS procedures. You must create a file (called an XML stream) that contains the formats and pass the file reference to the procedure with the FMTLIBXML= option. As explained on page 176, the following statement creates an XML stream named *ClmsFmts*:

```
%Make_XMLStream(name=ClmsFmts);
```

Fitting the Model

The following statements use the GAMPL procedure to fit the generalized additive model:

```
ods graphics on;
proc gampl data=ClaimSeverity plots=components fmtlibxml=ClmsFmts
           seed=757931;
   class AreaType(ref='Rural') Homeowner(ref='No') VehicleType(ref='Small')
         WorkStatus(ref='Not Working') / param=ref;
   model ClaimAmount = param(AreaType Homeowner VehicleType WorkStatus)
                       spline(AgePolicyHolder) /
                       distribution=gamma link=log;
run;
```

The PARAM option specifies the main effects of the classification variables AreaType, Homeowner, VehicleType, and WorkStatus. The SPLINE option specifies a smooth nonparametric effect for AgePolicyHolder that is represented by a thin-plate regression spline.

The simplicity of the MODEL statement belies the complexity of the algorithms for estimating the parameters of the linear effects, constructing basis expansions for splines (which involves determining the number and placement of the knots), and computing penalized likelihood estimates for spline coefficients (which involves a search for the optimal smoothing parameter). These steps are explained in Appendix G, "Algorithms for Generalized Additive Models."

The algorithms are not guaranteed to produce the best model. Convergence problems will occur if the model does not adequately describe the data; they can also occur due to technical limitations of the method for selecting the smoothing parameters (Wood 2006, Sec. 4.5). The performance iteration method, which is the default, usually converges. The outer iteration method, which you can request with the METHOD=OUTER option, is more robust, but it is also more expensive computationally. You should not expect the two methods to produce identical results.

Controlling the Construction of the Spline

By default, the procedure constructs the basis expansion for a spline effect from the unique points of the data values for the predictor. Although the default construction works well in this example, you can control it with SPLINE suboptions such as the following:

- `spline(AgePolicyHolder / df=15)` specifies 15 degrees of freedom, which determines the amount of smoothness or, equivalently, the amount of roughness.

- `spline(AgePolicyHolder / maxdf=20)` specifies 20 as the maximum number of degrees of freedom (the default is 10). The maximum is used to construct a low-rank approximation of the penalty matrix for the spline; see "Low-Rank Thin-Plate Regression Splines" on page 357.

- `spline(AgePolicyHolder / knots=list(20 to 85 by 5)` specifies a set of knots.

You can specify the maximum number of knots with the MAXKNOTS= option. If the number of unique data points exceeds this number, a subset with the maximum number is randomly selected from the data points by using the random number seed specified with the SEED= option in the procedure statement. The default maximum number is 2000.

The SEED= option specifies the random number seed for drawing a random subset of the observations to form the knots for the spline term and to construct a low-rank penalty matrix (it is not needed if you specify a list of knots). Keep in mind that the determination of the knots—and, ultimately, the fitted model—can vary with the seed. To assess the sensitivity to this variation, run the procedure with different seeds. A convenient way to do this is to specify SEED=0 (0 is the default value) so that the seed is derived from the time of day as given by the computer clock.

Programming Tip: Specify 0 with the SEED= option to explore sensitivity of the results to the random selection, and specify a positive number to reproduce the results.

Interpreting the Results

The output produced by the GAMPL procedure begins with Output 11.1, which shows that the performance iteration method and the generalized cross validation (GCV) criterion were used by default to fit the model. The performance iteration method is described on page 371; it determines the smoothing parameter for spline effects. The GCV criterion is described on page 370.

Output 11.1 Model Information

Model Information	
Description	**Value**
Data Source	WORK.CLAIMSEVERITY
Response Variable	ClaimAmount
Class Parameterization	Reference
Distribution	Gamma
Link Function	Log
Fitting Method	Performance Iteration
Fitting Criterion	GCV
Optimization Technique for Smoothing	Newton-Raphson
Random Number Seed	757931

Output 11.2 shows that all of the 30,360 observations that were read were used to fit the model.

Output 11.2 Number of Observations

Number of Observations Read	30360
Number of Observations Used	30360

Output 11.3 shows the reference levels and formatted values of the classification variables.

Output 11.3 Class Level Information

Class Level Information			
Class	**Levels**	**Reference Value**	**Values**
AreaType	4	Rural	City Rural Town Village
Homeowner	2	No	No Yes
VehicleType	8	Small	Crossover Large Luxury Midsized Pickup SUV Small Van
WorkStatus	3	Not Working	Full Time Not Working Part Time

Output 11.4 shows that the performance iteration method converged after five steps.

Output 11.4 Convergence Status

The performance iteration converged after 5 steps.

Output 11.5 shows the fit statistics for the model.

Output 11.5 Fit Statistics

Fit Statistics	
Penalized Log Likelihood	-63416
Roughness Penalty	0.00023900
Effective Degrees of Freedom	23.99999
Effective Degrees of Freedom for Error	30334
AIC (smaller is better)	126881
AICC (smaller is better)	126881
BIC (smaller is better)	127080
GCV (smaller is better)	0.59500

The total effective degrees of freedom for all of the effects in the model is 24.0. You can use this statistic to compare generalized additive models with generalized linear models. For instance, the selected model in the original example has 15 degrees of freedom; see Output 10.8. You can also use the information criteria for such comparisons because they penalize $-2\mathcal{L}(\beta; y)$ for the effective degrees of freedom. You can use GCV to compare generalized additive models fitted with penalized evaluation criteria as described on page 370.

Output 11.6 shows the parameter estimates for the linear effects in the model.

Output 11.6 Parameter Estimates for Linear Effects

			Standard		
Parameter	DF	Estimate	Error	Chi-Square	Pr > ChiSq
Intercept	1	0.994598	0.020816	2283.0634	<.0001
AreaType City	1	0.556531	0.015905	1224.4275	<.0001
AreaType Town	1	0.025552	0.016816	2.3089	0.1286
AreaType Village	1	0.042989	0.039274	1.1981	0.2737
Homeowner Yes	1	-0.210369	0.008937	554.1469	<.0001
VehicleType Crossover	1	0.016418	0.013907	1.3936	0.2378
VehicleType Large	1	0.128110	0.052799	5.8873	0.0153
VehicleType Luxury	1	0.321926	0.022540	203.9923	<.0001
VehicleType Midsized	1	-0.105387	0.018606	32.0823	<.0001
VehicleType Pickup	1	0.020257	0.015714	1.6617	0.1974
VehicleType SUV	1	-0.001970	0.018373	0.0115	0.9146
VehicleType Van	1	0.024416	0.022972	1.1297	0.2878
WorkStatus Full Time	1	-0.017475	0.008769	3.9716	0.0463
WorkStatus Part Time	1	-0.041464	0.011668	12.6288	0.0004
Dispersion	1	2.091213	2.754177		

With reference parameterization, requested by specifying PARAM=REF in the CLASS statement, you interpret the intercept as the average severity, assuming the classification variables are at the reference levels shown in Output 11.3 and the continuous variables are set to zero, so any spline effects are also set to zero. The estimate for each level of a classification effect is the increment (which can be positive or negative) in the average.

For instance, the estimate 0.556531 for Area Type City is the increase in average severity for that level compared with Area Type Rural, assuming the other classification effects are at their reference levels and the continuous variables are set to zero. The standard errors, chi-square values, and *p*-values are approximations because the distribution theory for generalized additive models is not exact.

Output 11.7 shows the effective degrees of freedom, the estimated smoothing parameter, and the roughness penalty for the smooth term. Here, the number of knots (68) is the number of values of AgePolicyHolder, which range from 23 to 90.

Output 11.7 Estimates for Smooth Effect

Estimates for Smoothing Components

Component	Effective DF	Smoothing Parameter	Roughness Penalty	Number of Parameters	Rank of Penalty Matrix	Number of Knots
Spline(AgePolicyHolder)	8.99999	2.061E-9	0.000239	9	10	68

Output 11.8 shows a plot of the spline component for AgePolicyHolder, which was requested with the PLOTS= option. The band is a 95% Bayesian posterior confidence band proposed by Wahba (1983) and Nychka (1988); it is tight because the number of observations is large.

Output 11.8 Spline Component Plot

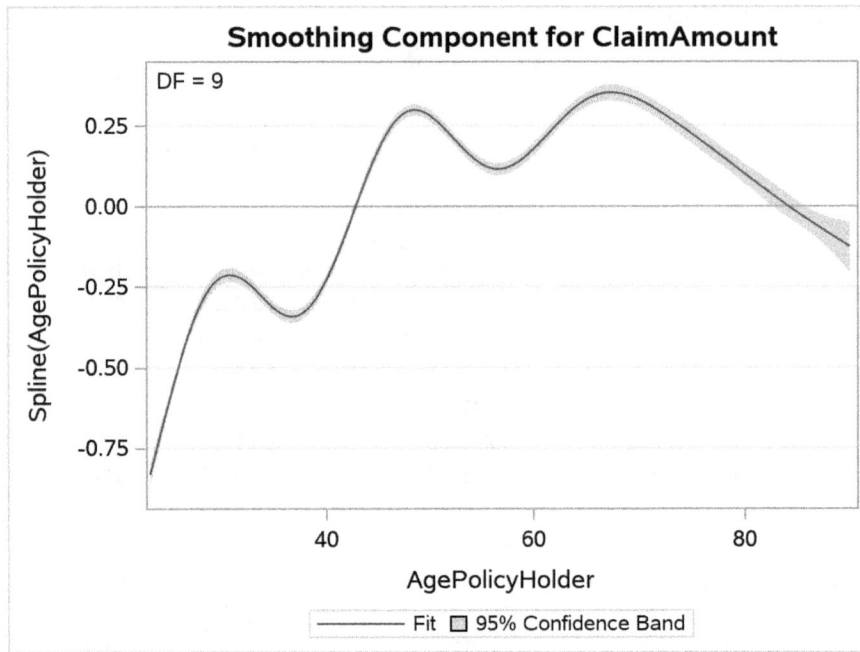

The effect of age has three peaks and two valleys; it increases for policy holders under 30 and decreases for those over 70. In general, graphs of this type stimulate discussion and interpretation; they can also help to identify unusual data points and suggest simpler parametric models.

Advantages of Splines over Categorization

Instead of using splines to model nonlinear effects, continuous predictors such as AgePolicyHolder are sometimes categorized or banded. The predictor range is broken into contiguous intervals, an indicator variable x_j is created for each interval, and the indicator variables replace the predictor in the model. For binary logistic regression with a logit link, categorization is appealing because $\exp(\hat{\beta}_j)$ can be interpreted as the effect of the jth interval on the odds of the event, and these estimates can be compared. However, as pointed out by Harrell (2015, p. 19), this approach can create more problems than it solves:

- Categorization assumes the dependency relationship is constant within intervals and discontinuous across intervals, which might not be the case, as in this example.

- Interval cutpoints are arbitrary and can lead to different results when reassigned.

- Categorization leads to invalid p-values and biased estimates of the β_js unless the cutpoints are assigned without knowledge of the response variable.

- In predictive applications, categorization complicates scoring unless the predictor values for new observations are also categorized, which might not be reasonable.

You can avoid these problems by modeling nonlinearity with spline effects.

Example: Modeling the Effect of Location on Claim Severity

In the preceding example, the effect of AreaType City shown in Output 11.6 was found to be significant. After seeing this result, an analyst decided to explore the effect of geographic location by fitting a generalized additive model in which the parametric effect of AreaType is replaced by a bivariate nonparametric effect for the longitude and latitude of the residence of the policy holder. These coordinates are provided by variables named LonAgePolicyHolder and LatAgePolicyHolder.

In order to focus the analysis, a subset of the observations in ClaimSeverity was selected for policy holders in the United States who live in a region of central North Carolina:

```
data ClaimSeverityNC;
   set ClaimSeverity;
   if ((LatPolicyHolder GE  34.8) AND (LatPolicyHolder LE 36.54) AND
       (LonPolicyHolder GE -81.0) AND (LonPolicyHolder LE -77.0)    );
run;
```

The data set ClaimSeverityNC has 23,696 observations.

Using this data set, the following statements fit a generalized additive model with a spline effect for AgePolicyHolder and a spline effect for LatPolicyHolder and LonPolicyHolder:

```
proc gampl data=ClaimSeverityNC plots(unpack)=components
           fmtlibxml=ClmsFmts seed=757931;
   class Homeowner(ref='No') VehicleType(ref='Small')
         WorkStatus(ref='Not Working') / param=ref;
   model ClaimAmount = param(Homeowner VehicleType WorkStatus)
                    spline(AgePolicyHolder)
                    spline(LonPolicyHolder LatPolicyHolder)
            / distribution=gamma link=log method=outer;
run;
```

The basis expansions and the smoothing parameters for both of the spline effects are determined algorithmically, and the outer iteration method is used to fit the model.

In addition to the spline effects, the model includes linear parametric effects for the classification variables Homeowner, VehicleType, and Workstatus. The formats for these variables are inherited from ClaimSeverity.

Output 11.9 shows the fit statistics for the model.

Output 11.9 Fit Statistics

Fit Statistics	
Penalized Log Likelihood	-50935
Roughness Penalty	9.62618
Effective Degrees of Freedom	38.85272
Effective Degrees of Freedom for Error	23657
AIC (smaller is better)	101938
AICC (smaller is better)	101938
BIC (smaller is better)	102251
GCV (smaller is better)	0.51080

As explained on page 24, the effective degrees of freedom (38.9) measures the flexibility of the model; it is greater than that of the previous model (24.0), which is to be expected since a bivariate spline effect replaced a categorical predictor. The information criteria and GCV in Output 11.9 are less than those in Output 11.5. Fitting the new model to the data in ClaimSeverity produces similar results (not shown), which indicate that it provides a better fit.

Output 11.10 shows the parameter estimates for the linear effects in the model.

Output 11.10 Parameter Estimates

Parameter Estimates

Parameter	DF	Estimate	Standard Error	Chi-Square	Pr > ChiSq
Intercept	1	1.419391	0.016803	7135.6966	<.0001
Homeowner Yes	1	-0.206382	0.010039	422.6227	<.0001
VehicleType Crossover	1	0.012620	0.015662	0.6493	0.4204
VehicleType Large	1	0.054078	0.058337	0.8593	0.3539
VehicleType Luxury	1	0.326280	0.025340	165.7997	<.0001
VehicleType Midsized	1	-0.100370	0.020977	22.8947	<.0001
VehicleType Pickup	1	0.009200	0.017688	0.2705	0.6030
VehicleType SUV	1	-0.018269	0.020655	0.7822	0.3765
VehicleType Van	1	0.028601	0.026069	1.2038	0.2726
WorkStatus Full Time	1	-0.016345	0.009876	2.7390	0.0979
WorkStatus Part Time	1	-0.040605	0.013101	9.6058	0.0019
Dispersion	1	2.115538	2.788188		

For each of the categorical variables, at least one level is significant.

Output 11.11 shows the effective degrees of freedom and related quantities for the smooth terms. These measures are explained on page 372 of Appendix G.

Output 11.11 Estimates for Smooth Effects

Estimates for Smoothing Components

Component	Effective DF	Smoothing Parameter	Roughness Penalty	Number of Parameters	Rank of Penalty Matrix	Number of Knots
Spline(AgePolicyHolder)	8.00019	0.9149	0.0193	9	10	68
Spline(LonPolicyHolder LatPolicyHolder)	18.85253	0.0517	9.6069	19	20	2000

Output 11.12 shows the results of tests for the null hypotheses that claim severity is not dependent on the spline effects. Both tests are significant, which is not surprising considering the number of observations. The p-values are analogous to the p-values for the parametric effects in Output 11.10.

Output 11.12 Tests for Smooth Effects

Tests for Smoothing Components

Component	Effective DF	Effective DF for Test	F Value	Pr > F
Spline(AgePolicyHolder)	8.00019	8	4077.53	<.0001
Spline(LonPolicyHolder LatPolicyHolder)	18.85253	19	4804.58	<.0001

Output 11.13 shows a plot of the spline component for AgePolicyHolder. This resembles the plot in Output 11.8, except that here the effect of age increases for policy holders over 80. This could be due to differences in the characteristics of older policy holders who are not included in ClaimSeverityNC, or it could simply be due to fewer data points at the upper end of the age range.

Output 11.13 Spline Component for AgePolicyHolder

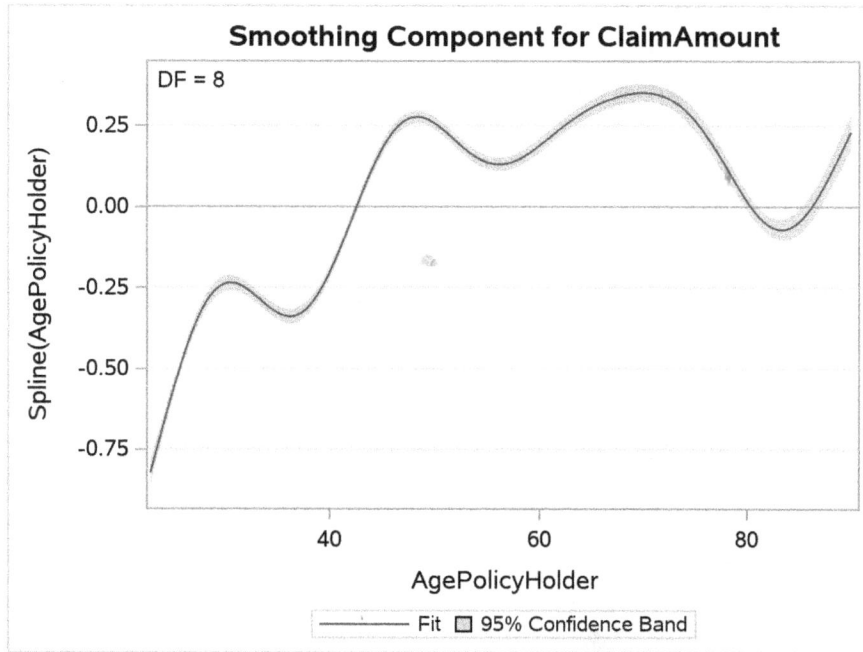

Output 11.14 shows the bivariate spline effect of the location of the policy holder. The axes are scaled in degrees of longitude and latitude.

Output 11.14 Spline Component for LatPolicyHolder and LonPolicyHolder

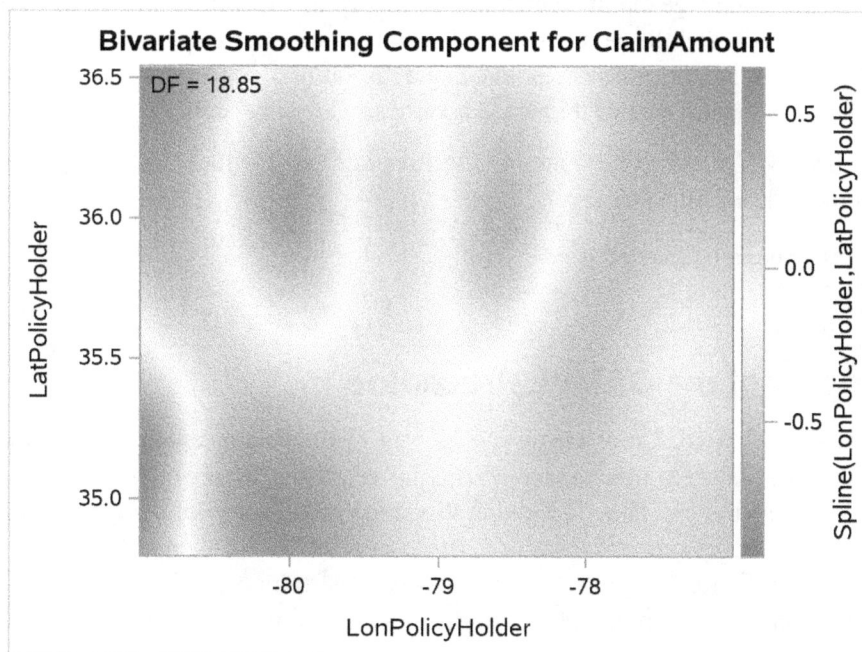

Annotating the Contour Plot

Output 11.14 reveals three areas in which the average claim amounts are clearly higher. You can identify these areas by annotating the contour plot with the locations of cities in central North Carolina. Appendix K provides a SAS program for this purpose and explains how you can annotate graphs produced by statistical procedures.

Output 11.15 shows the annotated plot.

Output 11.15 Annotated Spline Component Plot

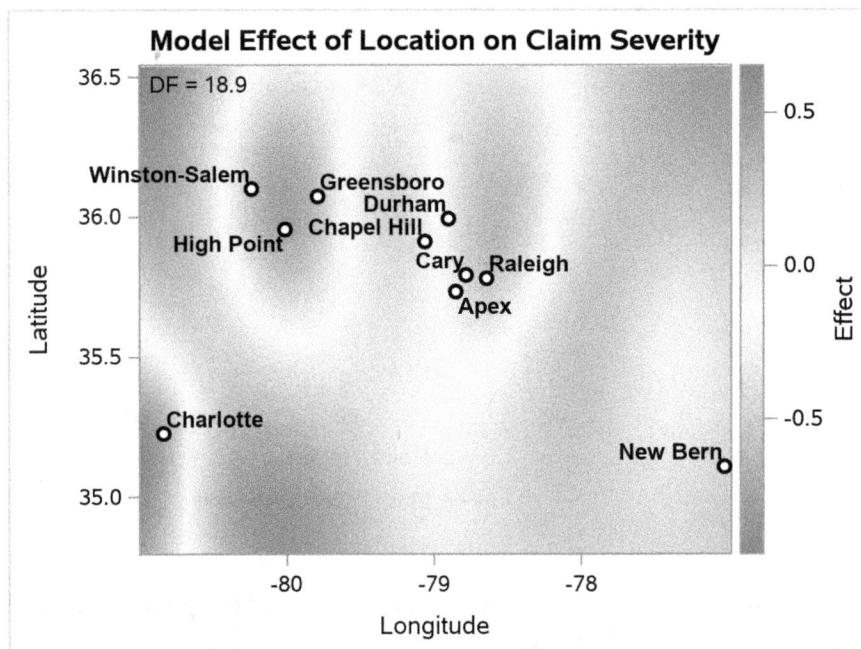

The plot reveals higher average claim amounts in the Charlotte area, the Triad area (Winston-Salem, High Point, Greensboro), and the Triangle area (Raleigh, Durham, Chapel Hill). The reason for the north-south elongation of these areas is that one degree of latitude is equal to 68.7 miles, whereas (at 35 degrees of latitude) one degree of longitude is only equal to 56.7 miles.

At this point, the XML stream that contains the user-defined formats is no longer needed. The following statement deletes the stream:

```
%Delete_XMLStream(ClmsFmts);
```

Further Examples of the GAMPL Procedure

At SAS Global Forum 2016, Carol Frigo and Kelsey Osterloo presented a paper in which they used the GAMPL procedure to incorporate geospatial variables in generalized additive models for pricing homeowner insurance. They found that this improves on traditional ratemaking done with generalized linear models (Frigo and Osterloo 2016). In a 2017 SAS Global Forum paper, Osterloo and Angela Wu used the LOESS and GAMPL procedures to incorporate household location and local crime risk in pure premium models for homeowner insurance (Osterloo and Wu 2017).

Introduction to the GAMMOD Procedure

The GAMMOD procedure in SAS Viya fits generalized additive models. It provides the same features as the GAMPL procedure in SAS/STAT (see page 226), it shares the same concepts (see page 227), and it provides results that agree closely. The computations in both procedures are multithreaded, and because the GAMMOD procedure was developed for SAS Viya, it can also run on a cluster of machines that distribute the data and the computations.

When you use the GAMMOD procedure, you specify the model with MODEL and CLASS statements that are the same as those for the GAMPL procedure. Likewise, the options for specifying the distribution and the link function are the same (see page 228), as are the options for selecting smoothing parameters (see page 229). Nonetheless, there are a few differences between the two procedures:

- The GAMMOD procedure provides a BY statement and a PLOTS= option, which are currently not available in the GAMPL procedure.

- The default link function for the gamma and inverse Gaussian distributions is the log link in the GAMMOD procedure and the reciprocal link in the GAMPL procedure.

- The FMTLIBXML= option, which you specify in the GAMPL procedure statement, does not apply in the GAMMOD procedure.

- Specifying the same value with the SEED= option in the procedure statements for the GAMMOD and GAMPL procedures will not produce identical results because random number generation is implemented differently.

- The DISPLAY statement replaces the ODS SELECT statement for specifying displayed output. The DISPLAYOUT statement, which creates CAS tables from displayed output, provides functionality comparable to that of the ODS OUTPUT statement.

- The STORE statement saves results you can process with the ASTORE procedure. In particular, you can use the SCORE statement in the ASTORE procedure to score observations with models built by the GAMMOD procedure (see page 384).

Example: Modeling the Frequency of Insurance Claims

This example revisits the one introduced on page 216 in Chapter 10, which uses the data set Claim-Frequency and the GENSELECT procedure to build a generalized linear model for NumberClaims, the frequency of insurance claims. The predictors selected in that example are AgePolicyHolder, AreaType, Deductible, NYoungDrvrs, StdHouseIncome, and VehicleOwned; see the selection summary in Output 10.25 on page 218. Table 10.9 on page 201 provides descriptions of these predictors.

Here, the linear effect in AgePolicyHolder is replaced with a spline effect in a generalized additive model that is otherwise the same as the generalized linear model. The new model is used to score or predict the response NumberClaims for observations in the test partition of ClaimFrequency created on page 207. The variable Role identifies the partitions with a value of 1 for training data and a value of 3 for test data.

Preliminary Steps

Working with the data set ClaimFrequency in the CAS (Cloud Analytic Services) environment requires the same preliminary steps explained in Chapter 10 on page 216.

User-defined formats are not directly available to a CAS server. The following statements re-create the formats defined on page 202 and make them visible to the CAS server:

```
proc format casfmtlib="casformats";
   value AType   1='City'  2='Town'  3='Village'  4='Rural';
   value Cite    1='None'  2='One'  3-5='Multiple';
   value Conv    0='None' 1='1 or more';
   ... additional VALUE statements ...
   value YN      1='Yes'  0='No';
run;
```

The CASFMTLIB= option adds a format library named *casformats* to the CAS session.

The following statement assigns the libref mycas to in-memory tables on the CAS server:

```
libname mycas cas;
```

Here, mycas refers to the active caslib. A caslib is associated with a data source; it is similar to a libref in SAS, but it operates on the CAS server and enables you to read and write tables from CAS. The active caslib is the default location for reading and writing in-memory data sets; it is created for you when you start a CAS session.

The next statements use the CASUTIL procedure to upload the data in ClaimFrequency to a CAS table named mycas.ClaimFrequency. These statements also assign formats to the classification variables.

```
proc casutil;
   format AreaType AType.      Citations Cite.        CreditScore Cred.
          Deductible Ded.      Education EdLev.       GarageParked YN.
          Homeowner YN.        MaritalStatus MStat.   MultipleVehicles YN.
          Rating RType.        TookCourse YN.         Transaction TType.
          VehicleOwned YN.     VehicleType VType.     VehicleUse VUse.
          WorkStatus WStat. ;
   load data=work.ClaimFrequency;
quit;
```

> **Programming Tip:** The FORMAT statement should be submitted before the LOAD statement.

The next statement creates a macro variable named ClassVars that saves the names of the categorical variables together with their reference levels. The levels are used by the reference method of parameterization, which you request with the PARAM=REF option in the CLASS statement.

```
%let ClassVars = AreaType(ref='Rural')          Citations(ref='None')
                 CreditScore(ref='300 to 499')  Deductible(ref='None')
                 Education(ref='No HS diploma')  GarageParked(ref='No')
                 Gender(ref='F')                 Homeowner(ref='No')
                 MaritalStatus(ref='Married')    MultipleVehicles(ref='No')
                 Rating(ref='U')                 TookCourse(ref='No')
                 Transaction(ref='New')          VehicleOwned(ref='No')
                 VehicleType(ref='Small')        VehicleUse(ref='Pleasure')
                 WorkStatus(ref='Not Working');
```

Including Observations for Scoring with the Input Data

Unlike the HPGENSELECT and GENSELECT procedures, the GAMMOD procedure does not provide a CODE statement that creates SAS code for scoring new data (see page 211). However, as explained in Appendix H, the GAMMOD procedure does provide a STORE statement you can use to score new data with the ASTORE procedure; see "Scoring with the ASTORE Procedure in SAS Viya" on page 384.

Alternatively, you can include the observations to be scored in the DATA= table and assign a missing value to their response values. The following statements make this assignment for observations in the test partition of ClaimFrequency. The variable NumberClaimsObs saves the observed values of NumberClaims.

```
data mycas.ClaimFrequency;
   set mycas.ClaimFrequency(where=(Role IN (1,3)));
   NumberClaimsObs = NumberClaims;
   if Role EQ 3 then NumberClaims = . ;
run;
```

Fitting the Model

The following statements fit a model for claim frequency by using the observations in the training partition, for which the values of NumberClaims are nonmissing:

```
proc gammod data=mycas.ClaimFrequency plots=components seed=892443;
   class &ClassVars / param=ref;
   model NumberClaims = param(AreaType Deductible VehicleOwned)
                        param(NYoungDrvrs StdHouseIncome)
                        spline(AgePolicyHolder)
                      / distribution=poisson link=log offset=logExposure;
   output out=mycas.PredClaimFrequency copyvars=(Role NumberClaimsObs)
          pred=NumberClaimsPred;
run;
```

The MODEL statement specifies a Poisson distribution, log link, and offset variable as in the MODEL statement for the GENSELECT procedure on page 216. Here, the PARAM options specify linear parametric effects for the categorical predictors and continuous predictors, and the SPLINE option specifies a spline effect for AgePolicyHolder. The OUTPUT statement names a CAS table that saves the predicted response values for the test observations as the variable PredClaimFrequency and includes the variables Role and NumberClaimsObs.

Interpreting the Results

Output 11.16 shows that 10,180 observations (the training partition) were used to fit the model.

Output 11.16 Number of Observations

Number of Observations Read	15270
Number of Observations Used	10180

Output 11.17 shows the fit statistics for the model.

Output 11.17 Fit Statistics

Fit Statistics	
Penalized Log Likelihood	-14016
Roughness Penalty	2.14282
Effective Degrees of Freedom	14.85225
Effective Degrees of Freedom for Error	10164
AIC (smaller is better)	28059
AICC (smaller is better)	28059
BIC (smaller is better)	28167
UBRE (smaller is better)	0.24842

Output 11.18 shows the parameter estimates for the linear effects in the model. Since reference parameterization is used, you can interpret the estimates as explained on page 233.

Output 11.18 Parameter Estimates

Parameter Estimates					
Parameter	DF	Estimate	Standard Error	Chi-Square	Pr > ChiSq
Intercept	1	0.667672	0.037298	320.4412	<.0001
AreaType City	1	0.078114	0.036504	4.5790	0.0324
AreaType Town	1	-0.001694	0.038877	0.0019	0.9653
AreaType Village	1	0.159153	0.086398	3.3933	0.0655
Deductible 0	1	0.040160	0.024726	2.6381	0.1043
Deductible Low	1	-0.173437	0.036058	23.1355	<.0001
VehicleOwned Yes	1	0.084888	0.018793	20.4031	<.0001
NYoungDrvrs	1	0.052435	0.007554	48.1762	<.0001
StdHouseIncome	1	-0.057552	0.009562	36.2276	<.0001

Output 11.19 shows estimates for the smoothing component. The effective degrees of freedom for Spline(AgePolicyHolder) is 5.85.

Output 11.19 Estimates for Smooth Effect

Estimates for Smoothing Components						
Component	Effective DF	Smoothing Parameter	Roughness Penalty	Number of Parameters	Rank of Penalty Matrix	Number of Knots
Spline(AgePolicyHolder)	5.85225	22343.7	2.1428	9	10	68

Output 11.20 shows that the smooth component is statistically significant.

Output 11.20 Test for Smooth Effect

Tests for Smoothing Components				
Component	Effective DF	Effective DF for Test	Chi-Square	Pr > ChiSq
Spline(AgePolicyHolder)	5.85225	7	21.3995	0.0032

Output 11.21 shows a plot of the spline component for AgePolicyHolder, which exhibits nonlinearity. Unlike the plot in Output 11.8, this effect decreases with age.

Output 11.21 Component Plot

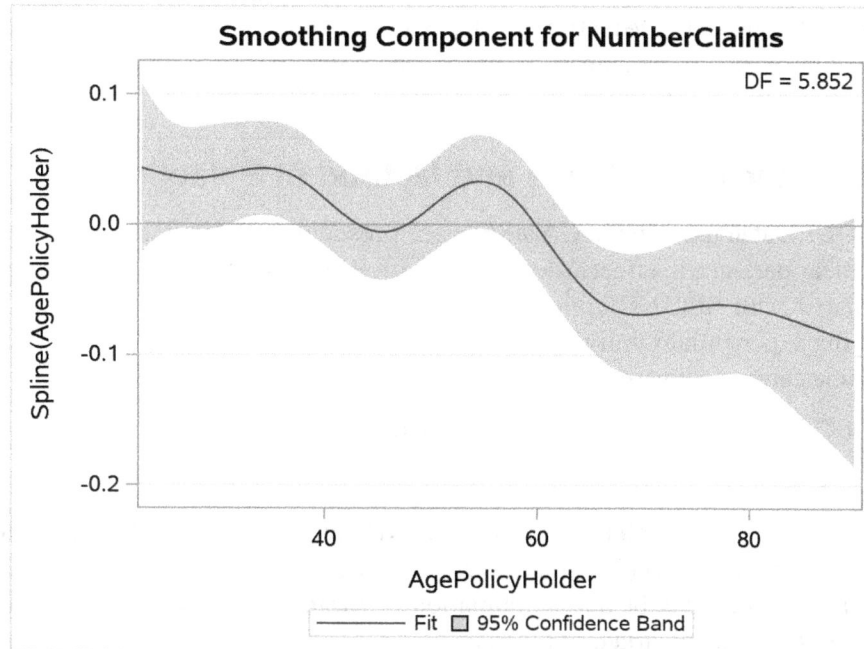

Smoothing Component for NumberClaims

Computing Prediction Error for the Test Data

The next statements compute and display the average square error (ASE) for the test observations:

```
data mycas.PredClaimFrequency;
   set mycas.PredClaimFrequency(where=(Role=3));
   SqError = (NumberClaimsObs - NumberClaimsPred)**2;
run;

proc means data=mycas.PredClaimFrequency n mean;
   output out=ASESummary (drop=_TYPE_ _FREQ_) mean=ASE n=N;
   var SqError;
run;

proc print data=ASESummary noobs label;
   label ASE = 'Average Squared Error' N = 'Number of Test Observations';
run;
```

Output 11.22 Average Squared Error

Average Squared Error	Number of Test Observations
1.59443	5090

The ASE is nearly the same as the ASE obtained by the generalized linear model for the test data, which is shown in Output 10.32 on page 221.

Introduction to the GAMSELECT Procedure

The GAMSELECT procedure in SAS Viya is primarily designed to build generalized additive models. It also fits models but lacks the versatility of the GAMPL and GAMMOD procedures, which are designed for that purpose. For a comparison of procedure features, see Table 11.9 on page 250.

Specifying the Candidate Effects and Method of Selection

You use the MODEL statement in the GAMSELECT procedure to specify candidate effects, which can be either linear parametric effects (designated with PARAM options) or nonparametric spline effects (designated with SPLINE options). You also use this statement to specify a response distribution in the exponential family, a link function, and an offset variable. You use the CLASS statement to name categorical variables.

The GAMSELECT procedure has a SELECTION statement, which provides two methods of model selection:

- The boosting method, which uses a componentwise implementation of the generic functional gradient descent algorithm (Friedman 2001; Bühlmann and Hothorn 2007). With this method, the candidate effects can be any combination of parametric effects and spline effects. The spline effects can be univariate or bivariate.

- The shrinkage method, which uses a penalized likelihood approach with penalties that induce sparsity. This approach draws on penalization techniques for fitting high-dimensional additive models proposed by Meier, Van de Geer, and Bühlmann (2009, Sec. 4.2), Suzuki and Sugiyama (2013), and Amato, Antoniadis, and De Feis (2016). With this method, the effects must include at least one spline effect. Selection is performed only on the spline effects, which must be univariate.

Appendix G explains the algorithms employed by the two methods, which are fundamentally different; see "Methods for Selecting Generalized Additive Models" on page 372.

The basic syntax of the GAMSELECT procedure is similar to that of the GAMPL and GAMMOD procedures, with the addition of SELECTION and PARTITION statements. For instance, the following statements build a generalized additive model from a set of candidate effects by applying the boosting method:

```
proc gamselect data=mycas.ClaimSeverity plots=components seed=892443;
   class Citations(ref='None') CreditScore(ref='300 to 499')
         Deductible(ref='None') / param=ref;
   model ClaimAmount = param(Citations CreditScore Deductible)
                       param(NYoungDrvrs)
                       spline(AgePolicyHolder)
                       spline(LonPolicyHolder LatPolicyHolder)
                     / distribution=gamma link=log;
   selection method=boosting;
run;
```

You can specify any number of PARAM options and any number of SPLINE options.

Specifying the Distribution and the Link Function

Table 11.6 lists response distributions you can specify with the DISTRIBUTION= option.

Table 11.6 Distributions and Default Link Functions

Response Distribution	DISTRIBUTION= keyword	Default Link Function	Characteristics of Response Data
Binary (Bernoulli)	BINARY	Logit	Binary, typically 1s and 0s
Binomial	BINOMIAL	Logit	Count of k events in n trials
Gamma	GAMMA	Log	Continuous over $(0, \infty)$
Inverse Gaussian	INVERSEGAUSSIAN	Log	Continuous over $(0, \infty)$
Normal (Gaussian)	NORMAL	Identity	Continuous over $(-\infty, \infty)$
Poisson	POISSON	Log	Count $k = 0, 1, \ldots$

The default link functions for the gamma and inverse Gaussian distributions are the same as those provided by the GAMMOD procedure but differ from those provided by the GAMPL procedure (see Table 11.3).

Table 11.7 lists link functions you can specify with the LINK= option.

Table 11.7 Link Functions

LINK=keyword	Link Function	$g(\mu) = \eta =$
CLOGLOG	Complementary log-log	$\log(-\log(1-\mu))$
IDENTITY	Identity	μ
INV	Inverse	$1/\mu$
INV2	Inverse square	$1/\mu^2$
LOG	Logarithm	$\log(\mu)$
LOGIT	Logit	$\log(\mu/(1-\mu))$
LOGLOG	Log-log	$-\log(-\log(\mu))$
PROBIT	Probit	$\Phi^{-1}(\mu)$

Table 11.8 lists alternative link functions available for each distribution.

Table 11.8 Alternative Link Functions

Distribution	LINK=keyword
Binary (Bernoulli)	PROBIT, CLOGLOG, LOGLOG
Binomial	PROBIT, CLOGLOG, LOGLOG
Gamma	INV
Inverse Gaussian	INV2
Normal (Gaussian)	LOG
Poisson	None

Example: Building a Model by Using the Boosting Method

This example revisits the one on page 201, which uses the data set ClaimSeverity and the HPGENSELECT procedure to build a generalized linear model by assuming a gamma distribution for the response variable ClaimAmount. Here, the GAMSELECT procedure is used to build a generalized additive model under the same assumption. However, spline effects are substituted for two of the original candidate effects:

- A univariate spline effect in AgePolicyHolder replaces the linear parametric effect of this variable.

- A bivariate spline effect in LonPolicyHolder and LatPolicyHolder replaces the linear parametric effect of AreaType.

The rest of the original candidate effects listed on page 203 are retained as linear parametric effects.

Formatting the Categorical Variables

Working with the data set ClaimSeverity in the CAS environment requires the same preliminary steps explained on page 240. The following statements upload the data to a CAS table named mycas.ClaimSeverity and assign formats to the classification variables:

```
proc casutil;
    format Citations Cite.       CreditScore Cred.       Deductible Ded.
           Education EdLev.       GarageParked YN.        Homeowner YN.
           MaritalStatus MStat.   MultipleVehicles YN.    Rating RType.
           TookCourse YN.         Transaction TType.      VehicleOwned YN.
           VehicleType VType.     VehicleUse VUse.        WorkStatus WStat. ;
    load data=work.ClaimSeverity;
quit;
```

Specifying the Effects and the Method of Selection

The following statements select a model for ClaimAmount:

```
proc gamselect data=mycas.ClaimSeverity plots=components seed=892443;
    class &ClassVars / param=ref;
    model ClaimAmount = param(Citations CreditScore Deductible Education
                             GarageParked Gender Homeowner MaritalStatus
                             MultipleVehicles Rating TookCourse
                             Transaction VehicleOwned VehicleType
                             VehicleUse WorkStatus )
                        param(NumberNoFault NYoungDrvrs StdHouseIncome)
                        spline(AgePolicyHolder / details)
                        spline(LonPolicyHolder LatPolicyHolder / details)
                        / distribution=gamma link=log;
    selection method=boosting(choose=validate);
    partition fraction(validate=0.25);
run;
```

In general, you can specify multiple candidate effects with a PARAM option but only one effect with a SPLINE option. Here, for convenience, the first PARAM option specifies the linear effects of categorical variables, and the second specifies the linear effects of continuous variables. The first SPLINE option specifies the univariate spline effect of a continuous variable, and the second specifies the bivariate spline effect of two continuous variables.

The boosting method is chosen here because it supports both univariate and bivariate spline terms, and because the candidate effects include a large number of parametric effects. The procedure computes the spline terms using penalized B-splines, which are explained on page 358 of Appendix F.

With the boosting method, you can control how a spline effect is constructed with suboptions that specify the degree and the knots, a fixed degrees of freedom, or a fixed smoothing parameter. For instance, `spline(AgePolicyHolder/df=8)` would specify eight degrees of freedom for the spline term for AgePolicyholder, which indirectly determines its smoothness.

In order to avoid overfitting, the selection criterion in this example is ASE computed from a validation data partition created by randomly selecting 25% of the observations, as specified in the PARTITION statement. Alternatively, you can specify the CHOOSE=CV suboption to request *m*-fold cross validation, which is explained on page 31. In addition, you can request early stopping of the selection process with the STOPHORIZON= suboption, which specifies the number of consecutive iterations at which the criterion must decrease.

The SEED= option specifies the initial seed for the random number generator that the GAMSELECT procedure uses to form knots if necessary (see page 231) and to randomly select observations for validation. Because random partitioning depends on how the data are distributed across machines and threads, the results might differ when you rerun the procedure with the same seed.

Interpreting the Results

Output 11.23 shows that the boosting algorithm executed 500 iterations. The selected model corresponds to the final iteration.

Output 11.23 Iteration Summary

Iteration Summary	
Iterations Executed	500
Selected Iteration	500
Number of Selected Effects	4

Output 11.24 shows the values of ASE computed from the training and validation partitions.

Output 11.24 Fit Statistics

Fit Statistics	
ASE (Train)	10.19335
ASE (Validate)	9.49565

Output 11.25 shows the effects in the selected model, the iteration at which each effect first entered the model, and the number of iterations for which the effect was selected. The spline effect for LonPolicyHolder and LatPolicyHolder was selected for update in most of the iterations.

Output 11.25 Selected Effects

	Selected Effects	
Effect	Entry Iteration	Times Selected
Spline(AgePolicyHolder)	1	90
Spline(LonPolicyHolder LatPolicyHolder)	5	379
VehicleType	33	12
Homeowner	44	19

These effects are comparable to those selected for the generalized linear model (see Output 10.6 on page 205), which are AgePolicyHolder, AreaType, VehicleType, Homeowner, and WorkStatus.

Output 11.26 shows the parameter estimates for the linear effects.

Output 11.26 Parameter Estimates

Parameter Estimates	
Parameter	Estimate
Intercept	1.381458
Homeowner Yes	-0.158874
VehicleType Crossover	0.014489
VehicleType Large	0.073886
VehicleType Luxury	0.242045
VehicleType Midsized	-0.057375
VehicleType Pickup	0.009071
VehicleType SUV	-0.012292
VehicleType Van	0.019113
Dispersion	0.478385

The signs of the estimates for the levels of Homeowner and VehicleType match those of the corresponding estimates in Output 11.10.

Output 11.27 shows details of the spline component for AgePolicyHolder, which were requested with the DETAILS suboption of the SPLINE option specified for this variable. This component has four degrees of freedom; it is clearly smoother than the component for AgePolicyHolder in Output 11.13, which has eight degrees of freedom.

Output 11.27 Details for Spline Component for AgePolicyHolder

Specifications for Spline(AgePolicyHolder)	
Number of Variables	1
Number of Knots	26
Number of Interior Knots	20
Order of Difference Penalty	2
Degree of B-Spline Transformation	3
Smoothing Parameter	36082
Degrees of Freedom	4

Output 11.28 shows the component plots for the two spline effects that were selected.

Output 11.28 Component Plots for Analysis of ClaimSeverity

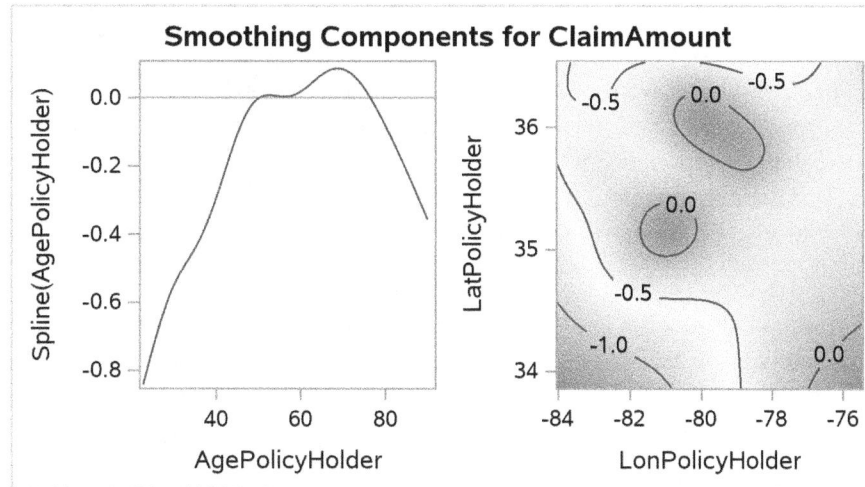

These plots differ from those in Output 11.13 and Output 11.14 because the latter were obtained by analyzing the observations in ClaimSeverityNC, which are a subset of those in ClaimSeverity. If you rerun the GAMSELECT statements on page 246 with the data set ClaimSeverityNC, the same effects are selected. Output 11.29 shows the component plots for the spline effects. Not surprisingly, they resemble those in Output 11.13 and Output 11.14.

Output 11.29 Component Plots for Analysis of ClaimSeverityNC

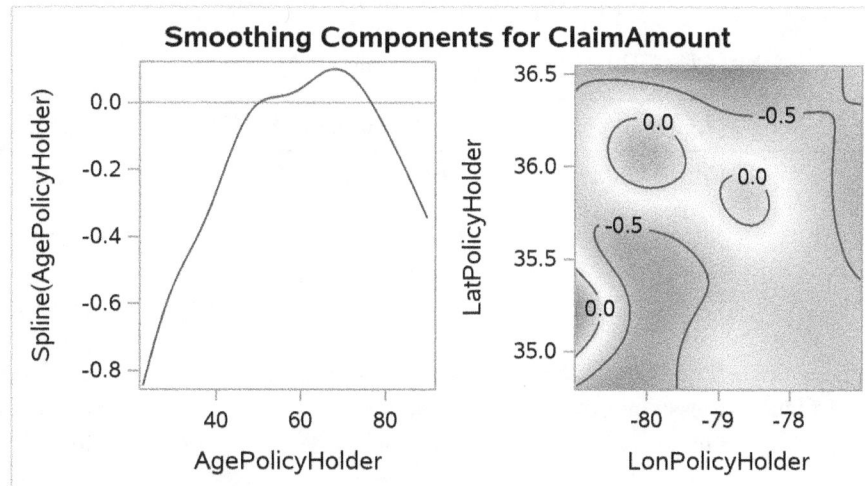

Further Examples of the GAMSELECT Procedure

At SAS Global Forum 2020, Michael Lamm and Weijie Cai presented a paper that uses simulated data to illustrate the boosting and shrinkage methods (Lamm and Cai 2020). This paper also compares the boosting method with the boosting method provided by the GRADBOOST procedure in SAS Viya, which fits a tree ensemble. For their simulated data, Lamm and Cai demonstrated that the boosting method provided by the GAMSELECT procedure does a better job of reconstructing the true model, especially in the tails of the predictors, and builds a smoother fitted model.

Summary

Generalized additive models have the same response distributions, link functions, and linear parametric effects as generalized linear models. They give you greater flexibility for exploration and modeling because they incorporate smooth, nonparametric effects that describe complicated nonlinear dependencies and are estimated with splines. Plots of spline effects reveal features of the data that would not otherwise be apparent, they invite discussion, and they sometimes suggest simpler parametric models.

The price for these added benefits is a sharp increase in computational work. Not only are there many more parameters to be estimated than with generalized linear models, but the right degree of smoothness must be determined for each spline term. The cost of fitting a model grows with the size and complexity of the data, and the cost of building a model is even greater.

The GAMPL procedure in SAS 9 and its counterpart in SAS Viya, the GAMMOD procedure, implement specialized algorithms and parallel computing techniques that deliver the scalability and performance necessary for fitting models with the large amounts of data now prevalent in business analytics and many areas of data science. If you are using SAS 9, you should use the GAMPL procedure instead of the older GAM procedure. The GAMSELECT procedure in SAS Viya uses distributed computing and two algorithmic methods, boosting and shrinkage, that provide the performance necessary for building models with very large data.

Table 11.9 summarizes the features of the GAM, GAMPL, GAMMOD, and GAMSELECT procedures.

Table 11.9 Procedures for Generalized Additive Modeling

Feature	GAM	GAMPL, GAMMOD	GAMSELECT
Primary purpose	Fitting models	Fitting models	Building models
Data size	Moderate	Large	Large
Computational execution	Single thread	Multiple threads, distributed (GAMMOD)	Multiple threads, distributed
Representation of nonparametric effects	Smoothing splines, loess smooth	Thin-plate regression splines	Penalized B-splines, natural cubic splines
Variables per spline term	One or two	Multiple	One or two (boosting), one (shrinkage)
Method of estimation for fixed smoothing	Local scoring	Penalized maximum likelihood	Likelihood techniques
Method of finding optimal smoothing	Optimization of GCV criterion one term at a time	Performance iteration, outer iteration; global evaluation criterion	Degrees of freedom (boosting), grid search (shrinkage)
Model degrees of freedom	Sum of traces of smoothing matrices	Trace of global degrees-of-freedom matrix	Computed only for components
Model fit statistics	Deviance	AIC, AICC, SBC, GCV	ASE

Table 11.9 *continued*

Feature	GAM	GAMPL, GAMMOD	GAMSELECT
Plots of smooth components	Yes Yes	Yes Yes	Yes Yes
Confidence bands for components	Yes	Yes	No
Tests for smooth components	Nonlinearity	Total contribution	None
Prediction limits	No	Yes	No
Common distributions in exponential family	Yes	Yes	Yes
Tweedie distribution	No	Yes	No
Negative binomial distribution	No	Yes	No
Link functions	Canonical only	Multiple	Multiple
Default link for gamma	Inverse	Log	Log
Default link for inverse Gaussian	Inverse square	Log	Log
Parameterizations for CLASS variables	GLM	GLM, reference (GAMPL); full set (GAMMOD)	Full set
Default parameterization	GLM	GLM	GLM
SPLIT option for CLASS variables	No	Yes (GAMMOD)	Yes
Model building methods	None	None	Boosting, shrinkage
Model selection criteria	None	None	ASE
Data partitioning	No	No	Yes

Chapter 12
Building Proportional Hazards Models

Contents

This chapter introduces the PHSELECT procedure in SAS Viya, which is designed for building proportional hazards models, also known as Cox models. The chapter also explains how you can build these models for discrete time data by using the HPLOGISTIC and LOGSELECT procedures, which were introduced in Chapter 9.

In a proportional hazards model, the observed response variable is the time until a subject experiences an event. The event, also called a failure, can have different interpretations depending on the application. In business analytics, a failure might be the loss of a customer; in medical research, a failure is typically the death of an individual due to a disease.

Models for time-to-event data are used to predict the probability that the lifetime T of a subject exceeds a given time t. The function $S(t) \equiv \Pr[T > t]$ is called the survival function, and time-to-event analysis is known as survival analysis. The survival function is the complement of the distribution function $F(t) = \Pr[T \leq t]$.

Proportional hazards models focus on the hazard function rather than the survival function. If T is continuous with a probability density function $f(t)$, the hazard function is

$$\lambda(t) \equiv \lim_{\Delta t \to 0^+} \frac{\Pr[t \leq T < t + \Delta t \mid T \geq t]}{\Delta t} = \lim_{\Delta t \to 0^+} \frac{F(t + \Delta t) - F(t)}{\Delta t \, \Pr[T \geq t]} = \frac{f(t)}{S(t)}$$

The numerator in the first term is the conditional probability that an event occurs in the interval $[t, t + \Delta t)$, given that a subject survives up to time t. This excludes the possibility that the subject experienced the event prior to t and is no longer at risk. The denominator adjusts the numerator for the length of time Δt. The ratio, after taking the limit, is not a probability but rather the instantaneous *risk* that an event occurs exactly at time t. This risk can be greater than one.

You can also interpret $\lambda(t)$ as the instantaneous *rate* of failure or the observed rate over a short period of time. For instance, consider the event that a bank customer is delinquent in repaying a loan, and suppose that $\lambda(t) = \lambda$ for 1,000 customers during one month. The entire group is at risk of delinquency for a total of 1,000 customer-months. If 18 customers are delinquent during the month, then the estimate of λ is $18/1000 = 0.018$ delinquencies *per customer-month*.

Like other models for survival analysis, proportional hazards models accommodate censoring, which occurs when a subject drops out of a study or survives through the end of the study. If the data are right censored, the response variable is $\min(T, C)$, where C denotes the censoring time.

The Proportional Hazards Model

The proportional hazards model assumes that the survival time for the ith subject has its own hazard function, which is expressed as

$$\lambda_i(t \mid \mathbf{x}_i) = \lambda_0(t) \exp(\beta_1 x_{i1} + \cdots + \beta_p x_{ip}), \quad i = 1, \ldots, n$$

where the baseline hazard function $\lambda_0(t)$ describes how the risk varies in time if the predictors are at their baseline levels The factor $\exp(\beta_1 x_{i1} + \cdots + \beta_p x_{ip})$ describes how the hazard function depends on the predictors. The ratio of the hazard functions for two groups of homogenous subjects, labeled A and B, depends only on differences in the values of their predictors:

$$\frac{\lambda_A(t \mid \mathbf{x}_i)}{\lambda_B(t \mid \mathbf{x}_i)} = \exp(\beta_1(x_{A1} - x_{B1}) + \cdots + \beta_p(x_{Ap} - x_{Bp}))$$

Because this ratio is constant with respect to time, the hazard functions are proportional to each other.

As in a generalized linear model, the predictors $x_{i1}, \ldots, x_{ip}$ represent main effects that consist of continuous or classification variables and can include interaction effects or constructed effects of these variables. Because the effects enter through a linear parametric form and $\lambda_0(t)$ is arbitrary and unspecified, the proportional hazards model is described as semiparametric.

The introduction of the model in a 1972 paper[†] by David Cox (then at Imperial College, London) was one of the most important breakthroughs in the field of modern statistics; it profoundly altered how statisticians thought about modeling failure times. Prior to 1972, censored failure times were often analyzed with standard regression models for lack of a better method. In addition to a modeling framework that handles censoring, the 1972 paper provided for the incorporation of time-dependent covariates that are measured multiple times during a study.

For inference about the regression parameters $\beta_1, \ldots, \beta_p$, Cox proposed a likelihood function that conditions on the times at which the failures occur and does not assume a parametric distribution. This is not a full likelihood function, but it leads to useful results much like the properties of maximum likelihood functions for logistic regression and generalized linear models (see Appendix D). In a 1975 paper, Cox justified his proposal by defining a partial likelihood function. This approach, combined with the proportional hazards model, is referred to as Cox regression.

Before long, the model became a standard tool for analysis of survival data, especially in clinical trials. Between 1978 and 2021, over 150,000 papers in medical research cited the 1972 paper (Firth et al. 2022, p. 40). Applications of the model continue to grow, not only in medical research but also in engineering, finance, sociology, and business analytics.

Sir David Cox was recognized globally for his fundamental contributions to the field of statistics; he received a knighthood in 1985, the Kettering Prize in 1990, and the International Prize in Statistics in 2017 (Hagerty 2022). One of the most interesting tributes published after his death in January 2022 at the age of 97 is a set of articles written by friends who recount the breadth of Sir David's accomplishments, the great clarity with which he communicated his work, and the admirable nature of his character (Firth et al. 2022).

[†] Sir David Cox later commented, "Nobody took much notice of the 1972 paper for a while, until various people started to write software which was widely useful," adding that this took six or seven years (Reid 1994). He himself tended to prefer parametric models in his own work with survival data, noting that accelerated life models are more interpretable in engineering applications.

Procedures for Proportional Hazards Models

The PHREG procedure is the primary procedure in SAS for fitting and analyzing proportional hazards models with specified effects. In addition to parameter estimates, *p*-values, and model fit statistics, it provides many features for postfit statistical analysis, such as estimation of contrasts in the model parameters and tests of hypotheses concerning the parameters.

The PHSELECT procedure does not replicate the inferential features of the PHREG procedure; it was designed for fitting and building predictive models, and it provides the following features:

- The ability to define candidate effects with MODEL and CLASS statements that are similar to those in the PHREG procedure.

- The ability to specify regression spline effects, polynomial effects, and other constructed effects in the set of candidate effects. This is available with the EFFECT statement.

- Model building with sequential selection methods and the group lasso method (see page 46).

- Model selection with information criteria (AIC, AICC, and SBC) that help to avoid overfitting by penalizing model complexity. This approach is discussed in "Criteria Based on Information Theory" on page 28.

- Model selection based on partitioning the data into training and validation sets. This approach is discussed in "External Validation Method for Estimating Prediction Error" on page 30.

- Cox regression diagnostics that are conditional on the selected model.

- Multithreaded computation for faster performance and the ability to perform computations with data distributed across multiple computers in a cloud environment.

Table 12.5 on page 268 compares the features of the PHSELECT and PHREG procedures. These two procedures belong to a family of procedures for survival analysis that are summarized in Table 12.1.

Table 12.1   Procedures for Survival Analysis

Procedure	Focus	Approach	Covariates	Censoring	Availability
LIFETEST	Survival function	Nonparametric	No	Right	SAS 9
ICLIFETEST	Survival function	Nonparametric	No	Interval	SAS 9
LIFEREG	Time to event	Parametric	Yes	Right, left, interval	SAS 9
SEVERITY	Loss	Parametric	Yes	Right, left, interval	SAS 9
QUANTLIFE	Time to event	Semiparametric	Yes	Right	SAS 9
PHREG	Hazard function	Semiparametric	Yes	Right	SAS 9
PHSELECT	Hazard function	Semiparametric	Yes	Right	SAS Viya
ICPHREG	Hazard function	Parametric	Yes	Interval	SAS 9
SURVEYPHREG	Hazard function	Semiparametric	Yes	Right	SAS 9
RMSTREG	Restricted mean survival time	Parametric	Yes	Right	SAS 9

Concepts of Proportional Hazards Models

This section briefly introduces prediction with proportional hazards regression as provided by the PHSELECT procedure. Countless papers and books have been written about inference with proportional hazards regression, especially in medical research and biostatistics. For comprehensive introductions, see the books by Allison (2010), Cox and Oakes (1984), Harrell (2015), Hosmer, Lemeshow, and May (2008), Kalbfleisch and Prentice (2002), Klein and Moeschberger (2003), and Lawless (2003).

The Number of Subjects at Risk

In time-to-event data, the number of subjects at risk changes over time, either because failures occur or because some failures can no longer be observed due to censoring. To understand this, consider the data shown in Figure 12.1 for five bank customers with loans, who are at risk of delinquency.

Figure 12.1 Time-to-Event Data for Customer Loans

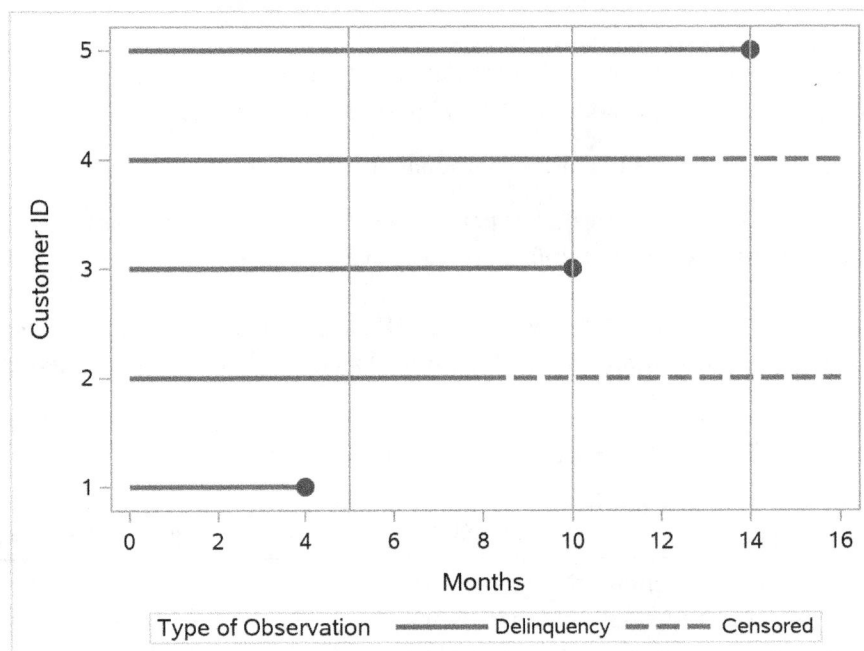

During the time interval [0,4), all five customers are at risk. Customer 1 is delinquent at $t = 4$, and Customer 2 becomes unknown to follow-up at $t = 8$, so four customers are at risk in [4,8). Customer 3 is delinquent at $t = 10$, and Customer 4 becomes unknown to follow-up at $t = 12$, so two customers are at risk in [10,12). Only Customer 5 is at risk in [12,14).

The number of subjects at risk is taken into account when estimating the hazard rate function or the survival function because it affects the total exposure to risk at time t. This is done by the product-limit estimator for the survivor function, a nonparametric method introduced by Edward Kaplan and Paul Meier in what is today the most frequently cited paper in statistics (Kaplan and Meier 1958). An explanation of this method, given in the next section, is helpful for understanding proportional hazards regression, which extends the estimator by allowing covariates.

The Product-Limit Estimator for the Survival Function

The product-limit or Kaplan-Meier estimator of $S(t)$ is computed from the ordered event times $0 < t_1 < t_2 < \cdots < t_k$ that correspond to k distinct failures (events) for a set of subjects. For $i = 1, \ldots, k$, suppose that Y_i is the number of subjects that have survived and are at risk until just prior to t_i. Also suppose that d_i is the number of failures that occur at t_i.

The product-limit estimator of $S(t)$ for $0 \le t < t_1$ is 1, because no failures have occurred during this time. Immediately before t_1, Y_1 subjects have survived, and there are d_1 failures at time t_1, so the probability of surviving beyond t_1 is $1 - d_1/Y_1$. In the loan example, the probability of surviving beyond $t_1 = 4$ is $1 - 1/5 = 0.8$.

The probability of surviving beyond t_2 is the product of two probabilities: the conditional probability of surviving beyond t_2 given survival beyond t_1 and the probability of surviving beyond t_1. In the example, censoring (but no failure) occurs at $t_2 = 8$, and so the probability of surviving beyond $t_2 = 8$ is $(1 - 0/4) \times (1 - 1/5) = 0.8$. In general, for $i = 1, \ldots, k$, the product-limit estimator of $S(t_i)$ is a product of a chain of conditional probabilities:

$$
\hat{S}(t_i) = \underbrace{\left(1 - \frac{d_i}{Y_i}\right)}_{\Pr[T > t_i \mid T > t_{i-1}]} \times \underbrace{\left(1 - \frac{d_{i-1}}{Y_{i-1}}\right)}_{\Pr[T > t_{i-1} \mid T > t_{i-2}]} \times \cdots \times \underbrace{\left(1 - \frac{d_1}{Y_1}\right)}_{\Pr[T > t_1]} = \prod_{j=1}^{i} \left(1 - \frac{d_j}{Y_j}\right)
$$

For all values of t, the product-limit estimator is

$$
\hat{S}(t) = \prod_{\{j \,:\, t_j \le t\}} \left(1 - \frac{d_j}{Y_j}\right), \quad 0 \le t \le \max_{1 \le i \le k} t_i
$$

Output 12.1 shows a plot of $\hat{S}(t)$ for the data in Figure 12.1 that was produced with the LIFETEST procedure.

Output 12.1 Estimate of Survival Function for Loan Delinquency

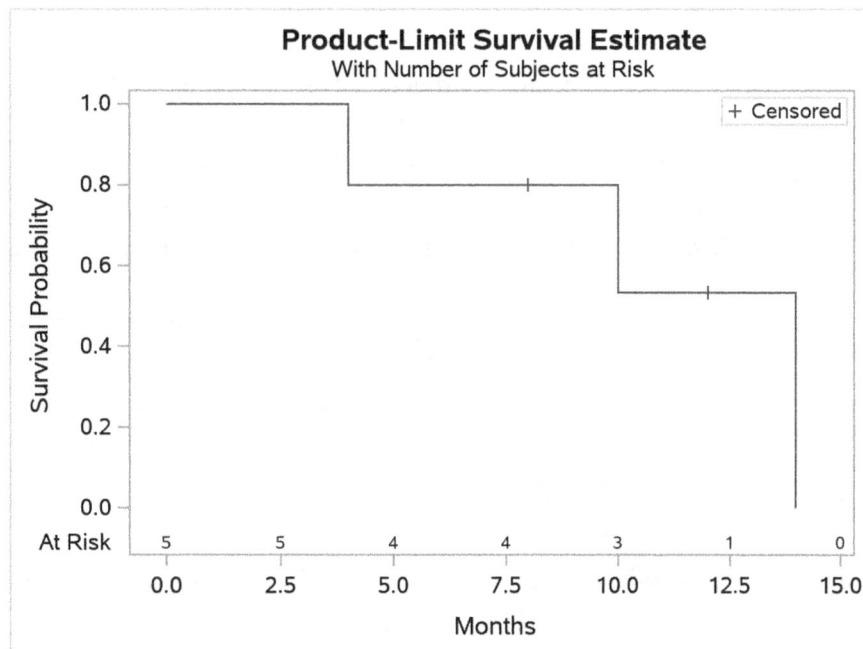

Parameter Estimation for the Proportional Hazards Model

The proportional hazards model produces an estimate of $S(t)$ that incorporates covariates providing subject-specific information. This approach starts by estimating the regression parameters $\boldsymbol{\beta} = (\beta_1, \ldots, \beta_p)'$ for the model (see page 254) with the partial likelihood, which eliminates the unknown baseline hazard function $\lambda_0(t)$.

Computation of the partial likelihood is complicated in the presence of ties in failure times, and the cost rises with the number of ties. The PHREG procedure implements two approximations, the Breslow likelihood and the Efron likelihood[†], in addition to an exact partial likelihood computed with an efficient numerical technique due to DeLong, Guirguis, and So (1994).

The PHSELECT procedure estimates $\boldsymbol{\beta}$ by maximizing the Breslow likelihood. Additional notation is needed to describe this likelihood. Let d_i denote the number of failures at time t_i, and let $\mathcal{D}_i$ denote the set of subjects that fail at t_i. Let $\mathcal{R}_i$ denote the set of subjects at risk immediately before t_i. Finally, let $\mathbf{x}_\ell(t)$ denote the vector of explanatory variables for the ℓth subject at time t. The Breslow log-likelihood function is

$$\mathcal{L}(\boldsymbol{\beta}; \mathbf{t}) = \sum_{j=1}^{k} \left\{ \boldsymbol{\beta}' \sum_{\ell \in \mathcal{D}_j} \mathbf{x}_\ell(t_j) - d_j \log \sum_{h \in \mathcal{R}_j} \exp(\boldsymbol{\beta}' \mathbf{x}_h(t_j)) \right\}$$

where $\mathbf{t} = (t_1, \ldots, t_k)$. When the data are stratified by secondary variables that are known to affect the hazard rate, this function is the sum of the log-likelihood functions for the individual strata.

The Survival Function for the Proportional Hazards Model

Given $\hat{\boldsymbol{\beta}}$, a profile likelihood method is used to estimate the baseline cumulative hazard function $H_0(t)$. The survival function corresponding to the proportional hazards model is

$$S(t; \mathbf{x}, \hat{\boldsymbol{\beta}}) = [S_0(t)]^{\exp(\tilde{\mathbf{x}}\hat{\boldsymbol{\beta}})}$$

where $\mathbf{x} = (\mathbf{x}_1, \ldots, \mathbf{x}_p)$. The baseline survival function $S_0(t) = \exp(-H_0(t))$ corresponds to a subject with average values of the continuous predictors and reference values of the categorical predictors (here $\tilde{\mathbf{x}}$ indicates the predictors are mean-centered or are offsets from reference values).

The sign of β_j indicates whether the risk associated with the predictor $\mathbf{x}_j$ is positive or negative. For instance, in the bank example, if the customer's credit score $\mathbf{x}_1$ is used to predict the hazard rate for loan delinquency, you would expect β_1 to be negative. It follows that for customers with above-average scores, $\tilde{\mathbf{x}}_1\beta$ is negative, $\exp(\tilde{\mathbf{x}}\beta)$ is less than one, and $S(t; x_1, \beta)$ is greater than $S_0(t)$. In other words, survivorship increases.

The PHSELECT procedure estimates $S(t; \mathbf{x}, \boldsymbol{\beta})$ by applying the Breslow estimator of $H_0(t)$ (Breslow 1974). With the estimated survival function, you can predict the probabilities of survival at specified times for a new subject with specified covariates.

[†]The Breslow likelihood originated in a contribution by Richard Peto to the discussion in Cox (1972) and a paper by Breslow (1974). The Efron likelihood was introduced by Efron (1977).

Introduction to the PHSELECT Procedure

The PHSELECT procedure in SAS Viya is recommended for building proportional hazards regression models with large data. Unlike the PHREG procedure, it was specifically designed for this purpose and offers extensive capabilities for effect selection together with a wide variety of selection and stopping criteria for customizing the selection.

Specifying the Candidate Effects

When you use the PHSELECT procedure to build a model, you specify the candidate effects in the MODEL and CLASS statements. As with other modeling procedures, the CLASS statement lists variables that should be treated as categorical. You specify the method of selection with the SELECTION statement.

For instance, the following statements (taken from a later example on page 261) request forward selection with the information criterion SBC:

```
proc phselect data=mycas.Retention;
   class Area CurrentPlan LifeChange;
   model Time* Status(0) = Age Area CurrentPlan LifeChange;
   selection method=forward(select=sbc stop=sbc);
run;
```

You specify the failure time variable after the keyword MODEL. If there is censoring in your data, you add an asterisk followed by the censoring variable. If the censoring variable takes one of the values listed in parentheses, the corresponding failure time is treated as censored. The procedure fits all of the effects in the MODEL statement if you specify METHOD=NONE or if you omit the SELECTION statement.

Selection Methods

Table 12.2 summarizes the methods available with the SELECTION statement.

Table 12.2   Effect Selection Methods in the PHSELECT Procedure

Method	Description	METHOD=*keyword*
Forward selection	Starts with no effects in the model and adds effects	FORWARD
Backward elimination	Starts with all effects in the model and deletes effects	BACKWARD
Fast backward elimination	Starts with all effects in the model and deletes effects without refitting the model; applies with SELECT=SL	BACKWARD(FAST)
Stepwise selection	Starts with no effects in the model and adds effects; effects already in the model do not necessarily stay	STEPWISE
Group lasso	Minimizes $-2\mathcal{L}(\beta; t)$ using a constraint that forces all parameters for the same effect to be included or excluded (Tibshirani 1997)	LASSO
No selection	Fits fully specified model	NONE

The PHSELECT procedure does not provide best subset selection. This approach is available in the PHREG procedure, but it is not feasible when the number of predictors is greater than around 40, and it does not apply to categorical predictors.

Controlling the Methods of Selection

The PHSELECT procedure provides three ways to control the operation of the methods in Table 12.2, which you specify with suboptions in parentheses after the METHOD= option:

- CHOOSE= specifies the criterion for choosing the model. This criterion is evaluated at each step of the selection process. The final selected model is the model with the best value of this criterion.

- SELECT= specifies the criterion for determining which effect enters or leaves at each step. This is the effect that gives the maximum improvement in the specified criterion.

- STOP= specifies the criterion for terminating the selection process. This suboption is ignored if you use the MAXSTEPS=k suboption to specify the maximum number of steps.

Table 12.3 lists criteria you can request with these suboptions.

Table 12.3 Criteria for Controlling Selection

Criterion	**Suboption** *keyword*
Akaike's information criterion (AIC)	AIC
Corrected Akaike's information criterion (AICC)	AICC
Schwarz Bayesian information criterion (SBC or BIC)	SBC
Significance level of score test	SL (not a CHOOSE= suboption)
$-2\mathcal{L}(\hat{\beta}; t)$ for validation data	VALIDATE (not a SELECT= suboption)

The default for the SELECT=, CHOOSE=, and STOP= suboptions is SBC. The significance level criterion is provided for consistency with the PHREG procedure. You can specify the levels for an effect to enter or stay with the SLENTRY= and SLSTAY= suboptions for the METHOD= option. However, this criterion is not recommended; see page 34.

The preferred approach for building a model that generalizes well to future data is to find a set of effects that minimizes prediction error when applied to validation or test data that the training process has not encountered. If you specify CHOOSE=VALIDATE, the PHSELECT procedure computes $-2\mathcal{L}(\hat{\beta}; t)$ from the validation data at each step, and it selects the model at the first step where this criterion is minimized. You can use the PARTITION statement to allocate part of the DATA= data set for validation. When there are not enough data to set aside for validation, consider using an information criterion; see "Criteria Based on Information Theory" on page 28.

No one combination of selection methods and criteria is uniformly the most effective. To learn how different methods perform, try various alternatives with your data. Performance varies depending on the size and shape of the data, the signal-to-noise ratios of effects, and issues such as missingness and collinearity.

The following example illustrates the use of the PHSELECT procedure.

Example: Predicting Customer Retention

The analytics center at a health insurance company conducts a study of younger customers enrolled in two plans (A and B) who are experiencing life changes. The goals are to identify factors that explain the risk of moving to a different insurance company and to predict the probability of retaining a customer from one to five years in the future.

Information about 38,445 customers is saved in a CAS table named Retention; each row corresponds to a single customer. The variable Time provides the length of time (in months) that an individual has been a customer; this variable is continuous. The times for 9,608 of these customers are censored, primarily because they changed from Plan A or Plan B to a different plan offered by the same company and, for administrative reasons, there was no follow-up. The variable Status is equal to 0 if Time is censored, and it is otherwise equal to 1.

The candidate predictors are shown in Table 12.4. All of these variables were recorded at the beginning of the study.

Table 12.4 Candidate Predictors for Customer Lifetime Model

Predictor	Type
Age	Continuous (years)
Area	Classification with levels Urban, Rural
CurrentPlan	Classification with levels A, B
Education	Continuous (years)
Income	Continuous (1,000 USD)
LifeChange	Classification with levels Married, New Job, Child, None
Satisfaction	Classification with levels Excellent, Good, Poor
Smoking	Classification with levels Yes, No, Quit

The variable Satisfaction indicates the customer's level of satisfaction with the current plan.

Building the Model

The following statements build a proportional hazards regression model for Time by using the forward selection method:

```
ods graphics on;
proc phselect data=mycas.Retention;
   class Area CurrentPlan LifeChange Satisfaction Smoking / param=glm;
   model Time*Status(0) = Age Area CurrentPlan Education Income LifeChange
                          Satisfaction Smoking;
   selection method=forward(choose=validate select=sbc stop=sbc) plots=all;
   partition fraction(validate=0.25 seed=244919);
   code file='ScoreCode.sas' timepoint=12 24 36 48 60;
run;
```

The CLASS statement identifies Area, CurrentPlan, LifeChange, Satisfaction, and Smoking as classification variables. The PARAM= option specifies GLM (less-than-full-rank) coding, which is explained in Appendix I.

The SELECTION statement requests the forward method, and the CHOOSE=VALIDATE option specifies $-2\mathcal{L}(\hat{\beta}; t)$ computed from validation data as the criterion for choosing the model. The PARTITION statement randomly selects 25% of the observations for validation.

The CODE statement writes SAS DATA step code for computing predicted survival probabilities to the file *ScoreCode.sas*. The TIMEPOINT= option specifies time points (in months) at which survival probabilities are to be predicted from the selected model.

Interpreting the Results

Output 12.2 shows the numbers of observed and censored events (customer departures) in the training and validation partitions.

Output 12.2 Numbers of Observations

	Number of Observations			
Role	Description	Total	Event	Censored
Training	Number of Observations Read	28844	21601	7243
Training	Number of Observations Used	28844	21601	7243
Validation	Number of Observations Read	9601	7236	2365
Validation	Number of Observations Used	9601	7236	2365
Total	Number of Observations Read	38445	28837	9608
Total	Number of Observations Used	38445	28837	9608

Here, during forward selection, effects that provide the best improvement in terms of minimizing $-2\mathcal{L}(\hat{\beta}; t)$ are added until no more effects improve the criterion or until the STOP=SBC criterion is satisfied. As shown in Output 12.3, the minimum value of $-2\mathcal{L}(\hat{\beta}; t)$ (labeled Validation M2LL) is reached at Step 3 when Education enters the model.

Output 12.3 Model Selection Summary

		Selection Summary		
Step	Effect Entered	Number Effects In	SBC	Validation M2LL
1	LifeChange	1	400227.421	118085.939
2	Satisfaction	2	400097.909	118042.830
3	Education	3	400088.292	118041.042*
4	Area	4	400082.582*	118043.766
5	Age	5	400091.000	118042.846
6	Income	6	400100.486	118042.986
7	CurrentPlan	7	400110.466	118042.975
* Optimal Value Of Criterion				

The process terminates at Step 7 because SBC reaches a minimum at Step 4 and because the stop horizon is three steps by default.

The selected model has one continuous predictor (Education) and two categorical predictors (LifeChange and Satisfaction), whose effects involve a total of eight parameters.

The plot in Output 12.4 visualizes the selection process.

Output 12.4 Coefficient Progression with Forward Selection

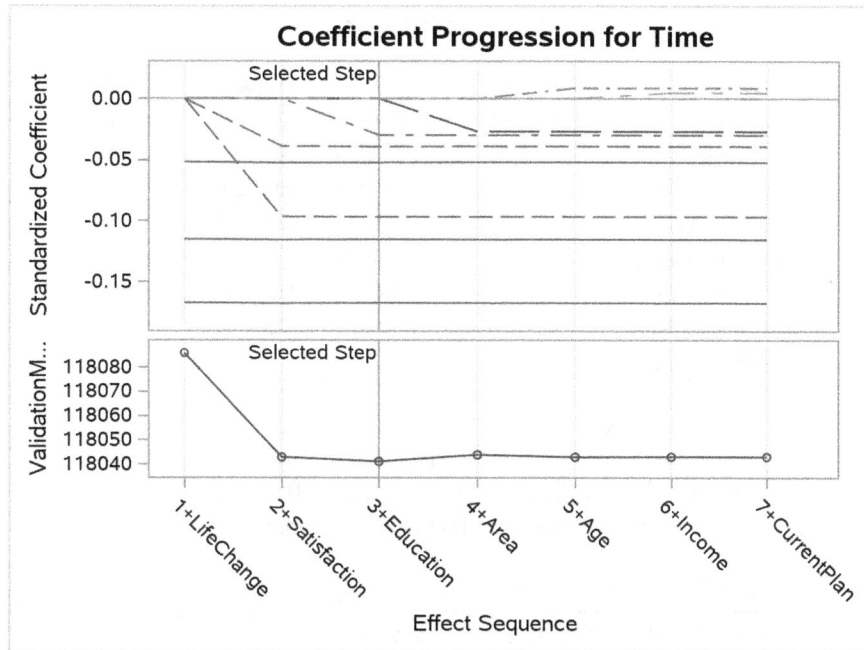

The criterion panel in Output 12.5 compares the selection with results based on other criteria. The variable Area would be selected by any of the information criteria, and it is a contender for inclusion. A model with seven variables would be selected by $-2\mathcal{L}(\hat{\beta}; t)$ computed from the training data. This model is not likely to generalize well to future data, as explained in "Assessment and Minimization of Prediction Error" on page 25.

Output 12.5 Criterion Panel with Forward Selection

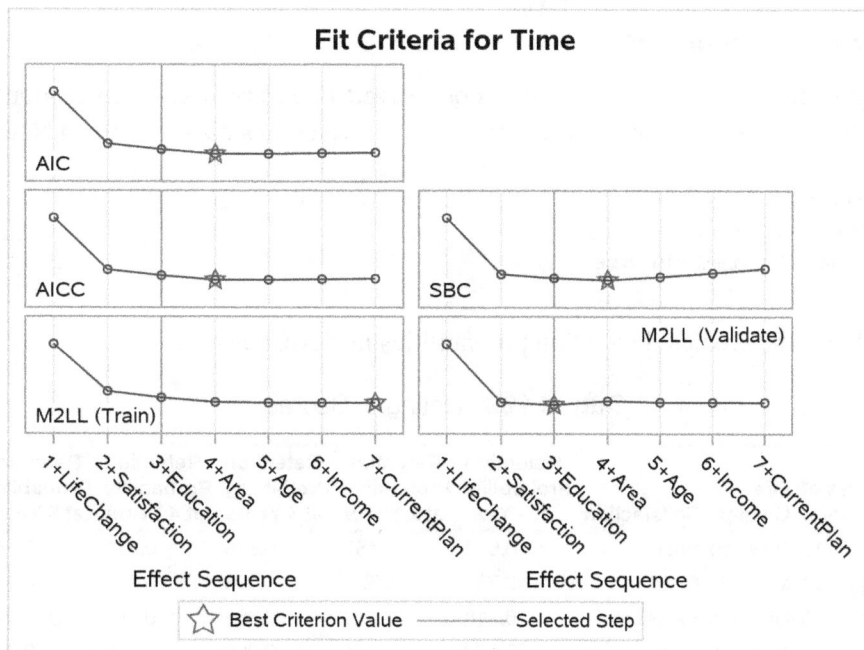

Output 12.6 shows the parameter estimates for the selected model.

Output 12.6 Parameter Estimates for Selected Model

Parameter Estimates

Parameter	DF	Estimate	Standard Error	Chi-Square	Pr > ChiSq
Education	1	-0.008648	0.001980	19.0725	<.0001
LifeChange Child	1	-0.385822	0.019396	395.6943	<.0001
LifeChange Married	1	-0.267121	0.019292	191.7090	<.0001
LifeChange New Job	1	-0.121000	0.019242	39.5436	<.0001
LifeChange None	0	0	.	.	.
Satisfaction Excellent	1	-0.206281	0.016711	152.3835	<.0001
Satisfaction Good	1	-0.083434	0.016622	25.1942	<.0001
Satisfaction Poor	0	0	.	.	.

There is no intercept estimate because the intercept is absorbed into the baseline hazard function. To assess a change in one of the predictors—for instance, from $\mathbf{x} = (x_1, x_2, \ldots, x_p)$ to $\mathbf{x}' = (x_1 + \delta, x_2, \ldots, x_p)$—consider the ratio of the hazard functions:

$$\frac{\lambda(t \mid \mathbf{x}')}{\lambda(t \mid \mathbf{x})} = \frac{\lambda_0(t) \exp(\beta_1(x_1 + \delta) + \beta_2 x_2 + \cdots + \beta_p x_p)}{\lambda_0(t) \exp(\beta_1 x_1 + \beta_2 x_2 + \cdots + \beta_p x_p)} = \exp(\beta_1 \delta)$$

Because of the proportional hazards assumption, this ratio depends only on $\beta_1 \delta$. For instance, the hazard ratio that corresponds to a five-year increase in Education is $\exp(-0.008648 \times 5) = 0.958$, or a decrease of 4.2% in the hazard rate. The estimate for LifeChange Child corresponds to a decrease of $100(1 - \exp(-0.385822)) = 32.0\%$ in the rate for LifeChange None. As explained on page 258, effects with negative coefficients are associated with an increase in the predicted survival time. The standard errors and p-values apply when the model is specified; they are not adjusted for the selection process and should be ignored here.

Predicting Survival Probabilities

The following statements use the generated code saved in *ScoreCode.sas* to compute retention probabilities for five new customers whose covariates are saved in a data set named NewCustomers:

```
data Predictions;
   set NewCustomers;
   %include 'ScoreCode.sas';
run;
```

Output 12.7 shows the predicted retention probabilities in NewCustomers.

Output 12.7 Listing of Scores

Years of Education	Life Change	Satisfaction	Retention Probability at 1 Year	Retention Probability at 2 Years	Retention Probability at 3 Years	Retention Probability at 4 Years	Retention Probability at 5 Years
13	New Job	Poor	0.677	0.452	0.306	0.211	0.145
14	Married	Good	0.735	0.535	0.393	0.293	0.218
8	New Job	Excellent	0.718	0.509	0.365	0.266	0.194
11	New Job	Poor	0.672	0.446	0.299	0.205	0.140
17	Child	Excellent	0.790	0.619	0.489	0.391	0.312

Model Building with Discrete Time

The proportional hazards model is designed for continuous failure time data; it assumes that no two events can occur simultaneously. In practice, however, event times are often tied, either because events naturally occur at discrete points in time or because event times are measured or grouped in discrete units.

Unfortunately, even a small number of ties adds expense to the computation of the partial likelihood. As noted on page 258, the PHREG procedure provides two approximations to the exact likelihood: the Breslow likelihood, which is also implemented by the PHSELECT procedure, and the Efron likelihood. With the PHREG procedure, you can request these approximations by specifying TIES=BRESLOW and TIES=EFRON in the MODEL statement.

Cox (1972) recognized the problem of ties and introduced a generalization of the proportional hazards model that applies to discrete time. This is really a different model. Here, the hazard function $\lambda(t \mid \mathbf{x})$ is the conditional *probability* of failure in an *interval* of time indexed by t, and it is related to the predictors as follows:

$$\log(\text{logit}(\lambda_i(t \mid \mathbf{x}))) = \beta_{0_t} + \beta_1 x_{it1} + \cdots + \beta_p x_{itp}, \quad i = 1, \ldots, n, \quad t = 1, 2, \ldots$$

You can request this model, referred to as a log-logit model, with the PHREG procedure by specifying TIES=DISCRETE in the MODEL statement. Currently, this model is not available in the PHSELECT procedure.

When you use the PHSELECT procedure with discrete data, keep in mind that the accuracy of the Breslow approximation decreases as the proportion of ties at time t increases in proportion to the number of subjects at risk (Farewell and Prentice 1980).

> **Programming Tip:** Check the results by refitting the selected model with the PHREG procedure and specifying TIES=DISCRETE.

Grouped-Data Version of the Proportional Hazards Model

Instead of using the PHSELECT procedure to build a proportional hazards model with discrete data, you can use the HPLOGISTIC procedure or the LOGSELECT procedure to build a grouped-data version of the proportional hazards model (Kalbfleisch and Prentice 1973; Prentice and Gloeckler 1978). The form of this model is

$$\log[-\log(1 - \lambda_i(t \mid \mathbf{x}))] = \beta_{0_t} + \beta_1 x_{it1} + \cdots + \beta_p x_{itp}, \quad i = 1, \ldots, n, \quad t = 1, 2, \ldots$$

where $\lambda(t \mid \mathbf{x})$ again denotes the conditional probability of failure in a time interval indexed by t. This is not the same as the log-logit model; it is a binary logistic regression model with the complementary log-log link function; see "Basic Concepts of Binary Logistic Regression" on page 161.

Allison (2010, Ch. 7) explains how you can fit this model by following a maximum likelihood approach that treats the survival history of each individual as a series of distinct observations, one at each time point. The first step is to create a new data set that contains one observation for each time point at which the subject was observed. The second step is to fit a logistic regression model to this data with the LOGISTIC procedure, specifying the link function with the LINK=CLOGLOG option in the MODEL statement and specifying the time variable as a predictor.

An advantage of this model is that the parameter estimates are directly comparable to those obtained from the proportional hazards model for ungrouped data; both estimate the same set of parameters $\beta_1, \ldots, \beta_p$. Although the estimates obtained with the two models will not be the same numerically, you can interpret them in the same way (see the explanation for the estimates in Output 12.6). The complementary log-log model also gives you estimates of the effect of time on the hazard function, and it handles time-dependent covariates.

The next example illustrates how you can build this model with the LOGSELECT procedure. You could also use the HPLOGISTIC procedure. Both procedures are explained in Chapter 9.

Example: Predicting Customer Retention (continued)

The following statements group the data in mycas.Retention by rounding the variable Time to the nearest year, and they create a table called mycas.RetentionYears that contains a row for each year during which the customer was observed.

```
data mycas.RetentionYears;
   set mycas.Retention;
   TimeYear = round(Time, 52) / 52 + 1;
   do Year=1 to TimeYear;
      LostCustomer = ( Year=TimeYear AND Status=1 );
      output;
   end;
run;
```

The variable LostCustomer is equal to one for a year in which a customer was lost. The next statements build a logistic regression model for the probability of losing a customer:

```
proc logselect data=mycas.RetentionYears;
   class Area CurrentPlan LifeChange Satisfaction Smoking Year / param=glm;
   model LostCustomer(event='1')=Age Area CurrentPlan Education Income
                        LifeChange Satisfaction Smoking Year
                        / link=cloglog;
   selection method=forward(select=sbc choose=validate stop=sbc);
   partition fraction(validate=0.25 seed=233411);
run;
```

Output 12.8 shows the selection summary.

Output 12.8 Model Selection Summary

Selection Details

	Selection Summary			
Step	Effect Entered	Number Effects In	SBC	Validation ASE
0	Intercept	1	58617.3159	0.2499
1	Year	2	57828.0176	0.2453
2	LifeChange	3	57633.0647	0.2434
3	Satisfaction	4	57566.3938*	0.2430
4	Education	5	57570.7454	0.2429
5	Area	6	57579.3831	0.2428*
6	CurrentPlan	7	57588.1756	0.2428
	* Optimal Value Of Criterion			

In addition to Education, LifeChange, and Satisfaction, which were selected by the PHSELECT procedure (see page 262), the LOGSELECT procedure selects Year and Area. Note that Area is the next effect that would have been selected by the PHSELECT procedure in Output 12.3.

Output 12.9 shows the parameter estimates for the selected model.

Output 12.9 Parameter Estimates

| | | | Parameter Estimates | | |
Parameter	DF	Estimate	Standard Error	Chi-Square	Pr > ChiSq
Intercept	1	0.787394	0.123669	40.5382	<.0001
Area Rural	1	-0.019740	0.013948	2.0030	0.1570
Area Urban	0	0	.	.	.
Education	1	-0.005078	0.002023	6.3031	0.0121
LifeChange Child	1	-0.275456	0.019746	194.6038	<.0001
LifeChange Married	1	-0.191129	0.019792	93.2519	<.0001
LifeChange New Job	1	-0.092435	0.019825	21.7399	<.0001
LifeChange None	0	0	.	.	.
Satisfaction Excellent	1	-0.158678	0.017108	86.0309	<.0001
Satisfaction Good	1	-0.064828	0.017053	14.4521	0.0001
Satisfaction Poor	0	0	.	.	.
Year 1	1	-0.967019	0.119293	65.7117	<.0001
Year 2	1	-0.510796	0.119598	18.2409	<.0001
Year 3	1	-0.569545	0.122808	21.5082	<.0001
Year 4	1	-0.730424	0.136906	28.4647	<.0001
Year 5	0	0	.	.	.

Here, a five-year increase in Education corresponds to a decrease of $100(1 - \exp(-0.005078 \times 5)) = 2.51\%$ in the hazard of losing a customer. Along with Education, LifeChange, and Satisfaction, Year clearly has an effect on retention. The estimate for Year 2 corresponds to an increase of $100(1 - \exp(-0.510796 - (-0.967019))) = 57.8\%$ in the hazard at Year 1.

Summary

The advantages of the proportional hazards model for time-to-event data are that it does not require the assumption of a parametric distribution for the survival time, nor does it assume a functional form for the baseline hazard function. The event times can be continuous or discrete.

For continuous data, the PHREG procedure provides extensive features for fitting proportional hazards models with specified effects and for postfit statistical analysis. The PHREG procedure provides some features for building models, but it does not incorporate methods that avoid overfitting, and it lacks the performance needed for working with large data. If you are building a predictive model, you should instead use the PHSELECT procedure, which is designed for that goal.

For discrete or grouped data, the PHREG procedure provides several methods that handle the problem of fitting proportional hazards models when there are ties. These methods are not available in the PHSELECT procedure. However, you can use either the HPLOGISTIC procedure or the LOGSELECT procedure to fit or build a complementary log-log model whose parameters have the same interpretation as those in a proportional hazards model.

Table 12.5 compares the features of the PHREG and PHSELECT procedures.

Table 12.5 Comparison of PHREG and PHSELECT Procedures

Feature	PHREG	PHSELECT
Primary purpose	Statistical analysis of fully specified models	Building predictive models with large data
MODEL and CLASS statements	Yes	Yes
Parameterization methods for classification variables	Full set	Full set
Default parameterization	REF	GLM
SPLIT option for CLASS variables	No	Yes
EFFECT statement for splines and other constructed effects	Yes	Yes
Time-dependent covariates	Yes	No
Model building methods	Sequential, best subsets	Sequential, lasso
Model selection criteria	Significance level for score test	AIC, AICC, SBC, validation
Data partitioning	No	Yes
Selection plots	No	Yes
Model fit statistics	$-2\mathcal{L}(\boldsymbol{\beta};t)$, AIC, SBC	$-2\mathcal{L}(\boldsymbol{\beta};t)$, AIC, AICC, SBC
p-values for parameters	Yes	Yes
Goodness-of-fit tests	Yes	No
Joint tests, Type 3 tests	Yes	Yes
Postfit analyses: contrasts, least squares means	Yes	No
Hazard ratios	Yes	No
Confidence limits for hazard ratios	Yes	No
Schemper–Henderson, concordance statistics for model assessment	Yes	No
Time-dependent ROC curves for model assessment	Yes	No
Competing risks models	Yes	No
Frailty models	Yes	No
Bayesian analysis of Cox models, piecewise exponential models, frailty models	Yes	No
Residual diagnostics	Yes	Yes
Influence statistics	Yes	Yes
Diagnostic and fit plots	Yes	No
Computational execution	Single thread	Multiple threads, distributed

Chapter 13
Building Classification and Regression Trees

Contents

This chapter introduces two procedures that build decision trees: the HPSPLIT procedure in SAS 9 and its newer counterpart in SAS Viya, the TREESPLIT procedure.

A decision tree is a set of rules that split the predictor space into nonoverlapping regions and assign a response value to each region.[†] Each rule consists of if-then statements about the predictors that define a particular region. The structure of these statements resembles the branches of a tree in which the leaves correspond to the regions. Decision trees for continuous responses are called regression trees, while decision trees for categorical responses are called classification trees.

Decision trees are methods of supervised learning and are called tree models because they can fit training data or predict responses for future data. However, they are fundamentally different from regression models discussed previously in this book because they are not probability models and do not have a linear form.

Algorithms for building decision trees determine the leaf regions by recursively partitioning the data. The partition at each step is based on a value, called the split point, of a particular predictor.

Example: Predicting Car Owner Interest in Telematics

To illustrate recursive partitioning, consider data from a survey that asked 500 car owners if they would be willing to adopt telematics, technology that tracks driving behavior and can reduce insurance rates. The response variable Telematics is categorical with two levels, Yes and No. The data include socioeconomic characteristics of the owners that might be good predictors of level Yes.

The algorithm begins with all the data and finds the predictor and split point that partition the observations into two sets whose proportions of the responses Yes and No are as *different* as possible. This predictor is the credit score of the owner, and the split point is 657.5. There are 148 observations with a credit score less than 657.5; these are assigned to a left branch, and the remaining 352 observations are assigned to a right branch. Figure 13.1 shows that Yes predominates in the left branch and No predominates in the right branch.

[†]The term decision tree is used in other ways. For instance, the DTREE procedure in SAS/OR produces tree diagrams of optimal decisions based on probabilities and rewards.

Figure 13.1 Responses in Left and Right Branches Formed by Splitting on Credit Score

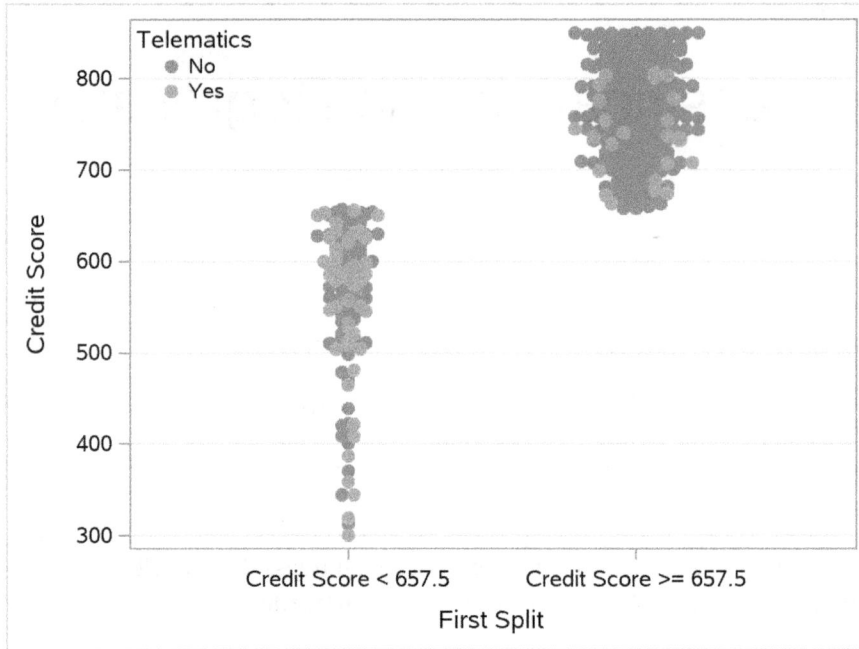

Next, the algorithm splits the left branch into two subbranches by finding another predictor and split point that partition the 148 observations into two sets whose response levels are again as different as possible. This predictor is the number of young drivers in the family. The 73 observations for which this number is 1, 2, 3, or 4 are assigned to a left subbranch corresponding to Yes, and the remaining 75 observations are assigned to a right subbranch corresponding to No.

The scatter plot in Figure 13.2 shows the partition corresponding to the left subbranch as a shaded rectangle and the partition corresponding to the right subbranch as an empty rectangle. Here, Yes predominates in the shaded rectangle, and No predominates in the empty rectangle.

Figure 13.2 Second Branch Based on Number of Younger Drivers

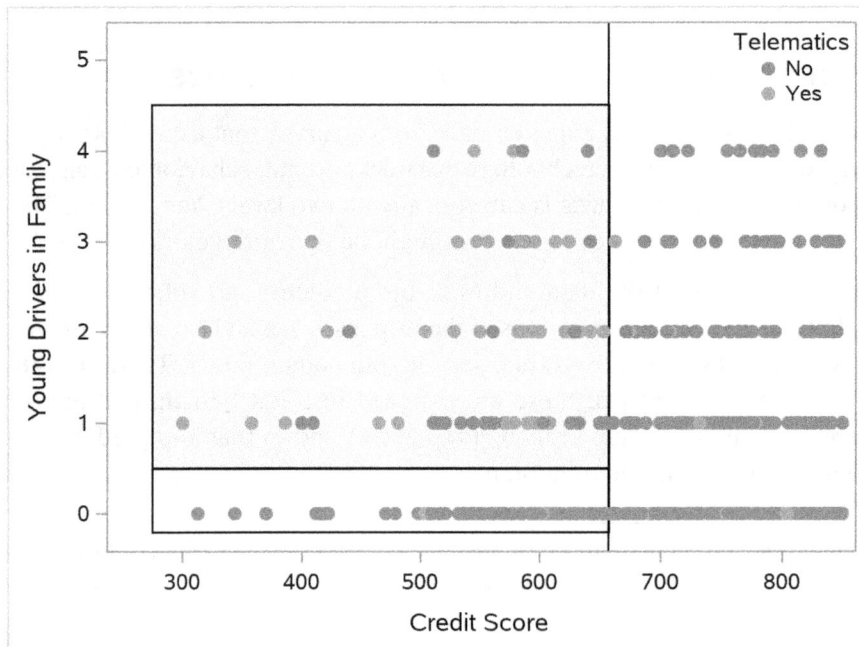

Recursive partitioning continues until a stopping criterion is satisfied. The regions at each step define the nodes of a tree, and the final regions determine the leaves of the tree, which are shown in Figure 13.3.

Figure 13.3 Classification Tree for Telematics Survey Data

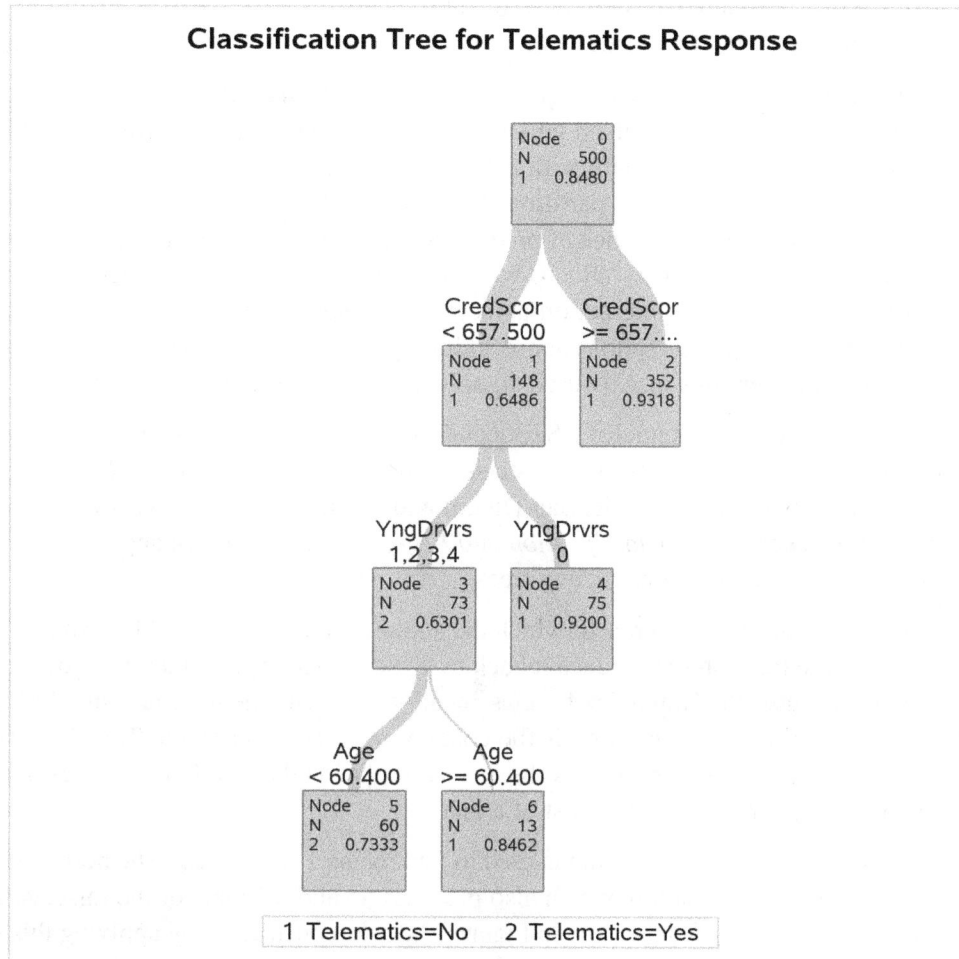

Classification Tree for Telematics Response

	Node	0
	N	500
	1	0.8480

CredScor < 657.500

	Node	1
	N	148
	1	0.6486

CredScor >= 657…

	Node	2
	N	352
	1	0.9318

YngDrvrs 1,2,3,4

	Node	3
	N	73
	2	0.6301

YngDrvrs 0

	Node	4
	N	75
	1	0.9200

Age < 60.400

	Node	5
	N	60
	2	0.7333

Age >= 60.400

	Node	6
	N	13
	1	0.8462

1 Telematics=No   2 Telematics=Yes

Decision trees are usually presented with the root node at the top. Figure 13.3 shows the complete tree for the telematics data. Node 0 (the root node) contains all 500 observations. Node 1 contains the observations plotted on the left in Figure 13.1, and Node 3 contains the observations plotted in the shaded rectangle in Figure 13.2. The width of each branch represents the number of observations in that branch. Nodes 2, 4, 5, and 6 are leaf (terminal) nodes. This example is discussed further beginning on page 276.

Rules for Decision Trees

The rule for each leaf in a decision tree is a series of if-then statements about the predictors and split points that define its path from the root node.

When the rules for a classification tree are applied to future observations, the predicted level for a leaf is the most frequent response among the training observations at that leaf. For a regression tree the predicted level is the mean response for the training observations at that leaf.

Origins of Decision Trees

The idea of splitting data in a progressive fashion to construct rules appeared in a 1959 paper by William Belson at the London School of Economics. The splitting variables he identified were jointly associated with the response and with subgroups of subjects that were matched by the rules.[†] Belson did not use the word "tree", but he illustrated the rules with a tree diagram (Belson 1959, p. 69).

Four years later, James Morgan and John Sonquist at the University of Michigan introduced automatic interaction detection (AID), which evolved into a class of techniques—among which CHAID is the best known—for classifying survey data with different types of response variables (Morgan and Sonquist 1963; Kass 1975, 1980). AID partitions the sample into disjoint subsets that best explain the response and are formed by a sequence of predictors and split points. Morgan and Sonquist used the word "automatic" because their techniques were implemented in computer programs, a novelty at that time. They used the term "interaction detection" because the techniques treat each subset individually without requiring assumptions about additivity or effects that characterize conventional regression models. Later versions of AID used significance tests as criteria for splitting.

In 1973, Leo Breiman (then at Technology Services Corporation) and Jerome Friedman (Stanford University) began to develop tree methods for classification that improved on AID. Together with Richard Olshen (University of California, San Diego) and Charles Stone (University of California, Berkeley), they wrote a book titled *Classification and Regression Trees*, which appeared in 1984 and laid out a systematic approach to constructing trees.

The main difference between this approach (which the authors abbreviated as CART) and AID is that it initially grows a large tree and then prunes it back to avoid overfitting. To measure goodness of fit during splitting, CART uses the Gini index for classification trees and the residual sum of squares for regression trees. The criterion for pruning is the cost complexity of a subtree T, which is defined as $\mathrm{CC}_\alpha(T) = \mathrm{R}(T) + \alpha|T|$, where $\mathrm{R}(T)$ is the error rate, $|T|$ is the number of leaves, and α is a complexity parameter that represents the cost of a leaf.

For a given value of α, weakest link pruning is used to find the best subtree T_α. The best value of α is determined by m-fold cross validation, which also provides a valid estimate of the misclassification rate for the final tree. The classification tree in Figure 13.3 was constructed by applying this method.

During the late 1990s, CART gained popularity as a tool for data mining along with other computationally intensive methods—such as generalized additive models—that find structure in high-dimensional data. SAS Enterprise Miner, which was introduced during this period, implemented classification and regression trees with algorithms that perform well with large data sets. The HPSPLIT and TREESPLIT procedures are likewise designed for scalability.

In addition to cost-complexity pruning, the procedures provide C4.5 pruning and reduced-error pruning, which were introduced by Ross Quinlan, a computer scientist now at Rulequest Research (Quinlan 1987, 1993).

[†]Belson had studied the effectiveness of a 1953 BBC television program that taught French to viewers making their first trip to France (Belson 1956a, b). By selecting test subjects from subgroups, he avoided bias when comparing results for those who had viewed and had not viewed the program. Belson later wrote a book about measuring the impact of television programming (Belson 1967). The issues he addressed are still relevant to the assessment of broadcast programming.

Advantages and Disadvantages of Decision Trees

The main advantage of decision trees over other models in this book is that they are easy to interpret and explain to clients. For instance, Figure 13.3 shows that car owners with credit scores under 657.5 who are over 60 and have young drivers in their families are likely interested to be in telematics. Of course, large decision trees can be more difficult to interpret.

Another advantage of decision trees is that they handle missing values in various ways. An observation with a missing value for a categorical predictor can be assigned to a branch for missing values, which helps you to learn whether such observations are different from those with nonmissing values (Hastie, Tibshirani, and Friedman 2009, p. 311). It is also possible to apply surrogate splitting rules, proposed by Breiman et al. (1984, p. 142). These do the assignment with alternative predictors whose values are not missing in observations where the primary predictor is missing. In recent years, experts have questioned the effectiveness of these rules, and so their use has diminished.

The main disadvantage of decision trees is that a small change in the data can result in a very different tree structure. As explained by Hastie, Tibshirani, and Friedman (2009, p. 312), this problem is inherent in the hierarchical nature of a tree because differences in top splits propagate to lower splits. Likewise, a change in a tuning parameter, such as the maximum number of branches, can alter the structure of the tree.

Because splitting is based on single predictors, many splits are typically needed to capture additive structures that involve only a few predictors; this impedes interpretation. The prediction surface for a decision tree is inherently rough because it is the sum of indicator functions for the leaf regions. With regression trees, this can lead to bias when the underlying function is assumed to be smooth. These issues motivated the development of multivariate adaptive regression splines, which are discussed in Chapter 14.

Procedures for Building Decision Trees

The HPSPLIT procedure in SAS 9 and the TREESPLIT procedure in SAS Viya build decision trees and provide the following features:

- Criteria for splitting nodes based on impurity (entropy, Gini index, residual sum of squares) and statistical tests (chi-square, F test, CHAID, FastCHAID).

- Cost-complexity pruning (weakest link pruning), C4.5 pruning, and reduced-error pruning.

- Selection of the best subtree based on m-fold cross validation or a validation partition.

- Various methods of handling missing values.

- Tree diagrams, plots for cost-complexity analysis, and plots of receiver operating characteristic (ROC) curves.

- Statistics for assessing model fit, including model-based (resubstitution) statistics and cross validation statistics.

- Measures of variable importance.

- Multithreaded computation for faster performance. The TREESPLIT procedure also performs computations with data distributed across multiple computers in a cloud environment.

Introduction to the HPSPLIT Procedure

The HPSPLIT procedure is a high-performance procedure like the HPLOGISTIC, HPGENSELECT, and GAMPL procedures (see page 163). However, because decision trees do not involve a linear model, the MODEL statement for the HPSPLIT procedure does not allow linear effects to be specified. Furthermore, the HPSPLIT procedure statement does not require that an XML stream for user-defined formats be specified with the FMTLIBXML= option.

Specifying the Candidate Variables

When you build a decision tree with the HPSPLIT procedure, the MODEL statement specifies the response variable and the variables that are candidates for splitting. The CLASS statement identifies the categorical variables. For instance, the following statements (taken from a later example on page 277) build the classification tree shown in Figure 13.3:

```
ods graphics on;
proc hpsplit data=Preliminary maxdepth=4 seed=533111
             plots=zoomedtree(depth=4 nodes=('0'));
   class Education MultipleVehicles NDrvConvict NumberAtFault
                 Telematics VehicleType YngDrvrs;
   model Telematics(event='Yes') = Age CredScor Education MultipleVehicles
                            NDrvConvict NumberAtFault VehicleType
                            YngDrvrs;
   grow gini;
   prune costcomplexity;
run;
```

The GROW statement specifies a criterion for growing a large initial tree, and the PRUNE statement specifies a method for pruning it to a size that is effective for prediction.

Criteria for Growing Trees

Table 13.1 summarizes the criteria available with the GROW statement. The default is entropy decrease for categorical responses and variance change for continuous responses.

Table 13.1 Criteria for Growing Decision Trees

Criterion	Response Type	keyword
CHAID based on chi-square or *F* tests	Categorical or continuous	CHAID
Chi-square statistic	Categorical	CHISQUARE
Entropy decrease	Categorical or continuous	ENTROPY
FastCHAID based on Kolmogorov–Smirnov splitter	Categorical or continuous	FASTCHAID
Gini index decrease	Categorical or continuous	GINI
Information gain ratio	Categorical or continuous	IGR
F statistic	Continuous	FTEST
Variance change	Continuous	RSS

Options for Splitting Nodes

Table 13.2 lists options for splitting nodes, which you specify in the HPSPLIT procedure statement.

Table 13.2 Options for Splitting Nodes

keyword	Description
ASSIGNMISSING=BRANCH	Creates a special branch for missing values, unknown levels, and levels with fewer observations than specified with the MINCATSIZE= option
ASSIGNMISSING=NONE	Excludes observations with missing values
ASSIGNMISSING=POPULAR	Assigns missing values to the most popular node
ASSIGNMISSING=SIMILAR	Assigns missing values to the most similar branch
MAXBRANCH=n	Maximum number of branches per node
MAXDEPTH=n	Maximum depth of tree to be grown
MINCATSIZE=	Number of observations a categorical predictor level must have to be considered in a split
MINLEAFSIZE=	Minimum number of observations that each branch of a split must have to be considered
SPLITONCE	Variables are split only once on a given branch

The defaults for these options are as follows:

- ASSIGNMISSING=NONE
- MAXBRANCH=2
- MAXDEPTH=ceil($10/\log_2(b)$), where b is the value of the MAXBRANCH= option
- MINCATSIZE=1
- MINLEAFSIZE=1

Methods of Pruning

Table 13.3 summarizes the methods available with the PRUNE statement. The default is cost-complexity pruning.

Table 13.3 Methods for Pruning Trees

Method	Type of Tree	keyword
C4.5 pruning (Quinlan 1993) based on upper confidence limits for the error rate	Classification trees	C45
Cost-complexity pruning (Breiman et al. 1984), (Quinlan 1987), (Zhang and Singer 2010)	Classification and regression trees	COSTCOMPLEXITY
Reduced-error pruning (Quinlan 1986)	Classification and regression trees	REDUCEDERROR

Example: Predicting Interest in Telematics

In the car insurance industry, policy pricing has traditionally relied on models that treat risk as a function of driver characteristics such as age and vehicle type, which place applicants into broad actuarial categories. The examples on page 201, page 207, and page 235 illustrate how generalized linear models and generalized additive models serve this goal.

Insurers and regulators would like to shift to more accurate pricing that is largely based on telematics—technology that monitors driving behavior and mileage through devices in vehicles. Models based on telematics data can qualify careful drivers for lower rates than they would otherwise receive under traditional models. Some insurers are pursuing arrangements with auto makers that will give vehicle owners convenient access to customized rates by seamlessly transmitting their data (Scism 2020).

Despite the attraction of lower rates, many consumers have privacy concerns about telematics. Currently, only a small percentage of auto policyholders in the United States participate in a telematics program. To understand which groups of consumers would be most likely to adopt telematics, an analytics center surveyed 5,886 vehicle owners who were not enrolled in a program. Table 13.4 lists socioeconomic variables that were saved in a data set named Respondents together with the response variable Telematics, whose values are Yes and No.

The data set Respondents is used by a later example on page 283. For simplicity, the example that follows uses a data set named Preliminary that resulted from a pilot survey of 500 owners over the age of 30 and contains a subset of the variables in Table 13.4.

Table 13.4 Candidate Predictor Variables in Examples

Variable	Description	Type
Age	Age of car owner	Continuous
CredScor	Credit score	Continuous
Deductible	Level of deductible	Categorical (3 levels)
Education	Educational attainment	Categorical (9 levels)
Exercise	Exercises or does sports	Categorical (2 levels)
Fuel	Car fuel	Categorical (3 levels)
Gender	Gender	Categorical (2 levels)
Interest	Main interest	Categorical (7 levels)
MaritalStatus	Marital status	Categorical (5 levels)
MultipleVehicles	More than one vehicle	Categorical (2 levels)
NDrvConvict	Number of driver convictions	Categorical (2 levels)
NumberAtFault	Number of at fault accidents	Categorical (3 levels)
PubLib	Uses public library	Categorical (2 levels)
Rating	Rating category	Categorical (4 levels)
Social	Uses social media	Categorical (2 levels)
Telematics	Willing to use telematics	Categorical (2 levels)
Transaction	Type of last transaction	Categorical (3 levels)
VehicleType	Vehicle type	Categorical (8 levels)
WorkStatus	Work status	Categorical (3 levels)
YngDrvrs	Number of drivers 16–21	Categorical (5 levels)

Formatting the Variables

The following statements define and assign formats for the categorical variables in Preliminary:

```
proc format;
   value Conv     0='None' 1='1 or more';
   value EdLev    1='No HS diploma' 2='HS diploma'    3='Some college'
                  4='Associate'      5='Bachelor'       6='Grad School'
                  7='Master'         8='Professional'  9='Doctorate';
   value VType    1='Crossover'  2='Pickup'  3='Small'  4='SUV'
                  5='Midsized'   6='Luxury'  7='Van'    8='Large';
   value WStat    1='Full Time'  2='Part Time'  3='Not Working';
   value YN       1='Yes'  0='No';
run;

data Preliminary; set Preliminary;
   format Education EdLev.  MultipleVehicles YN.  NDrvConvict Conv.
          Telematics YN.    VehicleType VType. ;
run;
```

Building the Classification Tree

The following statements use the HPSPLIT procedure to build a classification tree for Telematics:

```
ods graphics on;
proc hpsplit data=Preliminary maxbranch=2 maxdepth=4 nodes seed=533111
             plots=(wholetree zoomedtree(depth=4 nodes=('0')));
   class Education MultipleVehicles NDrvConvict NumberAtFault Telematics
         VehicleType YngDrvrs;
   model Telematics(event='Yes') = Age CredScor Education MultipleVehicles
                                   NDrvConvict NumberAtFault VehicleType
                                   YngDrvrs;
   grow gini;
   prune costcomplexity;
   code file='FinalTreeModel.sas';
run;
```

The tree, shown in Figure 13.3 on page 271, shows that vehicle owners under 60 with credit scores less than 657.5 and at least one young driver in the family are likely to be interested in telematics.

Output 13.1 summarizes the methods used to grow and prune the tree.

Output 13.1 Model Information

Model Information	
Split Criterion Used	Gini
Pruning Method	Cost-Complexity
Subtree Evaluation Criterion	Cost-Complexity
Number of Branches	2
Maximum Tree Depth Requested	4
Maximum Tree Depth Achieved	4
Tree Depth	3
Number of Leaves Before Pruning	16
Number of Leaves After Pruning	4
Model Event Level	Yes

The split criterion is the Gini index, which was requested with the GROW statement. As explained earlier, recursive partitioning subdivides the predictor space in such a way that response values for the observations within branch nodes are as similar or pure as possible. The HPSPLIT procedure provides two types of criteria for splitting a node: criteria that maximize a decrease in node impurity and criteria that are defined by a statistical test. The latter include the Gini index and entropy.

The Gini index measures the impurity of a node as

$$\sum_{k=1}^{K} \hat{p}_k(1 - \hat{p}_k) = 1 - \sum_{k=1}^{K} \hat{p}_k^2$$

where $\hat{p}_k$ is the proportion of observations in the node with the kth level of the response and K is the number of levels. Note that $1 - \hat{p}_k$ estimates misclassification error. Entropy measures impurity as

$$-\sum_{k=1}^{K} \hat{p}_k \log(\hat{p}_k)$$

Output 13.2 shows the misclassification rates for subtrees nested within a large tree that is initially grown by the procedure. The subtrees are indexed by their cost-complexity parameters, which are shown on the lower axis. The upper axis shows the number of leaves in each tree.

Output 13.2 Selection of Final Tree

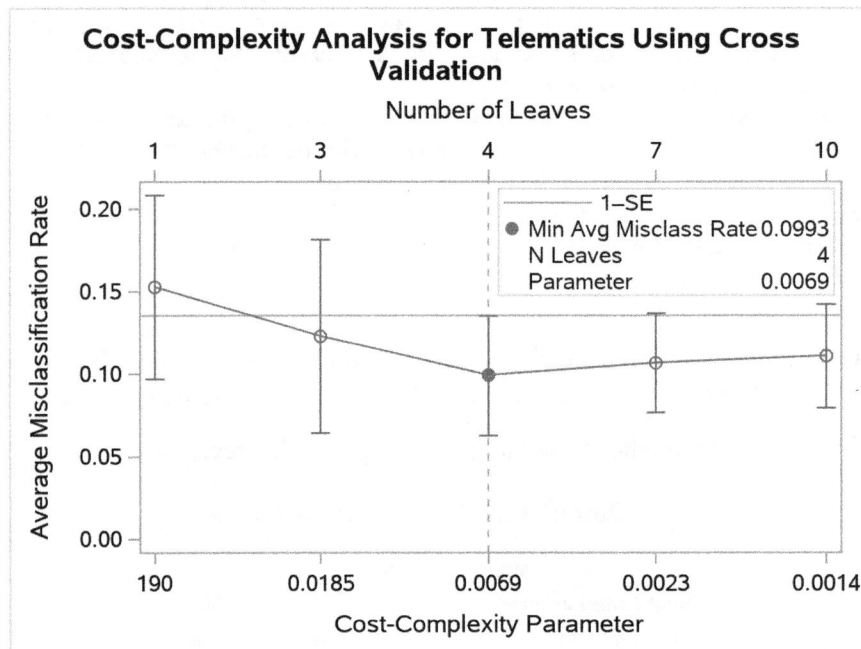

Here, because a validation partition is not provided, the misclassification rates for the subtrees are estimated by 10-fold cross validation. The minimum rate occurs at the parameter 0.0069, which leads to the selection of a subtree tree with four leaves. The horizontal line is positioned at one standard error above the minimum rate. Breiman's one-standard-error rule (1–SE rule) (Breiman et al. 1984, pp.78–80) would choose the subtree with three leaves, which is the smallest subtree whose rate is less than this level.

Cost-complexity plots often reveal multiple subtrees whose misclassification rates are close to the minimum and lie in a "long, flat valley region" (Breiman et al. 1984, p. 79).[†] In this situation, consider applying Breiman's 1–SE rule, and whenever possible apply knowledge of the problem. You can override the number of leaves selected by the procedure by specifying the LEAVES=*n* suboption for the C45, COSTCOMPLEXITY, and REDUCEDERROR options in the PRUNE statement.

Displaying the Tree and Details of the Nodes

The HPSPLIT procedure creates two types of tree diagrams: an overview of the entire tree, requested with the PLOTS=WHOLETREE option, and detailed views of subtrees, requested with the PLOTS=ZOOMEDTREE option. Output 13.3 shows the entire tree in this example.

Output 13.3 Overview of Entire Tree with 4 Leaves

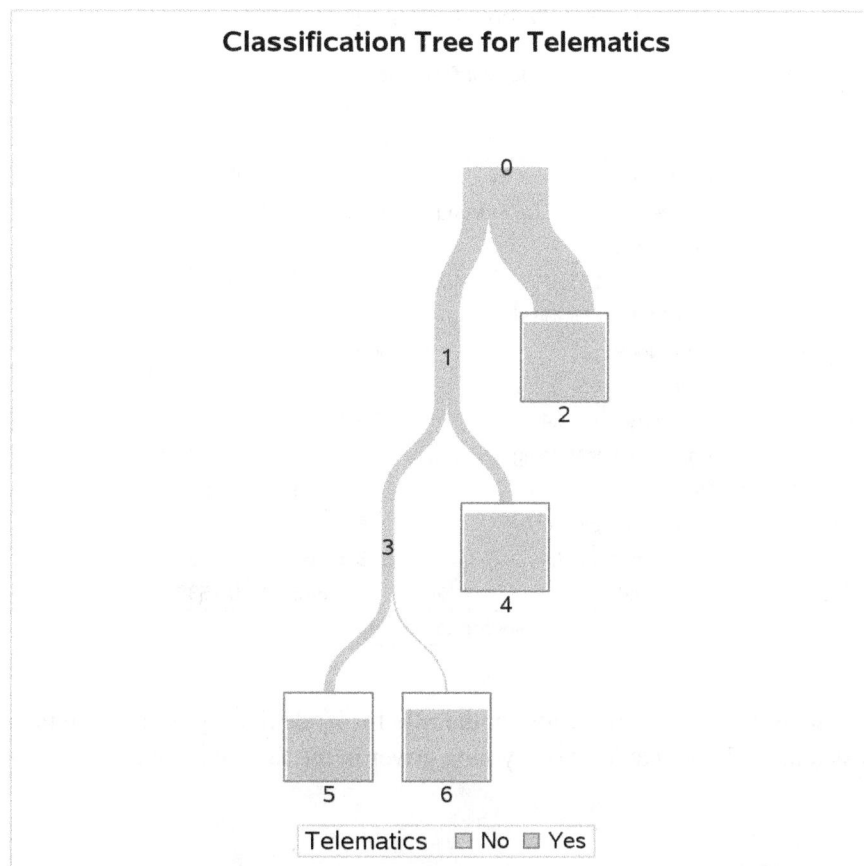

The color of the bar at each leaf indicates the most frequent level of Telematics among the training observations at that node. The height of the bar indicates the proportion of observations in the node with the most frequent level. When the tree model is applied to future data, this proportion estimates the probability that an observation assigned to this node has this level. The width of a branch indicates the proportion of observations in that branch.

[†]This is comparable to the situation that occurs in forward selection when multiple models are close to the "best" model in terms of the selection criterion; see the comments on page 119. Cost-complexity plots are analogous to coefficient progression plots such as the one on page 59.

Figure 13.3 on page 271 shows a detailed view of the same tree, which was requested by specifying a subtree with the DEPTH=4 and NODES=('0') suboptions for the PLOTS=ZOOMEDTREE option. Here, the complete tree is small enough that a complete view can be obtained by specifying a single subtree with four levels anchored at the root node. With larger trees, multiple subtrees will be needed, and you might need to rerun the procedure in order to create the right set.

Programming Tip: Use the overview tree diagram requested with PLOTS=WHOLETREE to identify the anchor nodes and depths for subtrees requested with PLOTS=ZOOMEDTREE.

Output 13.4, requested with the NODES option, displays the decision rule for each leaf node.

Output 13.4 Decision Rules for Leaf Nodes

		Node Information		
			Training Data	
ID	Path	Count	No	Yes
2	Root Node	500	0.8480	0.1520
	CredScor >= 657.5 or Missing	352	0.9318 *	0.0682
4	Root Node	500	0.8480	0.1520
	CredScor < 657.5	148	0.6486	0.3514
	YngDrvrs = 0 or Missing	75	0.9200 *	0.0800
5	Root Node	500	0.8480	0.1520
	CredScor < 657.5	148	0.6486	0.3514
	YngDrvrs = 1,2,3,4	73	0.3699	0.6301
	Age < 60.4 or Missing	60	0.2667	0.7333 *
6	Root Node	500	0.8480	0.1520
	CredScor < 657.5	148	0.6486	0.3514
	YngDrvrs = 1,2,3,4	73	0.3699	0.6301
	Age >= 60.4	13	0.8462 *	0.1538
	* Selected target level			

As indicated by the asterisk in the Yes column, the rule for Node 5 assigns car owners under 60 with credit scores less than 657.5 and at least one young driver in the family to Yes. The other rules assign owners to No.

Assessing the Tree Model

The confusion matrix in Output 13.5 shows how well the tree model classifies the training data.

Output 13.5 Model Information

Model-Based Confusion Matrix			
	Predicted		
Actual	No	Yes	Error Rate
No	408	16	0.0377
Yes	32	44	0.4211

The confusion matrix is also called the resubstitution matrix; it is obtained by applying the tree model to the training data and assigning a level to each observation based on the most frequent levels in the leaf nodes. The off-diagonal entries show how many times the model misclassified an observation.

Output 13.6 shows fit statistics for the tree model. The misclassification rate is the proportion of samples that were misclassified: $(16 + 32)/500 = 0.0096$. AUC is the area under the receiver operating characteristic (ROC) curve, and RSS is the residual sum of squares.

Output 13.6 Fit Statistics

			Model-Based Fit Statistics for Selected Tree					
N Leaves	ASE	Mis-class	Sensitivity	Specificity	Entropy	Gini	RSS	AUC
4	0.0826	0.0960	0.5789	0.9623	0.4296	0.1652	82.6186	0.7826

Output 13.7 shows the ROC curve. The construction is the same as that of the ROC curve for binary logistic regression; see page 166. Here, sensitivity and specificity are defined in terms of the event level Yes, which is specified in the MODEL statement.

Output 13.7 Receiver Operating Characteristic Curve for Training Data

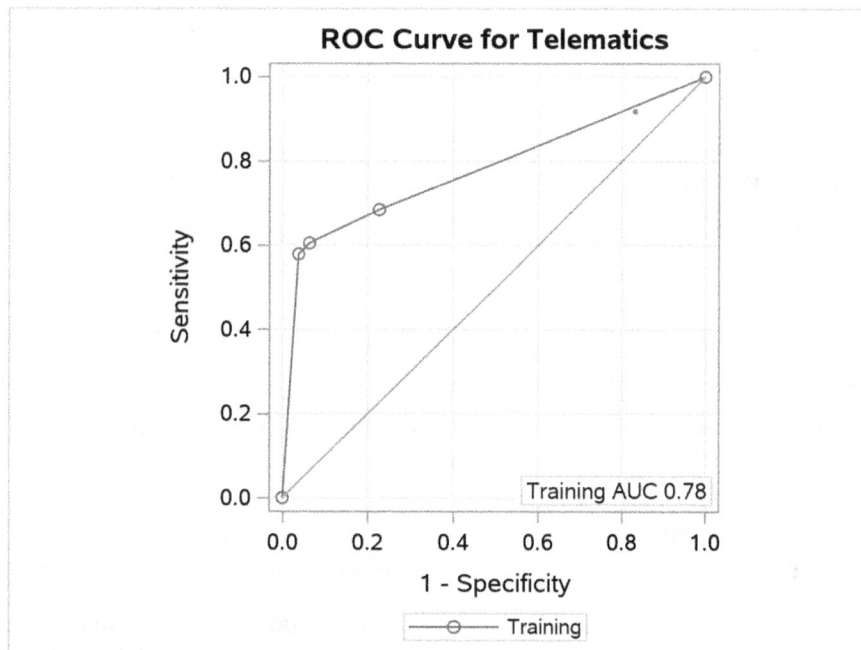

Computing Classification Probabilities for New Data

The following statements use the SAS DATA step code created by the CODE statement and saved in *FinalTreeModel.sas* to classify new observations supplied in the data set NewPreliminary:

```
data ClassifyTelematics;
   set NewPreliminary;
   %inc 'FinalTreeModel.sas';
run;
```

The data set ClassifyTelematics contains a variable P_TelematicsYes that provides the probability of level Yes and a variable P_TelematicsNo that provides the probability of level No.

Introduction to the TREESPLIT Procedure

The TREESPLIT procedure provides functionality comparable to that of the HPSPLIT procedure and shares the concepts explained on page 273. Because the TREESPLIT procedure was developed specifically for SAS Viya, it can run on a cluster of machines that distribute the data and the computations.

With the TREESPLIT procedure, you specify the candidate variables with MODEL and CLASS statements, the criterion for growing the tree with a GROW statement, and the pruning method with a PRUNE statement. These statements are similar to those of the HPSPLIT procedure (see page 274), except that the MODEL statement does not provide an EVENT= option for binary classification variables.

The TREESPLIT procedure provides a number of options not available in the HPSPLIT procedure. These include the following:

- The ASSIGNMISSING= option in the procedure statement provides two additional keywords, MACSMALL and USEINSEARCH. The ASSIGNMISSING=USEINSEARCH option, which is the default, treats a missing value of a predictor as a separate value. During training, no branch is selected if all the values are nonmissing. During scoring, if a predictor is missing or unknown, then the observation is assigned to the node with the most training observations. The ASSIGNMISSING=MACSMALL option specifies this behavior for categorical predictors.

- The BINMETHOD= and NUMBIN= options in the procedure statement provide ways to bin continuous predictors prior to training.

- The OUTMODEL= option in the procedure statement specifies a CAS table that saves the tree model. The INMODEL= specifies a previously saved model for use in scoring a new table.

The GROW statement in the TREESPLIT procedure does not provide the FastCHAID criterion, which is available with the HPSPLIT procedure (see Table 13.1).

The TREESPLIT procedure provides the following statements, which are not available in the HPSPLIT procedure:

- The AUTOTUNE statement searches for the best combination of values of the MAXDEPTH=, MINLEAFSIZE=, and NUMBIN= options in the procedure statement and the grow criterion.

- The CODE statement writes SAS DATA step code for computing predicted values to a file, to a catalog entry, or to a CAS table. The CODE statement for the HPSPLIT procedure only writes code to a file.

- The DISPLAY statement replaces the ODS SELECT statement for specifying displayed output. The DISPLAYOUT statement, which creates CAS tables from displayed output, provides functionality comparable to that of the ODS OUTPUT statement.

- The SAVESTATE statement saves an analytic store for the model, which you can use to score new data with the ASTORE procedure (see page 384 in Appendix H).

- The VIICODE statement writes SAS DATA step code to a file or to a catalog entry. This code creates new variables on the basis of detected variable interactions.

Example: Predicting Interest in Telematics (continued)

This example uses the data set Respondents, introduced on page 276, to identify groups of car owners who are willing to use telematics. It provides observations for 5,886 owners whose ages range from 22 to 80, and it contains 19 candidate predictors that are described in Table 13.4 on page 276. As in the previous example, the response variable Telematics has two levels, Yes and No.

Preliminary Steps

Working with these data in the CAS (Cloud Analytic Services) environment requires some preliminary steps. The following statements create formats for a number of the variables and make them visible to the CAS server:

```
proc format casfmtlib="casformats";
   value AType    1='City'  2='Town'  3='Village'  4='Rural';
   value Cite     1='None'  2='One'  3-5='Multiple';
   value Conv     0='None' 1='1 or more';
   value Cred     800-850='800 to 850'   750-799='750 to 799'
                  700-749='700 to 749'   650-699='650 to 699'
                  600-649='600 to 649'   550-599='550 to 599'
                  500-549='500 to 549'   300-499='300 to 499';
   value Ded      0='None' 1='Low' 2='High';
   value EdLev    1='No HS diploma'  2='HS diploma'    3='Some college'
                  4='Associate'        5='Bachelor'       6='Grad School'
                  7='Master'           8='Professional'  9='Doctorate';
   value FType    1='Gas'  2='Hybrid'  3='Electric'  ;
   value IType    1='Food'     2='Read'    3='Movies' 4='Games'
                  5='Sports'  6='Garden' 7='Other';
   value MStat    1='Married'     2='Widowed'  3='Divorced'
                  4='Separated'   5='Never Married';
   value RType    1='U'  2='V'  3='W'  4='X';
   value TType    1='New' 2='Modify' 3='Renew';
   value VType    1='Crossover'  2='Pickup'  3='Small'  4='SUV'
                  5='Midsized'     6='Luxury'  7='Van'     8='Large';
   value VUse     1='Pleasure'  2='Commuting';
   value WStat    1='Full Time'  2='Part Time'  3='Not Working';
   value YN       1='Yes'  0='No';
run;
```

The CASFMTLIB= option adds a format library named *casformats* to the CAS session.

The next statement assigns the libref mycas to in-memory tables on the CAS server:

```
libname mycas cas;
```

Here, mycas refers to the active caslib. A caslib is associated with a data source; it is similar to a libref in SAS, but it operates on the CAS server and enables you to read and write tables from CAS. The active caslib is the default location for reading and writing in-memory data sets; it is created for you when you start a CAS session.

The next statements use the CASUTIL procedure to upload the data in Respondents to a CAS table named mycas.Respondents. These statements also assign the formats to the variables.

```
proc casutil;
    format Deductible Ded.        Education EdLev.      Exercise YN.
           Fuel FType.            Interest IType.       MaritalStatus MStat.
           MultipleVehicles YN.   NDrvConvict Conv.     PubLib YN.
           Rating RType.          Social YN.            Telematics YN.
           Transaction TType.     VehicleType VType.    WorkStatus WStat. ;
    load data=work.Respondents;
quit;
```

Building the Classification Tree

The macro variable SplitCandidates saves the names of candidate predictors that are to be specified with the MODEL statement of the TREESPLIT procedure:

```
%let SplitCandidates = Age CredScor Deductible Education Exercise Fuel Gender
                       Interest MaritalStatus MultipleVehicles NDrvConvict
                       NumberatFault PubLib Rating Social Transaction
                       VehicleType WorkStatus YngDrvrs;
```

The macro variable ClassVars saves the names of categorical variables that are to be specified in the CLASS statement:

```
%let ClassVars = Deductible Education Exercise Fuel Gender Interest
                 MaritalStatus MultipleVehicles NDrvConvict NumberatFault
                 PubLib Rating Social Telematics Transaction VehicleType
                 WorkStatus YngDrvrs;
```

The following statements use the TREESPLIT procedure to build a classification tree for Telematics:

```
ods graphics on;
proc treesplit data=mycas.Respondents maxdepth=4 plots=(wholetree);
    class &ClassVars;
    model Telematics = &SplitCandidates;
    grow entropy;
    prune costcomplexity;
    output out=mycas.TelematicsPred copyvars=(Telematics) role=PartitionRole;
    partition fraction(validate=0.15 test=0.15 seed=16861);
run;
```

As in the example on page 277, the split criterion is the Gini index and the method of pruning is cost complexity. The MAXDEPTH= option specifies four as the maximum depth of the tree.

The OUTPUT statement names a CAS table that contains the results. A variable named P_TelematicsYes saves the probability of the level Yes, and a variable named P_TelematicsNo saves the probability of the level No.

Because there are sufficient observations in Respondents, the PARTITION statement is used to allocate 15% of the data for validation and 15% for testing while reserving 70% for training. The SEED= option specifies the seed for random partitioning.

Output 13.8 summarizes how the classification tree was built.

Output 13.8 Model Information

Model Information	
Split Criterion	Entropy
Pruning Method	Cost Complexity
Max Branches per Node	2
Max Tree Depth	4
Tree Depth Before Pruning	4
Tree Depth After Pruning	4
Number of Leaves Before Pruning	15
Number of Leaves After Pruning	7

Output 13.9 plots misclassification rates computed from the training and validation partitions for subtrees nested with the large tree that is initially grown.

Output 13.9 Pruning Plot

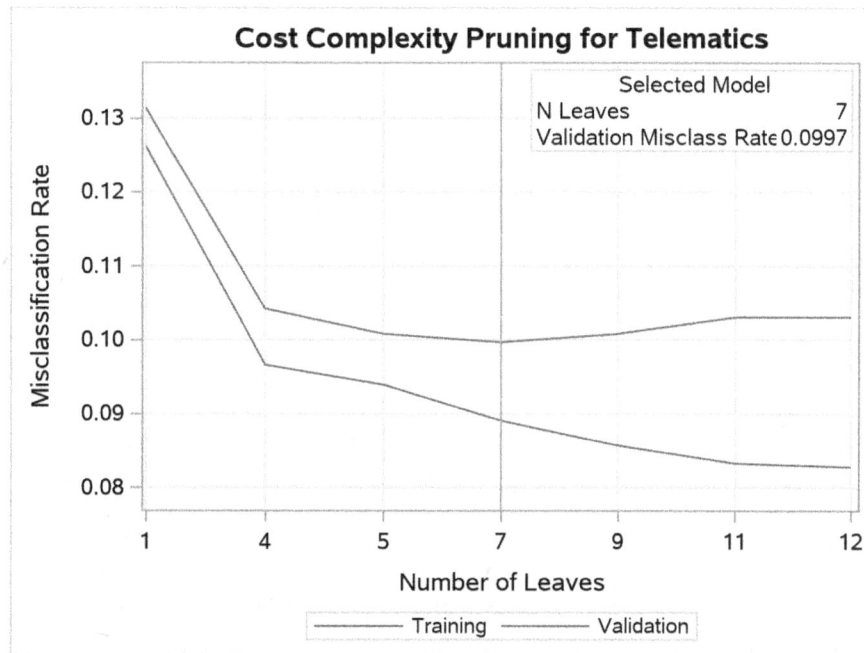

The procedure selects the subtree with seven leaves, which minimizes the misclassification rate for the validation data. The subtree with five leaves is also a reasonable selection. You could request it by specifying COSTCOMPLEXITY(LEAVES=5) in the PRUNE statement.

Output 13.10 shows the misclassification rates for the three partitions.

Output 13.10 Misclassification Rates Based on Resubstitution

Fit Statistics for Selected Tree		
	Number of Leaves	Misclassification Rate
Training	7	0.0891
Validation	7	0.0997
Test	7	0.0849

Displaying the Tree

Output 13.11, requested with the PLOTS=(WHOLETREE) option, shows the entire tree.

Output 13.11 Whole Tree Plot

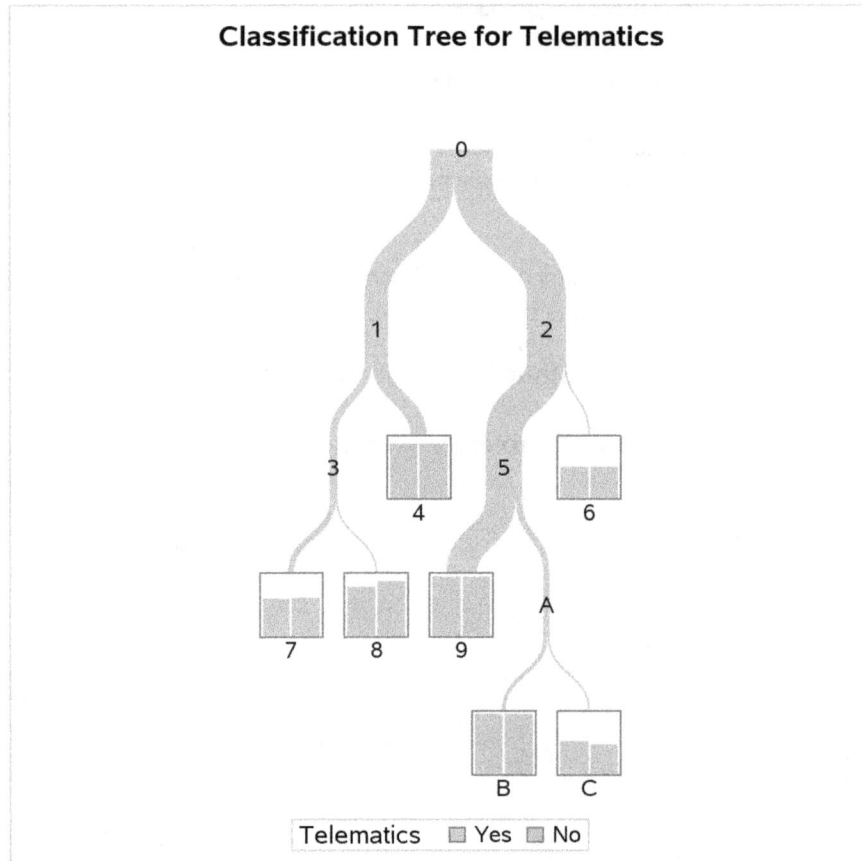

Classification Tree for Telematics

Telematics ☐ Yes ☐ No

There are two bars at each leaf node. The color of the left bar indicates the most frequent level of Telematics among the training observations in the node, and the color of the right bar indicates the most frequent level among the validation observations in the node. The heights of the bars indicate the proportions of observations in the node with the most frequent levels.

There are three leaf nodes in which the proportions of level Yes are in the majority: Nodes 7, 6, and C. To learn more about those nodes, you can request diagrams of the subtrees anchored at Nodes 1 and 2 by rerunning the procedure with the PLOTS=(ZOOMEDTREE) option as follows:

```
proc treesplit data=mycas.Respondents maxdepth=4 vii=3
                plots=(zoomedtree(depth=3 nodes=('1' '2'))) ;
    class &ClassVars;
    model Telematics = &SplitCandidates;
    grow entropy;
    prune costcomplexity;
    output out=mycas.TelematicsPred copyvars=(Telematics)
           role=PartitionRole;
    partition fraction(validate=0.15 test=0.15 seed=16861);
run;
```

Output 13.12 shows the subtree anchored at Node 1. The inset in the upper left indicates the location of the subtree in relation to the entire tree.

Output 13.12 Subtree Anchored at Node 1

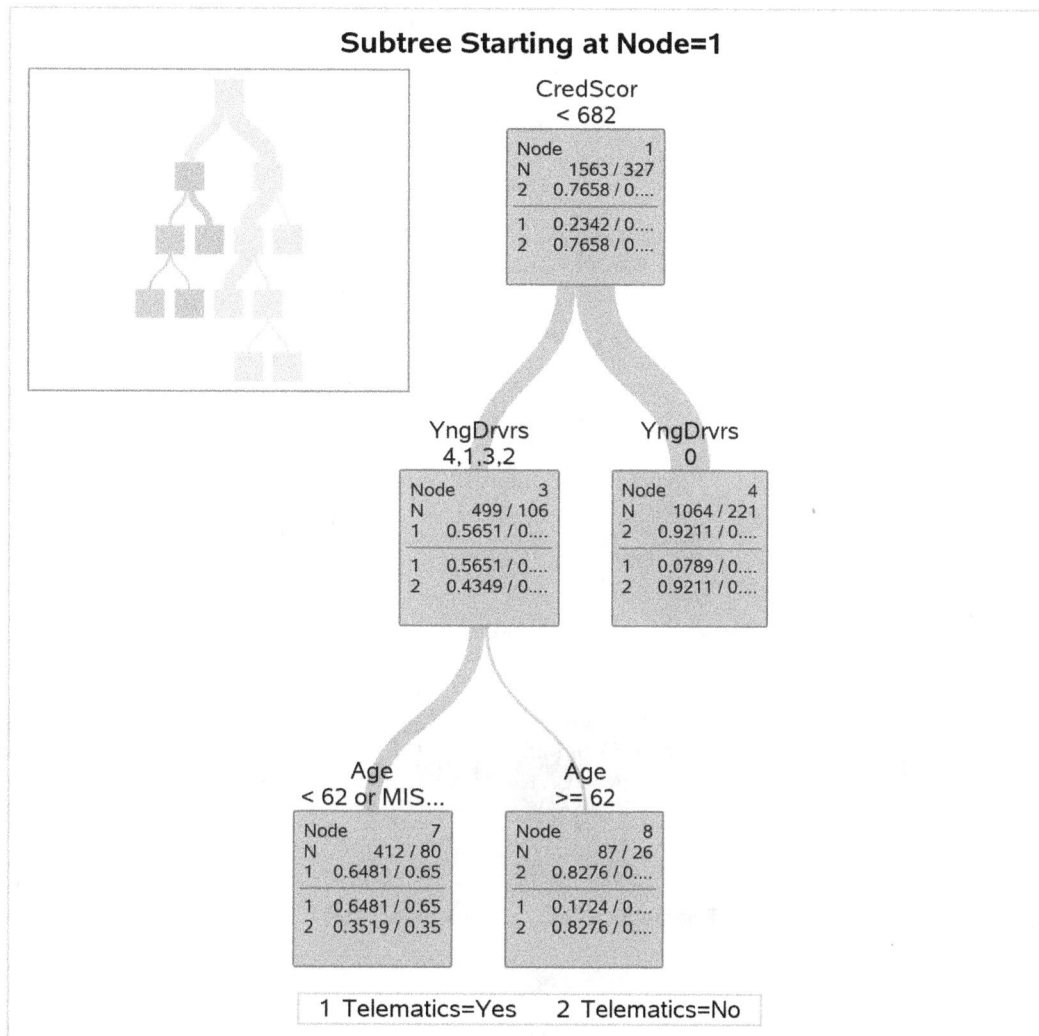

Node 7 is defined by vehicle owners who have credit scores less than 682, who have at least one young driver in the family, and who are under the age of 62. It is reasonable that owners in this category would adopt telematics to save on their insurance rates and to encourage safe driving habits in their families. This result is consistent with the interpretation of the tree that was built earlier with the data set Preliminary (see page 280).

Output 13.13 shows the subtree anchored at Node 2. Node 6 is defined by owners who are in graduate school and have credit scores greater than 682. This group is likely to be attracted by the lower rates available with telematics programs. Interestingly, Node C is defined by owners with advanced degrees who are over 61, enjoy gardening, and have credit scores greater than 682.

The analytics center produced the data set Respondents by selecting vehicle owners from several large databases. The selection is prone to bias because the observations are a judgment sample (also called a purposive sample)—not a random sample designed to represent the population of vehicle owners. This limitation needs to be kept in mind when the model is used to classify new data.

Output 13.13 Subtree Anchored at Node 2

Subtree Starting at Node=2

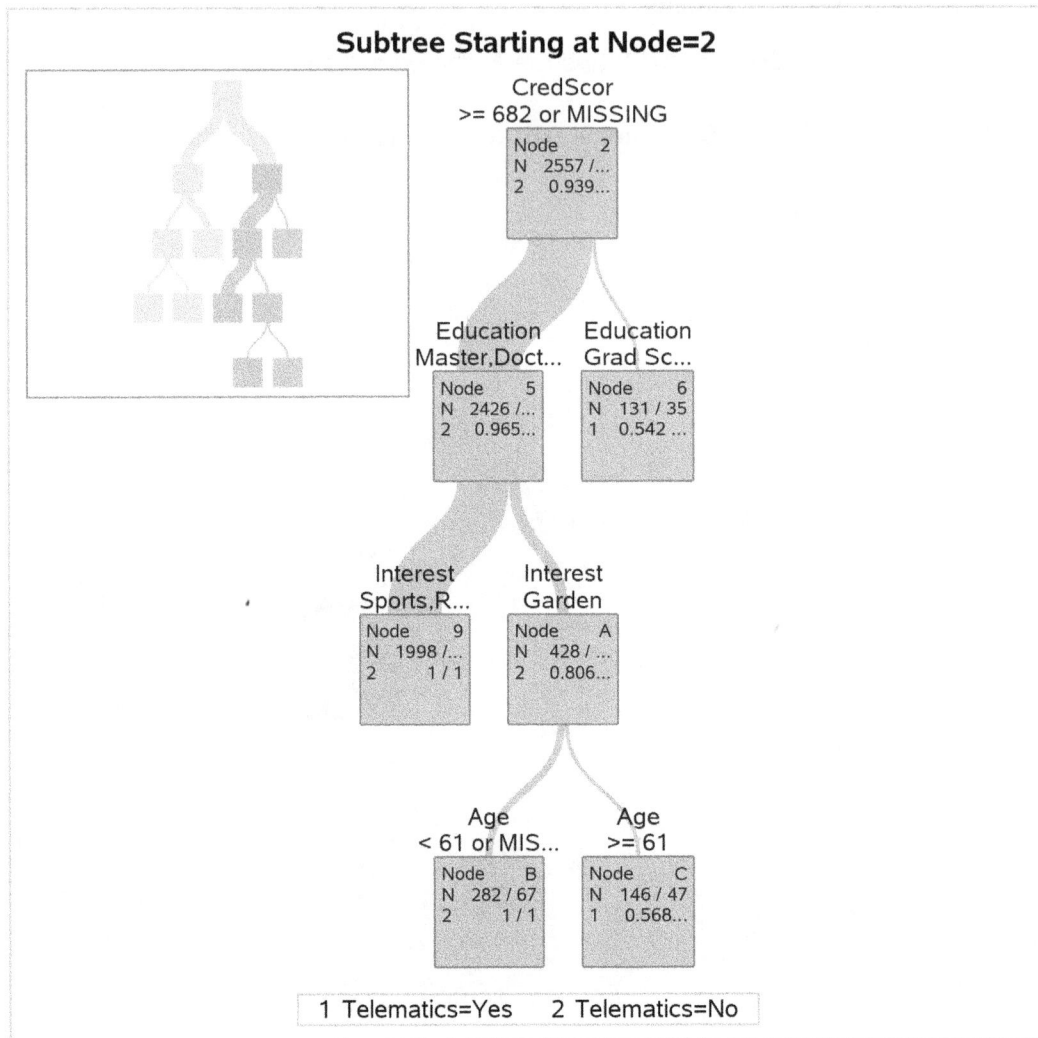

```
                    CredScor
                 >= 682 or MISSING
                  Node      2
                  N   2557 /...
                  2    0.939...
```

```
   Education              Education
 Master,Doct...           Grad Sc...
  Node     5              Node      6
  N   2426 /...           N   131 / 35
  2    0.965...           1    0.542 ...
```

```
   Interest               Interest
  Sports,R...              Garden
  Node     9              Node      A
  N   1998 /...           N   428 /...
  2      1 / 1            2    0.806...
```

```
     Age                    Age
  < 61 or MIS...          >= 61
  Node      B             Node      C
  N   282 / 67            N   146 / 47
  2      1 / 1            1    0.568...
```

| 1 Telematics=Yes | 2 Telematics=No |

Variable and Interaction Importance

Output 13.14 shows two measures of importance for variables in the tree model. Two-way and three-way interactions are included, as specified by the VII=3 option in the procedure statement.

The Count column provides the number of times a variable is used in a split; you can verify this by examining Output 13.12 and Output 13.13. The Count column also provides the number of times that two-way and three-way interactions appear in the tree.

For the variables, the Importance columns provide $\sum_{d=1}^{D} \Delta_d$, where Δ_d is the change in the residual sum of squares when a split is found at node d, and D is the number of nodes in which the variable was used for splitting.

For the interactions, the Importance columns provide generalizations of $\sum_{d=1}^{D} \Delta_d$. The Relative Importance measures scale the Importance measures relative to the largest measure. Importance values for the sets of variables and two-way and three-way interactions are not on the same scale and should only be compared within sets.

Output 13.14 Variable and Interaction Importance

			Variable Importance				
			Training		Validation		
Variable	2nd Order Interaction Variable	3rd Order Interaction Variable	Importance	Relative Importance	Importance	Relative Importance	Count
Age			94.6803	0.5896	27.2253	1.0000	2
YngDrvrs			160.59	1.0000	25.0911	0.9216	1
Education			64.0913	0.3991	16.3678	0.6012	1
CredScor			58.6966	0.3655	8.4098	0.3089	1
Interest			26.5123	0.1651	7.9777	0.2930	1
YngDrvrs	CredScor		3.7359	0.0233	3.9836	0.1463	1
Education	CredScor		2.0919	0.0130	2.9463	0.1082	1
Age	Interest		3.3453	0.0208	2.7741	0.1019	1
Age	YngDrvrs		1.2024	0.0075	1.5210	0.0559	1
Education	Interest		1.4137	0.0088	1.4874	0.0546	1
Age	Education	Interest	1.6863	0.0105	1.5814	0.0581	1
Age	YngDrvrs	CredScor	1.1482	0.0072	1.3902	0.0511	1
Education	Interest	CredScor	1.2159	0.0076	1.3220	0.0486	1

Here, the measures of variable importance add no practical value because the tree is so simple that it speaks for itself. The measures become useful with trees that are too large to visualize and involve many splits. With the VIICODE statement (not illustrated here), you can save SAS DATA step code that creates new variables from interactions whose importance is above a specified threshold. However, as shown by this example, there are different ways to define importance and no one method is the most informative.

Assessing the Tree Model with Classification Measures

Unlike the HPSPLIT procedure and other procedures that model binary responses, the TREESPLIT procedure does not provide an EVENT= option for specifying the event level, nor does it provide classification measures for assessing tree models for binary responses. Instead, you create an output table with the OUTPUT statement and pass it to the ASSESS procedure, a utility procedure that handles model assessment and comparison for supervised learning models in SAS Viya.

The following statements compute classification measures:

```
proc assess data=mycas.TelematicsPred(where=(PartitionRole=3)) ncuts=10;
   input P_TelematicsYes;
   target Telematics / event="Yes" level=nominal;
run;
```

The CAS table TelematicsPred was created by the OUTPUT statement for the TREESPLIT procedure on page 286. It contains a variable named PartitionRole with values 1, 2, and 3 for observations in the training, validation, and test partitions, respectively. The EVENT= option identifies the event level for Telematics. The INPUT statement specifies P_TelematicsYes as the variable that provides the probability of the event level. The NCUTS= option specifies the number of cutpoint values that are used to compute classification measures.

Output 13.15 shows the classification measures produced by the ASSESS procedure.

Output 13.15 Classification Measures (Partial Table)

					ROC Information					
Cutoff	TP	FP	FN	TN	FPR	FDR	TPR	FNR	TNR	AUC
0.0	106	777	0	0	1.0000	0.8800	1.0000	0.0000	0.0000	0.9115
0.1	95	79	11	698	0.1017	0.4540	0.8962	0.1038	0.8983	0.9115
0.2	94	63	12	714	0.0811	0.4013	0.8868	0.1132	0.9189	0.9115
0.3	94	63	12	714	0.0811	0.4013	0.8868	0.1132	0.9189	0.9115
0.4	94	63	12	714	0.0811	0.4013	0.8868	0.1132	0.9189	0.9115
0.5	94	63	12	714	0.0811	0.4013	0.8868	0.1132	0.9189	0.9115
0.6	56	28	50	749	0.0360	0.3333	0.5283	0.4717	0.9640	0.9115
0.7	0	0	106	777	0.0000	.	0.0000	1.0000	1.0000	0.9115
0.8	0	0	106	777	0.0000	.	0.0000	1.0000	1.0000	0.9115
0.9	0	0	106	777	0.0000	.	0.0000	1.0000	1.0000	0.9115
1.0	0	0	106	777	0.0000	.	0.0000	1.0000	1.0000	0.9115

The columns TP, FP, FN, and TN provide the numbers of true positives, false positives, false negatives, and true negatives, respectively. For definitions of these statistics, see Table 9.4 on page 166.

Columns FPR through TNR provide measures of classification accuracy that are defined as follows:

- FPR $= \mathrm{FP}/n_0$, where n_0 is the number of nonevents.
- TPR $= \mathrm{TP}/n_1$, where n_1 is the number of events. TPR is called the sensitivity.
- FNR $= \mathrm{FN}/n_1$.
- TNR $= \mathrm{TN}/n_0$. TNR is called the specificity.
- FDR $= 1 - (\mathrm{TPR} + \mathrm{TNR})/(n_1 + n_0)$. FDR is called the misclassification rate.

A drawback of these measures is that they assume equal misclassification costs for false positives and false negatives. In practice, the costs are typically unknown. Furthermore, these measures do not account for the prior distribution of the classes in the target population. Provost, Fawcett, and Kohavi (1998) discussed the disadvantages of using single accuracy measures to compare the performance of classifiers. They recommended ROC analysis as a better alternative.[†]

As explained on page 166, an ROC curve plots sensitivity as a function of $1 -$ specificity, and AUC is the area under the curve. Currently, the ASSESS procedure does not provide a plot of the ROC curve, but with the ROCOUT= option you can request a CAS table of the values for the curve. The `%ROCforASSESS` macro, available on the book website, uses this table to plot the curve, as illustrated by the following statements:

```
proc assess data=mycas.TelematicsPred(where=PartitionRole=(3)) ncuts=10
            rocout=mycas.ROCTest ;
   input P_TelematicsYes;
   target Telematics / event="Yes" level=nominal;
run;


%ROCforASSESS(Data= mycas.ROCTest , PartitionRole= 3 , Target= Telematics )
```

The plot is shown in Output 13.16.

[†]Harrell (2015, pp. 257–258) discusses these issues more deeply in the context of binary logistic regression and notes that making a classification rule from a probability model by applying a cutoff hinders decisions that would be better informed by the predicted probabilities.

Output 13.16 Receiver Operating Characteristic Curve for Test Partition

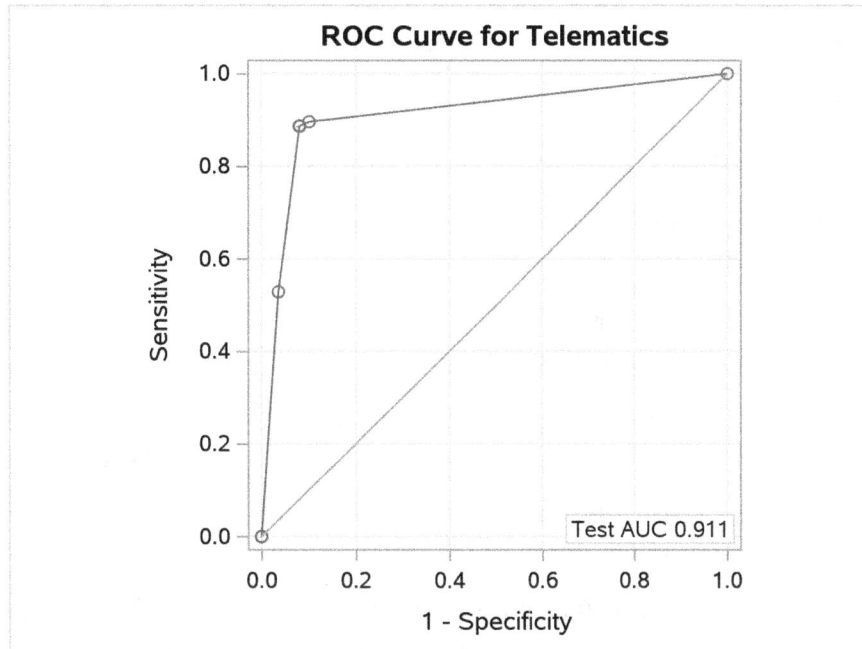

The AUC value 0.911 is high because the interaction effects in the data are unusually strong.

Assessing the Tree Model with Lift and Gain

Lift and gain are measures used by marketing analysts to differentiate competing models for binary classification. To compute these measures, the observations are sorted in decreasing order of the posterior probability values given by the model. The observations are then binned into deciles or half-deciles. A model with good discriminatory ability should predict a high percentage of events in the uppermost deciles, whereas a model with no ability should predict about 10% in each bin.

The following statements use the ASSESS procedure to compute measures for the model built on page 286 from the test observations in the CAS table TelematicsPred saved by the TREESPLIT procedure. The NBINS= option specifies binning into deciles.

```
proc assess data=mycas.TelematicsPred(where=(PartitionRole=3)) nbins=10;
   input P_TelematicsYes;
   target Telematics / event="Yes" level=nominal;
   ods output liftinfo=LiftMeasures;
run;
```

Output 13.17 shows a partial listing of the CAS table LiftMeasures produced by the procedure.

Output 13.17 Lift and Gain Information for P_TelematicsYes (Partial Table)

Depth	Number of Observations	Number of Events	Individual Captured Response Percent	Cumulative Captured Response Percent	Individual Lift	Cumulative Lift	Individual Response Percent	Cumulative Response Percent	Individual Gain
0	0	0.00	0.00	0.00	.	.	.	.	.
10	89	58.63	55.31	55.31	5.531	5.531	65.87	65.87	4.531
20	89	36.57	34.50	89.81	3.450	4.490	41.09	53.48	3.490

The columns of the table are defined as follows:

- Depth (Depth) identifies the deciles beginning with the second row of the table.

- Number of Observations (NObs) is the number of observations in each decile.

- Number of Events (NEvents) is the number of observed events in each decile.

- Individual Captured Response Percent (Resp) is the percentage of responses predicted by the model in each decile.

- Individual Lift (Lift) is the ratio of Individual Captured Response Percent to the baseline percentage response, which is 10% in each decile.

- Cumulative Lift (CumLift) is the ratio of Cumulative Captured Response Percent to the cumulative baseline percentage response. In the third row this is $89.81/(10 + 10) = 4.49$.

- Individual Response Percent (PctResp) is the percentage of events among the observations in each decile. In the second row this is $100 \times 58.63/89 = 65.87$.

- Cumulative Response Percent (CumPctResp) is the percentage of cumulative events among the cumulative observations. In the third row this is $100(58.63 + 36.57)/(89 + 89) = 53.46$.

- Individual Gain (Gain) indicates how much better (as a percentage) the model performs compared with tossing a coin. For each decile, Individual Gain is Cumulative Lift minus one (one is the cumulative lift for random classification).

The columns are saved as variables (indicated in parentheses) in the CAS table LiftMeasures created by the ODS OUTPUT statement. With the SGPLOT procedure, you can readily produce lift charts, such as the one in Output 13.18, which plots CumLift against Depth.

Output 13.18 Cumulative Lift for Tree Model Computed from Test Data

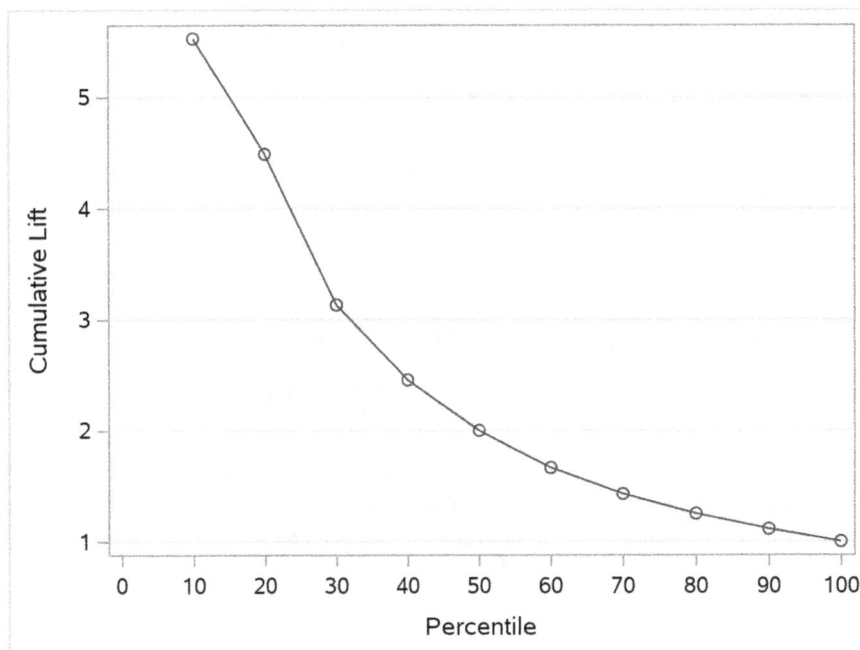

Summary

Decision trees have the ability to identify complex interactions, apply to both continuous and categorical predictors, and provide ways to handle missing data. Tree diagrams are also easy to explain and relate to domain knowledge in situations where they turn out to be simple.

A disadvantage of decision trees is that the structure of the tree can easily change if you perturb the training data or the tuning parameters. For instance, by rerunning the TREESPLIT statements on page 286 with different values of the SEED= option, which controls the random allocation of the training partition, you can produce trees that differ from the one in Output 13.11.

Of course, what matters most is not the visible structure of the tree but how well it does for classification and regression. The rules can have good predictive ability even when the structure is difficult to visualize, just as a complex regression model can be effective for prediction even though the interpretations of the parameters might not be obvious.

Compared with other methods for supervised learning, the flexibility of decision trees is limited by the roughness of their prediction surfaces, which are indicator functions for rectangular regions of the predictor space that are aligned orthogonally to the predictors. This deficiency motivated the development of multivariate adaptive regression splines, discussed next in Chapter 14.

Learning ensembles of trees provide better prediction accuracy than single decision trees. Two well-known ensemble methods—both of which lie outside the scope of this book—are random forests and gradient boosting. The FOREST procedure in SAS Viya implements Breiman's method of bootstrap aggregation (bagging), which averages trees grown from bootstrapped versions of the data (Breiman 1996, 2001a). The GRADBOOST procedure in SAS Viya builds predictive models by fitting a set of additive trees in an adaptive fashion and then averaging them. This approach is called gradient boosting (Friedman 2001).

Table 13.5 compares the features of the HPSPLIT and TREESPLIT procedures.

Table 13.5 Procedures for Building Classification and Regression Trees

Feature	HPSPLIT	TREESPLIT
Primary purpose	Building classification and regression trees	Building classification and regression trees
MODEL and CLASS statements	Yes	Yes
Binary event specification	Yes	No; in ASSESS
Criteria for growing trees		
CHAID based on chi-square or F tests	Yes	Yes
Chi-square statistic	Yes	Yes
Entropy decrease	Yes	Yes
FastCHAID	Yes	No
Gini index decrease	Yes	Yes
Information gain ratio	Yes	Yes
F statistic	Yes	Yes

Table 13.5 *continued*

Feature	HPSPLIT	TREESPLIT
Variance change	Yes	Yes
Methods for pruning trees		
C4.5	Yes	Yes
Cost complexity	Yes	Yes
Reduced error	Yes	Yes
Methods for handling missing values		
Creates special branch	Yes	Yes
Creates special branch; handles scoring when all training values are nonmissing	No	Yes
Assigns to most popular node	Yes	Yes
Assigns to most similar branch	Yes	Yes
Excludes	Yes	Yes
Methods for variable importance	Yes	Yes
Count	Yes	Yes
Surrogate count	Yes	Yes
Residual sum of squares	Yes	Yes
Relative importance	Yes	Yes
Random branch assignment	No	Yes
Methods for model assessment		
Misclassification rate	Yes	Yes
Average square error	Yes	No
Classification measures	Yes	No; in ASSESS
Estimation of subtree misclassification		
m-fold cross validation	Yes	Yes
Validation partition	Yes	Yes
Plots		
Tree diagrams	Yes	Yes
Subtree misclassification rates	Yes	Yes
ROC curves	Yes	No
Methods for saving and applying tree rules		
DATA step code	Yes	Yes
DATA step code with interactions	No	Yes
Analytic store	No	Yes
Autotuning	No	Yes
Computational execution	Multiple threads	Multiple threads, distributed

Chapter 14
Building Adaptive Regression Models

Contents

This chapter introduces the ADAPTIVEREG procedure in SAS 9 for building regression models with multivariate adaptive regression splines (MARS).

The MARS approach, which is well suited for building predictive models with a large number of predictors, was developed by Jerome Friedman at Stanford University (Friedman 1991).[†] It was intended to overcome the disadvantages of regression methods based on recursive partitioning—in particular, classification and regression trees (CART), which is discussed in Chapter 13. Recursive partitioning captures high-order interactions but lacks the ability to capture dependencies that are additive or that involve interactions among a small number of predictors. Furthermore, models produced by recursive partitioning are discontinuous. This is not necessarily a problem if the response is categorical, but it is a disadvantage for prediction when the regression surface $f(\mathbf{x})$ is assumed to be smooth.

MARS models are nonparametric, but like generalized linear models (see page 193) they incorporate continuous and categorical responses by providing a link function that connects the mean of the response to a linear predictor. For a MARS model, the linear predictor is

$$\mu = \beta_0 + \sum_{m=1}^{M} \beta_m B_m(\mathbf{x})$$

where $\mathbf{x} = (x_1, \ldots, x_p)'$. The functions $B_m(\mathbf{x})$ are the basis functions for a multivariate spline that approximates $f(\mathbf{x})$. They are constructed as products of piecewise linear functions:

$$B_m(\mathbf{x}) = \prod_{k=1}^{K_m} T_m(\mathbf{x}_{k,m}, t_{k,m}), \quad m = 1, \ldots, M$$

where $T_m(\mathbf{x}_{k,m}, t_{k,m}) \equiv [s_{km}(\mathbf{x}_{k,m} - t_{k,m})]_+ \equiv \max(s_{km}(\mathbf{x}_{k,m} - t_{k,m}), 0), k = 1, \ldots, K_m$. Here $\mathbf{x}_{k,m}$ is the predictor selected for the kth component of the mth basis function, s_{km} is ± 1, and $t_{k,m}$ is a value of $\mathbf{x}_{k,m}$ selected as a knot. The subscript $+$ stands for "positive part of."

The number of candidate models that can be formed in this fashion is enormous. With only 10 predictors and a sample size of 100, this number is already far too large for conventional model selection methods. Instead, MARS achieves computational feasibility with a two-stage algorithm that first overfits the data and then applies a backward deletion procedure. The next section illustrates a MARS model for a single predictor ($p = 1$).

[†]In the discussion of Friedman's paper, which appeared in the *Annals of Statistics*, Leo Breiman noted that it proposed useful methodology "[without] a single theorem, lemma, or proposition."

Example: Predicting Network Activity (revisited)

Figure 14.1 shows a MARS model and a CART model for the network activity data introduced on page 12. The MARS model (produced with the ADAPTIVEREG procedure) is piecewise linear and continuous. The CART model (produced with the HPSPLIT procedure) is a step function.

Figure 14.1 MARS and CART Models for Network Activity

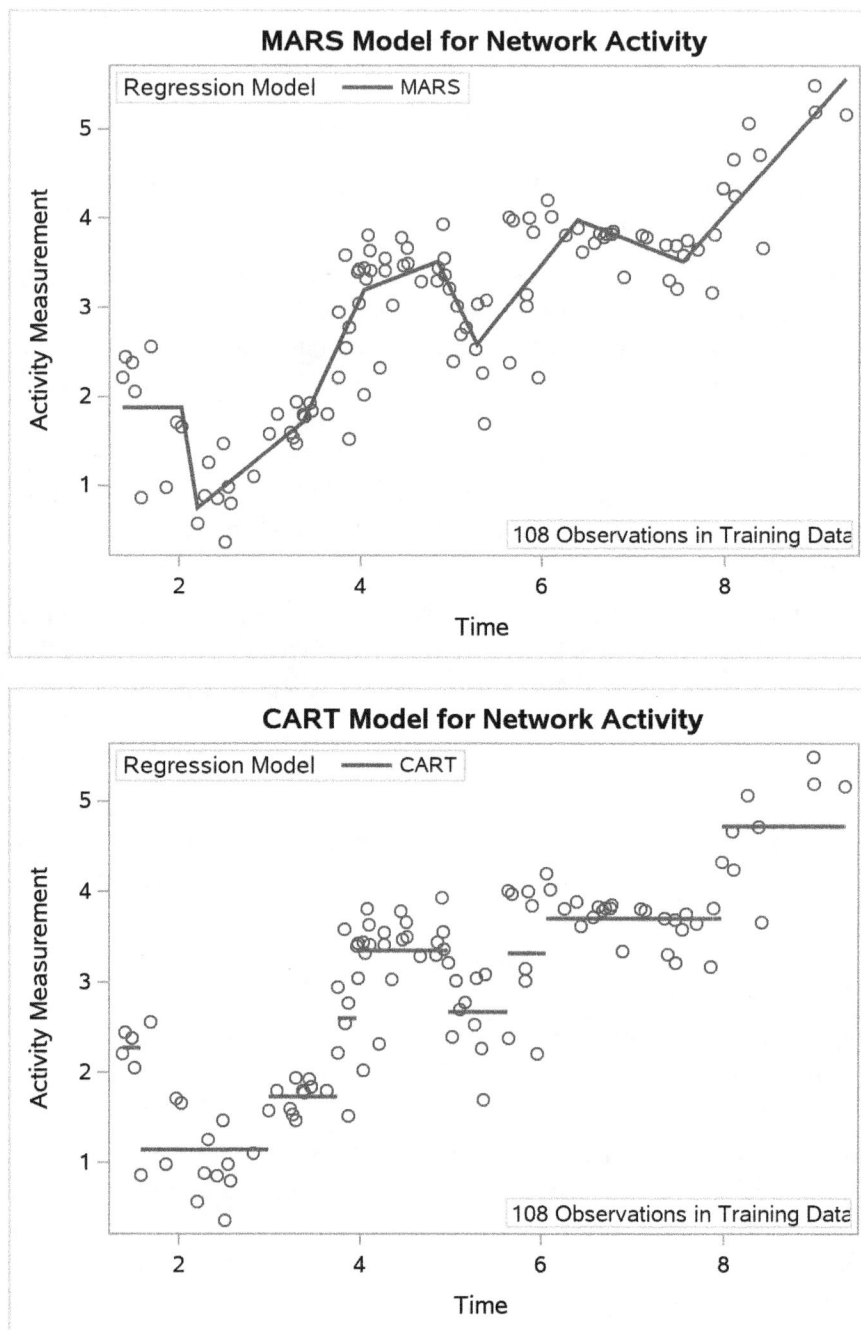

For comparison with a generalized additive model (produced with the GAMPL procedure), see Figure 11.1 on page 224. Generalized additive models are inherently smoother than MARS models.

The MARS Model Selection Strategy

The building blocks for MARS models are the piecewise linear functions $T_m(x_{k,m}, t_{k,m})$ that are defined on page 295. There are two versions of $T_m(x_{k,m}, t_{k,m})$ for each knot value $t_{k,m}$, as illustrated in Figure 14.2 for $t_{k,m} = 1$. The one on the left is the "plus" version; its reflection on the right is the "minus" version.

Figure 14.2 Building Block Functions for MARS Basis Functions

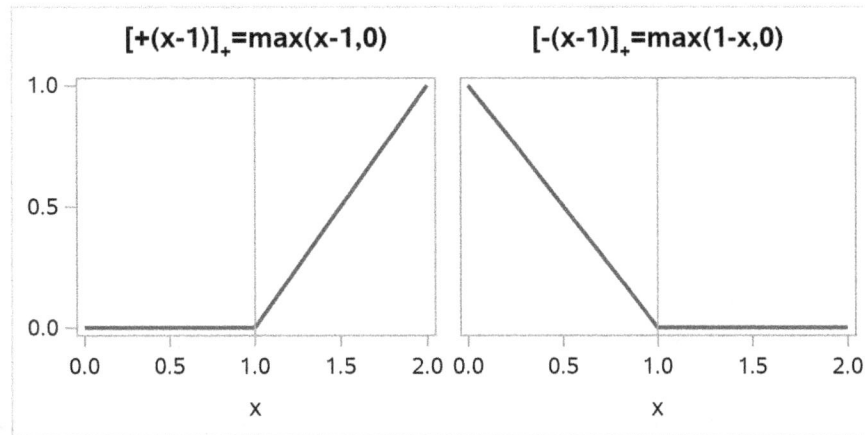

Because of their shapes, these functions are called hockey stick functions. Together with the constant function, they form a set of basis functions for univariate regression splines, which are discussed in Appendix F. This basis set is equivalent to the truncated power basis of order $d = 1$ (see page 353). It is easy to confuse the various sets of basis functions. Keep in mind that the MARS basis functions $B_m(x)$ are *constructed from* the $T_m(x_{k,m}, t_{k,m})$ functions; they *reduce to* the truncated power basis only in the special case $p = 1$.

Using the truncated power basis, Patricia Smith (then at Old Dominion University) developed an adaptive strategy for $p = 1$ that automatically selects the number and locations of the knots from the data (Smith 1982). This approach typically starts with many candidate knot locations—for instance, one at every interior value t_k of the predictor x_1—and treats the spline transformations of x_1 as candidates for standard stepwise selection. Smith (1982, Sec. 7) considered the construction of bivariate splines for two predictors by forming tensor products[†] of two univariate basis functions over a grid (either "plus" functions such as the one in Figure 14.2 or B-splines, discussed on page 355).

Although Smith's strategy was superseded by other smoothing methods, it served as a starting point for Friedman's development of the MARS strategy, which constructs the basis functions $B_m(x)$ as tensor products of the hockey stick functions. In place of stepwise selection (which is not feasible), MARS provides an algorithm that chooses a subset of the enormous number of possible products and only the number of knots needed for a good fit.

[†]The tensor product of d univariate functions $v^{(1)}(x_1), \ldots, v^{(d)}(x_d)$ that are defined on d copies of the real line $\mathcal{R}_1, \ldots, \mathcal{R}_d$ is a multivariate function $v(x_1, \ldots, x_d)$ defined on $\mathcal{R}_1 \times \ldots \times \mathcal{R}_d$ for which $v(x_1, \ldots, x_d) = v^{(1)}(x_1) \cdots v^{(d)}(x_d)$. The shorthand notation for the tensor product is $v = v^{(1)} \otimes \cdots \otimes v^{(d)}$. By the late 1970s, tensor products of B-splines were well established as a numerical method for approximating surfaces (De Boor 1978, 2001, Ch. 17) but not as a statistical method for approximating regression functions in higher dimensions. See Wood (2006, Sec. 4.1.8) for an explanation of tensor product smooths.

The MARS Algorithm

The MARS algorithm begins by initializing the basis function index m to 0 and defining the first basis function as $B_0(x) \equiv 1$. For $m \geq 1$, it constructs subsequent basis functions in two main steps:

1. For every predictor X_j not already represented in the tensor product for $B_m(x)$, a pair of hockey stick functions, $T^{(+)}(x_j, t_{obs}) = \max(x_j - t_{obs}, 0)$ and $T^{(-)}(x_j, t_{obs}) = \max(t_{obs} - x_j, 0)$, is formed at each observed value of X_j. These values are candidate knots.

   For each pair of functions, the following is done:

   (a) Candidates for the next two basis functions, $B_{m+1}(x)$ and $B_{m+2}(x)$, are constructed as products of $T^{(+)}(x_j, t_{obs})$ and $T^{(-)}(x_j, t_{obs})$ with each of the previous m basis functions. These candidates are tensor products of the form

   $$B_{m+1}^{can}(x) = B_\ell(x) \, T^{(+)}(x_j, t_{obs})$$
   $$B_{m+2}^{can}(x) = B_\ell(x) \, T^{(-)}(x_j, t_{obs})$$

   where $B_\ell(x) \in \{B_1(x), \ldots, B_{m-1}(x)\}$. $B_\ell(x)$ is called the *parent* of $B_{m+1}^{can}(x)$ and $B_{m+2}^{can}(x)$.

   (b) For each pair of candidate basis functions, a candidate model is constructed whose linear predictor is

   $$\mu^{can} = \beta_0 + \beta_1 B_1(x) + \cdots + \beta_m B_m(x) + \beta_{m+1} B_{m+1}^{can}(x) + \beta_{m+2} B_{m+2}^{can}(x)$$

   (c) Each candidate model is fitted, and a lack-of-fit criterion is computed.

2. The basis functions $B_{m+1}^{can}(x)$ and $B_{m+2}^{can}(x)$ for the candidate model that most decreases the criterion are chosen as $B_{m+1}(x)$ and $B_{m+2}(x)$. The index m is advanced to $m + 2$, and the algorithm returns to step 1.

The preceding steps define the first (forward) stage of the MARS algorithm, which continues until a prespecified number of basis functions are constructed for a model that deliberately overfits the data. At this point, there are $2m + 1$ basis functions in the model. The second (backward) stage of the algorithm then removes knots that make the least contributions to the fit. The forward and backward stages resemble the growing and pruning stages of the CART algorithm (see page 272).

The number of two-pair factors in the product for a basis function $B_m(x)$, which is denoted by K_m, is its interaction order. During the forward stage, the algorithm must enter basis functions of low interaction order before it can enter basis functions of higher interaction order. The former can be eliminated during the backward stage, but for small samples the algorithm (unlike the CART algorithm) favors models with low-order interactions. This is an advantage when the regression surface $f(x)$ is not dominated by high-order interactions (Friedman and Roosen 1995, p. 205). For large samples, the algorithm is more likely to include higher-order interactions.

For $m \geq 1$, each $B_m(x)$ contains at most one pair of hockey stick functions from each predictor. The MARS algorithm captures additive effects by creating particular basis functions, each of which multiplies (splits) $B_0(x)$ by pairs from distinct sets of one or more predictors.

The algorithm captures nonlinear effects in a single predictor x_j by splitting $B_0(x)$ more than once with $T(x_j, t_k)$ pairs placed at a series of knots t_k. These pairs form a truncated power basis for univariate regression splines, as explained on page 297. Figure 14.3 shows the pairs for the univariate MARS model illustrated in Figure 14.1.

Figure 14.3 Truncated Power Basis Pairs $T(\mathbf{x}_j, t_k)$ for MARS Model for Network Activity

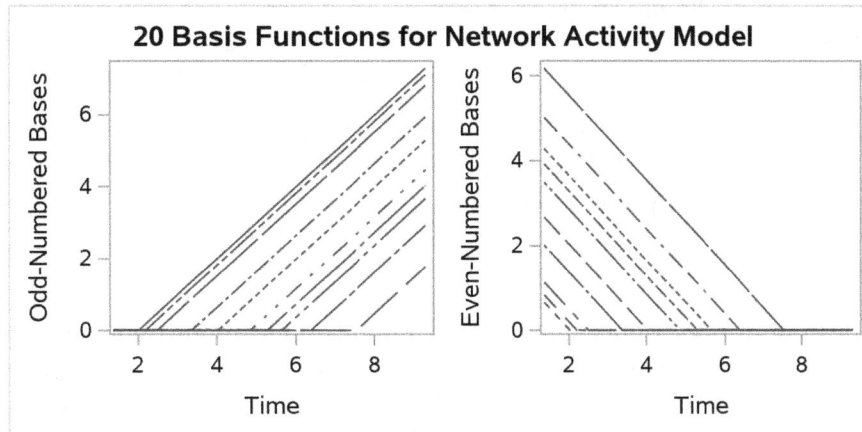

Categorical Predictors and Missing Values

In the preceding explanation, the predictors are assumed to be continuous. The MARS algorithm accommodates categorical predictors by representing their levels with indicator variables. Instead of searching for knot locations, it searches over levels and combines those that are similar. During the forward stage, the algorithm handles missing values in a predictor by introducing a companion indicator variable whose value is zero if the predictor is missing and one otherwise. This is similar to the way CART handles missing values by splitting them into separate branches.

Characteristics of MARS Models

MARS models are nonzero over small regions of the predictor space because the hockey stick functions are zero to the left or right of their knots. Figure 14.4 displays the tensor product of the two hockey stick functions shown in Figure 14.2.

Figure 14.4 Tensor Product of $\max(x - 1, 0)$ and $\max(1 - y, 0)$

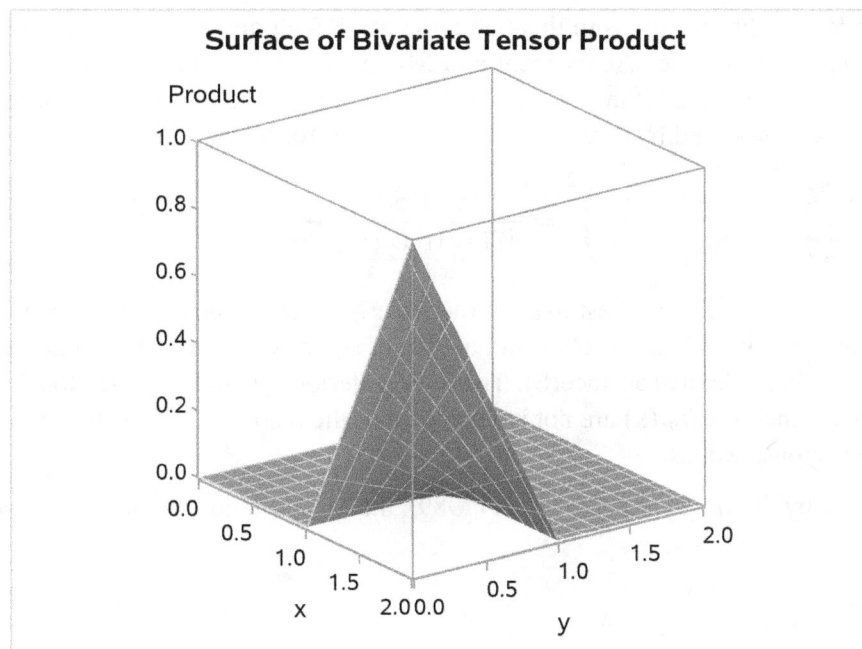

The product is nonzero only over the square where both functions are nonzero. In a MARS model, the interactions are specific to regions. This local property is important because the effective degrees of freedom for the model is spent sparingly, and its nonzero components are placed where they most matter in high dimensions (Hastie, Tibshirani, and Friedman 2009, p. 325).

Unlike the regions of a CART model, which are aligned perpendicular to the predictor axes, the regions of a MARS model can be oblique to the axes. MARS models are equivariant to changes in the signs of the predictors because the hockey stick functions always enter the model in pairs.

The ANOVA Representation

MARS models can be interpreted by regrouping their terms and representing them as a grand mean, main effects, two-way interactions, and higher-order interactions. This representation is reminiscent of the analysis of variance (ANOVA) for a general linear model, which decomposes the total variation of the response into components associated with main effects and interactions.

The ANOVA representation for a MARS model has the form

$$\hat{f}(\mathbf{x}) = \hat{\beta}_0 + \sum_{i:K_m=1} \hat{f}_i(\mathbf{x}_i) + \sum_{i,j:K_m=2} \hat{f}_{ij}(\mathbf{x}_i,\mathbf{x}_j) + \sum_{i,j,k:K_m=3} \hat{f}_{ijk}(\mathbf{x}_i,\mathbf{x}_j,\mathbf{x}_k) + \cdots$$

The first sum collects the contributions of basis functions that involve a single predictor ($K_m = 1$). The second sum collects the contributions of basis functions that involve exactly two variables ($K_m = 2$), and so on.

The univariate function $\hat{f}_i(\mathbf{x}_i)$ is a linear regression spline for predictor $\mathbf{x}_i$, which represents the univariate contribution of $\mathbf{x}_i$ to the model. If $\mathbf{x}_i$ does not appear in higher order terms, then its contribution to the model is additive. The bivariate function

$$f_{ij}^*(\mathbf{x}_i,\mathbf{x}_j) = f_i(\mathbf{x}_i) + f_j(\mathbf{x}_j) + f_{ij}(\mathbf{x}_i,\mathbf{x}_j)$$

is a tensor product regression spline that represents the joint contribution of $\mathbf{x}_i$ and $\mathbf{x}_j$.

The Modified Generalized Cross Validation Criterion

Like other model building methods in this book, the MARS algorithm deals with the problem of assessing prediction error; see "Assessment and Minimization of Prediction Error" on page 25. The backward stage of the algorithm uses a modification of the generalized cross validation (GCV) criterion, which was proposed by Craven and Wahba (1979) for linear smoothers:

$$\text{GCV} = \frac{1}{n} \sum_{i=1}^{n} \left(\frac{y_i - \hat{f}(\mathbf{x}_i)}{1 - \text{trace}(\mathbf{S})/n} \right)^2 = \frac{\text{RSS}}{n(1 - \text{trace}(\mathbf{S})/n)^2}$$

where $\mathbf{y}$ is the response, $\hat{f}(\cdot)$ is an estimate of the underlying regression function, $\mathbf{S}$ is a smoothing matrix such that $\hat{\mathbf{y}} = \mathbf{S}\mathbf{y}$, and RSS is the residual sum of squares. The effective degrees of freedom for a smoothing spline is defined as trace($\mathbf{S}$). The GCV criterion cannot be applied to a MARS model because the basis functions $B_m(\mathbf{x})$ are not independent of the response values; they are constructed by reusing the response values.

Drawing on work by Friedman and Silverman (1989), the MARS algorithm uses the modified GCV criterion

$$\frac{\text{RSS}}{n(1 - (M + d(M - 1)/2)/n)^2}$$

where M is the number of nonconstant basis functions and d represents the cost for each basis function optimization. The quantity d is specified; it acts as a smoothing parameter because larger values result in fewer knots and consequently a smaller and smoother final model (Friedman 1991, p. 20). Based on simulation studies, Friedman (1991, p. 21) suggested that the value of d should typically be in the range of two to four. Much higher values ranging from 20 to 200 have been found to work with large, complex data in data mining applications.

The expression $M + d(M - 1)/2$ can be viewed as the effective degrees of freedom for the model. However, it depends on a user specification, unlike the effective degrees of freedom for models constructed with the lasso method, ridge regression, and smoothing splines (see page 24).

Helpful References

The introduction to the MARS approach given here is limited to a brief overview of the main elements. The paper by Friedman (1991) is the definitive technical reference. A follow-up paper (Friedman and Roosen 1995) provides an introduction that explains the MARS algorithm and its extensions to different types of predictors and responses. A succinct description of the algorithm is given by Hastie, Tibshirani, and Friedman (2009, Sec. 9.4).

At SAS Global Forum 2013, Warren Kuhfeld and Weijie Cai presented a paper that provides a helpful introduction to the ADAPTIVEREG procedure (Kuhfeld and Cai 2013).

Features of the ADAPTIVEREG Procedure

The ADAPTIVEREG procedure provides the following features:

- Support for both continuous and categorical predictors.

- Support for response variables with distributions in the exponential family (Buja et al. 1991).

- Capability for forcing effects to be in the final model or restricting predictors to linear forms.

- Options for fast forward selection.

- Model selection based on leave-one-out cross validation, m-fold cross validation, or a validation partition.

- Partitioning of data into subsets for training, validation, and testing.

- Formation of candidate bases for predictors with missing values.

- Plots of the selection process, model fit, functional components, and fit diagnostics.

- Output data set with predicted values and residuals.

- Output data set with design matrix of formed basis functions.

- Measures of variable importance.

- Scoring with a SCORE statement.

- Multithreaded computation for faster performance.

Introduction to the ADAPTIVEREG Procedure

The ADAPTIVEREG procedure is the only procedure in SAS 9 that builds models with the MARS approach. There is currently no corresponding procedure in SAS Viya.

Specifying the Candidate Effects

The syntax of the ADAPTIVEREG procedure is surprisingly simple considering the complexity of the MARS algorithm. You specify the response variable and the candidate variables with MODEL and CLASS statements.

For instance, the following statements (taken from a later example on page 304) build a MARS model that predicts the event Yes for the binary response variable Telematics.

```
proc adaptivereg data=Preliminary;
   class Education MultipleVehicles NDrvConvict NumberAtFault VehicleType
         YngDrvrs;
   model Telematics(event='Yes') = Age CredScor Education MultipleVehicles
                                   NDrvConvict NumberAtFault VehicleType
                                   YngDrvrs /
                                   distribution=binomial link=logit
                                   dfperbasis=2 maxorder=2;
run;
```

You specify the distribution of the response and the link function with the DISTRIBUTION= and LINK= options in the MODEL statement. Although these options are similar to the DISTRIBUTION= and LINK= options in procedures for building generalized linear models and generalized additive models (see Chapter 10 and Chapter 11), MARS models are nonparametric. The estimates of $\beta_0, \beta_1, \ldots, \beta_{m+2}$ on page 298 are not obtained by maximizing a likelihood function. Instead, the ADAPTIVEREG procedure uses the distribution and link function to extend MARS models to generalized MARS models, which it fits by minimizing deviance as suggested by Buja et al. (1991, Sec. 2). The distribution and link function play a role in the computation of deviance, as explained on page 307.

Specifying the Tuning Parameters

The following options in the MODEL statement control the operation of the MARS algorithm:

- The ADDITIVE option requests a model that only includes main effects.

- The ALPHA=α option specifies the knot separation parameter, which controls the number of knots considered for each variable. For the number of observations between interior knots, Friedman (1991) used $-\frac{2}{5} \log_2 \left[-\log(1-\alpha)/pn_m \right]$, where p is the number of variables and n_m is the number of observations for which a parent basis function is positive. The default is ALPHA=0.05.

- The DFPERBASIS= option specifies the degrees of freedom charged per basis function. Larger values lead to fewer spline knots and smoother models. The default is DFPERBASIS=2.

- The MAXBASIS= option specifies the maximum number of basis functions $B_m(\mathbf{x})$ in the final model. The default is $\max(21, 1 + 2n_{\text{eff}})$, where n_{eff} is the number of nonintercept effects specified in the MODEL statement.

- The MAXORDER= option specifies the maximum order of interaction effects that can enter the model. The default is MAXORDER=2.

- The NOMISS option excludes observations with missing values. By default, missing values are handled with indicator variables.

- The VARPENALTY= option specifies the variable parsimony parameter γ, which penalizes the addition of new variables and favors the creation of new knots or interactions in existing variables. At each iteration of the forward stage, the improvement a model can achieve is reduced by a factor of $1 - \gamma$ for any variable that is introduced. The default is $\gamma = 0$. Friedman (1991) suggested 0.05 as a moderate penalty and 0.1 as a heavy penalty.

Specifying the Distribution and the Link Function

Table 14.1 lists response distributions you can specify with the DISTRIBUTION= option. For more about these distributions, see Appendix E.

Table 14.1   Distributions and Default Link Functions

Response Distribution	DISTRIBUTION= keyword	Default Link Function
Binary or binomial	BINOMIAL	Logit
Gamma	GAMMA	Inverse
Inverse Gaussian	INVERSEGAUSSIAN	Inverse square
Negative binomial	NEGBIN	Log
Normal (Gaussian)	NORMAL	Identity
Poisson	POISSON	Log

Table 14.2 lists link functions you can specify with the LINK= option.

Table 14.2   Link Functions

LINK=	Link Function	$g(\mu) = \eta =$
IDENTITY	Identity	μ
INVERSE	Inverse (reciprocal)	$1/\mu$
POWERMINUS2	Inverse square	$1/\mu^2$
LOG	Logarithm	$\log(\mu)$
LOGIT	Logit	$\log(\mu/(1 - \mu))$
PROBIT	Probit	$\Phi^{-1}(\mu)$

For the binary and binomial distributions, you can specify a logit or probit link function. For the gamma, inverse Gaussian, and normal distributions, you can specify a log link function instead of the default link function.

Example: Predicting Interest in Telematics (continued)

This example continues the one introduced on page 276, which builds CART models to predict the willingness of vehicle owners to use telematics; here, MARS models are built instead. The data from a study of 500 owners are provided in a data set named Preliminary. The variables are described in Table 13.4 on page 276. The response variable Telematics has two levels, Yes and No.

Formatting the Variables

The following statements define and assign formats for the categorical variables in Preliminary:

```
proc format;
    value Conv     0='None' 1='1 or more';
    value EdLev    1='No HS diploma' 2='HS diploma'    3='Some college'
                   4='Associate'     5='Bachelor'      6='Grad School'
                   7='Master'        8='Professional'  9='Doctorate';
    value VType    1='Crossover'  2='Pickup'  3='Small'  4='SUV'
                   5='Midsized'   6='Luxury'  7='Van'    8='Large';
    value WStat    1='Full Time'  2='Part Time'  3='Not Working';
    value YN       1='Yes'  0='No';
run;

data Preliminary; set Preliminary;
    format Education EdLev.  MultipleVehicles YN.  NDrvConvict Conv.
           Telematics YN.    VehicleType VType. ;
run;
```

Building a MARS Model with the Modified GCV Criterion

The following statements use the ADAPTIVEREG procedure to build a MARS model for Telematics:

```
ods graphics on;
proc adaptivereg data=Preliminary details=(bases bwdsummary) plots=selection;
    class Education MultipleVehicles NDrvConvict NumberAtFault Telematics
          VehicleType YngDrvrs;
    model Telematics(event='Yes') = Age CredScor Education MultipleVehicles
                                    NDrvConvict NumberAtFault VehicleType
                                    YngDrvrs / distribution=binomial link=logit;
run;
```

Interpreting the Results

Output 14.1 lists the tuning parameters, which are explained on page 302.

Output 14.1 Tuning Parameters for MARS Algorithm

Fit Controls	
Maximum Number of Bases	21
Maximum Order of Interaction	2
Degrees of Freedom per Knot	2
Knot Separation Parameter	0.05
Variable Parsimony Parameter	0
Missing Value Handling	Include

Output 14.2 shows that the second stage of the MARS algorithm began with the full model obtained by the first stage (which overfits the data) and deleted basis functions not needed to minimize the modified GCV criterion explained on page 300. The final selected model has 11 basis functions: Basis0, Basis13, Basis8, ..., Basis15, Basis5, and Basis1.

Output 14.2 Basis Selection for Final Model

	Backward Selection Summary			
Step	**Basis Removed**	**Number of Bases In**	**Deviance**	**GCV**
0		15	245.2715*	0.5528
1	Basis19	14	249.0235	0.5565
2	Basis10	13	249.0839	0.5520
3	Basis3	12	250.8695	0.5513
4	Basis17	11	251.7624	0.5486*
5	Basis13	10	262.4963	0.5673
6	Basis8	9	267.4522	0.5732
7	Basis2	8	271.2335	0.5765
8	Basis9	7	278.5340	0.5872
9	Basis6	6	292.8426	0.6123
10	Basis7	5	304.8152	0.6322
11	Basis11	4	328.9980	0.6768
12	Basis15	3	358.6262	0.7318
13	Basis5	2	361.7244	0.7322
14	Basis1	1	426.1627	0.8557

* Optimal Value of Criterion

Output 14.3 visualizes the selection with a plot that plays the same role as coefficient progression plots provided by procedures that build parametric models (for instance, see Output 5.5 on page 59).

Output 14.3 Basis Selection Plot

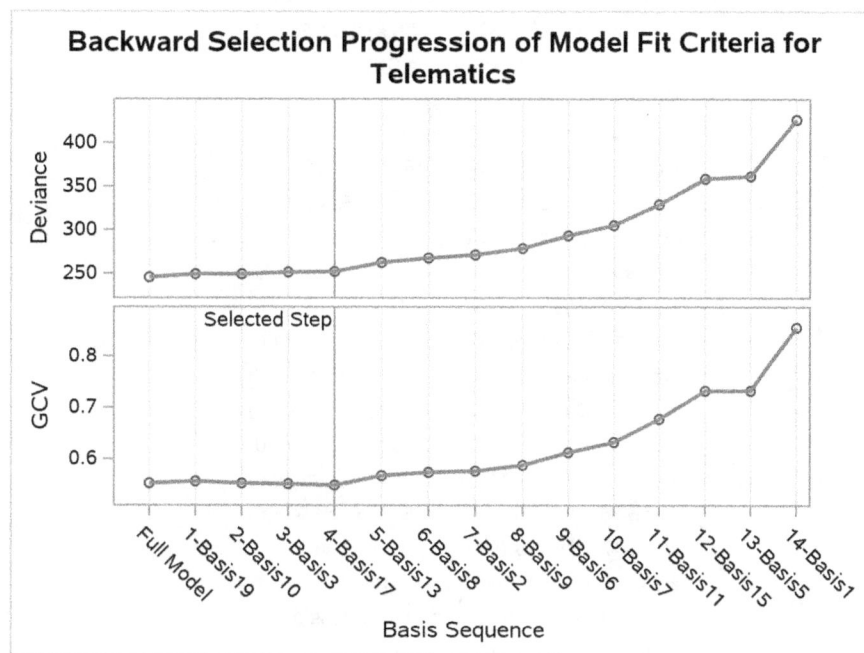

Backward Selection Progression of Model Fit Criteria for Telematics

Output 14.4 lists the basis functions $B_m(\mathbf{x})$ for the final model. The parent is the immediately preceding basis function in the chain of basis functions whose product with a hockey stick function forms $B_m(\mathbf{x})$; see step 1(a) on page 298. Basis0, the first function in the chain, is always $B_0(\mathbf{x}) \equiv 1$. Basis1 is $-0.1745\max(\text{CredScor} - 589, 0)$, and Basis2 is $0.00867\max(\text{CredScor} - 589, 0)$.

Output 14.4 Basis Functions for Selected Model

Name	Coefficient	Parent	Variable	Knot
Regression Spline Model after Backward Selection				
Basis0	0.1222		Intercept	
Basis1	-0.1745	Basis0	CredScor	589.00
Basis2	0.008670	Basis0	CredScor	589.00
Basis5	0.07780	Basis3	CredScor	633.00
Basis6	-0.01965	Basis3	CredScor	633.00
Basis7	0.000640	Basis1	Age	53.0000
Basis8	-0.00182	Basis1	Age	53.0000
Basis9	-0.08482	Basis4	Age	47.0000
Basis11	0.1432	Basis0	CredScor	571.00
Basis13	-0.1978	Basis0	CredScor	802.00
Basis15	-0.04254	Basis3	CredScor	509.00

You can interpret more complicated basis functions with the help of Output 14.5. For example, Basis5 is $0.07780\,\text{Basis3}\,\max(\text{CredScor} - 633, 0)$, where Basis3 is $I(\text{YngDrvrs} = 0)$ and $I(\cdot)$ is the indicator function. By substitution, Basis5 is $0.07780\,I(\text{YngDrvrs} = 0)\max(\text{CredScor} - 633, 0)$.

Output 14.5 Composition of Basis Functions

Name	Transformation
Basis Information	
Basis0	1
Basis1	Basis0*MAX(CredScor - 589,0)
Basis2	Basis0*MAX(589 - CredScor,0)
Basis3	Basis0*(YngDrvrs = 0)
Basis4	Basis0*NOT(YngDrvrs = 0)
Basis5	Basis3*MAX(CredScor - 633,0)
Basis6	Basis3*MAX(633 - CredScor,0)
Basis7	Basis1*MAX(Age - 53,0)
Basis8	Basis1*MAX(53 - Age,0)
Basis9	Basis4*MAX(Age - 47,0)
Basis10	Basis4*MAX(47 - Age,0)
Basis11	Basis0*MAX(CredScor - 571,0)
Basis12	Basis0*MAX(571 - CredScor,0)
Basis13	Basis0*MAX(CredScor - 802,0)
Basis14	Basis0*MAX(802 - CredScor,0)
Basis15	Basis3*MAX(CredScor - 509,0)
Basis16	Basis3*MAX(509 - CredScor,0)
Basis17	Basis13*(VehicleType = Small)
Basis18	Basis13*NOT(VehicleType = Small)
Basis19	Basis14*(Education = Professional)
Basis20	Basis14*NOT(Education = Professional)

Output 14.6 shows the ANOVA representation of the model (see page 300). The variable CredScore (the credit score of the owner) has a main effect on the response and is involved in interactions with YngDrvrs (the number of young drivers) and Age (the age of the owner). This result is consistent with the classification tree on page 271, which was obtained with the HPSPLIT procedure, but it is not as explicit as the rules provided by the tree.

Output 14.6 ANOVA Representation

ANOVA Decomposition					
				Change If Omitted	
Functional Component	Number of Bases	DF	Lack of Fit	GCV
CredScor	4	8	79.2363	0.1492
YngDrvrs CredScor	3	6	90.7975	0.1795
CredScor Age	2	4	20.4856	0.03486
YngDrvrs Age	1	2	10.5918	0.01834

Output 14.7 shows the number of basis functions in which each variable appears, which provides a measure of variable importance.

Output 14.7 Variable Importance

Variable Importance		
Variable	Number of Bases	Importance
CredScor	9	100.00
YngDrvrs	4	58.31
Age	3	12.30

Output 14.8 shows the fit statistics for the model.

Output 14.8 Fit Statistics

Fit Statistics	
GCV	0.54864
GCV R-Square	0.35887
Effective Degrees of Freedom	21
Log Likelihood	-125.88118
Deviance	251.76235

The GCV statistic is explained on page 300. The effective degrees of freedom (21) is equal to one (for the intercept) plus the specified number of degrees of freedom per knot (two) times the number of knots (ten).

The last two statistics in Output 14.8 are analogues of fit statistics for generalized linear models. The log-likelihood statistic is $\mathcal{L}(\hat{\beta}_{MARS}; y)$, where $\mathcal{L}(\beta; y)$, defined on page 325, is the log-likelihood function of the regression parameter $\beta = (\beta_0, \beta_1, \ldots, \beta_p)'$, and $\hat{\beta}_{MARS}$ is the estimate produced by the MARS algorithm. The log-likelihood function incorporates the distribution and link function specified in the MODEL statement. The deviance statistic is defined as $-2[\mathcal{L}(\hat{\mu}; y) - \mathcal{L}(y; y)]$, where $\mathcal{L}(y; y)$ is the maximum achievable log-likelihood, corresponding to a saturated baseline model with a parameter for each observation.

Building an Additive MARS Model

To gain interpretability—typically, at the expense of model accuracy—it is helpful to fit a MARS model that is additive. This means that no interactions are allowed between the basis functions constructed by the MARS algorithm. You can request an additive model by specifying the option ADDITIVE in the MODEL statement as follows:

```
proc adaptivereg data=Preliminary plots=components ;
   class Education MultipleVehicles NDrvConvict NumberAtFault Telematics
         VehicleType YngDrvrs;
   model Telematics(event='Yes') = Age CredScor Education MultipleVehicles
                                   NDrvConvict NumberAtFault VehicleType
                                   YngDrvrs / distribution=binomial link=logit
                                   additive ;
run;
```

Output 14.9 lists the basis functions for the final model. For each of these functions, the parent is the constant function Basis0.

Output 14.9 Parameter Estimates for Selected Additive Model

Regression Spline Model after Backward Selection					
Name	**Coefficient**	**Parent**	**Variable**	**Knot**	**Levels**
Basis0	0.2092		Intercept		
Basis3	-1.6619	Basis0	YngDrvrs		0
Basis5	0.5774	Basis0	CredScor	571.00	
Basis7	-0.4578	Basis0	CredScor	579.00	
Basis9	-0.1363	Basis0	CredScor	550.00	
Basis13	0.7169	Basis0	CredScor	789.00	
Basis15	-1.0311	Basis0	CredScor	802.00	
Basis17	-0.1877	Basis0	CredScor	776.00	

Output 14.10 shows plots, requested with the PLOTS= option, of the additive effects. Interest in telematics increases among vehicle owners with at least one younger driver in the family; it decreases gradually for credit scores greater than 570, and it decreases sharply for scores greater than 770.

Output 14.10 Plots of Additive Components

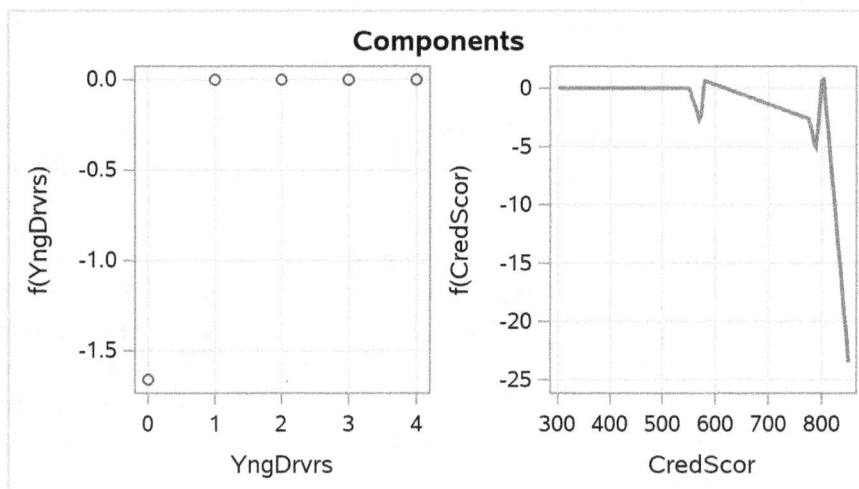

Output 14.11 shows the fit statistics. The GCV statistic and the deviance are both greater than the corresponding statistics in Output 14.8, indicating that the non-additive model provides a better fit.

Output 14.11 Fit Statistics for Additive Model

Fit Statistics	
GCV	0.64852
GCV R-Square	0.24216
Effective Degrees of Freedom	15
Log Likelihood	-152.54808
Deviance	305.09616

Example: Predicting Interest in Telematics (continued)

The example on page 283 uses the data set Respondents to build a classification tree for willingness to use telematics among vehicle owners whose ages range from 22 to 80. The data set provides observations for 5,886 vehicle owners and contains 19 candidate predictors, which are described on page 276. The response variable Telematics has two levels, Yes and No.

For comparison, this example builds a MARS model for the data in Respondents. Variable formats (not shown here) are created as on page 283. The following statements take advantage of the number of observations by partitioning the data into subsets for training, validation, and testing:

```
proc adaptivereg data=Respondents  seed=191277 ;
     class Education MultipleVehicles NDrvConvict NumberAtFault Telematics
           VehicleType YngDrvrs;
     model Telematics(event='Yes') = Age CredScor Education MultipleVehicles
                                     NDrvConvict NumberAtFault VehicleType
                                     YngDrvrs / dist=binomial link=logit
                                                     maxorder=3 ;
     output out=Results predicted=LinPred;
     partition fraction(validate=0.2 test=0.2);
  run;
```

The SEED= option provides the seed for random partitioning. The option MAXORDER=3 enables three-order interaction effects to enter the model.

Output 14.12 lists the fit statistics for the MARS model. The procedure applies validation deviance (see page 307) as the criterion for backward selection when the data are partitioned.

Output 14.12 Fit Statistics

Fit Statistics	
GCV	0.45692
GCV R-Square	0.41300
Effective Degrees of Freedom	21
Log Likelihood	-797.35868
Deviance (Train)	1594.71736
Deviance (Validate)	460.31142
Deviance (Test)	555.12130

Output 14.13 shows the ANOVA representation for the model. The interactions are consistent with those in the classification tree obtained with the TREESPLIT procedure on page 286.

Output 14.13 ANOVA Representation

	ANOVA Decomposition				
				Change If Omitted	
Functional Component	Number of Bases	DF	Lack of Fit	GCV	
YngDrvrs	1	2	709.98	0.2027	
Education	1	2	463.45	0.1321	
YngDrvrs Age	2	4	244.99	0.06900	
Education Age	1	2	73.9439	0.02064	
YngDrvrs CredScor	1	2	42.8536	0.01174	
YngDrvrs Education	1	2	12.2995	0.003000	
YngDrvrs CredScor Age	3	6	80.3708	0.02139	

The next statements use the model results saved with the OUTPUT statement to compute the misclassification rate for the model. The variable LinPred saves the values of the linear predictor μ. The predicted probabilities of the event Yes are obtained by applying the inverse of the logit link function to the values of LinPred. A cutoff of 0.5 is used to classify the observations.

```
data Results;
   set Results;
   if LinPred > 0 then Prob = 1 / (1 + exp( -LinPred ) );
   else                 Prob = exp( LinPred ) / ( 1 + exp( LinPred ) );
   PredTelematics = ( Prob GE 0.5 );
   MisClass = ( Telematics NE PredTelematics );
run;


proc sort data=Results; by _Role_; run;

proc means data=Results;
   var MisClass;
   output out=Summary(drop=_TYPE_ rename=(_FREQ_=N)) mean(MisClass)=Rate;
   by _Role_;
run;

proc print data=Summary noobs split='/';
   label N = 'Number of/Observations' Rate = 'Misclassification/Rate'
         _Role_ = 'Partition';
run;
```

The misclassification rate for the test partition (0.10745) shown in Output 14.14 is slightly greater than the rate (0.0849) obtained with the classification tree (see Output 13.10 on page 285).

Output 14.14 Misclassification Rates Based on Resubstitution

Partition	Number of Observations	Misclassification Rate
TEST	1182	0.10745
TRAIN	3532	0.10108
VALIDATE	1172	0.09215

Summary

The MARS approach was designed to automate the process of building a high-dimensional regression model by selecting the predictors, transformations of the predictors, and interaction effects. The MARS algorithm avoids the curse of dimensionality by judiciously placing the basis functions for multivariate splines in small regions of the predictor space. The algorithm avoids overfitting by growing an extra-large model and then tailoring it down by applying GCV to eliminate basis functions that are superfluous.

MARS models are nonparametric, unlike generalized linear models, which are parametric, and generalized additive models, which are semiparametric. MARS models are not additive, but the algorithm can enforce additivity so that the model captures main effects, unlike CART models. In fact, by eliminating interactions and replacing piecewise linear functions with indicator functions, the forward stage of the MARS algorithm becomes the same as the tree-growing stage of the CART algorithm (Hastie, Tibshirani, and Friedman 2009, Sec. 9.4).

This similarity is not a coincidence because the MARS approach was originally intended to overcome the limitations of models based on recursive partitioning—and the CART approach, in particular. Table 14.3 compares the two approaches.

Table 14.3 Comparison of MARS and CART Approaches to Model Building

Characteristic	MARS Approach	CART Approach
Types of effects	Captures main effects, interactions	Overemphasizes interactions
Prediction surface	Continuous	Step function
Ability to approximate	Not fully known	Universal approximator
Predictive ability	Very good	Good
Model interpretation	Difficult; ANOVA representation helps	Easy if tree is fairly small
Basis functions	Products of piecewise linear functions	Piecewise constant functions
Modeling strategy	Create extra-large model in forward stage; select model in backward stage	Grow extra-large tree; prune back to select final tree
Evaluation criterion	Modified GCV	Cost-complexity criterion
Tuning parameters	Maximum basis functions, maximum interaction order, variable parsimony, degrees of freedom per parameter	Maximum branches, maximum depth, minimum leaf size

Although the MARS approach is highly automated, it is not entirely automated because it involves a set of tuning parameters that determine the final model—more than other methods in this book. You must either specify these parameters or rely on default values provided by the ADAPTIVEREG procedure. There are no clear guidelines for choosing the parameter for degrees of freedom because the best value depends very much on the size and complexity of the data. Be sure to try different values and compare the resulting models by their fit statistics and measures of predictive accuracy. The efficiency of the MARS algorithm and the performance of the ADAPTIVEREG procedure make this convenient; if necessary you can apply options for faster computation.

Programming Tip: Establish tuning parameters by experimenting with different combinations and examining the results.

Part III

Appendices about Algorithms and Computational Methods

Appendix A
Algorithms for Least Squares Estimation

Contents

The general linear model, which is the focus of Part I of this book, has the form

$$\mathbf{y} = \beta_0 \mathbf{1} + \beta_1 \mathbf{x}_1 + \cdots + \beta_p \mathbf{x}_p + \boldsymbol{\epsilon} = \mathbf{X}\boldsymbol{\beta} + \boldsymbol{\epsilon}$$

where $\mathbf{X} = [\mathbf{1}\ \mathbf{x}_1 \cdots \mathbf{x}_p]$ is the model matrix, $\boldsymbol{\beta} = (\beta_0, \beta_1, \ldots, \beta_p)'$ is the parameter vector, and $\boldsymbol{\epsilon}$ is the vector of errors.

Assuming that the columns of $\mathbf{X}$ are linearly independent, the ordinary least squares (OLS) estimator of $\boldsymbol{\beta}$ minimizes the error sum of squares $\|\mathbf{y} - \mathbf{X}\boldsymbol{\beta}\|^2$. The minimum occurs at the value of $\boldsymbol{\beta}$ for which the derivative with respect to $\boldsymbol{\beta}$ of the sum of squares is zero, leading to the normal equations:

$$(\mathbf{X}'\mathbf{X})\hat{\boldsymbol{\beta}}_{\text{OLS}} = \mathbf{X}'\mathbf{y}$$

The solution can be written mathematically as

$$\hat{\boldsymbol{\beta}}_{\text{OLS}} = (\mathbf{X}'\mathbf{X})^{-1}\mathbf{X}'\mathbf{y}$$

However, forming and inverting $\mathbf{X}'\mathbf{X}$ is not the most accurate way to compute $\hat{\boldsymbol{\beta}}_{\text{OLS}}$, especially when $\mathbf{X}'\mathbf{X}$ is large or ill-conditioned. In general, accuracy is improved by avoiding computations that directly involve $\mathbf{X}'\mathbf{X}$.

This appendix describes several recommended algorithms for solving the normal equations. Each of these algorithms computes $\hat{\boldsymbol{\beta}}_{\text{OLS}}$ sequentially, and each—in its own way—orthogonalizes the predictors.

Orthogonalization replaces $\mathbf{x}_1, \mathbf{x}_2, \ldots, \mathbf{x}_p$ with p vectors $\mathbf{z}_1, \mathbf{z}_2, \ldots, \mathbf{z}_p$, that are orthogonal to each other ($\mathbf{z}'_j \mathbf{z}_k = 0$, $j \neq k$). This is necessary because the predictors in observational data are inevitably non-orthogonal or correlated. The Gram-Schmidt algorithm performs orthogonalization in a way that not only computes $\hat{\boldsymbol{\beta}}_{\text{OLS}}$ but also contributes insights about regression.

The books by Thisted (1988), Gentle (1998), Lange (1999), and Hastie, Tibshirani, and Friedman (2009) explain these algorithms from the perspectives of statistical computing and statistical learning. The books by Golub and Van Loan (1996), and Trefethen and Bau (1997), provide the perspective of numerical linear algebra.

The QR Decomposition

The QR decomposition of an $n \times (p + 1)$ matrix $\mathbf{X}$ factorizes the matrix as

$$\mathbf{X} = \mathbf{Q}_{n \times (p+1)} \mathbf{R}_{(p+1) \times (p+1)}$$

where $\mathbf{Q}$ is an orthogonal matrix ($\mathbf{Q'Q} = \mathbf{I}$) and $\mathbf{R}$ is an upper triangular matrix. In practice, the QR decomposition is obtained by applying a modified Gram-Schmidt procedure, a Householder transformation, or a Givens transformation (Gentle 1998, Ch. 3).

With the QR decomposition, the system of normal equations can be triangularized as follows:

$$
\begin{aligned}
\mathbf{X'X}\boldsymbol{\beta} &= \mathbf{X'y} \\
&\Downarrow \\
\mathbf{R'Q'QR}\boldsymbol{\beta} &= \mathbf{R'Q'y} \\
&\Downarrow \\
\mathbf{R'R}\boldsymbol{\beta} &= \mathbf{R'Q'y} \\
&\Downarrow \\
\mathbf{R}\boldsymbol{\beta} &= \mathbf{Q'y}
\end{aligned}
$$

The system $\mathbf{R}\boldsymbol{\beta} = \mathbf{Q'y}$ is triangular because the last row only involves β_1, the next-to-last row only involves β_1 and β_2, and so on. By applying back substitution, the system is readily solved for $\hat{\boldsymbol{\beta}}_{\text{OLS}}$. The ORTHOREG procedure in SAS/STAT fits specified general linear models by computing the $\mathbf{R}$ matrix in the QR decomposition.

The Singular Value Decomposition

The QR decomposition leads to another algorithm for factorizing $\mathbf{X}$ that is known as the singular value decomposition (SVD):

$$\mathbf{X}_{n \times p} = \mathbf{U}_{n \times p} \mathbf{D}_{p \times p} \mathbf{V'}_{p \times n}$$

The algorithm for this factorization begins by centering the predictors $\mathbf{x}_1, \ldots, \mathbf{x}_p$ by their means, which is equivalent to orthogonalizing them with respect to the intercept. The columns $\mathbf{u}_1, \ldots, \mathbf{u}_p$ of $\mathbf{U}$ are orthogonal to each other and span the column space of $\mathbf{X}$. In other words, each $\mathbf{x}_j$ can be represented as a linear combination of $\mathbf{u}_1, \ldots, \mathbf{u}_p$. The columns of $\mathbf{V}$ are orthogonal to each other and span the row space of $\mathbf{X}$.

The matrix $\mathbf{D}$ is a diagonal matrix whose elements $d_1 \geq d_2 \geq \ldots \geq d_p \geq 0$ are referred to as the singular values of $\mathbf{X}$. The number of nonzero singular values is equal to the rank of $\mathbf{X}$, which is the maximum number of linearly independent columns (or rows) of $\mathbf{X}$.

Based on the SVD, the OLS estimator can be expressed as $\hat{\boldsymbol{\beta}}_{\text{OLS}} = \mathbf{VD}^{-1}\mathbf{U'y}$ and the predicted response can be expressed as $\hat{\mathbf{y}} = \mathbf{UU'y}$. The SVD provides an algorithm for solving the normal equations that begins by computing $\mathbf{U'y}$ and solving the diagonal system $\mathbf{Dw} = \mathbf{U'y}$ for $\mathbf{w}$, where, of course, the inverse of the diagonal matrix $\mathbf{D}$ is easy to compute. It follows that $\hat{\boldsymbol{\beta}}_{\text{OLS}} = \mathbf{Vw}$.

The SVD is also useful for exploring multicollinearity in observed predictors (page 90), for understanding the behavior of ridge regression (page 98), and for obtaining principal components (page 109).

The Sweep Algorithm

The sweep algorithm was introduced in 1964 by Albert Beaton, then at the Educational Testing Service, as a computational method for fitting multiple regression models.

During the 1970s, James H. Goodnight at SAS Institute extended the sweep algorithm so it could be used to fit general linear models of less than full rank by computing the generalized inverse of $\mathbf{X}'\mathbf{X}$. He implemented the extended algorithm in the GLM procedure, which is the flagship procedure in SAS for statistical analysis of general linear models.

As noted by Goodnight (1979), the sweep algorithm is closely related to Gauss-Jordan elimination. This method solves the normal equations by forming the augmented matrix

$$\begin{bmatrix} \mathbf{X}'\mathbf{X} & \mathbf{X}'\mathbf{y}' \end{bmatrix}$$

and reducing the left matrix to the identity matrix by applying row operations to the augmented matrix. In general, row operations multiply a row by a constant and add a multiple of one row to another. In this case, performing row operations is equivalent to multiplying the augmented matrix on the left by $(\mathbf{X}'\mathbf{X})^{-1}$, which produces the matrix

$$\begin{bmatrix} \mathbf{I} & \hat{\boldsymbol{\beta}}_{\text{OLS}} \end{bmatrix}$$

The REG, GLMSELECT, and REGSELECT procedures use the sweep algorithm to build regression models and general linear models with best-subsets regression and sequential selection methods such as stepwise regression. In addition to computing the least squares estimate, the sweep algorithm furnishes information required to evaluate candidate predictors and to select a model.

The basic sweep operator replaces a symmetric $n \times n$ matrix $\mathbf{A} = [a_{ij}]$ with a symmetric $n \times n$ matrix $\tilde{\mathbf{A}} = [\tilde{a}_{ij}]$. A sweep of the kth diagonal element of $\mathbf{A}$ produces the elements

$$\tilde{a}_{kk} = -\frac{1}{a_{kk}}, \quad \tilde{a}_{ik} = \frac{a_{ik}}{a_{kk}}, \quad \tilde{a}_{kj} = \frac{a_{kj}}{a_{kk}}, \quad \tilde{a}_{ij} = a_{ij} - \frac{a_{ik}a_{kj}}{a_{kk}}, \quad i \neq k, \ j \neq k, \ k = 1, \ldots, n$$

Sweeping the diagonal entries of $\mathbf{X}'\mathbf{X}$ in the partitioned matrix

$$\begin{bmatrix} \mathbf{X}'\mathbf{X} & \mathbf{X}'\mathbf{y} \\ \mathbf{y}'\mathbf{X} & \mathbf{y}'\mathbf{y} \end{bmatrix}$$

produces the augmented matrix

$$\begin{bmatrix} -(\mathbf{X}'\mathbf{X})^{-1} & (\mathbf{X}'\mathbf{X})^{-1}\mathbf{X}'\mathbf{y} \\ \mathbf{y}'(\mathbf{X}'\mathbf{X})^{-1} & \mathbf{y}'\mathbf{y} - \mathbf{y}'(\mathbf{X}'\mathbf{X})^{-1}\mathbf{X}'\mathbf{y} \end{bmatrix} = \begin{bmatrix} -\frac{1}{\sigma^2}\text{Var}(\hat{\boldsymbol{\beta}}_{\text{OLS}}) & \hat{\boldsymbol{\beta}}_{\text{OLS}} \\ \hat{\boldsymbol{\beta}}'_{\text{OLS}} & \|\mathbf{y} - \hat{\mathbf{y}}\|_2^2 \end{bmatrix}$$

Here, $\text{Var}(\hat{\boldsymbol{\beta}}_{\text{OLS}})$ is the estimated variance matrix of $\hat{\boldsymbol{\beta}}_{\text{OLS}}$. The diagonal elements of this matrix are the estimated variances of the regression coefficients, and their square roots are the estimated standard deviations.

The quantity $\|\mathbf{y} - \hat{\mathbf{y}}\|_2^2$ is the sum of squares due to error, which gives the mean squared error, the R-square statistic, and the adjusted R-square statistic.

Unlike the REG, GLMSELECT, and REGSELECT procedures, the GLM procedure uses the sweep operator to detect linear dependencies among the columns of $\mathbf{X}$. The operator then produces a generalized inverse of $\mathbf{X}'\mathbf{X}$ and the corresponding solution to the normal equations, along with other statistical information.

The Gram-Schmidt Procedure

The Gram-Schmidt procedure provides a way to transform a set of m linearly independent vectors, $x_1, x_2, \ldots, x_m$, into a set of m orthonormal vectors, $z_1, z_2, \ldots, z_m$, that span the same space. This means that the set of all vectors that are linear combinations of $x_1, \ldots, x_p$ is the *same* as the set of all vectors that are linear combinations of $z_1, \ldots, z_p$.

Two vectors, a and b are orthonormal if they meet two conditions. The first is that both vectors are normalized so that $\|a\|_2 = \|b\|_2 = 1$. The second condition is that the two vectors are orthogonal to each other; in other words, their inner product, defined as $a'b$, is zero:

$$a'b = b'a = \sum_{i=1}^{m} a_i b_i = 0$$

The basic Gram-Schmidt procedure constructs $z_1, \ldots, z_m$ in the following sequence of steps:

$$y_1 = x_1, \quad z_1 = \frac{y_1}{\|y_1\|}$$

$$y_2 = x_2 - \frac{x_2' y_1}{y_1' y_1} y_1, \quad z_2 = \frac{y_2}{\|y_2\|}$$

$$y_3 = x_3 - \frac{x_3' y_1}{y_1' y_1} y_1 - \frac{x_3' y_2}{y_2' y_2} y_2, \quad z_3 = \frac{y_3}{\|y_3\|}$$

$$\vdots \quad \vdots \quad \vdots$$

$$y_m = x_m - \frac{x_m' y_1}{y_1' y_1} y_1 - \frac{x_m' y_2}{y_2' y_2} y_2 - \cdots - \frac{x_m' y_{m-1}}{y_{m-1}' y_{m-1}} y_{m-1}, \quad z_m = \frac{y_m}{\|y_m\|}$$

In the second step, the vector

$$\frac{x_2' y_1}{y_1' y_1} y_1$$

is called the projection of x_2 on the subspace generated by scalar multiples of y_1. The vector y_2 is the residual difference between the projection and x_2. It is simple to verify that y_2 is orthogonal to y_1:

$$y_1' y_2 = y_1' x_2 - \frac{x_2' y_1}{y_1' y_1} y_1' y_1 = 0$$

The vector y_2 is said to be *orthogonalized* with respect to y_1. The final vector y_m is orthogonalized with respect to all of the preceding vectors y_i.

The Gram-Schmidt procedure leads to the QR decomposition discussed on page 316. In the context of multiple regression, it provides an algorithm for computing $\hat{\beta}_{OLS}$ that does not involve the normal equations. Before describing this algorithm, the next two sections discuss orthogonalization in the simpler setting of univariate regression.

Orthogonalization in Univariate Regression without an Intercept

The model for simple linear regression with *no* intercept is $y = \beta_1 x_1 + \epsilon$, and the model matrix is $X = [x_1]$. The least squares estimate of β_1 is

$$\hat{\beta}_1 = \underset{\beta_1}{\operatorname{argmin}} \sum_{i=1}^{n}(y_i - x_{i1}\beta_1)^2 = \frac{\sum_{i=1}^{n} x_{i1} y_i}{\sum_{i=1}^{n} x_{i1}^2} = \hat{\beta}_1 = \frac{x_1' y}{x_1' x_1}$$

The predicted response $\hat{y} = \hat{\beta}_1 x_1 = (x_1' y) x_1 / (x_1' x_1)$ is the projection of y on the subspace generated by x_1. The residual $y - \hat{y}$ is orthogonal to $\hat{y}$.

Regressing y on x_1 with no intercept orthogonalizes y with respect to x_1 and is analogous to the orthogonalization in the second step of the Gram-Schmidt procedure.

Hastie, Tibshirani, and Friedman (2009, Sec. 3.2.3) use the phrase "regress b on a" to refer to a univariate regression of b on a without an intercept, where the coefficient is $\hat{\gamma} = a'b/a'a$ and the residual vector is $b - \hat{\gamma}a$. The vector b is adjusted for a or orthogonalized with respect to a.

Orthogonalization in Univariate Regression with an Intercept

The model for simple linear regression *with* an intercept is $y = \beta_0 + \beta_1 x_1 + \epsilon$, and the model matrix is $X = [1\, x_1]$. The least squares estimates of β_0 and β_1 can be obtained by solving the normal equations:

$$n\beta_0 + \beta_1 \sum_{i=1}^{n} x_{i1} = \sum_{i=1}^{n} y_i$$

$$\beta_0 \sum_{i=1}^{n} x_{i1} + \beta_1 \sum_{i=1}^{n} x_{i1}^2 = \sum_{i=1}^{n} x_{i1} y_i$$

The estimates are

$$\hat{\beta}_1 = \frac{\sum_{i=1}^{n}(x_{i1} - \bar{x}_1)(y_i - \bar{y})}{\sum_{i=1}^{n}(x_{i1} - \bar{x}_1)^2}$$

$$\hat{\beta}_0 = \bar{y} - \hat{\beta}_1 \bar{x}_1$$

where $\bar{y} = \frac{1}{n} \sum_{i=1}^{n} y_i$ and $\bar{x}_1 = \frac{1}{n} \sum_{i=1}^{n} x_{i1}$.

The Gram-Schmidt procedure provides a way to compute $\hat{\beta}_1$ without solving the normal equations. Applying the procedure to the columns of X produces the orthogonal vectors 1 and $x_1 - \bar{x}_1 1$. Regressing y on $x_1 - \bar{x}_1 1$ eliminates the intercept and yields the estimate

$$\hat{\beta}_1^{\text{noint}} = \frac{(x_1 - \bar{x}_1 1)' y}{(x_1 - \bar{x}_1 1)'(x_1 - \bar{x}_1 1)} = \frac{\sum_{i=1}^{n}(x_{i1} - \bar{x}_1) y_i}{\sum_{i=1}^{n}(x_{i1} - \bar{x}_1)^2}$$

The next section applies this method to multiple regression.

Orthogonalization in Multiple Regression

When multiple regression is used with data in which the explanatory variables are orthogonal to each other—as in the case of a balanced experimental design—the computation of $\hat{\boldsymbol{\beta}}_{\mathrm{OLS}}$ reduces to the computation of the regression coefficients for p univariate regression models. Since the columns of $\mathbf{X}$ are orthogonal after mean-centering, it follows that $\mathbf{x}'_j \mathbf{x}_k = 0$, $j \neq k$, and $\mathbf{X}'\mathbf{X}$ is a diagonal matrix with entries $\mathbf{x}'_j \mathbf{x}_j$ along the diagonal. The estimate of β_j is simply

$$\hat{\beta}_j = \frac{\mathbf{x}'_j \mathbf{y}}{\mathbf{x}'_j \mathbf{x}_j}, \quad j = 1, \dots, p$$

In this situation, the predictor $\mathbf{x}_j$ has no effect on the estimates of β_k for $k \neq j$.

When multiple regression is used with observational data, the predictors are almost never orthogonal to each other because they involve some amount of correlation. Algorithms such as those discussed earlier in this appendix are required to compute $\hat{\boldsymbol{\beta}}_{\mathrm{OLS}}$, typically by solving the system of normal equations.

The Gram-Schmidt procedure is different; it operates by orthogonalizing the columns of $\mathbf{X}$ and producing a set of p orthogonal vectors $\mathbf{z}_1, \mathbf{z}_2, \dots, \mathbf{z}_p$ that span the same space. When $\mathbf{y}$ is regressed on $\mathbf{z}_p$, the regression coefficient turns out to be the least squares regression coefficient for the last column $\mathbf{x}_p$:

$$\hat{\beta}_p = \frac{\mathbf{z}'_p \mathbf{y}}{\mathbf{z}'_p \mathbf{z}_p}$$

This result generalizes to each column of $\mathbf{X}$ since the columns can be rearranged so that any one of them comes last in the orthogonalization. The Gram-Schmidt procedure is presented as Algorithm 3.1 by Hastie, Tibshirani, and Friedman (2009, p. 54).

Since the predictors for a regression model can in principle be ordered so that any given one comes last, this result reveals that each $\hat{\beta}_j$ is the additional contribution of $\mathbf{x}_j$ to the response after $\mathbf{x}_j$ has been adjusted for all the other predictors.

Appendix B
Least Squares Geometry

Contents

This appendix describes two geometric aspects of ordinary least squares estimation that explain how it applies to fitting a general linear model. The first is the orthogonality of the model prediction ($\hat{\mathbf{y}}$) and its residual ($\mathbf{y} - \hat{\mathbf{y}}$). The second is the way in which the hat matrix $\mathbf{P}$ acts a projection matrix.

Orthogonality of Predictions and Residuals

The ordinary least squares estimator $\hat{\boldsymbol{\beta}}_{\text{OLS}}$ minimizes the squared distance

$$\| \mathbf{y} - \mathbf{X}\boldsymbol{\beta} \|_2^2 = (\mathbf{y} - \mathbf{X}\boldsymbol{\beta})'(\mathbf{y} - \mathbf{X}\boldsymbol{\beta})$$

where $\mathbf{y}$ is the response vector $(y_1, y_2, \ldots, y_n)'$, $\mathbf{X} = [\mathbf{1}\ \mathbf{x}_1 \cdots \mathbf{x}_p]$ is the model matrix, and $\boldsymbol{\beta} = (\beta_0, \beta_1, \ldots, \beta_p)'$ is the parameter vector.

The predicted response is

$$\hat{\mathbf{y}} = \mathbf{X}\hat{\boldsymbol{\beta}}_{\text{OLS}} = \mathbf{X}(\mathbf{X}'\mathbf{X})^{-1}\mathbf{X}'\mathbf{y} = \mathbf{P}\mathbf{y}$$

where $\mathbf{P} = \mathbf{X}(\mathbf{X}'\mathbf{X})^{-1}\mathbf{X}'$ is referred to as the hat matrix because it transforms $\mathbf{y}$ to $\hat{\mathbf{y}}$. This matrix has two important properties; it is symmetric ($\mathbf{P} = \mathbf{P}'$) and idempotent ($\mathbf{P}\mathbf{P} = \mathbf{P}$).

The vector of residual values is

$$\mathbf{r} = (y_1 - \hat{y}_1, y_2 - \hat{y}_2, \ldots, y_n - \hat{y}_n)' = \mathbf{y} - \hat{\mathbf{y}} = \mathbf{y} - \mathbf{P}\mathbf{y} = (\mathbf{I} - \mathbf{P})\mathbf{y}$$

In n-dimensional space, any two vectors $\mathbf{u} = (u_1, u_2, \ldots, u_n)'$ and $\mathbf{v} = (v_1, v_2, \ldots, v_n)'$ are orthogonal or perpendicular[†] to each other if their inner product is zero:

$$\mathbf{u}'\mathbf{v} = \mathbf{v}'\mathbf{u} = 0$$

The predicted response and the residual are orthogonal to each other because

$$\mathbf{y}'\mathbf{P}'(\mathbf{I} - \mathbf{P})\mathbf{y} = \mathbf{y}'(\mathbf{P}' - \mathbf{P}'\mathbf{P})\mathbf{y} - \mathbf{y}'\mathbf{P} - \mathbf{P}\mathbf{P})\mathbf{y} = 0$$

[†]The cosine of the angle between $\mathbf{u}$ and $\mathbf{v}$ is $\mathbf{u}'\mathbf{v}/(\|\mathbf{u}\|_2\ \|\mathbf{v}\|_2)$. If the inner product of $\mathbf{u}$ and $\mathbf{v}$ is zero, then the angle is 90 degrees. When the vectors represent a set of bivariate observations $(u_1, v_1), \ldots, (u_n, v_n)$ that have been standardized, the cosine is equal to their Pearson correlation.

The Hat Matrix as a Projection Matrix

In linear algebra, a projection matrix is a matrix that maps vectors into their orthogonal projections on a subspace; it must be square, symmetric, and idempotent.

The hat matrix satisfies these properties. It projects $\mathbf{y}$ from n-dimensional space to the p-dimensional subspace spanned by the columns of $\mathbf{X}$. This subspace is the set of all vectors $\mathbf{w}$ that are linear combinations of the predictors $\mathbf{x}_1, \ldots, \mathbf{x}_p$:

$$\mathbf{w} = [\, \mathbf{x}_1 \; \mathbf{x}_2 \; \cdots \; \mathbf{x}_p \,] \, \mathbf{c} = \mathbf{X}\mathbf{c}$$

where $\mathbf{c} = (c_1, c_2, \ldots, c_p)'$. This assumes the predictors are centered by their means so that they can be represented as vectors that are anchored at the origin.

Figure B.1 visualizes the subspace as a shaded plane and $\mathbf{y}$ as a point above the plane. The projection $\hat{\mathbf{y}}$ lies in the plane and is represented by a dashed line; it is as close to $\mathbf{y}$ as possible because it minimizes the distance $\|\mathbf{y} - \hat{\mathbf{y}}\|_2$.

Figure B.1 Least Squares Projection of $\mathbf{y}$ on Subspace Spanned by $\mathbf{x}_1, \ldots, \mathbf{x}_p$

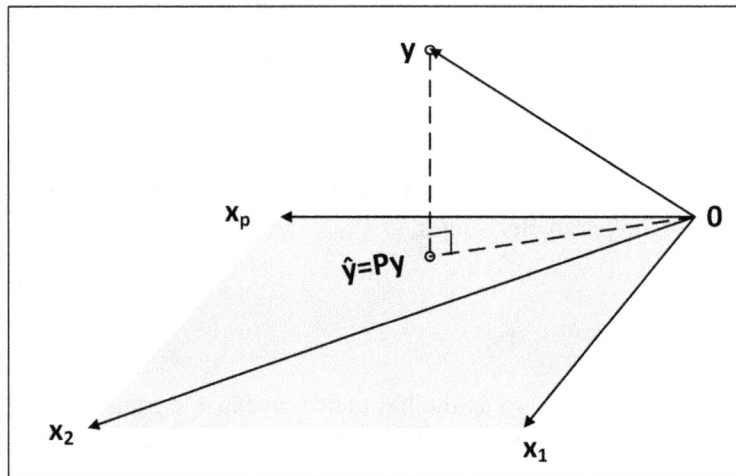

You can think of the projection as the light from a laser beam suspended in mid-air that is located at $\mathbf{y}$ and pointed down toward the floor. The light illuminates the closest point on the floor if you aim the laser perpendicular to the floor. The vertical dashed line in the figure represents the residual vector $\mathbf{r} = \mathbf{y} - \hat{\mathbf{y}}$. It is orthogonal to $\hat{\mathbf{y}}$ as established on page 321.

Knowing how the hat matrix operates as a projection is helpful for understanding how least squares regression minimizes the squared distance $\| \mathbf{y} - \mathbf{X}\boldsymbol{\beta} \|_2^2$. Moreover, the hat matrix is useful for analyzing regression data. The ith diagonal element of $\mathbf{P}$ (denoted by $\mathbf{P}_{ii}$) is related to the distance of the ith row of $\mathbf{X}$ from the center of the predictor space, $(\bar{x}_1, \bar{x}_2, \ldots, \bar{x}_p)$. Larger values of $\mathbf{P}_{ii}$ correspond to data points that are farther from the center.

The elements $\mathbf{P}_{ii}$ appear in the definitions of influence statistics, such as Cook's D and DFFITS, which are covered in standard courses on regression and are available in the REG procedure. The quantity $\sum_{i=1}^{n} \mathbf{P}_{ii}$, called the trace of $\mathbf{P}$, plays an important role in this book as a measure of model flexibility, which is introduced on page 22.

Appendix C
Akaike's Information Criterion

Contents

This appendix sketches the motivation for Akaike's information criterion, which is used by various procedures in this book. For in-depth explanations, see Burnham and Anderson (2002, Ch. 2), Cavanaugh and Neath (2019), Pawitan (2001, Sec. 13.6), and De Leeuw (1992).

The criterion, universally designated as AIC,[†] was proposed in the early 1970s by Hirotugu Akaike at the Institute of Statistical Mathematics in Tokyo. His initial paper (Akaike 1973), which he presented at an obscure conference in 1971, turned out to be a breakthrough in the field of statistics. Its deep insights bridged the problems of estimating the parameters of a model and determining the form of the model, and it contributed a practical approach to model building across a variety of frameworks, including regression and time series.

Forms of Akaike's Criterion

Suppose that $y_1, \ldots, y_n$ is a set of independent observations generated by an unknown distribution for a response variable whose probability density function is $f(y)$. Furthermore, suppose that the parametric density function $g(y|x, \boldsymbol{\theta})$ represents a model for the response conditional on the predictor x. The general form of Akaike's criterion for evaluating the model is

$$\text{AIC} = -2\mathcal{L}(\hat{\boldsymbol{\theta}}_{\text{MLE}}) + 2K$$

where K is the number of estimable parameters in $\boldsymbol{\theta}$, $\mathcal{L}$ is the log-likelihood function

$$\mathcal{L}(\boldsymbol{\theta} \mid \text{data, form of model } g) = \sum_{i=1}^{n} \log(g(y_i|x_i, \boldsymbol{\theta}))$$

and $\hat{\boldsymbol{\theta}}_{\text{MLE}}$ is the maximum likelihood estimate (MLE)

$$\hat{\boldsymbol{\theta}}_{\text{MLE}} = \underset{\boldsymbol{\theta}}{\text{argmax}} \, \mathcal{L}(\boldsymbol{\theta}) = \underset{\boldsymbol{\theta}}{\text{argmax}} \sum_{i=1}^{n} \log(g(y_i|x_i, \boldsymbol{\theta}))$$

[†]Akaike himself used the term "information criterion," which he abbreviated as IC. In a 1992 interview, he recalled that his assistant added the A in a FORTRAN program to avoid defining the criterion as an integer (Findley and Parzen 1995, p. 111).

In practice, the specific form of Akaike's criterion is derived from $g(y|x, \boldsymbol{\theta})$. For a general linear model with p predictors

$$y_i = \beta_0 + \beta_1 x_{i1} + \cdots + \beta_p x_{ip} + \epsilon_i, \quad i = 1, \ldots, n$$

it is assumed that ϵ_i has the normal distribution $N(0, \sigma^2)$ with mean 0 and variance σ^2. This assumption is made in order to define a likelihood function; it is not needed when the model is used for prediction rather than inference. It follows that y_i has the normal distribution $N(\mathbf{x}_i' \boldsymbol{\beta}, \sigma^2)$. The log-likelihood function is

$$\mathcal{L}(\boldsymbol{\beta}, \theta) = -\frac{n}{2} \log(2\pi\sigma^2) - \frac{1}{2\sigma^2} \sum_{i=1}^{n} (y_i - \theta)^2$$

and the maximum likelihood estimates for the parameters are related to the ordinary least squares (OLS) estimate and average square error (ASE) as follows:

$$\hat{\boldsymbol{\beta}}_{\text{MLE}} = (\mathbf{X}'\mathbf{X})^{-1} \mathbf{X}'\mathbf{y} = \hat{\boldsymbol{\beta}}_{\text{OLS}}$$

$$\hat{\sigma}^2_{\text{MLE}} = \frac{1}{n} \sum_{i=1}^{n} (y_i - \mathbf{x}_i' \hat{\boldsymbol{\beta}}_{\text{MLE}})^2 = \text{ASE}_{\text{train}}$$

The maximized log-likelihood is

$$\mathcal{L}(\hat{\boldsymbol{\beta}}_{\text{MLE}}, \hat{\sigma}^2_{\text{MLE}}) = -\frac{n}{2} \log(2\pi\hat{\sigma}^2_{\text{MLE}}) - \frac{n}{2}$$

With $K = p + 2$, the criterion reduces to

$$\text{AIC} = n \log(\hat{\sigma}^2_{\text{MLE}}) + 2p = n \log(\text{ASE}_{\text{train}}) + 2p$$

Motivation for Akaike's Criterion

The concept of maximizing likelihood applies to the estimation of unknown parameters for a model whose form is known, but it does not extend to the comparison of predictive models. Furthermore, if two models are nested (as in forward selection), the model with more parameters will always have a larger maximized log-likelihood, but it will not necessarily be better for prediction. Akaike dealt with these issues (which mirror problems of generalization discussed on page 25) by extending the principle of maximum likelihood.

The general form of Akaike's criterion is based on a connection between the maximized log-likelihood $\mathcal{L}(\hat{\boldsymbol{\theta}}_{\text{MLE}})$ and the relative Kullback-Leibler distance $I(f, g)$ from the model $g(y|x, \boldsymbol{\theta})$ to $f(x)$.[†] This distance, which is the information lost when $g(y|x, \boldsymbol{\theta})$ approximates $f(x)$, can be expressed as the difference between two expectations:

$$I(f, g) \equiv \int \log\left(\frac{f(y)}{g(y|x, \boldsymbol{\theta})}\right) f(y) dy = E_f[\log(f(y))] - E_f[\log(g(y|x, \boldsymbol{\theta}))]$$

When a set of candidate models $g_r(y|x, \boldsymbol{\theta}_r), r = 1, \ldots, R$, is compared by the models' distances to $f(x)$, the first expectation can be ignored. Akaike (1973) recognized the importance of estimating the second expectation. This cannot be done by comparing the maximized log-likelihoods $\mathcal{L}(\hat{\boldsymbol{\theta}}_r)$, which are biased upward because the same data are used to compute $\hat{\boldsymbol{\theta}}_r$. Akaike showed that his criterion estimates the second expectation and approximately corrects for the bias.

[†]Akaike recalled that this connection occurred to him while he was standing on a train he was taking to work (Findley and Parzen 1995, p. 111).

Appendix D
Maximum Likelihood Estimation for Generalized Linear Models

Contents

This appendix explains various computational aspects of maximum likelihood estimation[†] that are implemented for generalized linear models by the HPGENSELECT and GENSELECT procedures and for logistic regression models by the HPLOGISTIC and LOGSELECT procedures.

The Log-Likelihood Function

As explained on page 193, a generalized linear model consists of three components: a distribution for y_i in the exponential family, a linear predictor

$$\eta_i = \beta_0 + \beta_1 x_{i1} + \cdots + \beta_p x_{ip}, \quad i = 1, \ldots, n$$

and a link function $g(\cdot)$ that connects μ_i, the mean of the response distribution, with the linear predictor:

$$g(\mu_i) = \eta_i$$

The distribution $f(y_i)$ has the canonical form given on page 333. Starting with this form, the log-likelihood function of the regression parameter $\boldsymbol{\beta} = (\beta_0, \beta_1, \ldots, \beta_p)'$ can be expressed as

$$\mathcal{L}(\boldsymbol{\beta}; \mathbf{y}) = \sum_{i=1}^{n} \log f(y_i) = \sum_{i=1}^{n} \frac{y_i \theta_i - b(\theta_i)}{\phi} + \sum_{i=1}^{n} c(y_i, \phi)$$

Here, the functions $b(\cdot)$ and $c(\cdot, \cdot)$ are determined by the specified distribution, θ_i is the canonical parameter, and ϕ is the dispersion parameter. Although $\boldsymbol{\beta}$ is not apparent on the right-hand side, it enters through the link function.

[†]Maximum likelihood is one of the most important concepts in the field of statistics. It was introduced as a computational approach by Ronald Fisher in a six-page paper published in 1912, the year he graduated from Cambridge University. Fisher expanded the approach into a fundamental concept between the years of 1912 and 1922, when he used the term *maximum likelihood* in a landmark paper (Fisher 1922). See Aldrich (1997) for the story of this achievement.

The maximum likelihood estimator of $\boldsymbol{\beta}$ is

$$\hat{\boldsymbol{\beta}}_{\text{MLE}} = \underset{\boldsymbol{\beta}}{\text{argmax}}\{\mathcal{L}(\boldsymbol{\beta};\mathbf{y})\}$$

To make this notation more understandable, consider the case of binary logistic regression with the logit link function $g(\mu_i) = \log(\mu_i/(1-\mu_i))$. The response y_i has a Bernoulli distribution for which $P(y_i = 1) = \pi_i$ and $P(y_i = 0) = 1 - \pi_i$. This distribution is a member of the exponential family with the canonical parameter $\theta_i = \log(\pi_i/(1-\pi_i))$, the dispersion parameter $\phi \equiv 1$, $b(\theta_i) = \log(1 + \exp(\theta_i))$, and $c(y_i, \phi) = 0$. Since the mean of the distribution is $\mu_i = \pi_i$, the link function is

$$g(\pi_i) = \log\frac{\pi_i}{1-\pi_i} = \beta_0 + \beta_1 x_{i1} + \cdots + \beta_p x_{ip} = \mathbf{x}_i'\boldsymbol{\beta}, \quad i = 1,\ldots,n$$

where the vector $\mathbf{x}_i'$ is the ith row of the model matrix $\mathbf{X}$. It follows by substitution that

$$
\begin{aligned}
\mathcal{L}(\boldsymbol{\beta};\mathbf{y}) &= \sum_{i=1}^{n} y_i \log\left(\frac{\pi_i}{1-\pi_i}\right) - \sum_{i=1}^{n}\log\left(1 + \frac{\pi_i}{1-\pi_i}\right) \\
&= \sum_{i=1}^{n} y_i \mathbf{x}_i'\boldsymbol{\beta} - \sum_{i=1}^{n}\log(1 + \exp(\mathbf{x}_i'\boldsymbol{\beta}))
\end{aligned}
$$

The Likelihood Equations

Maximizing the function $\mathcal{L}(\boldsymbol{\beta};\mathbf{y})$ requires finding its derivative with respect to $\boldsymbol{\beta}$. As a function of $\boldsymbol{\beta}$, this derivative is called the score function, and it is expressed as the gradient vector

$$\mathbf{u} \equiv \left(\frac{\partial\mathcal{L}(\boldsymbol{\beta};\mathbf{y})}{\partial\beta_0}, \frac{\partial\mathcal{L}(\boldsymbol{\beta};\mathbf{y})}{\partial\beta_1}, \ldots, \frac{\partial\mathcal{L}(\boldsymbol{\beta};\mathbf{y})}{\partial\beta_p}\right)'$$

It can be shown that

$$\frac{\partial\mathcal{L}(\boldsymbol{\beta};\mathbf{y})}{\partial\beta_j} = \sum_{i=1}^{n}\frac{(y_i - \mu_i)x_{ij}}{\text{Var}(Y)}\frac{\partial\mu_i}{\partial\eta_i} = \sum_{i=1}^{n}\frac{(y_i - \mu_i)x_{ij}}{V(\mu_i)}\frac{\partial\mu_i}{\partial\eta_i}, \quad j = 0,\ldots,p$$

where $V(\mu)$ denotes the variance function for the distribution (see page 194). For example, the variance function for the Bernoulli distribution is $V(\mu) = \mu(1-\mu)$.

Setting these derivatives to zero gives the likelihood equations:

$$\sum_{i=1}^{n}\frac{(y_i - \mu_i)x_{ij}}{V(\mu_i)}\frac{\partial\mu_i}{\partial\eta_i} = 0, \quad j = 0,\ldots,p$$

Here again, the parameters $\beta_1,\ldots,\beta_p$ enter through the link function. The likelihood equations involve no aspects of the distribution other than the mean and the variance, which enters through $V(\mu)$.

The question now becomes how to solve these equations for $\hat{\boldsymbol{\beta}}_{\text{MLE}}$, since they have no explicit analytical solution.

Computational Algorithms

The computation of $\hat{\beta}_{\text{MLE}}$ requires an iterative algorithm that passes through all n observations at every step. Nelder and Wedderburn (1972, Sec. 2) showed that the likelihood equations can be solved by an iterative weighted least squares (IWLS) algorithm that is closely related to the Newton-Raphson algorithm for nonlinear optimization; the IWLS algorithm is explained on page 367. By default, the HPLOGISTIC, LOGSELECT, HPGENSELECT, and GENSELECT procedures apply a modification of the Newton-Raphson algorithm that uses a ridged Hessian matrix.

The standard Newton-Raphson algorithm starts with an initial value $\beta^{(0)}$ for the solution and approximates the objective function $\mathcal{L}(\beta; \mathbf{y})$ with a second-degree polynomial in a neighborhood of $\beta^{(0)}$. It then finds the value $\beta^{(1)}$ that maximizes this polynomial. The algorithm continues by generating a sequence of values $\beta^{(t)}, t = 2, 3, \ldots$, that maximize the local polynomial approximations of $\mathcal{L}(\beta; \mathbf{y})$ until the changes in $\mathcal{L}(\beta^{(t)}; \mathbf{y})$ fall within a small convergence criterion.

To make this more precise, let $\mathbf{u}(t)$ denote the gradient evaluated at $\beta = \beta^{(t)}$. Also, let $\mathbf{H}$ denote the Hessian matrix, also called the (negative of the) *observed Fisher information matrix*, with entries

$$h_{jk} = \frac{\partial^2 \mathcal{L}(\beta; \mathbf{y})}{\partial \beta_j \partial \beta_k}, \quad 0 \le j, k \le p$$

and let $\mathbf{H}(t)$ denote the Hessian matrix evaluated at $\beta = \beta^{(t)}$. Note that the components of $\mathbf{u}$ and $\mathbf{H}$ are functions of β, whereas the components of $\mathbf{u}(t)$ and $\mathbf{H}(t)$ are numerical values of these functions.

At step t, the log-likelihood function near $\beta^{(t)}$ is approximated by a Taylor series with first- and second-order terms:

$$\mathcal{L}(\beta; \mathbf{y}) \approx \mathcal{L}(\beta^{(t)}; \mathbf{y}) + \mathbf{u}(t)'(\beta - \beta^{(t)}) + \frac{1}{2}(\beta - \beta^{(t)})'\mathbf{H}(t)(\beta - \beta^{(t)})$$

The value $\beta^{(t+1)}$ that maximizes this approximation is determined by setting the derivative of the approximation to $\mathbf{0}$ and solving for β. The solution is

$$\beta^{(t+1)} = \beta^{(t)} - \mathbf{H}(t)^{-1}\mathbf{u}(t)$$

Computing $\beta^{(t+1)}$ requires that $\mathbf{H}(t)$ be positive definite, which means all of its eigenvalues must be positive (see page 90). If this is not the case, the ridged version of the Newton-Raphson algorithm adds a small constant to the diagonal elements of $\mathbf{H}(t)$. If $\mathcal{L}(\beta^{(t+1)}; \mathbf{y})$ is not greater than $\mathcal{L}(\beta^{(t)}; \mathbf{y})$, then the step size $\beta^{(t+1)} - \beta^{(t)}$ is halved.

An advantage of this algorithm is that the sequence $\beta^{(t)}$ converges at a quadratic rate. For t sufficiently large and for each j,

$$|\beta_j^{(t+1)} - \hat{\beta}_j| \le C|\beta_j^{(t)} - \hat{\beta}_j|^2$$

where C is some positive constant. However, depending on n and p, $\mathbf{H}(t) \equiv [h(t)_{jk}]$ can be expensive to compute because each of its elements is a sum:

$$h(t)_{jk} = \sum_{i=1}^{n} \frac{\partial^2 \ell_i(\beta; \mathbf{y})}{\partial \beta_j \partial \beta_k}\bigg|_{\beta=\beta(t)} \quad 0 \le j, k \le p$$

Here, ℓ_i is the contribution to the log-likelihood made by the ith observation.

The algorithm given by Nelder and Wedderburn is a variation of the Newton-Raphson algorithm that performs a weighted least squares regression at each step; it opened the door for early applications of generalized linear models because the computations could be carried out with existing programs for least squares computations.

The Nelder-Wedderburn algorithm also differs from the Newton-Raphson algorithm by replacing $\mathbf{H}$ with the *expected Fisher information matrix*:

$$\mathcal{I} \equiv -E(H) = -E\left(\frac{\partial^2 \mathcal{L}(\boldsymbol{\beta}; \mathbf{y})}{\partial \beta_j \partial \beta_k}\right)$$

In this respect, the Nelder-Wedderburn algorithm closely resembles the Fisher scoring algorithm[†] for computing maximum likelihood estimates.

With a canonical link function (see page 336), the Newton-Raphson and Fisher scoring algorithms coincide. With other link functions, they produce the same estimates of $\boldsymbol{\beta}$ but can lead to slightly different estimates of the covariance matrix of $\hat{\boldsymbol{\beta}}_{\mathrm{MLE}}$. With the Newton-Raphson algorithm, this estimate is $\widehat{\mathrm{Cov}}(\hat{\boldsymbol{\beta}}_{\mathrm{MLE}}) = -\hat{H}^{-1}$, which is computed by evaluating $-\mathbf{H}$ at $\boldsymbol{\beta} = \hat{\boldsymbol{\beta}}_{\mathrm{MLE}}$. The standard errors of $\hat{\beta}_1, \ldots, \hat{\beta}_p$ are given by the square roots of the diagonal elements of $\widehat{\mathrm{Cov}}(\hat{\boldsymbol{\beta}}_{\mathrm{MLE}})$.

The HPLOGISTIC and LOGSELECT procedures differ from the LOGISTIC procedure in that the latter—by default—computes $\hat{\boldsymbol{\beta}}_{\mathrm{MLE}}$ with the Fisher scoring algorithm. The LOGISTIC procedure provides the Newton-Raphson algorithm as an option.

There is no one algorithm that always finds $\hat{\boldsymbol{\beta}}_{\mathrm{MLE}}$ in a reasonable amount of time. When a unique estimate exists (see page 329), the performance of the algorithm depends on the size of the data and the configuration of the model matrix. For this reason, the procedures provide a variety of algorithms, listed in Table D.1, that you can request with the TECHNIQUE= option in the procedure statement.

Table D.1 Algorithms Available in the HPLOGISTIC and LOGSELECT Procedures

Algorithm	Required Derivatives	TECHNIQUE= keyword
Conjugate gradient	first order	CONGRA
Double dogleg	first order	DBLDOG
Dual quasi-Newton	first order	QUANEW
Nelder-Mead simplex	none	NMSIMP
Newton-Raphson with line search	second order	NEWRAP
Newton-Raphson with ridging	second order	NRRIDG (default)
Trust region	second order	TRUREG

First-order algorithms compute the gradient vector; second-order algorithms additionally compute the Hessian matrix. For more information about the tradeoffs between these algorithms, see "Choosing an Optimization Algorithm" in the chapter on the HPLOGISTIC procedure in the *SAS/STAT 15.1 User's Guide*.

[†]This algorithm was introduced by Ronald Fisher. It was applied by Fisher in an appendix to a 1935 paper on probit analysis by Chester Bliss, an American biologist who contributed to the field of statistics. This work was a forerunner of generalized linear models.

Existence of Maximum Likelihood Estimates

The LOGISTIC, HPLOGISTIC, and LOGSELECT procedures, which build logistic regression models, detect two data patterns, called complete separation and quasi-complete separation, for which $\hat{\beta}_{\text{MLE}}$ does not exist.

Figure D.1, based on an example from So (1995), illustrates complete separation with 10 observations and two predictors, x_1 and x_2. The response values y_i have two levels, 1 and 2, which are completely separated by the line $x_2 = -6 + 2x_1$.

Figure D.1 Complete Separation of Response Levels

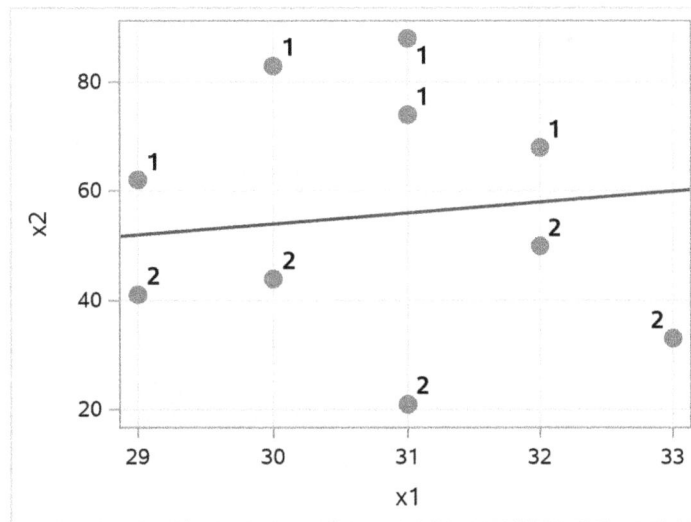

In general, complete separation occurs when there is a vector **b** for which

$$
\begin{aligned}
\mathbf{b}'\mathbf{x(i)} \;>\; 0 \quad \text{if} \;\; y_i = 1 \\
\mathbf{b}'\mathbf{x(i)} \;<\; 0 \quad \text{if} \;\; y_i = 2
\end{aligned}
$$

for $i = 1, 2, \ldots, n$. In Figure D.1, this vector is $\mathbf{b} = (6, -2, 1)'$.

The following statements attempt to fit a binary logistic regression model for the data in Figure D.1:

```
proc hplogistic data=CompleteSeparation;
   model y(event='1') = x1 x2 / link=logit;
run;
```

Output D.1 indicates that the Newton-Raphson algorithm converged but that complete separation was detected, which might seem counterintuitive. This means that the estimate of β produced by the algorithm is, in fact, a **b** vector.

Output D.1 Convergence Status

The HPLOGISTIC Procedure

Convergence criterion (ABSGCONV=1E-7) satisfied. Complete separation detected.

When there is complete separation, the objective function at step t goes to 0 as t increases. This is evident in the iteration history shown in Output D.2. Note that the column labeled "Objective Function" displays the values of the *negative* log-likelihood function normalized by n.

Output D.2 Iteration History

		Iteration History		
Iteration	Evaluations	Objective Function	Change	Max Gradient
0	4	0.1618383755	.	1.561166
1	2	0.0744746749	0.08736370	0.685177
2	2	0.0290297022	0.04544497	0.282078
3	2	0.0107297135	0.01829999	0.107336
4	2	0.0039632138	0.00676650	0.039951
5	2	0.001467005	0.00249621	0.014774
6	2	0.0005433974	0.00092361	0.005448
7	2	0.0002012759	0.00034212	0.002006
8	2	0.0000745322	0.00012674	0.000738
9	2	0.000027589	0.00004694	0.000271
10	2	0.0000102083	0.00001738	0.0001
11	2	3.7756236E-6	0.00000643	0.000037
12	2	1.3958442E-6	0.00000238	0.000013
13	2	5.1581904E-7	0.00000088	4.949E-6
14	2	1.905337E-7	0.00000033	1.818E-6
15	2	7.0350113E-8	0.00000012	6.679E-7
16	2	2.59647E-8	0.00000004	2.454E-7
17	2	9.579353E-9	0.00000002	9.012E-8

Figure D.2 illustrates quasi-complete separation with data that are nearly the same as those in Figure D.1. Because the observation at (30, 44) has been moved to (30, 64), there is no line that separates the two response groups. The line $x_2 = 4 + 2x_1$ connects points in both groups, but it completely separates the remaining points.

Figure D.2 Quasicomplete Separation of Response Levels

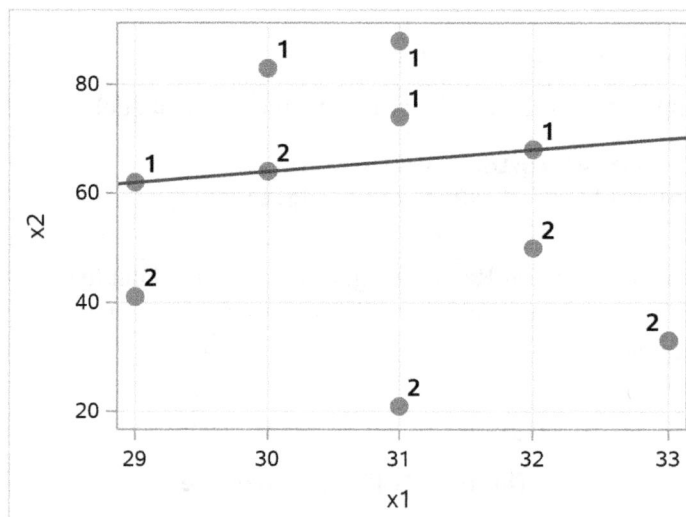

Quasi-complete separation occurs when there is a vector **b** for which

$$\mathbf{b}'\mathbf{x}(\mathbf{i}) \geq 0 \quad \text{if } y_i = 1$$
$$\mathbf{b}'\mathbf{x}(\mathbf{i}) \leq 0 \quad \text{if } y_i = 2$$

for $i = 1, 2, \ldots, n$. In Figure D.2, this vector is $\mathbf{b} = (-4, -2, 1)'$. When there is quasi-complete separation, $\mathcal{L}(\boldsymbol{\beta}^{(t)}; \mathbf{y})$ does not decrease to 0, but the standard errors of $\hat{\beta}, \ldots, \hat{\beta}_p$ become inflated.

The following statements attempt to fit a binary logistic regression model for the data in Figure D.2:

```
proc hplogistic data=QuasiSeparation;
   model y(event='1') = x1 x2 / link=logit;
run;
```

Output D.3 indicates that the algorithm converged but quasi-complete separation was detected. The standard errors are two orders of magnitude greater than the estimates.

Output D.3 Convergence Status and Parameter Estimates

Convergence criterion (FCONV=2.1073424E-8) satisfied. Quasi-complete separation detected.

Parameter Estimates

Parameter	Estimate	Standard Error
Intercept	-18.0541	3987.85
x1	-3.9160	1993.86
x2	2.1273	996.93

Programming Tip: When you fit or build a logistic regression model, check the Convergence Status table or the SAS log for occurrences of separation.

The problems of separation tend to occur with small data. Although complete separation can occur with many types of data, quasi-complete separation is not likely with continuous data. Allison (2008) points out that quasi-complete separation occurs when a predictor x_j is a categorical variable with two levels and there is a zero in the 2×2 table formed by x_j and the response variable.

Separation has been studied in the context of statistical inference, beginning with the work of Albert and Anderson (1984) and Santner and Duffy (1986). If your goal is inference, it is recommended that you fit the model and request postfit analysis with the LOGISTIC procedure. The paper by Paul Allison (Allison 2008) and his SAS Press book on logistic regression (Allison 2012, Sec. 3.4) provide practical recommendations for dealing with separation. These include the use of exact methods and Firth's method of penalized likelihood estimation (see Firth 1993 and Heinze and Schemper 2002), which you can request with the EXACT and FIRTH options in the LOGISTIC procedure.

In the context of model building, SAS Usage Note 22599[†] recommends using forward or stepwise regression rather than backward elimination to avoid separation. If separation occurs at a particular step, the note suggests using the model at the previous step. Backward elimination is not recommended because it begins by fitting the most complex model, which maximizes the chance of encountering separation when there is sparseness in the data.

[†]This note is available at https://support.sas.com/kb/22/599.html.

Approximate Computation of Information Criteria

The information criteria for generalized linear models are given by the following equations:

$$\text{AIC} = -2\mathcal{L}(\hat{\boldsymbol{\beta}}_{\text{MLE}}) + 2p$$

$$\text{AICC} = \begin{cases} -2\mathcal{L}(\hat{\boldsymbol{\beta}}_{\text{MLE}}) + 2pn/(n-p-1) & \text{when } n > p+2 \\ -2\mathcal{L}(\hat{\boldsymbol{\beta}}_{\text{MLE}}) + 2p(p+2) & \text{otherwise} \end{cases}$$

$$\text{BIC} = -2\mathcal{L}(\hat{\boldsymbol{\beta}}_{\text{MLE}}) + p\log(n)$$

where p denotes the number of parameters in the candidate model, n denotes the number of observations, and $\mathcal{L}(\hat{\boldsymbol{\beta}}_{\text{MLE}})$ is the log-likelihood function evaluated at the maximum likelihood estimate of the regression parameters. These criteria are likelihood-based analogues of the information criteria for general linear models on page 28.

When you build a model with the HPLOGISTIC, LOGSELECT, HPGENSELECT, or GENSELECT procedures and specify AIC, AICC, or BIC with the SELECT= suboption for the METHOD= option, the criteria are computed from an approximation of the log-likelihood function at every step where the model is not refitted. This approximation is also used when you request the fast backward elimination method with the HPLOGISTIC and LOGSELECT procedures by specifying METHOD=BACKWARD(FAST), which greatly reduces the cost of building logistic regression models with large data.

The approximation is based on a paper by Lawless and Singhal (1978) that proposed a version of all subsets regression for nonnormal responses.[†] Their approach screens the submodels of a full model by testing them with the likelihood ratio statistic $\Lambda = -2[\mathcal{L}(\hat{\boldsymbol{\beta}}_{\text{submodel}}) - \mathcal{L}(\hat{\boldsymbol{\beta}}_{\text{full}})]$. For large n, this statistic has a χ^2 distribution with q degrees of freedom, where q is the difference between the number of parameters in the full model and the submodel. Because Λ is expensive to compute, Lawless and Singhal (1978) approximated it with a statistic, denoted by Λ', that can be computed efficiently with matrix sweep operations and is adequate for model screening.

The procedures use Λ' to compare the information criteria for candidate models without the expense of refitting the model every time a predictor is removed. In particular, the difference between two AIC values (plus $2q$) has the same form as Λ, and so it can be approximated by Λ'. As a result, the values of AIC for candidate models will differ slightly from those computed by other software. For the final selected model, the procedures compute information criteria by refitting the model.

Although Lawless and Singhal (1978) treated Λ' as a test statistic for model selection, the procedures treat it as the numerical difference between the information criteria for a submodel and a full model— with no reference to hypothesis testing or significance levels. There are theoretical connections between hypothesis testing for model comparison and the information-theoretic approach, but the two frameworks are fundamentally different, as explained by Burnham and Anderson (2002, Sec. 3.5.5 and 6.9.3).

[†]All subsets regression is available in the REG procedure, which implements the algorithm of Furnival and Wilson (1974) (see page 74), and in the LOGISTIC procedure (see page 189). The LOGISTIC procedure implements an adaptation of the Furnival-Wilson algorithm that finds the models with the highest chi-square statistic (score statistic) of a given size.

Appendix E
Distributions for Generalized Linear Models

Contents

When you use the HPGENSELECT and GENSELECT procedures to fit or build a generalized linear model, you specify a response distribution from a theoretical class of distributions known as the exponential family. A number of well-known continuous and discrete distributions are members of this family.

The first section of this appendix explains how the exponential family is defined and why it is useful. The second and third sections describe the member distributions that are available in the procedures.

The Exponential Family

A distribution is a member of the exponential family if its probability density function or probability mass function can be expressed as

$$f(y) = \exp\left(\frac{y\theta - b(\theta)}{\phi} + c(y, \phi)\right)$$

where $b(\cdot)$ and $c(\cdot, \cdot)$ are known functions. There are different definitions of the exponential family with varying degrees of generality. This particular expression is one of the more basic definitions; it is referred to as the canonical form, and it is related to the exponential dispersion model that was introduced by Jørgensen (1987). The parameter θ is called the *canonical parameter* or *natural parameter*, and the parameter ϕ is called the *dispersion parameter*.

The exponential family includes familiar distributions whose conventional parametric equations seem unrelated until they are cast into the canonical form. For example, the normal distribution with mean μ and standard deviation σ qualifies as a member of the exponential family because its probability density function can be rewritten as follows:

$$
\begin{aligned}
f(y) &= \frac{1}{\sqrt{2\pi}\sigma} \exp\left[-\frac{1}{2}\left(\frac{y - \mu}{\sigma}\right)^2\right] \\
&= \exp\left[-\frac{y^2}{2\sigma^2} + \frac{y\mu}{\sigma^2} - \frac{\mu^2}{2\sigma^2} - \frac{1}{2}\log(2\pi\sigma^2)\right] \quad \text{for} \ -\infty < y < \infty
\end{aligned}
$$

Here, the natural parameter is $\theta = \mu$, the dispersion parameter is $\phi = \sigma^2$, and the functions in the canonical form are $b(\theta) = \theta^2/2$ and

$$c(y, \phi) = \frac{-1}{2}\left[\frac{y^2}{\phi} + \log(2\pi\phi)\right]$$

Likewise, the Poisson distribution with mean μ qualifies as a member because its probability mass function can be rewritten as follows:

$$f(y) = e^{-\mu}\frac{\mu^y}{y!} = \exp\left[y\log(\mu) - \mu - \log(y!)\right] \quad \text{for } y = 0, 1, 2, \ldots$$

Here, the natural parameter is $\theta = \mu$, and the functions in the canonical form are $b(\theta) = \exp(\theta)$ and $c(y, \phi) = -\log(y!)$.

Because ϕ is trivially equal to 1, the Poisson distribution does not have a proper dispersion parameter. Similarly, four other distributions in the exponential family lack a dispersion parameter: the binary, binomial, multinomial, and zero-inflated Poisson distributions.

Practical Benefits

The exponential family plays a fundamental role in statistical theory that lies far outside the scope of this book, but it provides two benefits in the application of generalized linear models.[†] First, it includes a variety of well-known distributions; these are summarized starting on page 337. Second, for each of the distributions in the exponential family, the mean (expectation) and variance have a simple relationship that can motivate the selection of an appropriate response distribution.

If Y has a distribution in the exponential family, it can be shown that

$$\mu \equiv E(Y) = \frac{\partial}{\partial\theta}\,b(\theta)$$

and

$$\text{Var}(Y) = \frac{\phi}{w_i}\frac{\partial^2}{\partial\theta^2}b(\theta) = \frac{\phi V(\mu)}{w_i}$$

where $V(\mu)$ is called the *variance function* associated with the distribution.

In the case of the normal distribution, the variance function is $V(\mu) = 1$, and so the variance is $\phi = \sigma^2$, which is functionally independent of the mean. For the Poisson distribution, the variance function is $V(\mu) = \mu$, and so the variance is equal to the mean.

The variance function gives you a basis for comparing and selecting distributions that is not obvious from the conventional parametric equations for $f(y)$. Table E.1 lists the variance functions for distributions that are available in the procedures.

[†]The exponential family predates the introduction of generalized linear models. It has a rich history in the theory of statistical inference, beginning with the work of Darmois, Koopmans, and Pitman in the 1930s, and it is intertwined with the concept of sufficiency, which was introduced by Ronald Fisher in 1922. See Pawitan (2001, Ch. 4) and Cox (2006, Ch. 2).

Table E.1 Variance Functions for Distributions in the Exponential Family

Type	Distribution	Variance Function $V(\mu)$
Continuous	normal	1
Continuous	gamma	μ^2
Continuous	exponential	μ^2
Continuous	inverse Gaussian	μ^3
Continuous	Tweedie	$\mu^p, \quad 1 < p < 2$
Discrete	binary (Bernoulli)	$\mu(1 - \mu)$
Discrete	binomial	$\mu(1 - \mu)/n$
Discrete	negative binomial	$\mu(1 + k\mu)$
Discrete	geometric	$\mu + \mu^2$
Discrete	Poisson	μ

For distributions with a proper dispersion parameter, the HPGENSELECT and GENSELECT procedures compute an estimate of ϕ that is displayed in the table of regression parameter estimates. However, you can specify a fixed value for ϕ with the DISPERSION= option in the MODEL statement for the HPGENSELECT procedure and with the PHI= option in the MODEL statement for the GENSELECT procedure.

The GENMOD procedure differs from the HPGENSELECT and GENSELECT procedures in that it uses a scale parameter related to the dispersion parameter ϕ rather than ϕ itself. When you use the GENMOD procedure, the scale parameter is displayed in the Parameter Estimates table.

Alternatively, you can specify a fixed scale parameter with the SCALE= option in the MODEL statement. The definition of the GENMOD scale parameter depends on the distribution and is indicated in the sections that follow.

The Log-Likelihood Function

In a generalized linear model, the observations are assumed to be independent, and $f(y)$ represents the distribution of y_i, the value of the response variable Y for the ith observation. The canonical parameter θ is assumed to vary across observations and is denoted by θ_i, whereas the dispersion parameter ϕ is treated as a constant.

Because the mean corresponding to y_i is a function of θ_i, the likelihood contribution of the ith observation is denoted as $f(y_i, \mu_i, \phi)$, and the log-likelihood function of the model is expressed as

$$\mathcal{L}(\boldsymbol{\mu}, \phi; \mathbf{y}) = \sum_{i=1}^{n} \log(f(y_i, \mu_i, \phi))$$

where $\boldsymbol{\mu} = (\mu_1, \ldots, \mu_n)'$. The sum need not include terms that do not depend on the parameters. For instance, the log-likelihood function for a Poisson distribution is

$$\mathcal{L}(\boldsymbol{\mu}; \mathbf{y}) = \sum_{i=1}^{n} [y_i \log(\mu_i) - \mu_i]$$

When you fit or build a generalized linear model, you specify a link function $g(\cdot)$ along with the response distribution. The link function relates μ_i to the linear structure of the predictors:

$$g(\mu_i) = g\left(\frac{\partial}{\partial\theta}\,b(\theta)\right) = \beta_0 + \beta_1 x_{i1} + \cdots + \beta_p x_{ip} \quad i = 1, \ldots, n$$

When it is more important to emphasize its dependence on the regression parameters, the log-likelihood function is denoted as $\mathcal{L}(\boldsymbol{\beta}; \mathbf{y})$, where $\boldsymbol{\beta} = (\beta_0, \beta_1, \ldots, \beta_p)'$. In particular, the maximum likelihood estimate of $\boldsymbol{\beta}$ is $\hat{\boldsymbol{\beta}}_{\mathrm{MLE}} = \underset{\boldsymbol{\beta}}{\mathrm{argmax}}\{\mathcal{L}(\boldsymbol{\beta}; \mathbf{y})\}$.

An important quantity related to the log-likelihood is the model *deviance*, whose interpretation is similar to that of the residual sum of squares $\|\mathbf{y} - \mathbf{X}\hat{\boldsymbol{\beta}}_{\mathrm{OLS}}\|_2^2$ for a general linear model. The definition of deviance is

$$D(\hat{\boldsymbol{\beta}}) \equiv \sum_{i=1}^{n} 2[\mathcal{L}(\mathbf{y}; \mathbf{y})) - \mathcal{L}(\hat{\boldsymbol{\beta}}_{\mathrm{MLE}})$$

where $\mathcal{L}(\mathbf{y}; \mathbf{y}))$ denotes the maximum attainable log likelihood, corresponding to a saturated model that has a parameter for every observation. The deviance is also denoted as $D(\hat{\boldsymbol{\mu}})$. For instance, the deviance for model with a Poisson distribution is

$$D(\hat{\boldsymbol{\mu}}) = \sum_{i=1}^{n} 2\left[y_i\left(\log\left(\frac{y_i}{\hat{\mu}_i}\right)\right) - (y_i - \hat{\mu}_i)\right]$$

The *scaled deviance* $D^*(\hat{\boldsymbol{\mu}})$ is defined as $D(\hat{\boldsymbol{\mu}})/\phi$.

Canonical Links for Distributions

For a given response distribution in the exponential family, if $g(\cdot)$ is the functional inverse of the derivative of $b(\theta)$, then $g(\mu_i)$ is equal to the canonical parameter θ_i, and $g(\cdot)$ is called the *canonical link* associated with the distribution. In this case, the log-likelihood function for estimating the regression parameters simplifies to

$$\mathcal{L}(\boldsymbol{\beta}; \mathbf{y}) = \sum_{j=1}^{p} \beta_j \sum_{i=1}^{n} \frac{x_{ij}\, y_i}{\phi_i} - \sum_{i=1}^{n}\left[\frac{b(\theta_i)}{\phi_i} - c(y_i, \phi_i)\right]$$

For example, if Y has a Bernoulli distribution, the canonical link is the logit link, and the log-likelihood function simplifies to the form for binary logistic regression on page 162.

You might wonder if there is any reason to prefer the canonical link. In fact, the simplification of $\mathcal{L}(\boldsymbol{\beta}; \mathbf{y})$ that results from a canonical link is immaterial to the algorithms for computing the maximum likelihood estimate of $\boldsymbol{\beta}$ (see page 328). McCullagh and Nelder (1989, Sec. 2.2) pointed out that canonical links lead to desirable statistical properties in small samples, but in practice there is no a priori reason to prefer a canonical link.

Programming Tip: Specify link functions that are interpretable or that scale the response in a way that is motivated by subject matter knowledge.

Continuous Distributions in the Exponential Family

The following continuous distributions in the exponential family are available in the GENMOD, HPGENSELECT, and GENSELECT procedures. The canonical link function is denoted by $g_{can}(\mu)$.

When you fit a generalized linear model with the GENMOD procedure, it includes the estimate for a scale parameter in the Parameter Estimates table. This parameter is generally not the same as the dispersion parameter ϕ. Here, the scale parameter estimated by the GENMOD procedure is denoted by *GENMOD scale*.

Normal Distribution

You can request the normal distribution with the DISTRIBUTION=NORMAL option in the MODEL statement. The main characteristics of this distribution are

$$
\begin{aligned}
f(y) &= \frac{1}{\sqrt{2\pi}\sigma} \exp\left[-\frac{1}{2}\left(\frac{y-\mu}{\sigma}\right)^2\right] \quad \text{for} -\infty < y < \infty \\
E(Y) &= \mu \\
\mathrm{Var}(Y) &= \sigma^2 \\
\phi &= \sigma^2 \\
V(\mu) &= 1 \\
g_{can}(\mu) &= \mu \\
\text{GENMOD scale} &= \sigma
\end{aligned}
$$

Figure E.1 illustrates the probability density function $f(y)$ for three combinations of μ and σ.

Figure E.1 Examples of Normal Distributions

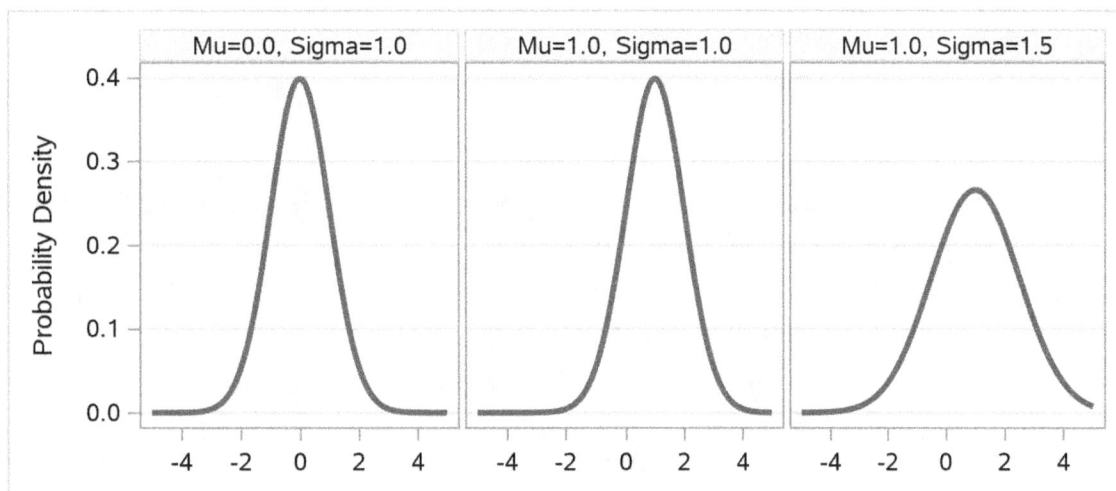

For further details of the normal distribution, see Johnson, Kotz, and Balakrishnan (1994, Ch. 13).

Inverse Gaussian Distribution

You can request the inverse Gaussian distribution with the DISTRIBUTION=IGAUSSIAN option in the MODEL statement. The main characteristics of this distribution are

$$
\begin{aligned}
f(y) &= \frac{1}{\sqrt{2\pi y^3}\sigma} \exp\left[-\frac{1}{2y}\left(\frac{y-\mu}{\mu\sigma}\right)^2\right] \quad \text{for } 0 < y < \infty \\
E(Y) &= \mu \\
\text{Var}(Y) &= \sigma^2\mu^3 \\
\phi &= \sigma^2 \\
V(\mu) &= \mu^3 \\
g_{\text{can}}(\mu) &= 1/\mu^2 \\
\text{GENMOD scale} &= \sigma
\end{aligned}
$$

Figure E.2 illustrates the probability density function $f(y)$ for three combinations of μ and σ.

Figure E.2 Examples of Inverse Gaussian Distributions

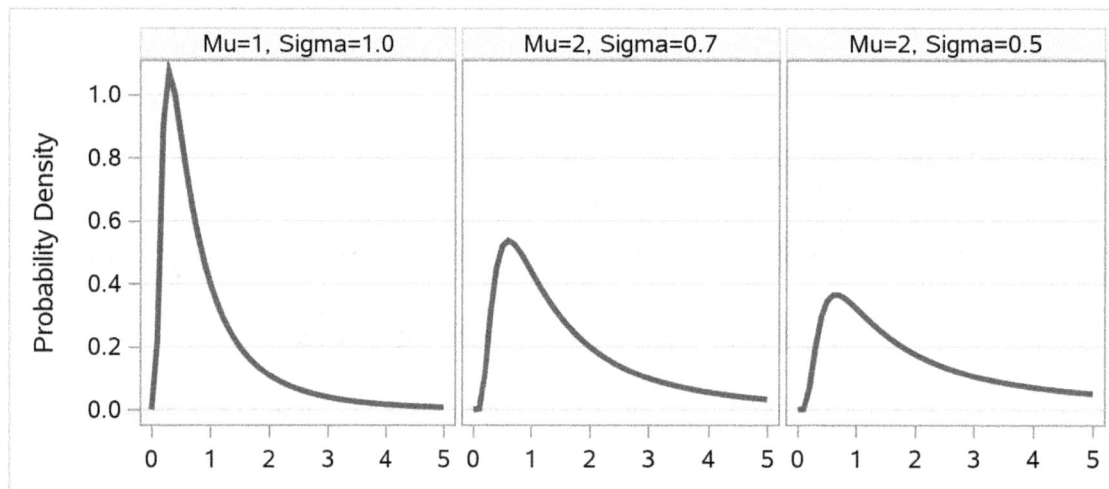

The densities have sharper peaks and wider tails compared with densities of gamma distributions that have the same means and variances.

For further details of the inverse Gaussian distribution, also known as the Wald distribution, see Johnson, Kotz, and Balakrishnan (1994, Ch. 15).

Gamma Distribution

You can request the gamma distribution with the DISTRIBUTION=GAMMA option in the MODEL statement (see the example on page 203). The main characteristics of this distribution are

$$
\begin{aligned}
f(y) &= \frac{1}{\Gamma(\alpha)y}\left(\frac{y\alpha}{\mu}\right)^{\alpha}\exp\left(-\frac{y\alpha}{\mu}\right) \quad \text{for } 0 \le y < \infty \\
\mathrm{E}(Y) &= \mu \\
\mathrm{Var}(Y) &= \frac{\mu^2}{\alpha} \\
\phi &= \alpha^{-1} \\
V(\mu) &= \phi\mu^2 \\
g_{\mathrm{can}}(\mu) &= -1/\mu \\
\text{GENMOD scale} &= \alpha
\end{aligned}
$$

The parameter α is referred to as the shape parameter or the index parameter. The exponential distribution and the chi-square distribution are special cases of the gamma distribution.

Figure E.3 illustrates the probability density function $f(y)$ for three combinations of μ and α.

Figure E.3 Examples of Gamma Distributions

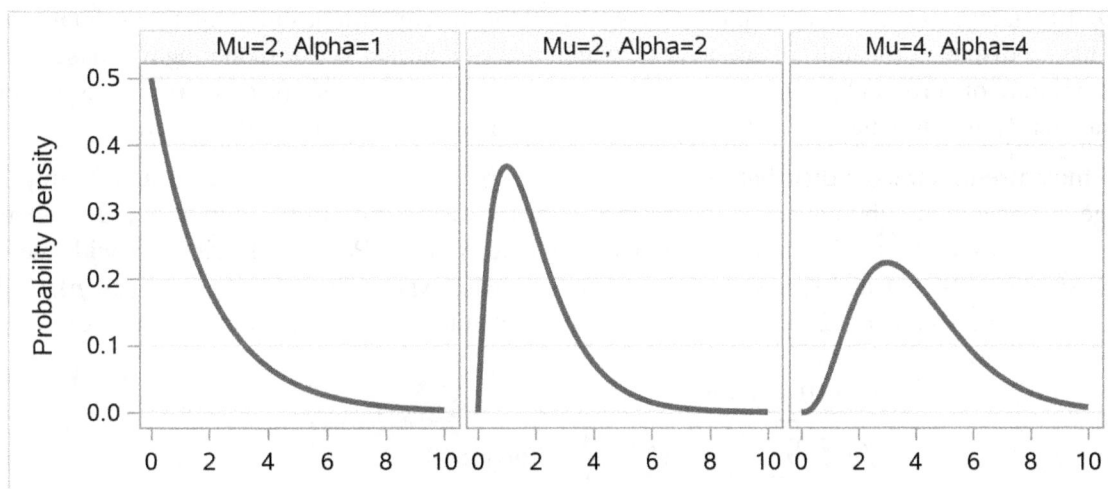

The example on page 203 illustrates the use of the HPGENSELECT procedure to build a generalized linear model in which the response is assumed to have a gamma distribution.

For further details of the gamma distribution, see Johnson, Kotz, and Balakrishnan (1994, Ch. 17).

Exponential Distribution

You can request the exponential distribution with the DISTRIBUTION=EXPONENTIAL option in the MODEL statement. The main characteristics of this distribution are

$$
\begin{aligned}
f(y) &= \frac{1}{\mu} \exp\left(\frac{-y}{\mu}\right) \quad \text{for } 0 \le y < \infty \\
\mathrm{E}(Y) &= \mu \\
\mathrm{Var}(Y) &= \mu^2 \\
\phi &\equiv 1 \\
V(\mu) &= \phi\mu^2 \\
g_{\mathrm{can}}(\mu) &= -1/\mu \\
\text{GENMOD scale} &= 1
\end{aligned}
$$

The exponential distribution is the special case of the gamma distribution for which $\alpha = 1$. The left panel in Figure E.3 illustrates an exponential distribution with $\mu = 2$. For further details of the exponential distribution, see Johnson, Kotz, and Balakrishnan (1994, Ch. 19).

Tweedie Distribution

You can request the Tweedie distribution with the DISTRIBUTION=TWEEDIE option in the MODEL statement (see the example on page 212). This distribution has nonnegative support and can have a discrete probability mass at zero, which makes it attractive for modeling responses that are a mixture of zeros and positive values (Tweedie 1984). In addition to the mean μ and dispersion parameter ϕ, the Tweedie distribution has a power parameter p that controls the variance.

The most useful Tweedie distributions are those for which p is strictly between 1 and 2. In this range, a Tweedie distribution can be characterized as the distribution of the sum of N independent and identically distributed random variables Y_i, where N has a Poisson distribution with mean $\lambda = \mu^{2-p}/(\phi(2-p))$, and Y_i has a gamma distribution with expected value $\mathrm{E}(Y_i) = \phi(2-p)\mu^{p-1}$ and shape parameter $\alpha = (2-p)/(p-1)$. The main characteristics of this distribution are

$$
\begin{aligned}
f(0) &= \Pr(N = 0) = \exp(-\lambda) \\
f(y) &= e^{-y/\gamma} e^{-\lambda} \sum_{n=1}^{\infty} \frac{\gamma^{-n\alpha}}{\Gamma(n\alpha)} y^{n\alpha-1} \frac{\lambda^n}{n!} \quad \text{for } y > 0 \\
\mathrm{E}(Y) &= \mu = \lambda\alpha\gamma \\
\mathrm{Var}(Y) &= \lambda\alpha\gamma^2 + \lambda\alpha^2\gamma^2 \\
\phi &= \frac{\lambda^{1-p}(\alpha\gamma)^{2-p}}{2-p} \\
V(\mu) &= \mu^p \\
g_{\mathrm{can}}(\mu) &= \mu^{1-p}/(1-p)
\end{aligned}
$$

Figure E.4 illustrates the probability density function $f(y)$ for three combinations of p and μ. The bars indicate the probability masses at zero, which vary with p.

Figure E.4 Examples of Tweedie Distributions

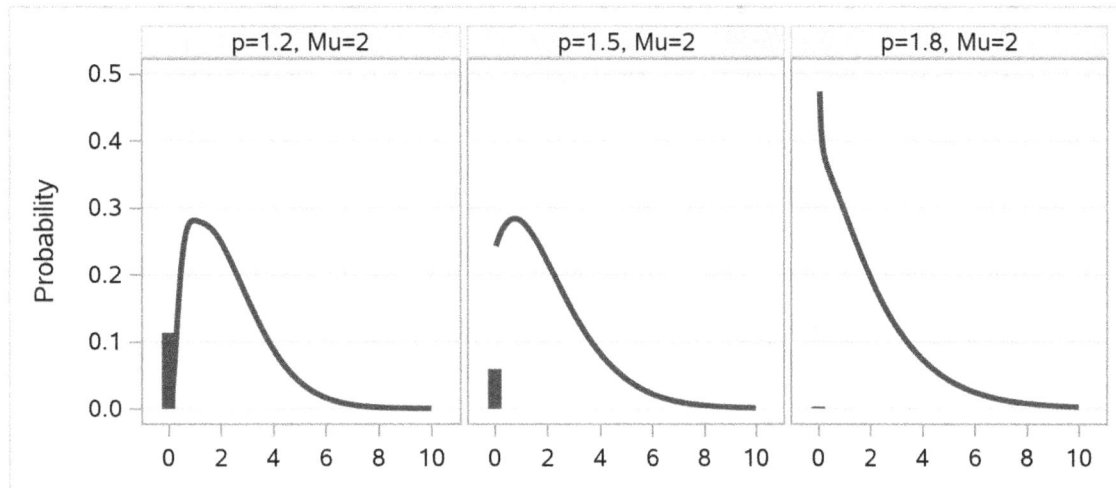

Four well-known distributions are special cases of the Tweedie distribution. For $p = 0$, the Tweedie distribution becomes a normal distribution; for $p = 1$, it becomes a Poisson distribution; for $p = 2$, it becomes a gamma distribution; and for $p = 3$, it becomes an inverse Gaussian distribution. The Tweedie distribution is not defined when p is between 0 and 1. Except for the four special cases, $f(y)$ does not have a closed form.

The GENMOD, HPGENSELECT, and GENSELECT procedures evaluate $f(y)$ with methods proposed by Dunn and Smyth (2005, 2008). For numerical stability, the procedures require p to be greater than or equal to 1.1.

Computing the maximum likelihood estimate of p in a reasonable amount of time is challenging, and it can be difficult to obtain a good starting value. Because no one method works well in every situation, the procedures provide four different methods, listed in Table E.2, which you can request with the OPTMETHOD= suboption for the DIST=TWEEDIE option.

Table E.2 Computational Methods for Estimating p

Method	OPTMETHOD=
Extended quasi-likelihood[†] for sample, followed by extended quasi-likelihood for full data	EQL
Extended quasi-likelihood for sample, followed by Tweedie log-likelihood for full data (default)	EQLLHOOD
Four-stage approach: extended quasi-likelihood and Tweedie log-likelihood for sample, followed by extended quasi-likelihood and Tweedie log-likelihood for full data	FINALLHOOD
Tweedie log-likelihood for full data	LHOOD

[†]The quasi-likelihood function, introduced by Wedderburn (1974), involves only the mean and variance of the distribution rather than its full form; it has properties similar to those of the log-likelihood function and is simpler to compute. The extended quasi-likelihood function, defined by Nelder and Pregibon (1987), enables the comparison of different variance functions.

Discrete Distributions in the Exponential Family

The following discrete distributions in the exponential family are available in the GENMOD, HPGEN-SELECT, and GENSELECT procedures, with two exceptions. Zero-inflated negative binomial and zero-inflated Poisson distributions are available only in the GENMOD and HPGENSELECT procedures. Canonical links are denoted by $g_{can}(\mu)$.

Binary (Bernoulli) Distribution

You can request the binary distribution with the DISTRIBUTION=BINARY option in the MODEL statement. The binary distribution, also known as the Bernoulli distribution, is the special case of the binomial distribution for which $n = 1$.

The main characteristics of the binary distribution are

$$
\begin{aligned}
f(y) &= pI_{y=1} + (1 - p)I_{y=0} \\
E(Y) &= \mu = p \\
Var(Y) &= \mu(1 - \mu) \\
\phi &\equiv 1 \\
V(\mu) &= \mu(1 - \mu) \\
g_{can}(\mu) &= \log(\mu/(1 - \mu))
\end{aligned}
$$

The Bernoulli distribution does not have a true dispersion parameter because $\phi \equiv 1$.

Figure E.5 illustrates the probability mass function $f(y)$ for three values of p.

Figure E.5 Examples of Binary Distributions

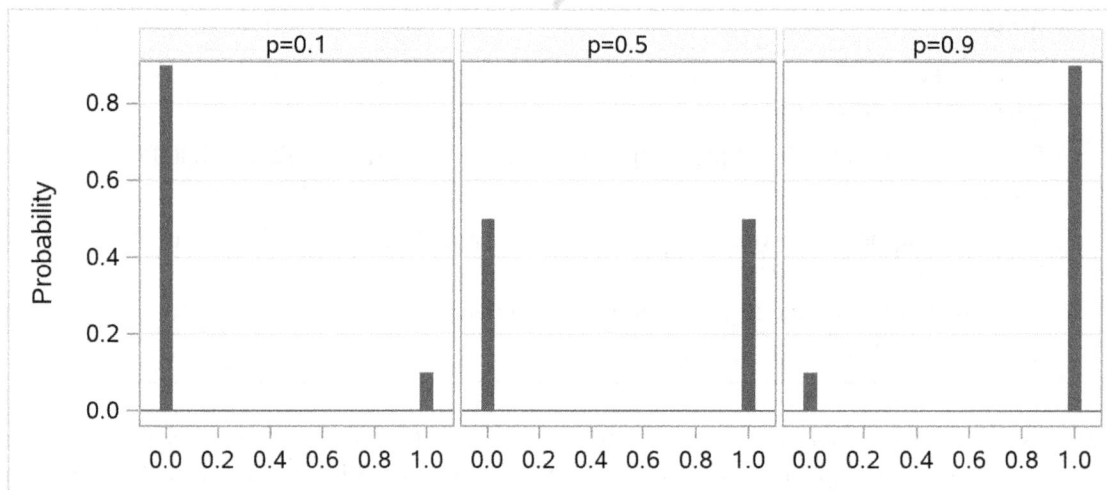

Binomial Distribution

You can request the binomial distribution with the DISTRIBUTION=BINOMIAL option in the MODEL statement. The response variable should be listed in a CLASS statement as well as the MODEL statement, and it must have exactly two levels. Alternatively, with the events/trials syntax in the MODEL statement, which is illustrated on page 197, you can request the binomial distribution by specifying a variable that contains the number of events and a second variable that contains the number of trials.

For the binomial distribution, the response is the binomial proportion $Y = $ events / trials. The main characteristics of this distribution are

$$
\begin{aligned}
f(y) &= \binom{n}{k} \mu^k (1 - \mu)^{n-k} \quad \text{for } y = \frac{k}{n}, \; k = 0, 1, 2, \ldots, n \\
\mathrm{E}(Y) &= {} = \mu \\
\mathrm{Var}(Y) &= \frac{\mu(1 - \mu)}{n} \\
\phi &\equiv 1 \\
V(\mu) &= \frac{\mu(1 - \mu)}{n} \\
g_{\mathrm{can}}(\mu) &= \log(\mu/(1 - \mu))
\end{aligned}
$$

The binomial distribution does not have a true dispersion parameter because $\phi \equiv 1$.

The variance function is typically expressed as $V(\mu) = \mu(1 - \mu)$, and the binomial trials parameter n is treated as a weight w.

Figure E.6 illustrates the probability mass function $f(y)$ for $n = 10$ and three values of p.

Figure E.6 Examples of Binomial Distributions

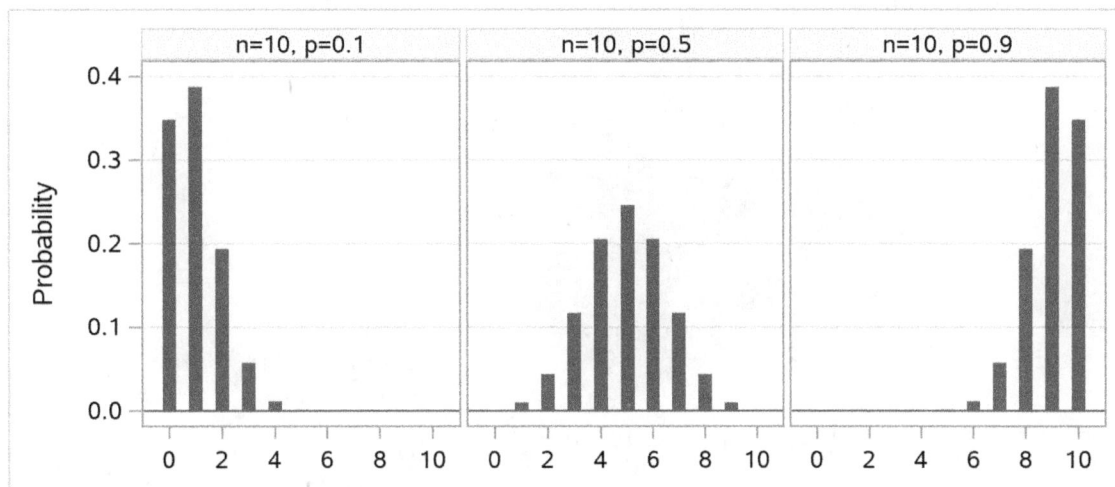

For further details of the binomial distribution, see Johnson, Kotz, and Kemp (1992, Ch. 3).

Multinomial Distribution

The GENMOD, HPGENSELECT, and GENSELECT procedures assume the response variable has a multinomial distribution if it is categorical (listed in a CLASS statement) and has more than two levels. The multinomial distribution generalizes the binomial distribution and is defined as follows.

Suppose there are n independent trials in which k mutually exclusive events, $E_1, E_2, \ldots, E_k$, are observed, and the probability of E_j is p_j. If N_j is the number of occurrences of E_j, with $\sum_{j=1}^{k} N_j = n$, the joint distribution of $N_1, N_2, \ldots, N_k$ is the multinomial distribution:

$$
\begin{aligned}
f(y_1, y_2, \ldots, y_k) &= \frac{n!}{y_1! y_2! \cdots y_k!} p_1^{y_1} p_2^{y_2} \cdots p_k^{y_k} \\
E(N_j) &= n p_j \quad \text{for } j = 1, 2, \ldots, k \\
\text{Var}(N_j) &= n p_j (1 - p_j) \\
\text{Cov}(N_i, N_j) &= -n p_i p_j
\end{aligned}
$$

The multinomial distribution is a member of the multivariate discrete exponential family (Johnson, Kotz, and Balakrishnan 1997, p. 12).

The probability mass function can be expressed in terms of the first $k - 1$ components. Figure E.7 illustrates the function for the trinomial distribution with $k = 3$, $n = 10$, $p_1 = 0.2$, $p_2 = 0.4$, and $p_3 = 0.4$.

Figure E.7 Example of a Multinomial Distribution with $k = 3$

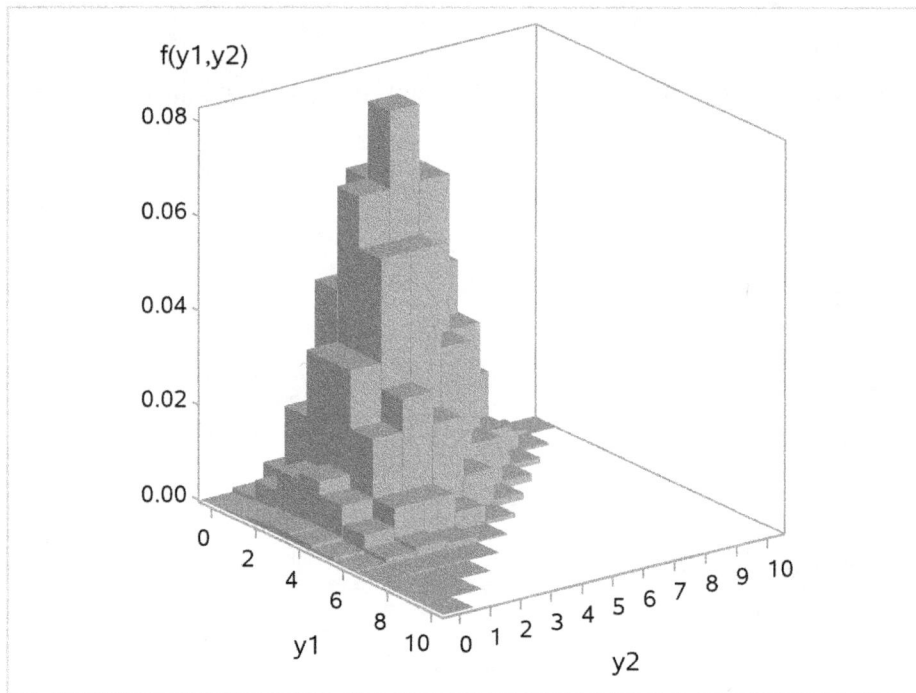

Note that N_1 and N_2 are negatively correlated ($\rho = -0.08$) because the support of their joint distribution is restricted to a triangular section of the plane.

The HPGENSELECT and GENSELECT procedures build models for multinomial responses with two types of levels:

- By default, the procedures treat the levels as ordered and use the cumulative logit link. You can request cumulative versions of the probit, complementary log-log, and log-log links.

- The procedures treat the levels as nominal and unordered if you request the generalized logit link by specifying LINK=GLOGIT. This is the only link function for the nominal case.

For further details of the multinomial distribution, see Johnson, Kotz, and Balakrishnan (1997, Ch. 35).

Negative Binomial Distribution

You can request the negative binomial distribution with the DISTRIBUTION=NEGATIVEBINOMIAL option in the MODEL statement. The main characteristics of this distribution are

$$
\begin{aligned}
f(y) &= \frac{\Gamma(y + 1/k)}{\Gamma(y + 1)\Gamma(1/k)} \frac{(k\mu)^y}{(1 + k\mu)^{y+1/k}} \quad \text{for } y = 0, 1, 2, \ldots \\
E(Y) &= \mu \\
\text{Var}(Y) &= \mu + k\mu^2 \\
\phi &\equiv 1 \\
V(\mu) &= \mu(1 + k\mu) \\
g_{\text{can}}(\mu) &= \log(\mu/k(1 + \mu/k))
\end{aligned}
$$

Figure E.8 illustrates the probability mass function $f(y)$ for $k = 2$ and three values of μ.

Figure E.8 Examples of Negative Binomial Distributions

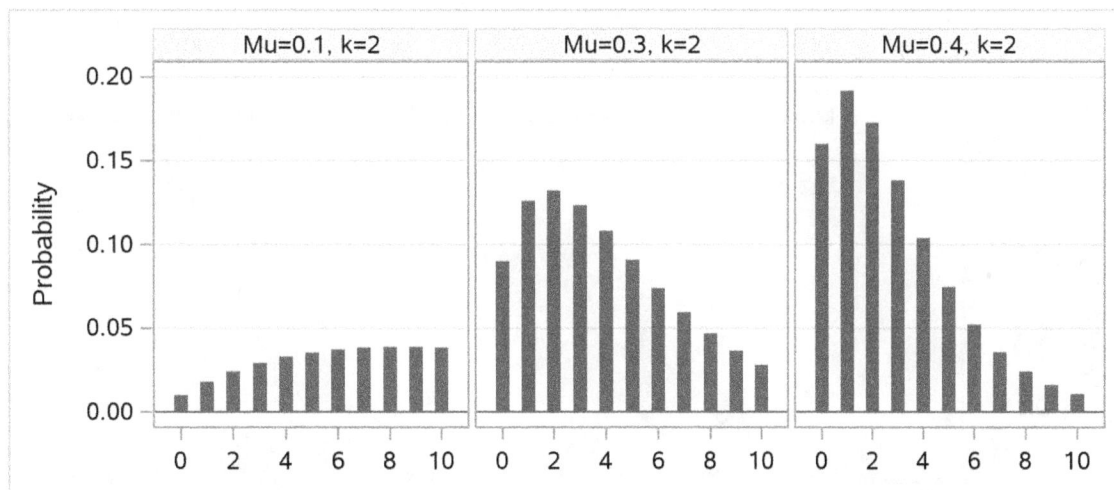

For further details of the negative binomial distribution, see Johnson, Kotz, and Kemp (1992, Ch. 5).

Zero-Inflated Negative Binomial Distribution

With the HPGENSELECT procedure, you can request the zero-inflated negative binomial distribution by specifying the DISTRIBUTION=ZINB option in the MODEL statement.

The zero-inflated negative binomial distribution extends the negative binomial distribution; it models overdispersion when the frequency of zero counts in the data exceeds the number expected based on the negative binomial distribution.

The main characteristics of the zero-inflated negative binomial distribution are

$$
f(y) = \begin{cases} \omega + (1-\omega)(1+k\mu)^{-\frac{1}{k}} & \text{for } y = 0 \\ (1-\omega)\frac{\Gamma(y+1/k)}{\Gamma(y+1)\Gamma(1/k)}\frac{(k\mu)^y}{(1+k\mu)^{y+1/k}} & \text{for } y = 1, 2, \ldots \end{cases}
$$

$$\phi \equiv 1$$

$$\text{dispersion} = k$$

$$\mu = \text{E}(Y) = (1-\omega)\mu$$

$$\text{Var}(Y) = (1-\omega)\mu(1+\omega\mu+k\mu) = \mu + \left(\frac{\omega}{1-\omega} + \frac{k}{1-\omega}\right)\mu^2$$

The distribution lacks a variance function because it is not a member of the exponential family.

The assumption underlying the zero-inflated negative binomial distribution is that the data are generated by two independent processes. The first process generates count data that are adequately modeled by a negative binomial distribution with parameter λ (see page 348). Based solely on this model, the probability of a zero count is $(1 + k\mu)^{-1/k}$. The second process generates additional zeros with a probability of ω, which is called the *zero-inflation probability*. In practice, these zeros represent events generated by the first process that are under-reported; they can also represent individuals or entities that do not participate in the process.

Figure E.9 illustrates $f(y)$ for $\omega = 0.1$ and the same values of μ and k shown in Figure E.8.

Figure E.9 Examples of Zero-Inflated Negative Binomial Distributions

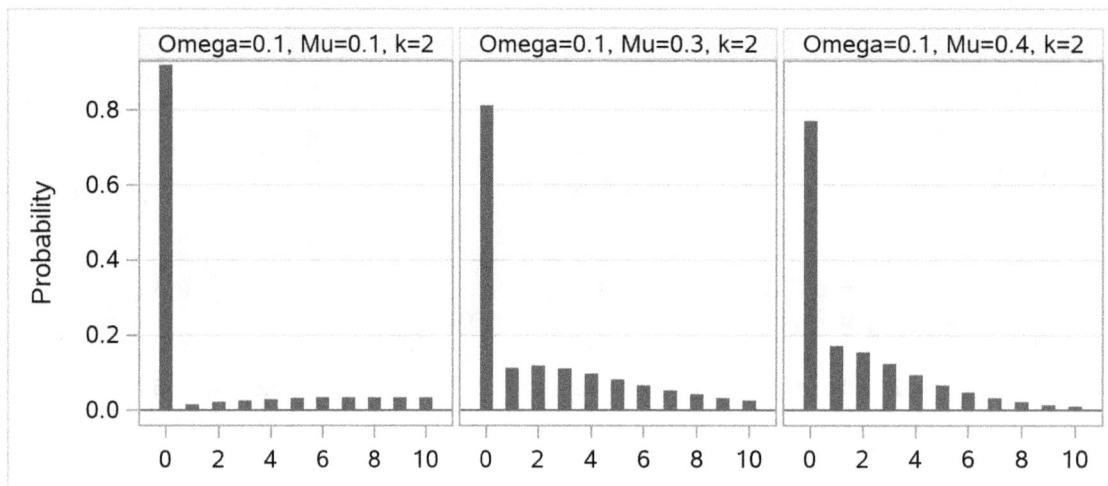

When you use the HPEGENSESLECT procedure to build a generalized linear model with a zero-inflated negative binomial distribution, the negative binomial mean of the response variable depends on the candidate predictors specified in the MODEL statement. The zero-inflation probability depends on the predictors specified in the ZEROMODEL through a logit link function.

See Lambert (1992), Long (1997), Cameron and Trivedi (1998), and Ridout, Hinde, and Demétrio (1998) for more information about zero-inflated models. Helpful examples of fitting and diagnosing zero-inflated count data models with the GENMOD procedure are available at https://support.sas.com/rnd/app/stat/examples/GENMODZIP/roots.htm.

Geometric Distribution

You can request the geometric distribution with the DISTRIBUTION=GEOMETRIC option in the MODEL statement of the GENSESLECT procedure (but not the HPGENSELECT procedure). The geometric distribution is a special case of the negative binomial distribution for which $k = 1$. The main characteristics of the geometric distribution are

$$
\begin{aligned}
f(y) &= \frac{\mu^y}{(1+\mu)^{y+1}} \quad \text{for } y = 0, 1, 2, \ldots \\
\mathrm{E}(Y) &= \mu \\
\mathrm{Var}(Y) &= \mu + \mu^2 \\
\phi &\equiv 1 \\
V(\mu) = &= \mu + \mu^2 \\
g_{\mathrm{can}}(\mu) &= \log(\mu/1 + /mu/))
\end{aligned}
$$

Figure E.10 illustrates the probability mass function $f(y)$ for the same values of μ as in Figure E.8.

Figure E.10 Examples of Geometric Distributions

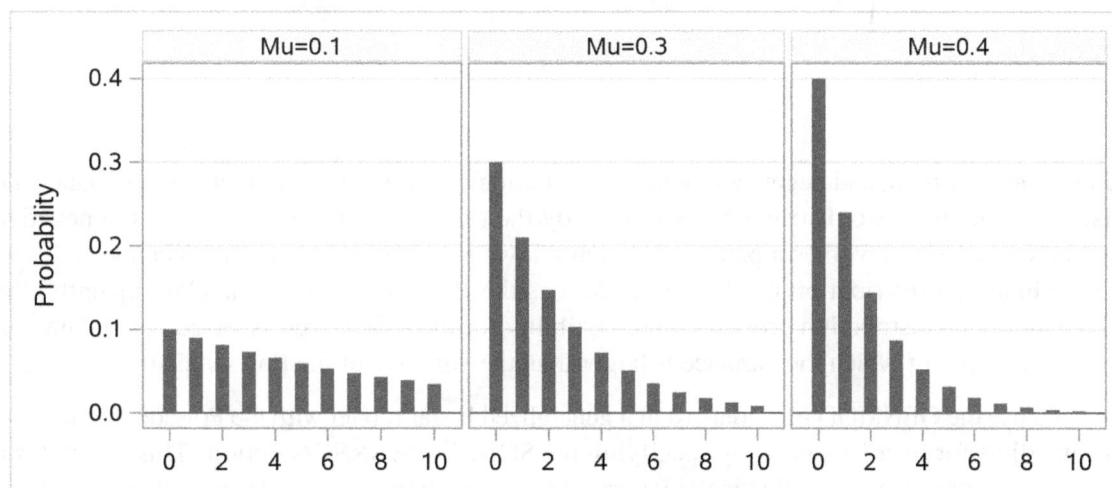

For further details of the geometric distribution, see Johnson, Kotz, and Kemp (1992, p. 201).

Poisson Distribution

You can request the Poisson distribution with the DISTRIBUTION=POISSON option in the MODEL statement (see the example on page 217). The main characteristics of this distribution are

$$
\begin{aligned}
f(y) &= \frac{\lambda^y e^{-\lambda}}{y!} \quad \text{for } y = 0, 1, 2, \dots \\
\mathrm{E}(Y) &= \mu = \lambda \\
\mathrm{Var}(Y) &= \mu \\
\phi &\equiv 1 \\
V(\mu) = &= \mu \\
g_{\mathrm{can}}(\mu) &= \log(\mu)
\end{aligned}
$$

The Poisson distribution does not have a true dispersion parameter because $\phi \equiv 1$.

Figure E.11 illustrates the probability mass function $f(y)$ for three values of λ.

Figure E.11 Examples of Poisson Distributions

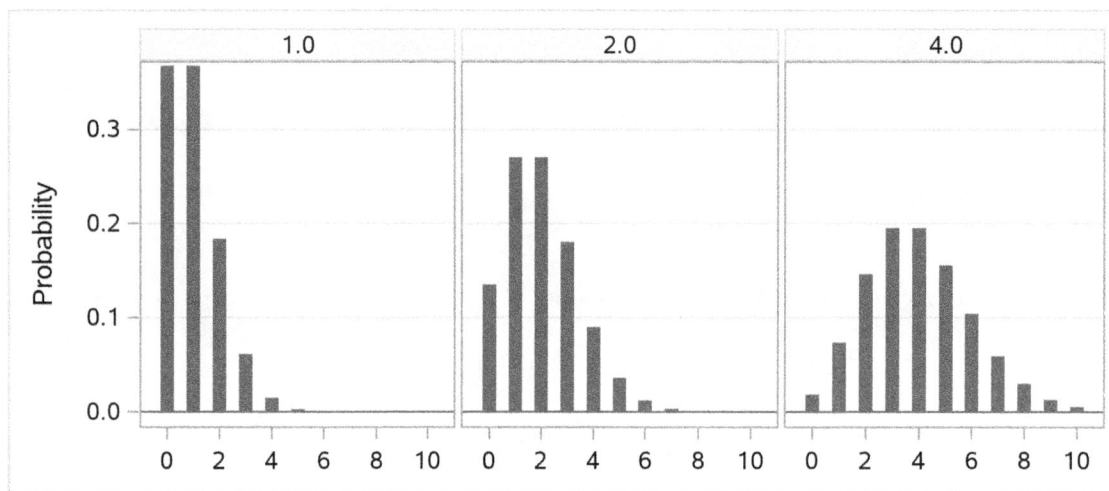

The Poisson, binomial, and negative binomial distributions are often used to model count data. The variances of the first two distributions are fixed by their means, but the variance of the negative binomial distribution involves a parameter k that allows it to vary more freely. When $k = 0$, the negative binomial distribution has the same form as the Poisson distribution. Consequently, the negative binomial distribution provides more flexibility for modeling overdispersed count data—in other words, data for which the variance is larger than the variance of the Poisson distribution.

When you use the GENMOD procedure to fit a generalized linear model with the Poisson distribution, you can adjust for overdispersion by specifying the SCALE=PEARSON option. This computes a scaling factor for the variance that is the Pearson Q statistic divided by its degrees of freedom; see Stokes, Davis, and Koch (2012, Sec. 12.5). This option is not available in the HPGENSELECT and GENSELECT procedures.

For further details of the Poisson distribution, see Johnson, Kotz, and Kemp (1992, Ch. 4).

Zero-Inflated Poisson Distribution

With the HPGENSELECT procedure, you can request the zero-inflated Poisson distribution by specifying the DISTRIBUTION=ZIP option in the MODEL statement.

The zero-inflated Poisson distribution extends the Poisson distribution; it models overdispersion when the frequency of zero counts in the data exceeds the number expected based on the Poisson distribution.

The main characteristics of the zero-inflated Poisson distribution are

$$
\begin{aligned}
f(y) &= \begin{cases} \omega + (1-\omega)e^{-\lambda} & \text{for } y = 0 \\ (1-\omega)\frac{\lambda^y e^{-\lambda}}{y!} & \text{for } y = 1, 2, \ldots \end{cases} \\
E(Y) &= \mu = (1-\omega)\lambda \\
\text{Var}(Y) &= (1-\omega)\lambda(1+\omega\lambda) = \mu + \frac{\omega}{1-\omega}\mu^2 \\
\phi &\equiv 1
\end{aligned}
$$

The distribution lacks a variance function because it is not a member of the exponential family.

The assumption underlying the zero-inflated Poisson distribution is that the data are generated by two independent processes. The first process generates count data that are adequately modeled by a Poisson distribution with parameter λ (see page 348). Based solely on this model, the probability of a zero count is $\exp(-\lambda)$. The second process generates additional zeros with a probability of ω, which is called the *zero-inflation probability*. In practice, these zeros represent events generated by the first process that are under-reported; they can also represent individuals or entities that do not participate in the process.

Figure E.12 illustrates the probability mass function $f(y)$ for $\omega = 0.1$ and the same values of λ that are shown in Figure E.11.

Figure E.12 Examples of Zero-Inflated Poisson Distributions

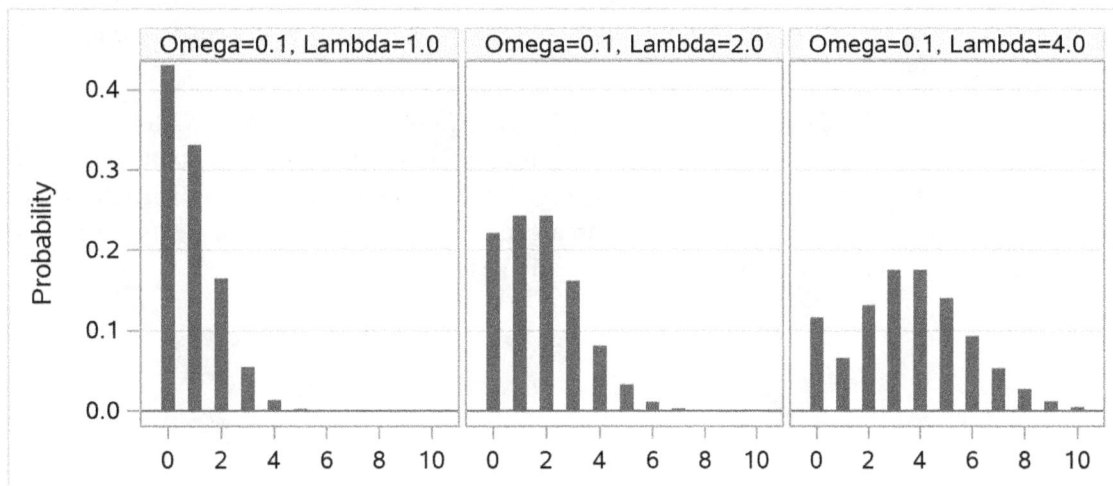

When you use the HPEGENSESLECT procedure to build a generalized linear model with a zero-inflated Poisson distribution, the Poisson mean of the response variable depends on the candidate predictors specified in the MODEL statement. The zero-inflation probability depends on the predictors specified in the ZEROMODEL through a logit link function. See the example on page 208.

See Lambert (1992), Long (1997), Cameron and Trivedi (1998), and Ridout, Hinde, and Demétrio (1998) for more information about zero-inflated models. Helpful examples of fitting and diagnosing zero-inflated count data models with the GENMOD procedure are available at https://support.sas.com/rnd/app/stat/examples/GENMODZIP/roots.htm.

Distributions Outside of the Exponential Family

The definition of an exponential family given on page 333 has been extended in various ways. Consequently, some well-known distributions not listed in Table E.1 are considered to be members of some form of exponential family. Three such distributions are available in the procedures:

- The multinomial distribution, available in the HPGENSELECT and GENSELECT procedures, is a member of a multivariate extension of the exponential family defined on page 333. This distribution is useful for modeling categorical response data with multiple levels that can be nominal or ordered.

- The zero-inflated negative binomial and zero-inflated Poisson distributions, available in the HPGENSELECT procedure, are each a mixture of two distributions that belong to the family defined on page 333. These distributions are useful for modeling response data in which the frequency of zeros exceeds the mean-variance relationships given in Table E.1.

The means and variances of these distributions do not have simple relationships.

For reasons that are not apparent, the GENSELECT procedure provides options for specifying four response distributions (beta, generalized Poisson, t, and Weibull) that are not members of an exponential family and are highly limited in their implementation. For instance, the option for the beta distribution cannot be used if the endpoints of the distribution are unknown, which is often the case in practice. The option for the Weibull distribution cannot be used with censored data, which are prevalent in reliability analysis.

You can use the RELIABILITY procedure in SAS/STAT to fit regression models to life data that are complete, right censored, left censored, or interval censored. You can specify a Weibull, exponential, extreme value, normal, lognormal, logistic, log-logistic, or generalized gamma distribution. The procedure fits a location-scale model rather than a generalized linear model; it treats the location parameter as a linear function of the explanatory variables.

Appendix F
Spline Methods

Contents

This appendix introduces the types of splines that are mentioned in this book and provides an overview of spline methods that are available in various procedures.

For more detailed introductions to spline methods used in statistical learning, see Wahba (1990), Hastie and Tibshirani (1990, Ch. 2), Wood (2006, Chs. 3 and 4), Hastie, Tibshirani, and Friedman (2009, Ch. 15), and James et al. (2021, Ch. 7). You will also find helpful explanations of splines and spline bases in the chapter about Shared Concepts and Topics in the *SAS/STAT 15.1 User's Guide*, as well as chapters about specific procedures that implement spline techniques.

Basic Terminology

Univariate splines assume a model of the form

$$y_i = f(x_i) + \epsilon_i, \quad i = 1, \ldots, n$$

for a set of n data points, $(x_1, y_1), \ldots, (x_n, y_n)$, where the random errors ϵ_i are independent and identically distributed with $E(\epsilon_i) = 0$. Univariate splines are one of many nonparametric methods for estimating $f(\cdot)$ that also include orthogonal polynomials, k-nearest-neighbors regression, kernel smoothing, local polynomial regression (loess), and wavelets.

A spline of order d is a function $S(x)$ that consists of pieces of polynomials with degree d that are connected smoothly by q knots located at $x_1^* < x_2^* < \cdots < x_q^*$. The function can be expressed as

$$S(x) = \begin{cases} P_0(x) & x < x_1^* \\ P_i(x) & x_i^* \leq x < x_{i+1}^*, \quad i = 1, \ldots, q-1 \\ P_q(x) & x \geq x_q^* \end{cases}$$

where each $P_i(x)$ is a polynomial of degree d. The knots do not need to be located at data points.

A spline of order 1 is a piecewise linear function in which the lines connect at the knots, and a spline of order 2 is a piecewise quadratic curve whose values and slopes coincide at the knots. A spline of order 3 is a piecewise cubic curve whose values, slopes, and curvature coincide at the knots; when plotted, it is so smooth that the knots are usually not visible. In general, a spline of order d has $d-1$ continuous derivatives, provided that at each knot there is a match between the values of adjacent polynomials and the values of their derivatives up to order $d-1$.

The Knot Selection Problem

The selection of the number of knots and their locations can make a large difference in the fit, and it is particularly challenging when the data are limited, noisy, and complex. In theory, q should increase with n for the estimate of $f(\cdot)$ to converge at an optimal rate.

Many knots are preferable when you are building a predictive model with large data. A common approach is to space the knots equally between the extremes of the data.

A small number of knots suffices when n is small and the goal is to characterize the nonlinearity of a variable with broad strokes. For use with natural cubic splines (page 354), Stone (1986) suggested ordering $x_1, x_2, \ldots, x_n$ as $x_{(1)} \leq x_{(2)} \cdots \leq x_{(n)}$ and placing five knots at $x_1^* = x_{(1)}$, $x_2^* = x_{(i_2)}$, $x_3^* = x_{(i_3)}$, $x_4^* = x_{(i_4)}$, and $x_5^* = x_{(n)}$, where i_2, i_3, and i_4 are chosen so that the logits of $1/(n+1)$, $i_2/(n+1)$, $i_3/(n+1)$, $i_4/(n+1)$, and $n/(n+1)$ are equally spaced. Another approach is to place the knots at specified percentiles.

Harrell (2015, p. 28) indicates that $q = 5$ is a good choice when $n \geq 100$ and recommends placing the knots at the percentiles 5, 27.5, 50, 72.5, and 95. This avoids letting outliers influence the placement.

The knot selection problem occurs with regression splines and is avoided by smoothing splines.

Types of Splines

The splines used by the procedures in this book fall into two types: regression splines and smoothing splines. These terms can be confusing because both types of splines are used to construct regression models and both types produce smooth estimates of $f(\cdot)$. Nonetheless, the two types have distinct characteristics:

- Regression splines have much in common with ordinary least squares regression, where the coefficients are estimated by minimizing the sum of squares of the residuals between the observed and predicted values of the response. In both situations, the prediction of the response vector $\mathbf{y} = (y_1, \ldots, y_n)'$ is the projection of $\mathbf{y}$ on the subspace spanned by the predictors (see page 16 in Chapter 2), and this subspace is represented by a set of basis functions. In both situations, the degrees of freedom is fixed.

- Smoothing splines have more in common with ridge regression and the elastic net (see Chapter 6), where the coefficients are estimated by minimizing the sum of squares of the residuals with one or two penalty terms that constrain the sizes of the coefficients. For a smoothing spline, a single penalty term constrains the roughness (wiggliness) of the spline. The penalization parameter can be determined by using cross validation or an information criterion, as illustrated for ridge regression on page 103 and the elastic net on page 108.

The next two sections describe regression splines and smoothing splines in more detail.

Regression Splines

In ordinary least squares regression, the dimension of the space spanned by the predictors $(\mathbf{x}_1, \ldots, \mathbf{x}_p)$ is equal to the maximum number of linearly independent columns in the model matrix $\mathbf{X}$; see "Model Flexibility and Degrees of Freedom" on page 22. Each basis function is a linear combination of the predictors, and the number of basis functions is equal to the dimension of the space. With a set of basis functions, the regression model $\mathbf{y} = \mathbf{X}\boldsymbol{\beta}$ can be expressed in ways that simplify the computation of the ordinary least squares estimator $\hat{\boldsymbol{\beta}}_{\text{OLS}} = (\mathbf{X}'\mathbf{X})^{-1}\mathbf{X}'$.

Similar concepts apply to least squares estimation of the coefficients in a regression spline. Given a spline of order d with q distinct knots, the dimension of the linear space spanned by the polynomial pieces is $q + d + 1$. Consequently, with a set of $q + d + 1$ basis functions $b_j(x)$, the spline function $S(x)$ can be represented as

$$S(x) = \sum_{j=1}^{q+d+1} \beta_j b_j(x)$$

This expression is called a linear basis expansion in x. For a given set of basis functions, it defines a regression model $\mathbf{y} = \mathbf{X}\boldsymbol{\beta}$, where $\boldsymbol{\beta} = (\beta_1, \ldots, \beta_{q+d+1})'$ and the elements of the model matrix are $\mathbf{X}_{ij} = f_j(x_i)$, $i = 1, \ldots, n$, and $j = 1, \ldots, q + d + 1$. The least squares estimator of $\boldsymbol{\beta}$ is

$$\hat{\boldsymbol{\beta}} = \underset{\boldsymbol{\beta}}{\text{argmin}} \, \| \mathbf{y} - \mathbf{X}\boldsymbol{\beta} \|_2^2 = (\mathbf{X}'\mathbf{X})^{-1}\mathbf{X}'\mathbf{y}$$

Since $\hat{\mathbf{y}} = \mathbf{X}(\mathbf{X}'\mathbf{X})^{-1}\mathbf{X}'\mathbf{y}$, the fit is linear in $\mathbf{y}$, and so a regression spline is a linear smoother. As in ordinary least squares regression (see page 322), the fit is a projection of $\mathbf{y}$ on the subspace that is spanned by the columns of $\mathbf{X}$. The degrees of freedom of a regression spline is the dimension of the projection space, which is the number of basis functions.

Choosing an appropriate set of basis functions $b_j(x)$ is important for computing $\hat{\boldsymbol{\beta}}$ efficiently, especially when building a predictive model with large data, where splines are building blocks in computationally intensive methods. Functions with a simple form can aid the interpretation of a spline estimate in an explanatory model, and an obvious choice is the set of power functions $b_j(x) = x^j$, which reduce the spline function to a global polynomial with no knots. However, polynomials with high degrees tend to be numerically unstable, and they can have undulations at unexpected places. Because each data point affects the fit of the entire curve, a good fit at one end of the data can induce a poor fit at the other end.

These problems are avoided by truncated power bases, B-spline bases, and natural cubic spline bases, which are discussed in the next three subsections.

Truncated Power Basis

The truncated power function for a knot x_i^* is defined as

$$t_i(x) = \begin{cases} 0 & x < x_i^* \\ (x - x_i^*)^d & x \geq x_i^* \end{cases}$$

Figure F.1 shows examples of these functions for $d = 1$ and $d = 3$ with a knot at $x = 1$.

Figure F.1 Truncated Power Functions with Knot at $x = 1$

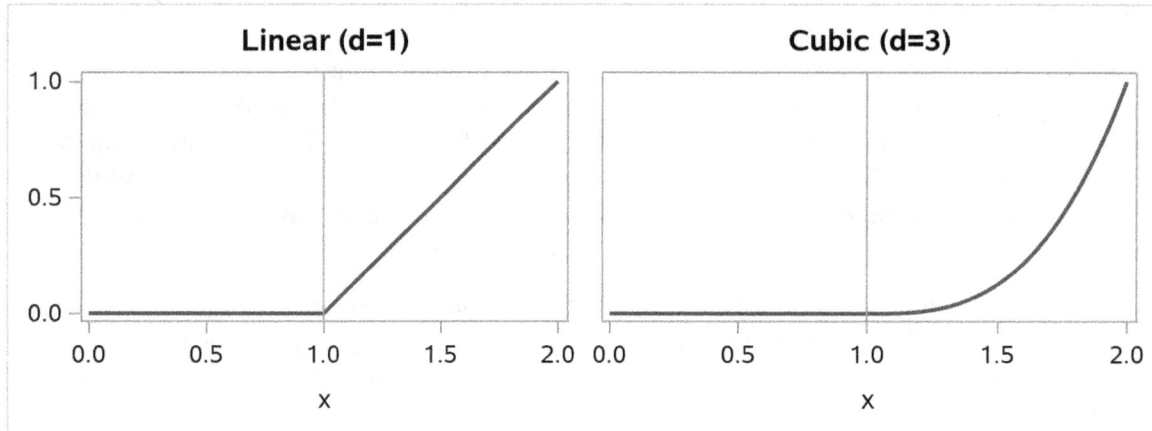

The truncated power basis for a regression spline of order d with q knots consists of truncated power functions $t_i(x)$ for each of the q knots together with the $d + 1$ power functions $1, x, x^2, \ldots, x^d$. This basis is easy to interpret, but it can lead to precision problems in the evaluation of the spline because the functions grow large as x increases. This issue is avoided by the natural cubic spline basis and the B-spline basis.

Natural Cubic Spline Basis

Natural cubic splines are cubic splines that are required to be linear beyond the extreme knots. They are sometimes called restricted cubic splines. The space of unrestricted cubic splines with q knots has dimension $q + 4$. With the restriction that the cubic polynomials be linear polynomials for $x < x_1^*$ and $x > x_q^*$, the dimension of the space is reduced by 4, and so a basis for the natural cubic splines consists of q functions. Hastie, Tibshirani, and Friedman (2009, Sec. 5.2.1) describe a construction of this basis.

Figure F.2 shows a natural cubic spline basis defined on [0, 1] with four equally spaced internal knots at 0.2, 0.4, 0.6, and 0.8. It consists of four basis functions that are all linear beyond the extreme knots at 0.2 and 0.8.

Figure F.2 Natural Cubic Spline Basis with Four Equally Spaced Knots

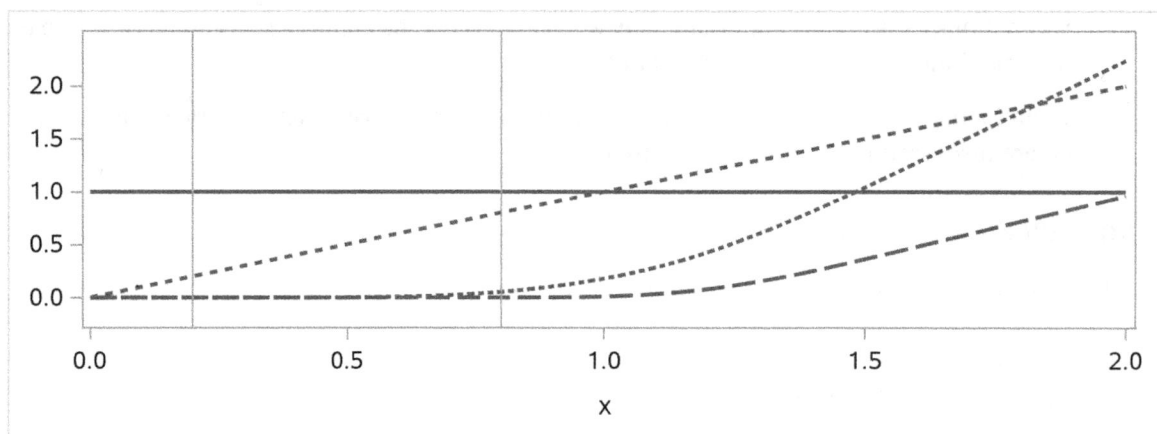

B-Spline Basis

As explained by De Boor (1978, p. 90), the basis functions for a B-spline of order d with q knots can be constructed recursively, starting with the basis functions for $d = 1$:

$$B_{j,1}(x) \equiv \begin{cases} 1 & x_j^* \leq x < x_{j+1}^* \\ 0 & \text{otherwise} \end{cases}$$

$$B_{j,d}(x) = \frac{x - x_j^*}{x_{j+d-1}^* - x_j^*}\Bigg) B_{j,d-1}(x) + \left(1 - \frac{x - x_{j+1}^*}{x_{j+d}^* - x_j^*}\right) B_{j+1,d-1}(x), \quad d > 1$$

Here $B_{j,d}(x)$ depends only on $d + 1$ knots $x_j^*, \ldots, x_{j+d}^*$ that are internal to the data. An additional d knots, called boundary knots, are placed on the left of these knots, and $\max(d, 1)$ boundary knots are placed on their right. The basis functions are nonzero over an interval that spans at most $d + 2$ knots, and so computations with a B-spline basis are numerically stable. Figure F.3 shows a linear B-spline basis defined on $[0, 1]$ with four internal knots at 0.2, 0.4, 0.6, and 0.8. This basis consists of six functions, each of which is nonzero over an interval that spans at most three knots.

Figure F.3 Linear B-Spline Basis with Four Equally Spaced Interior Knots

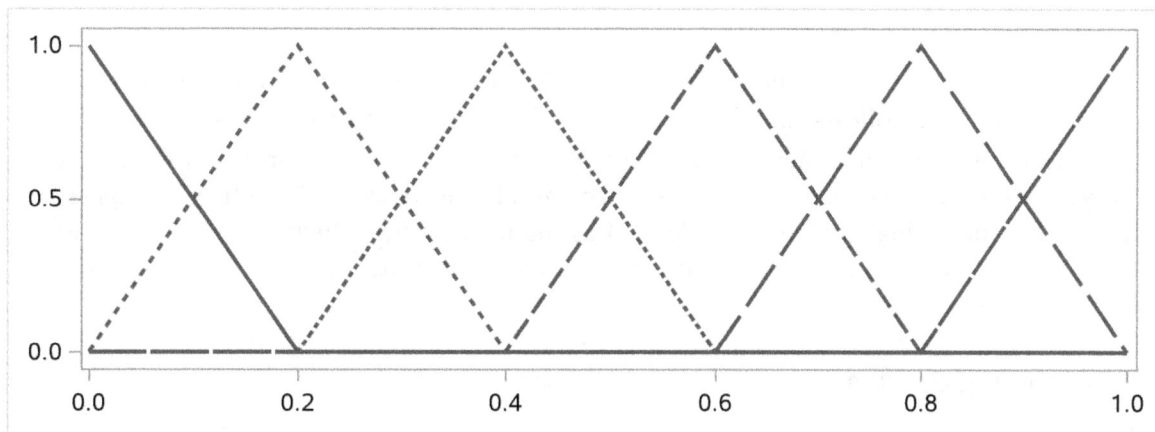

Figure F.4 shows the cubic B-spline basis used to produce the model with seven interior knots for the network activity data in Figure 2.1 on page 12.

Figure F.4 Cubic B-Spline Basis for Network Activity Data

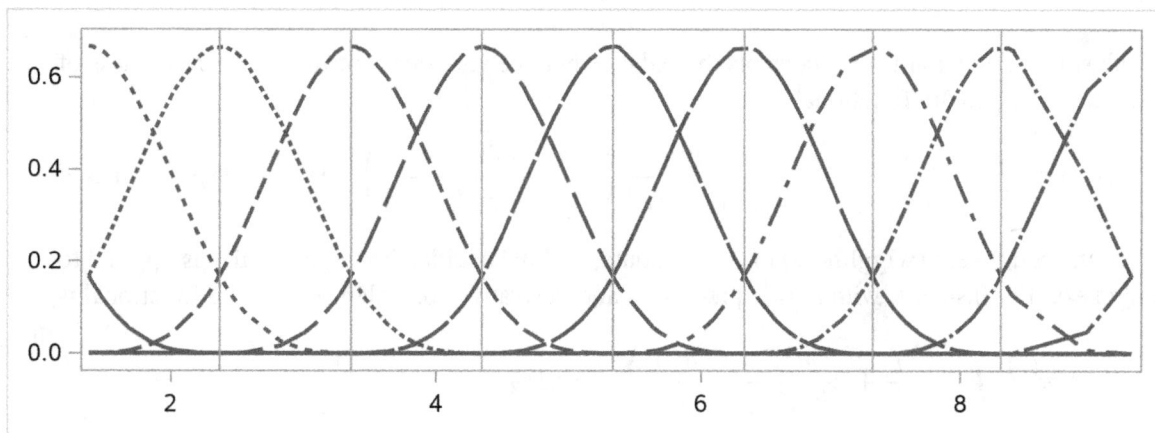

Smoothing Splines

Smoothing splines trade the problem of knot selection for the problem of selecting a regularization parameter that is called the smoothing parameter.

In a 1967 paper that is now a classic, Christian Reinsch showed that among all functions $f(x)$ with two continuous derivatives, a natural cubic spline with knots at the unique values of $x_1, x_2, \ldots, x_n$ minimizes the penalized sum of squares

$$\sum_{i=1}^{n} \{y_i - f(x_i)\}^2 + \lambda \int \{f''(t)\}^2 dt \quad \lambda \geq 0$$

where λ is called the smoothing parameter. If λ is equal to 0, the spline interpolates the data. As λ increases, it controls the balance between goodness of fit and roughness, and the penalty term causes the coefficients of the spline to shrink toward those of a least squares fit (Hastie, Tibshirani, and Friedman 2009, Sec. 5.4).

Using the basis for a natural cubic spline (see page 354), a smoothing spline can be expressed as $f(x) = \sum_{j=1}^{q} \beta_j b_j(x)$, and the minimization criterion can be expressed as

$$(\mathbf{y} - \mathbf{N}\boldsymbol{\beta})'(\mathbf{y} - \mathbf{N}\boldsymbol{\beta}) + \lambda \boldsymbol{\beta}' \boldsymbol{\Omega}_q \boldsymbol{\beta}$$

where $\mathbf{N}$ is an $n \times q$ matrix with elements $\mathbf{N}_{ij} = b_j(x_i)$ and $\boldsymbol{\Omega}_q$ is a $q \times q$ matrix with elements $\boldsymbol{\Omega}_{jk} = \int b_j''(t) b_k''(t)$. It follows that $\hat{\boldsymbol{\beta}} = (\mathbf{N}'\mathbf{N} + \lambda \boldsymbol{\Omega}_q)^{-1} \mathbf{N}'\mathbf{y}$, which is the estimator for a generalized form of ridge regression. Since $\hat{\mathbf{y}} = \mathbf{N}(\mathbf{N}'\mathbf{N} + \lambda \boldsymbol{\Omega}_q)^{-1} \mathbf{N}'\mathbf{y}$ can be expressed as $\hat{\mathbf{y}} = \mathbf{S}_\lambda \mathbf{y}$, a smoothing spline—like a regression spline—is a linear smoother. The effective degrees of freedom for a smoothing spline can be defined as the trace of $\mathbf{S}_\lambda$, which provides a way to parameterize the spline and compare it with other smoothing methods (Hastie, Tibshirani, and Friedman 2009, p. 154).

Thin-Plate Smoothing Splines

Thin-plate smoothing splines (Duchon 1976, 1977; Wahba 1990) provide a way to estimate a smooth function $f(x_1, \ldots, x_d)$ of d predictors from a set of n observations $(\mathbf{x}_1, y_1), \ldots, (\mathbf{x}_n, y_n)$, where the vector $\mathbf{x}_i$ has a component for each predictor. Thin-plate smoothing splines are constructed by finding the estimate $\hat{f}$ that minimizes the penalized least squares function:

$$\sum_{i=1}^{n} (y_i - f(\mathbf{x}_i))^2 + \lambda J_{m,d}(f)$$

where the smoothing parameter λ controls the balance between goodness of fit and the roughness of the estimate. The penalty functional

$$J_{m,d}(f) \equiv \int \cdots \int_{\mathcal{R}^d} \sum_{\nu_1 + \cdots + \nu_d = m} \frac{m!}{\nu_1! \cdots \nu_d!} \left(\frac{\partial^m f}{\partial x_1^{\nu_1} \cdots \partial x_d^{\nu_d}} \right)^2 dx_1 \cdots dx_d, \quad 2m > d$$

measures the roughness (wiggliness) of the estimate, and m specifies how the penalty is applied to the roughness. For instance, with $d = 2$ predictors and derivatives of order $m = 2$, the functional is

$$J_{2,2}(f) \equiv \int \int \left(\frac{\partial^2 f}{\partial x_1^2} + 2\frac{\partial^2 f}{\partial x_1 \partial x_2} + \frac{\partial^2 f}{\partial x_2^2} \right)^2 dx_1 dx_2$$

Derivatives whose order is less than m are not penalized. When λ is zero, the estimate interpolates the data. For positive values of λ, the minimizing function has the form

$$f_\lambda(\mathbf{x}) = \sum_{i=1}^{n} \delta_i \, \eta_{m,d}(\|\mathbf{x} - \mathbf{x}_i\|) + \sum_{j=1}^{M} \alpha_j \phi_j(\mathbf{x})$$

where $\boldsymbol{\delta} = (\delta_1, \ldots, \delta_n)'$ and $\boldsymbol{\alpha} = (\alpha_1, \ldots, \alpha_M)'$ are parameter vectors to be estimated and where the functions $\phi_j(\mathbf{x})$ are linearly independent polynomials that span the vector space of polynomials in $\mathcal{R}^d$ that are of degree less than m. Because $J_{m,d}(f) = 0$ for polynomials in this space, they are not penalized. The number of such polynomials is $M = \binom{m+d-1}{d}$.

The function $\eta_{m,d}$ models local nonlinearity that is not expressed by the polynomials; it is a smoothly increasing function of the Euclidean distance between any $\mathbf{x}$ value and an observed $\mathbf{x}_i$ value:

$$\eta_{m,d}(r) = \begin{cases} \dfrac{(-1)^{m+1+d/2}}{2^{2m-1}\pi^{d/2}(m-1)!(m-d/2)!} r^{2m-d} \log(r) & \text{if } d \text{ is even} \\[2em] \dfrac{\Gamma(d/2-m)}{2^{2m}\pi^{d/2}(m-1)!} r^{2m-d} & \text{if } d \text{ is odd} \end{cases}$$

The coefficients δ_i must satisfy the constraint $\mathbf{T}'\boldsymbol{\delta} = \mathbf{0}$. In other words, $\boldsymbol{\delta}$ must be in the null space of $\mathbf{T}'$, whereas $\boldsymbol{\alpha}$ is in the range space of $\mathbf{T}$.[†]

The least squares estimates of $\boldsymbol{\alpha} = (\alpha_1, \ldots, \alpha_M)'$ and $\boldsymbol{\delta} = (\delta_1, \ldots, \delta_n)'$ can be computed by solving the minimization problem

$$\min_{\boldsymbol{\delta}, \boldsymbol{\alpha}} \|\mathbf{y} - \mathbf{T}\boldsymbol{\alpha} - \mathbf{E}\boldsymbol{\delta}\|^2 + \lambda \boldsymbol{\delta}'\mathbf{E}\boldsymbol{\delta} \quad \text{subject to } \mathbf{T}'\boldsymbol{\delta} = \mathbf{0}$$

where the elements of the $n \times n$ penalty matrix $\mathbf{E}$ are $\mathbf{E}_{ij} = \eta_{m,d}(\|\mathbf{x}_i - \mathbf{x}_j\|)$.

Wood (2006, p. 156) points out that thin-plate smoothing splines are attractive in several ways. They have built-in knot positions and basis functions, they apply to any number of predictor variables, and they provide flexibility in the measure of roughness as well as a parameter for balancing between data fitting and smoothness. A major drawback is the high cost of estimating a large number of unknown parameters, which (except for the case $d = 1$) involves $O(n^3)$ operations.

Low-Rank Thin-Plate Regression Splines

Low-rank thin-plate regression splines, proposed by Wood (2003), reduce the computational cost of thin-plate smoothing splines by replacing the $n \times n$ penalty matrix $\mathbf{E}$ with a low-rank approximation. The idea is to change and truncate the basis for the $\boldsymbol{\delta}$ parameter space with minimal change to the model fit.

Because $\mathbf{E}$ is symmetric and nonnegative definite, it can be represented as $\mathbf{E} = \mathbf{V}\mathbf{D}\mathbf{V}'$, where $\mathbf{D}$ is the diagonal matrix of eigenvalues d_i of $\mathbf{E}$, and $\mathbf{V}$ is the matrix of eigenvectors that correspond to the eigenvalues (see the explanation of eigenvalue decomposition on page 90).

[†]The set of $n \times 1$ vectors that are linear combinations of the columns of an $n \times p$ matrix $\mathbf{A}$ is called the range space of $\mathbf{A}$. The set of all $m \times 1$ vectors that are orthogonal to vectors in the range space is called the null space of $\mathbf{A}'$. Any $n \times 1$ vector $\mathbf{v} \neq \mathbf{0}$ can be expressed as $\mathbf{v} = \mathbf{v}_R + \mathbf{v}_N$, where $\mathbf{v}_R$ in the range space of $\mathbf{A}$, $\mathbf{v}_N$ is in the null space of $\mathbf{A}'$, and $\mathbf{v}_R'\mathbf{v}_N = 0$.

The low-rank approximation of $\mathbf{E}$ is the $n \times k$ matrix $\tilde{\mathbf{E}}_k = \mathbf{V}_k \mathbf{D}_k \mathbf{V}_k'$, where $\mathbf{D}_k$ is a diagonal matrix that contains the k most extreme eigenvalues in descending order of their absolute values and the columns of $\mathbf{V}_k$ are the eigenvectors that correspond to the eigenvalues in $\mathbf{D}_k$.

Since the columns of $\mathbf{V}_k$ are an orthogonal basis for the n-dimensional space of $\delta_1, \ldots, \delta_n$, there is a $k \times 1$ vector $\boldsymbol{\delta}_k$ such that $\boldsymbol{\delta} = \mathbf{V}_k \boldsymbol{\delta}_k$. By substituting $\tilde{\mathbf{E}}_k$ for $\mathbf{E}$ and noting that $\tilde{\mathbf{E}}_k \boldsymbol{\delta} = \mathbf{V}_k \mathbf{D} \mathbf{V}_k' \boldsymbol{\delta} = \mathbf{V}_k \mathbf{D} \mathbf{V}_k' \mathbf{V}_k \boldsymbol{\delta}_k = \mathbf{V}_k \mathbf{D} \boldsymbol{\delta}_k$, the minimization problem on page 357 becomes

$$\operatorname*{argmin}_{\boldsymbol{\delta}_k, \boldsymbol{\alpha}} \| \mathbf{y} - \mathbf{T}\theta - \mathbf{V}_k \mathbf{D}_k \boldsymbol{\delta}_k \|^2 + \lambda \boldsymbol{\delta}_k' \mathbf{D}_k \boldsymbol{\delta}_k \quad \text{subject to } \mathbf{T}' \mathbf{V}_k \boldsymbol{\delta}_k = 0$$

Wood (2003, Sec. 2.1) justified this substitution by showing that the basis change and truncation used to obtain $\tilde{\mathbf{E}}_k$ minimize changes to the model fit and the penalty.

By obtaining an orthogonal column basis $\mathbf{Z}_k$ such that $\mathbf{T}' \mathbf{V}_k \mathbf{Z}_k = 0$ and by representing $\boldsymbol{\delta}_k$ as $\mathbf{Z}_k \tilde{\boldsymbol{\delta}}$, the constrained minimization problem can be recast as an unconstrained problem:

$$\operatorname*{argmin}_{\tilde{\boldsymbol{\delta}}, \boldsymbol{\alpha}} \| \mathbf{y} - \mathbf{T}\theta - \mathbf{V}_k \mathbf{D}_k \mathbf{Z} \tilde{\boldsymbol{\delta}} \|^2 + \lambda \tilde{\boldsymbol{\delta}}' \mathbf{Z}' \mathbf{D}_k \mathbf{Z} \tilde{\boldsymbol{\delta}}$$

The cost of solving this problem is only $O(k^3)$, which opens the door for using low-rank thin-plate regression splines in generalized additive models and other computationally intensive applications involving large data.

Penalized B-Splines

Smoothing splines can be constructed with B-splines as the basis functions, but the penalty term on page 356 is not easy to evaluate. During the 1990s, Paul Eilers and Brian Marx popularized B-splines penalized by second order (or higher order) differences of the coefficients β_j for adjacent B-splines. This construction makes it feasible to use a rich B-spline basis without being overly concerned about the number or placement of splines and focus instead on controlling the smoothness of the spline.

Given a set of n data points, $(x_1, y_1), (x_2, y_2), \ldots, (x_n, y_n)$, the optimization problem for computing the spline coefficients is

$$\min_{\beta_1, \ldots, \beta_m} \left\{ \sum_{i=1}^{n} \left[(y_i - \sum_{j=1}^{m} \beta_j B_j(x_i) \right]^2 + \lambda \sum_{j=k+1}^{m} \left(\Delta^k \beta_j \right)^2 \right\}, \quad \lambda > 0$$

where m is the number of B-splines, Δ is the finite difference operator ($\Delta\beta_j \equiv \beta_j - \beta_{j-1}$), k is the difference order, and the parameter λ controls the smoothness. This formulation reduces the dimension of the problem from the number of observations (the dimension for smoothing splines) to the number of B-splines. For $k = 2$, the second summation is the analogue of $\int \{f''(t)\}^2 dt$ in the objective function for smoothing splines given on page 356.

Eilers and Marx (1996) showed that this combination of B-splines and difference penalties, which they called P-splines, has many attractive properties. P-splines avoid boundary effects, they extend to generalized linear models, and as λ becomes large, the fit approaches a polynomial of degree $k - 1$ if the degree of the B-splines is at least k. The solution to the minimization problem is obtained by solving the linear system $\mathbf{N}' \mathbf{y} = (\mathbf{N}' \mathbf{N} + \lambda \mathbf{D}_k' \mathbf{D}_k) \boldsymbol{\beta}$, where $\mathbf{D}_k$ is the matrix representation of the operator Δ_k and the finite difference coefficients are arranged along the diagonal of Δ_k. Typically, λ is obtained by cross validation.

Spline Functionality in Procedures

This section provides a tour of spline functionality available in various procedures.

Procedures with the EFFECT Statement

The EFFECT statement, which is available in a number of procedures, enables you to define spline effects, polynomial effects, and other model effects represented by special collections of columns in the design matrix. The effects you specify with the EFFECT statement are referred to as *constructed effects* to distinguish them from model effects formed from continuous or classification variables, which you specify with the MODEL and CLASS statements. The EFFECT statement extends the syntax of the MODEL and CLASS statements. You can use it to specify the effects in a fitted model or to specify the candidate effects in model selection.

In SAS 9, the EFFECT statement is available in the GLMSELECT and QUANTSELECT procedures for model building, which are discussed in Chapter 5 and Chapter 8 of this book. The statement is also available in the following procedures for statistical analysis: GLIMMIX, HPMIXED, LOGISTIC, ORTHOREG, PHREG, PLS, QUANTLIFE, QUANTREG, ROBUSTREG, SURVEYLOGISTIC, and SURVEYREG.

In SAS Viya, the EFFECT statement is available in the GENSELECT, LOGSELECT, PHSELECT, PLSMOD, QTRSELECT, and REGSELECT procedures, which are discussed in this book. The statement is also available in the MODELMATRIX and LMIXED procedures.

Example: Predicting Network Activity

The following statements use the EFFECT statement in the GLMSELECT procedure to fit a B-spline model with seven knots to the network activity data introduced on page 12. The first step creates a data set used for scoring and plotting:

```
data ScorePlot;
   do Time = 1.2 to 9.0 by 0.1; output; end;
run;

proc glmselect data=Network;
   effect Spline7 = spline(Time / basis=bspline details degree=3
                                   knotmethod=equal(7));
   model Activity = Spline7 / selection=none;
   score data=ScorePlot out=ScoreSpline7 pred=PredSpline7;
run;
```

The EFFECT statement defines a constructed effect named Spline7. The SPLINE option specifies a regression spline effect whose columns are the univariate spline expansions of the variables listed in the parentheses, which must be continuous. You can request a B-spline basis or a truncated power function basis with the BASIS= option, and you specify the degree of the spline with the DEGREE= option. The KNOTMETHOD= option specifies how to construct the k knots. Here, seven equally spaced knots are positioned between the extremes of the data.

The analysis of variance table in Output F.1 shows that the model has 10 degrees of freedom.

Output F.1 Analysis of Variance Table

Least Squares Model (No Selection)

Source	DF	Sum of Squares	Mean Square	F Value	Pr > F
Analysis of Variance					
Model	10	110.24313	11.02431	48.87	<.0001
Error	97	21.88307	0.22560		
Corrected Total	107	132.12620			

The knot information table in Output F.2 lists the locations of the seven interior knots and six boundary knots for the B-spline basis functions that were constructed; the knot details table (requested with the DETAILS option) shows their supports. The basis functions are plotted in Figure F.4.

Output F.2 Knot Placements and Supports

Knots for Spline Effect Spline7

Knot Number	Boundary	Time
1	*	-0.60614
2	*	0.38536
3	*	1.37686
4		2.36836
5		3.35986
6		4.35137
7		5.34287
8		6.33437
9		7.32587
10		8.31737
11	*	9.30887
12	*	10.30037
13	*	11.29187

Basis Details for Spline Effect Spline7

Column	Support		Support Knots
1	-0.60614	2.36836	1-4
2	-0.60614	3.35986	1-5
3	0.38536	4.35137	2-6
4	1.37686	5.34287	3-7
5	2.36836	6.33437	4-8
6	3.35986	7.32587	5-9
7	4.35137	8.31737	6-10
8	5.34287	9.30887	7-11
9	6.33437	10.30037	8-12
10	7.32587	11.29187	9-13
11	8.31737	11.29187	10-13

The following statements create the plot of the spline model that is shown in Output F.3:

```
proc sort data=Network;        by Time;  run;
proc sort data=ScoreSpline7;  by Time;  run;

data Combine;
   merge Network ScoreSpline7; by Time;
run;

title "Regression Model for Network Activity";
proc sgplot data=Combine;
   scatter x=Time y=Activity    / markerattrs=(symbol=circle color=blue);
   series  x=Time y=PredSpline7 / lineattrs=(thickness=2px)
                                  legendlabel="B-Spline with 7 Knots"
                                  name="Spline7";
   keylegend "Spline7"          / title="Regression Model"
                                  linelength=0.7cm
                                  location=inside across=1;
   inset "108 Observations in Training Data" / position=bottomright border;
   label Time     = "Time"
         Activity = "Activity Measurement";
run;
```

Output F.3 Spline Fit for Network Activity Data

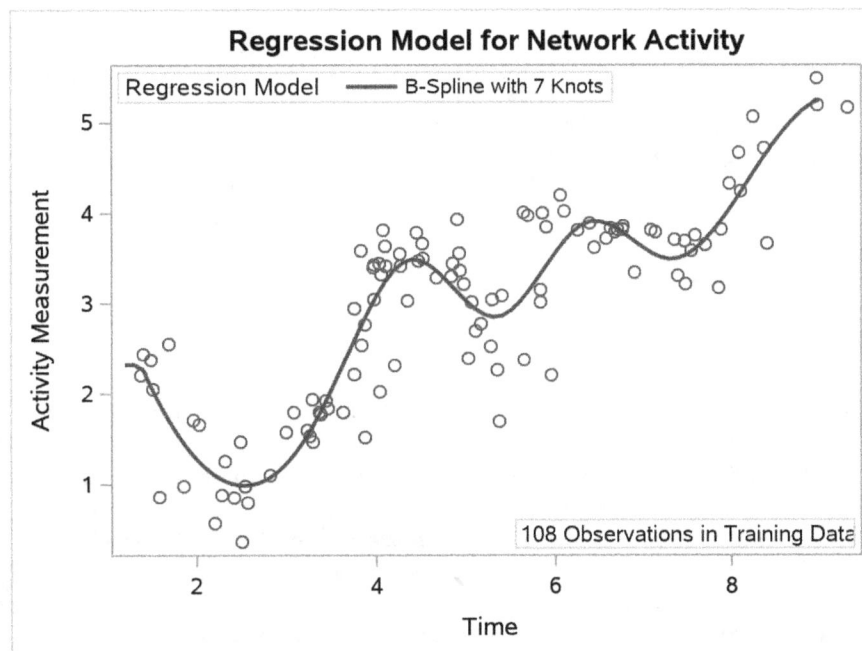

Example: Predicting the Close Rate for Retail Stores

This example revisits the one on page 56, which uses the GLMSELECT procedure to build a general linear model for close rate using the data set Stores. Here, the candidate variables X2 and X4 are represented with spline effects:

```
proc glmselect data=Stores;
   class Region(param=reference ref='Midwest' split)
         Training(param=reference ref='None');
   effect SplineX2 = spline(X2 / basis=bspline details degree=3
                                 knotmethod=equal(10));
   effect SplineX4 = spline(X4 / basis=bspline details degree=3
                                 knotmethod=equal(10));
   model CloseRate = Region Training X1 SplineX2 X3 SplineX4 X5-X20 L1-L6 P1-P6 /
      selection=forward(choose=sbc select=sbc stop=sbc);
run;
```

Output F.4 shows that both spline effects were selected. This is to be expected since X2 and X4 were originally selected (see Output 5.6 on page 60).

Output F.4 Selected Effects

Selected Model

Effects: Intercept Region_South SplineX2 SplineX4 L1 L3 L4 L5 L6 P1 P2 P3 P4 P5 P6

The parameter estimates for the spline effects are not shown here because they are not interpretable. The next statements create a plot of the spline effect for X2, which is shown in Output F.5:

```
/* Step 1: Refit selected model without SplineX2 and save residuals */
data Stores; set Stores; Region_South = ( Region='South' ); run;
proc glmselect data=Stores;
   class Region_South(param=reference ref='0')
         Training(param=reference ref='None');
   effect SplineX4 = spline(X4 / basis=bspline details degree=3
                                 knotmethod=equal(10));
   model CloseRate = Region_South Training SplineX4 L1 L3 L4 L5 L6 P1-P6 /
      selection=none;
   output out=PredStores residual=Residual;
run;


/* Step 2: Create grid of X2 values */
data ScorePlot; do X2 = -0.5 to 0.5 by 0.01; output; end; run;


/* Step 3: Fit residuals with SplineX2 and save predicted values */
proc glmselect data=PredStores;
   effect SplineX2 = spline(X2 / basis=bspline details degree=3
                                 knotmethod=equal(10));
   model Residual = SplineX2;
   score data=ScorePlot out=ScoreSpline pred=PredSpline;
run;


/* Step 4: Plot predicted values for grid */
proc sgplot data=ScoreSpline;
   series x=X2 y=PredSpline/ lineattrs=(thickness=2px);
   xaxis grid;
   inset "500 Stores in Training Data" / position=bottomright border;
   label PredSpline = "Spline Effect of X2";
run;
```

Output F.5 Spline Component for X2

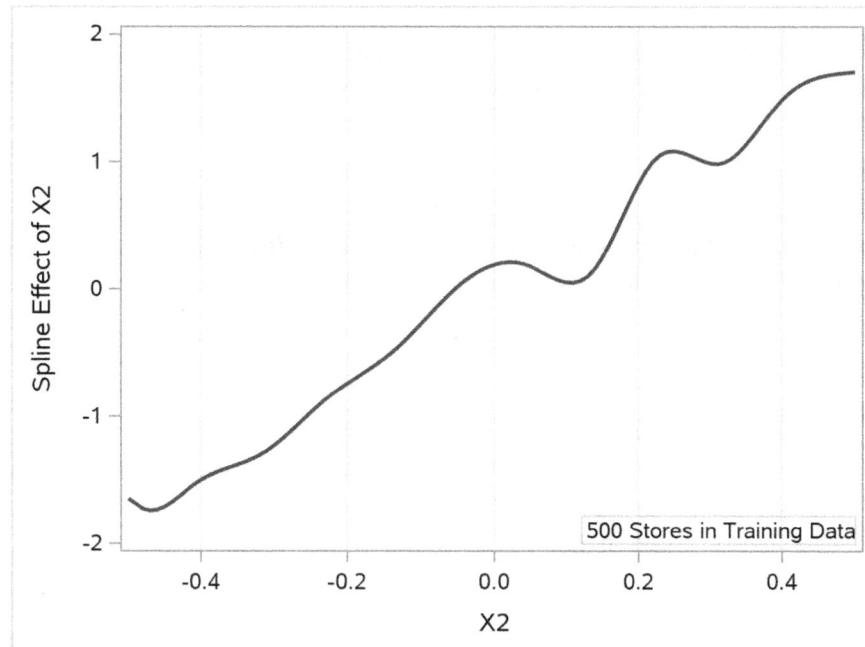

The plot reveals that the effect of X2 on close rate is linear with two undulations near X2=0.1 and X2=0.3. If these are actual effects, incorporating the spline term in the model could make a slight improvement in its predictive accuracy.

The TRANSREG Procedure

The TRANSREG procedure fits general linear models in which continuous variables—including the response variable—can be transformed with splines or with other methods, such as Box–Cox transformations.

You can specify spline transformations directly, or you can request optimal transformations that are computed iteratively by alternating between least squares estimation of the model parameters given the current scoring of the data and least squares estimation of the scoring parameters given the current set of model parameters (Young 1981).[†]

The MODEL statement provides many options for transforming variables. Penalized B-splines and smoothing splines are available for specified transformations, and B-splines and monotonic B-splines are available for optimal transformations. For penalized splines, there are options for determining the smoothing parameter λ by using generalized cross validation and information criteria.

[†]For regression models with spline transformations, the TRANSREG procedure produces results that are somewhat comparable to those obtained with the alternating conditional expectation (ACE) method of Breiman and Friedman (1985). However, ACE is based on a fundamentally different approach. Hastie and Tibshirani (1990, Ch. 7) explain the method, noting that it operates on the joint distribution of the response and the predictors and is more of a method for correlation than for regression.

The TPSPLINE Procedure

The TPSPLINE procedure fits nonparametric regression models by using thin-plate smoothing splines to estimate the response surface and by using penalized least squares to estimate the regression parameters. The smoothing parameter is determined by generalized cross validation.

Penalized least squares is computationally intensive. Performance degrades with the number of unique design points, which determines the number of parameters to be estimated. Furthermore, the number of variables must be kept small to avoid the curse of dimensionality (see page 366). For large data, generalized additive models offer a practical alternative.

Procedures for Generalized Additive Models

As explained in Chapter 11, the GAM, GAMPL, and GAMMOD procedures fit generalized additive models, and the GAMSELECT procedure builds generalized additive models. These procedures use different types of splines, as listed in Table F.1.

Table F.1 Splines for Generalized Additive Models

Procedure	Spline Used to Create Basis Expansions
GAM	Cubic smoothing splines for one variable, thin-plate smoothing splines for two variables
GAMPL	Thin-plate regression splines for multiple variables
GAMMOD	Thin-plate regression splines for multiple variables
GAMSELECT	Penalized B-splines and natural cubic splines

The ADAPTIVEREG Procedure

The ADAPTIVEREG procedure, discussed in Chapter 14, fits multivariate adaptive regression splines using the approach introduced by Friedman (1991), which combines regression splines and model selection methods. Continuous predictors are transformed with linear truncated power splines (see Figure F.1 on page 354).

The SGPLOT and SGPANEL Procedures

The SGPLOT procedure creates many kinds of plots that can be overlaid on a single set of axes. You can use the PBSPLINE statement to display a model fit constructed with penalized B-splines. This statement is also available in the SGPANEL procedure, which creates plots arranged in panels according to the values of one or more classification variables.

The PBSPLINE statement should not be confused with the SPLINE statement, which is available in both procedures and creates a series plot in which the points are interpolated with a quadratic Bézier spline.

Appendix G
Algorithms for Generalized Additive Models

Contents

This appendix describes algorithms used by the GAM, GAMPL, GAMMOD, and GAMSELECT procedures to fit or build generalized additive models. For in-depth explanations, see the books by Hastie and Tibshirani (1990), Hastie et al. (2009), and Wood (2006, 2017).

Additive Models

The general form of the unknown regression surface for p predictors is

$$E[y|x_1, x_2, \ldots, x_p] = f(x_1, x_2, \ldots, x_p)$$

Additive models assume that

$$E[y|x_1, x_2, \ldots, x_p] = \mu + f_1(x_1) + f_2(x_2) + \cdots + f_p(x_p)$$

where the univariate functions $f_j(x_j)$ are typically smooth functions estimated with one-dimensional smoothers. Additive models can only approximate the regression surface but are useful as first-order approximations in exploratory analysis and enable the roles of the predictors to be examined independently with plots of the estimated functions (Hastie and Tibshirani 1990, Sec. 4.3).

The assumption of additivity in the predictor effects is crucial because local smoothing methods—which include kernel smoothers, local polynomial regression (loess), and splines—begin to lose their effectiveness when used to fit data with more than one or two dimensions.

As p increases, the data become sparse in such a way that the observations closest to a given point are no longer local; local neighborhoods become empty because the data are near the boundary of the data space. The sample size n needed for estimation with reasonably small variances grows exponentially with p, and the computational expense of the methods grows accordingly. These problems manifest the curse of dimensionality (Hastie, Tibshirani, and Friedman 2009, Sec. 2.5).

Additive models circumvent the curse by restricting $f_1(\cdot), \ldots, f_p(\cdot)$ to be functions of a single variable. Functions that represent second-order effects and interactions can be included, but the curse of dimensionality cannot be avoided if functions representing many higher order effects are included.

The Backfitting Algorithm for Additive Models

The fundamental and best known method for estimating the functions $f_j(\cdot)$ in an additive model is the backfitting algorithm, which exploits additivity by solving the following equations:

$$f_j(x_j) = E[y - \beta_0 - \sum_{k \neq j} f_k(x_k) \mid x_j], \quad j = 1, \ldots, p$$

The algorithm initializes with the assignments $\hat{\beta}_0 = \frac{1}{n} \sum_{i=1}^{n} y_i$ and $\hat{f}_j(\cdot) \equiv 0, j = 1, \ldots, p$. It then proceeds through the predictor functions one at a time, making the following replacements:

$$\hat{f}_j(\cdot) \quad S_j \left\{ \left(y_i - \hat{\beta}_0 - \sum_{k \neq j} \hat{f}_k(x_{ik}), x_{ij} \right) : i = 1, \ldots, n \right\}$$

Here $S_j\{(y_i, x_{ij}) : i = 1, \ldots, n\}$ denotes the application of a scatterplot smoothing operator to the points inside the braces. For example, this can be a smoothing spline (see page 356 in Appendix F). The cycle is repeated until the estimates $\hat{f}_1(\cdot), \ldots, \hat{f}_p(\cdot)$ change less than a specified convergence criterion.

The backfitting algorithm accommodates linear predictors $f_j(x_j) = \beta_j x_j$ by using linear regression smoothers, and it accommodates categorical predictors by fitting their levels with histogram smoothers. The backfitting algorithm can also accommodate functions of two or more variables by applying higher-dimensional smoothers such as bivariate thin-plate smoothing splines.

Local Scoring for Generalized Additive Models

Local scoring and other methods for fitting generalized additive models are considerably more complex than the backfitting method for additive models because they incorporate a link function and a response distribution while constructing smooth estimates of the functions $\hat{f}_j(\cdot)$ with an appropriate degree of smoothness. Essentially, local scoring adds a wrapper or outer loop to the backfitting algorithm.

The local scoring algorithm extends the iteratively weighted least squares (IWLS) algorithm for fitting a generalized linear model, which was introduced by Nelder and Wedderburn (1972). The next section explains the IWLS algorithm as a preliminary step toward explaining local scoring.

The IWLS Algorithm for Generalized Linear Models

The IWLS algorithm starts with an initial estimate of the parameter vector $\boldsymbol{\beta} = (\beta_0, \beta_1, \ldots, \beta_p)'$ for a generalized linear model. Let $\hat{\boldsymbol{\beta}}_{(t)}$ denote the estimate at step t, let $\hat{\boldsymbol{\eta}}_{(t)} = \mathbf{X}\hat{\boldsymbol{\beta}}_{(t)}$ denote the vector of linear predictors $\eta_{(t)i}, i = 1, \ldots, n$, and let $\hat{\boldsymbol{\mu}}_{(t)}$ denote the vector of predicted means $\hat{\mu}_{(t)i}$, which are computed with the inverse link function $\mu_{(t)i} = g^{-1}(\eta_{(t)i})$. The adjusted dependent variable is defined as the vector $\mathbf{z}_{(t)}$ whose ith component is

$$z_{(t)i} = \hat{\eta}_{(t)i} + (y_i - \hat{\mu}_{(t)i}) \left(\frac{d\eta}{d\mu} \right) \Bigg|_{\mu = \hat{\mu}_{(t)i}}, \quad i = 1, \ldots, n$$

Here the vertical bar indicates that the derivative is evaluated at $\hat{\mu}_{(t)i}$. This variable is a linearized version of the link function applied to the response variable; it serves as the dependent variable in a weighted regression used to compute the estimate of $\boldsymbol{\beta}$ at step $t + 1$. The weight matrix $\mathbf{W}_t$ is diagonal with elements $w_{(t)i}$ along the diagonal; these are defined by their inverses

$$w_{(t)i}^{-1} = \left(\frac{d\eta}{d\mu} \right)^2 \Bigg|_{\mu = \hat{\mu}_{(t)i}} V(\hat{\mu}_{(t)i}), \quad i = 1, \ldots, n$$

where $V(\cdot)$ is the variance function that corresponds to the distribution (see Table 10.2 on page 194). At step $t + 1$, the estimate

$$\hat{\boldsymbol{\beta}}_{(t+1)} = (\mathbf{X}'\mathbf{W}_t\mathbf{X})^{-1}\mathbf{X}'\mathbf{W}_t\mathbf{z}_{(t)}$$

is used to form $\hat{\boldsymbol{\eta}}_{(t+1)}$ and a new weight matrix W_{t+1}. This process is repeated until the estimates of $\boldsymbol{\beta}$ converge to the maximum likelihood estimate.

You might wonder why the usual parametric form of the response distribution does not enter the IWLS algorithm. As explained in Appendix E, distributions in the exponential family share a canonical form that involves only their means and variances, and so it is these parameters—not the conventional parameters—that matter for maximum likelihood estimation. The variance of a distribution in the exponential family is equal to $\phi V(\mu)$, where ϕ is called the dispersion parameter and $V(\mu)$ is called the variance function. For instance, this function is $V(\mu) = \mu^2$ for a gamma distribution and $V(\mu) = \mu$ for a Poisson distribution. This function enters the algorithm in the construction of $\mathbf{W}_t$.

The IWLS algorithm can be implemented using only routines for weighted least squares regression, which contributed to the early success of generalized linear models. It is viewed as a version of the Newton–Raphson algorithm[†] for computing the maximum likelihood estimate of $\boldsymbol{\beta}$ by taking the derivative of the log-likelihood function $\mathcal{L}(\boldsymbol{\beta}; \mathbf{y})$ with respect to $\boldsymbol{\beta}$ and computing the maximum likelihood estimate $\hat{\boldsymbol{\beta}}_{\text{MLE}}$ for which the derivative is zero. The derivative is referred to as the score function, as explained in "The Likelihood Equations" on page 326. This approach involves the second derivative and a related quantity known as expected Fisher information. For this reason, the IWLS algorithm resembles the Fisher scoring algorithm, which is explained further on page 327.

In summary, the IWLS algorithm consists of a single loop within which the adjusted dependent variable and the weight matrix are recomputed at each step.

[†]By default, the HPLOGISTIC, LOGSELECT, HPGENSELECT, and GENSELECT procedures apply a different version of the Newton–Raphson algorithm that uses a ridged Hessian matrix and observed Fisher information.

The Local Scoring Algorithm for Generalized Additive Models

The name "local scoring algorithm" refers to the way in which the algorithm generalizes Fisher scoring by applying local smoothing (Hastie and Tibshirani 1990, Sec. 6.3). The algorithm begins with the assignments $\hat{\beta}_{(1)0} = \frac{1}{n} \sum_{i=1}^{n} y_i$ and $\hat{f}_{(1)j}(\cdot) \equiv 0, j = 1, \ldots, p$. It then proceeds in two loops that are nested.

The Outer and Inner Loops

The outer loop resembles the loop of the IWLS algorithm; it constructs an adjusted response variable $\mathbf{z}_{(t)}$, also referred to as a pseudo-response variable, with components

$$z_{(t)i} = \hat{\eta}_{(t)i} + (y_i - \hat{\mu}_{(t)i}) \left(\frac{d\eta}{d\mu} \right)\Bigg|_{\mu = \hat{\mu}_{(t)i}}, \quad i = 1, \ldots, n$$

where

$$\hat{\eta}_{(t)i} = \beta_{(t)0} + \sum_{j=1}^{p} f_{(t)j}(x_{ij})$$

and $\hat{\mu}_{(t)i} = g^{-1}(\hat{\eta}_{(t)i})$. Then the inverse weights are computed:

$$w_{(t)i}^{-1} = \left(\frac{d\eta}{d\mu} \right)^2 \Bigg|_{\mu = \hat{\mu}_{(t)i}} V(\hat{\mu}_{(t)i}), \quad i = 1, \ldots, n$$

The weights $w_{(t)i}$ form the diagonals of a weight matrix $\mathbf{W}_{(t)}$ used to fit a weighted additive model for $\mathbf{z}_{(t)}$. This is done by backfitting as described on page 366, which involves an inner loop over the functions $f_j(x_j)$ and produces new estimates $\hat{\beta}_{(t+1)0}$ and $\hat{f}_{(t+1)j}(\cdot), j = 1, \ldots, p$. These quantities are then used to compute a new additive predictor $\hat{\eta}_{(t+1)i}$, a new set of fitted values $\hat{\mu}_{(t+1)i}$, and a new adjusted dependent variable $\mathbf{z}_{(t+1)}$.

The entire process is repeated until the changes in the estimated functions fall below convergence criteria. Some special cases are worth noting:

- If the link function is the identity $g(\mu_i) = \mu_i$, then only the weights change in the outer loop, and so the fit is an iteratively weighted additive fit. If in addition the response distribution is normal, then the outer loop reduces to a single step and the local scoring algorithm simplifies to the backfitting algorithm.

- If some of the functions in the additive predictor are linear ($f_j(x_j) = \beta_j$), then simple linear regression smoothers are applied to these functions in the inner loop, and the coefficients ($\hat{\beta}_j$) are computed as least squares estimates. These converge to maximum likelihood estimates as the result of reweighting in the outer loop.

Local Scoring in the GAM Procedure

The GAM procedure implements the local scoring algorithm. For each smooth effect in the model, you specify a univariate smoothing spline, a bivariate smoothing spline, or a loess smoother. The smoothing parameters for the smooth effects are determined independently of each other, either by specifying the degrees of freedom for the smoother or by applying generalized cross validation.

Penalized Likelihood for Generalized Additive Models

In contrast to the GAM procedure, the GAMPL and GAMMOD procedures fit generalized additive models by using penalized maximum likelihood estimation. This method differs from local scoring in four key aspects:

- Smooth terms are approximated by low-rank thin-plate regression splines, which were proposed by (Wood 2003) and are explained on page 357 of Appendix F.

- Fitting is based on a global design matrix.

- Regression parameters are simultaneously constrained by a roughness penalty matrix.

- Smoothing parameters are determined simultaneously by optimizing global criteria.

Suppose that the additive predictor for the model consists of a linear predictor with parameters $\boldsymbol{\beta}_L = (\beta_{L1}, \ldots, \beta_{Lq_L})'$ and p smooth effects. Furthermore, suppose that the jth effect is represented by a penalized spline of the form

$$f_j(\mathbf{x}_j) = \sum_{k=1}^{q_j} \beta_{jk} b_{jk}(\mathbf{x}_j)$$

for which $\boldsymbol{\beta}_j = (\beta_{j1}, \ldots, \beta_{jq_j})'$ denotes the coefficients of the basis functions. The roughness (wiggliness) of the spline can be measured by the quadratic form $\boldsymbol{\beta}'_j \tilde{\mathbf{S}}_j \boldsymbol{\beta}_j$, where $\tilde{\mathbf{S}}_j$ is a matrix of known coefficients.

After a reparameterization that centers the smoothed functions and provides model identifiability, the predictor can be expressed as $\boldsymbol{\eta} = \mathbf{X}\boldsymbol{\beta}$, where the model matrix is $\mathbf{X} = [\mathbf{X}_L : \tilde{\mathbf{X}}_1 : \ldots : \tilde{\mathbf{X}}_p]$ and the parameter vector is $\boldsymbol{\beta}' = [\boldsymbol{\beta}'_L : \boldsymbol{\beta}'_1 : \ldots : \boldsymbol{\beta}'_p]$. The generalized additive model can then be written as $g(\boldsymbol{\mu}) = (g(\mu_1), \ldots, g(\mu_n))' = \mathbf{X}\boldsymbol{\beta}$.

Algorithms for Penalized Likelihood Estimation

The penalized log-likelihood function for the model is

$$\mathcal{L}_p(\boldsymbol{\beta}; \mathbf{y}) = \mathcal{L}(\boldsymbol{\beta}; \mathbf{y}) - \frac{1}{2}\boldsymbol{\beta}'\mathbf{S}_\lambda\boldsymbol{\beta}$$

where the first term on the right is the log-likelihood for a generalized linear model, the second term is the roughness penalty, and the roughness penalty matrix $\mathbf{S}_\lambda$ is a block diagonal matrix:

$$\mathbf{S}_\lambda = \begin{bmatrix} 0 & 0 & \cdots & & 0 \\ 0 & \lambda_1\mathbf{S}_1 & \cdots & & 0 \\ & & \ddots & & \\ \vdots & \vdots & & \lambda_j\mathbf{S}_j & \vdots \\ & & & & \ddots \\ 0 & 0 & \cdots & & \lambda_p\mathbf{S}_p \end{bmatrix}$$

The vector of smoothing parameters $\boldsymbol{\lambda} = (\lambda_1, \ldots, \lambda_p)'$ controls the amount of roughness. Penalization avoids overfitting when the sets of basis functions for the smooth terms are large. The parameters for the linear term are not penalized.

For fixed $\boldsymbol{\lambda}$, the penalized maximum likelihood estimate of $\boldsymbol{\beta}$ can be obtained by setting the derivatives of $\mathcal{L}_p(\boldsymbol{\beta}; \mathbf{y})$ to zero and solving for $\boldsymbol{\beta}$:

$$\frac{\partial \mathcal{L}_p(\boldsymbol{\beta}; \mathbf{y})}{\partial \boldsymbol{\beta}} = \frac{\partial \mathcal{L}(\boldsymbol{\beta}; \mathbf{y})}{\partial \boldsymbol{\beta}} - \mathbf{S}_{\boldsymbol{\lambda}} \boldsymbol{\beta} = 0$$

Maximizing the penalized likelihood is equivalent to minimizing the penalized deviance, $D(\hat{\boldsymbol{\beta}}) + \boldsymbol{\beta}' \mathbf{S}_{\boldsymbol{\lambda}} \boldsymbol{\beta}$, where the deviance $D(\hat{\boldsymbol{\beta}})$ is the analogue of the residual sum of squares for a general linear model; see page 336.

Wood (2006, Sec. 4.3) describes an algorithm called penalized iteratively reweighted least squares (P-IRLS) that computes $\hat{\boldsymbol{\beta}}$. The P-IRLS algorithm resembles the IWLS algorithm described on page 367; at step $t + 1$ it incorporates the penalty matrix $\mathbf{S}_{\boldsymbol{\lambda}}$ by computing

$$\hat{\boldsymbol{\beta}}_{(t+1)} = (\mathbf{X}'\mathbf{W}\mathbf{X} + \mathbf{S}_{\boldsymbol{\lambda}})^{-1} \mathbf{X}'\mathbf{W}\mathbf{y}$$

After the final step, the smoothing matrix (also called the influence matrix) is formed as

$$\mathbf{H}_{\boldsymbol{\lambda}} = \mathbf{W}^{1/2} \mathbf{X} (\mathbf{X}'\mathbf{W}\mathbf{X} + \mathbf{S}_{\boldsymbol{\lambda}})^{-1} \mathbf{X}'\mathbf{W}^{1/2}$$

The P-IRLS algorithm is closely related to the Newton–Raphson algorithm (see page 327), which is the default method used by the GAMPL and GAMMOD procedures.

Model Evaluation Criteria

The procedures find the smoothing parameters λ_k for the fitted model by minimizing one of three evaluation criteria defined as follows for an additive model:

- Generalized cross validation (GCV), proposed by Craven and Wahba (1979):

$$\mathcal{V}_g(\boldsymbol{\lambda}) = \frac{n \|\mathbf{y} - \mathbf{H}_{\boldsymbol{\lambda}} \mathbf{y}\|_2^2}{[\mathrm{tr}(\mathbf{I} - \gamma \mathbf{H}_{\boldsymbol{\lambda}})]^2}, \quad \gamma \geq 1$$

- Unbiased risk estimator (UBRE), proposed by Craven and Wahba (1979):

$$\mathcal{V}_u(\boldsymbol{\lambda}) = \frac{1}{n} \|\mathbf{y} - \mathbf{H}_{\boldsymbol{\lambda}} \mathbf{y}\|_2^2 - \frac{2}{n} \sigma^2 \mathrm{tr}(\mathbf{I} - \gamma \mathbf{H}_{\boldsymbol{\lambda}}) + \sigma^2, \quad \gamma \geq 1$$

where σ^2 is known.

- Generalized approximate cross validation (GACV), proposed by Xiang and Wahba (1996):

$$\mathcal{V}_a(\boldsymbol{\lambda}) = \frac{1}{n} \|\mathbf{y} - \mathbf{H}_{\boldsymbol{\lambda}} \mathbf{y}\|_2^2 \left(1 + 2\gamma \frac{\mathrm{tr}(\mathbf{H}_{\boldsymbol{\lambda}})}{\mathrm{tr}(\mathbf{I} - \mathbf{H}_{\boldsymbol{\lambda}})}\right), \quad \gamma \geq 1$$

Here, γ is a tuning parameter that can be specified to produce smoother models; the default is $\gamma = 1$.

GCV avoids the computational expense of leave-one-out cross validation (LOOCV), which is discussed in "Cross Validation Methods for Estimating Prediction Error" on page 31. It also avoids an invariance problem with LOOCV that arises with additive models when the objective function for estimating β has the form

$$\|\mathbf{y} - \mathbf{X}\boldsymbol{\beta}\|_2^2 + \sum_{j=1}^{p} \lambda_j \boldsymbol{\beta}_j' \mathbf{S}_j \boldsymbol{\beta}_j$$

If the smoothing parameters λ_j are fixed and $\mathbf{y} - \mathbf{X}\boldsymbol{\beta}$ is replaced by the rotation $\mathbf{Q}(\mathbf{y} - \mathbf{X}\boldsymbol{\beta})$, where $\mathbf{Q}$ is an orthogonal matrix, the estimator of $\boldsymbol{\beta}$ does not change, but the value of LOOCV is different. GCV is derived by applying a special rotation that results in an influence matrix $\mathbf{H}$ whose diagonal elements $\mathbf{H}_{ii}$ all have the same value, $\mathrm{tr}(\mathbf{H})/n$. This prevents a small number of high-leverage observations from overly influencing the criterion.

The criterion UBRE is intended for additive models where σ^2 is known or an unbiased estimate is available; it is an unbiased estimate of the expected mean squared error of prediction that generalizes Mallows' C_P statistic, which is discussed on page 26. For a general linear model with parameters $\beta_0, \ldots, \beta_p$,

$$\frac{n\mathcal{V}_u(0)}{\sigma^2} = \frac{\|\mathbf{y} - \mathbf{H}_\lambda \mathbf{y}\|_2^2}{\sigma^2} - 2tr(\mathbf{I} - \mathbf{H}) + n = \frac{\mathrm{SSE}}{\sigma^2} + 2(p+1) - n = C_P$$

where SSE is the sum of squares for error.

GACV was proposed for determining the smoothing parameter λ_j for a spline term in a generalized linear model, where estimation of the regression parameters is based on maximizing a log-likelihood that is penalized for the roughness of the spline.

Searching for the Optimal λ

The GAMPL and GAMMOD procedures provide two different methods that search for the optimal smoothing parameters.

The *performance iteration method* was proposed by Gu and Wahba (1991), Gu (1992), and Wood (2004). It initializes the smoothing parameter to $\boldsymbol{\lambda} = (1, \ldots, 1)'$ and the regression parameter to $\boldsymbol{\beta} = (g(\bar{y}), 0, \ldots, 0)'$. At step t, an adjusted response variable, a linear predictor, and an adjusted weight are formed for the ith observation as in the local scoring algorithm described on page 368. Then an optimization technique is used to find the best smoothing parameter for step $t + 1$. The Newton–Raphson method involves derivatives of the evaluation criteria with respect to λ_j, which are given by Wood (2004). The process continues until convergence criteria are met.

The *outer iteration method* adapts a Newton–Raphson method proposed by O'Sullivan, Yandell, and Raynor (1986, Sec. 2.3) for minimizing a penalized likelihood in the framework of generalized linear models. As described by Wood (2006, Sec. 4.7), the outer iteration method directly minimizes the evaluation criteria on page 370, which are extended to generalized additive models by replacing the error measure $\|\mathbf{y} - \mathbf{H}_\lambda \mathbf{y}\|_2^2$ with the scaled deviance $D^*(\hat{\boldsymbol{\mu}})$, which is defined on page 336. For instance, $\mathcal{V}_g(\boldsymbol{\lambda})$ is extended to

$$\mathcal{V}_g^o(\boldsymbol{\lambda}) = \frac{nD^*(\hat{\boldsymbol{\mu}})}{[\mathrm{tr}(\mathbf{I} - \gamma\mathbf{H}_\lambda)]^2}, \quad \gamma \geq 1$$

The outer iteration method initializes the smoothing parameter by taking one step of the performance iteration method. Then it applies a Newton–Raphson algorithm nested inside of an outer Newton–Raphson algorithm. Given a set of smoothing parameters $\lambda_1, \ldots, \lambda_p$ at each step of the outer algorithm, the inner algorithm estimates β by minimizing the penalized deviance D_p or—in the case of the negative binomial distribution—by maximizing the penalized likelihood. This involves the first and second derivatives of the regression coefficients with respect to the logs of $\lambda_1, \ldots, \lambda_p$, which are given by Wood (2006, Sec. 4.7). The outer algorithm searches for the best smoothing parameters by minimizing one of the extended criteria. This involves first and second derivatives of the criterion with respect to λ. The process continues until convergence criteria are met.

Wood (2006, Sec. 4.5) points out that the performance iteration method can fail to converge and explains the reasons for this. The outer iteration method does not have this problem, but it is computationally more expensive.

Effective Degrees of Freedom

As explained on page 22, the degrees of freedom for a general linear model fitted with least squares estimation is defined as the trace of the hat matrix

$$\mathbf{P} = \mathbf{X}(\mathbf{X}'\mathbf{X})^{-1}\mathbf{X}'$$

The effective degrees of freedom for a fitted generalized additive model is defined by Wood (2006, Sec. 4.4) as the trace of the degrees of freedom matrix

$$\mathbf{F} = (\mathbf{X}'\mathbf{W}\mathbf{X} + \mathbf{S}_\lambda)^{-1}\mathbf{X}'\mathbf{W}\mathbf{X}$$

where $\mathbf{W}$ is the adjusted weight matrix at the final step of the P-IRLS algorithm (see page 369). The degrees of freedom for the jth spline term in the model is then the trace of the submatrix of $\mathbf{F}$ that corresponds to β_j.

These definitions allow for reductions in degrees of freedom that result from penalization. If the smoothing parameters are all zero, the degrees of freedom for the model is the dimension of β minus the number of linear constraints needed for model identifiability. If the smoothing parameters are all large, the model is inflexible, and so the degrees of freedom is small.

Methods for Selecting Generalized Additive Models

The GAMSELECT procedure provides two methods of fitting and selecting generalized additive models:

- The boosting method uses a componentwise implementation of the generic functional gradient descent algorithm (Friedman 2001; Bühlmann and Hothorn 2007).

- The shrinkage method uses a penalized likelihood approach with penalties that induce sparsity.

With the boosting method, the model can have any combination of parametric effects and spline effects; the spline terms can be univariate or bivariate. With the shrinkage method, the model must have at least one spline term; selection is performed only on the spline effects, and the spline terms must be univariate. The algorithms used by these methods are completely different.

The Boosting Method

Boosting is a general approach to supervised learning that improves the predictive ability of weak learners, such as individual trees, by combining them into a strong ensemble learner that reduces bias and variance. There are many types of boosting.

The Adaptive Boosting (AdaBoost) algorithm for binary classification, proposed by Yoav Freund and Robert Schapire, is considered the first practical boosting method (Freund and Schapire 1997; Schapire and Freund 2012). It fits a sequence of decision trees in which data weights are adjusted after each fit in order to correct for incorrect classification, and it gained prominence because of its speed and performance.

In the late 1990s, Leo Breiman showed that AdaBoost can be viewed as a steepest descent algorithm in function space. Such algorithms are called functional gradient descent algorithms. Subsequently, Friedman, Hastie, and Tibshirani (2000) and Friedman (2001) introduced gradient boosting, a statistical framework that takes a stagewise modeling approach and accommodates regression and classification with different loss functions. Instead of weight-based adjustment, gradient boosting constructs sequential base learners, such as regression trees, in such a way that each improves on its predecessor.

To be clear, the GAMSELECT procedure does not implement the gradient tree boosting algorithm[†] that is described by Hastie, Tibshirani, and Friedman (2009, p. 361). Instead, the procedure implements a variant of gradient boosting that estimates the components, $f_j(\mathbf{x}_j), j = 1, \ldots, p$, of a generalized additive model. This differs from the penalized likelihood method described on page 369, which computes $\hat{f}_j(\mathbf{x}_j)$ by maximizing a likelihood function over a parametric space that includes parameters for spline components as well as parameters for linear effects. Instead, the boosting algorithm used by the GAMSELECT procedure solves for $\hat{f}_j(\mathbf{x}_j)$ in function space.

This algorithm begins at step $m = 1$ with an initial estimate $\hat{f}^0(\mathbf{x})$ for the regression surface function $f(\mathbf{x})$ (see page 365) that is an intercept-only model. At each of the subsequent steps, the algorithm computes the functional derivatives

$$u_i = \left. \frac{\partial \mathcal{L}(y_i, f)}{\partial f(\mathbf{x}_i)} \right|_{f = \hat{f}^{(m-1)}(\mathbf{x}_i)}, \quad i = 1, \ldots, n$$

Here $\mathcal{L}(y_i, f)$ denotes the likelihood as a function of f rather than the regression parameter $\boldsymbol{\beta}$, and the right-hand side is the gradient for the negative likelihood or loss function evaluated at the previous estimate $\hat{f}^{m-1}(\mathbf{x})$. If, for instance, the response distribution is normal and the link function is the identity, then the loss function is the squared loss $\frac{1}{2}[y_i - f(\mathbf{x}_i)]^2$, and the right-hand side is simply the residual $y_i - \hat{f}^{(m-1)}(\mathbf{x})$. For this reason, $u_1, \ldots, u_n$ are called pseudo residuals.

For each of the p components, the algorithm fits a model, denoted by $\gamma_j^m(\mathbf{x}_j)$, using the pseudo-observations $(u_i, x_{ij}), i = 1, \ldots, n$. This is done by weighted least squares with observation weights w_i computed by using the variance function for the distribution as in the IWLS algorithm. If the jth component corresponds to a parametric effect, $\gamma_j^m(\mathbf{x}_j)$ is a linear model. If the jth component corresponds to a spline term, $\gamma_j^m(\mathbf{x}_j)$ is estimated using penalized B-splines (see page 358).

[†]The GRADBOOST procedure in SAS Viya does gradient boosting by fitting a decision tree at each iteration and constructing a tree ensemble that serves as a predictive model. For a comparison of the GRADBOOST and GAMSELECT procedures, see Lamm and Cai (2020).

By default, a smoothing parameter value is selected so that a univariate spline term has four degrees of freedom and a bivariate spline term has six degrees of freedom.

Given $\hat{\gamma}_1^m, \ldots, \hat{\gamma}_p^m$, the algorithm finds

$$j^* = \operatorname*{argmin}_{j=1,\ldots,p} \sum_{i=1}^n w_i \left(u_i - \hat{\gamma}_j^m(\mathbf{x}_{ij}) \right)^2$$

and updates the estimated component functions as follows:

$$\hat{f}_j^m(\mathbf{x}) = \begin{cases} \hat{f}_j^{(m-1)}(\mathbf{x}) + \nu\hat{\gamma}_j^m & \text{if } j = j^* \\ \hat{f}_j^{(m-1)}(\mathbf{x}) & \text{if } j \neq j^* \end{cases}$$

Here ν denotes the update step size, which is 0.1 by default. The algorithm then increments m and checks the stopping criterion.

The updating of the components maintains the additivity of the estimated model $\hat{f}^m(\mathbf{x})$ at step m. Small degrees of freedom for the spline terms and a small step size favor a finely detailed exploration of the model space. The total number of steps is $m_{\text{end}} + 1$, where m_{end} denotes the step at which the stopping criterion is satisfied.

Among the models obtained during the steps, the final selected model $\hat{f}(\mathbf{x})$ is the model that minimizes the average square error (ASE) for the training data. The effects in the final model are the effects selected in at least one iteration. To avoid overfitting, you can specify an early stopping criterion, or you can apply k-fold cross validation of the ASE. You can also base the selection on ASE computed for a validation partition.

The Shrinkage Method

The shrinkage method is based on likelihood estimation penalized by sparsity-inducing norms. It uses univariate natural cubic splines to estimate the p component functions in the model, and it constructs a B-spline basis representation for each spline; see "Natural Cubic Spline Basis" on page 354 and "B-Spline Basis" on page 355.

The basis coefficients for the splines are model parameters, denoted here by $\boldsymbol{\beta}_1, \ldots, \boldsymbol{\beta}_p$. Because the parameters fall into groups—one for each spline term—the shrinkage method is designed to operate like the group lasso method for general linear models, which selects groups that correspond to classification effects (see page 46). However, unlike the group lasso method, the shrinkage method does not apply shrinkage to linear parametric effects.

The shrinkage method penalizes the minimization of the negative log-likelihood function with three terms, P_1, P_2, and P_3, which are controlled by tuning parameters $\boldsymbol{\lambda} = (\lambda_1, \lambda_2, \lambda_3)$. For fixed $\boldsymbol{\lambda}$, the objective function is

$$\frac{-\mathcal{L}(\boldsymbol{\beta}_1,\ldots,\boldsymbol{\beta}_p)\phi}{n} + \underbrace{\lambda_1 \sum_j \phi_j \sqrt{\boldsymbol{\beta}_j' \mathbf{B}_j' \mathbf{B}_j \boldsymbol{\beta}_j / n}}_{P_1 \text{ induces sparsity}} + \underbrace{\lambda_2 \sum_j \psi_j \sqrt{\boldsymbol{\beta}_j' \boldsymbol{\Omega}_j \boldsymbol{\beta}_j}}_{P_2 \text{ induces sparsity}} + \underbrace{\lambda_3 \sum_j \boldsymbol{\beta}_j' \boldsymbol{\Omega}_j \boldsymbol{\beta}_j}_{P_3 \text{ induces smoothness}}$$

The columns of $\mathbf{B}_j$ are the B-spline basis expansion of $\mathbf{x}_j$, and $\mathbf{\Omega}_j$ is a diagonal matrix whose elements are the squared second derivatives of the basis functions. The parameter ϕ is the dispersion parameter for the response distribution; see "The Exponential Family" on page 333. Multiplying $\mathcal{L}(\boldsymbol{\beta}_1, \ldots, \boldsymbol{\beta}_p)$ by ϕ cancels the dispersion parameter in the expression for the log-likelihood function (see page 336), which focuses the minimization on estimation of the model parameters.

The penalization terms in the objective function play different roles:

- The term P_1 generalizes the unsquared ℓ_2 norm that induces sparsity in the group lasso. This term induces sparsity by forcing $\boldsymbol{\beta}_j$ to shrink toward $\mathbf{0}$ as λ_1 increases.

- The term P_2 forces $\boldsymbol{\beta}_j' \mathbf{\Omega}_j \boldsymbol{\beta}_j$ to shrink toward 0 if λ_2 is sufficiently large. The expression $\boldsymbol{\beta}_j' \mathbf{\Omega}_j \boldsymbol{\beta}_j$ represents the curvature or roughness of the spline; it penalizes the minimization criterion for smoothing splines (see page 356). Here, however, this expression appears as an *unsquared* ℓ_2 norm, and so as λ_2 increases, it induces sparsity by shrinking the curvature of the spline to a linear effect in β_j.

- The term P_3 induces smoothness rather than sparsity because the expression $\boldsymbol{\beta}_j' \mathbf{\Omega}_j \boldsymbol{\beta}_j$ appears as a *squared* ℓ_2 norm. It resembles the penalty term for ridge regression (see page 98). As λ_3 decreases, the fitted model becomes rougher, and as λ_3 increases, the fitted model becomes smoother.

For fixed $\boldsymbol{\lambda}$, the GAMSELECT procedure solves the minimization problem by an iterative approach that constructs a pseudo response variable $\mathbf{z}_{(t)}$ and a weight matrix $\mathbf{W}_{(t)}$ at step t as described in "The Local Scoring Algorithm for Generalized Additive Models" on page 368. The estimates $\hat{\boldsymbol{\beta}}_j(t+1)$ at the next step are computed as

$$\underset{\boldsymbol{\beta}_{1(t+1)}, \ldots, \boldsymbol{\beta}_{p(t+1)}}{\text{argmin}} \left\{ \frac{1}{2n} \Big(\mathbf{z}_{(t)} - \sum_j \mathbf{B}_j \boldsymbol{\beta}_{j(t+1)} \Big)' \mathbf{W}_{(t)} \Big(\mathbf{z}_{(t)} - \sum_j \mathbf{B}_j \boldsymbol{\beta}_{j(t+1)} \Big) + P_1 + P_2 + P_3 \right\}$$

This approach is also used in the performance iteration method, which is described on page 371.

The multipliers ϕ_j and ψ_j in the objective function on page 374 are parameters you can use to tailor the penalties for individual spline terms as in the adaptive lasso method (see page 45). These parameters allow different degrees of sparsity and smoothness to be applied to different components in an adaptive fashion.

The shrinkage method performs a grid search of combinations of tuning parameters, estimates $\boldsymbol{\beta}_1, \ldots, \boldsymbol{\beta}_p$ for each combination, and evaluates the model from the training data or the validation data.

Elements of the shrinkage method are drawn from penalization techniques for high-dimensional additive model fitting that were proposed by Meier, Van de Geer, and Bühlmann (2009, Sec. 4.2); Suzuki and Sugiyama (2013); and Amato, Antoniadis, and De Feis (2016). The latter reviews developments in this field.

Part IV

Appendices about Common Topics

Appendix H
Methods for Scoring Data

Contents

Scoring is the process of applying a model to predict outcomes or responses. In order for those predictions to be valid, the data must satisfy the assumptions of the model and must not have been used to train the model. Scoring is commonly done with production data in applications such as fraud detection, credit risk reduction, and customer retention. Scoring is also done with test data in order to assess, validate, and compare models that are being built, and it is done with resampled data to compute bootstrap estimates.

SAS provides many different approaches to scoring. Some involve writing a SAS program, while others—for instance, SAS Model Manager and SAS Model Studio—are implemented in environments that support the entire process of model deployment.

There are a variety of ways to score data with the regression models discussed in this book, depending on the complexity of the model and the features of the procedure used to build the model. As SAS has evolved, methods for scoring have been added to the modeling procedures in SAS/STAT, and even more methods are now available in SAS Viya.

Selecting the best scoring method for a particular application can bewilder even the most experienced SAS user because not every method is available with every modeling procedure. Furthermore, the syntax for these method is confusing; depending on the method, the keywords SCORE and STORE each mean different things.

This appendix guides you through the various methods, which are summarized in Table H.1.

Table H.1 Scoring Methods Applicable with Regression Model Building Procedures

Method	Procedures	Scoring Done By	Platform
Missing response	All	Modeling procedure	SAS 9, SAS Viya
Test partition	Many	Modeling procedure	SAS 9, SAS Viya
SCORE statement	Some	Modeling procedure	SAS 9
SCORE procedure	REG	SCORE procedure	SAS 9
PLM procedure	GLMSELECT	PLM procedure	SAS 9
ASTORE procedure	All except PHSELECT	ASTORE procedure	SAS Viya
CODE statement	Many	DATA step	SAS 9, SAS Viya

Types of Scoring Methods

Scoring methods in SAS fall into two main categories:

- Methods in which the scoring model is run internally by the same procedure you use to fit or build the regression model. Here, methods of this type are referred to as *internal methods*.

- Methods in which the scoring model produced by the regression procedure is saved and run externally, either by another procedure designed specifically for scoring or by a program. The program can be a SAS program or—if you are using SAS Viya—it can be a program in another language such as Python. Here, methods of this type are referred to as *external methods*.

Internal methods are further differentiated by whether the scoring data—the new observations that are to be scored—are included with the input data set you specify with the DATA= option for the regression procedure or whether they are provided in an external SAS data set.

Figure H.1 shows how the scoring methods are categorized.

Figure H.1 Internal and External Scoring Methods

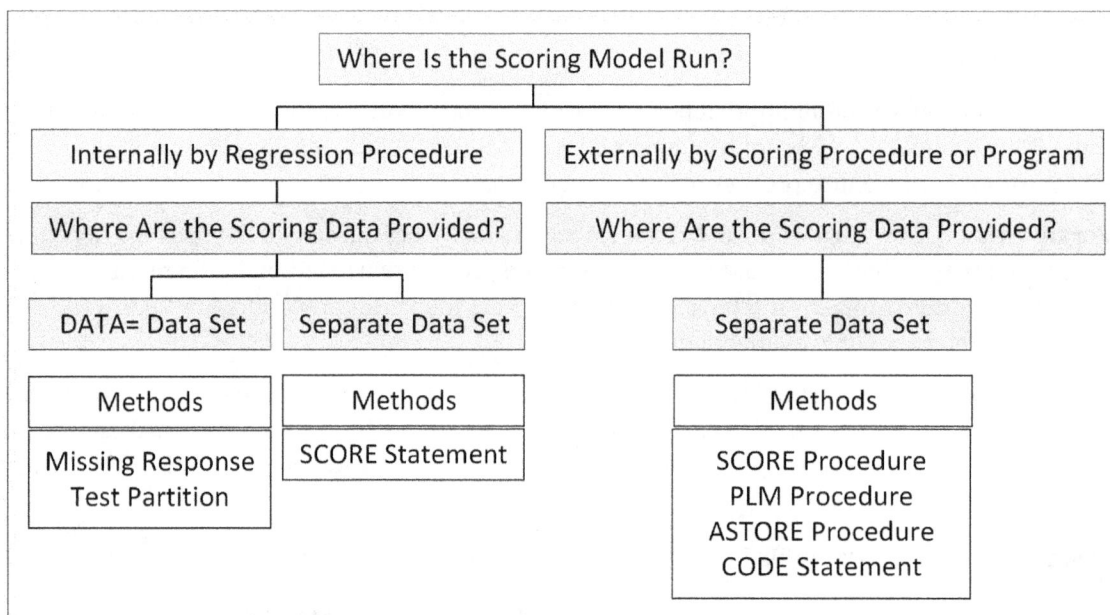

Internal Scoring Methods

The next three subsections describe the internal scoring methods:

- Missing Response
- Test Partition
- SCORE Statement

Scoring with the Missing Response Method

With the missing response method, the regression procedure runs the scoring model internally. You include the observations to be scored—with their response values set to missing—in the input data set specified with the DATA= option. The procedure does not use these observations to train the model; instead, it scores them and saves them, together with the training observations, in an output data set specified in an OUTPUT statement.

The advantage of this method is its availability in all of the model building procedures discussed in this book. The disadvantage is you must rerun the procedure and rebuild the model whenever you need to score new data. This is not practical if the training data are large, if the model building process is computationally expensive, or if scoring is done on a computing platform different from the one where the procedure is run.

The example on page 239 of Chapter 11 illustrates the missing response method for scoring test data and computing the average squared error with a generalized additive model fitted with the GAMMOD procedure in SAS Viya. Due to the complexity of such models, the only alternative to the missing response method is the ASTORE method, which is illustrated in the example on page 385. With the GAM procedure or the GAMPL procedure in SAS 9, the missing response method is the only choice. Also see the example for the GLMSELECT procedure on page 83.

Scoring with the Test Partition Method

Nearly all of the model building procedures in this book provide a PARTITION statement that designates observations for training, validation, and testing; see "Terminating Selection Based on ASE Computed from Validation Data" on page 63. Although this facility is neither intended nor recommended for scoring external data, it can serve this purpose if you include the observations to be scored in the input data set and designate them as a test partition. Thus, the test partition method is an internal method like the missing response method.

The test partition method is used by the `%Bootstrap632Plus` macro, which computes estimates of the prediction error for a logistic regression model; see "Bootstrap Assessment of Prediction Error" on page 172. The macro pairs bootstrap samples with data copies in the input data set for the HPLOGISTIC procedure; it treats the pairs as BY groups, and it uses the PARTITION statement to designate the bootstrap samples as training data and the data copies as test data for scoring. This approach is highly efficient because it requires only two invocations of the HPLOGISTIC procedure.

Scoring with the SCORE Statement in SAS 9

Scoring with the SCORE statement, available in some model building procedures, is more convenient than the missing response method because it applies the model to a separate input data set that supplies the scoring observations. You specify this data set with the SCORE statement.

The disadvantage of the SCORE statement—as with the missing response method–is that you must rerun the procedure whenever you have new observations to be scored. Furthermore, the SCORE statement is not provided by every model building procedure in SAS 9. It is available with the ADAPTIVEREG and GLMSELECT procedures, as well as several procedures that fit regression models, including the GAM, LOESS, LOGISTIC, and TPSPLINE procedures. The SCORE statement is not provided with model building procedures in SAS Viya.

Example: Scoring Close Rate Data for Retail Stores

This example illustrates the SCORE statement in the GLMSELECT procedure with the data set Stores, which is used on page 56 to build a model for the close rates of 500 stores. The next statements rebuild the model and score data for additional stores that are provided in a data set named NewStores. The output data set CloseRateScores contains the predicted values and the observations in NewStores.

```
proc glmselect plots=coefficients data=Stores;
   class Region(param=reference ref='Midwest' split)
         Training(param=reference ref='None');
   model CloseRate = Region Training X1-X20 L1-L6 P1-P6 /
      selection=forward(choose=sbc select=sbc stop=sbc);
   score data=NewStores out=CloseRateScores ;
run;

proc print data=CloseRateScores(obs=3) noobs;
   var StoreID x1-x3 l1-l2 p1-p2 Region Training p_CloseRate;
run;
```

Output H.1 shows a partial listing of CloseRateScores. The variable p_CloseRate contains the predicted values.

Output H.1 Partial Listing of CloseRateScores

StoreID	X1	X2	X3	L1	L2	P1	P2	Region	Training	p_CloseRate
601	-0.340	-0.268	0.376	0.451	0.633	0.094	-0.122	East	None	58.3912
602	0.466	0.225	-0.069	0.021	0.093	0.496	0.107	East	InProgress	60.5080
603	0.436	0.469	-0.250	0.193	0.557	-0.225	-0.316	East	None	62.1660

External Scoring Methods

The next four subsections describe the external scoring methods.

- SCORE procedure
- PLM procedure
- ASTORE procedure
- CODE statement

Scoring with the SCORE Procedure in SAS 9

Scoring with the SCORE procedure is the oldest external scoring method in SAS. You provide the predictor variables for the observations to be scored in a DATA= data set, and you provide the parameter estimates for a regression model in a SCORE= data set. The SCORE procedure computes the predicted values as linear combinations of the two inputs ($\hat{y} = \hat{\beta}_1 x_1 + \cdots + \hat{\beta}_p x_p$), and it saves them in an OUT= data set.

You can automatically create a SCORE= data set by fitting or building a model with the REG procedure and saving the parameter estimates in an OUTEST= data set. The OUTEST= data set has exactly the right variables that the SCORE procedure expects in a SCORE= data set.

With other regression procedures in this book, you can create a parameter estimates data set with an ODS OUTPUT statement such as

```
ods output ParameterEstimates=MyParmEst;
```

However, a data set of this type must be transposed before it can serve as a SCORE= data set. Furthermore, this approach works only with models whose parameters correspond to simple linear predictors. For example, it does not work with models built by the GLMSELECT procedure in which predictors show up in cross-product or interaction terms.

Nonetheless, there are situations in which the SCORE procedure comes in handy for writing a SAS program that does scoring, as illustrated by the next two examples.

Example: Scoring with a Principal Components Regression Model

The %PLSRegScore macro, described on page 113, uses the SCORE procedure to score data with a principal components regression model constructed with the PLS procedure. The macro uses the TRANSPOSE procedure and a DATA step with four lines to transform the parameter estimates data set created by the PLS procedure into a SCORE= data set. The macro code is available on the book website.

Example: *m*-Fold Cross Validation for All Subsets Regression

The %AllSubsetsCV macro, described on page 75, uses *m*-fold cross validation to estimate the average squared error of prediction as a function of model size for all subsets regression, which is performed by the REG procedure. In this situation, the SCORE procedure provides a convenient way to score the data for each fold. The macro code is available on the book website.

Scoring with the PLM Procedure in SAS 9

The PLM procedure in SAS/STAT performs a variety of postfitting statistical analyses by processing a SAS item store, which is a binary representation of information rather than a SAS data set. A number of SAS/STAT procedures for statistical analysis of fitted models, such as the GENMOD, GLIMMIX, GLM, LOGISTIC, and PHREG procedures, provide a STORE statement you can use to create an item store that saves information about the model. The GLMSELECT procedure is the only model building procedure that provides this statement.

Scoring is just one of the tasks the PLM procedure can perform. For models that are specified rather than built, it can also test hypotheses, compute confidence intervals, and produce prediction plots. The advantage is that you can reanalyze a fitted model any number of times without the computational expense of refitting the model.

Example: Scoring Close Rate Data for Retail Stores (continued)

This example illustrates the STORE statement in the GLMSELECT procedure with the same data sets used in the example on page 382. The following statements rebuild the model and score observations for additional stores provided by the data set NewStores.

```
proc glmselect plots=coefficients data=Stores;
   class Region(param=reference ref='Midwest' split)
         Training(param=reference ref='None');
   model CloseRate = Region Training X1-X20 L1-L6 P1-P6 /
      selection=forward(choose=sbc select=sbc stop=sbc);
   store out=CloseRateModel;
run;

proc plm  restore=CloseRateModel ;
   score data=NewStores out=PLMCloseRateScores
         Predicted=PredCloseRate LCL=LowerPredLimit UCL=UpperPredLimit /
         alpha=0.05;
run;

proc print data=PLMCloseRateScores(obs=3) noobs;
   var StoreID x1-x3 Region Training LowerPredLimit UpperPredLimit PredCloseRate;
run;
```

To score new data with the PLM procedure, you use the RESTORE= option to specify the item store that contains the fitted model, and you use a STORE statement to specify the data set to be scored, as discussed on page 381. Along with scoring, the PLM procedure has the capability to compute upper and lower prediction limits. Output H.2 shows a partial listing of the OUT= data set. The predicted values are saved in a variable named PredCloseRate and match those of p_CloseRate in Output H.1.

Output H.2 Partial Listing of CloseRateScores

StoreID	X1	X2	X3	Region	Training	LowerPredLimit	UpperPredLimit	PredCloseRate
601	-0.340	-0.268	0.376	East	None	56.5235	60.2588	58.3912
602	0.466	0.225	-0.069	East	InProgress	58.6324	62.3837	60.5080
603	0.436	0.469	-0.250	East	None	60.2974	64.0346	62.1660

Scoring with the ASTORE Procedure in SAS Viya

The ASTORE procedure in SAS Viya does scoring much like the PLM procedure in SAS 9—by applying a binary store previously created by an analytic procedure that contains the context and results of the work performed by the procedure. In the case of a regression procedure, the store contains the model information needed to compute predicted values and other postfit statistics. The following procedures in SAS Viya provide a STORE statement you can use to create a model store: GAMMOD, GAMSELECT, GENSELECT, LOGSELECT, QTRSELECT, and REGSELECT. The TREESPLIT procedure provides a SAVESTATE statement with similar functionality.

An advantage of scoring with a store in SAS Viya is that it is not limited by the complexity of the model. For instance, you can create stores that save information for generalized additive models, as illustrated in the next example. Another advantage is that you can score data by calling the aStore action[†] with the native CAS Language (CASL) or with open source languages such as Python and R.

[†]The use of actions lies outside the scope of this book. An action performs a basic unit of work for the Cloud Analytics Services (CAS) distributed computing engine in SAS Viya. Actions are building blocks for procedures in SAS Viya, and procedures provide interfaces to actions.

Example: Scoring Claim Frequency Data

This example is a continuation of the one on page 239 in Chapter 11, which uses the GAMMOD procedure to fit a generalized additive model for the frequency of insurance claims. The data are provided in a CAS table named mycas.ClaimFrequency, which is partitioned into 10,180 observations for training and 5,090 observations for testing. The variable Role identifies the training observations with a value of 1 and the test observations with a value of 3.

On page 241, the response variable NumberClaims is assigned a missing value for observations in the test partition, and so the GAMMOD procedure scores these observations internally before saving them in the output CAS table mycas.PredClaimFrequency. The statements on page 243 use this table to compute the average squared error (ASE) for prediction shown in Output 11.22.

Here, instead of applying the missing response method, the training data and the test data are first separated into two CAS tables:

```
data mycas.ClaimFrequencyTrain;
   set mycas.ClaimFrequency(where=(Role=1));
run;

data mycas.ClaimFrequencyTest;
   set mycas.ClaimFrequency(where=(Role=3));
   ObservedNumberClaims = NumberClaims;
run;
```

The following statements use the training data to refit the generalized additive model:

```
ods graphics on;
proc gammod data=mycas.ClaimFrequencyTrain plots=components seed=892443;
   class &ClassVars / param=ref;
   model NumberClaims = param(AreaType Deductible VehicleOwned)
                        param(NYoungDrvrs StdHouseIncome)
                        spline(AgePolicyHolder)
                      / distribution=poisson link=log offset=logExposure;
   store mycas.ClaimsModel;
run;
```

The STORE statement saves the model information in an analytic store named mycas.ClaimsModel.

The next statements use the analytic store to score the observations in mycas.ClaimFrequencyTest:

```
proc astore;
   setoption alpha 0.05;
   setoption COMPUTE_STANDARD_ERROR 1;
   setoption COMPUTE_LINEAR_PREDICTOR 1;
   setoption COMPUTE_CONFIDENCE_LIMIT 1;
   setoption COMPUTE_COMPONENTWISE_STATS 1;
   score data=mycas.ClaimFrequencyTest
         out=mycas.ScoreOut copyvars=(ObservedNumberClaims)
          rstore=mycas.ClaimsModel ;
quit;
```

The SETOPTION statements specify statistics that are to be included in the output table, which is named mycas.ScoreOut.

The next statements use the CASUTIL procedure to obtain information about the columns in mycas.ScoreOut:

```
proc casutil;
    contents casdata="ScoreOut" incaslib="casdata";
quit;
```

The information is displayed in Output H.3.

Output H.3 Column Information for ScoreOut

	Column Information for SCOREOUT in Caslib CASDATA					
Column	Label	Type	Length	Formatted Length	Format Width	Format Decimal
P_NumberClaims	Predicted: NumberClaims	double	8	12	0	0
XBETA	Linear Predictor	double	8	12	0	0
STD	Bayesian Posterior Standard Deviation	double	8	12	0	0
LCLM	Lower Bound of 95% Confidence Band	double	8	12	0	0
UCLM	Upper Bound of 95% Confidence Band	double	8	12	0	0
_XBETA_AgePolicyHolder	Linear Predictor for Spline(AgePolicyHolder)	double	8	12	0	0
_STD_AgePolicyHolder	Bayesian Posterior Standard Deviation for Spline(AgePolicyHolder)	double	8	12	0	0
_LCLM_AgePolicyHolder	Lower Bound of 95% Confidence Band for Spline(AgePolicyHolder)	double	8	12	0	0
_UCLM_AgePolicyHolder	Upper Bound of 95% Confidence Band for Spline(AgePolicyHolder)	double	8	12	0	0
ObservedNumberClaims		double	8	12	0	0

The next statements list the first three observations in mycas.ScoreOut, which are shown in Output H.4.

```
proc print data=mycas.ScoreOut(obs=3) noobs;
run;
```

Output H.4 First Three Observations of ScoreOut

P_NumberClaims	_XBETA_	_STD_	_LCLM_	_UCLM_	_XBETA_AgePolicyHolder	_STD_AgePolicyHolder
0.80312	-0.21924	0.031874	0.75449	0.85490	-0.067552	0.023441
1.00203	0.00203	0.030587	0.94372	1.06394	-0.059870	0.022152
0.37822	-0.97227	0.027791	0.35817	0.39939	0.040671	0.019383

_LCLM_AgePolicyHolder	_UCLM_AgePolicyHolder	ObservedNumberClaims
-0.11350	-0.021608	0
-0.10329	-0.016452	1
0.00268	0.078661	0

The final set of statements computes ASE from the data in mycas.ScoreOut:

```
data mycas.ScoreOut;
    set mycas.ScoreOut;
    SqError = (ObservedNumberClaims - P_NumberClaims)**2;
run;
```

```
proc means data=mycas.ScoreOut n mean;
   output out=ASESummary (drop=_TYPE_ _FREQ_) mean=ASE n=N;
   var SqError;
run;

proc print data=ASESummary noobs label;
   label ASE = 'Average Square Error' N = 'Number of Test Observations';
run;
```

Output H.5 shows the value of ASE, which is identical to the value in Output 11.22.

Output H.5 Average Square Error

Average Square Error	Number of Test Observations
1.59443	5090

Scoring with the CODE Statement in SAS 9 and SAS Viya

In contrast to the external scoring methods discussed so far, the CODE statement, which is available in many model building procedures, packages the model by generating SAS programming statements you can save in a file and use to score new data in a DATA step. The new data must have the same predictor variables (with the same names) as the training data.

In SAS 9, the CODE statement is available in the GLMSELECT, HPLOGISTIC, HPSPLIT, LOGISTIC, QUANTSELECT, and REG procedures. In SAS Viya, the CODE statement is available in the GENSELECT, LOGSELECT, PHSELECT, QTRSELECT, REGSELECT, and TREESPLIT procedures.

The advantages of the CODE statement method are its convenience and portability; you can include the file in a DATA step with a %INCLUDE statement, and you can score data on any platform where you can run SAS. Furthermore, you can view and interpret the code, and you can even modify it (Gibbs and Tobias 2019).

The CODE statement is not available in procedures that build highly complex models by incorporating spline effects; these include the ADAPTIVEREG and GAMPL procedures in SAS 9 and the GAMMOD and GAMSELECT procedures in SAS Viya.

Example: Scoring Close Rate Data for Retail Stores (continued)

This example illustrates the CODE statement in the GLMSELECT procedure with the same data sets used on page 382. The following statements rebuild the model and score the data in NewStores.

```
proc glmselect plots=coefficients data=Stores;
   class Region(param=reference ref='Midwest' split)
         Training(param=reference ref='None');
   model CloseRate = Region Training X1-X20 L1-L6 P1-P6 /
      selection=forward(choose=sbc select=sbc stop=sbc);
   code file='ScoringCode.sas';
run;
```

```
data DSCloseRateScores;
   set NewStores;
    %include 'ScoringCode.sas';
run;

proc print data=DSCloseRateScores(obs=3) noobs;
   var StoreID x1-x3 l1-l2 p1-p2 Region Training P_CloseRate;
run;
```

Output H.6 shows a partial listing of the data set DSCloseRateScores. The predicted values are saved in P_CloseRate and match those of p_CloseRate in Output H.1.

Output H.6 Partial Listing of CloseRateScores

StoreID	X1	X2	X3	L1	L2	P1	P2	Region	Training	P_CloseRate
601	-0.340	-0.268	0.376	0.451	0.633	0.094	-0.122	East	None	58.3912
602	0.466	0.225	-0.069	0.021	0.093	0.496	0.107	East	InProgress	60.5080
603	0.436	0.469	-0.250	0.193	0.557	-0.225	-0.316	East	None	62.1660

Summary

Among the scoring methods presented here, no one method is best for every situation; each has advantages and disadvantages. In SAS 9, the most convenient method is the CODE statement method; it requires no preprocessing of the training data and generates SAS statements you can conveniently include in a DATA step program that does the scoring. In SAS Viya, the most versatile method is scoring with the ASTORE procedure; it is not limited by the complexity of the model.

Appendix I
Coding Schemes for Categorical Predictors

Contents

Parametric and semiparametric regression models are stated in matrix form as

$$y = \beta_0 1 + \beta_1 x_1 + \cdots + \beta_p x_p + \epsilon = X\beta + \epsilon$$

where $X = [1 \; x_1 \cdots x_p]$ is the design matrix. As explained on page 16, the columns of X express the effects of the predictors. Model building procedure form the design matrix from candidate predictors and effects you specify with MODEL, CLASS, and EFFECT statements.

Procedures with a CLASS statement provide the ability to include categorical (classification) predictors and effects in the model. They also provide different ways to represent the levels of a categorical predictor as a set of columns called dummy variables. These various representations are called parameterizations or coding schemes. Because no one parameterization is best for every situation, this appendix explains several that are useful for building predictive models.

Why Does Parameterization Matter?

If you have had a course on regression analysis or linear models that focused on statistical analysis, you likely learned about confidence intervals and hypothesis tests for linear functions of the parameters, such as differences and contrasts, that apply to a population. In that context—which lies outside the scope of this book—the particular parameterization you choose affects which *linear functions* you can estimate from the data. The choice is particularly critical in the analysis of interactions for complex designs, especially if some cells are missing.

When you build a regression model for prediction, the parameters play a supporting role as model coefficients. Confidence intervals and tests are not relevant because the focus is generalization to future data rather than inference about a population. Nonetheless, the parameter estimates are useful because they help you understand features of the data that the model uses to make predictions. Parameterization affects which *features* the parameter estimates measure.

Specifying the Parameterization and Level Order

You specify the parameterization with the PARAM= option in the CLASS statement, either globally (after a slash) for all the variables or individually for each variable. For instance, in the example on page 56, the following statements request reference parameterization for Region and Training:

```
proc glmselect plots=coefficients data=Stores;
   class Region param=reference ref='Midwest' split)
         Training (param=reference ref='None') ;
   model CloseRate = Region Training X1-X20 L1-L6 P1-P6 /
      selection=forward(choose=sbc select=sbc stop=sbc);
run;
```

Table I.1 lists three parameterizations commonly used for building regression models. Other parameterizations are available for specialized applications.

Table I.1   Commonly Used Parameterizations

PARAM= keyword	Description	Type
EFFECT	Effect parameterization	Full rank
GLM	GLM (general linear model) parameterization	Less than full rank
REFERENCE	Reference parameterization	Full rank

GLM parameterization is the default for the procedures discussed in this book. The high-performance procedures (see page 163) only provide GLM and reference parameterization, while the GLMSELECT and QUANTSELECT procedures allow additional parameterizations. In SAS Viya, GLM parameterization is the default, and the alternatives are the same for all procedures.

Programming Tip: To learn which parameterizations are provided by a procedure, consult the section for the CLASS statement in the procedure chapter in the documentation.

The sort order for the levels determines which parameters in the model correspond to each level in the data. By default, the procedures order the levels by their formatted values. In SAS 9, you can specify the ordering with the ORDER= option in the procedure statement. In SAS Viya, this option appears in the CLASS statement. Table I.2 lists the available orderings.

Table I.2   Level Orderings

ORDER= keyword	How the Levels Are Ordered
DATA	By appearance in input data set (SAS 9 only)
FORMATTED	By internal values for numeric predictors with no explicit format; by formatted values for other predictors
FREQ	By descending frequency count in input data set
INTERNAL	By unformatted values

Note that the concept of data order does not apply to CAS tables in SAS Viya.

Specifying Effect Splitting

In the CLASS statement on page 390, the SPLIT option is specified for Region but not for Training. This enables the columns of the design matrix that correspond to Region to enter the model independently of each other during forward selection. However, the columns that correspond to Training must enter as a set.

In general, when you apply the SPLIT option to a classification variable, the columns of the design matrix that correspond to any effect that contains this variable can enter or leave the model independently of the other design columns for that effect.

In SAS 9, the SPLIT option is available in the GLMSELECT and QUANTSELECT procedures but not in the high-performance procedures discussed in this book. In SAS Viya, the SPLIT option is available in all of the model building procedures.

You can apply the SPLIT option to all of the variables in a CLASS statement by specifying it after the slash (/).

> **Programming Tip:** In procedures where the SPLIT option is available, you can use it with any sequential selection method and with any parameterization.

Useful Parameterizations

The next sections explain the parameterizations listed in Table I.1. The following statements create a small subset of the data set Stores (see page 56) named Stores8 that is used for illustration:

```
data Stores8;
   set Stores(keep=CloseRate x2 Region);
   if _N_ in ( 1 2 125 126 280 281 360 361 );
run;

proc print data=Stores8; run;
```

Output I.1 shows that Stores8 contains two observations for each of the four levels of Region.

Output I.1 Listing of Stores8

Obs	X2	CloseRate	Region
1	-0.268	57.86	Midwest
2	0.225	60.28	Midwest
3	-0.057	59.85	South
4	-0.399	61.85	South
5	-0.468	59.37	West
6	-0.005	62.81	West
7	-0.048	60.82	East
8	-0.140	62.08	East

GLM Parameterization

For a categorical predictor with G distinct levels, GLM parameterization generates G columns in the design matrix that represent the main effect of the predictor. Each column is an indicator variable for one of the levels. GLM parameterization also generates a column of 1's for the intercept parameter. Because the $G + 1$ columns are not linearly independent, the matrix does not have full rank, and so GLM coding is called a less-than-full-rank or singular parameterization.

In order to illustrate this coding, the following statements use the GLMSELECT procedure to fit a model for the data in Stores8 with the continuous predictor (X2) and the categorical predictor (Region). The PARAM= option requests GLM coding.

```
proc glmselect data=Stores8 outdesign=GLMDesign;
   class Region / param=glm show;
   model CloseRate = x2 Region / selection=none;
run;
```

Output I.2, requested with the SHOW option, provides the level coding.

Output I.2 GLM Level Coding for Region

Class Level Coding				
	Design Variables			
Region Level	1	2	3	4
East	1	0	0	0
Midwest	0	1	0	0
South	0	0	1	0
West	0	0	0	1

For convenience, the next statements augment the design matrix, which was requested with the OUTDESIGN= option and saved in GLMDesign, with the values of Region.

```
data RegionOnly; set Stores8; keep Region; run;
data Augment; merge GLMDesign RegionOnly; run;
proc print data=Augment noobs; run;
```

Output I.3 shows the augmented matrix.

Output I.3 Design Matrix with GLM Parameterization

Region	Intercept	X2	Region_East	Region_Midwest	Region_South	Region_West
Midwest	1	-.26782	0	1	0	0
Midwest	1	0.22493	0	1	0	0
South	1	-.05684	0	0	1	0
South	1	-.39888	0	0	1	0
West	1	-.46757	0	0	0	1
West	1	-.00538	0	0	0	1
East	1	-.04847	1	0	0	0
East	1	-.14040	1	0	0	0

Output I.4 shows the parameter estimates.

Output I.4 Parameter Estimates with GLM Parameterization

Parameter Estimates			
Parameter		DF	Estimate
Intercept		1	61.895482
X2		1	3.401708
Region	East	1	-0.122881
Region	Midwest	1	-2.755708
Region	South	1	-0.268363
Region	West	0	0

With GLM coding, parameters can only be estimated for $G - 1$ levels. Here, the parameter for level West is not estimated because it happens to be last in the sort order. The intercept is the baseline predicted response assuming that X2 is zero and the level of Region is West. The estimate for level Midwest (-2.755708) is the decrease in the baseline response when the level of Region is Midwest.

In summary, GLM coding gives you estimates for as many parameters *as can be estimated from the data*. The next sections describe coding schemes that create a full-rank design matrix by imposing assumptions about the parameters that are external to the data.

Effect Parameterization

With effect parameterization, you can designate one of the levels for each categorical predictor as a reference level; the default is the last level in the sort order. For the other levels, this parameterization first generates indicator variables with values 0 and 1 as columns in the design matrix. Then for all observations in the reference group, it resets the values of the indicator variables to -1.

The following statements request effect coding. The REF= option specifies West as the reference level.

```
proc glmselect data=Stores8 outdesign=EffectDesign;
   class Region(ref='West') / param=effect;
   model CloseRate = x2 Region / selection=none;
run;
```

Output I.5 shows the augmented design matrix.

Output I.5 Design Matrix with Effect Parameterization

Region	Intercept	X2	Region_East	Region_Midwest	Region_South
Midwest	1	-.26782	0	1	0
Midwest	1	0.22493	0	1	0
South	1	-.05684	0	0	1
South	1	-.39888	0	0	1
West	1	-.46757	-1	-1	-1
West	1	-.00538	-1	-1	-1
East	1	-.04847	1	0	0
East	1	-.14040	1	0	0

Output I.6 shows the parameter estimates.

Output I.6 Parameter Estimates with Effect Parameterization

Parameter Estimates			
Parameter		DF	Estimate
Intercept		1	61.108743
X2		1	3.401708
Region	East	1	0.663857
Region	Midwest	1	-1.968970
Region	South	1	0.518375

The intercept is the baseline predicted response assuming that X2 is zero and the level of Region is the reference level West. For each of the non-reference levels, the parameter estimate represents the difference in the effect of the level compared with the average effect of all the levels. This is why, for instance, the estimate obtained here for level Midwest differs from the estimate obtained with GLM coding in Output I.4. The parameter estimate for the reference level has the same interpretation. It is not provided because it is redundant; it is simply the sum of the other parameter estimates multiplied by −1.

Reference Parameterization

With reference parameterization (as with effect parameterization), you designate one of the levels for each categorical predictor as a reference level; the default is the last level in the sort order. For the other levels, reference parameterization first generates indicator variables with values 0 and 1 as columns in the design matrix. Then for all observations in the reference group, it resets the values of the indicator variables to 0.

The following statements request reference coding. The REF= option specifies West as the reference level.

```
proc glmselect data=Stores8 outdesign=ReferenceDesign;
    class Region(ref='West') / param=reference;
    model CloseRate = x2 Region / selection=none;
run;
```

Output I.7 shows the augmented design matrix.

Output I.7 Design Matrix with Reference Parameterization

Region	Intercept	X2	Region_East	Region_Midwest	Region_South
Midwest	1	-.26782	0	1	0
Midwest	1	0.22493	0	1	0
South	1	-.05684	0	0	1
South	1	-.39888	0	0	1
West	1	-.46757	0	0	0
West	1	-.00538	0	0	0
East	1	-.04847	1	0	0
East	1	-.14040	1	0	0

Output I.8 shows the parameter estimates.

Output I.8 Parameter Estimates with Reference Parameterization

Parameter Estimates		DF	Estimate
Intercept		1	61.895482
X2		1	3.401708
Region	East	1	-0.122881
Region	Midwest	1	-2.755708
Region	South	1	-0.268363

The intercept is the baseline predicted response assuming that X2 is zero and the level of Region is the reference level West. For each of the non-reference levels, the parameter estimate represents the difference in the effect of the level compared with the effect of the reference level. This is why the estimate obtained here for level Midwest differs from the estimates obtained with GLM coding in Output I.4 and effect coding in Output I.6.

Other Parameterizations

The parameterizations described here are only a subset of the coding schemes that are available with statistical procedures in SAS 9 and SAS Viya. For full details, see the section "Parameterization of Model Effects" in the chapter "Shared Concepts and Topics" in the *SAS/STAT User's Guide*.

Chapter 12 of the 2017 SAS Press book *Applying Data Science: Business Case Studies Using SAS* by Gerhard Svolba provides a helpful explanation of coding schemes for regression models.

Summary

The preceding examples demonstrate that the various coding schemes lead to parameter estimates that differ numerically and have different interpretations. However, the predicted values produced by models with different schemes for the same categorical predictors are the same.[†]

Although GLM coding is the default parameterization for the model building procedures in this book, it is not the default for all statistical modeling procedures in SAS/STAT. For instance, effect parameterization is the default for the LOGISTIC procedure, while reference parameterization is the default for the PHREG procedure.

Programming Tip: For consistency, if you use a statistical modeling procedure to explore a model obtained with a model building procedure, use the same parameterization in both models.

[†]The reason is that the design matrices are full-rank linear transformations of each other. However, with models that are selected rather than specified, the predicted values might differ if the model building process only selects portions of categorical effects that are coded differently. For instance, this can occur if you use the SPLIT option or if interaction effects are permitted to enter or leave the model without their corresponding main effects (see page 58).

Appendix J
Essentials of ODS Graphics

Contents

The majority of graphs in this book were created automatically by model building procedures, either by default or by requesting specific plots with a PLOTS= option provided by the procedure. In some cases, graphs were created with the SGPLOT procedure, a general-purpose procedure for statistical graphics.

The convenience of creating high-quality graphs and the consistency of their appearance are benefits of ODS Graphics, a system for producing graphs that extends the Output Delivery System (ODS) in SAS 9 and SAS Viya. ODS manages the display of procedure output—both tables and graphs—in a variety of destinations, such as HTML and RTF.

In order to create graphs, the one thing you need to know about ODS Graphics is how to enable it. In SAS Studio and the SAS windowing environment, it is enabled by default. In other environments, you can enable it with the following statement:

```
ods graphics on;
```

You can place this statement once at the beginning of your SAS session or program. You do *not* need to place it before each procedure (this is a common misconception). In this book, the statement is placed once at the beginning of the first example in each chapter.

Because ODS Graphics consumes additional resources, you might consider disabling it if you are only interested in computational or tabular results. You can do this with the following statement:

```
ods graphics off;
```

By learning more about ODS Graphics, you can take advantages of features that control the appearance of graphs and access graphs as individual image files. This appendix provides a brief explanation of these features.

Managing the Display of Graphs and Tables

Graphs and tables are integrated in an output destination specified with an ODS statement such as

```
ods html;
```

The LISTING destination is the destination originally provided by the SAS windowing environment. For a list of the available destinations, see the section "ODS Destination Statements" in Chapter 21, "Statistical Graphics Using ODS," in the *SAS/STAT User's Guide*.

Only some of the output produced by a procedure might be relevant to your work. You can use ODS SELECT and ODS EXCLUDE statements to select or exclude graphs and tables from your output. You refer to graphs and tables by their names, which you can find in the "ODS Graphics" and "ODS Table Names" subsections of the "Details" section of each procedure chapter in the *SAS/STAT User's Guide*. For instance, in the example on page 169 the following statements build a model and restrict the displayed output to the table of association statistics shown in Output 9.4:

```
proc hplogistic data=Train;
    model y(event='1') = x1-x&nVars / association ctable=ROCValues;
    selection method=stepwise(choose=validate select=sbc stop=validate
                              maxsteps=20);
    partition fraction(validate=0.2 test=0.2 seed=15531);
     ods select Association;
run;
```

Creating SAS Data Sets from Graphs and Tables

It is often necessary to capture the information in graphs and tables as SAS data sets for subsequent processing with a SAS program. The ODS OUTPUT statement is indispensable for this purpose. The DISPLAYOUT statement in SAS Viya creates CAS tables from displayed output.

This book uses the ODS OUTPUT statement in situations where creating a SAS data set from a table provides a convenient way to extend the functionality of a procedure. For instance, the HPLOGISTIC procedure does not create a plot of the receiver operating characteristic (ROC) curve. As a workaround, the example on page 169 creates a SAS data set named AssocStat that contains the statistics displayed in the Association Statistics table in Output 9.4:

```
proc hplogistic data=Train;
    model y(event='1') = x1-x&nVars / association ctable=ROCValues;
    selection method=stepwise(choose=validate select=sbc stop=validate
                              maxsteps=20);
    output out=trainOut(keep=y ModelPred1) copyvars=(y) p=ModelPred1;
    partition fraction(validate=0.2 test=0.2 seed=15531);
     ods output Association=AssocStat;
run;
```

The example then uses the data set to create the plot with the SGPLOT procedure (see Output 9.5).

You can place the ODS OUTPUT statement before the procedure statement, but placing it after—as shown here—is good practice because it clarifies that the statement is part of the procedure step. The ODS OUTPUT statement should not be confused with the OUTPUT statement, which creates a data set that saves predicted values for the observations.

Accessing Individual Graphs

If you are writing a paper or creating a presentation, you will need to access your graphs individually. You can do this interactively or programmatically.

If you are running SAS interactively and you are viewing RTF output, you can copy and paste your graphs from the viewer into a Microsoft Word document or a Microsoft PowerPoint slide. If you are viewing HTML output, you can copy and paste your graphs from the viewer, or you can right-click on the graph and save it to a file.

If you are writing a program, you can add statements that save your graphs in image files (such as PNG files) for later inclusion in a paper or presentation. You specify the graphics image format and the filename in the ODS GRAPHICS statement. For example, you can specify the following statements before a procedure step that produces multiple graphs:

```
ods graphics on / imagefmt=png imagename="MyPlot";
ods html path = "D:\MyAnalysis" gpath = "D:\MyAnalysis\MyGraphs";
```

The graphs are saved in the directory *MyGraphs* as PNG files that are named *MyPlot.png*, *MyPlot1.png*, and so on.

The section "Image File Types" in Chapter 21, "Statistical Graphics Using ODS," in the *SAS/STAT User's Guide* provides details about the file types available for various destinations, how they are named, and how they are saved.

Specifying the Size and Resolution of Graphs

When you are creating graphs for a paper or presentation, two factors to consider are the size of your graphs and their resolution. For best results, you should specify the size of the graph as it will appear in the document. You can specify the size in the ODS GRAPHICS statement, as illustrated by the following examples:

```
ods graphics on / width=6in;
ods graphics on / height=4in;
ods graphics on / width=4.5in height=3.5in;
```

When you specify only one dimension, most graphs are produced with a width-to-height aspect ratio of 4/3.

The default resolution of graphs created for the HTML and LISTING destinations is 100 DPI (dots per inch), whereas the default for the RTF destination is 200 DPI. You can change the resolution by specifying the IMAGE_DPI= option in the destination statement, as in the following example:

```
ods html image_dpi=300;
```

An increase in resolution often improves the quality of the graphs, but it also increases the size of the image file. The section "Graph Size and Resolution" in Chapter 21, "Statistical Graphics Using ODS," in the *SAS/STAT User's Guide* provides more information about graph size and resolution.

Specifying the Style of Graphs and Tables

ODS styles control the overall appearance of your graphs and tables. For graphs, they specify colors, fonts, line patterns, symbol markers, and other attributes.

You specify an ODS style with the STYLE= option in the ODS destination statement. For example, the following statement sets the style for the HTML destination:

```
ods html style=HTMLBlue;
```

When you specify a style in the ODS LISTING statement, it applies only to graphs; SAS monospace format is used for tables.

It is possible—though rarely necessary—to modify the specifications of a style by editing the style template. For more information, see the section "ODS Styles" in Chapter 21, "Statistical Graphics Using ODS," in the *SAS/STAT User's Guide*. Also see the *SAS Output Delivery System: User's Guide*.

Distinguishing Groups in Graphs

When you create graphs that involve groups of points, lines, or curves, you can distinguish the groups with a combination of colors, markers, and line patterns or only with colors. You might prefer the latter for graphs in a presentation and the former for graphs in a black-and-white publication.

The distinction, called attribute priority, is a feature of the style:

- An ATTRPRIORITY=NONE style distinguishes groups by colors, markers, and lines. For instance, in the coefficient progression plot in Output 10.27 on page 218, the lines are distinguished by both colors and line patterns.

  Most ODS styles are ATTRPRIORITY=NONE styles. They are compromise styles in the sense that some graph elements are intentionally overdistinguished to facilitate black-and-white printing.

- An ATTRPRIORITY=COLOR style distinguishes groups of observations by colors and not by lines or symbols. Styles of this type include HTMLBLUE, PEARL, PEARLJ, and SAPPHIRE.

If you want to control the markers or lines that are displayed for groups of observations when you are using an ATTRPRIORITY=COLOR style, specify the ATTRPRIORITY=NONE option in the ODS GRAPHICS statement.

For instance, the style used to create this book is an ATTRPRIORITY=COLOR style. In order to differentiate the lines in a coefficient progression plot with both colors and patterns, the example on page 217 specifies

```
ods graphics on / attrpriority=none;
```

The plot is shown in Output 10.27.

For more information, see the sections "Attribute Priorities" and "Overriding How Groups Are Distinguished" in Chapter 21, "Statistical Graphics Using ODS," in the *SAS/STAT User's Guide*.

Modifying Graphs by Editing Graph Templates

You might occasionally need to modify a graph by editing its template. A graph template is a program, written in the Graph Template Language (GTL), that specifies the layout and details of a graph. Graphs produced by ODS Graphics are constructed from two underlying components: a data object created by a procedure at run time and a compiled graph template that is designed to work with this data object. Templates are complete descriptions of how graphs are to be produced, and so they tend to be lengthy and complex.

Ordinarily, you do not need to know anything about templates or the GTL because SAS provides a template for every graph produced by a statistical procedure. However, with a moderate understanding of the GTL, you can edit graph templates to make changes that are applied whenever you rerun the procedure. For instance, you can customize titles and axis labels. Appendix K explains the process of editing a template. For more information, see Chapter 22, "ODS Graphics Template Modification," in the *SAS/STAT User's Guide*.

Creating Graphs by Writing Graph Templates

A second reason for learning about the GTL is that you can use it to create highly customized displays by writing your own graph templates. For instance, this approach was used to produce Figure 14.4 on page 299. See Kuhfeld (2016) for additional examples.

Creating Graphs with Statistical Graphics Procedures

SAS provides the following general-purpose statistical graphics procedures for data exploration and analysis:

- The SGPLOT procedure, which creates a variety of plots that can be overlaid. The ROC plot on page 170 is just one of a number of graphs in this book that were created with this procedure.

- The SGSCATTER procedure, which creates scatter plot matrices and related displays.

- The SGPANEL procedure, which creates panels of plots arranged by values of classification variables. For instance, the distribution plots in Appendix E were created with this procedure.

These procedures, collectively known as the "SG procedures," produce density plots, dot plots, needle plots, series plots, horizontal and vertical bar charts, histograms, and box plots. They also display loess fits, polynomial fits, penalized B-spline fits, reference lines, bands, and ellipses.

The SG procedures are documented in the *SAS ODS Graphics: Procedures Guide*. The 2011 SAS Press book *Statistical Graphics Procedures by Example* by Sanjay Matange and Dan Heath is an indispensable resource for getting started with these procedures. Also recommended are two online books by Warren Kuhfeld that give examples of the SG procedures, compare them with the GTL, and discuss plot annotation (Kuhfeld 2015, 2016).

Appendix K
Modifying a Procedure Graph

Contents

You might occasionally need to modify a graph produced by a statistical procedure. For instance, you might want to customize the title and the axis labels, or you might want to annotate the graph with additional information. You can do this by modifying the template that SAS supplies for the graph.

A graph template is a program, written in the Graph Template Language (GTL), that specifies the layout and details of a graph. Ordinarily, you do not need to know anything about templates because they are applied internally by procedures at run time. However, by following the steps illustrated in this appendix, you can access, modify, and save the template for a graph. Your graph will then be modified whenever you rerun the procedure.

Example: Enhancing a Contour Plot

In Chapter 11, the example on page 235 uses the GAMPL procedure to fit a generalized additive model for the severity of insurance claims in a region of North Carolina. In order to explore the effect of geographic location, the model includes a bivariate spline effect for the latitude and longitude of the policyholder in addition to a univariate spline effect for the age of the policyholder. The following statements fit the original model:

```
ods graphics on;
proc gampl data=ClaimSeverityNC plots(unpack)=components
          fmtlibxml=ClmsFmts seed=757931;
    class Homeowner(ref='No') VehicleType(ref='Small')
          WorkStatus(ref='Not Working') / param=ref;
    model ClaimAmount = param(Homeowner VehicleType WorkStatus)
                        spline(AgePolicyHolder)
                        spline(LonPolicyHolder LatPolicyHolder)
              / distribution=gamma link=log method=outer;
run;
```

As requested with the PLOTS= option, the GAMPL procedure creates a bivariate spline component plot, which is shown in Output K.1.

Output K.1 Spline Component for LatPolicyHolder and LonPolicyHolder

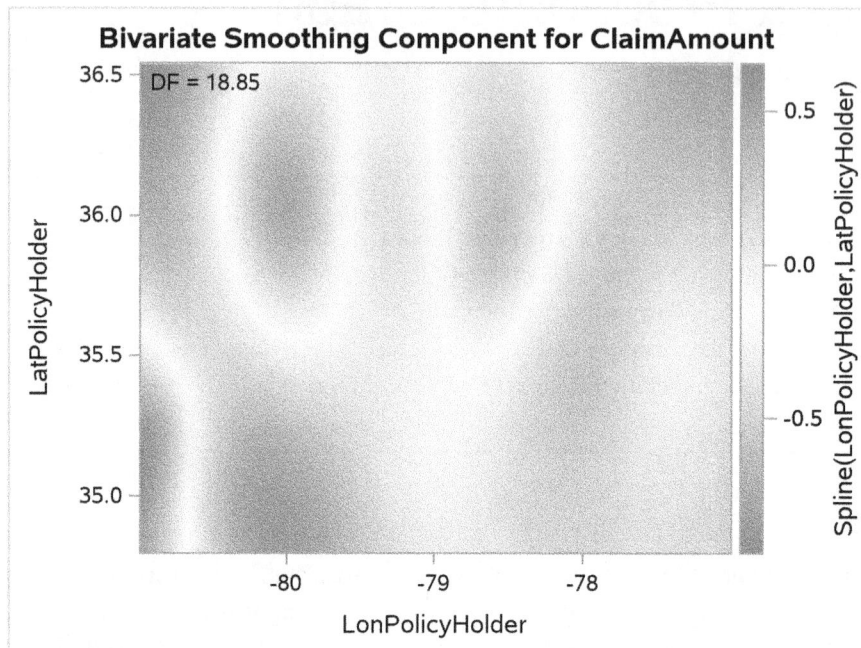

This example enhances the plot in two ways. First, it replaces the default text in the title, axis labels, and legend label—which uses SAS variable names—with text that is more recognizable for a presentation. This is done by modifying the template for the graph.

Second, the example adds the locations of nine North Carolina cities in order to make the shaded regions more interpretable. This is done by enabling annotation and reading the latitudes and longitudes of the cities from an annotation data set.

The SGRENDER procedure produces the final plot, shown in Output K.2, by applying the modified template to the values in the original plot and adding the city locations.

Capturing the Data in the Procedure Plot

As a preliminary step, the following statements capture the values displayed in the plot originally produced by the procedure by adding an ODS OUTPUT statement:

```
proc gampl data=ClaimSeverityNC plots(unpack)=components
           fmtlibxml=ClmsFmts seed=757931;
    ods output  SmoothingComponentPlot = ComponentPlots
                SmoothingEstimates      = SmoothEst;
    class Homeowner(ref='No') VehicleType(ref='Small')
          WorkStatus(ref='Not Working') / param=ref;
    model ClaimAmount = param(Homeowner VehicleType WorkStatus)
                        spline(AgePolicyHolder)
                        spline(LonPolicyHolder LatPolicyHolder)
           / distribution=gamma link=log method=outer;
run;
```

The ODS OUTPUT statement saves the values for the univariate and bivariate spline component plots in a data set named ComponentPlots, and it saves the smoothing estimates for the components in a data set named SmoothEst.

The next statements create a data set named ContourPlot that contains the variables and observations in ComponentPlots that correspond to the bivariate spline component plot:

```
data ContourPlot;
   keep p_s2x1x2 s2x2 s2x1;
   set ComponentPlots(where=(p_s2x1x2 NE . ));
run;
```

The variables S2X1, S2X2, and P_S2X1X2 are the *x*-variable, the *y*-variable, and the *z*-variable, respectively.

The next statements create a macro variable named EffectiveDF that saves the effective degrees of freedom for the bivariate spline component:

```
data SmoothEst;
   set SmoothEst(where=(Component='Spline(LonPolicyHolder LatPolicyHolder)'));
   call symputx('EffectiveDF', put(EDF, BEST4.), 'g' );
run;
```

Determining the Template Name

In order to modify a template used by a procedure, you first need to know the name of the template. A convenient way to determine this is with the ODS TRACE statement, which writes a record of each output object to the SAS log:

```
 ods trace on;
proc gampl data=ClaimSeverityNC plots(unpack)=components
           fmtlibxml=ClmsFmts seed=757931;
   ods output SmoothingComponentPlot = ContourPlot
              SmoothingEstimates      = SmoothEst;
   class Homeowner(ref='No') VehicleType(ref='Small')
         WorkStatus(ref='Not Working') / param=ref;
   model ClaimAmount = param(Homeowner VehicleType WorkStatus)
                       spline(AgePolicyHolder)
                       spline(LonPolicyHolder LatPolicyHolder)
            / distribution=gamma link=log method=outer;
run;
 ods trace off;
```

The statement produces the following record for the contour plot:

```
Output Added:
-------------
Name:         SmoothingComponentPlot
Label:        Spline(LonPolicyHolder,LatPolicyHolder)
Template:     HPSTAT.GAMPL.Graphics.SmoothingComponent2d
Path:         GAMPL.SmoothingComponentPlots.SmoothingComponentPlot
```

The complete name of the template is **HPSTAT.GAMPL.Graphics.SmoothingComponent2d**.

Accessing and Displaying the Template

With the template name, you can use the TEMPLATE procedure to save the source code for the template in a specified file:

```
proc template;
    source HPSTAT.GAMPL.Graphics.SmoothingComponent2d / file='SourceCode.txt';
```

By default, the procedure writes the source code to the SAS log. The template is displayed as follows:

```
define statgraph Hpstat.GAMPL.Graphics.SmoothingComponent2d;
    notes "Bivariate Smoothing Component Plot";
    dynamic _STATLINE _X1VAR _X2VAR _PRED _DEPNAME _SHORTXLABEL _SHORTYLABEL
            _CONTOURLEVEL _PLOTHEAD _YLABEL _XLABEL _byline_ _bytitle_
            _byfootnote_;
    BeginGraph;
        ENTRYTITLE "Bivariate Smoothing Component for " _DEPNAME;
        ENTRYTITLE _STATLINE / textattrs=GRAPHVALUETEXT;
        layout overlay / xaxisopts=(linearopts=(thresholdmin=0 thresholdmax=0)
                                    offsetmin=0 offsetmax=0 label=_XLABEL
                                    shortlabel=_SHORTXLABEL)
                         yaxisopts=(linearopts=(thresholdmin=0 thresholdmax=0)
                                    offsetmin=0 offsetmax=0 label=_YLABEL
                                    shortlabel=_SHORTYLABEL);
            ContourPlotParm z=_PRED y=_X2VAR x=_X1VAR / contourtype=gradient
                                                        name="ContourLevels"
                                                        gridded=false;
            continuousLegend "ContourLevels" / title=_CONTOURLEVEL;
            entry _PLOTHEAD / autoalign=(topleft topright top bottomleft
                                        bottomright bottom);
        endlayout;
        if (_BYTITLE_)
            entrytitle _BYLINE_ / textattrs=GRAPHVALUETEXT;
        else
            if (_BYFOOTNOTE_)
                entryfootnote halign=left _BYLINE_;
            endif;
        endif;
    EndGraph;
end;
```

The template definition begins with a DEFINE STATGRAPH statement and ends with an END statement. The DYNAMIC statement defines variables whose values are supplied by the procedure at run time. Here, these values supply variable names and text displayed in the plot. For instance, _DEPNAME is the name of the dependent variable, _XLABEL is the label of the *x*-axis, and _PLOTHEAD provides the text DF=18.85 that indicates the effective degrees of freedom.

Embedded in every graph template is a block of statements enclosed by BEGINGRAPH and ENDGRAPH statements. This block contains ENTRYTITLE statements that provide titles and footnotes, and it contains at least one block of statements enclosed by LAYOUT and ENDLAYOUT statements that define the layout and components of the graph. Here, the COUNTOURPLOTPARM statement creates the contour plot, and the CONTINOUSLEGEND statement adds a thermometer legend.

Modifying the Template Code

The following statements use the TEMPLATE procedure to create a template named **AnnotatedPlot** that modifies the original template **SmoothingComponent2d**:

```
proc template;
   define statgraph AnnotatedPlot / store=sasuser.templat;
   notes "Modified Bivariate Smoothing Component Plot";
   BeginGraph;
      ENTRYTITLE "Model Effect of Location on Claim Severity"
                 / textattrs=GRAPHTITLETEXT;
      layout overlay / xaxisopts=(linearopts=(thresholdmin=0 thresholdmax=0)
                                  offsetmin=0 offsetmax=0 label="Longitude")
                       yaxisopts=(linearopts=(thresholdmin=0 thresholdmax=0)
                                  offsetmin=0 offsetmax=0 label="Latitude");
         ContourPlotParm z=p_s2x1x2 y=s2x2 x=s2x1 / contourtype=gradient
                                                    name="ContourLevels"
                                                    gridded=false;
         continuousLegend "ContourLevels" / title="Effect";
         entry "DF = &EffectiveDF." / autoalign=(topleft topright top
                                      bottomleft bottomright bottom);
         annotate;
      endlayout;
   EndGraph;
   end;
run;
```

The title, axis labels, and legend labels are replaced with text strings, and the X=, Y=, and Z= options in the COUNTOURPLOT statement are assigned the names of variables in CountourPlot. This eliminates the dynamic variables, so the new template can be used independently of the GAMPL procedure. The new template also includes an ANNOTATE statement; this enables annotation instructions to be read from a SAS data set when the template is used by the SGRENDER procedure to create a graph. The template is saved in a template store in the SASUSER library.

Creating an Annotation Data Set with City Information

This step creates an annotation data set named CityLabels that contains the latitudes, longitudes, and names of nine cities in North Carolina. The following statements define a macro named **%MyLabel** that places a circle at the latitude and longitude of a city:

```
%SGANNO;
%macro MyLabel(City=, Lat=, Lon=, Anchor=,);;
   %SGTEXT( label="&City.", x1=&Lon, y1=&Lat,
            anchor="&Anchor.", justify="right",
            drawspace="datavalue", x1space="datavalue", y1space="datavalue",
            textcolor="black", textfont="Arial", textweight="bold",
            textstyle="normal", textsize=9, width=300, widthunit="pixel",
            border="false",layer="front" )
   %SGOVAL( height=9, width=9, x1=&Lon, y1=&Lat,
            drawspace="datavalue", x1space="datavalue", y1space="datavalue",
            display="all", linecolor="black", fillcolor="white",
            heightunit="pixel", widthunit="pixel", layer="front" )
%mend MyLabel;
```

The macro calls two SG annotation macros, `%SGTEXT` and `%SGOVAL`, that are compiled by issuing the `%SGANNO` macro. These macros are documented in *SAS ODS Graphics: Procedures Guide*. The next statements create an annotation data set named CityLabels with the locations of nine cities:

```
data CityLabels;
    %MyLabel(City=Raleigh,        Lon=-78.6382, Lat=35.7796, Anchor=bottomleft )
    %MyLabel(City=Cary,           Lon=-78.7811, Lat=35.7915, Anchor=bottomright)
    %MyLabel(City=Apex,           Lon=-78.8503, Lat=35.7327, Anchor=topleft    )
    %MyLabel(City=Durham,         Lon=-78.8986, Lat=35.9940, Anchor=bottomright)
    %MyLabel(City=Chapel Hill,    Lon=-79.0558, Lat=35.9132, Anchor=bottomright)
    %MyLabel(City=Winston-Salem,  Lon=-80.2442, Lat=36.0999, Anchor=bottomright)
    %MyLabel(City=High Point,     Lon=-80.0053, Lat=35.9557, Anchor=topright   )
    %MyLabel(City=Greensboro,     Lon=-79.7920, Lat=36.0726, Anchor=bottomleft )
    %MyLabel(City=Charlotte,      Lon=-80.8431, Lat=35.2271, Anchor=bottomleft )
    %MyLabel(City=New Bern,       Lon=-77.0441, Lat=35.1085, Anchor=bottomright)
run;
```

The next statements use the SGRENDER procedure to produce the enhanced contour plot from the data set ContourPlot by applying the instructions in the template `AnnotatedPlot` and by annotating the contour plot with the city locations in the data set CityLabels:

```
proc sgrender data=ContourPlot template=AnnotatedPlot sganno=CityLabels;
run;
```

Output K.2 shows the enhanced graph.

Output K.2 Annotated Spline Component Plot

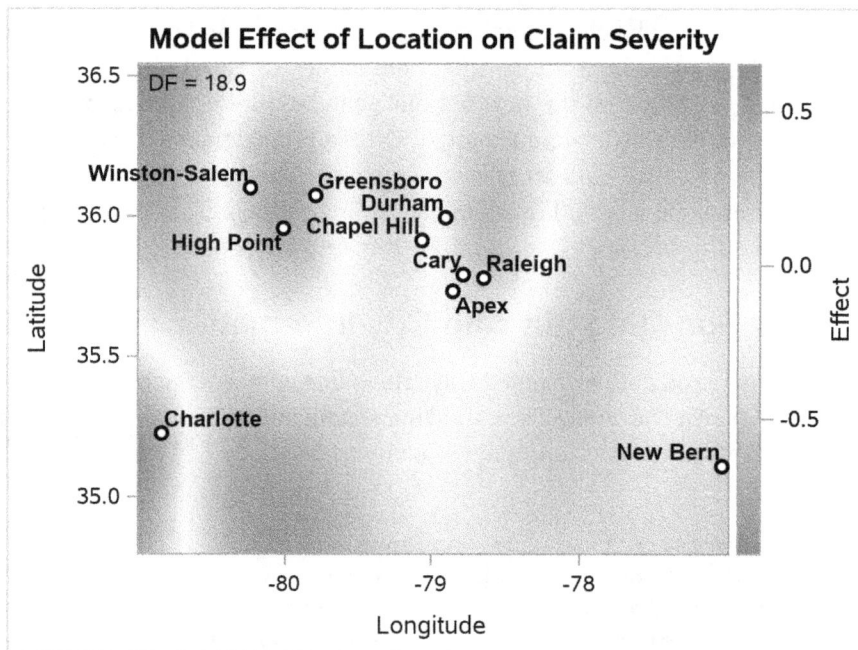

The final statements delete `AnnotatedPlot` since it is no longer needed:

```
proc template;
    delete AnnotatedPlot / store=sasuser.templat;
run;
```

Summary

You can modify the titles, labels, footnotes, and other text in a procedure graph by modifying its template. This involves the following steps:

1. Use the ODS TRACE statement to determine the template name.

2. Use the SOURCE statement in the TEMPLATE procedure to list the template.

3. Edit the template by replacing dynamic variables used for text with quoted strings.

4. Use the TEMPLATE procedure to compile the modified template, *keeping the name of the original template*, and save it in a template store in the SASUSER library.

When you rerun the procedure, it will access the template in SASUSER rather than the SAS-supplied template, and your modifications will be displayed in the graph.

The GTL syntax is documented in *SAS 9.4 Graph Template Language User's Guide* and *SAS 9.4 Graph Template Language Reference*. You do not need to understand the full syntax in order to make the basic types of modifications described here, but by learning more of it you will be able to make extensive modifications and write your own templates.

The example in this appendix does more; it enhances the original graph with information that was not available to the procedure. Consequently, the template must be modified so that it can be used by the SGRENDER. Here, this is done by eliminating all of the dynamic variables and enabling annotation. The DATA= data set used by the SGRENDER procedure contains the values that were displayed by the GAMPL procedure; it was captured with an ODS OUTPUT statement. The SGANNO= data set contains city locations; it was created with SG annotation macros.

For additional examples, see the chapter "ODS Graphics Template Modification" in the *SAS/STAT User's Guide*. For an explanation of SG annotation, see Kuhfeld (2015).

Appendix L
Marginal Model Plots

Contents

Marginal model plots, proposed by Cook and Weisberg (1997), provide a way to compare the values predicted by a regression model with the observed response values. Smoothed values of the predicted response and the observed response are plotted as curves against each of the predictors; an additional plot displays the predicted values on the horizontal axis. Agreement between the curves in every plot is evidence that the model provides a good fit. Disagreement in a particular plot might suggest the need for a spline transformation of the predictor.

An advantage of marginal model plots over residual plots is that they apply to generalized linear models and generalized additive models, as well as general linear models. However, marginal model plots—like other diagnostic tools that plot all the observations—do not easily extend to data with more than a few hundred observations and more than a dozen or so predictors.

This appendix explains how you can create marginal model plots with the `%Marginal` macro in SAS.

Example: Claim Rates for Mortgages

In the mortgage insurance industry, analysts create models to predict conditional claim rates for specific types of loans. Understanding how claim rates depend on predictors is critical because the model is used to assess risk and allocate funds for potential claims.

Claim rates for 8,500 mortgages are saved in a data set named Claims. The response variable Rate is the number of claims per 10,000 contracts in a policy year; it is assumed to follow a Poisson distribution whose mean depends on the predictors listed in Table L.1.

Table L.1 Predictors for Claim Rate

Predictor	Description
Age	Age of loan
LoanValue	Amount of loan
PayIncmRatio	Payment-to-income ratio
Price	Price of house
RefInctvRatio	Refinance incentive ratio
RefInd	Indicator if loan is refinanced
UnempRate	Unemployment rate

The following statements use the GAMPL procedure, described in Chapter 11, to fit a generalized additive model for Rate:

```
ods graphics;
proc gampl data=Claims plots=components;
   class RefInd;
   model Rate = param(LoanValue RefInd PayIncmRatio RefInctvRatio UnempRate)
                spline(Age) spline(Price) / distribution=poisson log=link;
   output out=PredValues p=PredRate;
   id Rate Age LoanValue PayIncmRatio Price RefInctvRatio RefInd UnempRate;
run;
```

The MODEL statement specifies spline effects in Age and Price to characterize the nonlinearity in these predictors. The OUTPUT statement saves the predicted values in a data set named PredValues that includes the variables listed in the ID statement.

Output L.1 shows plots of the spline components for Age and Price.

Output L.1 Spline Component Plots

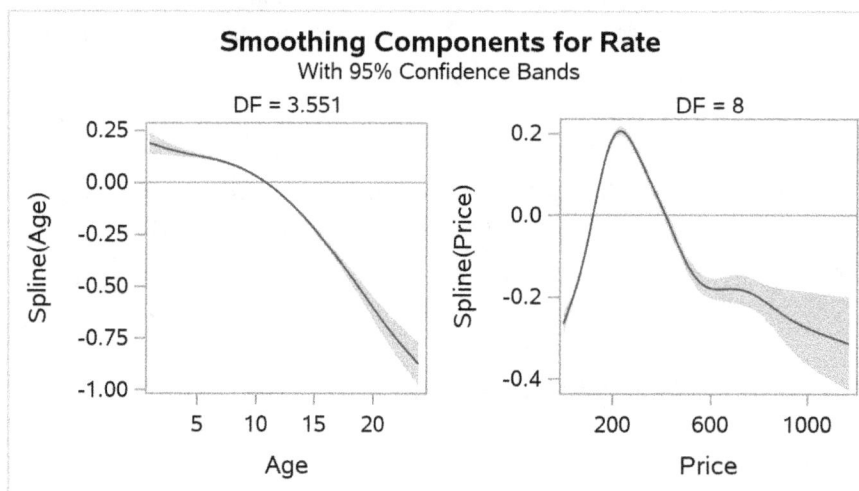

To avoid overplotting points in the marginal model plot, the next statement draws a random sample of 200 observations from PredValues and saves them in a data set named SamplePred.

```
proc surveyselect data=PredValues out=SamplePred method=srs seed=59931 sampsize=200;
run;
```

The next statement invokes the %Marginal macro:

```
%Marginal(data=SamplePred,
          independents=Age LoanValue PayIncmRatio Price RefInctvRatio
                       RefInd UnempRate,
          dependent=Rate,
          predicted=PredRate)
```

The INDEPENDENTS= option specifies the predictors used to fit the model. The DEPENDENT= option specifies the response variable, and the PREDICTED= option specifies the predicted response.

Output L.2 shows the marginal model plots.

Output L.2 Marginal Model Plots

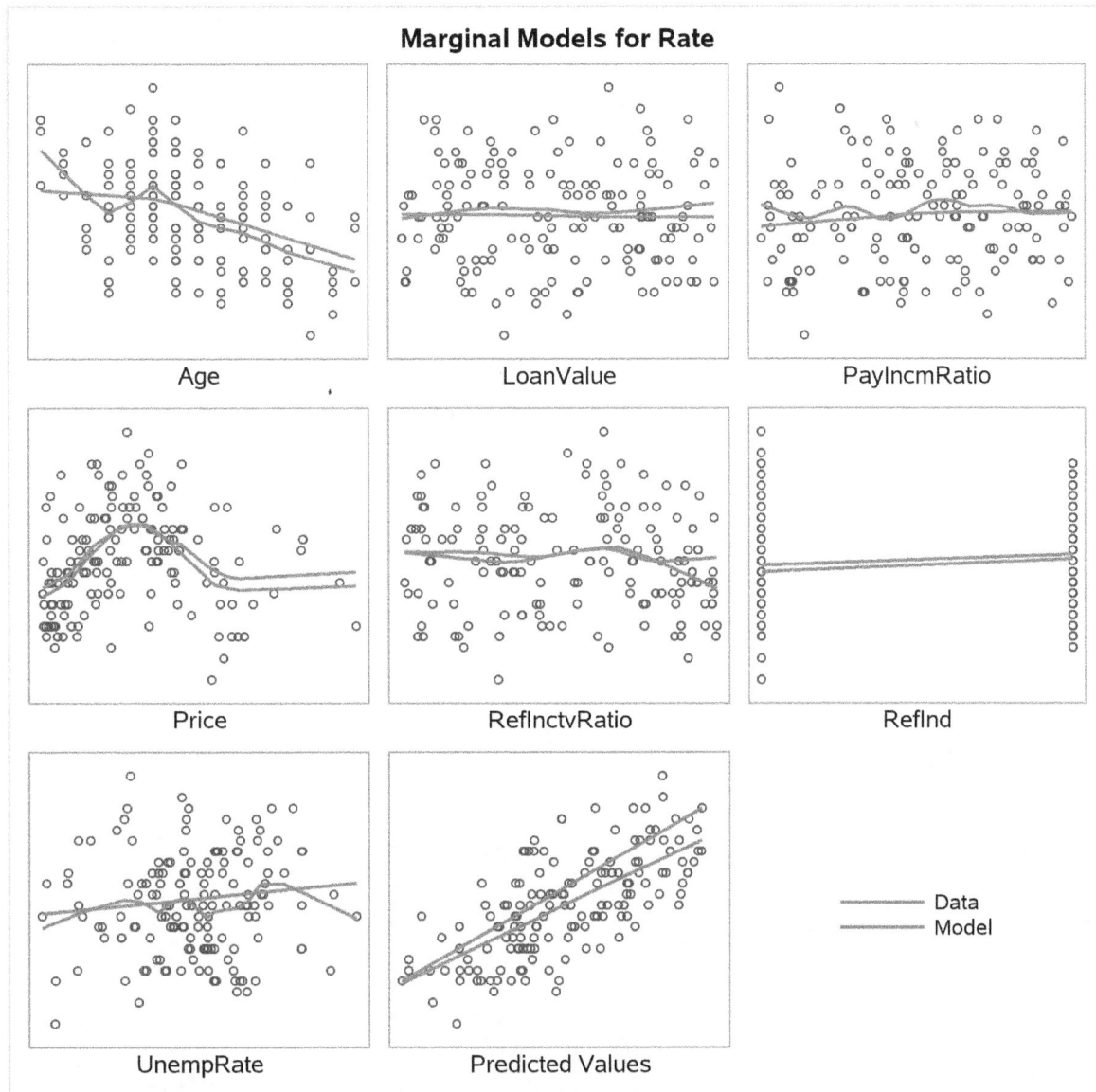

Marginal Models for Rate

The agreement of the curves in each of the plots indicates the model is a good fit. The curves in the plots for Age and Price echo the nonlinearity of the spline components in Output L.1.

The %Marginal Macro

The `%Marginal` macro is a gem buried deep in the documentation for SAS/STAT; it is explained in an example provided in the chapter on "ODS Graphics Template Modification" in the *SAS/STAT 15.1 User's Guide*. The macro displays multiple panels when there are too many plots to fit in a single panel. You can specify the number of rows and columns in a panel, as well as the design height for the graph. You can also specify the smoothing method for the curves; the default is loess.

Glossary

algorithm
a well-defined set of instructions for solving a particular problem.

bias
systematic error in the results produced by a model.

binary logistic regression model
a regression model for the probability of an event of interest (such as the repayment of a loan).

binary response
a response variable with two levels or labels (such as Yes and No), one of which corresponds to an event of interest.

black box model
a model whose internal operation is impenetrable.

categorical variable
a variable whose values are categories measured on a nominal scale (such as geographic region) or an ordinal scale (such as educational level).

classification
In machine learning, the use of algorithms to predict the categories of observations.

collinearity
strong correlations among predictors that make it difficult to determine which ones are important.

constructed effect
an effect in a regression model, such as a polynomial or spline effect, that is derived from predictor variables in the data.

continuous variable
a variable that can assume any number of values measured on a continuous scale (such as loan amount).

correlation coefficient
a measure of the strength of the linear relationship between two variables.

cross validation

a method for determining the predictive performance of a model on data previously not encountered.

decision tree

a supervised learning method for classification or regression that constructs a set of rules for predicting the response.

dependent variable

the response variable, target variable, or Y variable in a regression model.

design matrix

the matrix whose columns are the predictors in a linear regression model.

dimensionality reduction

reducing the number of predictors to a level more suitable for building a model.

expectation

the average value of a variable based on its distribution.

explanatory variable

a covariate, independent variable, predictor variable, or X variable, in a regression model.

false negative

an error that occurs in binary classification when a model misclassifies a positive response as negative.

false positive

an error that occurs in binary classification when a model misclassifies a negative response as positive.

feature

an input to a machine learning algorithm. In this book, features for building regression models are variables in the data or effects constructed from these variables.

feature engineering

the process of identifying variables and constructing effects for possible inclusion in a model.

feature selection

the process of determining features that are informative or relevant for use in a model.

fully specified model

a model whose variables and effects are chosen by the analyst, typically with the help of subject matter knowledge or previous research.

generalization
the ability of a model to predict previously unseen data produced by the same process that generated the training data.

goodness of fit
the extent to which a model fits the data, typically a measure computed from the discrepancies between the observed values of the response and the values predicted by the model.

hold-out sample
a subset of observations that is reserved for testing a model and is not used to build the model.

indicator variable
a variable with values 0 and 1 that represents a level of a categorical variable in a model matrix; also referred to as a dummy variable.

inference
in statistics, the use of estimation, confidence intervals, and hypothesis tests to answer questions about the data-generating process in ways that quantify uncertainty due to variability in the data.

In machine learning, the application of a model to new data in a production environment for tasks such as prediction.

interaction effect
an effect in a regression model that represents the linear dependence of the response on combinations of levels of two or more predictors.

interval target
a continuous response variable.

linear regression model
a model that expresses the conditional average of a continuous response variable as a linear function of the predictors.

logistic regression model
a regression model for the probabilities of outcomes or events.

machine learning
a branch of computer science that trains algorithms to discover patterns in data and to perform classification and prediction without the need for human intervention.

main effect
the effect of a predictor variable on the response averaged across the levels of other predictors in a regression model.

model

in statistics, a mathematical description of the data-generating process that makes assumptions about the relationships and probability distributions of the variables and serves to explain the process or predict future observations.

In machine learning, code used for prediction that is produced by algorithms which capture the relationships between the variables from large amounts of data.

model building

the process of constructing a model by applying a variety of methods such as model selection, shrinkage methods, methods for model averaging, methods for constructing spline effects, and methods for building trees.

model matrix

the matrix whose columns are the predictors in a linear regression model.

model parameters

unknown quantities in a model such as the coefficients of the predictors in a linear regression model.

model selection

the process of selecting the variables or effects in a model from a set of candidates.

model validation

the process of assessing how well a model performs.

nominal target

a categorical response variable.

overfitting

building an overly flexible model that fits the details of the training data so closely that it performs poorly when used to predict new data.

***p*-value**

the probability—assuming a statistical model—that a result (such as the difference in means between two groups) is equal to or more extreme than its observed value purely by chance. A *p*-value is not the probability that the model is correct.

polynomial effect

an effect in a regression model that represents the nonlinear dependence of the response on a continuous predictor with a polynomial transformation.

predictive model

a model used to predict response values in future observations.

predictor
a covariate, explanatory variable, independent variable, or X used for explaining or predicting the outcome in a regression model.

residuals
the differences between the observed and predicted values of a response variable.

response variable
the dependent variable, target variable, or Y variable that represents the outcome in a regression model.

scoring
the process of applying a model to predict or classify the response for new observations.

selected model
a model whose variables and effects are determined from the data by an algorithm or model building method.

specified model
a model whose variables and effects are chosen by the analyst, typically with the help of subject matter knowledge or previous research.

spline effect
an effect in a regression model that represents the nonlinear dependence of the response on a continuous predictor with a spline transformation defined by pieces of polynomials.

supervised learning
an approach that learns the relationship $y = f(\mathbf{x})$ between a set of inputs $\mathbf{x}$ and a labeled output y by applying algorithms to observations of the form $(\mathbf{x}_1, y_1), \ldots, (\mathbf{x}_n, y_n)$. Classification and regression are two types of supervised learning.

training a model
fitting or building a model with good predictive ability.

tuning parameter
a value specified by the analyst that controls the operation of an algorithm.

underfitting
building a model that is insufficiently flexible to capture the relationship between the predictors and the response.

References

Agresti, A. (2013). *Categorical Data Analysis*. 3rd ed. Hoboken, NJ: John Wiley & Sons.

Agresti, A. (2015). *Foundations of Linear and Generalized Linear Models*. Hoboken, NJ: Wiley.

Akaike, H. (1973). "Information Theory and an Extension of the Maximum Likelihood Principle." In *Breakthroughs in Statistics, Volume I: Foundations and Basic Theory*, edited by S. Kotz, and N. L. Johnson, 610–624. New York: Springer-Verlag.

Akaike, H. (1974). "A New Look at the Statistical Model Identification." *IEEE Transactions on Automatic Control* AC-19:716–723.

Akaike, H. (1979). "A Bayesian Extension of the Minimum AIC Procedure of Autoregressive Model Fitting." *Biometrika* 66:237–242.

Albert, A., and Anderson, J. A. (1984). "On the Existence of Maximum Likelihood Estimates in Logistic Regression Models." *Biometrika* 71:1–10.

Aldrich, J. (1997). "R. A. Fisher and the Making of Maximum Likelihood, 1912–1922." *Statistical Science* 12:162–176.

Allen, D. M. (1971). "Mean Square Error of Prediction as a Criterion for Selecting Variables." *Technometrics* 13:469–475.

Allen, D. M. (1974). "The Relationship between Variable Selection and Data Augmentation and a Method of Prediction." *Technometrics* 16:125–127.

Allison, P. (2008). "Convergence Failures in Logistic Regression." In *Proceedings of the SAS Global Forum 2008 Conference*. Cary, NC: SAS Institute Inc. https://support.sas.com/resources/papers/proceedings/pdfs/sgf2008/360-2008.pdf.

Allison, P. D. (2010). *Survival Analysis Using the SAS System: A Practical Guide*. 2nd ed. Cary, NC: SAS Institute Inc.

Allison, P. D. (2012). *Logistic Regression Using SAS: Theory and Application*. 2nd ed. Cary, NC: SAS Institute Inc.

Amato, U., Antoniadis, A., and De Feis, I. (2016). "Additive Model Selection." *Statistical Methods and Applications* 25:519–564.

Beaton, A. E. (1964). *The Use of Special Matrix Operations in Statistical Calculus*. Princeton, NJ: Educational Testing Service.

Belson, W. A. (1956a). "Learning and Attitude Changes Resulting from Viewing a Television Series, 'Bon Voyage'." *British Journal of Educational Psychology* 26:31–38.

Belson, W. A. (1956b). "A Technique for Studying the Effects of a Television Broadcast." *Journal of the Royal Statistical Society, Series C* 5:195–202.

Belson, W. A. (1959). "Matching and Prediction on the Principle of Biological Classification." *Journal of the Royal Statistical Society, Series C* 8:65–75.

Belson, W. A. (1967). *The Impact of Television: Methods and Findings in Program Research.* London: Crosby Lockwood & Son.

Bliss, C. I. (1935). "The Calculation of the Dosage-Mortality Curve." *Annals of Applied Biology* 22:134–167.

Boulesteix, A.-L., and Strimmer, K. (2006). "Partial Least Squares: A Versatile Tool for the Analysis of High-Dimensional Genomic Data." *Briefings in Bioinformatics* 8:32–44.

Breiman, L. (1992). "The Little Bootstrap and Other Methods for Dimensionality Selection in Regression: X-Fixed Prediction Error." *Journal of the American Statistical Association* 87:738–754.

Breiman, L. (1995). "Better Subset Regression Using the Nonnegative Garrote." *Technometrics* 37:373–384.

Breiman, L. (1996). "Bagging Predictors." *Machine Learning* 24:123–140.

Breiman, L. (2001a). "Random Forests." *Machine Learning* 45:5–32.

Breiman, L. (2001b). "Statistical Modeling: The Two Cultures." *Statistical Science* 16:199–231.

Breiman, L., Friedman, J., Olshen, R. A., and Stone, C. J. (1984). *Classification and Regression Trees.* Belmont, CA: Wadsworth.

Breiman, L., and Friedman, J. H. (1985). "Estimating Optimal Transformations for Multiple Regression and Correlation." *Journal of the American Statistical Association* 77:580–619. With discussion.

Breiman, L., and Spector, P. (1992). "Submodel Selection and Evaluation in Regression: The X-Random Case." *International Statistical Review* 60:291–319.

Breslow, N. E. (1974). "Covariance Analysis of Censored Survival Data." *Biometrics* 30:89–99.

Buckland, S. T., Burnham, K. P., and Augustin, N. H. (1997). "Model Selection: An Integral Part of Inference." *Biometrics* 53:603–618.

Bühlmann, P., and Hothorn, T. (2007). "Boosting Algorithms: Regularization, Prediction and Model Fitting." *Statistical Science* 22:477–505. https://doi.org/10.1214/07-STS242.

Buja, A., Duffy, D., Hastie, T. J., and Tibshirani, R. (1991). "Discussion: Multivariate Adaptive Regression Splines." *Annals of Statistics* 19:93–99.

Burnham, K. P., and Anderson, D. R. (2002). *Model Selection and Multimodel Inference.* 2nd ed. New York: Springer-Verlag.

Cameron, A. C., and Trivedi, P. K. (1998). *Regression Analysis of Count Data.* Cambridge: Cambridge University Press.

Cavanaugh, J. E., and Neath, A. A. (2019). "The Akaike Information Criterion: Background, Derivation, Properties, Application, Interpretation, and Refinements." *WIREs Computational Statistics* 1–11. https://doi.org/10.1002/wics.1460.

Chatfield, C. (1995). "Model Uncertainty, Data Mining and Statistical Inference." *Journal of the Royal Statistical Society, Series A* 158:419–466.

Chiang, S., and Rao, V. R. (2022). "Choosing the Best Antiseizure Medication—Can Artificial Intelligence Help?" *JAMA Neurology* Editorial. Published online August 29. `https://doi.org/10.1001/jamaneurol.2022.2441`.

Cohen, R. (2006). "Introducing the GLMSELECT Procedure for Model Selection." In *Proceedings of the Thirty-First Annual SAS Users Group International Conference.* Cary, NC: SAS Institute Inc. `http://www2.sas.com/proceedings/sugi31/207-31.pdf`.

Cohen, R. (2009). "Applications of the GLMSELECT Procedure for Megamodel Selection." In *Proceedings of the SAS Global Forum 2009 Conference.* Cary, NC: SAS Institute Inc. `http://support.sas.com/resources/papers/proceedings09/259-2009.pdf`.

Cohen, R., and Rodriguez, R. N. (2013). "High-Performance Statistical Modeling." In *Proceedings of the SAS Global Forum 2013 Conference.* Cary, NC: SAS Institute Inc. `http://support.sas.com/resources/papers/proceedings13/401-2013.pdf`.

Cook, R. D., and Weisberg, S. (1997). "Graphics for Assessing the Adequacy of Regression Models." *Journal of the American Statistical Association* 92:490–499.

Cox, D. R. (1958). "The Regression Analysis of Binary Sequences." *Journal of the Royal Statistical Society, Series B* 20:215–242.

Cox, D. R. (1972). "Regression Models and Life-Tables." *Journal of the Royal Statistical Society, Series B* 34:187–220. With discussion.

Cox, D. R. (1975). "Partial Likelihood." *Biometrika* 62:269–276.

Cox, D. R. (2006). *Principles of Statistical Inference.* New York: Cambridge University Press.

Cox, D. R., and Oakes, D. (1984). *Analysis of Survival Data.* London: Chapman & Hall.

Cramer, J. S. (2002). "The Origins of Logistic Regression." Tinbergen Institute Discussion Paper TI 2002–119/4. `https://papers.tinbergen.nl/02119.pdf`.

Craven, P., and Wahba, G. (1979). "Smoothing Noisy Data with Spline Functions." *Numerical Mathematics* 31:377–403.

Daniel, C., and Wood, F. (1971). *Fitting Equations to Data.* New York: John Wiley & Sons.

De Boor, C. (1978). *A Practical Guide to Splines.* New York: Springer-Verlag.

De Boor, C. (2001). *A Practical Guide to Splines.* Rev. ed. New York: Springer-Verlag.

De Jong, S. (1993). "SIMPLS: An Alternative Approach to Partial Least Squares Regression." *Chemometrics and Intelligent Laboratory Systems* 18:251–263.

De Leeuw, J. (1992). "Introduction to Akaike (1973) Information Theory and an Extension of the Maximum Likelihood Principle." In *Breakthroughs in Statistics, Volume I: Foundations and Basic Theory*, edited by S. Kotz, and N. L. Johnson, 599–609. New York: Springer-Verlag.

DeLong, D. M., Guirguis, G. H., and So, Y. C. (1994). "Efficient Computation of Subset Selection Probabilities with Application to Cox Regression." *Biometrika* 81:607–611.

Delwiche, L. D., and Slaughter, S. J. (2019). *The Little SAS Book: A Primer.* 6th ed. Cary, NC: SAS Institute Inc.

Denby, L., Landwehr, J., and Mallows, C. L. (2013). "A Conversation with Colin L. Mallows." *International Statistical Review* 81:338–360.

Dobson, A. (1990). *An Introduction to Generalized Linear Models.* London: Chapman & Hall.

Domingos, P. (2012). "A Few Useful Things to Know about Machine Learning." *Communications of the ACM* 55:78–87.

Dorsey, E. R., Okun, M. S., and Tanner, C. M. (2021). "Bad Air and Parkinson Disease: The Fog May Be Lifting." *JAMA Neurology* May 21. Editorial, published online.

Duchon, J. (1976). "Fonctions-spline et espérances conditionnelles de champs gaussiens [Spline functions and conditional expectations of Gaussian fields]." *Annales scientifiques de l'Université de Clermont-Ferrand 2, Série Mathématique* 14:19–27.

Duchon, J. (1977). "Splines Minimizing Rotation-Invariant Semi-norms in Sobolev Spaces." In *Constructive Theory of Functions of Several Variables*, edited by W. Schempp and K. Zeller, 85–100. New York: Springer-Verlag.

Dunn, P. K., and Smyth, G. K. (2005). "Series Evaluation of Tweedie Exponential Dispersion Model Densities." *Statistics and Computing* 15:267–280.

Dunn, P. K., and Smyth, G. K. (2008). "Series Evaluation of Tweedie Exponential Dispersion Model Densities by Fourier Inversion." *Statistics and Computing* 18:73–86.

Efron, B. (1977). "The Efficiency of Cox's Likelihood Function for Censored Data." *Journal of the American Statistical Association* 72:557–565.

Efron, B. (1983). "Estimating the Error Rate of a Prediction Rule: Improvement on Cross-Validation." *Journal of the American Statistical Association* 78:316–331.

Efron, B. (1986). "How Biased Is the Apparent Error Rate of a Prediction Rule?" *Journal of the American Statistical Association* 81:461–470.

Efron, B. (1998). "R. A. Fisher in the 21st Century." *Statistical Science* 13:95–114.

Efron, B., Hastie, T. J., Johnstone, I. M., and Tibshirani, R. (2004). "Least Angle Regression." *Annals of Statistics* 32:407–499. With discussion.

Efron, B., and Tibshirani, R. (1997). "Improvements on Cross-Validation: The .632+ Bootstrap Method." *Journal of the American Statistical Association* 92:548–560.

Efron, B., and Tibshirani, R. J. (1993). *An Introduction to the Bootstrap.* New York: Chapman & Hall.

Efroymson, M. A. (1960). "Multiple Regression Analysis." In *Mathematical Models for Digital Computers*, edited by A. Ralston, and H. S. Wilf, vol. 1, 191–203. New York: John Wiley & Sons.

Eilers, P. H. C., and Marx, B. D. (1996). "Flexible Smoothing with *B*-Splines and Penalties." *Statistical Science* 11:89–121. With discussion.

Evans, E., and Mathews, A. W. (2019). "Researchers Find Racial Bias in Hospital Algorithm." *Wall Street Journal* October 25. https://www.wsj.com/articles/researchers-find-racial-bias-in-hospital-algorithm-11571941096.

Fan, J., and Li, R. (2001). "Variable Selection via Nonconcave Penalized Likelihood and Its Oracle Properties." *Journal of the American Statistical Association* 96:1348–1360.

Farewell, V. T., and Prentice, R. L. (1980). "The Approximation of Partial Likelihood with Emphasis on Case-Control Studies." *Biometrika* 67:273–278.

Findley, D. F., and Parzen, E. (1995). "A Conversation with Hirotugu Akaike." *Statistical Science* 10:104–117.

Firth, D. (1991). "Generalized Linear Models." In *Statistical Theory and Modelling*, edited by D. V. Hinkley, N. Reid, and E. J. Snell, 55–82. London: Chapman & Hall.

Firth, D. (1993). "Bias Reduction of Maximum Likelihood Estimates." *Biometrika* 80:27–38.

Firth, D., Reid, N., Mayo, D. G., Battey, H., Tibshirani, R., Cortina Borja, M., Stander, J., and Sebastiani, G. (2022). "Remembering Sir David Cox, 1924–2022." *Significance* 30–41. April. https://rss.onlinelibrary.wiley.com/doi/epdf/10.1111/1740-9713.01632.

Fisher, R. A. (1912). "On an Absolute Criterion for Fitting Frequency Curves." *Messenger of Mathematics* 41:155–160.

Fisher, R. A. (1922). "On the Mathematical Foundations of Theoretical Statistics." *Philosophical Transactions of the Royal Society of London, Series A* 222:309–368.

Fox, J. (2016). *Applied Regression Analysis and Generalized Linear Models.* 3rd ed. Thousand Oaks, CA: Sage.

Frank, I., and Friedman, J. (1993). "A Statistical View of Some Chemometrics Regression Tools." *Technometrics* 35:109–135.

Freedman, D. A. (1983). "A Note on Screening Regression Equations." *American Statistician* 37:152–155. https://www.jstor.org/stable/2685877.

Frees, E. W. (2010). *Regression Modeling with Actuarial and Financial Applications.* Cambridge: Cambridge University Press.

Freund, Y., and Schapire, R. E. (1997). "A Decision-Theoretic Generalization of On-Line Learning and an Application to Boosting." *Journal of Computer and System Sciences* 55:119–139.

Friedman, J. H. (1991). "Multivariate Adaptive Regression Splines." *Annals of Statistics* 19:1–67.

Friedman, J. H. (2001). "Greedy Function Approximation: A Gradient Boosting Machine." *Annals of Statistics* 29:1189–1232.

Friedman, J. H., Hastie, T., and Tibshirani, R. (2000). "Additive Logistic Regression: A Statistical View of Boosting." *Annals of Statistics* 28:337–407. With discussion.

Friedman, J. H., and Roosen, C. B. (1995). "An Introduction to Multivariate Adaptive Regression Splines." *Statistical Methods in Medical Research* 4:197–217.

Friedman, J. H., and Silverman, B. W. (1989). "Flexible Parsimonious Smoothing and Additive Modeling." *Technometrics* 31:3–21.

Frigo, C., and Osterloo, K. (2016). "exSPLINE That: Explaining Geographic Variation in Insurance Pricing." In *Proceedings of the SAS Global Forum 2016 Conference*. Cary, NC: SAS Institute Inc. http://support.sas.com/resources/papers/proceedings16/8441-2016.pdf.

Furnival, G. M., and Wilson, R. W. (1974). "Regression by Leaps and Bounds." *Technometrics* 16:499–511.

Garthwaite, P. H. (1994). "An Interpretation of Partial Least Squares." *Journal of the American Statistical Association* 89:122–127.

Geisser, S. (1975). "The Predictive Sample Reuse Method with Applications." *Journal of the American Statistical Association* 70:320–328.

Gentle, J. E. (1998). *Numerical Linear Algebra for Applications in Statistics*. New York: Springer.

Gibbons, D. I., and McDonald, G. C. (1980). "Examining Regression Relationships between Air Pollution and Mortality." Presentation at the annual meeting of the American Statistical Association, August 11–14, Houston. Formerly available from General Motors Research Laboratories as Research Publication GMR-3278.

Gibbs, P., and Tobias, R. (2019). "SCORE! Techniques for Scoring Predictive Regression Models Using SAS/STAT Software." In *Proceedings of the SAS Global Forum 2019 Conference*. Cary, NC: SAS Institute Inc. https://www.sas.com/content/dam/SAS/support/en/sas-global-forum-proceedings/2019/3337-2019.pdf.

Goldburd, M., Khare, A., Tevet, D., and Guller, D. (2020). *Generalized Linear Models for Insurance Rating*. Casualty Actuarial Society.

Golub, G. H., and Van Loan, C. F. (1996). *Matrix Computations*. 3rd ed. Baltimore: Johns Hopkins University Press.

Goodnight, J. H. (1979). "A Tutorial on the Sweep Operator." *American Statistician* 33:149–158.

Gorman, J. W., and Toman, R. J. (1966). "Selection of Variables for Fitting Equations to Data." *Technometrics* 8:27–51. https://www.jstor.org/stable/1266260.

Gu, C. (1992). "Cross-Validating Non-Gaussian Data." *Journal of Computational and Graphical Statistics* 1:169–179.

Gu, C., and Wahba, G. (1991). "Minimizing GCV/GML Scores with Multiple Smoothing Parameters via the Newton Method." *SIAM Journal on Scientific Computing* 12:383–398.

Haaland, D. M., and Thomas, E. V. (1988). "Partial Least-Squares Methods for Spectral Analyses. 1. Relation to Other Quantitative Calibration Methods and the Extraction of Qualitative Information." *Analytical Chemistry* 60:1193–1202.

Hagerty, J. R. (2022). "British Statistician Won Global Acclaim for His Methods." *Wall Street Journal* Published online Jan. 28. `https://www.wsj.com/articles/british-statistician-won-global-acclaim-for-his-methods-11643382040`.

Hakeem, H., Feng, W., Chen, Z., Choong, J., Brodie, M. J., Fong, S.-L., Lim, K.-S., Wu, J., et al. (2022). "Development and Validation of a Deep Learning Model for Predicting Treatment Response in Patients with Newly Diagnosed Epilepsy." *JAMA Neurology* Published online August 29. `https://doi.org/10.1001/jamaneurol.2022.2514`.

Hao, L., and Naiman, D. Q. (2007). *Quantile Regression*. London: Sage Publications.

Harrell, F. E., Califf, R. M., Pryor, D. B., Lee, K. L., and Rosati, R. A. (1982). "Evaluating the Yield of Medical Tests." *Journal of the American Medical Association* 247:2543–2546.

Harrell, F. E., Jr. (2015). *Regression Modeling Strategies: With Applications to Linear Models, Logistic Regression, and Survival Analysis*. 2nd ed. New York: Springer.

Hastie, T. J., and Tibshirani, R. J. (1986). "Generalized Additive Models." *Statistical Science* 1:297–318.

Hastie, T. J., and Tibshirani, R. J. (1987). "Generalized Additive Models: Some Applications." *Journal of the American Statistical Association* 82:371–386.

Hastie, T. J., and Tibshirani, R. J. (1990). *Generalized Additive Models*. New York: Chapman & Hall.

Hastie, T. J., Tibshirani, R. J., and Friedman, J. H. (2009). *The Elements of Statistical Learning: Data Mining, Inference, and Prediction*. 2nd ed. New York: Springer-Verlag.

Hastie, T. J., Tibshirani, R. J., and Wainwright, M. (2015). *Statistical Learning with Sparsity: The Lasso and Generalizations*. Boca Raton, FL: CRC Press.

He, X. (2017). "A Conversation with Roger Koenker." *International Statistical Review* 85:46–60.

Heinze, G., and Dunkler, D. (2017). "Five Myths about Variable Selection." *Transplant International* 30:6–10.

Heinze, G., and Schemper, M. (2002). "A Solution to the Problem of Separation in Logistic Regression." *Statistics in Medicine* 21:2409–2419.

Heinze, G., Wallisch, C., and Dunkler, D. (2017). "Variable Selection: A Review and Recommendations for the Practicing Statistician." *Biometrical Journal* 60:431–449.

Hocking, R. R. (1976). "The Analysis and Selection of Variables in a Linear Regression." *Biometrics* 32:1–50.

Hocking, R. R. (1983). "Developments in Linear Regression Methodology: 1959–1982." *Technometrics* 25:219–230.

Hoerl, A. E. (1962). "Application of Ridge Analysis to Regression Problems." *Chemical Engineering Progress* 58:54–59.

Hoerl, A. E., and Kennard, R. W. (1970a). "Ridge Regression: Applications to Nonorthogonal Problems." *Technometrics* 12:69–82.

Hoerl, A. E., and Kennard, R. W. (1970b). "Ridge Regression: Biased Estimation for Non-orthogonal Problems." *Technometrics* 12:55–67.

Hoerl, R. W. (1985). "Ridge Analysis 25 Years Later." *American Statistician* 39:186–192.

Hoerl, R. W. (2020). "Ridge Regression: A Historical Context." *Technometrics* 62:420–425. https://doi.org/10.1080/00401706.2020.1742207.

Hoeting, J. A., Madigan, D., Raftery, A. E., and Volinsky, C. T. (1999). "Bayesian Model Averaging: A Tutorial." *Statistical Science* 14:382–417.

Hosmer, D. W., Jr., Lemeshow, S., and May, S. (2008). *Applied Survival Analysis: Regression Modeling of Time-to-Event Data.* 2nd ed. Hoboken, NJ: John Wiley & Sons.

Hotelling, H. (1936). "Relations between Two Sets of Variables." *Biometrika* 28:321–377.

Hurvich, C. M., and Tsai, C.-L. (1989). "Regression and Time Series Model Selection in Small Samples." *Biometrika* 76:297–307.

James, G., Witten, D., Hastie, T. J., and Tibshirani, R. J. (2021). *An Introduction to Statistical Learning: With Applications in R.* 2nd ed. New York: Springer.

James, W., and Stein, C. (1961). "Estimation with Quadratic Loss." In *Proceedings of the Fourth Berkeley Symposium on Mathematical Statistics and Probability*, 361–379. Berkeley: University of California Press.

Johnson, N. L., Kotz, S., and Balakrishnan, N. (1994). *Continuous Univariate Distributions.* 2nd ed. Vol. 1. New York: John Wiley & Sons.

Johnson, N. L., Kotz, S., and Balakrishnan, N. (1997). *Discrete Multivariate Distributions.* New York: John Wiley & Sons.

Johnson, N. L., Kotz, S., and Kemp, A. W. (1992). *Univariate Discrete Distributions.* 2nd ed. New York: John Wiley & Sons.

Jørgensen, B. (1987). "Exponential Dispersion Models." *Journal of the Royal Statistical Society, Series B* 49:127–162. With discussion.

Kalbfleisch, J. D., and Prentice, R. L. (1973). "Marginal Likelihoods Based on Cox's Regression and Life Model." *Biometrika* 60:267–278.

Kalbfleisch, J. D., and Prentice, R. L. (2002). *The Statistical Analysis of Failure Time Data.* 2nd ed. Hoboken, NJ: John Wiley & Sons.

Kaplan, E. L., and Meier, P. (1958). "Nonparametric Estimation from Incomplete Observations." *Journal of the American Statistical Association* 53:457–481.

Kass, G. V. (1975). "Significance Testing in Automatic Interaction Detection (A.I.D.)." *Journal of the Royal Statistical Society, Series C* 24:178–189.

Kass, G. V. (1980). "An Exploratory Technique for Investigating Large Quantities of Categorical Data." *Journal of the Royal Statistical Society, Series C* 29:119–127.

Klein, J. P., and Moeschberger, M. L. (2003). *Survival Analysis: Techniques for Censored and Truncated Data.* 2nd ed. New York: Springer-Verlag.

Koenker, R. (2005). *Quantile Regression.* New York: Cambridge University Press.

Koenker, R., and Bassett, G. W. (1978). "Regression Quantiles." *Econometrica* 46:33–50.

Kuhfeld, W. F. (2015). *Advanced ODS Graphics Examples.* Cary, NC: SAS Institute Inc. `http://support.sas.com/documentation/prod-p/grstat/9.4/en/PDF/odsadvg.pdf`.

Kuhfeld, W. F. (2016). *Basic ODS Graphics Examples.* Cary, NC: SAS Institute Inc. `http://support.sas.com/documentation/prod-p/grstat/9.4/en/PDF/odsbasicg.pdf`.

Kuhfeld, W. F., and Cai, W. (2013). "Introducing the New ADAPTIVEREG Procedure for Adaptive Regression." In *Proceedings of the SAS Global Forum 2013 Conference.* Cary, NC: SAS Institute Inc. `https://support.sas.com/resources/papers/proceedings13/457-2013.pdf`.

Lambert, D. (1992). "Zero-Inflated Poisson Regression with an Application to Defects in Manufacturing." *Technometrics* 34:1–14.

Lamm, M., and Cai, W. (2020). "Introducing the GAMSELECT Procedure for Generalized Additive Model Selection." In *Proceedings of the SAS Global Forum 2020 Conference.* Cary, NC: SAS Institute Inc. `https://www.sas.com/content/dam/SAS/support/en/sas-global-forum-proceedings/2020/4283-2020.pdf`.

Lange, K. (1999). *Numerical Analysis for Statisticians.* New York: Springer-Verlag.

Lankham, I., and Slaughter, M. (2021). "A Framework for Simple and Efficient Bootstrap Validation in SAS, with Examples." In *Proceedings of the 2021 SAS Global Forum Conference.* Cary, NC: SAS Institute Inc. `https://communities.sas.com/t5/SAS-Global-Forum-Proceedings/A-Framework-for-Simple-and-Efficient-Bootstrap-Validation-in-SAS/ta-p/726298`.

Lave, L. B., and Seskin, E. P. (1970). "Air Pollution and Human Health." *Science* 169:723–733.

Lave, L. B., and Seskin, E. P. (1977). *Air Pollution and Human Health.* Baltimore: Johns Hopkins University Press.

Lawless, J. F. (2003). *Statistical Model and Methods for Lifetime Data.* 2nd ed. New York: John Wiley & Sons.

Lawless, J. F., and Singhal, K. (1978). "Efficient Screening of Nonnormal Regression Models." *Biometrics* 34:318–327.

Lee, T., Duling, D., Liu, S., and Latour, D. (2008). "Two-Stage Variable Clustering for Large Data Sets." In *Proceedings of the SAS Global Forum 2008 Conference.* Cary, NC: SAS Institute Inc.

Long, J. S. (1997). *Regression Models for Categorical and Limited Dependent Variables.* Thousand Oaks, CA: Sage Publications.

Lukacs, P. M., Burnham, K. P., and Anderson, D. R. (2010). "Model Selection Bias and Freedman's Paradox." *Annals of the Institute of Statistical Mathematics* 62:117–125.

Mallows, C. L. (1973). "Some Comments on C_P." *Technometrics* 15:661–675.

Mallows, C. L. (1995). "More Comments on C_P." *Technometrics* 37:362–372.

Marquardt, D. W. (1970). "Generalized Inverses, Ridge Regression, Biased Linear Estimation, and Nonlinear Estimation." *Technometrics* 12:591–612.

Martens, H. (2001). "Reliable and Relevant Modelling of Real World Data: A Personal Account of the Development of PLS Regression." *Chemometrics and Intelligent Laboratory Systems* 58:85–95.

Matange, S., and Heath, D. (2011). *Statistical Graphics Procedures by Example: Effective Graphs Using SAS*. Cary, NC: SAS Institute Inc.

McCullagh, P., and Nelder, J. A. (1989). *Generalized Linear Models*. 2nd ed. London: Chapman & Hall.

McCulloch, C. E., Searle, S. R., and Neuhaus, J. M. (2008). *Generalized, Linear, and Mixed Models*. 2nd ed. Hoboken, NJ: Wiley.

McDonald, G. C., and Schwing, R. C. (1973). "Instabilities of Regression Estimates Relating Air Pollution to Mortality." *Technometrics* 15:463–481.

Meier, L., Van de Geer, S., and Bühlmann, P. (2009). "High-Dimensional Additive Modeling." *Annals of Statistics* 37:3779–3821.

Miller, A. J. (2002). *Subset Selection in Regression*. Vol. 95 of Monographs on Statistics and Applied Probability. 2nd ed. Boca Raton, FL: Chapman & Hall/CRC.

Montgomery, D. C., Peck, E. A., and Vining, G. G. (2012). *Introduction to Linear Regression Analysis*. 5th ed. Hoboken, NJ: Wiley.

Morgan, J. N., and Sonquist, J. A. (1963). "Problems in the Analysis of Survey Data, and a Proposal." *Journal of the American Statistical Association* 58:415–434.

Neath, A. A., and Cavanaugh, J. E. (2012). "The Bayesian Information Criterion: Background, Derivation, and Applications." *WIREs Computational Statistics* 4:199–203. https://doi.org/10.1002/wics.199.

Nelder, J. A., and Pregibon, D. (1987). "An Extended Quasi-Likelihood Function." *Biometrika* 74:221–232. https://www.jstor.org/stable/2336136.

Nelder, J. A., and Wedderburn, R. W. M. (1972). "Generalized Linear Models." *Journal of the Royal Statistical Society, Series A* 135:370–384.

Nesterov, Y. (2013). "Gradient Methods for Minimizing Composite Objective Function." *Mathematical Programming* 140:125–161.

Nychka, D. (1988). "Bayesian Confidence Intervals for Smoothing Splines." *Journal of the American Statistical Association* 83:1134–1143.

Obermeyer, Z., Powers, B., Vogeli, C., and Mullainathan, S. (2019). "Dissecting Racial Bias in an Algorithm Used to Manage the Health of Populations." *Science* 336:447–453.

O'Brien, R. M. (2007). "A Caution Regarding Rules of Thumb for Variance Inflation Factors." *Quality and Quantity* 41:673–690.

Osborne, M. R., Presnell, B., and Turlach, B. A. (2000a). "A New Approach to Variable Selection in Least Squares Problems." *IMA Journal of Numerical Analysis* 20:389–404.

Osborne, M. R., Presnell, B., and Turlach, B. A. (2000b). "On the LASSO and Its Dual." *Journal of Computational and Graphical Statistics* 9:319–337. `https://doi.org/10.2307/1390657`.

Osterloo, K., and Wu, W. (2017). "Geospatial Analysis: Linear, Nonlinear, or Both?" In *Proceedings of the SAS Global Forum 2017 Conference*. Cary, NC: SAS Institute Inc. `https://support.sas.com/resources/papers/proceedings17/1128-2017.pdf`.

O'Sullivan, F., Yandell, B. S., and Raynor, W. T., Jr. (1986). "Automatic Smoothing of Regression Functions in Generalized Linear Models." *Journal of the American Statistical Association* 81:96–103.

Pawitan, Y. (2001). *In All Likelihood: Statistical Modelling and Inference Using Likelihood*. Oxford: Clarendon Press.

Pearson, K. (1901). "On Lines and Planes of Closest Fit to Systems of Points in Space." *Philosophical Magazine* 6:559–572.

Pope, P. T., and Webster, J. T. (1972). "The Use of an F-Statistic in Stepwise Regression Procedures." *Technometrics* 14:327–340.

Prentice, R. L., and Gloeckler, L. A. (1978). "Regression Analysis of Grouped Survival Data with Applications to Breast Cancer Data." *Biometrics* 34:57–67.

Provost, F. J., Fawcett, T., and Kohavi, R. (1998). "The Case against Accuracy Estimation for Comparing Induction Algorithms." In *Proceedings of the Fifteenth International Conference on Machine Learning*, 445–453. San Francisco: Morgan Kaufmann.

Quinlan, J. R. (1986). "Induction of Decision Trees." *Machine Learning* 1:81–106.

Quinlan, J. R. (1987). "Simplifying Decision Trees." *International Journal of Man-Machine Studies* 27:221–234.

Quinlan, J. R. (1993). *C4.5: Programs for Machine Learning*. San Francisco: Morgan Kaufmann.

Raftery, A. E., Madigan, D., and Hoeting, J. A. (1997). "Bayesian Model Averaging for Linear Regression Models." *Journal of the American Statistical Association* 92:179–191.

Rawlings, J. O., Pantula, S. G., and Dickey, D. A. (1998). *Applied Regression Analysis: A Research Tool*. 2nd ed. New York: Springer-Verlag.

Reid, N. (1994). "A Conversation with Sir David Cox." *Statistical Science* 9:439–455.

Reinsch, C. H. (1967). "Smoothing by Spline Functions." *Numerische Mathematik* 10:177–183.

Ridout, M. S., Hinde, J. P., and Demétrio, C. G. B. (1998). "Models for Count Data with Many Zeros." In *Proceedings of the Nineteenth International Biometric Conference*, 179–192. Cape Town, South Africa.

Rothamsted Research (2019). "Surprising Birthplace of Modern Data Analysis Celebrates 100 Years." https://www.rothamsted.ac.uk/news/surprising-birthplace-modern-data-analysis-celebrates-100-years.

Rudin, C. (2019). "Stop Explaining Black Box Machine Learning Models for High Stakes Decisions and Use Interpretable Models Instead." *Nature Machine Intelligence* 1:206–215.

Rudin, C., and Radin, J. (2019). "Why Are We Using Black Box Models in AI When We Don't Need To? A Lesson from an Explainable AI Competition." *Harvard Data Science Review.* https://hdsr.mitpress.mit.edu/pub/f9kuryi8.

Rudin, C., Wang, C., and Coker, B. (2020). "The Age of Secrecy and Unfairness in Recidivism Prediction." *Harvard Data Science Review.* https://hdsr.mitpress.mit.edu/pub/7z10o269/release/7.

Santner, T. J., and Duffy, D. E. (1986). "A Note on A. Albert and J. A. Anderson's Conditions for the Existence of Maximum Likelihood Estimates in Logistic Regression Models." *Biometrika* 73:755–758.

Sauerbrei, W. (1999). "The Use of Resampling Methods to Simplify Regression Models in Medical Statistics." *Journal of the Royal Statistical Society, Series C* 48:313–329. https://www.jstor.org/stable/2680827.

Sauerbrei, W., Perperoglou, A., Schmid, M., Abrahamowicz, M., Becher, H., Binder, H., Dunkler, D., Harrell, F. E., Jr., et al. (2020). "State of the Art in Selection of Variables and Functional Forms in Multivariable Analysis—Outstanding Issues." *Diagnostic and Prognostic Research* 4:3.

Savage, L. J. (1976). "On Rereading R. A. Fisher." *Annals of Statistics* 4:441–500.

Sawa, T. (1978). "Information Criteria for Discriminating among Alternative Regression Models." *Econometrica* 46:1273–1282.

Schapire, R. E., and Freund, Y. (2012). *Boosting: Foundations and Algorithms.* Cambridge, MA: MIT Press.

Schwarz, G. (1978). "Estimating the Dimension of a Model." *Annals of Statistics* 6:461–464.

Scism, L. (2020). "Car Insurers Struggle to Track Driving Behavior. GM May Have a Better Way to Do It." *Wall Street Journal* November 19. https://www.wsj.com/articles/car-insurers-struggle-to-track-driving-behavior-gm-may-have-a-better-way-to-do-it-11605791475.

Searle, S. R. (1971). *Linear Models.* New York: John Wiley & Sons.

Senn, S., and Nelder, J. (2003). "A Conversation with John Nelder." *Statistical Science* 18:118–131.

Sheather, S. J. (2009). *A Modern Approach to Regression with R.* New York: Springer.

Simonoff, J. S. (2003). *Analyzing Categorical Data.* New York: Springer-Verlag.

Smith, P. L. (1982). *Curve Fitting and Modeling with Splines Using Statistical Variable Selection Techniques.* Technical report, NASA Langley Research Center.

Smith, T. C., and Smith, B. (2019). "Integrating Case Studies in a Health Analytics Curriculum." In *Proceedings of the SAS Global Forum 2019 Conference.* Cary, NC: SAS Institute Inc. `https://www.sas.com/content/dam/SAS/support/en/sas-global-forum-proceedings/2019/3282-2019.pdf`.

So, Y. (1995). "A Tutorial on Logistic Regression." In *Proceedings of the Twentieth Annual SAS Users Group International Conference.* Cary, NC: SAS Institute Inc. `https://support.sas.com/rnd/app/stat/papers/logistic.pdf`.

Stein, C. (1956). "Inadmissibility of the Usual Estimator for the Mean of a Multivariate Normal Distribution." In *Proceedings of the Third Berkeley Symposium on Mathematical Statistics and Probability*, 197–206. Berkeley: University of California Press.

Stein, C. M. (1981). "Estimation of the Mean of a Multivariate Normal Distribution." *Annals of Statistics* 9:1135–1151.

Steyerberg, E. W. (2019). *Clinical Prediction Models: A Practical Approach to Development, Validation, and Updating.* 2nd ed. Cham, Switzerland: Springer.

Stigler, S. M. (1981). "Gauss and the Invention of Least Squares." *Annals of Statistics* 9:465–474.

Stokes, M. E., Davis, C. S., and Koch, G. G. (2012). *Categorical Data Analysis Using SAS.* 3rd ed. Cary, NC: SAS Institute Inc.

Stone, C. T. (1986). "Comment: General Additive Models." *Statistical Science* 1:312–314.

Stone, M. (1974). "Cross-Validatory Choice and Assessment of Statistical Predictions." *Journal of the Royal Statistical Society, Series B* 36:111–147.

Stuart, E. A., Polsky, D., Grabowski, M. K., and Peters, D. (2020). "10 Tips for Making Sense of COVID-19 Models for Decision-Making." Johns Hopkins Bloomberg School of Public Health. April 27. `https://www.jhsph.edu/covid-19/articles/10-tips-for-making-sense-of-covid-19-models-for-decision-making.html`.

Suzuki, T., and Sugiyama, M. (2013). "Fast Learning Rate of Multiple Kernel Learning: Trade-Off between Sparsity and Smoothness." *Annals of Statistics* 41:1381–1405.

Svolba, G. (2017). *Applying Data Science: Business Case Studies Using SAS.* Cary, NC: SAS Institute Inc.

Thibodeau, L. A., Reed, R. B., Bishop, Y. M. M., and Kammerman, L. A. (1980). "Air Pollution and Human Health: A Review and Reanalysis." *Source: Environmental Health Perspectives* 34:165–183.

Thisted, R. A. (1988). *Elements of Statistical Computing: Numerical Computation.* London: Chapman & Hall.

Thompson, M. L. (1978). "Selection of Variables in Multiple Regression: Part I. A Review and Evaluation." *International Statistical Review* 46:1–19.

Tibshirani, R. (1996). "Regression Shrinkage and Selection via the Lasso." *Journal of the Royal Statistical Society, Series B* 58:267–288.

Tibshirani, R. (1997). "The Lasso Method for Variable Selection in the Cox Model." *Statistics in Medicine* 16:385–395.

Tibshirani, R. (2011). "Regression Shrinkage and Selection via the Lasso: A Retrospective." *Journal of the Royal Statistical Society, Series B* 73:273–282.

Trefethen, L. N., and Bau, I., D. (1997). *Numerical Linear Algebra.* Philadelphia: SIAM.

Tweedie, M. C. K. (1984). "An Index Which Distinguishes between Some Important Exponential Families." In *Statistics: Applications and New Directions—Proceedings of the Indian Statistical Institute Golden Jubilee International Conference*, edited by J. K. Ghosh and J. Roy, 579–604. Calcutta: Indian Statistical Institute.

Volovici, V., Syn, N. L., Ercole, A., Zhao, J. J., and Liu, N. (2022). "Steps to Avoid Overuse and Misuse of Machine Learning in Clinical Research." *Nature Medicine* 28:1996–1999.

Wahba, G. (1983). "Bayesian 'Confidence Intervals' for the Cross Validated Smoothing Spline." *Journal of the Royal Statistical Society, Series B* 45:133–150.

Wahba, G. (1990). *Spline Models for Observational Data.* Philadelphia: SIAM.

Wedderburn, R. W. M. (1974). "Quasi-likelihood Functions, Generalized Linear Models, and the Gauss-Newton Method." *Biometrika* 61:439–447.

Wold, H. (1966). "Estimation of Principal Components and Related Models by Iterative Least Squares." In *Multivariate Analysis*, edited by P. R. Krishnaiah, 391–420. New York: Academic Press.

Wold, S. (2001). "Personal Memories of the Early PLS Development." *Chemometrics and Intelligent Laboratory Systems* 58:83–84.

Wood, S. (2003). "Thin Plate Regression Splines." *Journal of the Royal Statistical Society, Series B* 65:95–114.

Wood, S. (2004). "Stable and Efficient Multiple Smoothing Parameter Estimation for Generalized Additive Models." *Journal of the American Statistical Association* 99:673–686.

Wood, S. (2006). *Generalized Additive Models.* Boca Raton, FL: Chapman & Hall/CRC.

Wood, S. (2008). "Fast Stable Direct Fitting and Smoothness Selection for Generalized Additive Models." *Journal of the Royal Statistical Society, Series B* 70:495–518.

Wood, S. (2011). "Fast Stable Restricted Maximum Likelihood and Marginal Likelihood Estimation of Semiparametric Generalized Linear Models." *Journal of the Royal Statistical Society, Series B* 73:3–36.

Wood, S. (2012). "On *p*-Values for Smooth Components of an Extended Generalized Additive Model." *Biometrika* 1–8. http://biomet.oxfordjournals.org/content/early/2012/10/18/biomet.ass048.abstract.

Wood, S. N. (2017). *Generalized Additive Models: An Introduction to R.* 2nd ed. Boca Raton, FL: Chapman & Hall/CRC.

Xiang, D., and Wahba, G. (1996). "A Generalized Approximate Cross Validation for Smoothing Splines with Non-Gaussian Data." *Statistica Sinica* 6:675–692.

Yao, Y. (2017). "Fast Quantile Process Regression." Paper presented at the 2017 International Conference on Robust Statistics, Wollongong, NSW, Australia.

Young, F. W. (1981). "Quantitative Analysis of Qualitative Data." *Psychometrika* 46:357–388.

Yuan, M. (2006). "GACV for Quantile Smoothing Splines." *Computational Statistics and Data Analysis* 50:813–829. `http://econpapers.repec.org/article/eeecsdana/v_3a50_3ay_3a2006_3ai_3a3_3ap_3a813-829.htm`.

Yuan, M., and Lin, L. (2006). "Model Selection and Estimation in Regression with Grouped Variables." *Journal of the Royal Statistical Society, Series B* 68:49–67.

Zhang, C.-H. (2010). "Nearly Unbiased Variable Selection under Minimax Concave Penalty." *Annals of Statistics* 38:894–942.

Zhang, H., and Singer, B. H. (2010). *Recursive Partitioning and Applications.* 2nd ed. New York: Springer.

Zou, H. (2006). "The Adaptive Lasso and Its Oracle Properties." *Journal of the American Statistical Association* 101:1418–1429.

Zou, H., and Hastie, T. (2005). "Regularization and Variable Selection via the Elastic Net." *Journal of the Royal Statistical Society, Series B* 67:301–320.

Zou, H., Hastie, T., and Tibshirani, R. (2007). "On the 'Degrees of Freedom' of the Lasso." *Annals of Statistics* 35:2173–2192.

Zou, H., and Zhang, H. H. (2009). "On the Adaptive Elastic-Net with a Diverging Number of Parameters." *Annals of Statistics* 37:1733–1751.

Subject Index

Syntax Index

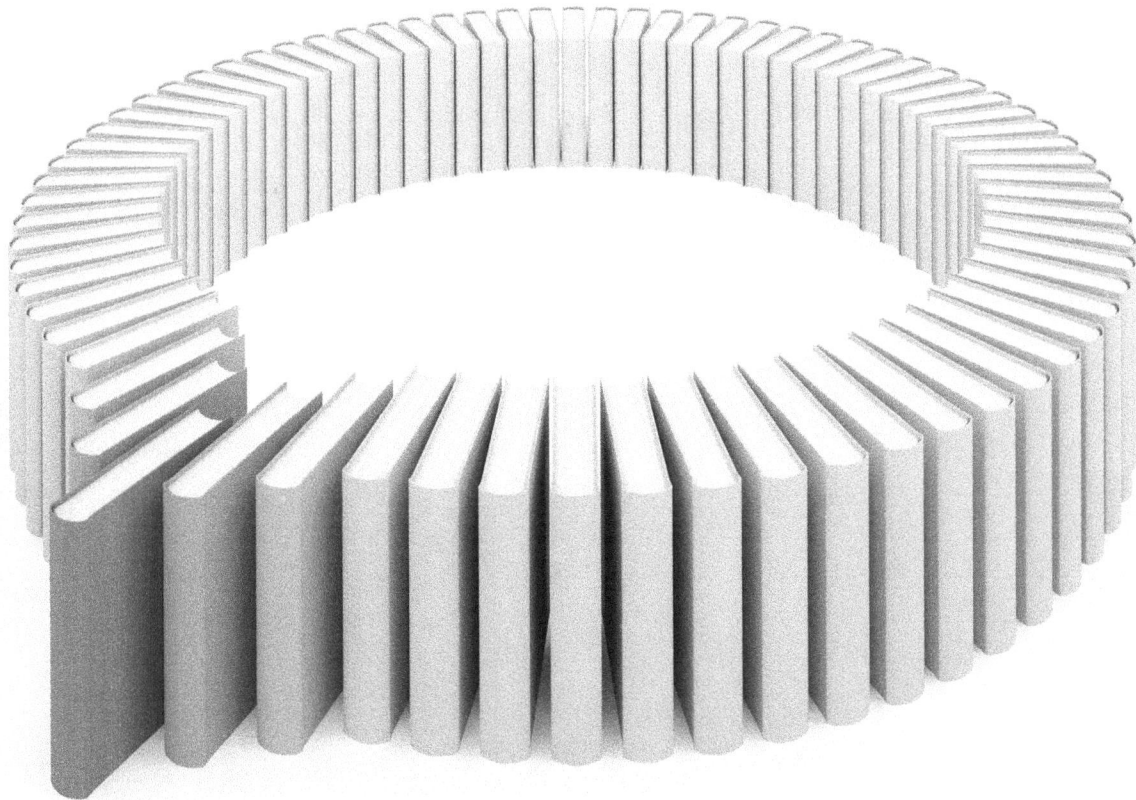

www.ingramcontent.com/pod-product-compliance
Lightning Source LLC
Chambersburg PA
CBHW081224220326
41598CB00037B/6869